www.wadsworth.com

wadsworth.com is the World Wide Web site for Wadsworth and is your direct source to dozens of online resources.

At *wadsworth.com* you can find out about supplements, demonstration software, and student resources. You can also send email to many of our authors and preview new publications and exciting new technologies.

wadsworth.com
Changing the way the world learns®

Sixth Edition

Criminal Investigation

Wayne W. Bennett
Former Chief of Police
Boulder City, Nevada
Edina, Minnesota

Kären M. Hess
Normandale Community College
Bloomington, Minnesota

WADSWORTH

THOMSON LEARNING

Australia • Canada • Mexico • Singapore • Spain
United Kingdom • United States

WADSWORTH

THOMSON LEARNING

Executive Editor, Criminal Justice: Sabra Horne
Development Editor: Barbara Yien
Assistant Editor: Ann Tsai
Editorial Assistant: Cortney Bruggink
Marketing Manager: Jennifer Somerville
Project Editor: Jennie Redwitz
Print Buyer: Karen Hunt
Permissions Editor: Bob Kauser
Production Service Coordinator: Andrea Bednar,
                 Shepherd, Inc.

Text Designer: Carolyn Deacy
Photo Researcher: Mary Reeg
Copy Editor: Carol Hoke
Illustrator: Jeni McAtee
Cover Designer: Harold Burch
Cover Image: Tony Cordoza, Photonica
Cover Printer: Phoenix Color Corporation
Compositor: Shepherd, Incorporated
Printer: R. R. Donnelley, Willard
Index: Christine M. H. Orthmann

Library of Congress Cataloging-in-Publication Data
Bennett, Wayne.
  Criminal investigation / Wayne W. Bennett,
Kären M. Hess.—6th ed.
    p. cm.
  Includes index
  ISBN 0-534-57654-0
  1. Criminal investigation. I. Hess, Kären M., II. Title.

HV8073 .B43 2001
363.25—dc21   00-026683

Instructor's Edition ISBN: 0-534-57655-9

Wadsworth/Thomson Learning
10 Davis Drive
Belmont, CA 94002-3098
USA

For more information about our products, contact us:
Thomson Learning Academic Resource Center
1-800-423-0563
http://www.wadsworth.com

International Headquarters
Thomson Learning
International Division
290 Harbor Drive, 2nd Floor
Stamford, CT 06902-7477
USA

UK/Europe/Middle East/South Africa
Thomson Learning
Berkshire House
168-173 High Holborn
London WC1V 7AA
United Kingdom

Asia
Thomson Learning
60 Albert Street, #15-01
Albert Complex
Singapore 189969

Canada
Nelson Thomson Learning
1120 Birchmount Road
Toronto, Ontario M1K 5G4
Canada

Contents in Brief

SECTION FIVE

Other Challenges to the Criminal Investigator 427

Appendixes

Contents

SECTION FOUR

Investigating Crimes against Property 345

CHAPTER 14

Burglary 347

CHAPTER 15

Larceny/Theft, Fraud, White-Collar and Environmental Crime 361

Other Challenges to the Criminal Investigator 427

CHAPTER 20
Drug Buyers and Sellers 491

Appendixes

APPENDIX A
Death Scene Checklist 524

APPENDIX B
Associations that Provide Support in
Investigating Computer-Related Crimes 527

APPENDIX C
Sample Form for Reporting Bias Crimes 529

Preface

The complex responsibilities of criminal investigation must be fulfilled under constantly changing conditions and in a way that protects the rights of all citizens. Changes in technology and society continually present new challenges to investigators, requiring them to be knowledgeable in a wide variety of areas.

This sixth edition of *Criminal Investigation* focuses on technologic innovations in every aspect of investigative work. These innovations are highlighted by a thunderbolt icon.

The text provides fundamental information that serves as an overview of the entire field as well as a solid foundation for specialized course work. Although the content of each chapter could easily be expanded into an entire book or course, this text can provide only the basic concepts of each area. In Section One you are introduced to the broad field of criminal investigation, to the elements of an effective, efficient investigation and to the equipment, technology and procedures that facilitate investigation (Chapter 1). Important court cases and decisions are cited and explained throughout the text.

In Section Two you become acquainted with the various investigative responsibilities: photographing and sketching crime scenes (Chapter 2), taking notes and writing reports (Chapter 3), searching crime scenes and suspects (Chapter 4), identifying and collecting physical evidence (Chapter 5), obtaining information (Chapter 6), identifying and arresting suspects (Chapter 7) and testifying in court (Chapter 8).

Sections Three, Four and Five illustrate how these responsibilities are carried out in specific types of investigations. Section Three discusses the basics of investigating crimes against the person: robbery (Chapter 9), assault (Chapter 10), sex offenses (Chapter 11), crimes against children (Chapter 12) and homicide (Chapter 13). Section Four discusses crimes against property: burglary (Chapter 14), larceny/theft, white-collar crime and environmental crime (Chapter 15), motor vehicle theft (Chapter 16) and arson (Chapter 17). Section Five discusses other investigative challenges: computer crimes (Chapter 18), organized crime, gang-related crime, bias/hate crime and ritualistic crime (Chapter 19) and drugs and drug-related crimes (Chapter 20).

How to Use This Text

Criminal Investigation is a carefully structured learning experience. The more actively you participate in it, the greater your learning will be. You will learn and remember more if you first familiarize yourself with the total scope of the subject. Read and think about the Table of Contents, which provides an outline of the many facets of criminal investigation. Then follow these steps for triple-strength learning as you study each chapter.

1. Read the objectives at the beginning of the chapter. These are stated as "Do You Know?" questions. Assess your current knowledge of the subject of each question. Examine any preconceptions you may hold. Look at the key terms, and watch for them when they are used.

2. Read the chapter, underlining, highlighting or taking notes—whatever is your preferred study method.

   a. Pay special attention to all highlighted information:

   - - - - - - - -

   Cast shoe or tire tread impressions found in dirt and sand or snow.

   - - - - - - - -

   The key concepts of the text are highlighted in this way and answer the "Do You Know?" questions.

b. Pay special attention to all words in bold print. The key terms of the chapter appear this way the first time they are used.

3. When you have finished reading the chapter, read the summary—your third exposure to the chapter's key information. Then return to the beginning of the chapter and quiz yourself. Can you answer the "Do You Know?" questions? "Can You Define?" the key terms?

4. Finally, in Sections Three, Four and Five, complete the Application exercises at the end of each chapter. These exercises ask you to apply the chapter concepts in actual or hypothetical cases. Then read the Discussion Questions and be prepared to contribute to a class discussion of the ideas presented in the chapter.

By following these steps, you will learn more information, understand it more fully and remember it longer. Good learning!

Acknowledgments

A number of professionals from academia and the field have reviewed the previous editions of *Criminal Investigation* and provided valuable suggestions. We thank them all: Joel J. Allen, Western Illinois University; Thomas Allen, University of South Dakota; Frank Anzelmi; Greg Arnold, Manatee Community College; Robert Barthol, Chabot College; Walt Copley, Metropolitan State College of Denver; Edward Creekmore, Northland Community College; Stanley Cunningham, Western Illinois University; Andrew Dantschich, St. Petersburg Junior College; Wayne Dunning, Wichita State University; Cass Gaska, Henry Ford Community College; Bruce Gordon, University of Cincinnati; Keith Haley, University of Cincinnati; George Henthorn, Central Missouri State University; John Hicks, Hocking Technical College; Robert R. Ives, Rock Valley College; George Keefer; Robert A. Lorinskas, Southern Illinois at Carbondale; Jane E. McClellan; Michael Meyer, University of North Dakota; Jane Kravits Munley, Luzerne County Community College; James F. Newman, Rio Hondo Community College; William L. Pelkey, Eastern Kentucky University; Ronald A. Pricom, New Mexico State University; Charles Quarles, University of Mississippi; Walter F. Ruger, Nassau Community College; Jospeh R. Terrill, Hartford Community College; Charles A. Tracy, Portland State University; Bob Walker, Trinity Valley Community College; and Richard Weber, Jamestown Community College. The following reviewers contributed numerous suggestions to the Sixth Edition:

Alison McKenney Brown
Wichita State University

Joseph Bunce
Montgomery College

William Castleberry
University of Tennessee

Edmund Grosskopf
Indiana State University

Gayle Mericle
Western Illinois University

Michael Meyer
University of North Dakota

Robert Neville
College of the Siskiyous

Thomas O'Connor
North Carolina Wesleyan College

We greatly appreciate the input of these people. Sole responsibility for all content, however, is our own.

Thank you also to A. E. "Al" Hansen for providing some of the text's sketches and to Dorothy Bennett for assistance in the photo program. We extend a special thank you to Christine Hess Orthmann for her careful preparation of the revised manuscript, the index and the supplemental materials. Additional special thanks go to Sabra Horne, executive editor; Barbara Yien and Ann Tsau, assistant editors; Jennie Redwitz, production editor at Wadsworth Thomson Learning; and to Andrea Bednar our production editor at Shepherd Inc. Finally, we thank our families and colleagues for their continuing support and encouragement throughout the development of *Criminal Investigation,* Sixth Edition.

Wayne W. Bennett
Kären M. Hess

About the Authors

Wayne W. Bennett is a graduate of the FBI National Police Academy, holds an LLB degree in law and has served as the Director of Public Safety for the Edina, Minnesota, Police Department and as Chief of Police of the Boulder City, Nevada, Police Department. He is coauthor of *Management and Supervision in Law Enforcement,* Third Edition, and is currently working on an *Introduction to Criminal Justice* text for Wadsworth/Thomson Learning.

Kären M. Hess holds a PhD in English and in instructional design from the University of Minnesota and a PhD in criminal justice from Pacific Western University. Other Wadsworth Thomson Learning texts Dr. Hess has coauthored are *Criminal Procedure, Corrections in the Twenty-First Century: A Practical Approach, Introduction to Law Enforcement and Criminal Justice* (Sixth Edition), *Introduction to Private Security* (Fifth Edition), *Juvenile Justice* (Third Edition), *Management and Supervision in Law Enforcement* (Third Edition), *The Police and the Community: Strategies for the 21st Century* (Second Edition), *Police Operations* and *Seeking Employment in Criminal Justice and Related Fields* (Third Edition).

This text is based on the practical experience of Wayne W. Bennett, who has spent 45 years in law enforcement and has taught various aspects of criminal investigation over the past 30 years as well as the expertise of Kären M. Hess, who has been developing instructional programs for 25 years. The text has been reviewed by numerous experts in the various areas of criminal investigation as well.

Introduction

Criminal investigation is a complex, sophisticated field, each aspect of which could constitute a book in itself. This text includes the most basic aspects of criminal investigation. Section One presents an overview of criminal investigation and general guidelines to follow or adapt in specific circumstances, as well as basic considerations in the preliminary investigation.

Investigators must be thoroughly familiar with crimes and their elements, modus operandi information, the major goals of investigation, the basic functions of investigating officers and the investigators' relationships with other individuals and agencies.

The most critical phase in the majority of criminal investigations is the preliminary investigation. The decisions made, the responsibilities assumed and the tasks performed apply to a wide variety of crimes and must be part of every investigator's repertoire.

Investigators do not operate in a vacuum but must relate to constitutional safeguards set forth in the U.S. Constitution's Fourth, Fifth, Sixth and Fourteenth Amendments. They must also understand case law determining the parameters within which they perform the investigative process. How these constitutional safeguards and case law specifically affect investigations is emphasized throughout the text.

Chapter 1

Criminal Investigation: An Overview

Can You Define?

civil liability

community policing

crime

criminal intent

criminal investigation

criminal statute

criminalistics

elements of the crime

emergency

fact

felony

forensic science

inference

intuition

investigate

misdemeanor

modus operandi (MO)

opinion

ordinance

predication

res gestae statement

Do You Know?

What criminal investigation is?

What the major goals of criminal investigation are?

What basic functions investigators perform?

What characteristics are important in investigators?

Who usually arrives at a crime scene first?

What should be done initially?

What to do if a suspect is still at a crime scene? Has recently fled the scene?

How the crime scene and evidence are protected and for how long?

What responsibilities are included in the preliminary investigation?

What the meaning and importance of *res gestae* statements are?

How to determine whether a crime has been committed?

What basic components are included in an investigative plan?

Who is responsible for solving crimes?

With whom investigators must relate?

How to avoid civil lawsuits?

Introduction

On April 19, 1995, Trooper Charlie Hanger of the Oklahoma Highway Patrol was traveling north on Interstate 35 when he saw a 1977 Mercury Marquis with no license plate. Hanger pulled the car over, and the only occupant, a white male, got out. While Hanger was questioning the driver about the license plate, the trooper noticed a bulge in the man's clothing. When asked, the man admitted he had a gun and was arrested. The driver—Timothy McVeigh—was later found responsible for the bombing of a federal building in Oklahoma City that killed 168 people and left hundreds injured. Some would say that the arrest was just plain luck. Harris (1999, p. 15) argues otherwise: "Luck—if you insist on using that term—is when preparation meets opportunity."

An observant police officer can initiate an important criminal investigation, sometimes without realizing it at first. Criminal investigation combines art and science and requires extraordinary preparation and training.

A **criminal investigation** is usually initiated by personal observation or information from a citizen. Patrol officers may see a suspicious action or person, or a citizen may report suspicious actions or people. Such information is received at police headquarters by telephone, teletype, radio or direct report when a person steps up to a police complaint desk. A police dispatcher relays the information to a patrol officer by radio or teleprint, and the officer responds.

The initial response is crucial to the success of an investigation. Although it is popularly believed that cases are won or lost in court, more cases actually are lost during the first hour of an investigation—the initial response period—than in court.

Because no two crimes are identical, even if they are committed by the same person, each investigation is unique. The great range of variables in individual crimes makes it impossible to establish fixed rules for conducting an investigation. Nevertheless, some general guidelines help to ensure that investigations are thorough and effective. Investigators modify and adapt these guidelines to fit each case.

Investigators need not have superhuman reasoning ability. They must, however, proceed in an orderly, systematic way, gathering facts to analyze and evaluate. Geberth (1998, p. 194) states: "Major case investigations are successfully completed by a combination of brainstorming, intuition and educated guesswork." This chapter introduces decisions to be made and the actions to be taken. Subsequent chapters explain each step of the preliminary investigation more fully.

This chapter begins with a discussion of criminal investigation, its goals and basic functions, followed by an examination of the characteristics of an effective investigator. Next, it describes basic considerations in the preliminary investigation, including the initial response, the point of arrival, setting priorities, handling emergency situations, protecting the crime scene and beginning the investigation. The chapter then discusses the follow-up investigation, computer-aided investigation and investigative productivity and follows with an explanation of the numerous individuals and agencies with which investigators must interact. The chapter concludes with a discussion of how to avoid civil liability. ■

Criminal Investigation Defined

An *investigation* is a patient, step-by-step inquiry or observation, a careful examination, a recording of evidence or a legal inquiry. The word **investigate** is derived from the Latin word *vestigare,* meaning "to track or trace," a derivation easily related to police investigation.

- - - - - - - -

A criminal investigation is the process of discovering, collecting, preparing, identifying and presenting evidence to determine *what happened and who is responsible.*

- - - - - - - -

If a crime is suspected or is known to have been committed, the police conduct an investigation. They may investigate alone or seek help from medical and technical specialists or specialists representing private groups, for example, insurance claims adjustors and consumer fraud investigators. Investigators from federal, state or county police agencies may also assist.

Other Terms Defined

The first determination in a criminal investigation is whether a crime has, in fact, been committed. Does the evidence support a specific offense? A legal arrest cannot be made for an act that is not defined by statute or ordinance as a crime.

Although everyone has a notion of what crime is, investigators must have a very precise understanding of what it means. Specific definitions of such terms as *crime, felony, misdemeanor, criminal statute* and *ordinance* are found in case law:

- A **crime** is an act in violation of penal law and an offense against the state. The broader use of the term includes both felonies and misdemeanors. A

Criminal investigators must discover, collect, identify and present evidence. Here, investigators collect evidence from a stolen vehicle found overturned in Waynesville, North Carolina, on September 30, 1999. The owner of the vehicle had been found murdered, along with four other family members, in a home near where the vehicle was wrecked. A suspect was later apprehended.

crime is a violation of a public right or law. It is an act or omission forbidden by law and punishable by a fine, imprisonment or even death. This is in contrast to torts or private harms.

- A **felony** is a serious crime, graver than a misdemeanor; it is generally punishable by death or imprisonment of more than one year in a penitentiary.

- A **misdemeanor** is a crime or offense that is less serious than a felony and punishable by fine or imprisonment of up to one year in an institution other than a penitentiary.

- A **criminal statute** is a legislative act relating to a crime and its punishment.

- An **ordinance** is an act of the legislative body of a municipality or county relating to all the rules gov-

erning the municipality or county, inclusive of misdemeanor crimes.

Crimes and their penalties are established and defined by state and federal statutes and local ordinances.[1] An act that is not declared a crime by statute or ordinance is not a chargeable offense, no matter how wrong it may seem. Designated crimes and their punishments change as society's attitudes change. In the past, for example, behavior associated with alcoholism was considered criminal, but today many states regard alcoholism as an illness. However, driving while intoxicated is now

_____

[1] Some states, such as Illinois, do not consider violations of city ordinances to be crimes.

considered a much more serious offense than it was previously. Conversely, our society has designated as crimes certain acts, such as computer fraud, that were unknown in earlier times.

Crimes fall into two general categories—felonies and misdemeanors—depending on the severity of an act and its recommended punishment. The more serious society considers a crime, the more severe the penalty. Investigations involve both types of crimes. Misdemeanors are sometimes further subdivided into gross and petty misdemeanors, based on the value of the property involved.

Because definitions of crimes and their penalties vary considerably depending on whether they occur at the municipal, county, state or federal level, investigators must be familiar with their area's criminal statutes and ordinances. For example, in some states, such as Michigan, shoplifting is a felony. In most states the value of the shoplifted property determines whether it is a misdemeanor or a felony.

Statutes and ordinances list specific conditions, called the **elements of the crime,** that must occur for an act to be called a specific kind of crime. For example, a state statute might define burglary as occurring when (1) an accused enters a building (2) without the consent of the rightful owner (3) with the intent to commit a crime. An investigation must prove each element, even if the suspect has confessed. Many crimes have as an element **criminal intent,** that is, purposely performing an unlawful act or knowing an act to be illegal. Sections Three and Four of this text discuss the elements of major crimes. Knowing these elements is essential to gathering evidence to prove that a crime has been committed.

In addition to proving that a crime has been committed, investigators must determine who committed it. Investigation is often aided by knowing how criminals usually operate, that is, their **modus operandi,** or **MO.** For example, it was relatively easy to recognize the "work" of Jack the Ripper. Morrison (1999, p. 103) suggests:

> Most police officers utilize the MO point of view to investigate a crime. They may not actually put it on paper, but they do estimate probabilities by looking at the suspect's habits, techniques and pecularities of behavior in serial crimes or of people arrested in the past. A certain amount of weight is assigned to each variable.

According to Geberth (p. 194): "Experienced detectives have solved innumerable cases by recognizing a particular modus operandi from a case in the past or a perpetrator's distinctive signature." Morrison notes:

> Along with many other factors, detectives still maintain a mental list of the peculiar details of every crime scene and the matching traits of known perpetrators of previous crimes. . . .
>
> Given the fact that most criminals today do not face long prison sentences and are, unfortunately, out on the streets all too soon repeating their offenses, it would seem likely that MO files should be in demand. In many cases, these offenders return to their original methods of criminal attack only a few hours after their release (1997b, p. 80).

Modus operandi information can provide clues in less obvious cases as well. For example, if several burglaries are committed between 11 A.M. and 1 P.M. in one area of a community and all involve broken glass in a door, one might infer that the same individual committed the crimes. A similar time, area and method of entry would further support this assumption. Although the burglaries may be unrelated, the probability is low. One might further assume that the burglar would not commit armed robbery or other crimes unless surprised while committing a burglary.

Such assumptions are *not certainties,* however. Although it was formerly thought that each criminal followed a certain MO and rarely changed from one type of crime to another or to committing the same type of crime in a different way, it is now known that some criminals commit several types of crimes and may change the type according to need, opportunity, inability to repeat certain types of crimes or greater sophistication. For example, a narcotics user may commit larceny, burglary or robbery to obtain money for drugs. A burglar may become too old to commit burglaries and may turn to shoplifting. Or a burglar may first steal checks and a check writer and then turn to forgery to cash the checks. Never eliminate suspects simply because their known MO does not fit the crime being investigated.

Goals of Criminal Investigations

The goal of criminal investigation would obviously seem to be to solve cases, to discover "whodunit." In reality, the goals of criminal investigation are not quite so simple.

- - - - - - - -

The goals of criminal investigation are to:

■ Determine whether a crime has been committed.

■ Legally obtain information and evidence to identify the responsible person.

■ Arrest the suspect.

■ Recover stolen property.

■ Present the best possible case to the prosecutor.

- - - - - - - -

While committing crimes, people may make mistakes. They almost always leave some type of evidence. They may overlook tangible evidence such as a jacket, pen, purse, piece of paper or card that connects them with a crime scene. Such evidence may be left for many reasons: carelessness, panic, underestimation of police capabilities, emotional or mental instability or the influence of drugs or alcohol. More often, however, criminals leave *trace evidence,* less-visible evidence such as fingerprints, small particles of glass or dirt, a faint footprint, body hairs or clothing fibers.

Investigators search for evidence using methods discussed fully in Chapter 4. Sometimes, however, little or no evidence exists. Thus, not all crimes are solvable. For example, a theft committed by a transient who enters a house through an open door, takes food (larceny), eats it and then leaves the area unseen is a crime not likely to be solved. A burglary committed by a person wearing gloves and whose footprints are washed away by a hard rain before police arrive will be more difficult to solve than if it had not rained. Often fingerprints are found but cannot be matched with any prints on file. Many cases have insufficient evidence, no witnesses and no informants to provide leads.

Learn to recognize when a case is unsolvable but only after all leads are exhausted. An FBI agent once remarked, "Any average person with training can pursue hot leads; it is the investigator who can develop leads when the trail grows cold who is the superior investigator." A successful investigation is one in which:

■ A logical sequence is followed.

■ All physical evidence is legally obtained.

■ All witnesses are effectively interviewed.

■ All suspects are legally and effectively interrogated.

■ All leads are thoroughly developed.

■ All details of the case are accurately and completely recorded and reported.

Investigators systematically seek evidence to identify the individual who committed a crime, locate the individual and obtain sufficient evidence to prove in court that the suspect is guilty beyond a reasonable doubt. Procedures to accomplish these goals are the focus of the remainder of this text. However, determining the truth is more important than obtaining a conviction or closing a case.

Basic Functions

Successful investigation involves a balance between scientific knowledge acquired by study and experience and the skills acquired by the artful application of learned techniques. Police portrayals in mystery stories and on radio and television seldom depict police investigations accurately.

Police investigations involve great attention to details, an exceptionally suspicious nature at the appropriate time, considerable training in the classroom and the field, an unusual ability to obtain information from diverse types of personalities under adverse circumstances and endless patience and perseverance.

- - - - - - - -

Investigators perform the following functions:

■ Provide emergency assistance.

■ Secure the crime scene.

■ Photograph, videotape and sketch.

■ Take notes and write reports.

■ Search for, obtain and process physical evidence.

■ Obtain information from witnesses and suspects.

■ Identify suspects.

■ Conduct raids, surveillances, stakeouts and undercover assignments.

■ Testify in court.

- - - - - - - -

These basic functions are discussed in Section Two. What is important at this point is to realize the complexity of and interrelationships among the various functions performed by investigators and the skills they must develop.

Criminal investigation has become more scientific over the years and more thoroughly grounded in natural laws and scientific principles. Nonetheless, investigators are frequently required to practice the "art" of investigation; that is, to rely on skill acquired by experience, study and observation rather than on scientific principles. They must develop the ability to see relationships between apparently unrelated facts and to question the apparently unquestionable.

Characteristics of an Effective Investigator

A good investigator is imaginative, creative, patient and persistent. Peak et al. suggest:

> In addition to performing the usual investigative functions, investigators must be able to think logically, comprehend and understand complex masses of data, communicate and relate well with other members of the agency, and understand the concepts of organized crime, intelligence collecting and civil liberties. They must also have self-discipline, patience, attention to detail, knowledge of the law and some understanding of scientific techniques. Deductive and inductive reasoning and decision-making abilities are also assets (1998, p. 165).

A good investigator also reads a lot about a variety of subjects. Regardless of title, pay or rank, investigative officers are more effective when they possess specific intellectual, psychological and physical characteristics.

Intellectual Characteristics

Investigators must absorb training and apply it to their work. They must know the elements of the crime, understand and be able to apply investigative techniques and be able to work with many different types of people. Exceptional intelligence is not a requisite trait of an effective investigator; objectivity, logic and common sense are more important.

- - - - - - - -

Effective investigators obtain and retain information, apply technical knowledge, and remain open minded, objective and logical.

- - - - - - - -

Investigators obtain vast amounts of information. They meet and talk with people from all walks of life—factory workers, professionals, males, females, adults and juveniles—and must adjust their approach to each. In addition, each crime scene must be absorbed and recalled, sometimes months or years later. Thus, accurate, complete, well-organized reports and records are essential.

Investigators also develop knowledge of and skill in investigative techniques such as interviewing and interrogating, photographing and sketching, searching, report writing and numerous other areas discussed in Section Two. Knowledge of and skill in investigative techniques are acquired through continuous training and experience, including academic classroom experiences, personal experiences, street learning and learning from others in the field.

The abilities to obtain and retain information and to use investigative techniques effectively are worth little without the ability to reason through a case. The mental process involved in investigation is extremely complex. Logic is indispensible and often involves *reverse thinking,* that is, working the case "backward." Why did an event happen? When? How? Who is culpable? Investigators must examine all possible cause-and-effect relations, find links and draw conclusions—but only after they thoroughly explore all alternatives.

Decision making is continual and, to be effective, must be based on facts. When investigators review information and evidence, they concentrate on what is known (facts) rather than on what is only probable (inferences), and they eliminate personal opinions as much as possible. With sufficient facts, investigators can make valid inferences, from which they can logically draw definite conclusions.

A **fact** is an action, an event, a circumstance or an actual thing done. In contrast, an **inference** is a process of reasoning by which a fact may be deduced. **Opinion** is personal belief. For example, an investigator called to the scene of a shooting finds a dead man with a revolver in his hand (fact) and a suicide note on the table (fact). The officer might *infer* that the man committed suicide. He or she might also hold the *opinion* that people who commit suicide are cowards. This opinion is irrelevant to the investigation. The inference, however, is critical. If the officer formulates a theory about the death based on suicide and sets out to prove the theory correct, much information and evidence may be ignored.

Although investigators must draw inferences and form theories, they must also remain open minded and willing to consider alternatives. Preconceived ideas hinder good investigation. Objectivity is essential in investigation. Whenever an inference is drawn, its validity should be tested by examining the facts on which it is based. All alternatives should be considered; otherwise, valuable time may be lost, evidence may disappear or the case may simply remain unsolved.

The hazards of drawing premature conclusions are illustrated by a homicide case in which lie-detection tests were given to two main suspects. Suspect A was given two polygraph tests by separate operators. Both tests indicated that he was deceptive on critical questions concerning the case. Suspect B was given a lie-detection voice-stress test that indicated he was truthful on the same questions. Based on these results, the investigators concentrated on discovering evidence to link Suspect A to the crime and ignored Suspect B. After six months of following up leads that turned into dead ends, the investigators resumed their investigation of Suspect B and discovered enough evidence to persuade him to confess to the crime.

The point of this illustration is *not* that lie-detection tests are invalid. In fact, correlation between positive test results and suspect involvement or guilt is very high. The point is that no one fact should dominate an entire investigation. All alternatives should be considered. In our illustrative case, Suspect B had taken six tranquilizers before taking the test, which made interpretation more difficult. Suspect A may have been involved in an unrelated homicide or may simply have been extremely nervous because he was a prime suspect. Perseverance eventually revealed the truth despite evidence apparently to the contrary.

Psychological Characteristics

Certain psychological characteristics are indispensible to effective investigation.

- - - - - - - -

Effective investigators are emotionally well balanced, detached, inquisitive, suspecting, discerning, self-disciplined and persevering.

- - - - - - - -

Investigation is highly stressful and involves many decisions. Therefore, it requires emotional stability. Officers who are overly defensive or overly sensitive may fall victim to stress. Investigators must also absorb abuse and at the same time show kindness and empathy. Further, they must remain detached and uninvolved; otherwise the problems of those with whom they are in contact will decrease their objectivity. Personal involvement with individuals associated with a case under investigation not only hinders the investigation but also poses a direct threat to the investigator's emotional well-being.

Although remaining detached and objective, effective investigators are intimately involved with every aspect of the case. They do not accept things at face value; rather, they question what they hear and see. They use their knowledge of human nature to determine the truth of what is said. People often lie or tell half-truths, but this does not necessarily mean they are criminals.

With experience, investigators develop a sense for who is telling the truth, who has important information and who is acting suspiciously. The ability to distinguish the ordinary from the extraordinary and the normal from the suspicious is a hallmark of an effective investigator.

In addition, investigators must be self-disciplined and able to organize their time. Success often depends on an investigator's developing efficient work habits, setting priorities and using time wisely. Closely related to self-discipline is the willingness to persevere, to "stick with it" as long as is reasonable. Investigation often involves hours or even days of waiting and watching, of performing tedious, boring assignments that may or may not yield information or evidence helpful to the case. Thus, patience and perseverance are often the key to successful investigation.

Investigators often experience cases in which facts, reason and logic seem to lead nowhere. Yet, when the case is about to be closed, by chance, additional clues surface. An obscure newspaper item, an anonymous phone tip, an overheard remark at a social function or even a series of events having no apparent connection with the case may provide leads for further investigation. Many cases are solved when investigators develop leads and pursue both relevant and seemingly irrelevant information. This is where the art of investigation supersedes the science of investigation.

Perseverance, coupled with inquisitiveness and intuition, are indispensable in difficult cases. Although some deny the existence or worth of intuition, hundreds of experienced investigators attest to its value. **Intuition** is a "sudden knowing" without conscious reasoning or apparent logic. Based on knowledge and experience, it is commonly referred to as *street sense*. It is the urge to proceed with no apparent valid reason, a "gut feeling" developed through experience.

For example, while I (W. Bennett) was director of public safety for a suburban community, a series of car thefts occurred in a neighborhood shopping center. One day a patrol sergeant came into my office to discuss the matter. I suggested we go to a gravel pit near the shopping center to look around. We did so, and, as luck would have it, several youths were in the gravel pit painting a car. We talked with them and then checked the car's registration, as it had not been reported stolen. When we contacted the registered owner, he said his wife had taken the car to the shopping center. Because the youths had no logical explanation for their actions, we took them to the station for questioning. It turned out they were responsible for the theft of more than a dozen vehicles from the shopping center. The case was solved by a combination of my hunch about the gravel pit and

Most police academies teach new recruits self-defense techniques.

the pure happenstance that the hunch occurred at precisely the same time as one of the thefts.

Although perseverance is desirable, it should not be confused with a stubborn refusal to admit a case is not likely to be solved. Additionally, investigators must exercise good judgment that incorporates a good sense of timing.

Farrar (1999, p. 68) stresses that intuition should not be overlooked as part of an investigator's "arsenal." He recounts an instance when he became aware of a beam of light shining in his passenger window. Because he was tired, he ignored his initial instinct that it "just didn't look right" (JDLR) and drove on. But he kept looking over his shoulder and finally was compelled to investigate. Following the beam of light, he discovered a passenger car 200 feet from the freeway jammed into some trees. The driver was obviously dead, but the passenger was alive. Farrar radioed for help. His advice: "JDLR is a powerful response. Trust your instincts. You might prolong your own life or that of another human being."

Physical Characteristics

Age, height and weight, unless they are extreme, are not important characteristics for investigators. However, some physical characteristics are important.

Effective investigators are physically fit and have good vision and hearing.

Good health and a high energy level are beneficial because the hours spent performing investigative duties can be long and demanding. In addition to being physically fit, investigators are aided by keen vision and hearing. If uncorrected, color blindness, nearsightedness, night blindness and farsightedness may impair investigative effectiveness. Hearing is especially important when darkness limits vision. Keen hearing helps to estimate the nearness of a suspect, the movement of animals or people, the direction of gunfire or other detonations and the direction of foot sounds. In addition, investigators may have to listen to words during sobbing, moans and hysteria; hear a very weak voice from a seriously wounded or dying person; listen to more than one person talking at a time; or conduct an interview while a plane is flying overhead, machinery is operating or heavy traffic is passing by.

All these intellectual, psychological and physical characteristics may be needed in the preliminary investigation of a crime.

The Preliminary Investigation: Basic Considerations

An investigation starts with a direction to proceed to a scene. Department policy defines not only who is to respond but also the duties of these individuals, as well as those of evidence technicians, investigators, supervisors and command personnel. The first officer who responds is in charge until relieved by another officer. The same basic procedures are followed regardless of whether the first officer at the scene is a patrol officer, an investigator or the chief of police.

The initial response is usually by a patrol officer assigned to the area where a crime has occurred.

The Initial Response

After notification, either through direct observation or departmental communications, officers go to the scene as rapidly and safely as circumstances permit. A crime response survey conducted by the Law Enforcement Assistance Administration (LEAA) revealed that a response time of one minute or less is necessary to increase the probability of arrest at the scene. Most police departments, however, cannot assure their citizens of such a short response time, even for emergencies. To provide a one-minute response time, police agencies would need much smaller patrol areas, much larger staffs, computer-dispatched vehicles and personnel and, thus, much larger budgets.

It is important to arrive at a crime scene rapidly because:

■ The suspect may still be at or near the scene.

■ Injured persons may need emergency care.

■ Witnesses may still be at the scene.

■ A dying person may have a confession or other pertinent information to give.

■ Weather conditions may change or destroy evidence.

■ Someone may attempt to alter the crime scene.

The responding officers proceed to the scene as quickly as safety allows. Officers who injure themselves or someone else on the way to a call may create more serious problems than exist at the crime scene. They may, in fact, open themselves, their department and even their city to a civil lawsuit.

The seriousness of a crime and whether it is in progress are important factors in the rapidity of response. The driving speed and use of emergency lights and siren depend on the information furnished. A siren speeds arrival, but it also prompts the criminal to flee the scene. On the other hand, in a violent crime against a person, a siren alerts the offender but may prevent further vio-

Police officers planning routes to high-crime areas. Preplanning can be critical to rapid response time.

lence. Sometimes the victim, to avoid attracting attention, requests that no sirens and red lights be used.

The route taken is also discretionary. Officers should know which streets are under construction in their areas and avoid them. They must also choose between the fastest route and the route the suspect might use to leave the scene. When approaching a scene, officers should observe people leaving the scene and make mental descriptions of them. If two officers are in the patrol vehicle, one may write descriptions of people and vehicles observed leaving the scene. Many officers use tape recorders for such observations. This equipment permits either a single officer or the second person in a two-officer car to record while proceeding to the scene.

If other officers are available, they are alerted to cover escape routes rather than go directly to the scene. While driving to the scene, officers formulate a plan of action based on the type of crime and its location.

An immediate response may be crucial because, even if no immediate arrest is made, the amount of information that can be obtained is directly related to the speed of response. Initial information is often the most important and accurate. Many departments are developing necessary guidelines for rapid responses, replacing the assumption that all calls for service should be responded to as rapidly as possible.

Other departments are finding that sending several vehicles to a crime scene may not be the most effective approach. The Phoenix Police Department, for example, responds to a scene where a crime has "just occurred" by sending only two vehicles. Other units proceed to major intersections to observe traffic coming from the direction of the crime scene, called the "Bullseye." Success depends on broadcasting the suspects' descriptions rapidly and getting to the major intersections quickly. The Phoenix Police Department found that "Operation Bullseye" resulted in catching the suspects about 80 percent of the time. In addition, armed robberies, a crime well suited for this approach, decreased by 30 percent.

The Point of Arrival

When the first officers arrive, the scene may be either utter confusion or deserted. Regardless of the situation, the officers must take charge immediately and form a plan for proceeding.

People at a crime scene are usually excited, apprehensive and perplexed. They may be cooperative or uncooperative, confused or lucid. Therefore, officers must be flexible and understanding. Discretion and good judgment are essential because the greatest potential for solving the case lies with those present at the scene, even though many details of the crime may not be known at this stage.

More decisions are made in less time at the point of arrival than at any other stage in the investigation, and this is when officers obtain the majority of leads for subsequent action.

Setting Priorities

Circumstances at the scene often dictate what is done first. The priorities are as follows:

--- --- --- --- --- ---

- Handle emergencies first.
- Secure the scene.
- Investigate.

--- --- --- --- --- ---

Adapt the following guidelines to fit specific circumstances.

A police officer waves away press and onlookers from the scene of a shooting outside the White House.

Handling Emergency Situations

Sometimes emergencies dictate procedure. An **emergency** might include a dangerous suspect at or near the scene or a gravely injured person. For example, if you arrive at a crime scene and the suspect begins to shoot at you, apprehending the suspect obviously becomes your first priority. In other instances, a person may be so seriously injured that without immediate care, death is probable. Such emergencies take precedence over all other procedures.

Good judgment and the number of available officers dictate what should occur first if more than one emergency exists. Sometimes the decision is difficult. For example, if a victim is drowning, a suspect is running away and only one officer is at the scene, the officer must make a split-second decision. Usually, saving life takes precedence. However, if the officer can do nothing to save the victim, the best alternative is to pursue the suspect. Apprehension may save other victims.

Responding to emergency situations causes one's adrenaline to flow. At the same time, you must plan your approach. One officer facing a life-or-death situation said he thought of a quotation: "Death must be a beautiful moment; otherwise they wouldn't save it until last." Holding this thought, he carried out his immediate responsibilities without hesitation.

You should also attempt to think like the suspect. Decide which escape routes you would use and block them. The information you have about the situation will help you decide whether using lights and siren is advantageous to you or to the suspect. Think what you would do if you were the suspect and you were cornered at the crime scene. If it is daytime, you may be visible and the suspect not. If it is nighttime, you may be able to take advantage of a darker area for your approach.

Flexibility is essential. Assess the situation because each incident is different and requires different approaches and techniques. Be cognizant that more than one suspect may be present. Check your equipment on the way to the scene. Provide the dispatcher with all pertinent information. Maintaining some distance can facilitate observation and give you time to make decisions that will enhance your safety.

A Suspect at or Near the Scene
If a call is made rapidly enough and officers can respond quickly, they may observe the crime in progress and arrest the suspect at the scene.

> Any suspect at the scene should be detained, questioned and then released or arrested, depending on circumstances.

Departmental policy determines whether the first officer at the scene thoroughly interrogates a suspect. Before any interrogation, an officer must read the Miranda warning (a legality discussed in Chapter 6) to the suspect. Even if the policy is that officers do not interrogate suspects, officers often use discretion. For example, they may have to take a dying declaration or a suspect's spontaneous confession. If this occurs, a statement is taken immediately because the suspect may refuse, or be unable, to cooperate later. A more formal interrogation and written confession can be obtained later at the police department.

The suspect is removed from the scene as soon as possible to minimize the destruction of evidence and to facilitate questioning. The sooner suspects are removed, the less they can observe of the crime scene and possible evidence against them.

If the Suspect Has Recently Fled
If the suspect has just left the scene, immediate action is required. If the information is provided early enough, other units en route to the scene might make an arrest.

> If a suspect has recently left the scene, obtain a description of the suspect, any vehicles, direction of travel and any items taken. Dispatch the information to headquarters immediately.

As soon as practical, obtain more detailed information about the suspect's possible whereabouts, friends, descriptions of stolen items and other relevant information regarding past criminal records and modus operandi.

If a Person Is Seriously Injured
Emergency first aid to victims, witnesses and suspects is often a top priority of arriving officers. Sustaining life and minimizing injuries may override all other considerations. Call for medical assistance and then do whatever is possible until help arrives. Observe and record the condition of the injured person, the type of injury, its location and the victim's general condition.

If a person is injured so severely that he or she must be removed from the scene, instruct attending medical personnel to listen to any statements or utterances the victim makes and to save all clothing for evidence. If the injured person is a suspect, a police officer almost always accompanies the suspect to the hospital. The humanitarian priority of administering first aid may have to become second priority if a dangerous suspect is still at or near the scene because others may be injured or killed.

If a Dead Body Is at the Scene
A body at the crime scene may immediately become the center of attention, and even a suspect might be overlooked. If the victim is obviously dead, leave the body just as it is found but protect it and its surroundings. Identifying the body is not an immediate concern. Preserving the scene is more important because it may later yield clues about the dead person's identity, the cause of death and the individual responsible.

Protecting the Crime Scene

Securing the crime scene is a major responsibility of the first officers to arrive. Everything of a nonemergency nature is delayed until the scene is protected.

At outdoor scenes, weather conditions such as heat, wind, rain, snow or sleet can alter or destroy physical evidence. In addition, people may accidentally or intentionally disturb the scene. Additions to the scene can be as disconcerting to later investigation as the removal of evidence.

Explain to bystanders that protecting the crime scene is critical and that the public must be excluded. Treat them courteously but firmly. A delicate part of public relations is dealing with the family of someone who has been killed. Explain what you are doing and why. Help them understand that you must take certain steps to discover what happened and who is responsible.

Crime scene protection can be as simple as locking a door to a room or building, or it can involve roping off a large area outdoors. Within a room, you can use chairs or boxes to cordon off an area. Many officers carry rope in their vehicle for this purpose and attach a sign that says, "CRIME SCENE—DO NOT ENTER."

Station a guard to maintain security. If all officers are busy with emergency matters, ask a citizen to help protect the area temporarily. In such cases, record the citizen's name, address and phone number in your notes. Give the person specific instructions and minimal duties. The citizen's main duty is to protect the crime scene by barring entrance and to keep passersby moving along. You might instruct the citizen this way: "Do not let any person into this area except police who identify themselves with a badge. Keep spectators moving away from the scene." Relieve the citizen from guard duty as soon as possible and thank him or her for the assistance.

Sometimes other officers arriving at the scene can cause problems by ignoring posted warnings and barriers. *Ironically, police officers with no assigned responsibilities at a scene are often the worst offenders.* Inform arriving officers and everyone present at the scene of what has happened and what you want them to do. Ask other officers to help preserve the scene, interview witnesses or search for evidence.

- - - - - - - - -

Take all necessary measures to secure the crime scene—including locking, roping, barricading and guarding—until the preliminary investigation is completed.

- - - - - - - - -

Protect evidence from destruction or alteration by the elements by covering it until photographing and measuring can be done. Sometimes investigators must move evidence before they can examine it. For example, a vehicle covered with snow, dust or other materials can be moved into a garage. In one case a car used in a kidnapping was found four days later in a parking lot. Snow that had fallen since the kidnapping covered the car. To process the car's exterior for fingerprints, investigators took the car to a garage to let the snow melt and the surface dry.

Conducting the Preliminary Investigation

After all emergency matters have been handled and the crime scene has been secured, the actual preliminary investigation can begin. This includes several steps, whose order depends on the specific crime and the types of evidence and witnesses available.

- - - - - - - - -

Responsibilities during the preliminary investigation include:

- Measuring, photographing, videotaping and sketching the scene.
- Searching for evidence.
- Identifying, collecting, examining and processing physical evidence.
- Questioning victims, witnesses and suspects.
- Recording all statements and observations in notes.

- - - - - - - - -

Each of these procedures is explained in Section Two. At this point you are concerned with the total picture, the overview. In simple cases one officer may perform all these procedures; in complex cases responsibilities may be divided among several officers. Everything that occurs at a crime scene is recorded with photographs, videotape, sketches and complete, accurate notes. This record is the basis not only of future reports but also for future investigation and prosecution of the case.

Information may be volunteered by victims, witnesses or suspects at or very near to the time of the criminal actions. Unplanned statements about the "things done" by people present are called *res gestae* statements.

- - - - - - - - -

***Res gestae* statements** are spontaneous statements made at the time of a crime, concerning and closely related to actions involved in the crime. They are often considered more truthful than later, planned responses.

- - - - - - - - -

Res gestae statements are generally an exception to the hearsay rule because they are usually very closely related to facts and are, therefore, admissible in court.

Record *res gestae* statements in your notes, and have the person making them sign or initial them so there is no question of your misunderstanding or of the person later denying having made the statement.

Field Tests Numerous field tests can help investigators in the preliminary examination and are less expensive than full laboratory examinations. They save investigators' time by identifying evidence that may have little chance of yielding positive results in the laboratory. The purpose of these tests is to discover clues, and they are used on only a small number of specific items of evidence located at crime scenes. If a field test is affirmative, the evidence is submitted to a laboratory for a more detailed, expert examination whose results can then be presented in court.

Investigators often want to know if evidence discovered is what they think it is—for example, a bloodstain or an illegal substance. Field test kits help in this determination. Investigators can use field tests to develop and lift fingerprints; discover flammable substances through vapor and fluid examination; detect drugs, explosive substances on hands or clothing, imprints of firearms on hands or bullet-hole residue; and conduct many other tests. Local, state and federal police laboratories can furnish information on currently available field test kits and may also provide training in their use.

Determining Whether a Crime Has Been Committed and When
As soon as possible during the preliminary investigation, it is necessary to determine whether a crime has, in fact, been committed.

- - - - - - - -

Determine whether a crime has been committed by knowing the elements of each major offense, the evidence that supports them and ascertaining whether they are present. Try to determine when the event occurred.

- - - - - - - -

Individual elements of various offenses are discussed in Sections Three and Four.

Observe the condition of the scene and talk to the complainant as soon as possible. After discussing the offense with the victim or complainant, determine whether a specific crime has been committed. It is common for crime victims to misclassify what has occurred. For example, they may report a burglary as a robbery. In addition, state statutes differ in their definitions of the elements of certain crimes. For example, in some states entering a motor vehicle with intent to steal is larceny. In other states it is burglary. Determining when the event occurred is critical for checking alibis and reconstructing the modus operandi.

If no crime has been committed, explain the circumstances to the complainant. If it is a civil rather than a criminal situation, suggest where the victim can obtain assistance.

Establishing a Command Center
In complex cases involving many officers, a command center may be set up where information about the crime is gathered and reviewed. This center receives summaries of communications, police reports, autopsy results, laboratory reports, results of interviews, updates on discovered evidence and tips. Personnel at the center keep files of news releases and news articles and prepare an orderly, chronological progress report of the case for police command, staff and field personnel. If the investigation becomes lengthy, the command center can be moved to police headquarters.

Dealing with the News Media
A close, almost symbiotic relationship exists between the police and the news media. They depend upon each other. The media serve the public's right to know within legal and reasonable standards, a right protected by the First Amendment. The public is always hungry for news about crime. The police, on the other hand, are responsible for upholding the Sixth and Fourteenth Amendment guarantees of the right to a fair trial and the protection of a suspect's rights. This often necessitates confidentiality. Further, making some information public would impair or even destroy many investigations. On the other hand, the police rely on the media to disseminate news about wanted suspects or to seek witnesses from the community. Many cases are solved because of information from citizens. Furthermore, notes Rosenthal (1998, p. 44): "The media are crucially important to the image of a department. Without proper media training, the public image of a department suffers."

Thus the media and the police must understand and respect each other's roles and responsibilities. Citizens' First Amendment rights must be balanced against safe and competent law enforcement and an individual's right to privacy. Media access to police information is neither comprehensive nor absolute. In general, the media have no right to enter any area to which the public does not have access, and all rules at cordoned-off crime scenes are as applicable to the media as they are to the general public. On the other hand, police may not construct a "cocoon" of secrecy. Neither should regard the other as the enemy. Rosenthal (1999b, p. 16) states that: "Law enforcement can and *should* work *with* the media, so the media don't work *on* law enforcement. Cooperation works, confrontation doesn't."

Despite the need for cooperation, complaints from both sides are prevalent. News reporters complain that police withhold important information and are uncooperative. The police, on the other hand, may complain that reporters interfere with cases, lack sensitivity, frequently

A Los Angeles police officer and a television cameraman photograph one of several police vehicles that were shot up during a botched bank robbery.

report inaccurately and tend to sensationalize. Shemeligian (1996, p. 31) notes: "There is an innate distrust of journalists by police officers, and it's strong enough to, for example, prevent a small-town police department from broadcasting details about a major crime on the radio—just to thwart reporters." A tragic example of this desire to keep details from the media was seen in the 1993 kidnapping and murder of 12-year-old Polly Klaas in northern California. Shemeligian (p. 31) reports:

> Two hours after Klaas was kidnapped from her home in Petaluma, two Sonoma County Sheriff's deputies spotted suspect Richard Allen Davis leaning up against his car in a woodsy area 27 miles north of Petaluma.
>
> Davis later told officers that he had taken Polly up a hill and left her while he had tried to get his car freed from a ditch. Police still do not know whether Polly was alive at the time.
>
> When the officers approached, they noticed that Davis, who was smoking, had bits of brush in his hair and on his clothing. He was sweating profusely on his forehead.
>
> Davis said he was lost. The deputies didn't believe him, but a warrant check turned up nothing.
>
> Then according to news reports of the ongoing murder trial of Davis, the deputies helped pull the suspect's car free.
>
> "The deputies didn't know a kidnapping had occurred because the Petaluma Police Department had

asked other police agencies not to send out information by radio, where the media could overhear," writes *Sacramento Bee* reporter Patrick Hoge.

> Davis later told detectives that he waited a while and then drove back to the woodsy area to retrieve Polly.

Most members of the media understand the restrictions at a crime scene and cooperate. It is necessary to exercise firmness with those who do not follow instructions and even to exclude them if they jeopardize the investigation. Give only facts—not opinions. Give the name of someone who has been killed *only* after a careful identity check and notification of relatives. Do not release any information on the cause of death; the medical examiner determines this. Do not express legal opinions about the specific crime or the perpetrator.

Rosenthal (1999a, p. 25) suggests: "Be accurate with information. If you don't know something, don't fill in the blanks. There's nothing wrong with saying, 'I don't know.' Be truthful with reporters. They know there are certain parts of operations that can't be talked about."

Some departments use public information officers (PIOs). Other departments assign the highest-ranking officer at the time of an incident or use written information releases. Woodall (1998, p. 72) observes: "If there is a written media policy in place, confusion, interference and misunderstandings between the agency and the media can be avoided."

The Follow-Up Investigation

Preliminary investigations that satisfy all the criteria for good investigation do not necessarily yield enough information to prosecute a case. Despite a thorough preliminary investigation, many cases require a follow-up investigation. A need for a follow-up investigation does not necessarily reflect poorly on those who conducted the preliminary investigation. Often factors exist that are beyond the officers' control: Weather can destroy evidence before officers arrive at a scene; witnesses can be uncooperative; and evidence may be weak or nonexistent, even after a very thorough preliminary investigation.

The follow-up phase builds on what was learned during the preliminary investigation. It can be conducted by the officers who responded to the original call or, most often, by detectives or investigators, depending on the seriousness and complexity of the crime and the size of the department. If investigators take over a case begun by patrol officers, coordination is essential.

Investigative leads that may need to be pursued include checking the victim's background; talking to informants; determining who would benefit from the crime and who had sufficient knowledge to plan the crime; tracing weapons and stolen property; and searching modus operandi, mug shot and fingerprint files. Specific follow-up procedures for the major offenses are discussed in Sections Three, Four and Five.

Investigative Planning

Bowker (1999, p. 23) maintains that a properly formulated investigative plan:

- Focuses on the investigative process to ensure that all offense elements are addressed.

- Limits unnecessary procedures and step duplication.

- Coordinates the investigative activities of numerous personnel on large cases.

- Provides stability to the investigation if staff changes occur.

- Enhances communication with prosecuting officials by providing an outline of the investigation and identifying strengths and weaknesses in the case.

- Provides a framework for the final report.

- Becomes a training aid for inexperienced staff members.

A written investigative plan contains four basic components—predication, elements to prove, preliminary steps and investigative steps.

Predication is a brief statement justifying the opening of a case. Bowker (p. 23) notes three features of predication: the basic allegation, the source of the allegation and the date the allegation was made. *Elements to prove* include all the specific components detailed in state or federal statutes and any special jurisdictional issues that define a criminal violation. *Preliminary steps* are the methods investigators use to obtain basic background information on the complainant, the victim and the suspect. *Investigative steps* consider the basic parameters required to establish that a crime has occurred and include the individuals who will be interviewed and the records that will be obtained and examined. Bowker (p. 24) observes that: "Investigative steps should parallel the elements that need to be proven."

Bowker concludes that: "Investigators should seriously consider keeping copies of investigative plans on computer. Once they develop a plan for a particular case, they can continue to use it as a model, or boilerplate, for similar cases" (p. 25).

Computer-Aided Investigation

Computers have significantly affected police operations. In addition to their obvious contribution to record keeping and statistical analysis, computers are becoming increasingly important in criminal investigations.

Diaz (1999, p. 53) notes three important computer functions that assist investigators:

- Quickly and efficiently access existing information such as fingerprint records and DNA tests, parking tickets and pawnshop tickets.

- Capture new information and store it compactly for instant transmission anywhere in the world.

- Analyze data for patterns (as in various forms of crime mapping) and manipulate digital representations to enhance video images, eliminate clutter from sound recordings, create three-dimensional images, re-create and visually track a sequence of events or analyze blood splatter patterns.

One software program, PowerCase, is an effective case management tool with applications for investigations involving homicides, drug-related offenses, fraud and other crimes (Kanable, 1999, p. 58). It keeps track of evidence gathering and stores witness statements and other reports. Furthermore, Kanable reports (p. 60): "Among the new strengths of PowerCase3 is incident linking, which enables investigators to extend their research across multiple investigations. . . . Another new feature is the ability to support multi-media attachments. Examples include storing and linking photographs, video clips and audio clips to documents, creating a permanent record of interviews."

In addition to innovative software, the Internet has become an invaluable tool to law enforcement. Morrison (1997a, p. 56) comments on the "gold mine waiting at the end of the Web—much of it available for free. There's so much information available to investigators on the Internet these days, that one might not even have to leave his or her office to collect info that might have once taken him or her all over the city on a wild goose chase." Dobeck (1997, p. 35) asserts: "To continue to be effective in the 21st century, law enforcement must meet the challenge of cyberspace and learn to take advantage of the dedicated law enforcement resources and information available through the Internet."

And although some agencies have yet to realize the full potential of Internet access, many others are already capitalizing on the multiple benefits of being online. Strandberg (1998c, p. 59) observes

that: "Law enforcement agencies are developing websites at an incredible rate, and opening their doors wide to the global electronic community." Such websites enable departments to promote their crime prevention programs, provide crime prevention tips to the general public and let people know about the officers serving in their community, an aspect which one lieutenant says "puts a human touch on our officers and lets people see that we aren't that different from everyone else" (Strandberg, 1998c, p. 59).

The Internet offers hundreds of thousands of websites to aid informed investigators. Morrison (1998, pp. 27–28) maintains that:

> Once you have loaded these sites into your bookmarks or favorites list, you can access them in a matter of seconds. . . .
> www.lawguru.com offers searchable law directories for most states. . . .
> www.mapquest.com will take you anywhere you need to go. . . .
> www.switchboard.com has some interesting information on locating people, businesses and e-mail addresses.
> There are some sites where you will find hard to get information such as unlisted telephone numbers, pay phone traces, etc. www.sourceresource.com is a good example. The fees range from $45.00 to $69.00. If you consider the amount paid on the street for information everyday by law enforcement, these prices are bargains.

Wolf (1998, p. 31) gives a vivid example of how the Internet was used to capture Leslie Rogge. Rogge escaped from federal custody in Idaho in 1985 and for 11 years eluded capture, living undetected in South America. Then, in 1995, the FBI started using the Internet to search for wanted fugitives. Rogge's photo was added to the FBI's "Ten Most Wanted" homepage. A Guatemalan Internet surfer recognized Rogge's picture and contacted the authorities. The FBI became the first to capture a fugitive with its website.

Another crime-fighting tool finding its way into law enforcement is the computer scanner. Stockton (1998, p. 71) reports that: "Scanners can take conventional photos and convert them to electronic files. Those files in turn can be used to quickly make wanted bulletins or press releases. They can also be sent, in seconds, to other law enforcement agencies across the country."

continued

Innovations in computer technology have expanded beyond the station house and desk top into the hands of officers on the street. Strandberg (1998a, p. 30) notes: "Every year, the hardware . . . gets faster, more feature packed—and less expensive. . . . Ruggedized computers are standard laptop computers designed for the real world. . . . Known as the 'Rambos' of laptops, these computers can survive drops, car chases and much more." Wireless communication, the next wave of information technology, also enhances officer safety by relaying data rapidly, accurately and securely (p. 32). Officers are also able to complete and submit reports from their patrol cars using report-writing software and wireless transmission systems, thus allowing them to stay in the field without having to continuously report back to the office (Dees, 1999, p. 87). Such technology enhances officer efficiency and productivity.

arrests in relationship to schools, liquor stores or landmarks; target accident prone intersections and much more.

Criminal investigation frequently relies on data collected by more than one officer and more than one agency. Data collected during criminal investigations can be extremely valuable to the problem-oriented policing that many departments are adopting. Investigators can analyze data to determine groups of problems rather than isolated incidents. Once specific underlying problems are identified, departments can seek alternative approaches to reduce or eliminate the incidence of particular crimes.

The subject of problem-solving policing is beyond the scope of this text, but it is an important trend that deserves attention. The information obtained today during routine criminal investigations may provide the basis for vitally important new knowledge in the future.

Crime Analysis and Problem-Oriented Policing

Computers are also being used to analyze data. Strandberg (1998b, p. 41) reports:

> Analysis of crime is one of the things computers are very well suited for, crunching numbers and evaluating objective trends, and one of the most effective ways of analyzing crime involved mapping the crime and examining trends. This was once done with a huge map on the wall and with pushpins, but with today's hardware and software, it can now be done on the computer, with incredible results.

Such digital mapping can highlight problem areas, thus enabling managers and captains to more effectively redraw patrol areas to balance the workload in high-crime areas (Sherman, 1998, p. 75).

Developments in technology have enabled even the smallest law enforcement agencies to participate in the latest methods of crime analysis. Collins (1997, p. 80) notes that mapping software permits small agencies to use big-city crime analysis techniques:

> Digital maps . . . help [with] flexible, dynamic beat staffing; establish incident patterns; locate parolees and other registrants; map drug

Investigative Productivity

Productivity has been of interest in the police field for some time. Major opposition to a focus on productivity in police work may arise because of alleged "quota systems" in issuing traffic citations. Productivity involves considerably more than issuing citations, however. Nearly all jobs have some standard of productivity, even though the job may not involve a production line.

A screening process to eliminate criminal investigations with low potential for being solved can often increase productivity. Many police departments screen investigations with a form that asks specific questions. If the answers to these questions are negative, the department either gives the case low priority for assignment or does not assign it at all.

Criminal investigation personnel have traditionally been evaluated by the number and type of cases assigned to them, the number of cases they bring to a successful conclusion, and the number of arrests and the amount of property they recover. The evaluations should also assess how well the officers use investigative resources and how well they perform overall within the department and in the community.

An advantage of continuous evaluation of productivity is that updating case status is possible at any time. Such information is useful not only for investigating but also for developing budgets, making additional case assignments, identifying modus operandi similarities among cases and responding to public inquiries.

The Investigative Function: The Responsibility of All Police Personnel

Early police organizations were one-unit/one-purpose departments with everyone performing generalized functions. However, over time, departments perceived a need for specialization. The first detective bureaus in the United States were established in Detroit in 1866 and then in New York in 1882. Investigation became specialized because of the following factors:

■ The need to know about criminals and their modus operandi

■ The amount of training necessary for learning and developing investigative techniques

■ The frequency with which investigators had to leave their assigned shifts and areas during an investigation

■ Patrol forces' heavy workloads

■ A general administrative philosophy that supported specialization as a means of increasing efficiency and therefore solving more crimes

In larger police departments, specialization developed first in investigative functions before it did in other areas such as traffic, crime prevention, juveniles and community relations. In departments with specialized investigative units, the investigative and patrol functions often experienced difficulty separating their respective duties. Duties often overlapped, decreasing efficient coordination.

Many of these difficulties have been overcome, but many others remain. Regardless of whether a department has specialists or generalists, their goal is the same: solving crimes.

- - - - - - - -

The ultimate responsibility for solving crimes lies with all police personnel. It must be a cooperative, coordinated departmental effort.

- - - - - - - -

All levels of police administration and operations contribute to successful investigations. Administrative decisions affect the selection and assignment of personnel as well as the policies regulating their performance.

In most larger departments, the investigative division remains a separate unit under its own command and supervisory personnel. The officer in charge reports directly to the chief of police or a chief of operations. Department policy specifies the roles of and the relationships among the administrative, uniformed patrol and investigative divisions. When these roles are clearly defined, the department can better achieve its common goals, with the investigative division fulfilling its assigned responsibilities in coordination with all other departments.

Today, however, researchers are studying the extent to which specialization should remain, its effectiveness, the number of personnel that should be assigned to specialized investigative functions and the selection and training required for such specialization. The following factors appear to support the training of all officers to perform investigative duties:

■ Increasing competition for tax monies

■ Possession of highly sophisticated equipment by some criminals

■ More criminals using multiple modus operandi

■ "Withdrawal syndrome" within the general public (The desire to remain uninvolved necessitates specialized training in interviewing techniques.)

■ Overwhelming workload of cases assigned to investigative personnel

■ More intelligent, better-educated police recruits

■ More police training available

In addition, most police officers' daily activities are investigative, even though the matters they investigate may not involve crimes. Therefore, the trend is for a few specialists to direct an investigation and for all officers to assume a more active role in investigating crimes. This role gives patrol officers more responsibility when responding to a call to proceed to a crime scene. It also enables them to conduct as much of the follow-up investigation as their shift and assigned areas of patrol permit. The importance of the patrol officer's investigative role cannot be overemphasized.

Traditionally, uniformed patrol has been considered the backbone of the police department and has been responsible for the initial response to a crime. Because they are the first to arrive, patrol officers are in an ideal position to do more than conduct the preliminary investigation. Experiments have shown that initial investigations by patrol officers can be as effective as those conducted by specialists. This is partly because the officers deal with the entire case.

This new challenge for patrol officers—involvement in the entire investigative process—creates interest in crime prevention as well as investigation. In addition, giving patrol officers increased responsibility for investigating crimes frees up detectives to concentrate on offenses that require detailed investigations as well as on cases that require them to leave the community to conduct special interviews or to pursue leads. The result is better investigation by the patrol officer of the more frequent, less-severe crimes.

Interrelationships with Others

Investigators do not work in a vacuum but rely heavily on assistance from numerous other individuals and agencies.

Investigators interrelate with uniformed patrol officers, dispatchers, the prosecutor's staff, the defense counsel, supervisors, physicians, the coroner or medical examiner, laboratories and citizens, including victims.

Uniformed Patrol

As noted, patrol officers are a vital part of the investigative process because they are usually the first to arrive at a crime scene. What patrol officers do or fail to do at the scene greatly influences the outcome of an investigation. The patrol officer, as the person daily in the field, is closest to potential crime and has probably developed contacts who can provide information.

A potential pitfall is lack of direct, personal communication between uniformed and investigative personnel, which can result in attitudinal differences and divisiveness. Communication problems can be substantially reduced by using a simple checklist describing the current investigative status of any cases jointly involving patrol and investigators. The form should include information such as that illustrated in Figure 1.1.

Patrol officers want to know what happens to the cases they begin. Officers who have been informed of the status of "their" cases report a feeling of work satisfaction not previously realized, increased rapport with investigative personnel and a greater desire to make good initial reports on future cases.

Dispatchers

In most cases, a police dispatcher is the initial contact between a citizen and a police agency. Most citizens call a police agency only a few times during their lives, and their permanent impression of the police may hinge on this contact and the citizens' perceptions of the police agency's subsequent actions.

This dispatcher of Putnam County, Florida, Sheriff's headquarters relays messages to officers on the road.

In addition, the information obtained by the dispatcher is often critical to the officer, the victim, other citizens and the success of the investigation. The accuracy of the information dispatched to the field officer or investigator may determine the success or failure of the case. In critical incidents, it can also make the difference between life, death or injury to the officer, the victim or others. The responding officer needs to know the exact nature and location of the incident. A direct radio, computer or phone line should be cleared until the officer arrives at the scene. All pertinent descriptions and information should be dispatched directly to the responding officer.

Prosecutor's Staff

Cooperation between investigators and the prosecutor's staff depends on the personalities involved, the time available, a recognition that it is in everyone's best interest to work together and an acceptance of everyone's investigative roles and responsibilities. Given sufficient time and a willingness to work together, better investigations and prosecutions result. When investigators have concluded

STATUS REPORT

To:
From:
Case #:
Date:

_____ Offense sent to prosecution	_____ Added offenses
_____ Cleared by arrest	_____ Not cleared by arrest
_____ Refused prosecution	_____ Unfounded
_____ Suspect developed	_____ Suspect released
_____ Suspect in custody	_____ Suspect known
_____ Property recovered	_____ No property recovered
_____ Case still open	_____ Case closed
_____ Good patrol report	_____ Incomplete patrol report
_____ Need further information; please call:	_____

FIGURE 1.1

Sample Checklist for Case Status Report

an investigation, they should seek the advice of the prosecutor's office. At this point the case may be prosecuted, new leads may be developed, or the case may be dropped, with both the investigator and the prosecutor's office agreeing that it would be inefficient to pursue it further.

The prosecutor's staff can give legal advice on statements, confessions, evidence, the search and necessary legal papers and may also provide new perspectives on the facts in the case. The prosecutor's office can review investigative reports, review evidence that relates to the elements of the offense, advise whether the proof is sufficient to proceed and assist in further case preparation.

Defense Counsel

Our legal system is based on the adversary system: the accused against the accusor. Although both sides seek the same goal—determining truth and obtaining justice—the adversarial nature of the system requires that contacts between the defense counsel and investigators should occur only on the advice of the prosecutor's office. Inquiries from the defense counsel should be referred to the prosecutor's office. If the court orders specific documents to be provided to the defense counsel, investigators must surrender the material, but they should seek the advice of the prosecution staff before releasing any documents or information.

Physicians, Coroners and Medical Examiners

If a victim at a crime scene is obviously injured and a doctor is called to the scene, saving life takes precedence over all aspects of the investigation. However, the physician is there for emergency treatment, not to protect the crime scene, so investigators must take every possible precaution to protect the scene during the treatment of the victim.

Physicians and medical personnel should be directed to the victim by the route through the crime scene that is least destructive of evidence. They should be asked to listen carefully to anything the victim says and to hold all clothing as evidence for the police.

The coroner or medical examiner is called if the victim has died. Coroners or medical examiners have the authority to investigate deaths to determine whether they were natural, accidental or the result of a criminal act. They can also provide information on the time of death and the type of weapon that might have caused the death.

Depending on the individual case, investigators and the medical examiner or coroner may work as a team, with an investigator present at the autopsy. The medical examiner or coroner may obtain samples of hair, clothing, fibers, blood and body organs or fluids as needed for later laboratory examination.

Garrison (1998, p. 97) notes: "A trained, experienced, full-time medical examiner is the backbone of any criminal investigation involving death. If the ME is too overworked, too understaffed or too politically inclined, the whole investigative process suffers."

Crime Laboratories

Crime laboratories employ specialists trained in **forensic science** or **criminalistics,** the application of physical and biological sciences and technology to the scientific examination of physical evidence. These laboratories examine many types of evidence, including documents, computers, paints, hairs, fibers, blood and other body fluids, safe insulation and various types of impressions. Examiners may use chemistry, radio engineering, cryptanalysis and physics. They may also use standards and reference files such as fraudulent check files and bank robbery files.

All law enforcement agencies now have access to highly sophisticated criminalistic examinations through local, state and federal laboratories and private laboratories. In larger cities the laboratory is usually located within the police department or in the same building. Smaller departments often use the forensic departments and crime laboratories of larger cities or the state crime lab facilities. When using the facilities of larger cities, smaller departments are usually charged a fee. Use of the state crime lab facilities is usually free. However, because of budget restrictions, some state laboratories now charge a fee. The state crime laboratory is usually located either in the state's largest city or in the state capital and can be used by all police agencies of the state. The FBI Laboratory in Washington, DC, is also available to all law enforcement agencies.

Selection of a laboratory is based on its capabilities and equipment, the quality of its work, distance, cost and availability of personnel to testify in court. Investigators need to be familiar with the laboratory facilities available in their particular area and the procedures and forms they require. There are 330 crime labs across the United States, and the level of expertise among lab technicians varies significantly. Pilant (1997, pp.35–36) points out:

> Training is doubly important in agencies where officers wear more than one hat. . . . There is a big margin between the well-trained, well-equipped metro agencies and the small agencies that don't have resources, where the guy who is the patrol officer is also the crime scene technician and the booking guy. If they are faced with a major crime, evidence collection is key. They need to have the training to handle it. You don't want them to miss something because they don't know the new techniques.

Some equipment is specifically designed for entry-level users, because many departments are financially unable to provide their lab technicians with extensive training, and they are unable to hire the work out to more sophisticated labs. For example:

> The MultiScope Fourier Transform-Infrared (FT-IR) Microscope . . . is an entry-level, problem-solving tool for forensics laboratories that need a rapid, simple method for screening, inspecting and identifying a wide range of micro-samples. . . . The MultiScope FT-IR miscroscope has fewer and simpler controls based on those of a standard laboratory optical microscope. Simple set-up makes it easy for entry-level users ("Forensics," 1999, p. 52).

Labs of all sizes and capabilities may also receive assistance from the Forensic Science Information Resource System, established in 1985 to help the FBI laboratory and the hundreds of state and local crime laboratories. The library contains more than 10,000 scientific and technical reference books and more than 350 journals. Indirectly, all law enforcement officers benefit by this increased knowledge available to crime laboratories. (Information about the vast services of this library can be obtained from: Librarian, Federal Bureau of Investigation, Room 3589, 10th and Pennsylvania Avenue NW, Washington, DC 20535.)

When no government-operated laboratories are available or they cannot perform required tests, private consultants or laboratories in the region must be used.

Private Laboratories

Many agencies hire private laboratories to examine crime evidence. Private laboratories can handle drug, fingerprint, toolmark, firearms, trace evidence, explosives and fire cases. Their turnaround time is usually much faster than that at state crime labs, and their results are usually accepted by the courts.

Citizens

Investigators are only as good as their sources of information. They seldom solve crimes without citizen assistance. In fact, citizens frequently provide the most important information in a case.

Witnesses to a crime should be contacted immediately to minimize their time involved and inconvenience. Information about the general progress of the case should be relayed to those who have assisted. This will maintain their interest and increase their desire to cooperate at another time.

Citizens can help or hinder an investigation. Frequently, citizens who have been arrested in the past have information about crimes and the people who commit them. The manner and attitude with which such citizens are contacted will increase or decrease their cooperation with the police, as discussed in Chapter 6.

In 1829 in England, Sir Robert Peel stated: "The police are the public and the public are the police." Scholars have pointed to this philosophy as the modern day roots of **community policing.** Miller and Hess note (1998, p.xxii):

> Community policing . . . is a philosophy, a belief that working together, the police and the community can accomplish what neither can accomplish alone. The *synergy* that results from community policing can be powerful. It is like the power of a finely tuned athletic team, with each member contributing to the total effort.

Victims

Almost every crime has a victim, and in many instances the victim receives the least attention and assistance. Even so-called victimless crimes often have innocent victims who are not directly involved in a specific incident. The victim is often the reporting person (complainant) and often has the most valuable information.

Police should keep victims informed of investigative progress unless releasing the information would jeopardize prosecution of the case or unless the information is confidential. The Federal Victimization Bill provides matching-fund assistance to states for victims of some crimes. Numerous states also have victimization funds that can be used for funeral or other expenses according to predetermined criteria. Police agencies should maintain a list of federal, state and local agencies, foundations and support groups that provide assistance to victims. Police should tell victims how to contact community support groups. For example, most communities have support groups for victims of sexual offenses—if not locally, then at the county or state level.

Investigating officers should also give victims information on future crime prevention techniques and temporary safety precautions. They should help victims understand any court procedures that involve them. Officers should tell victims whether local counseling services are available and whether there is a safe place where they can stay if this is an immediate concern.

In larger departments, psychological response teams are available. In smaller agencies, a chaplains' corps or clergy from the community may assist with death notifications and the immediate needs of victims.

Major-Case Task Forces

A *multidisciplinary* approach to case investigation uses specialists in various fields from within a particular jurisdiction. A *multijurisdictional* investigation, in contrast, uses personnel from different police agencies. Many metropolitan areas consist of 20 or more municipalities surrounding a core city. In a number of metropolitan areas, multijurisdictional major-case squads or metro crime teams have been formed, drawing the most talented investigative personnel from all jurisdictions. In addition, the services of federal, state or county police agency personnel may be used.

In some major cases—for example, homicides involving multijurisdictional problems, serial killers, police officer killings or multiple sex offenses—it is advisable to form a major-case task force from the jurisdictions that have major interests in the case. All evidence from the joint case is normally sent to the same laboratory to maintain continuity and consistency.

On the federal level, the Violent Criminal Apprehension Program (VICAP) has been created within the FBI to study and coordinate investigation of crimes of interstate and national interest. INTERPOL is an organization that coordinates information on international cases. Through INTERPOL all evidence concerning cases of mutual interest is collected, analyzed and provided to the member jurisdictions.

Many agencies are developing special investigation units, focusing resources and training efforts on specific local crime problems. Lesce (1998, pp.175–176) reports:

> The areas of interest to Special Investigations are wide. Among them are oversight of outlaw motorcycle gangs, extremist groups of both left and right wing coloration, and overtly criminal organizations. . . .
>
> Another important function is liaison. Analysts and agents maintain contact with national and international law enforcement bodies such as the International Police Organization (INTERPOL), the Law Enforcement Intelligence Unit (LEIU), the Financial Crimes Enforcement Network (FinCEN), and the National White Collar Crime Center (NWCCC).

Other areas commonly investigated by special units include drug trafficking and gaming enforcement.

A Fresno Violent Crime Suppression Unit (VCSU) officer detains a suspect as a Fresno police officer in traditional uniform cuffs him after an early-morning raid on a suspected drug house. The Fresno police instituted the VCSU after several years of increasing violent crime and shootings at the police.

Avoiding Civil Liability

Civil liability refers to a person's degree of risk of being sued. Anyone who acts under the authority of law and who violates another person's constitutional rights can be sued. Walsh (1997, p. 66) notes: "Civil suits against law enforcement agencies and their officers are clearly at an all-time high, and there is no decline in sight."

Officers must face the unfortunate reality that being sued goes with wearing the uniform. "It is a fact of life today that if you are an active police officer, a lawsuit with your name on it as 'defendant' is likely to be waiting for you just around the corner" (Young, 1996b, p. 8). Young (1996a, p. 8) further suggests: "Members of police departments throughout the country are so liability-conscious today that a state of 'lawsuit paranoia' hampers, constricts and otherwise handicaps the effective operation of law enforcement agencies."

One of the best ways to avoid lawsuits or to defend yourself if sued is to keep complete, accurate records of all official actions you take. Young (1996b, pp. 8, 10) suggests eight additional ways to avoid or minimize lawsuits.

- - - - - - - -

To avoid or minimize lawsuits:

■ Know the law.

■ Know your department's policies.

■ Become the best police officer possible.

■ Develop and fine-tune your policing skills further through education.

■ Sharpen your effectiveness in all aspects of human relations.

■ Officially report understaffing and equipment or vehicle needs and malfunctions.

■ Double-check a supervisor's orders and evaluate fellow officers' performance.

■ Unless it is a priority, do not get involved when off duty.

- - - - - - - -

Summary

A criminal investigation is the process of discovering, collecting, preparing, identifying and presenting evidence to determine what happened and who is responsible.

The goals of police investigation vary from department to department, but most investigations aim to:

■ Determine whether a crime has been committed.

■ Legally obtain sufficient information and evidence to identify the responsible person.

■ Locate and arrest the suspect.

■ Recover stolen property.

■ Present the best possible case to the prosecutor.

Among the numerous functions performed by investigators are providing emergency assistance; securing the crime scene; photographing, videotaping and sketching;

taking notes and writing reports; searching for, obtaining and processing physical evidence; obtaining information from witnesses and suspects; identifying suspects; conducting raids, surveillances, stakeouts and undercover assignments; and testifying in court.

All investigators—whether patrol officers or detectives—are more effective when they possess certain intellectual, psychological and physical characteristics. Effective investigators obtain and retain information, apply technical knowledge, and remain open minded, objective and logical. They are emotionally well balanced, detached, inquisitive, suspecting, discerning, self-disciplined and persevering. Further, they are physically fit and have good vision and hearing.

The first officer to arrive at a crime scene is usually a patrol officer assigned to the area. In any preliminary investigation, it is critical to establish priorities. Handle emergencies first and then secure the scene. Any suspect at the scene should be detained, questioned and then either released or arrested, depending on circumstances. If a suspect has recently left the scene, obtain a general description of the suspect, any vehicles, direction of travel and any items taken. Dispatch the information to headquarters immediately.

After emergencies are dealt with, the first and most important function is to protect the crime scene and evidence. Take all necessary measures to secure the crime scene—including locking, roping, barricading and guarding—until the preliminary investigation is completed.

Once the scene is secured, proceed with the preliminary investigation, which includes measuring, photographing, videotaping and sketching the scene; searching for evidence; identifying, collecting, examining and processing physical evidence; questioning victims, witnesses and suspects; and recording all statements and observations in notes. *Res gestae* statements are spontaneous statements made at the time of a crime, concerning and closely related to actions involved in the crime. They are often considered more truthful than later, planned responses. The crime scene is preserved through these records.

As soon as possible, determine whether a crime has been committed by knowing the elements of each major offense and the evidence that supports them and then ascertaining whether they are present. Also try to determine when the event occurred.

A properly formulated written investigative plan is vital and contains four basic components—predication, elements to prove, preliminary steps and investigative steps.

Even in police departments that have highly specialized investigation departments, the ultimate responsibility for solving crimes lies with all police personnel. It must be a cooperative, coordinated departmental effort. Cooperation and coordination of efforts is also required outside the police department. Investigators must interrelate not only with uniformed patrol officers but also with dispatchers, the prosecutor's staff, the defense counsel, physicians, the coroner or medical examiner, laboratories and citizens, including victims. Criminal investigation is, indeed, a mutual effort.

To avoid or minimize lawsuits, (1) know the law, (2) know your department's policies, (3) become the best police officer possible, (4) develop and fine-tune your policing skills further through education, (5) sharpen your effectiveness in all aspects of human relations, (6) officially report understaffing and equipment or vehicle needs and malfunctions, (7) double-check a supervisor's orders and evaluate fellow officers' performance and, (8) unless it is a priority, do not get involved when off duty.

Checklist

Preliminary Investigation

- Was a log kept of all actions taken by officers?
- Were all emergencies attended to first (First aid; detaining suspects; broadcasting information regarding suspects)?
- Was the crime scene secured and the evidence protected?
- Were photographs or videotapes taken?
- Were measurements and sketches made?
- Was all evidence preserved?
- Were witnesses interviewed as soon as possible and statements taken?

Questions

- How was the complaint received?
- What were the date and time it was received?
- What was the initial message received? (State the offense and location.)
- Where were you when the message was received?
- Who was with you at the time?

- Did you observe any suspicious persons or vehicles while en route to the scene?

- What time did you arrive at the scene?

- How light or dark was it?

- What were the weather conditions? Temperature?

- Were there other notable crime-scene conditions when you arrived?

- How did you first enter the scene? Describe in detail the exact position of doors or windows—open, closed, locked, glass broken, ajar, pried or smashed. Were the lights on or off? Shades up or down?

- Was the heating or air-conditioning on or off? Was a television, radio or stereo on?

- Were dead or injured persons at the scene?

- What injuries to persons did you observe? Was first aid administered?

- What type of crime was committed?

- Was the time the crime occurred estimated?

- Who was the first contact at the scene? Name, address and telephone number.

- Who was the victim? Name, address, telephone number. Was the victim able to give an account of the crime?

- What witnesses were at the scene? Names, addresses and telephone numbers.

- Were unusual noises heard—shots, cars, screams, loud language, prying or breaking noises?

- Had clocks stopped?

- Were animals at the scene?

- Was an exact description of the suspect obtained? Physical description, jewelry worn, unusual voice or body odors; unusual marks, wounds, scratches, scars; nicknames used; clothing; cigarettes or cigars smoked; weapon used or carried; direction of leaving the scene?

- Was a vehicle involved? Make, model, color, direction, unusual marks?

- Were items taken from the scene? Exact description?

- What was done to protect the crime scene physically?

- What officers were present during the preliminary investigation?

- Were specialists called to assist? Who?

- Was the coroner or medical examiner notified?

- What evidence was discovered at the scene? How was it collected, identified, preserved? Were field tests used?

Discussion Questions

1. What are the advantages of assigning all investigations to specialists? What disadvantages does this pose? Which approach do you support?

2. Of all the suggested characteristics required for an effective investigator, which three are the most critical? Are these qualifications more stringent than those required for a patrol officer?

3. What is the role of the victim in investigating crime?

4. What misconceptions regarding investigation are conveyed by television shows and movies?

5. What do you believe is the most important goal of a criminal investigation?

6. What major factors must responding officers consider while proceeding to a crime scene?

7. How important is response time to the investigation of a crime? How is the importance affected by the type of crime?

8. What determines who is in charge at a crime scene? What authority does this officer have?

9. Controversy exists over which emergency takes precedence: an armed suspect at or near the scene or a severely injured person. Which do you think should take priority? Why?

10. What balance should be maintained between freedom of the media to obtain information during a crime investigation and the right to privacy of the individuals involved?

References

Bowker, Arthur L. "Investigative Planning: Creating a Strong Foundation for White-Collar Crime Cases." *FBI Law Enforcement Bulletin,* Vol.68, No.6, June 1999, pp. 22–25.

Collins, Carolen. "Small Agencies Get Big City Crime Analysis." *Law and Order,* December 1997, pp. 80–81.

Dees, Tim. "Technology Makes Mobile Computing Affordable." *Law and Order,* February 1999, pp. 83–87.

Diaz, Tom. "Computer-Enhanced Investigations." *The Police Chief,* Vol. LXVI, No. 9, September 1999, pp. 50–56.

Dobeck, Michael. "Taking Advantage of the Internet." *The Police Chief,* January 1997, pp. 35–38.

Farrar, Arthur James. "It Just Didn't Look Right." *Police,* Vol. 23. No 9, September 1999, p. 68.

"Forensics, AFIS and Investigations Showcase." *Law Enforcement Technology*, March 1999, pp. 52–56.

Garrison, Dean. "Cooperation in Crime Scene Investigations." *Law and Order,* Vol. 46, No. 9, September 1998, pp. 95–97.

Geberth, Vernon. "Detective Rotation: An Enigma." *Law and Order,* October 1998, p. 194.

Harris, Wesley. "Luck vs. Good Police Work." *Law and Order,* April 1999, p. 115.

Kanable, Rebecca. "A Power Tool for Case Management." *Law Enforcement Technology,* January 1999, pp. 58–60.

Lesce, Tony. "Developing Special Investigations Units." *Law and Order,* October 1998, pp. 175–178.

Miller, Linda S. and Hess, Kären M. *The Police in the Community: Strategies for the 21ˢᵗ Century.* Belmont, CA: West/Wadsworth Publishing Company, 1998.

Morrison, Richard D. "Cyber-Investigator—The New Detective?" *Law Enforcement Technology,* 1997a, pp. 56–58.

Morrison, Richard D. "The MO—A Lost Tool?" *Law Enforcement Technology,* June 1997b, pp. 80–81.

Morrison, Richard D. "Cyber Cops Use Internet." *Law and Order,* February 1998, pp. 27–28.

Morrison, Richard D. "Do the Math, Solve the Crime." *Law Enforcement Technology,* Vol. 26, No. 8, August 1999, pp. 103–104.

Peak, Ken; Evans, Stan; Adams, Frank; and Ashby, Harlan. "Recruiting and Testing Criminal Investigators: A Job Related Approach." *The Police Chief,* Vol. LXV, No. 4, April 1998, pp. 165–168.

Pilant, Lois. "Spotlight on Crime Laboratory Developments." *The Police Chief,* June 1997, pp. 31–37.

Rosenthal, Rick. "Media Tips from IACP/Salt Lake City." *Law and Order,* December 1998, p. 44.

Rosenthal, Rick. "Lessons from Littleton." *Law and Order,* Vol. 47, No. 6, June 1999a, pp. 25–26.

Rosenthal, Rick. "The Quill and Badge Award." *Law and Order,* January 1999b, pp. 16–18.

Shemeligian, Bob. "Police Shouldn't Fear the Media." *Las Vegas Review Journal,* April 21, 1996, p. 31.

Sherman, Fraser. "Digital Mapping–What's the Advantage?" *Law Enforcement Technology,* April 1998, pp. 75–77.

Stockton, Dale. "Computer Scanners–A Great Crime Fighting Tool." *Law and Order,* June 1998, pp. 71–74.

Strandberg, Keith W. "Law Enforcement Computers and Software: Part I." *Law Enforcement Technology,* April 1998a, pp. 30–34.

Strandberg, Keith W. "Law Enforcement Computers and Software: Part II." *Law Enforcement Technology,* May 1998b, pp. 40–45.

Strandberg, Keith W. "Websites for Law Enforcement." *Law Enforcement Technology,* January 1998c, pp. 59–60.

Walsh, Peter. "Awareness of Conflicts of Interest is Crucial." *Police,* January 1997, pp. 24–25, 66.

Wolf, James. "Taking a Megabyte Out of Crime." *Law and Order,* Vol. 46, No. 4, April 1998, pp. 31–32.

Woodall, Everett. "Why Have a Written Media Relations Policy." *The Poice Chief,* Vol. LXV, No. 6, June 1998, pp. 71–73.

Young, Robert A. "The Current Police Phobia: Civil Liability." *Law Enforcement News,* February 29, 1996a, p. 8.

Young, Robert. "'Liability Blues': 8 Ways to Avoid Civil Suits." *Law Enforcement News,* March 15, 1996b, pp. 8, 10.

Basic Investigative Responsibilities

As Berg (1999, p. 8) points out: "Police can learn a few lessons from legendary basketball coach John Wooden," who believed that constantly practicing, mastering and executing the basics were the keys to a team's success. Berg contends:

> Officers, detectives and sergeants should constantly evaluate their fundamentals. Are reported crimes being thoroughly investigated or merely reported? Are neighborhoods being canvassed for that one witness who may give us the little piece of information we need to identify the suspect? Have we searched thoroughly for evidence, including fingerprints, and have we protected evidence and gathered it in an expert manner? Are we completing well written reports that contain all of the information that will make a subsequent follow-up successful? Are we doing a comprehensive job investigating at a crime scene or do we always expect the experts and the specialists to "figure it out?"
>
> Essentially, how well do our front-line patrol investigators, detectives and our sergeants execute the fundamentals of high-quality police work at the scene of a crime? As John Wooden taught us so many years ago, you don't get to cut the net down after the final game if you don't understand the most basic fundamentals of the game and perform them consistently well. So it is with front-line police work.

The basic investigative techniques introduced in Chapter 1 are central to the successful resolution of a crime. Investigators must be skilled in taking photographs and sketching crime scenes (Chapter 2), taking notes and writing reports (Chapter 3), searching (Chapter 4), obtaining and processing physical evidence (Chapter 5), obtaining information through interviews and interrogation (Chapter 6), identifying and arresting suspects and conducting raids, surveillances, stakeouts and undercover assignments (Chapter 7) and testifying in court (Chapter 8).

Although these techniques are discussed separately, they actually overlap and often occur simultaneously. For example, note taking occurs at almost every phase of the investigation, as does obtaining information. Further, the techniques require modification to suit specific crimes as discussed in Sections Three, Four and Five. Nonetheless, investigation of specific crimes must proceed from a base of significant responsibilities applicable to most investigations. This section provides that base.

Chapter 2

Investigative Photography and Crime-Scene Sketches

Do You Know?

What purposes are served by crime-scene photography?

What the advantages and disadvantages of using photography are?

What the minimum photographic equipment for an investigator is?

What errors in technique to avoid?

What to photograph at a crime scene and in what sequence?

What types of photography are used in criminal investigations?

What basic rules of evidence photographs must meet?

What purposes are served by the crime-scene sketch?

What should be sketched?

What materials are needed to make a rough sketch?

What steps to take in making a rough sketch?

How plotting methods are used in sketches?

When a sketch or a scale drawing is admissible in court?

Introduction

Photography plays an important role in documenting evidence and presenting cases in court. It is also useful in crime-prevention and investigation training. Some departments rely almost exclusively on their own specially trained photographers. Other departments rely on their investigators to perform this function. Often both photographs and sketches must accompany written notes to provide a clear picture of the crime scene.

This chapter discusses both crime-scene photography and sketching. It begins by looking at the advantages and disadvantages of photographs, the basic photographic equipment needed, training in investigative photography and errors to avoid. Next is an explanation of what to photograph or videotape and the role of instant photography. This is followed by a description of other types of investigative photography and suggestions on how to identify, file and maintain continuity of the photographs or videos. The discussion concludes with an explanation of the rules of evidence governing admissibility of photographic evidence in court.

The second portion of the chapter—crime-scene sketching—begins with a description of a rough crime-scene sketch and the steps involved in creating it. This is followed by an explanation of how to file the sketch and how it is used in creating the finished scale drawing. The discussion on crime-scene sketching concludes with the legal admissibility of sketches and drawings. ■

Investigative Photography: An Overview

Although the officers' initial responsibility upon arriving at a scene is to handle emergency matters and then to protect the scene, one of the first investigative tasks is to take photographs or to videotape the crime scene and all evidence. Photographing usually precedes sketching, note taking and searching. Do not touch or move any evidence until pictures have been taken of the general area and all evidence.

The basic purpose of crime-scene photography is to record the scene permanently. Pictures taken immediately, using proper techniques to reproduce the entire crime scene, provide a factual record of high evidentiary value. Wexler (1999, p. 23) observes that: "Crime scene photographs provide a permanent visual record of the crime scene as it was first found and depict what was seen and collected by the investigators. The photos serve as key elements in follow-up investigations and court proceedings."

- - - - - - - -

Photographs and videotapes reproduce the crime scene in detail for presentation to the prosecution, defense, witnesses, judge and jury in court. They are used in investigating, prosecuting and police training.

- - - - - - - -

Crime-scene photos are sometimes acquired from the media, but not always without controversy. After violence broke out at the Woodstock '99 concert, New York state police posted this photo and 13 others on the Internet, hoping that the public could help identify suspects. The posting of the photos generated protests because they were reprinted without permission from the Associated Press and Syracuse Online, which owned rights to the photos. The photos were later removed and replaced with photos taken by state employees.

Although most crime-scene photographs are taken by investigators, they may also be acquired from commercial or amateur photographers, attorneys, news media personnel or the coroner's staff. For example, in an arson case at a church, photographs came from three outside sources. The pastor hired a photographer to take pictures for historical purposes and to assess damage; an insurance company photographer took pictures; and a television reporter had in-progress movies. These pictures, along with those taken by police personnel, provided an excellent record of the fire in progress, where it was started and the resulting damage.

Videotape is now well established as an investigative tool. Lightweight, handheld video camcorders are easy to use at a crime scene. Taking videos is similar to taking still pictures. The police photographer starts at the entry, obtaining wide shots, and then records details. Zoom lenses allow close shots without disturbing the crime scene, and close-ups are possible with macro lenses. The photographer can use the sound capability to describe the procedure being used to make the video and to explain what is being taped. Videotapes can also be made of witness testimony, depositions, evidence, lineups and even trials.

After a crime scene is secure, an important step is photographing/ videotaping the scene, including any evidence located. Here an officer videotapes confiscated drugs, money and weapons.

Advantages and Disadvantages of Photographs

One advantage of photographs is that they can be taken immediately, an important factor in bad weather or when many people are present. For example, a picture of a footprint in the dirt outside a window broken during a burglary can be important if it rains before a casting can be made. The same is true when a large number of people present might alter the scene.

Another obvious advantage of crime-scene photographs is that they accurately represent the crime scene in court. The effect of pictures on a jury cannot be overestimated. Photographs are highly effective visual aids that corroborate the facts presented.

- - - - - - - -

Advantages of photographs: They can be taken immediately, accurately represent the crime scene and evidence, create interest and increase attention to testimony.

- - - - - - - -

Although photographs of a crime scene accurately represent what was present, they include everything at the scene, both relevant and irrelevant. So much detail may distract viewers of photographs.

- - - - - - - -

Disadvantages of photographs: They are not selective, do not show actual distances and may be distorted and damaged by mechanical errors in shooting or processing.

- - - - - - - -

Despite these disadvantages, photography is a valuable investigative technique. A vast array of modern equipment has greatly enhanced its usefulness in investigation.

Basic Photographic Equipment

Crime-scene photography uses both common and special-function cameras and equipment, depending on the crime investigated and the investigator's preferences.

- - - - - - - -

At a minimum, have available and be skilled in operating a 35 mm camera, an instant-print camera, a press camera, a fingerprint camera and video equipment.

- - - - - - - -

Investigators commonly have individual preferences about the equipment to use in a given situation. Some have switched from 35 mm and press cameras to professional roll-film cameras. Generally, equipment should meet several photographic needs.

Versatile *35 mm cameras* provide negatives for enlargements. Many models have an automatic built-in flash (which can be turned off) and can imprint the date directly on the photo. Many also allow the film to be rewound before the entire roll is shot.

Single-use law enforcement cameras are another option "developed specifically for use by the first officer on the scene, regardless of photographic training or skill. This fixed-focus flash camera comes preloaded with both film and battery . . . [and] provides good photographs at normal distances, even under adverse conditions" (Lesce, 1998, p. 80).

Instant-print cameras such as those made by Polaroid and Impulse provide low-cost-per-image pictures. Color or black-and-white film may be used. Instant photography provides immediate confirmation of the quality and accuracy of the picture at a time when it is possible to take another shot. The cameras are simple to operate, which lessens the need for training. Every officer on the force can use an instant camera. Giulliano (1998, p. 42) reports that instant-print cameras have good optics and great res-

olution and color and can be used to document small evidence such as bullet holes and minute paint transfers. He also notes that such cameras are useful for taking on-the-spot photo lineups and in documenting crime scenes such as drug laboratories: "When you enter these labs, you have to wear a body suit and a face shield. . . . You can't really look through the camera's viewfinder, but it has a light-focusing system so [you] don't have to." And the photographer can tell immediately whether the photo is good.

Digital cameras allow instant viewing of results. "Digital photography offers significant advantages over conventional photography for some applications. . . . The most significant is the ability to see immediately that the desired information has been captured" (Wong, 1999, p. 6). For example, one officer who took 30 digital photos at a crime scene was able to see, through the camera's view screen, that he needed to reshoot 10 pictures that had reflections or were not adequately lit ("Digital Photography Aids . . .," 1998, p. 68).

Other advantages to digital cameras include elimination of the time and expense involved in the processing of photographic film. "Advances in digital imaging have created a wide array of opportunities to improve the efficiency and cost-effectiveness of crime scene photography" ("Digital Imaging Benefits Police," 1999, p. 37). The head of a forensic identification unit states ("Digital Detectives," 1998, p. 45) that: "Timeliness is critical in police work. Crime scenes get cold fast and the sooner we can develop leads, the better. Digital imaging lets us do that." Stockton (1997, p. 30) notes other advantages:

Pictures recorded in digital form provide electronic images, which are quickly adaptable as e-mail attachments, computer-produced "Wanted" posters or an electronic database: digital images can even be incorporated into a written report alongside an officer's narrative.

Digital cameras can bypass the need for outside processing, thereby allowing unsurpassed confidentiality for sensitive situations.

Morrison (1999, p. 88) adds: "Combined with computer power, digital cameras are a substantial leap forward. Overall, digital pictures offer high reso-

lution, high-quality images that last forever and take up little storage space." Furthermore, because of the ease with which such data can be sent online, "digital photography also increases the likelihood of sharing images with agencies outside the city" ("Montgomery Police Save . . .," 1998, p. 96).

One concern about digital photography is the possibility of altering the images. Blitzer (1996, p. 14) comments:

Not too long ago, a cover of *Scientific American* magazine showed Marilyn Monroe walking arm-in-arm with Abraham Lincoln. Every day we see extraordinary special effects . . . [due to] new digital technologies [that] make it relatively easy to manipulate images; in turn, this ease makes digital imaging technology suspect in the courtroom. . . .

However, it is still the integrity of the witness that is in question, not the technology in the lab. The best way to alleviate suspicions about the witness's integrity is to be able to say, "We have standard procedures, and we followed them in preparing these images."

Biehl (1999, p. 12) stresses: "To submit digital images as admissible evidence, a law enforcement agency beginning to acquire digital technology should also enforce standard operating procedures." Strandberg (1998, p. 18) states:

Because of the ease of manipulating digital images, digital photography must follow a specific process for photographs to be admissible in court. The images must be captured in a .TIF format and the images must be removed from the camera quickly and transferred to a write-only, stable media that cannot be altered.

continued

To overcome this concern, some manufacturers are designing digital cameras with image formats that make it impossible for a photo to be altered ("Digital Detectives," p. 46). Digital cameras have other disadvantages as well. Mossberg (1999, p. 4K) points out:

> Despite the hype, digital photography suffers from four main drawbacks compared with standard film photography. First, the equipment is usually more expensive. Second, photos from mainstream digital cameras still aren't as rich and detailed as regular snapshots. Third, you have to use a personal computer to view and print digital pictures, which cuts out non-PC owners. . . . And, finally, it's a tremendous pain to get the pictures out of the camera and into the PC.

Stockton (p. 31) notes other drawbacks of digital cameras, including their vulnerability to rough treatment or exposure to the elements and the difficulty in producing adequate images at night. Nonetheless, digital photography is growing in popularity, with increasing diversity in its applications. For example, one city is planning to digitally photograph all school-age children as part of a Child Safety program ("Digital Photography Aids . . .," p. 69).

DeFranco (1999, p. 82) describes another advance combining digital photography and computer software that allows investigators to take two digital photographs of 180 degrees each and "sew" them together on a computer to create one 360-degree picture. According to Paynter (1999, p. 88): "The images can transport witnesses of a crime back through the crime scene to refresh their memory before testifying and can show a judge and jury the scene as it looked on the day of the crime." The panoramic view of the crime scene is interactive, allowing viewers to walk through it as though they were there. It is, in effect, a virtual crime scene.

Press cameras provide excellent photographs of a general scene as well as of smaller areas or small pieces of evidence. The ground glass of their lenses permits perfect focusing and shows exactly what portion of the scene will appear in the photograph. The 4" × 5" negative allows enlargement for detailed court presentation.

Fingerprint cameras are specially constructed to take pictures of fingerprints without distortion. They provide their own light through four bulbs, one in each corner. Removing a bulb from any corner provides slanted lighting to show fingerprint ridge detail. This camera can also photograph trace evidence such as bloodstains and toolmarks.

Videotape cameras are used to record alleged bribery, payoffs and narcotics buys. Permanently installed units frequently photograph crimes actually being committed such as bank robberies or shoplifting. Videotaping crime scenes is now commonplace. The cameras have become much less expensive, much more portable and much easier to operate. They have the advantage of immediacy and elimination of a middle processing step in the chain of evidence. In addition, most can operate with quite limited light.

Camcorders and videotaping equipment have been used for in-station recording of bookings and for DWI-suspect tests for some time. Use of video cameras for crime-scene investigations is now prevalent. Many police departments have purchased video equipment to record crime scenes and criminal acts such as vandalism, drug deals and thefts. When violations and arrests are videotaped and the tapes are submitted in court as evidence, convictions have increased.

According to Pilant (1999) aerospace experts are able to extract information from video evidence from ATM films, cameras located in banks or shopping malls, or from media footage. They can help investigators identify suspects, reconstruct crime scenes, and get clearer shots of license plates and vehicles. Pilant notes that one shopping center's enhancement of a shopping mall video helped identify a man who kidnapped and molested an eight-year-old girl.

Videotapes have become a form of crime prevention and control as well as an investigative aid, as discussed later in this chapter. Some police departments have mounted video cameras on their patrol vehicles' dashboards, an application that offers many benefits, including the following (Pult, 1998, p. 2B):

■ Increasing DUI conviction rates

■ Enhancing an officer's integrity

■ Providing additional safety to officers

■ Reducing conflicts with offenders

■ Documenting traffic violations

■ Reducing court time for officers

■ Reducing overtime for officers by enabling them to process their cases faster

■ Lowering liability in police misconduct cases and helping eliminate unfounded lawsuits

■ Documenting probable cause and physical evidence

This videorecorder can be used for taping DUIs, drug arrests and traffic stops. The tapes can also be used for training.

In addition to use in patrol cars, new applications of video equipment are being developed all the time. Stockton (1999, p. 78) describes a body-mounted camera known as CopCam. This device works in conjuction with a camera and recording unit in the patrol car, allowing officers to record an entire scene "up close and personal." In another technological advance, Page (1998, p. 70) reports: "Police . . . may soon be aided and protected to a degree thanks to a new video camera so small it can be hidden in a police shield. . . . [The] tiny camera device will allow police officers to discreetly videotape every field interrogation, routine traffic stop and domestic disturbance to which they are dispatched."

In addition to providing realistic accounts of traffic violations, DUI apprehensions, felony arrests and drug buys, the videotapes are useful for training.

Specialized cameras such as binocular cameras and trip cameras (cameras that set themselves off) are helpful in surveillance.

Film for the various cameras may be black-and-white or color. Although more expensive, color film is often preferred because it is more realistic and accurate. Film can also be special purpose such as infrared film. Literature furnished with the camera gives detailed information about the type of film to use.

It is difficult to describe color and sometimes impossible to describe varying shades of color accurately. Therefore, color film has a clear advantage. Officers and witnesses can more easily recognize objects in color photographs. Color photographs can bring out faintly visible stains and preserve the original colors of objects that fade because of weather or age. Color photographs are especially helpful in showing the nature and extent of physical injuries. More extensive uses of color photography in police work are being developed each year, and improved film and processing are assisting in the admissibility of color photographs in court.[1]

Accessories, depending on the cameras used, include an exposure meter, flash attachments, flood lamps and high-intensity spotlights. Lighting equipment can also assist in illuminating the scene as officers search for minute evidence. An adjustable tripod for mounting the camera at any angle makes for better photographs in most instances.

---

[1]Defense attorneys sometimes object to color photographs on the grounds that they are inflammatory. This concern is discussed later in the chapter.

Lenses and filters are available for different purposes. Normal lenses are best for evidence, but sometimes special lenses are needed. For example, a telephoto lens can capture a distant subject, whereas a wide-angle lens can cover an entire room in a single shot. Various filters can eliminate certain colors from a photograph.

Selection of a camera and accessories is determined by budget, local needs and investigator preference. Sometimes investigators can borrow equipment from local schools or community organizations or share it with other agencies. In some communities, citizens lend special-purpose equipment to the police department.

Darkroom facilities are an additional consideration. Smaller departments often share a darkroom with another agency such as a fire department. Larger departments usually have their own darkrooms. If a commercial developer is used, it may take too long to get pictures back, confidential information may be revealed, and the commercial developer may be required to testify in court. For these reasons, a police department may find it advantageous to have its own darkroom facilities or to share them with another agency.

Training in Investigative Photography

Investigators can master most photographic equipment by reading the accompanying manuals and practicing. Some equipment, however, requires special training. Photographic training includes instruction in the operation of all available photographic equipment; shooting techniques; anticipated problems; and identifying, filing and maintaining continuity of photographic evidence. Learn the nomenclature and operation of your available photographic equipment. Sometimes camera and equipment manufacturers or outlets provide such training.[2]

Professional commercial photographers in the community can sometimes assist in training or serve as consultants. They can provide information on photographic techniques and special problems such as lighting, close-ups, exposures and use of filters. Training programs also include instructions on identifying and filing photo-

graphs and on establishing and maintaining the continuity of a chain of evidence.

Errors to Avoid

To obtain effective photographs, be familiar with your equipment and check it before you use it.

- - - - - - - -

Take photographs before anything is disturbed. Avoid inaccuracies and distortions.

- - - - - - - -

If something has been moved, do *not* put it back. It is legally impossible to return an object to its original position. To minimize distortion or misrepresentation, maintain proper perspective and attempt to show the objects in a crime scene in their relative size and position. Take pictures from eye level, the height from which people normally observe objects.

What to Photograph or Videotape

Take sufficient photographs and/or videotape to reconstruct the entire scene. This usually requires a series of shots, including the entrance point, the crime commission area and the exit point. If possible, show the entire scene of the crime in a pictorial sequence. This helps relate the crime to other crimes.

Move the camera to cover the entire crime-scene area, but plan the sequence of shots to least disturb the scene. The initial photographs showing the entire crime scene should use a technique called **overlapping.** Photograph the scene clockwise and take the first picture with a specific object on the right. For the second photo, make sure that same object is on the left side of the photograph. Continue in this way until you have covered the entire scene.

- - - - - - - -

First photograph the general area, then specific areas and finally specific objects of evidence. Take exterior shots first because they are the most subject to alteration by weather and security violations.

- - - - - - - -

This progression of shots will reconstruct the commission of a crime:

---

[2]The Polaroid Corporation provides training on law enforcement photography and publishes a photography newsletter for law enforcement called *Instant Evidence!* In addition, Polaroid has a technical assistance hotline: 1-800-225-1618.

1. Take *long-range* pictures of the locality, points of ingress and egress, normal entry to the property and buildings, exterior of the buildings and grounds and street signs or other identifiable structures that will establish location.

2. Take *medium-range* pictures of the immediate crime scene and the location of objects of evidence within the area or room.

3. Take *close-range* pictures of specific evidence such as hairs, fibers, footprints and bloodstains. The entire surface of some objects may be photographed to show all the evidence; for example, a table surface may contain bloodstains, fingerprints, hairs and fibers.

Markers can be useful. A **marker** is anything used in a picture to show accurate or relative size. It is usually a ruler, but it can be some other object of a known size, such as a coin.

Using a marker introduces something foreign to the crime scene. The same is true of chalk marks drawn around a body or placed on walls to illustrate bullet direction. Therefore, first take a picture of the scene or object without the marker; then add the marker and take a second photograph.

Different crimes require different types of photographs. In arson cases, photograph the point of origin and any incendiary devices. In burglaries, photograph the points of entry and exit, toolmarks, fingerprints and other trace evidence. In assaults, photograph injuries, and do so in color if possible. In homicides or suicides, photograph the deceased, including pictures of the clothing worn; take a full-length picture showing height, position of the body and all extremities; and evidence near the body. Photograph injured parts of the body to show the location and extent of injuries and any postmortem lividity (discussed in Chapter 13).

Cameras can also be used in combination with radar to document the speed of motorists. These cameras provide a photograph of both the car and the driver along with the date, time, speed and location.

Types of Investigative Photography

In addition to crime-scene photography, certain types of photography play vital roles in investigation.

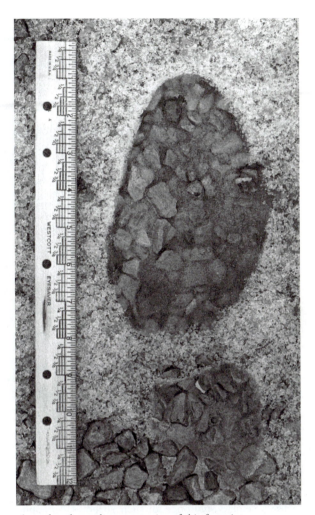

A marker shows the accurate size of this footprint.

Types of investigative photography include crime-scene, surveillance, aerial, night, laboratory, lineup and mugshot photography.

Surveillance Photography

Surveillance photography establishes the identity of a subject or records criminal behavior without the photographer's presence being known to the subject. The photographs or videotapes can help identify a suspect's associates, destroy an alibi, plan a raid or develop a surveillance plan. Banks and stores frequently use surveillance cameras to help identify robbers and burglars. Numerous bank robbers have been identified through photographs taken by surveillance cameras installed in the bank.

This new high-resolution digital camera can capture enough detail for a photorealistic 5 × 7-inch print. It has a total output resolution of one million pixels and can capture 16 to 20 pictures on a four-megabyte card included with the camera.

Photographs taken during a stakeout are usually taken with a single-reflex camera with several telephoto lenses. Sometimes infrared film is used. It may be necessary to use a van—preferably borrowed because it is best to use a vehicle only once for such purposes. An appliance repair van or any van that would commonly be seen in the area is desirable.

Digital technology has also had an impact on surveillance techniques, helping to overcome some of the problems commonly encountered with surveillance photography. Wimmer (1998, p. 56) notes: "Conditions such as poor lighting, high scene contrasts and the need to create greater picture definition have created many problems in the past for anyone designing or installing a surveillance system." To address some of these challenges, the digital-signal-processed (DSP) surveillance camera has been introduced. Features such as motion detection, camera tilting and remote setup are also available with DSP cameras (p. 87).

Concealing a camera can be a problem. You might use a bag, briefcase, suitcase or coat pocket with an opening. You can also conceal the camera by using rooftops or windows of buildings or vehicles in the area. A camera kept away from a vehicle window is rarely seen by people outside the vehicle. Keep the camera loaded and adjusted to the required light so you can take pictures instantly.

Surveillance photography is often called **trap photography** because the photos prove that an incident occurred and can help identify suspects and weapons. These photos corroborate witness testimony and identification. The fact that the photos exist often induces guilty pleas without court appearances, thus saving investigators' time.

Battery-operated cameras can be moved to different locations. You can reduce the amount of film needed by using such things as bait-money pull switches or by placing activation buttons in several locations where employees can reach them easily. Lighting conditions determine whether color or black-and-white film is appropriate. Hidden camcorders can be used at drug-buy scenes.

Surveillance photography can also be a crime prevention/detection tool. For example, the Newark Police Department has video cameras mounted in six different areas of the two-square-mile downtown area. An officer observes what is taking place in each area from a central location. Burglaries and street robberies have decreased, and the police have successfully presented the videos as evidence in court.

Aerial Photography

Investigators often use aerial photography to cover extensive areas. For example, it can be used in a bank robbery to show roads leading to and from the bank. It is also useful when police know that a crime is going to be committed but not when. Aerial photography shows routes to the scene as well as how to block escape routes, avoid detours during pursuit and set up roadblocks. It is essential in locating dead-end streets—information that can be very important if a chase ensues. Aerial pictures can also help establish the location of a crime scene, especially in large rural areas or mountainous sectors.

Aerial photos can be enlarged or presented on slides to show the relationships of streets and roads. For example, in the John F. Kennedy assassination investigation, the entire area was photographed, including all points from which shots might have been fired.

Aerial photographs are often available in commercial photographers' files, engineering offices or highway-planning agencies. The vast areas covered by highways and engineering projects usually require aerial mapping. Federal, state, county and municipal agencies also may have aerial photos. If none are available, a local photographer can be hired to provide them. Many larger departments and county sheriffs' offices have helicopters that might be available.

Night Photography

Taking pictures at night presents special problems, particularly that of illuminating a scene. Adequate light can be obtained by increasing exposure time, using a photoflash for small areas and a flash series for larger areas or using floodlights. Floodlights also aid in locating evidence and decrease the chance of evidence being accidentally destroyed.

State-of-the-art night-vision devices/cameras are dramatically better than earlier ones. Their range extends up to a mile. Because they are quite expensive and used infrequently, they are often shared with other federal, state or county law enforcement agencies.

As in other areas of investigative photography, night photography is benefitting from advances in technology. Siuru (1997, p. 38) reports:

Add a new technology—laser radar—to the increasing menu of techniques to see the bad guys in the dark. . . .

Advanced Ranging Imaging Sensor (ARIS) is a scannerless laser radar imaging system that simultaneously generates both two-dimensional reflectance images and three-dimensional radar images. . . . ARIS uses diffused, infrared energy from a scannerless laser transmitter to flood-light the entire surveillance scene to produce instantaneous three-dimensional images.

Laboratory Photography

Not all investigative photography is done in the field. Sometimes objects are photographed in a laboratory with special equipment that is too large, delicate or expensive to use in the field. For example, infrared film photographs can reveal the contents of unopened envelopes, bloodstains, alterations to documents, variations in types of ink and residue near where a bullet has passed through clothing. X-ray cameras can detect loaded dice.

Microphotography—taking pictures through a microscope—helps identify minute particles of evidence such as a hair or fiber. For example, a digital microscope camera was used to compare two pieces of evidence recently submitted to the U.S. Postal Service National Forensic Laboratory ("Microscopy . . .," 1999, p. 62):

The first was a minute remnant of a circuit board from the debris of an improvised explosive device. The second, a larger, undamaged piece of circuit board was discovered by a postal inspector in the workshop of a suspect.

Using comparison microscopy, one edge of the piece recovered from the improvised explosive device matched the circuit board found in the workshop. This proved conclusively that, at one time, both pieces were part of the same circuit board. The forensic analyst then documented this match using a digital microscope camera.

In contrast, **macrophotography** enlarges a subject. For example, a fingerprint or a toolmark can be greatly enlarged to show the details of ridges or striations.

Laser-beam photography can reveal evidence indiscernible to the naked eye. For example, it can reveal the outline of a footprint in a carpet even though the fibers have returned to normal position.

Ultraviolet-light photography uses the low end of the color spectrum, which is invisible to human sight, to make visible impressions of bruises and injuries long after their actual occurrence. Bite marks, injuries due to beatings, cigarette burns, neck strangulation marks and other impressions left from intentional injuries can be reproduced and used as evidence in criminal cases by scanning the presumed area of injury with a fluorescent or blue light. The damage impression left by the injury is then photographed. In addition, the type of weapon used in committing a crime can often be determined by examining its impression, developed by using ultraviolet light.

Mug Shots

Although investigators seldom take **mug shots** themselves, these photographs are often significant in criminal investigations. Mug shots originated in nineteenth-century France when Alphonse Bertillon developed a method of identification that used an extensive system of measurements to describe people. The Bertillon identification system included a written description, the complete measurements of the person and a photograph. The pictures of people in police custody were kept in department files for identification and became known as *mug shots.* Gathered in files and displayed in groups, they were called a **rogues' gallery.**

Opinions differ regarding the preferred poses for mug shots. Some agencies believe the front and profile of the head are sufficient; others prefer full-length, stand-up pictures. No matter what the pose, mug shots should include the facial features and the clothing worn at the time of arrest because a defendant's appearance may change between the time of arrest and trial. Mug shots can be filed by age, sex and height to make them more readily accessible for viewing.

Mug shots can be carried in the field to identify suspicious persons or to show to crime victims to assist in identifying their attacker. They are also used for "wanted" circulars distributed to other police agencies and the public. The use of mug shots in suspect identification is discussed in Chapter 7.

Video imaging systems have greatly increased the ease of taking and using mug shots. Marchand (1997, p. 18) states: "Mug shots have traditionally been stored in large books . . . [and] keeping the mug books up to date is difficult." However, most agencies today are using a new photographic mug-shot imaging system. Marchand reports: "Newer imaging systems blend mug shots with computer technology. Today, in some departments, one can sit down in front of a computer workstation, enter information on the suspect's race, approximate age, height and weight, and view a series of images on the screen. This system stores digitized images in computer memory."

Video-imaging systems enable booking officers to enter mug shots directly into computer arrest or incident files, allowing for faster, more accurate booking because officers can preview a shot before storing it. If unacceptable, it can be retaken.

In addition, photo mug-shot systems can increase the productivity of the booking process and reduce its cost. It also eliminates storage and filing costs ("Photo Mugshot System," 1999, p. 98).

One of the newest technologies in mug shots is a software program that allows a human head to be re-created in three dimensions, which is how witnesses see suspects. As Pilant (p. 60) observes: "Imaging systems are in the vanguard of the new police technologies. They provide another tool to make police officers more effective and more efficient, and—in many cases—to ensure a successful prosecution."

Lineup Photographs

The computer's capacity to sort through a database of mug shots and bring up all the "hits" within specific categories can assist in generating photographic lineups. After entering characteristics of a known suspect, an offi-

A video-imaging system allows officers to sort a database using specific characteristics—race, sex, hair color, height, age, distinguishing characteristics—in fact, any feature that can be visually described.

cer can select six to twelve other "hits" to be used for presentation with the suspect's photo. In addition, videotapes or photographs of people included in lineups may be taken to establish the fairness of the lineup.

Identifying, Filing and Maintaining Continuity of Evidence

Photographs must be properly identified, filed and kept secure to be admissible as evidence.

Identifying In the field notes, the photographs taken should be dated and numbered in sequence. Include the case number, type of offense and subject of the picture. To further identify the photograph with the crime scene and the subject, record the photographer's name, location and direction of the camera, lens type, approximate distance in feet to the subject, film and shutter speed, lighting, weather conditions and a brief description of the scene in the picture.

The photos should also be marked like any other evidence relating to the crime scene using a procedure called **backing.** This includes writing on the back of the photo your initials, the date the photo was taken, what the photo depicts and the direction of north.

Filing File the picture and negatives for easy reference. Pictures in the case file are available to others. Therefore, it is usually best to put them in a special photograph file, cross-referenced by case number.

Maintaining Security Record the chain of custody of the film and photographs in the field notes or in a special file. Mark and identify the film as it is removed from the camera. Each time the film changes possession, record the name of the person accepting it. If a commercial firm develops the film, take it to the company in person or send it by registered mail with a return receipt.

Admissibility of Photographs in Court: Rules of Evidence

Photographs must be taken under certain conditions and must meet specific criteria to be admissible in court.

Photographs must be material, relevant, competent, accurate, free of distortion and noninflammatory.

A **material photograph** relates to a specific case and subject. Material evidence is relevant and forms a substantive part of the case presented or has a legitimate and effective influence on the decision of the case. A **relevant photograph** helps explain testimony. A **competent photograph** accurately represents what it purports to represent, is properly identified and is properly placed in the chain of evidence and secured until court presentation.

Testimony reports the exact conditions under which the photographs were taken, the equipment and type of film used and where the film was processed. Photographs must be accurate and free of distortion. If nothing has been removed from or added to the scene, the photograph will be accurate. Inaccuracies do not necessarily render the photograph inadmissible as evidence as long as they are fully explained and the court is not misled about what the picture represents.

Likewise, distortion will not necessarily disqualify a photograph as evidence if no attempt is made to misrepresent the photograph and if the distortion is adequately explained. For example, an amateur photographer may have taken the picture from an unusual camera height to produce a dramatic effect, not knowing the picture would later be useful as evidence in a criminal investigation.

Color distortion is a frequent objection. Because most objects have color, black-and-white photographs are technically distorted. Therefore, color photographs usually constitute better evidence. However, color can also be distorted by inadequate lighting or faulty processing. Nevertheless, the photograph can still be useful, especially if the object's shape is more important than its color.

Although color photographs are less distorted and are usually better evidence than black-and-white photographs, they have often been objected to as being inflammatory—for example, showing in gruesome, vivid color a badly beaten body. To be ruled inadmissible, color photographs must be judged by the court to be so inflammatory that they will unduly influence the jury. Sometimes taking both color and black-and-white pictures is advisable. The black-and-white pictures can be introduced as evidence; the color pictures can be used for investigatory purposes only.

Objections to enlargements have also been raised. Such objections can be nullified by producing the original negative along with the enlargement to prove that no alterations have been made.

In addition to admissible photographs and videotapes, investigators usually must prepare a crime-scene sketch.

Crime-Scene Sketches: An Overview

An investigator's scene **sketch** can be more descriptive than hundreds of words and is often an extremely important investigative aid. The crime-scene sketch accomplishes the following:

- Accurately portrays the physical facts.
- Relates to the sequence of events at the scene.
- Establishes the precise location and relationship of objects and evidence at the scene.
- Helps to create a mental picture of the scene for those not present.
- Is a permanent record of the scene.
- Is usually admissible in court.

A crime-scene sketch assists in (1) interviewing and interrogating people, (2) preparing the investigative report and (3) presenting the case in court.

The sketch supplements photographs, notes, plaster casts and other investigative techniques.

Artistic ability is helpful but not essential in making crime-scene sketches. Still, many police officers avoid making sketches. To overcome this hesitance, practice by drawing familiar scenes such as your home, office or police station. Use graph paper to make sketching easier.

The most common types of sketches are those drawn at the crime scene, called *rough sketches,* and those completed later by an investigator or a drafter, called *scale* (or *finished*) *drawings.* Both describe the crime scene pictorially and show the precise location of objects and evidence.

The Rough Sketch

A **rough sketch** is the first pencil-drawn outline of a scene and the location of objects and evidence within this outline. It is not usually drawn to scale, although distances are measured and entered in the appropriate locations.

Sketch all serious crime and accident scenes after photographs are taken and before anything is moved. Sketch the entire scene, the objects and the evidence.

It is better to include too much rather than too little, but do not include irrelevant objects that clutter and confuse the sketch.

The area to be sketched depends on the crime scene. If it involves a large area, make a sketch of nearby streets, vegetation and entrance and exit paths. If the scene is inside a house or apartment building, show the scene's location in relation to the larger structure. If the scene involves only a single room, sketch only the immediate crime scene, including an outline of the room, objects and the evidence within it.

Do not overlook the possible availability of architectural drawings of the house or building. These are often on file with local engineering, assessing or building departments or with the architect who drew the original plans.

Sketching Materials

Materials needed for rough sketches should be assembled and placed in their own kit or in the crime-scene investigation kit.

Materials for the rough sketch include paper, pencil, long steel measuring tape, carpenter-type ruler, straightedge, clipboard, eraser, compass, protractor and thumbtacks.

Paper of any type will do, but plain white or graph paper is best. No lines interfere if you use plain white. On the other hand, graph paper provides distance ratios and allows for more accurate depictions of the relationships between objects and evidence at the scene. When sketching, use a hard lead pencil to avoid smudges. Keep two or three pencils on hand.

Use a 50- to 150-foot steel measuring tape for measuring long distances. Steel is preferable because it does not stretch and is therefore more accurate than cloth tape. Use a carpenter-type ruler to take short and close-quarter measurements and a straightedge to draw straight lines. A clipboard will give a firm, level drawing surface.

Use a compass to determine true north, especially in areas and buildings laid out in other than true directions. Use a protractor to find the proper angles when determining coordinates.

Thumbtacks are helpful to hold down one end of the tape when you measure. You can also use them to fasten paper to a drawing surface if no clipboard is available.

Steps in Sketching the Crime Scene

Once photographs have been taken and other priority steps in the preliminary investigation performed, you can begin sketching the crime scene. First, make an overall judgment of the scene. Remember not to move, remove, touch or pick up anything until it has been photographed, located on the rough sketch and described in detail in your notes. Then handle objects only in accordance with the techniques for preserving evidence.

To sketch a crime scene:

■ Observe and plan.

■ Measure distances.

■ Outline the area.

■ Locate objects and evidence within the outline.

■ Record details.

■ Make notes.

■ Identify the sketch with a legend and a scale.

■ Reassess the sketch.

Step One: Observe and Plan

Before starting to sketch, observe the scene as many times as you need to feel comfortable with it. Take in the entire scene mentally so you can recall it later. Plan in advance how to proceed in an organized way to avoid destruction of evidence. Ask yourself, "What is relevant to the crime? What should be included in the sketch?"

State troopers take accurate measurements inside a secured crime-scene area.

The size of the area determines how many sketches you make. For example, part of the crime may have taken place indoors and another part outdoors a considerable distance away. To include the entire area would make the scale too small. Therefore, make two sketches.

Decide Where to Start The overview also helps you determine where to start sketching and measuring. If the scene is a room, stand in the doorway and start the sketch there. Then continue clockwise or counterclockwise. The photographs, sketch and search are all made in the same direction. Usually it does not matter which direction is selected, but try to use the one that is least disturbing to evidence.

Step Two: Measure and Outline the Area

All measurements must be accurate. A steel tape is best for measuring because it does not stretch. Do not estimate distances or use paces or shoelength measurement. Use conventional units of measurements such as inches, feet or yards. Do not move any objects while measuring.

If another officer is helping you take measurements, reverse the ends of the tape so both of you can observe the actual distance on the tape. Legally, it is *hearsay* for officers to testify to what they did not actually observe. If a third officer is taking notes, that officer can testify to only the measurements given to him or her unless he or she actually saw the tape measurement. However, all officers may testify from the same notes if they review and initial them as they are made.

Do not measure from movable objects. Use *fixed locations* such as walls, trees, telephone poles, building corners, curbs and so on. Measure from wall to wall, not baseboard to baseboard.

Once the outside measurements have been made, sketch the outline, maintaining some distance ratio. Use the longest measurement first and orient the sketch paper to this distance, positioning the sketch so *north is toward the top of the paper.* Place the outside limits in the sketch using dimension lines such as this:

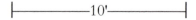

Determine the **scale** by taking the longest measurement at the scene and dividing it by the longest measurement of the paper used for sketching. For example, if your paper is 10 inches and the longest measurement at the scene is 100 feet, let 1 inch equal 10 feet. Use the largest, simplest scale possible.

Table 2.1 presents suggested scales for sketches. Graph paper makes it easier to draw to scale. Each square can equal one square foot or one square inch, depending on the size of the scene. The outline sketch of a room might look like Figure 2.1, whereas the outline sketch of an outdoor scene might look like Figure 2.2.

Next measure and sketch the doors and windows. Record their measurements and indicate whether the

Table 2.1	Suggested Scales for Sketches	
Indoor Areas		*Outdoor Areas*
1/2" = 1' (small rooms)		1/2" = 10' (large buildings and grounds)
1/4" = 1' (large rooms)		1/8" = 10' (large land areas)
1/8" = 1' (very large rooms)		

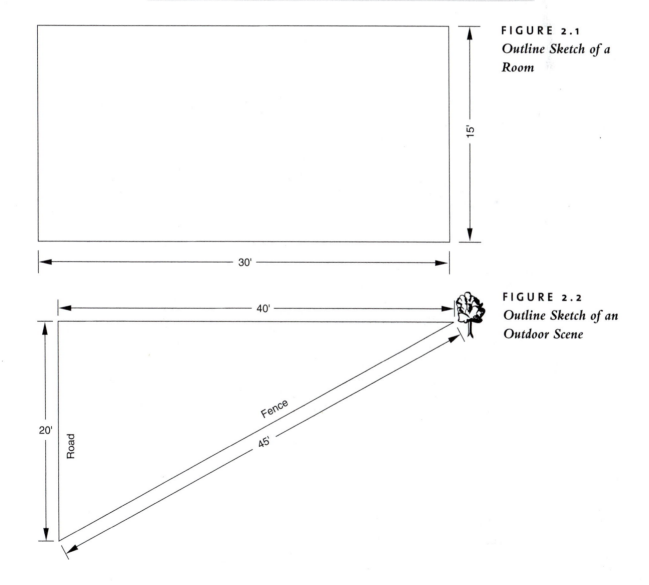

FIGURE 2.1
Outline Sketch of a Room

15'

30'

FIGURE 2.2
Outline Sketch of an Outdoor Scene

40'

20'

Road

Fence

45'

FIGURE 2.3
Outline Sketch of
Room with Door and
Windows

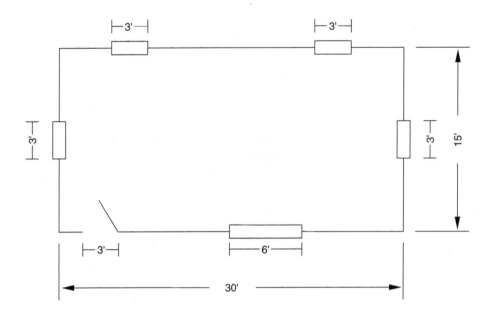

Step Three: Plot Objects and Evidence

- - - - - - - -

Plotting methods are used to locate objects and evidence on the sketch. They include the use of rectangular coordinates, a baseline, triangulation and compass points.

- - - - - - - -

To plot objects and evidence accurately, determine fixed points from which to measure.

Rectangular-Coordinate Method The rectangular-coordinate method is a common way to locate objects and evidence in a room. The **rectangular-coordinate method** uses two adjacent walls as fixed points from which distances are measured at right angles. Locate objects by measuring from one wall at right angles and then from the adjacent wall at right angles. This method is restricted to square or rectangular areas (see Figure 2.4).

Baseline Method Another way to measure by coordinates is to run a baseline from one fixed point to another. The **baseline method** establishes a straight line from one fixed point to another, from which measurements are taken at right angles. Take measurements along either side of the baseline to a point at right angles to the object to be located. An indoor baseline method sketch might look like Figure 2.5 or 2.6. Outdoors, it might look like Figure 2.7.

doors open in or out. To measure windows, use the width and height of the actual window opening; do not include the window frame. The outline of a room with doors and windows added might look like Figure 2.3.

Sketch the location of physical objects within the perimeter. Use approximate shapes for large objects and symbols for small ones. Place items of evidence in the sketch at the same time you place objects. Use numbers to designate objects and letters to designate evidence. Include such items as points of entry or exit of a bullet, body, hair, gun, fibers, bloodstains and so on. Use exact measurements to show the location of evidence within the room and in relation to all other objects.

Opinions differ on whether to include the location of evidence in this sketch. If evidence is placed within the sketch, some courts have withheld introduction of the sketch until the evidence has been approved. If the evidence is placed only in the finished scale drawing, the sketch can be introduced and used by witnesses to corroborate their testimony.

While sketching, check measurements frequently. Make corrections if needed, but make no changes after leaving the scene. Measurements may or may not be placed in the sketch itself, depending on how many objects are located in the available space. Measurements can be placed in your notes and later entered in the scale drawing.

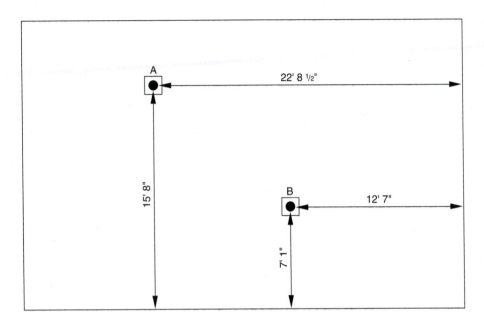

FIGURE 2.4
Rectangular–Coordinate Method

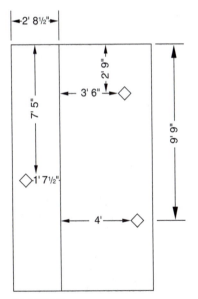

FIGURE 2.5
Center Baseline Method

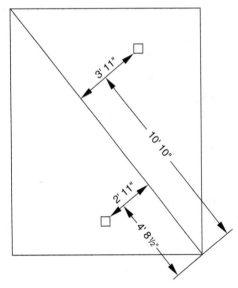

FIGURE 2.6
Diagonal Baseline Method

Sometimes the distance between two locations is important. For example, the distance from the normal route to a door might be very important if evidence is found in a room. The 34-foot measurement in Figure 2.7 illustrates this need in an outdoor setting.

Triangulation Method Triangulation is commonly used in outdoor scenes but can also be used indoors. **Tri-**

angulation uses straight-line measures from two fixed objects to the evidence to create a triangle with the evidence in the angle formed by the two straight lines. The degree of the angle formed at the location of the object or evidence can then be measured with a protractor. The angle can be any degree, in contrast to the rectangular-coordinate and baseline methods, in which the angle is always a right angle (90°).

FIGURE 2.7
Outdoor Baseline Method

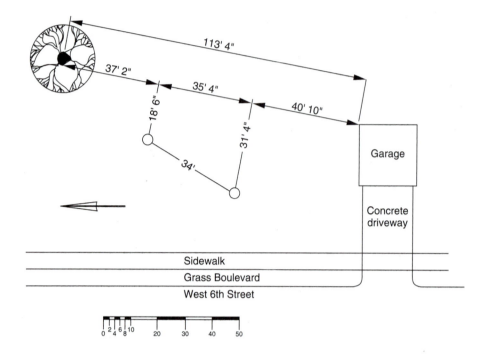

Always select the best fixed points possible, with emphasis on their permanence. Fixed points may be closet doors, electrical outlets, door jambs or corners of a structure. It is sometimes impossible to get to the corners of a room for accurate measurements due to obstacles. Triangulation is illustrated in Figure 2.8.

Compass Point Method The **compass point method** uses a protractor to measure the angle formed by two lines. In Figure 2.9, for example, Object *A* is located 10'7" from origin *C* and at an angle of 59° from the vertical line through point *C*. Object *B* is 16'7" from origin C at an angle of 47° from the vertical.

Cross-Projection Method For some interior crime scenes, it is useful to show the relationship between evidence on the floors and the walls. This can be done by sketching the room as though the viewer is straight above it, looking down. In effect, the room is flattened out much like a box cut down at the four corners and opened out flat. A **cross-projection sketch** presents the floor and walls as though they were one surface. Objects of evidence on both the floor and the walls can be meas-

ured to show their relationship on a single plane, as shown in Figure 2.10.

Step Four: Take Notes

After you have completed your sketch, take careful notes regarding all relevant factors associated with the scene that are not sketchable, such as lighting conditions, colors and people present.

Step Five: Identify the Scene

Prepare a **legend** containing the case number, the type of crime, name of the victim or complainant, location, date, time, the investigator, anyone assisting, scale of the sketch, direction of north and name of the person making the sketch (see Figure 2.11).

Step Six: Reassess the Sketch

Before leaving the scene, make sure you have recorded everything you need on the sketch. Make sure nothing

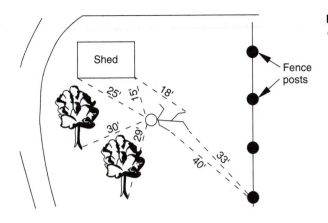

FIGURE 2.8
Triangulation Method

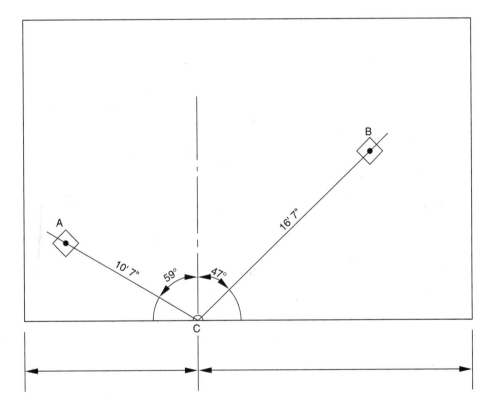

FIGURE 2.9
*Compass Point
Method*

has been overlooked or incorrectly diagrammed. Once you have left, nothing should be added to the sketch. Compare the scene with the sketch. Are all measurements included? Have all relevant notations been made? Have you missed anything? Figure 2.12 is a completed rough sketch of a crime scene.

File the Sketch

Place the rough sketch in a secure file. It is a permanent record for all future investigations of the crime. It may be used later to question witnesses or suspects and is the foundation for the finished scale drawing. The

FIGURE 2.10
Cross-Projection Sketch

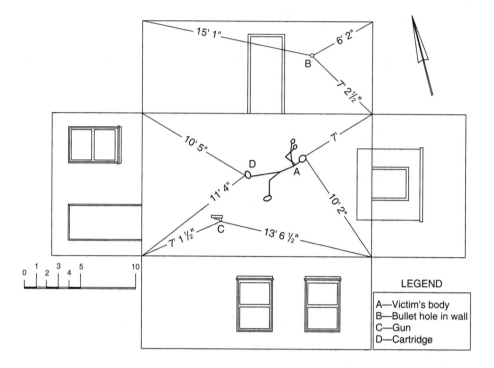

FIGURE 2.11
Sample Legend

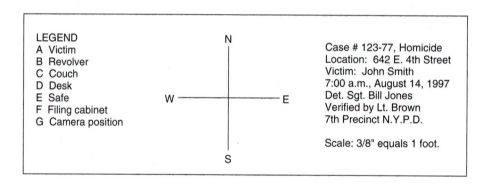

better the rough sketch is, the better the finished drawing will be.

Keep the rough draft in its original form even after the scale drawing is completed because it may be needed for testifying. Otherwise the defense may claim that changes were made in preparing the scale drawings.

The Finished Scale Drawing

Given a well-drawn rough sketch, the finished scale drawing can be completed. The **finished scale drawing** is done in ink on a good grade of paper and is drawn to scale, using exact measurements. The materials used for making scale drawings are listed in Table 2.2.

The artistic refinements of the scale drawing do not permit it to be made at the crime scene. Instead it is made at the police station by the investigator or by a drafter. If anyone other than the investigator prepares the finished scale drawing, the investigator must review it carefully and sign it along with the drafter.

The finished drawing can be simple or complex, but it must represent the actual distances, objects and evidence contained in the rough sketch. Color designations and plastic overlays to illustrate other phases of the investigation are often added. The drawing can be

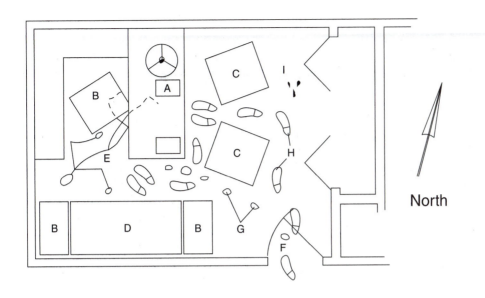

FIGURE 2.12
Completed Crime Scene Sketch

North

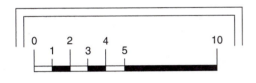

0   1   2   3   4   5   10

LEGEND

A—Lamp   F—Door suspect entered
B—Tables   G—Bloodstains
C—Chairs   H—Muddy footprints
D—Sofa   I—Cigarette butts
E—Victim

Table 2.2	Materials for Making Scale Drawings

Materials	Uses
Drawing kit	Contains tools for finer drawing
Triangular scale rule	Accurate scaling
Templates (assorted shapes, sizes)	Curves, oddly shaped objects
Indelible ink	For permanency of finished drawing
Drafting table	Ease, perfection in drawing
T-square	Accurate, straight lines, right angles
Drafting paper	Higher-quality absorption of inks, better display
Colors	Show areas of comparison

duplicated for other investigators and distributed to the prosecuting attorney. It is usually placed on white mounting board for display in court. A finished scale drawing is illustrated in Figure 2.13.

Computer-Assisted Drawing

Drawing software for investigators has improved significantly over the past decade. Benefits of computer-aided drawing programs include their accuracy, repeatability, simplicity and ability of files to be inserted into other documents to enhance reports. Dees (1997, p. 13) asserts that: "CAD-produced documents are more portable, more legible, and easier to duplicate and revise."

Dees (1999, p. 60) describes a three-dimensional architectural design and drawing program for Windows:

> 3D EyeWitness crime scene diagramming software from DesignWare . . . can create a much more detailed and more accurate diagram than most skilled draftsmen could create, and in less time. . . .
>
> The complete drawing, or any portion of it, can be zoomed in or out . . . and examined from any angle, by rotating it on the screen. . . .
>
> The software handles traffic diagrams with ease, and has a complete library of symbols used in reconstruction.

Dees (p. 60) also notes: "The Crime Zone, from the CAD Zone company, is a package with similar features. . . . The Crime Zone has many traditional crime scene icons and drawing tools." Such computer-assisted drawing programs are:

- Easy to learn
- Easy to use
- Flexible
- Fast

Figure 2.14 compares a typical hand-drawn diagram with one drawn with a CAD software program.

Visatex Corporation has developed software that generates professional crime-scene drawings as well as automated drawings and calculations for automobile accident reconstruction. Visatex's Compuscene™ software allows officers to select images of common household and office items and furniture, various vehicles and weapons and human figures and to show critical distances and dimensions automatically. Final scale drawings can be saved for easy modification or future reference. The drawings can be rescaled automatically and enlarged to 4' × 4' for courtroom presentation. In fact, some officers bypass the rough sketch entirely, going directly to the finished sketch via computer. As Jones (1999, p. 12) notes: "Quick yet accurate diagrams drawn in the field on laptops are eliciting confessions and producing higher conviction rates."

Today, the traditional two-dimensional sketches and drawings are being made even more realistic by using three-dimensional computer crime-scene sketches. A "3-D" crime scene is illustrated in Figure 2.15.

Legal Admissibility of Sketches and Drawings

- - - - - - -

An admissible sketch is one drawn or personally witnessed by an investigator that accurately portrays a crime scene.

- - - - - - -

As with all other evidence, the investigator must be prepared to testify about the information contained in the sketch, the conditions under which it was made and the process used to construct it.

- - - - - - -

A scale drawing also is admissible if the investigating officer drew it or approved it after it was drawn and if it accurately represents the rough sketch. The rough sketch must remain available as evidence.

- - - - - - -

Well-prepared sketches and drawings help judges, juries, witnesses and other people to visualize crime scenes.

FIGURE 2.13
Finished Scale Drawing

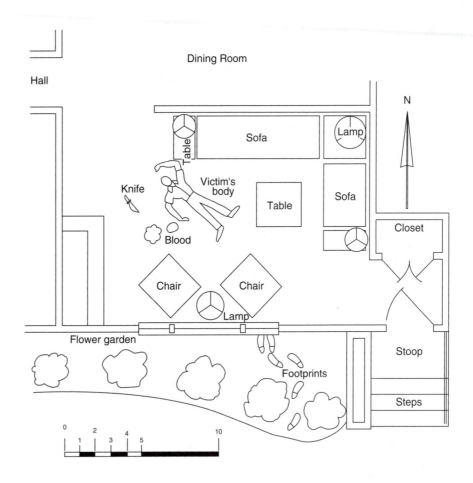

FIGURE 2.14

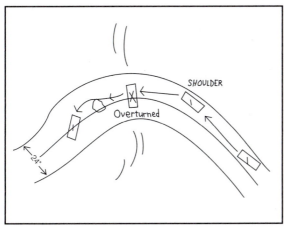

Typical Hand-Drawn Diagram

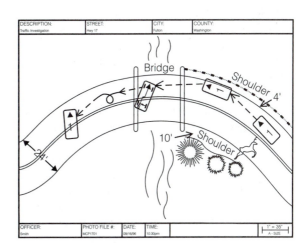

Courtroom Quality Diagrams
Drawn with the Crime Zone

Comparison of a Hand-Drawn and Computer-Generated Crime-Scene "Sketch"

Reprinted by permission of the CAD Zone, Inc.

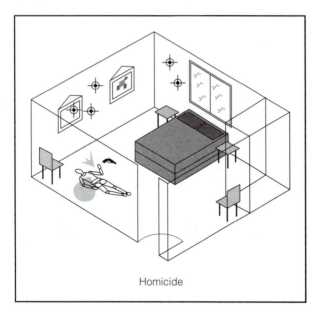

FIGURE 2.15
"3-D" Crime Scene

Reprinted by permission of the CAD Zone, Inc.

Summary

Photography, one of the first investigative techniques to be used at a crime scene, helps to establish that a crime was committed and to trace the occurrence of the crime. Photographs and videotapes reproduce the crime scene in detail for presentation to the prosecution, defense, witnesses, judge and jury in court. They are used in investigation, prosecution and police training.

Photography has become increasingly important in criminal investigation because it can immediately preserve evidence, accurately represent the crime scene and evidence, create interest and increase attention to testimony. However, photographs also have disadvantages: They are not selective, do not show actual distances and may be distorted and damaged by mechanical errors in shooting or processing. At a minimum, have available and be skilled in operating a 35 mm camera, an instant-print camera, a press camera, a fingerprint camera and video equipment.

Take photographs of the entire crime scene before anything is disturbed and avoid inaccuracies and distortions. First photograph the general area, then specific areas and finally specific objects of evidence. Take exterior shots first. Investigative photography includes crime-scene surveillance, aerial, night, laboratory, mug shot and lineup.

After photographs are taken, they must be properly identified, filed and kept secure to be admissible as evidence. In addition, rules of evidence dictate that photographs be material, relevant, competent, accurate, free of distortion and noninflammatory.

In addition to photographs, crime-scene sketches are often used. A crime-scene sketch assists in (1) interviewing and interrogating people, (2) preparing the investigative report and (3) presenting the case in court. Photographs, sketches and written notes are often needed to provide a clear picture of the scene.

Sketch the scene of a serious crime or accident after photographing it and before moving anything. Include all relevant objects and evidence. Materials needed for making the rough sketch include paper, pencil, long steel measuring tape, carpenter-type ruler, straightedge, clipboard, eraser, compass, protractor and thumbtacks. The steps involved in sketching include (1) observing and planning; (2) measuring distances and outlining the general area; (3) locating, measuring and recording objects and evidence within the outline; (4) taking notes; (5) identifying the scene; and (6) reassessing the sketch.

Plotting methods useful in locating objects and evidence include rectangular coordinate, baseline, triangulation and compass point. A cross-projection sketch shows the floor and walls in the same plane.

After completing the sketch, record in your notes the lighting conditions, colors, people present at the scene and all other information that cannot be sketched. Then place a legend in the lower corner of the sketch, outside the room or area outline. Identify the scene completely—the location, type of crime and case number. Include the scale and an arrow indicating north pointing to the top of the sketch. Include the name of the person making the sketch. Before leaving the scene, make sure nothing has been overlooked. Keep the sketch secure because it is the basis for the finished scale drawing and may be needed as evidence in court.

The finished scale drawing is done in ink on a good grade of paper and is drawn to scale using exact measurements. Both the rough sketch and the scale drawing are admissible in court if they are made or personally witnessed by the investigator and accurately portray the crime scene. The original rough sketch must remain available as evidence.

Checklist
Police Photography

- Photograph the entire scene and specific objects before moving anything.

- Include markers where needed to indicate size of evidence.

- Record equipment and techniques used, lighting conditions, and so on, in notes.
- Check for other sources of available photographs.

Questions

- Do the photographs taken at the crime scene depict the scene as you saw it?
- Do they show the exact appearance and condition of the scene as it appeared on your arrival?
- Have exterior pictures been taken to show entrances to the scene and the outside appearance of the crime scene?
- Have close-up shots been taken of the entry and exit points?
- Were aerial photos taken of the crime scene that show routes into and out of the scene area?
- Were interior pictures taken showing the entire layout of the facility in which the crime occurred?
- Do the photographs show the criminal act itself; for example, in a burglary, do the pictures show pry marks on the door, a broken window or shattered glass on the ground or floor?
- Were detailed pictures taken of how the crime was committed? The tools with which it was committed? Any weapon used?
- Do photographs show the victim? Injuries? Were wounds, scratches, bruises or other marks recorded in color as soon as possible after the commission of the crime? A day or two later as well?
- Were pictures taken of the deceased at the scene? Exact position, clothing worn, wounds?
- Were pictures taken at the autopsy?
- Do photographs show the property attacked?
- Were detailed pictures taken of all items of evidence before they were collected, showing exact condition and position at the scene?
- Was anything moved before the picture was taken? (If so, was it recorded in your notes?)
- Were photographs a true and accurate representation of relevant material?
- Are laboratory photos available for scientific tests conducted?
- Were photographs taken of the suspect to show appearance and condition at the time of the crime? Close-up photos of clothing worn?
- Were all pictures used for identifying suspects placed in special envelopes for later court testimony?

- If a lineup was conducted, were pictures taken of the lineup to show the people selected and their appearance in relation to each other?
- If a motor vehicle was involved, were detailed pictures taken of the vehicle's exterior and interior, color, license plate and any damaged areas?
- What types of photographs are available: moving pictures, black-and-white, color, videotapes?
- Are there crime-in-progress pictures from on-the-scene cameras such as bank surveillance cameras, or were pictures taken by media photographers?
- Have photographs been suitably mounted for presentation in court?
- Have all relevant notes been recorded in the notebook?

Sketching the Crime Scene

- Is your sketching kit readily available?
- Is the kit completely equipped?
- Have you formed a plan for making the sketch?
- Have you selected the simplest, largest scale?
- Have you sketched the outline of the room or area first?
- Have you used the appropriate plotting method to locate objects and evidence?
- Have you then added objects and evidence, including measurements?
- Have you recorded in your notes information that cannot be sketched?
- Have you prepared a legend for the sketch that includes identifying information, the scale and the direction of north?
- Have you reassessed the sketch and compared it with the scene?
- Have you kept the sketch secure?
- Have you prepared or had someone else prepare a finished scale drawing if needed?

Discussion Questions

1. In what types of crimes are photographs likely to be important to the investigation?
2. List the basic equipment you would want for a normal crime-scene photographic assignment. Compare it with others' preferences.

3. What sources outside your police department might contribute photographs of a crime scene?

4. How are investigative photographs developed and filed in your police department?

5. In what nationally known cases have photographs played a significant role?

6. In what well-known cases have rough sketches or scale drawings been important evidence?

7. What basic sketching materials would you want in an investigative kit?

8. What method of taking measurements for an outdoor sketch do you prefer? What are the advantages and disadvantages of this method?

9. By which plotting method could you best locate your precise position in your surroundings at this moment?

10. Who is responsible for making the crime-scene sketch? Should more than one officer sketch the scene?

References

Berg, Gregory R. "Crime Scene Investigations–Time to Get Back to the Basics." *Law Enforcement News,* Vol. XXV, No. 508, March 31, 1999, p. 8.

Biehl, Craig. "Ensuring Integrity of Digital Imaging." *The Police Chief,* Vol. LXVI, No. 6, June 1999, p. 12.

Blitzer, Herbert. "Forensic Imaging Options: Worth a Thousand Words." *The Police Chief,* October 1996, p. 14.

Dees, Tim. "Help for the Graphically Impaired." *Law and Order,* July 1997, pp. 13–14.

Dees, Tim. "Investigative Software." *Law and Order,* Vol. 47, No. 6, June 1999, pp. 55–61.

DeFranco, Liz Martinez. "IPIX the Crime Scene." *Law Enforcement Technology,* Vol. 26, No. 9, September 1999, pp. 82–85.

"Digital Detectives." *Law and Order,* February 1998, pp. 44–47.

"Digital Imaging Benefits Police." *Law and Order,* June 1999, pp. 37–39.

"Digital Photography Aids Investigations." *Law and Order,* June 1998, pp. 68–69.

Giulliano, Joseph. "Cameras Document Evidence." *Law and Order,* November 1998, p. 42.

Jones, Bobby. "Diagrams that Convict." *Law and Order,* Vol. 47, No. 7, July 1999, p. 12.

Lesce, Tony. "Single-Use Law Enforcement Camera." *Law and Order,* June 1998, p. 80.

Marchand, David. "Multi-Composite Suspect Rendering." *The Police Chief,* February 1997, pp. 18–20.

"Microscopy and Digital Photography." *Law Enforcement Technology,* March 1999, pp. 62–64.

"Montgomery Police Save Time and Money with Digital Cameras." *Law Enforcement Technology,* October 1998, pp. 94–96.

Morrison, Richard D. "Digital Point-and-Shoot Camera System." *Law Enforcement Technology,* Vol. 26, No. 6, June 1999, pp. 88–90.

Mossberg, Walter. "Digital Photography." *Las Vegas Review Journal,* January 31, 1999, p. 4K.

Page, Douglas. "Picture This: Oak Ridge National Laboratory (ORNL) Has Developed a Police Shield that Doubles as a Video Camera." *Law Enforcement Technology,* June 1998, pp. 70–73.

Paynter, Ronnie L. "Roll a Winner with D.I.C.E. (Digital Interactive Crime Environment)." *Law Enforcement Technology,* Vol. 26, No. 9, September 1999, pp. 88–90.

"Photo Mugshot System." *Law Enforcement Technology,* Vol. 26, No. 8, August 1999, pp. 98–101.

Pilant, Lois. "Spotlight on Computer Imaging." *The Police Chief,* Vol. LXVI, No. 5, May 1999, pp. 56–60.

Pult, Glenn. "Cost Makes Video Cameras Long Shot for Police." *Las Vegas Review Journal,* February 9, 1998, p. 2B.

Siuru, William D., Jr. "Seeing in the Dark." *Law Enforcement Technology,* January 1997, p. 38.

Stockton, Dale. "Going Digital." *Law and Order,* August 1997, pp. 30–35.

Stockton, Dale. "Police Video Up Close and Personal." *Law and Order,* Vol. 47, No. 8, August 1999, pp. 44–46.

Strandberg, Keith W. "On the Cutting Edge." *Law Enforcement Technology,* August 1998, pp. 18–23.

Wexler, Sanford. "Every Crime Scene Tells a Story." *Law Enforcement Technology,* Vol. 26, No. 8, August 1999, pp. 22–25.

Wimmer, Robert A. "Understanding the Ins and Outs of Digital Cameras." *Security Technology and Design,* August 1998, pp. 56–66, 87.

Wong, Jeff. "Digital Photography." *Law and Order,* January 1999, p. 6.

Investigative Notes and Reports

Do You Know?

Why notes are important in an investigation?

When to take notes?

What to record in investigative notes?

How to record the notes?

What the characteristics of effective notes are?

Where to file notes if they are retained?

How notes are used in court and what problems can arise?

What steps are involved in writing an investigative report?

What types of investigative reports may be required?

Why reports are important to an investigation?

How the narrative should be structured?

What the characteristics of effective investigative reports are?

Introduction

Most people who go into law enforcement are amazed at the amount of paperwork and writing that is required. Paperwork can constitute up to 70 percent of an investigator's job; thus typing and computer skills are essential. Strandberg (1998, p. 82) asserts:

> Writing is a constant fact of life for law enforcement. Reports, memos, updates, evaluations—all of these and more have to be written to drive the information machine that is law enforcement.
>
> Unfortunately, a great deal of law enforcement writing is mired in stilted language, unclear reporting, inconsistencies and mistakes, jargon and inappropriate word choice. This directly impacts how the justice system works.

One police science instructor describes the current status of law enforcement writing this way: "It is one of the areas where police have traditionally had a big, big problem" (Strandberg, p. 82). This chapter begins with a discussion of field notes: when to take them, what to record and where to record. Next is a discussion of various methods of taking notes, the characteristics of effective notes and filing notes. This is followed by an explanation of using notes in court. Then a discussion is presented on how to go from field notes to a police report, the types of reports that might be required and the importance of such reports. Next is a step-by-step method for organizing the field notes and actually writing the reports, followed by a description of the characteristics of effective reports and a way to evaluate your reports. The chapter concludes with a look at taping and dictating report writing and computerized report writing. ■

Field Notes

Note taking is not unique to the police profession. News reporters take notes to prepare stories; physicians record information furnished by patients to follow the progress of a case; lawyers and judges take notes to assist in interviewing witnesses and making decisions; students take notes in class and as they read. Quite simply, notes are brief records of what is seen and/or heard.

- - - - - - - - -

Investigative notes are a permanent written record of the facts of a case to be used in further investigation, in writing reports and in prosecuting the case.

- - - - - - - - -

Note taking and report writing are often regarded as unpleasant, boring tasks. Yet no duty is more important, as many officers have found, much to their embarrassment, when they did not take notes, or they took incomplete notes. For example, detailed notes can make or break a conviction, as Dahlinger and Simpson (1997, p. 97) point out: "Successful prosecution of drinking and driving offenses requires careful documentation of the officer's observations of the drinking suspect." When a defense attorney challenges in court the reliability or validity of various breath or blood measurements of alcohol content, the case often hinges on the thoroughness of an officer's written report.

Accurate notes not only aid later recall but also are used for preparing sketches and reports. Notes are important throughout an entire investigation.

When to Take Notes

- - - - - - - -

Start to take notes as soon as possible after receiving a call to respond and continue recording information as it is received throughout the investigation.

- - - - - - - -

Sometimes it is physically impossible to take notes immediately, for example, while driving a vehicle or in complete darkness. At other times, taking notes immediately will hinder obtaining information if it intimidates a witness or suspect. Whether to take out your notebook immediately in the presence of a person being questioned is a matter of personal insight and experience.

When people are excited, want to get their name in the newspaper or want to get your attention, you can usually record information immediately. Most people are willing to give information if you are friendly and courteous and you explain the importance of the information. In such cases no delay in taking notes is required.

On the other hand, reluctant witnesses and suspects may not talk if you record what they say. In such cases, obtain the information first and record it later. You must sense when it is best to delay writing notes. Specific methods of obtaining information from willing and unwilling people are discussed in Chapter 6.

If someone gives you an exact wording of what was said by a person committing a crime, have the witness initial that portion of your notes after reading it to help ensure that it is accurate. If possible, have people who give you information take time to write a statement in their own handwriting. This avoids the possibility they may later claim they did not make the statement or were misunderstood or misquoted.

What to Record

Take notes on everything you do in an official investigative capacity. Record all facts, regardless of where they may lead. Information establishing a suspect's innocence is as important as that establishing guilt.

Enter general information first: the time and date of the call, the location, officer assigned and arrival time at

Witnesses are important sources of information regarding crimes committed in their neighborhoods.

the scene. Police departments using centrally dispatched message centers may automatically record date, time and case numbers. Even if this is done, make written notes of this initial information because recording tapes may not be kept for extended periods or they may become unusable. The tapes and notes corroborate each other.

Record all information that helps to answer the questions: Who? What? Where? When? How? and Why?

As you take notes, ask yourself specific questions such as these (Hess and Wrobleski, 1996, pp. 24–25, reprinted by permission):

When: did the incident happen? was it discovered? was it reported? did the police arrive on the scene? were suspects arrested? will the case be heard in court?

Where: did the incident happen? was evidence found? stored? do victims, witnesses and suspects live? do suspects frequent most often? were suspects arrested?

Who: are suspects? accomplices?

Complete descriptions would include the following information: sex, race, coloring, age, height, weight, hair (color, style, condition), eyes (color, size, glasses), nose (size, shape), ears (close to head or protruding), distinctive features (birthmarks, scars, beard), clothing, voice (high or low, accent), other distinctive characteristics such as walk.

Who: were the victims? associates? was talked to? were witnesses? saw or heard something of importance? discovered the crime? reported the incident? made the complaint? investigated the incident? worked on the case? marked and received the evidence? was notified? had a motive?

What: type of crime was committed? was the amount of damage or value of the property involved? happened (narrative of the actions of suspects, victims and witnesses; combines information included under "How")? evidence was found? preventive measures had been taken (safes, locks, alarms, etc.)? knowledge, skill or strength was needed to commit the crime? was said? did the police officers do? further information is needed? further action is needed?

How: was the crime discovered? does this crime relate to other crimes? did the crime occur? was evidence found? was information obtained?

Why: was the crime committed (was there intent? consent? motive?)? was certain property stolen? was a particular time selected?

Make notes that describe the physical scene, including general weather and lighting conditions. Witnesses may testify to observations that would have been impossible, given the existing weather or lighting. Accurate notes on such conditions will refute false or incorrect testimony.

Record everything you observe in the overall scene: all services rendered, including first aid; description of the injured; location of wounds; who transported the victim and how. Record complete and accurate information regarding all photographs taken at the scene. As the search is conducted, record the location and description of evidence and its preservation. Record information to identify the type of crime and what was said and by whom. Include the name, address and phone number of every person present at the scene and all witnesses.

The amount of notes taken depends on the type of offense, the conditions of the case, your attitude and ability and the number of other officers assigned to the case. Make sure you take enough notes to completely describe what you observe and do during an investigation. This will provide a solid foundation for a detailed report and for court testimony. If in doubt about whether to include a specific detail, record it.

Do *not* jot down information unrelated to the investigation, for example, the phone number of a friend, an idea for a poem or a doodle. If the defense attorney, judge or jury see your notes, such irrelevant material will reflect poorly on your professionalism.

Where to Record Notes

Use a notebook to record all facts observed and learned during an investigation. Despite the availability of sophisticated recorders and computers, the notebook remains one of the simplest, most economical and most basic investigative tools. Notes taken on scraps of paper, on the backs of envelopes or on napkins are apt to be lost, and they also reflect poorly on an officer's professionalism.

Divide the notebook into sections for easy reference. One section might contain frequently used telephone numbers. Another section might contain frequently needed addresses. This information can be a permanent part of the notebook. Identify the notebook with your name, address, telephone number and the address and telephone number of your police department.

Opinions vary as to whether it is better to use a loose-leaf notebook or separate spiral-bound notebooks for each case. If you use a loose-leaf notebook, you can easily add paper for each case you are working on as the need arises, and you can keep it well organized. Most investigators favor the loose-leaf notebook because of its flexibility in arranging notes for reports and for testifying in court. However, use of a loose-leaf notebook opens the opportunity of challenge from the defense attorney that the officer has fabricated the notes, adding or deleting relevant pages. This can be countered by numbering each page, followed by the date and case number or by using a separate spiral notebook for each case.

Disadvantages of the latter approach are that the spiral notebook is often only partially used and therefore expensive and may be bulky for storage. Further, if other notes are kept in the same notebook, they also will be subject to the scrutiny of the defense. A final disadvantage is that if you need a blank sheet of paper for some reason, you should not take it from a spiral notebook because most of these notebooks indicate on the cover how many pages they contain. The defense can only conjecture about loose-leaf pages that might have been removed, but missing pages from a spiral notebook can be construed as evidence that something has been removed.

The decision to use a loose-leaf or spiral-bound notebook is sometimes a matter of department policy. In addition to the notebook, always carry pens and pencils. Use a pen for most notes because ink is permanent. You may want to use pencil for rough sketches that require minor corrections as you sketch.

How to Take Notes

Note taking is an acquired skill. Time does not permit a verbatim transcript. Learn to select key facts and record them in abbreviated form.

- - - - - - - -

Write brief, legible, abbreviated notes that others can understand.

- - - - - - - -

Notes provide the basis for the written report. Sometimes notes are dictated. In many instances a combination of notes and dictation are used.

Do not include words such as *a, and* and *the* in your notes. Omit all other unnecessary words. For example, if a witness said, "I arrived here after having lunch at Harry's Cafe, a delightful little place over on the west side, at about 1:30, and I found my boss had been shot," you would record: "Witness arrived scene 1:30 (after lunch at Harry's Cafe) to find boss shot." You would not know at the time if the fact that she had lunch at Harry's Cafe was important, but it might be, so you would include it.

Write or print legibly, especially when recording names, addresses, telephone numbers, license numbers, distances and other specific facts. If you make an error, cross it out, make the correction and initial it. Do *not* erase. Whether intentional or accidental, erasures raise credibility questions.

Whenever possible, use standard abbreviations such as *mph, DWI, Ave.* Do *not,* however, devise your own shorthand. For example, if you wrote, "Body removed by A. K.," the initials *A. K.* would be meaningless to others. If you become ill, injured or deceased, others must be able to read and understand your notes. This is necessary

to further the investigation even though some question regarding admissibility in court may arise.

Using a Tape Recorder

Some police departments use tape recorders extensively because of the definite advantage of recording exactly what was stated with no danger of misinterpreting, slanting or misquoting. However, tape recorders do not replace the notebook. Despite their advantages, they also have serious disadvantages. The most serious is that they can malfunction and fail to record valuable information. Weak batteries or background noise can also distort the information recorded. In addition, transcribing tapes is time consuming, expensive and subject to error. Finally, the tapes themselves, not the transcription, are the original evidence and thus must be retained and filed.

If information is taped, check the recorder before using it, record the appropriate heading before beginning the questioning, and always play the tape back to ensure that the information is recorded satisfactorily. Supplement the tape with notes of the key points.

Characteristics of Effective Notes

Effective notes describe the scene and the events well enough to enable a prosecutor, judge or jury to visualize them.

- - - - - - - -

Effective notes are complete, accurate, specific, factual, clear, well organized and legible.

- - - - - - - -

The basic purpose of notes is to record the *facts* of a case. Recall the discussion of the importance of objectivity in an investigation. Use this same objectivity in note taking. For example, you might include in your notes the *fact* that a suspect reached inside his jacket and your *inference* that he was reaching for a gun. Your *opinion* on the merits of gun-control laws, however, has no place in your notes. If you have a specific reason for including an opinion, clearly label the statement as an opinion. Normally, however, restrict your notes to the facts you observe and learn and the inferences you draw. If, for example, you see a person whom you consider to be nervous and you make a note to that effect, you are recording an inference. If, on the other hand, you record specific observations such as "The man kept looking over his shoulder, checking his watch and wiping perspiration from his forehead," then you are recording facts on which you based your inference. You may not remember six months or a year later why you inferred that the man was nervous.

Record facts accurately. An inaccurately recorded name can result in the loss of a witness or suspect. Inaccurate measurements can lead to wrong conclusions. Have people spell their names for you. Repeat spellings and numbers for verification. Recheck measurements.

Be as specific as possible. Rather than saying, "tall," "fast" or "far," say "6'8"," "80 mph" or "50 feet." Little agreement may exist on what is tall, fast or far.

Notes are usually taken rapidly, increasing the chance of errors. Take enough time to write legibly and clearly. Legibility and clarity are not synonymous. *Legibility* refers to the distinctness of your letters and numbers. *Clarity* refers to the distinctness of your statements. For example, lack of clarity is seen in a note that states, "When victim saw suspect he pulled gun." *Who* pulled the gun: the victim or the suspect? The same lack of clarity is seen in the statements "When suspect turned quickly I fired" (Did the suspect turn quickly, or did the officer fire quickly?) and "When the suspect came out of the house, I hit him with the spotlight." Make certain your notes are clear and can be interpreted only one way.

Effective notes are also well organized. Make entries from each case on separate pages and number the pages. Keep the pages for each case together and record the case number on each page.

Filing Notes

Some officers destroy all their field notes after they have written their reports. They believe that notes simply duplicate what is in the report and may in fact contain information no longer pertinent when the report is written. Some police departments also have this as a policy. If department policy is to keep the notes, place them in a location and under a filing system that makes them available months, even years, later. Department policy usually determines where and how notes are filed.

- - - - - - - -

If notes are retained, file them in a secure location readily accessible to investigators.

- - - - - - - -

Store notes in an official police department case file or any secure location where they are available on short demand. Some departments file notes with the original file in the official records department. Others permit an officer to keep the original notes and file only the report made from the notes. Wherever notes are filed, they must be secure.

No one filing system is best. Notes may be filed alphabetically by the victim's name or by case number or in chronological order. As long as the system is logical, the notes will be retrievable. Appeals have been granted as long as 20 years after convictions, with the defendant being granted a new trial. Because of this, many officers retain their notes indefinitely.

Using Notes in Court

Properly introduced *original* notes made by the testifying officer can be used in a criminal proceeding. Notes may be used by a person other than the officer who wrote them if the other person was present when they were written, witnessed the writing and initialed the notes at the time.

Officers may refer to their notes to refresh their memories, but if they do so, the defense counsel may examine them and read or show them to the judge or jury. The defense may criticize the conditions under which the notes were taken, their readability, spelling errors and other discrepancies. Such attempts to discredit the value of the officer's testimony can be embarrassing, especially if attention is called to unrelated material such as doodling.

> Original notes are legally admissible in court, and officers may use them to refresh their memories. Officers should take to court only those notes that pertain to the particular case.

Best evidence, in the legal sense, is the original, best and highest evidence; the highest available degree of proof that can be produced. The best-evidence rule specifies that whenever possible, the original notes are to be used. However, a copy of the original may be used to testify from if the reason for failing to produce the original is clearly explained. For example, the original notes may have been destroyed, lost, stolen or become unreadable. If you are not using original notes during your testimony, be sure to state this.

The difficulties that can arise when original notes are not used are illustrated by the case of an investigator who inspected a car believed to be involved in a hit-and-run accident. As the vehicle was raised on a hoist, the investigator made notes regarding a piece of fabric caught on the head of a bolt and a hair located at another spot. Because these notes were smudged and stained from wetness and oil drippings, the investigator typed the notes and later testified from these typed notes. When asked by defense counsel whether the notes were original, the officer said yes. The defense council then asked where and how the notes were made. Hearing the investigator's explanation, he immediately challenged the notes as not original. Fortunately, the investigator could produce the original notes and was allowed to testify from them after they were properly introduced. The officer did not intentionally introduce false evidence, but the notes were *not* original, and the alert defense attorney took the opportunity to attempt to discredit the important testimony.

If your notes are original, factual and accurate, you should have them with you, to refer to them and to testify from them. The use of notes in court is probably their most important legal application. They can help discredit a suspect's or a defense witness's testimony; support evidence already given by a prosecution witness, strengthening that testimony; and defend against false allegations by the suspect or defense witnesses. Notes give you an advantage because others rarely make written notes and, therefore, must testify from memory.

Reports

Notes provide a foundation for the investigative report written for each case. Five basic steps are involved in writing a report (Hess and Wrobleski, p. 42):

> Steps in report writing:
> 1. Gather the facts: Investigate, interview, interrogate.
> 2. Record the facts immediately: Take notes.
> 3. Organize the facts.
> 4. Write the report.
> 5. Evaluate the report: Edit and proofread; revise if necessary.

The first two steps have already been completed before you sit down to write the report. If they have not, it is unlikely that your report will be adequate. Before looking at the remaining steps, however, consider the types of police reports you might be required to write, as well as the importance of such reports.

Types of Reports

Although the types of reports and the forms used vary widely among police departments, most departments use at least three types.

> Investigators usually complete (1) an initial or preliminary report, (2) supplemental or progress reports and (3) a closing or final report.

The initial or preliminary report is completed after the preliminary investigation. This may be followed by a series of supplemental reports to keep the appropriate individuals apprised of progress in the case. The closing or final report is prepared before prosecution of the case.

Some departments have attempted to standardize report writing by using forms. However, most forms still require a narrative account of the investigation. Law enforcement report forms vary greatly in format. Many report forms contain boxes for placement of descriptive information and addresses and phone numbers of the persons involved. (See Figure 3.1.) It is unnecessary to duplicate this information in the narrative unless it is needed for clarity—simply because it tends to interrupt the flow of words and clutter the narrative. Conversely,

GENERAL	3. Specific Offense & NRS/BC Ord. 181.26 Theft-Motor Vehicle	1. D.R. Number 90-0906	2. Reference D.R. Number 90-0704	4. Offense Reported: ☒ Dispatch ☐ Citizen ☐ On view ☐ Station Rpt.	5. Teleserve ☐ Yes ☐ No

LOC. — 13. Physical Address and/or Location of Occurrence (address, city, state): 1423 Shady Beach Rd. Boulder City, Nevada 89005 — 14. Reporting Zone: 14 — 8. NCIC Trans. No.: 6034

TIME — 9. Date–Time Occurred on or between: Month Feb, Day 15th, Year 1999, Time 0213 — 10. Date–Time Reported: Month, Day, Year, Time

CODE: V - Victim   L - Legal Owner   RO - Registered Owner   LIST FIRM NAME AND CORPORATE NAME IF DIFFERENT

VICTIMS

11. Code	12. Name (Last, First, Middle) Timothy Reinke	13. Sex M	14. Race W	15. Age 34	16. Date of Birth 9-12-56	17. Occupation Desk Clerk

18. Address Residence: 4401 Jersey Avenue, Boulder City, Nevada — Zip Code 89005 — SS 476-08-1406 — Telephone (x=Day) ( ) 239-1082 [ ]
Business — ( ) [ ]

11. Code	12. Name (Last, First, Middle)	13. Sex	14. Race	15. Age	16. Date of Birth	17. Occupation

18. Address Residence — Zip Code — SS — Telephone (x=Day) ( ) [ ]
Business — ( ) [ ]

11. Code	12. Name (Last, First, Middle)	13. Sex	14. Race	15. Age	16. Date of Birth	17. Occupation

18. Address Residence — Zip Code — SS — Telephone (x=Day) ( ) [ ]
Business

20. Additional Persons Listed? Yes ☐ No ☒

CODES: RP-Reporting Party W-Witness LP-Last Person in Possession L-Legal Owner D-Discovered Crime PA-Person Accepting Document
P- Person Securing Premise

WITNESSES

21. Code	22. Name (Last, First, Middle)	23. DOB	24. Address	Zip Code	25. Telephone (X=Day) Include Area Code
	None		Res. Bus.		
			Res. Bus.		
			Res. Bus.		
			Res. Bus.		
			Res. Bus.		

VEHICLE

26. Vehicle Year 1988	27. Vehicle Make Plymouth	28. Vehicle Model Station Wagon	29. Vehicle Style 4 dr.	30. Vehicle Colors – Top/Bottom blue

31. Vehicle License No. 592-AHU	32. License Type Passenger	33. License Year 1999	34. License State Nevada	35. Vehicle License Colors – Prime/Numerals Gray-Blue

Plates taken off vehicle? ☐ Yes ☒ No — 37. Vehicle I.D. No./Motorcycle Frame No. 3461426 — 37. Vehicle Engine No. 643129 — 38. Vehicle Insured By Farmers Insurance

39. Additional Vehicle Identifiers (damage, chrome wheels, etc.) Dent right front fender

40. Evidence Obtained: ☒ Fingerprints ☐ Vehicle ☐ Stains ☒ Other Prints ☒ Photos ☐ Blood/Semen ☐ None ☐ Weapon/Tools ☐ Hair ☐ Other

INVEST.

41. INVESTIGATION
☒ Dusted for latents ☒ Photo/Impression Taken ☐ Diagram of Scene ☐ Witnesses Contacted
☐ Tool Marks Noted ☐ Scene Photographed ☒ Neighbors Checked ☒ Victim Contacted
☒ Vehicle Shoe Tracks ☐ Photos of Victim ☒ Area Checked ☐ Scene Processed

SUSPECT

PRIMARY	Yes	No	SECONDARY	Yes	No	SECONDARY	Yes	No
42. Was a suspect arrested?	☐	☒	47. Can a suspect be described?	☐	☒	50. Is there significant physical evidence?	☒	☐
43. Can a suspect be named?	☐	☒	48. Is there a significant M.O. present?	☐	☒	51. Are all elements of crime present?	☒	☐
44. Can a suspect be located?	☐	☒	49. Is stolen property traceable?	☐	☒	52. Can suspect vehicle be identified?	☒	☐
45. Was there a witness to the crime?	☒	☐						
46. Can suspect be identified?	☐	☒						

53. Is there a significant reason to believe the crime may be solved?   Yes ☒ No ☐

If fingerprint match can be found-several suspect possibilities known

CERT.

54. Reporting Party Signature: I affirm this information is true and correct.

☒ Open ☐ Closed   Copy to: ☐ CSO ☒ Dept. F.U. ☐ D.A. ☐ Other ☐ CA ☐ JO F.U. ☐ Patrol F.U. ☐ Records

55. Officer Signature, Number and Division #8 Patrol	56. Supervisor Initials and Date 2-15-99	57. Detective Assigned Clifford Sharr	58. Page___ Of

FIGURE 3.1
Offense Report Form

narrative reports that are not contained within box-style law enforcement reports should include descriptive information, addresses and phone numbers within the body of the narrative. Note the underlined information in this excerpt from a narrative:

> The victim, Harry Brown, <u>1925 West State St., Milwaukee, Wisconsin, phone: 955-4331,</u> told me that taken during the burglary was his diamond ring, <u>one-third karat diamond stone, 14-karat gold setting, with the initials R. S. G. inside the band, valued at $575.00.</u>

If the underlined information was reported on a box-style report form, it could be deleted from the narrative report—unless that information was needed for clarity.

Importance of Reports

Servino (1999, p. 23) recalls that Wilson and McLaren wrote in *Police Administration* nearly 30 years ago:

> Almost everything that a police officer does must be reduced to writing. What is written is often the determining factor in whether a suspect is arrested in the first place, and if he is arrested, whether he is convicted and sentenced. The contents of written reports, in fact, often have great bearing in life-and-death situations. To say that officers need to be proficient in report writing is an understatement.

Garner (1997, p. 32) stresses: "The best investigation is only as good as the report completed about it. Molden (1996, p. 13) emphasizes: "The more complex our society becomes, the more litigious and demanding the criminal justice system, the greater will be the need for detailed, accurate and complete reporting by officers." Your reports are *used,* not simply filed away. If investigative reports were not required for efficient law enforcement, you would not have to write them.

> Reports are a permanent written record of important facts that can be used to examine the past, keep other police officers informed, continue investigations, prepare court cases, provide the court with relevant facts, coordinate law enforcement activities, plan for future law enforcement services and evaluate law enforcement officers' performance.

What you write may be read by many different people: other officers, your supervisor, lawyers, judges, citizens or reporters. You must communicate to these numerous readers what happened, when and how. Well-written reports not only further the cause of justice; they also reflect positively on your education, your competence and your professionalism.

Most law enforcement officers submit their reports for prosecution with concern over the outcome but without much thought about the wheels they've started in motion. This is understandable, for they've done their jobs, and many more cases wait to be investigated. But, what happens when they haven't really done their jobs—when their reports are distorted or incomplete (as many are) because of poor writing? The results not only cost the taxpayers in wasted man-hours, but they also breed disaster in the courtroom.

To cite an all-too-common example, in one recent criminal case the reporting officer, using the passive voice, wrote the following in his report: "The weapon was found in the bushes where the suspect had thrown it." He did not clarify this statement elsewhere in his report. Expectedly, the prosecuting attorney subpoenaed the reporting officer to testify at the preliminary hearing. Unfortunately, the reporting officer's testimony revealed that his partner, not he, had observed the suspect's action and had retrieved the weapon. The partner was unavailable to testify on short notice. Without his testimony the necessary elements of the crime could not be established and the case was dismissed and had to be refiled. The man-hours expended at the time of the dismissal, by witnesses, secretaries, clerks, attorneys and the judge, were virtually wasted because the whole process had to be repeated. The reporting officer could have avoided the problem at the onset through use of the active voice which would have provided clarification. Sadly, this basic writing error is not an isolated example; it, and others like it, slip through the system daily, causing delays in the judicial process and depleting dwindling budgets.[1]

Field Training Officers' Opinions about Reports

Molden (p. 13) reported on a survey of 148 field training officers in Los Angeles County by the National Association

----

[1]Reprinted with permission from the preface by Floyd T. Stokes in *For the Record: Report Writing in Law Enforcement,* 4th edition. By Kären M. Hess and Henry M. Wrobleski, Bloomington, MN: Innovative Systems–Publishers, 1996, p. i.

of Field Training Officers. In this survey respondents expressed "serious concerns" about law enforcement trainees' ability to write reports. In response to the question, "What concerns do you have with trainees?," the greatest number of responses indicated report writing. Likewise, in response to the question, "In what areas do academies need to improve?" the greatest number answered report writing.

With the importance of effective police reports in mind, consider now the third step in creating such reports: organizing the information from your field notes.

Organizing Information

According to Clark (1996, p. 98), the key to writing good reports is "strict adherence to basic format, *organization* and correct word usage." [emphasis added]

First make an informal outline. As Lewis (1999, p. 136) points out: "Writing is slower than thinking. You will leave out thoughts as your mind races ahead of your pen. Outline important points so thoughts will not be left out." Next, list what you want to include under each heading in the outline. Review your notes and number each statement to match a heading in your outline. For example, if section III.C. of the outline is headed "Description of Suspect #2," write *III.C.* in the margin wherever Suspect #2 is described in your notes. List the facts of the investigation in **chronological order** beginning with the response to the call and concluding with the end of the investigation. If the report is long (over four pages), use headings to guide the reader, for example, "Initial Response," "Crime Scene Conditions," "Photographs Taken," "Evidence," "Witnesses," "Suspects," etc. After you complete the outline and determine where each note fits, you are ready to write the report.

Writing the Report: Structuring the Narrative

The following discussion of structuring the narrative is from *For the Record: Report Writing in Law Enforcement* by Hess and Wrobleski (pp. 51–52, reprinted by permission):

> The law enforcement **narrative** is essentially a technical report structured in chronological order describing a sequence of investigative events. Those events are:

1. You, the reporting officer, receive information by either viewing something or by being told something, e.g., by examining a crime scene or by interviewing a victim or witness.

2. You act on the information you receive, e.g., by collecting evidence, by talking to other witnesses, etc.

3. Your actions cause you to receive additional information, e.g., new witnesses to talk to, other areas to search, etc.

4. You act on the new information you receive.

This process continues until you have exhausted all leads, completed the investigation or turned the case over to another entity, such as the detective division.

The narrative should first set the stage. Give the date, time, how you came to be involved and the type of incident. For example:

> *On 9–12–99 at about 0750 hours, I was dispatched to the Downtown Marina regarding the report of a felony theft. Upon arrival at about 0800 hours, I talked to the victim, Norman Smith.*

The next paragraph of the narrative should explain what information you received. For example:

> *Smith said he arrived at the Downtown Marina at about 0730 hours to work on his boat. When he went to his walled boat dock, he discovered the dock's door was open and his boat and motor were missing. He did not go inside the dock but immediately phoned the police. He had locked the door the night before at about 1930 hours when he left the dock. The boat and motor were in the dock at that time. He had no idea how the boat and motor were taken. (See Property Loss Section for full description of the missing items.)*

The following paragraph should explain what you did about the information you received. For example:

> *I checked the open door and saw that the lock appeared to be broken and that the knob had marks on it. The marks appeared similar in pattern to pipewrench jaws. I searched the area and located a 14-inch pipewrench on the dock behind the door. I saw no other items of evidence.*

The narrative should then explain what you did about the new information you received. For example:

> *I collected the door knob and pipewrench as physical evidence. I photographed the scene. I radioed a description of the boat and motor to dispatch for entry into the NCIC computer system. I checked the area for witnesses but found none. I booked the collected items and negatives into the evidence section (refer to the evidence sheet for details).*

The final paragraph of the narrative should explain the disposition of your investigation. For example:

> *Case referred to the detective division for follow-up.*

Usually the narrative is structured as follows:

1. The opening paragraph of a police report states the time, date, type of incident and how you became involved.

2. The next paragraph contains what you were told by the victim or witness. For each person talked to, use a separate paragraph.

3. Next record what you did based on the information you received.

4. The final paragraph states the disposition of the case.

Steps 2 and 3 may be repeated several times in a report on an incident where you talk to several witnesses/victims.

Characteristics of Effective Reports

In addition to an accurate, complete, well-structured narrative, an effective report exhibits several other characteristics.

An effective report uses paragraphs, the past tense, first person and active voice. It is factual, accurate, objective, complete, concise, clear, mechanically correct, written in standard English, legible and reader focused.

Paragraphs

The discussion on structuring the narrative assumed that the writer *uses paragraphs* to guide the reader. Keep the paragraphs short (usually 100 words or less). Discuss only one subject in each paragraph.

Paragraphs are reader friendly, guiding the reader through your report. Most paragraphs should be five to six sentences, although they may be a single sentence or up to 10 or 15 sentences on occasion. Start a new paragraph when you change speakers, locations, time or ideas, for example, observations, descriptions and statements.

Past Tense

Write in the past tense throughout the report. **Past tense** writing uses verbs that show events have already occurred. Your report contains what *was* true at the time

you took your notes. Use of present tense can cause tremendous problems later. For example, suppose you wrote "John Doe *lives* at 100 South Street and *works* for Ace Trucking Company." One year later you find yourself on the witness stand with a defense attorney asking you: "Now, Officer, your report says that John Doe lives at 100 South Street. Is that correct?" You may not know, and you would have to say so. The next question: "Now, Officer, your report says John Doe works for Ace Trucking Company. Is *that* correct?" Again, you may be uncertain and be forced into an "I don't know" response. Use of the past tense in your report avoids this problem.

First Person

Use the first person to refer to yourself. **First person** in English uses the words *I, me, my, we, us* and *our.* The sentence "*I* responded to the call" is written in the first person. This is in contrast to "*This officer* responded to the call," which uses the third person. Whether you remember your English classes and discussions of first-, second- and third-person singular and plural is irrelevant. Simply remember to refer to yourself as *I* rather than as *this officer.*

Active Voice

In the **active voice** the subject of the sentence performs the actions, for example, "I wrote the report." This is in contrast to the *passive* voice, in which the subject does nothing, for example, "The report was written by me." The report did not do anything. The problem with the passive voice is that often the *by* is left off, for example, "The report was written." Later, no one knows who did the writing. Passive voice results in a "whodunit" which can have serious consequences in court, as illustrated in the scenario on page 65.

Objective

Be objective. Keep to the facts. Include all facts, even those that may appear to be damaging to your case, and use words with no emotional overtones. Word choice is an often overlooked—yet very important—aspect of report writing. Consider, for example, the difference in effect achieved by these three sentences:

The man cried.   The man wept.   The man blubbered.

Only the first sentence is truly objective. The second sentence makes the reader feel sympathetic toward the man. The third makes the reader unsympathetic. Likewise, a writer who uses the word *nigger* to refer to a black person reveals bias. An alert defense attorney will capitalize on words with emotional overtones and attempt to show bias. Even the use of *claimed* rather than *stated* can be used to advantage by a defense attorney, who might suggest that the officer's use of *claimed* implies that the officer did not believe the statement.

Also, use the correct word. Do not confuse words that are similar, or you can be made to appear ridiculous. For example, this sentence in an officer's report would probably cast suspicion on the officer's intelligence: "During our training we spent four hours learning to resemble a firearm and the remainder of the time learning defective driving."

Avoid **conclusionary language.** Show, don't tell. Do not, for example, write "The man *could* not walk a straight line." You do not know what another person can or cannot do. The objective way to report this would be "The man *did* not walk a straight line." Even better would be "The man stepped 18 inches to the right of the line twice and 12 inches to the left of the line three times."

Phrases such as "he saw what happened" or "he heard what happened" are also conclusionary. People can be looking directly at something and not see it either because they are simply not paying attention or because they have terrible vision. The same is true of hearing. Again, you do not know what another person sees or hears. Your report should say "He *said* he saw what happened," or "He looked directly at the man committing the crime."

Another common conclusionary phrase found in police reports is "The check was signed by John Doe." Unless you saw John Doe sign the check, the objective statement would be "The check was signed John Doe." The little two-letter word *by* can create tremendous problems for you on the witness stand!

One area in which complete, accurate *objective* reporting is critical is where use of force is involved. Peak (1996, p. 13) suggests that an officer's documentation of his use of force is likely to improve once he realizes that a well-written report is his best defense against excessive force claims. Peak offers the following advice:

> The report should address why it was necessary for the officer to use force, what force was used, why the force used was reasonable, and the consequences that resulted from its use.
>
> The report should obviously describe any observable injuries sustained by the suspect, any complaints of injury made by the suspect and the officer's response. It is equally important to document the officer's observations and any statements made by the suspect that tend to show that the suspect was not injured. For example:
>
> I assisted Johnson to his feet and looked him over. I saw no evidence of injuries. I asked if he wanted to

see a doctor, and he said, "No." I saw him walk without difficulty, and he had no difficulty entering or exiting my squad. He did not complain of any injuries while in my custody.

Concise

Be concise. Avoid wordiness. Length alone does not ensure quality. Some reports can be written in half a page; others require 12 or even 20 pages. No specific length can be prescribed, but strive to include all relevant information in as few words as possible. For example, do not say "The car was blue in color"; say "The car was blue." Other wordy phrases to avoid are listed in Table 3.1. Avoiding wordiness does not mean eliminating details; it means eliminating empty words and phrases.

Clear

Make certain your sentences can be read only one way. Consider, for example, the following unclear sentences:

- When completely plastered, officers who volunteer will paint the locker room.
- Miami police kill a man with a machete.
- Three cars were reported stolen by the Los Angeles police yesterday.
- Police begin campaign to run down jaywalkers.
- Squad helps dog bite victim.

Rewrite such sentences so that only one interpretation is possible. For example, the first sentence might read: "Officers who volunteer will paint the locker room after it is completely plastered." The second sentence might read: "Miami police kill a man who was brandishing a machete."

Another way to increase clarity is to use diagrams and sketches. These are especially helpful in investigative reports of accidents, homicides and burglaries. The diagrams need not be works of art, but they should be in proportion and help the reader follow the description in the report.

Grammatically and Mechanically Correct

Mistakes in spelling, punctuation, capitalization and grammar give the impression that the writer is careless, uneducated or stupid—maybe all three! Use a dictionary and a grammar book if in doubt about how to write something. The dictionary can tell you not only how to spell a word but also whether it should be capitalized and how it should be abbreviated.

A word on spelling: If you are a poor speller, do not let it bother you. As W. C. Fields said, "Anyone who can

Table 3.1	Concise Writing

Wordy	Concise
made a note of the fact	noted
square in shape	square
despite the fact that	although
at a high rate of speed	rapidly
in the state of California	in California
with reference to	about
in the amount of	for
subsequent to	after
is of the opinion	believes
in spite of	despite
month of February	February
red in color	red
in the event that	if
the perpetrator of the crime	the suspect
at that point in time	then

spell a word only one way is an idiot." In fact, many intelligent people are poor spellers. Why? Because the English language consists of words from numerous countries, each country with its own spelling rules. This results in a hodgepodge of spelling rules. For example, in no other language does the combination of written letters *ough* have six different sounds: d*ough*, b*ough*t, b*ough*, r*ough*, thr*ough*, and hicc*ough*. Nor does any other language have 13 different ways to spell the sound *sh*, the sound people make when they want someone to be quiet: *ch*aperon, con*sc*ious, fu*ch*sia, is*s*ue, man*s*ion, mi*ss*ion, na*ti*on, nau*se*ous, o*ce*an, p*sh*aw, *sch*ist, *sh*oe, *s*ugar, suspi*ci*on. No wonder people have difficulty mastering English spelling.

To make spelling less difficult, consider using a *speller/divider*. These little reference books contain thousands of the most commonly used words—showing their spelling and how they are divided. The reader is not distracted by definitions, information on the history of the word, synonyms and so on. The most important advantage is that one speller/divider page has as many words on it as 15 to 20 dictionary pages. Bookstores and office-supply stores carry these handy little books.

Whether you use a dictionary or a speller/divider, when you look up a word, it is a good idea to make a check mark beside it in the margin. The next time you look up that same word, make another check. As the row of checks gets longer, you can easily see how much time

you are wasting looking up the same word. Do something about that word. Either learn it, or write it some place where you can easily locate it, such as the inside cover of your dictionary or speller/divider. This can save you much time and effort in the future.

Legible

Write or print legibly. Ideally, reports should be typed. However, this often is impossible. Many officers prefer to print their reports to increase readability. Whether the reports are typed, written or printed, make certain that others can read them easily.

Reader Friendly

Always *consider who the reader is.* Among possible readers of police reports, in addition to other police officers, are judges, lawyers, juries, coroners, parole officers, child-welfare-agency personnel and insurance people. Given these varied backgrounds and individuals with limited familiarity with law enforcement terminology, the necessity for reader-focused reports becomes obvious.

One way to be reader friendly is to be certain the narrative portion of your report can stand alone. That calls for eliminating such phrases as *the above*. A reader-friendly report does not begin, "On the above date at the above time, I responded to the above address to investigate a burglary in progress."

Using such phrases presents two problems. First, if readers take time to look "above" to find the information, their train of thought is broken. It is difficult to find where to resume reading, and time is wasted. Second, if readers do *not* take time to look "above," important information is not conveyed, and it is very likely that the reader, perhaps subconsciously, will be wondering what would have been found "above." If information is important enough to refer to in your report, include it in the narrative. Do not take the lazy approach and ask your reader to search for the information "above."

Evaluating Your Report

Once you have written your report, evaluate it. Do not simply add the final period, staple the pages together and turn it in. Reread it. Make certain it says what you want it to and contains no content or composition errors. Ask yourself if the report is accurate, factual, organized, objective, complete, concise, clear, in past tense and active voice, mechanically correct, written in standard English and legible.

The California Highway Patrol relies heavily on computers to generate reports.

Taping and Dictating Reports

Taping or dictating reports is common in some departments. Reports that need quick attention might be red tagged, and records personnel type all red-tagged cases first.

In effect, taping or dictating reports shifts the bulk of writing/transcribing time to the records division. According to some, report dictation may cut reporting time down to a fraction of the time required for handwritten reports (Dees, 1999, p. 15). Even with taping or dictating, however, officers must still take final responsibility for what is contained in the report. Do not assume that what you think you spoke into a dictation machine is what will end up on

paper. Following are some humorous illustrations of how some dictated sentences can be misinterpreted:

He called for a toe truck.

Smith was arrested for a mister meaner.

Jones was a drug attic.

The victim was over rot.

Johnson died of a harder tack.

Another disadvantage sometimes associated with dictated reports is cited by DiMiceli of the California Peace Officer Standards and Training Commission:

Less preparation time results in longer reports, often with extraneous stuff due to long-winded officers. Something about dictating prompts verbosity.

Other problems noted included delays in getting the final product ready for filing or action (Dees, pp. 15–16).

Computerized Report Writing

Computers have made significant contributions to efficiency in report writing. Hess (1999, p. 43) states: "If the pen is mightier than the sword, in modern times the word processor is mightier than the Glock." The hardware available for word processing has become smaller and faster. It is easier to use and much more portable. Software too has kept pace. In addition to sophisticated spelling- and grammar-checking programs, other programs have been developed to help in the actual preparation of police reports.

Pen-based computers also make report writing easier. Pen computing uses a special "pen" to write on a computer screen. "The greatest advantage of pen-based computers," notes Coumoundouros (1995, p. 50), "is ease of use. . . . Code entry is very easy with pen-based computers, which typically display a list from which the user can select the proper code by pressing the pen next to it."

Baker and Smith (1997, p. 27) explain:
> The pen-based computers . . . include forms developed for use by officers in completing traffic citations and crash reports. The automation of these forms offers many possibilities to improve accuracy and efficiency. For example, as many as 17 forms may be required to process a traffic crash involving alcohol, and each requires the same basic information about the driver. Because they exist in an electronic format, the officer can choose which forms are needed and have the common information automatically entered in each. . . .
>
> The pen-based computers will ultimately give officers the ability to query federal, state and local traffic and criminal records, receiving information via the handheld unit.

A software program frequently used in conjunction with pen-based computing is Advanced Law Enforcement Response Technology (ALERT). In one case, an officer who responded to a six-vehicle accident that involved two commercial vehicles, sent seven people to three different hospitals and required writing multiple tickets for DUI used ALERT to greatly simplify the report-writing process. According to Pilant (1999, p. 12):
> The paperwork alone would have generated at least 35 forms, all of which required filling in the same information— for example, name, date of birth, and driver's license number. Instead, using a handheld mobile computer that communicates with the system [ALERT] in his car, [the officer] entered the basic information once and assigned it to as many forms as he needed.

Another advance is Computer-Assisted Report Entry (CARE). This live-entry system centers around a CARE operator who leads officers through preformatted screens and questions, allowing them to complete reports in a matter of minutes. The CARE system has reduced report-writing times and improved the quality, accuracy and timeliness of police reports. In addition, Uniform Crime Reporting information is automatically aggregated.

Computerized report writing offers other advantages described by Hawkins and Olon (1995, p. 16):
> Because certain fields *require* an answer, for example, the investigator is forced to enter necessary information. The narratives have also greatly improved with the development of a **template** setting out a logical order of investigative events. Any subsequent investigation is added simply by starting the new paragraph with the date and time the additional investigation was begun. [emphasis added]

Although computerized report writing has greatly increased officers' efficiency, it cannot correct sloppy data entry. Officers are responsible for the accuracy and clarity of the data. Adams (1998, p. 17) cautions: "Although computer technology can make writing easier, faster and better, it is not a panacea for lazy, inept, unimaginative writers. Technology is far from foolproof. To a spell check program 'there,' 'their,' and 'they're' are equally correct regardless of context."

Summary

Investigative notes and reports are critical parts of a criminal investigation. Notes are a permanent written record of the facts of a case to be used in further investigation, in writing reports and in prosecuting the case. Start to take notes as soon as possible after receiving an initial call to respond, and continue recording information as it is received throughout the investigation.

Record all relevant information concerning the crime, the crime scene and the investigation, including information that helps answer the questions: Who? What? Where? When? How? and Why? Write brief, abbreviated notes that others can understand. Make them complete, accurate, specific, factual, clear, well organized and legible. After you have written your report, file your notes in a secure location readily accessible to you or destroy them according to department policy. Original notes are legally admissible in court and may be used to testify from or to refresh your memory. Take to court only those notes that pertain to the case.

Good notes are the foundation for effective reports. The five steps in writing a report are to (1) gather facts, (2) take notes, (3) organize the notes, (4) write the report and (5) evaluate it. Investigators usually complete an initial or preliminary report, supplemental or progress reports and a closing or final report. These provide a permanent written record of important facts that can be used to examine the past, keep other police officers informed, continue investigations, prepare court cases, provide the court with relevant facts, coordinate law enforcement activities, plan for future law enforcement services and evaluate law enforcement officers' performance.

A police report's narrative might be structured as follows:

- The opening paragraph of a police report states the time, date, type of incident and how you became involved.

- The next paragraph contains what you were told by the victim or witnesses. For each person you talked to, use a separate paragraph.

- Next, record what you did based on the information you received.

- The final paragraph states the disposition of the case.

An effective report uses paragraphs, the past tense, first person and active voice. It is factual, accurate, objective, complete, concise, clear, mechanically correct, written in standard English, legible and reader focused.

Checklist
Note Taking

- Is my notebook readily available?
- Does it contain an adequate supply of blank paper?
- Is it logically organized?
- Have I recorded all relevant information legibly?
- Have I identified each page of notes with case number and page number?
- Have I included sketches and diagrams where appropriate?
- Have I filed the notes securely?

Report Writing

- Have I made a rough outline and organized my notes?
- Have I included all relevant information?
- Have I included headings?
- Have I proofread the paper to spot content and composition errors?
- Have I submitted all required reports on time?

Discussion Questions

1. When else do you take notes in your life? How do these notes differ from those taken during an investigation?

2. What do you think is the ideal size for an investigative notebook?

3. What can you do if your writing is illegible?

4. What is the *most* important use of notes? Of reports?

5. Critics of having witnesses read and initial investigative notes contend that witnesses may not be able to read them, that it takes too much time to discuss the notes with witnesses and that the practice inhibits officers from recording all observations. How would you counter such arguments, or do you agree with them?

6. Do you think notes should be retained or destroyed after a report has been written?

7. Does your police department use standard forms? If so, for what types of reports?

8. Have you ever found yourself in a position where you realized that you did not take sufficient notes? Explain.

9. What factors influence the decision of whether to take notes immediately or to wait? When should notes be taken? Not taken?

10. If two investigators take notes and conflicting facts occur in the two sets of notes, how is this resolved? Should more than one person take notes?

References

Adams, Kenneth. "The New Technology of Writing." *ACJS Today,* Vol. XVII, Issue 2, September/October 1998, p. 17.

Baker, William T. and Smith, David M. "ALERT: Police Vehicle Technology for the 21st Century." *The Police Chief,* September 1997, pp. 23-33.

Clark, Lance A. "A Way with Words." *Police,* February 1996, p. 98.

Coumoundouros, John. "Computerized Report Entry Systems." *The Police Chief,* September 1995, pp. 50–52.

Dahlinger, Charles W. and Simpson, C. Dennis. "Documented Observations: Detailed Notes and DUI Prosecution." *Law and Order,* June 1997, pp.97-99.

Dees, Tim. "Dictating Reports and Preparing for Disaster." *Law and Order,* Vol. 47, No. 7, July 1999, pp. 15–16.

Garner, Gerald. "Reporting What You Did." *Police,* May 1997, p. 32.

Hawkins, Michael L. and Olon, Nancy L. "Computerized Reporting and Case Management." *The Police Chief,* July 1995, p. 16.

Hess, Kären M. "The ABCs of Effective Reports: Observe the Basics." *Police,* March 1999, pp. 43-44.

Hess, Kären M. and Wrobleski, Henry M. *For the Record: Report Writing in Law Enforcement,* 4th edition. Bloomington, MN: Innovative Systems–Publishers, Inc., 1996.

Lewis, Scott. "Writing Tips for Adult Learners." *Law and Order,* Vol. 47, No. 7, July 1999, pp. 135–136.

Molden, Jack. "Basic Report Writing." *Law and Order,* February 1996, pp. 13–14.

Peak, Kevin P. "Reporting the Use of Force." *The Police Chief,* May 1996, pp. 10–13.

Pilant, Lois. "Going Mobile in Law Enforcement Technology." *National Institute of Justice Journal,* January 1999, pp. 11-16.

Servino, Carol. "Command English." *The Police Chief,* Vol. LXVI, No. 5, May 1999, p. 23.

Strandberg, Keith W. "Toward Better Report Writing." *Law Enforcement Technology,* June 1998, pp. 82-84.

Searches

Do You Know?

Which constitutional amendment restricts investigative searches?

What is required for an effective search?

What the preconditions and limitations of a legal search are?

When a warrantless search is justified?

What basic restriction is placed on all searches?

What precedents are established by the *Carroll, Chambers, Chimel, Mapp, Terry* and *Weeks* decisions?

What the characteristics of a successful crime-scene search are?

What is included in organizing a crime-scene search?

What physical evidence is?

What search patterns are used in exterior searches? Interior searches?

What plain-view evidence is?

How to search a vehicle, a suspect and a dead body?

How dogs can be used in searches?

What the exclusionary rule is and how it affects investigators?

What the fruit-of-the-poisonous-tree doctrine, the inevitable-discovery doctrine and the good-faith doctrine are?

Introduction

Searching is a vital task in most criminal investigations because through searching, evidence of crime and against criminals is obtained. Equally vital, however, is an investigator's understanding of the laws relating to searches. Every search must be firmly based on an understanding of the restrictions under which police officers must operate.

To **search** is to go over or look through for the purpose of finding something. A search is not haphazard; it is directed and organized. It is an examination of a

Shannon Mann joins a group of more than 25 volunteers in a search for evidence related to the disappearance of 19-year-old Minnesota resident Kathlyn (Katie) Poirier. On May 26, 1999, Poirier was working alone during a night shift at a convenience store. A security camera captured the image of a man leading Poirier out of the store, with his hands near her neck. A suspect was later arrested, but as of press time, Poirier had not been found.

person's house or other buildings or premises or of a person for the purpose of discovering contraband or illicit or stolen property or some evidence of guilt that can be used in prosecuting a criminal action with which a person is charged.

Investigators make many kinds of searches. They search crime scenes, suspects, dead bodies, vehicles, hotel rooms, apartments, homes and offices. The same basic principles apply to most searches.

This chapter begins with a discussion of investigative searches, the Fourth Amendment and the legal requirements for a search. This is followed by a description of the crime-scene search and specific search patterns that might be used. Next, an explanation is given of specific types of searches, including searches of buildings, trash or garbage cans, vehicles, suspects and dead bodies. This is followed by a discussion of the use of dogs in searches. The chapter concludes with the consequences imposed by the exclusionary rule if the legal requirements are not met. ■

Legal Searches and the Fourth Amendment

An understanding of the Fourth Amendment of the U.S. Constitution and its relevance for searches and seizures is critical for any investigator. The Fourth Amendment to the U.S. Constitution states:

> The right of the people to be secure in their persons, houses, papers, and effects, against unreasonable searches and seizures, shall not be violated, and no Warrants shall issue, but upon probable cause, supported by Oath or affirmation, and particularly describing the place to be searched, and the persons or things to be seized.

The Fourth Amendment to the U.S. Constitution forbids unreasonable searches and seizures.

Decades ago police officers went to the home of Ted Chimel with an arrest warrant charging him with burglarizing a coin shop. They told Chimel they wanted to "look around." Although Chimel objected, the officers insisted they had the right to search because they had a legal arrest warrant. The officers opened kitchen cabinets and drawers, searched closets, looked behind furniture in every room and even searched the garage. Their hour-long search turned up several coins that they took as evidence. On the basis of this evidence, Chimel was convicted in a California court, but he appealed on the grounds that the coins had been seized illegally. In a historic decision (*Chimel v California,* 1969), the U.S. Supreme Court reversed the California decision by ruling that the conviction had been based on illegally obtained evidence.

The courts are bound by rules and can admit evidence only if it is obtained constitutionally. Thus the legality of a search must always be kept in mind during an investigation.

To conduct an effective search, know the legal requirements for searching, the items being searched for and the elements of the crime being investigated; be organized, systematic and thorough.

The courts have adopted guidelines to assure law enforcement personnel that if they adhere to certain rules, their searches or seizures will be reasonable.

A search can be justified and therefore considered legal if any of the following conditions are met:

- A search warrant has been issued.
- Consent is given.
- The search is incidental to a lawful arrest.
- An emergency exists.

If any *one* of these *preconditions* exists, a search will be considered "reasonable" and therefore legal.

Search with a Warrant

Technically—according to the Fourth Amendment—all searches are to be conducted under the authority of a warrant. Crawford (1999, p. 27) states: "To obtain a valid search warrant, officers must meet two critical requirements of the Fourth Amendment: 1) establish probable cause to believe that the location contains evidence of a crime and 2) particularly describe that evidence."

Probable cause is more than reasonable suspicion. Probable cause to search requires that a combination of facts makes it more likely than not that items sought are where the police believe them to be. Probable cause is what would lead a person of "reasonable caution" to believe that something connected with a crime is on the premises or person to be searched.

A search warrant must contain the reasons for requesting it, the names of the people presenting affidavits, what specifically is being sought and the signature of the judge issuing it. The warrant must be based on facts and sworn to by the officer requesting the warrant. An address and description of the location must be given, for example, "100 S. Main Street," "the ABC Liquor Store" or "1234 Forest Drive, a private home." Figure 4.1 is an example of a search warrant.

The search warrant can be issued to search for and seize the following:

- Stolen or embezzled property
- Property designed or intended for use in committing a crime
- Property that indicates that a crime has been committed or that a particular person has committed a crime

Once a warrant is obtained, it should be executed promptly. Usually the officer serving the warrant knocks on the particular door, states the purpose of the search and gives a copy of the warrant to the person who has answered the knock. Bulzomi (1997, p. 28) notes this "knock and announce" rule is based in English common law and "deals with the right to privacy, specifically in one's home. . . . It is clear that the framers of the Fourth Amendment were familiar with the abusive search and seizure practices used by the British government and adopted the amendment as a response to such practices." Nonetheless, the courts have recognized there are some instances in which safe and effective law enforcement requires that certain exceptions be made to the knock-and-announce rule.

A **no-knock warrant** may be issued if evidence might be easily destroyed or if there is advance knowledge of explosives or other specific danger to an officer. Wallentine (1998, p. 38) adds: "When officers see obvious signs that the suspects are aware of the officers' presence, and are taking steps to prevent or delay the officers' entry or destroy evidence, officers may enter without waiting for a response." Furthermore, officers may enter by force to exe-

FIGURE 4.1
Search Warrant

SEARCH WARRANT   2-1

STATE OF MINNESOTA, COUNTY OF ____Hennepin____   ____Justice____ COURT

TO:__Edina Police Department any officer__

_____ (A) PEACE OFFICER(S) OF THE STATE OF MINNESOTA.

WHEREAS, ____Patrick Olson____ has this day on oath, made application to the said Court

applying for issuance of a search warrant to search the following described (premises) (motor vehicle) (person):

__716 Sunshine Avenue, a private residence,__

located in the city of ____Edina____, county of ____Hennepin____ STATE OF MINN.

for the following described property and things: (attach and identify additional sheet if necessary)

    One brown, 21" Panasonic Television,
    Serial Number, 63412X

WHEREAS, the application and supporting affidavit of ____Patrick Olson____
(was) (were) duly presented and read by the Court, and being fully advised in the premises.

NOW, THEREFORE, the Court finds that probable cause exists for the issuance of a search warrant upon the following grounds: (Strike inapplicable paragraphs)

1. The property above-described was stolen or embezzled.
2. The property above-described was used as a means of committing a crime.
3. The possession of the property above-described constitutes a crime.
4. The property above described is in the possession of a person with intent to use such property as a means of committing a crime.
5. The property above described constitutes evidence which tends to show a crime has been committed, or tends to show that a particular person has committed a crime.

The Court further finds that probable cause exists to believe that the above-described property and things (are) (will be) (at the above-described premises) (in the above-described motor vehicle) (on the person of _____).

The Court further finds that a nighttime search is necessary to prevent the loss, destruction or removal of the objects of said search.

The Court further finds that entry without announcement of authority or purpose is necessary (to prevent the loss, destruction or removal of the objects of said search) (and) (to protect the safety of the peace officers).

NOW, THEREFORE, YOU,__a peace officer of the Edina Police____
Department

THE PEACE OFFICERS(S) AFORESAID, ARE HEREBY COMMANDED (TO ENTER WITHOUT ANNOUNCEMENT OF AUTHORITY AND PURPOSE) (IN THE DAYTIME ONLY) (IN THE DAYTIME OR NIGHTTIME)   TO SEARCH (THE DESCRIBED PREMISES) (THE DESCRIBED MOTOR VEHICLE) (THE PERSON OF_____

_____) FOR THE ABOVE DESCRIBED PROPERTY AND THINGS.   AND TO SEIZE SAID PROPERTY AND THINGS AND (TO RETAIN THEM IN CUSTODY SUBJECT TO COURT ORDER AND ACCORDING TO LAW) (DELIVER CUSTODY OF SAID PROPERTY AND THINGS TO _____

_____).

BY THE COURT:

                                    Oscar Kuntson
Dated____4-14____, 20_00_   JUDGE OF   COURT
                                    Justice Court

COURT - WHITE COPY • PROS. ATTY. - YELLOW COPY • PEACE OFFICER - PINK COPY • PREMISES/PERSON - GOLD COPY

---

cute a search warrant if no one is there to admit them. Even with a search warrant, certain limitations must be observed.

-- -- -- -- -- --

A search conducted with a warrant must be limited to the specific area and specific items named in the warrant.

-- -- -- -- -- --

During a search conducted with a warrant, items not specified in the warrant may be seized if they are similar to the items described, if they are related to the particular crime described or if they are contraband.

Search with Consent

Searching without a warrant is allowed if consent is given by a person having authority to do so. This might be a spouse or roommate, a business partner if the search is at a place of business, the owner of a car and the like. As with a search warrant, however, searches conducted with consent have limitations.

Consent to search must be voluntary, and the search must be limited to the area for which consent is given.

The consent must not be in response to an officer's claim of lawful authority or phrased as a command or threat. It must be a genuine request for permission to search. A genuine affirmative reply must also be given; a simple nodding of the head or opening of a door is not sufficient. Silence is *not* consent.

Some officers use a prepared consent form to be signed by the person giving consent. If consent is given, the person granting it must be legally competent to do so. Further, the person may revoke the consent at any time during the search. If this occurs, officers are obligated to discontinue the search.

If the police believe the person giving consent has authority, they may act on this belief, even though it later turns out the person did not have authority. Any of several people occupying a location may usually give consent for the entire premises.

Search Following an Arrest

Every lawful arrest is accompanied by a search of the arrested person to protect the arresting officers and others and to prevent destruction of evidence. Any weapon or dangerous substance or evidence discovered by the search may be seized. Limitations on a search incidental to arrest are found in the **Chimel decision.**

The *Chimel* decision established that a search incidental to a lawful arrest must be made simultaneously with the arrest and must be confined to the area within the suspect's immediate control.

A person's **immediate control** means within the person's reach. The Court noted that using an arrest to justify a thorough search would give police the power to conduct "general searches," which were declared unconstitutional nearly 200 years ago.

If law enforcement officers take luggage or other personal property into their exclusive control and there is no longer any danger that the arrestee might gain access to the property to seize a weapon or destroy evidence, a search of that property is no longer an incident of the arrest and a search warrant should be obtained.

Buie v Maryland (1990) expanded the area of a premises search following a lawful arrest to ensure officers' safety. In this case the Supreme Court added authority for the police to search areas immediately adjoining the place of arrest. Such a **protective sweep** is justified when reasonable suspicion exists that another person might be present who poses a danger to the arresting officers. Colbridge (1998, p. 29) notes the protective sweep is an important law enforcement tool but its scope "should be limited in both its intensity and duration. It is narrowly confined to a cursory visual inspection of those places in which a person might be hiding."

Search in an Emergency Situation

In situations where police officers believe there is probable cause but no time to secure a warrant—for example, if shots are being fired or a person is screaming—they may act on their own discretion.

A warrantless search in the absence of a lawful arrest or consent is justified only in emergencies where probable cause exists and the search must be conducted immediately.

Hawley (1996, p. 25) explains that: "Exigent circumstances that create the need for an immediate search arise when there is a danger of violence or injury to officers or others, a risk of the subject's escape or the probability that evidence will be destroyed or concealed." In *Mincey v Arizona* (1978), the Supreme Court stated that the Fourth Amendment does not require police officers to delay a search in the course of an investigation if to do so would gravely endanger their lives or the lives of others. Once the danger has been eliminated, however, any further search should be conducted only after obtaining a search warrant.

Basic Limitation on Searches

All searches have one limitation.

The most important limitation on any search is that the scope must be narrowed. General searches are unconstitutional.

Having looked at the legal restrictions on searching, now consider the search itself, beginning with the search of a crime scene. Although each crime scene is unique, certain general guidelines apply.

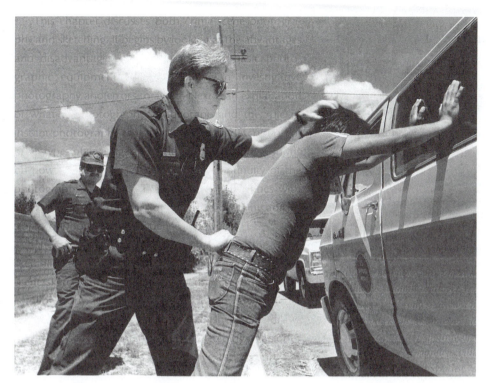

This officer is restricted to a patdown for weapons because no arrest has been made at this point as established by the Terry decision. Even with no arrest, however, officers remain on guard.

The Crime-Scene Search

A basic function of investigators is to conduct a thorough, legal search at the scene of a crime. Even though not initially visible, evidence in some form is present at most crime scenes. The goal of any search during an investigation, at the crime scene or elsewhere, is to discover evidence that helps to:

■ Establish that a crime *was* committed and *what* the specific crime was.

■ Establish *when* the crime was committed.

■ Identify *who* committed the crime.

■ Explain *how* the crime was committed.

■ Suggest *why* the crime was committed.

— — — — — — — —

A successful crime-scene search locates, identifies and preserves all evidence present.

— — — — — — — —

Evidence found at a scene assists in re-creating a crime in much the same way that bricks, properly placed, result in the construction of a building. A meticulous, properly conducted search usually results in the discovery of evidence. The security measures taken by the first officer at the scene determine whether evidence is discovered intact or after it has been altered or destroyed. During a search, do not change or contaminate physical evidence in any way, or it will be declared inadmissible. Maintain the chain of custody of evidence from the initial discovery to the time of the trial as discussed in the next chapter.

Organizing the Crime-Scene Search

After emergencies have been attended to, the scene has been secured, witnesses have been located and separated for interviewing, and photographing and sketching have been completed, a search plan must be formulated. Also, a search headquarters needs to be established away from the scene to prevent destruction of evidence.

— — — — — — — —

Organizing a search includes dividing the duties, selecting a search pattern, assigning personnel and equipment and giving instructions.

— — — — — — — —

Proper organization results in a thorough search with no accidental destruction of evidence. However, even the best-organized search may not yield evidence. Evidence may have been destroyed before the search or removed by the criminal. In a few, rare instances, evidence is simply nonexistent.

In a single-investigator search, one officer conducts the physical search and describes, identifies and preserves the evidence found. If two or more officers conduct the search, the highest-ranking officer on the scene usually assumes command. In accordance with department policy, the officer in charge assigns personnel based on their training. For example, if one officer has specialized training in photography, another in sketching and a third in fingerprinting, they are assigned to their respective specialities. Someone is assigned to each function required in the search. Often two officers are assigned to take measurements to ensure accuracy. These same two officers can collect, identify and preserve evidence as it is found. Evidence should never be removed from the scene without the permission of the search leader.

The search leader also determines the number of personnel needed, the type of search best suited for the area and the items most likely to be found. Personnel are assigned according to the selected search pattern. Members of the search party are given all known details of the crime and instructed on the type of evidence to seek and the members' specific responsibilities.

The search leader also determines whether anyone other than the person committing the crime has entered the scene. If so, the person is asked to explain in detail any contacts with the scene that might have contaminated evidence. If no one has entered the scene between the time the crime was committed and when the police arrived, and if the scene was immediately secured, the scene is considered to be a **true,** or **uncontaminated, scene;** that is, no evidence has been introduced into it or taken from it except by the person committing the crime.

Physical Evidence

Physical evidence ranges in size from very large objects to minute substances. Understanding what types of evidence can be found at various types of crime scenes is important to the search. Obviously not everything found at a scene is evidence.

- - - - - - - -

Knowing what to search for is indispensable to an effective crime-scene search. Evidence is anything material and relevant to the crime being investigated.

- - - - - - - -

The elements of the crime help to determine what will be useful as evidence. For example, a burglary requires an illegal entry; therefore, toolmarks and broken glass in a door or window are evidence that assists in proving burglary. A forcible rape requires a sexual act against a victim's will. Therefore, bruises, semen stains or witnesses hearing

screams would help to establish evidence of that crime. Specific types of evidence to seek are discussed in Chapter 5 and throughout Sections Three, Four and Five.

Besides knowing what types of evidence to search for, investigators must know where evidence is most likely to be found. For example, evidence is often found on or near the route used to and from a crime. A suspect may drop items used to commit a crime or leave shoe or tire prints. Evidence is also frequently found on or near a dead body.

The **"elephant-in-a-matchbox" doctrine** requires that searchers consider the probable size and shape of evidence they seek because, for example, large objects cannot be concealed in tiny areas. Ignoring this doctrine can result in a search that wastes resources, destroys potential evidence and leaves a place in shambles. It may also result in violating the Fourth Amendment requirements on reasonable searches.

Search Patterns

All **search patterns** have a common denominator: They are designed to locate systematically any evidence at a crime scene or any other area where evidence might be found. Most patterns involve partitioning search areas into workable sizes. The search pattern should be adapted to the area involved, the personnel available, the time limits imposed by weather and light conditions and the circumstances of the individual crime scene. Such patterns ensure thoroughness.

Exterior Searches

Exterior searches can cover small, large or vast areas. Regardless of the dimensions, the area to be searched can be divided into subareas and diagrammed on paper. As each area is searched, check it off. Be certain sufficient light is available. A search conducted with inadequate light can destroy more evidence than it yields. If weather conditions are favorable, delay nighttime searches until daylight if feasible.

- - - - - - - -

Exterior search patterns divide an area into lanes, concentric circles or zones.

- - - - - - - -

Lane-Search Pattern The **lane-search pattern** partitions the area into lanes, using stakes and string as illustrated in Figure 4.2. A **lane** is a narrow strip. An officer

FIGURE 4.2
Lane-Search Pattern

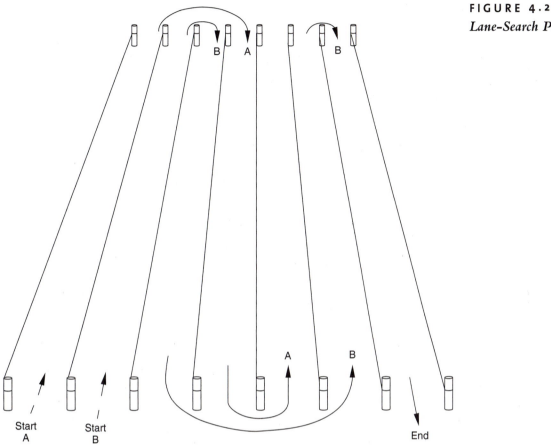

is assigned to each lane. Therefore, the number of lanes to use depends on the number of officers available to search.

These lanes can be imaginary. Officers' search widths vary from arm's length to shoulder-to-shoulder, either on foot or on their knees. Such searches use no string or cord to mark the lanes.

If only one officer is available for the search, the lane pattern can be adapted to what is commonly called the **strip-search pattern.** The officer starts at the beginning of the first lane, goes to the end and then begins at the end of the second lane, as illustrated in Figure 4.3.

For an extensive search, the lane pattern is often modified to form a **grid,** and the area is crisscrossed, as illustrated in Figure 4.4.

Circle-Search Pattern Another commonly used pattern is the **circle search,** which begins at the center of an area to be searched and spreads out in ever widening concentric circles (see Figure 4.5).

A wooden stake with a long rope is driven into the ground at the center of the area to be searched. Knots are tied in the rope at selected regular intervals. The searcher circles around the stake in the area delineated by the first knot, searching the area within the first circle. When this area is completed, the searcher moves to the second knot and repeats the procedure. The search is continued in ever widening circles until the entire area is covered.

Zone- or Sector-Search Pattern In the **zone** or **sector** search, an area is divided into equal squares on a map of the area, and each square is numbered. Search personnel are assigned to specific squares (see Figure 4.6).

Interior Searches

The foregoing exterior search patterns can be adapted to an interior crime scene. Of prime concern is to search thoroughly without destroying evidence.

Interior searches go from the general to the specific, usually in a circular pattern, covering all surfaces of a search area. The floor should be searched first.

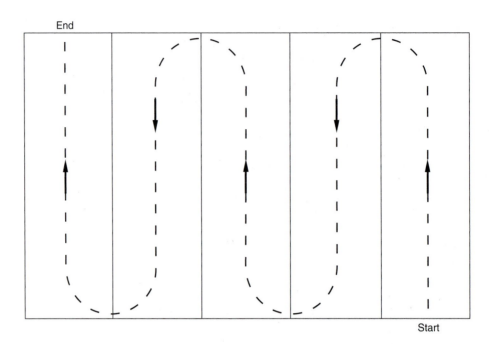

FIGURE 4·3 *Strip-Search Pattern*

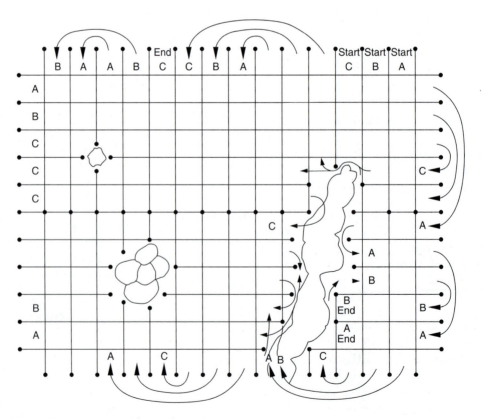

FIGURE 4·4 *Grid-Search Pattern*

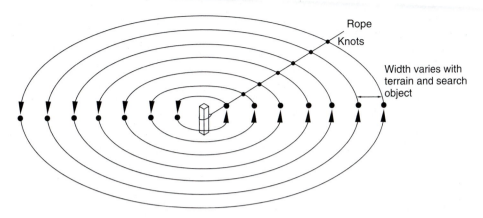

FIGURE 4·5   *Circle-Search Pattern*

A	B	C
A	B	C
A	B	C

FIGURE 4.6   *Zone- or Sector-Search Pattern*

In making an interior search, look closely at all room surfaces, including the floor, ceiling, walls and all objects on the floor and walls. Evidence can be found on any surface.

The floor usually produces the most evidence, followed by doors and windows. Although the ceiling is often missed in a search, it too can contain evidence such as stains or bullet holes. It can even contain such unlikely evidence as footprints. Footprints were found on the ceiling by an alert officer during the investigation of a bank burglary. Paperhangers had left wallpaper on the bank's floor during the night and had hung it on the

ceiling early the next morning before the burglary was discovered. During the night, one of the burglars had stepped on the wallpaper, leaving a footprint that was transferred in a faint outline to the ceiling.

An interior room search usually starts at the point of entry. The floor is searched first so that no evidence is inadvertently destroyed during the remainder of the search. The lane- or zone-search patterns are adaptable to an interior floor search.

After the floor search, the walls—including doors and windows—and then the ceiling are searched, normally using a clockwise or counterclockwise pattern around the room. Because doors and windows are points of entry and exit, soil, fingerprints, glass fragments and other evidence are often found there. Walls may contain marks, bloodstains or trace evidence such as hairs or fibers.

After a room is searched in one direction, it is often searched in the opposite direction because lighting is different from different angles. The same general procedures are followed in searching closets, halls or other rooms off the main room. The search is coordinated, and the location of all evidence is communicated to members of the search team.

General Guidelines

The precise search pattern used is immaterial as long as the search is systematic and covers the entire area. Assigning two officers to search the same area greatly increases the probability of discovering evidence. Finding evidence is no reason to stop a search. Continue searching until the entire area is covered.

Plain-View Evidence

The preceding limitations are intended to protect the rights of all citizens and to ensure due process of law. They are not intended to hamper investigations, nor do they preclude the use of evidence that is not concealed and that is accidentally found.

Plain-view evidence—unconcealed evidence seen by an officer engaged in a lawful activity—is admissible in court.

In *United States v Henry* (1958) the Court said: "If, however, while legitimately looking for such articles, the officer unexpectedly discovers evidence of another crime, he can seize that evidence as well." In both *Michigan v Tyler* (1978) and *Mincey v Arizona* (1978), the Court ruled that while officers are on the premises pursuing their legitimate emergency activities, any evidence in plain view may be seized. In other words, as Bourn (1996, p. 9) notes: "Police officers have the right to observe their surroundings—provided they have the right to be in those surroundings in the first place."

Evidence qualifies as plain-view evidence if (1) officers are engaged in a lawful activity when they discover the evidence, (2) an item is not concealed and (3) the discovery is accidental. An officer cannot obtain a warrant and fail to mention a particular object and then use "plain view" to justify its seizure. If the officer is looking for it initially, it must be mentioned in the warrant. Plain-view evidence itself is not sufficient to justify a warrantless seizure of evidence; probable cause must also exist.

Evidence may also be seized when its detection falls beyond the "plain view" rationale. Bourn (p. 24) explains: "The courts have applied the plain view rationale, even if an officer relies on a sense other than sight. For example, a customs officer who smells marijuana coming from a package has probable cause to make an arrest under a 'plain smell' rationale (*United States v Lueck*)."

Officers may seize any contraband they discover during a legal search. In *Boyd v United States* (1886), Justice Bradley stated: "The search for and seizure of stolen or forfeited goods or goods liable to duties and concealed to avoid payment thereof, are totally different things from a search or a seizure of a man's private books and papers. In one case the government is entitled to the property, and in the other it is not."

Building Searches

When executing a warrant to search a building, officers should first familiarize themselves with the location and the past record of the person living there. Check records for any previous police actions at that location. Decide on the least dangerous time of day for the suspect, the police and the neighborhood. For example, the time of day when children come home from school would not be a good time to execute a warrant.

Do not treat the execution of a search warrant as routine. Plan for the worst-case scenario. Think *safety* first and last. Arrive safely. Turn off your vehicle's dome light as you approach the building. Stay away from the headlights or turn them off. Use any available cover as you approach the building.

Have a plan before entering the building. Secure the outside perimeter and as many exits as possible—at a minimum, the front and rear doors. If possible, call for a backup before entering and search with a partner. Once inside, wait for your vision to adjust to interior light conditions. Keep light and weapons away from your body. Reduce the audio level of your radio, and turn off your beeper. Go quickly through doors into dark areas. When moving around objects, take quick peeks before proceeding. Avoid windows. Use light and cover to your advantage. Know where you are at all times and how to get back to where you were. Look for exits.

If the entire building is to be searched, use a systematic approach. Secure each area as it is searched.

Trash or Garbage Can Searches

Trash and garbage cans in alleys and on public sidewalks are often the depository for evidence of thefts, drugs and even homicides. In *California v Greenwood* (1988), the Supreme Court ruled that containers left on public property are open to search by police without a warrant. The U. S. Supreme Court ruled that such a search does not constitute a violation of the Fourth Amendment or a reasonable expectation of privacy: "It is common knowledge that plastic garbage bags left on a public street are readily accessible to animals, children, scavengers, snoops, and other members of the public," and therefore "no reasonable expectation of privacy" is violated by such a search. Trash or garbage containers on private property may not be searched without a warrant.

The most important factor in determining the legality of a warrantless trash inspection is the physical location of the retrieved trash. Police cannot trespass to gain access to the trash location, and the trash must not be located within the **curtilage,** which the Supreme Court has described as "the area to which extends the intimate activity associated with the 'sanctity of a man's home and the privacies of life'" (Hendrie, 1998, p. 26). In other words, curtilage is that portion of a residence that is not open to the public. It is reserved for private owner or family use, and an expectation of privacy exists. This is in contrast to sidewalks and alleys that are used by the public.

Hendrie (p. 25) notes the concept of curtilage comes from the English common law tradition of protecting the home from government intrusions. In his address before the English House of Commons in 1763, William Pitt stated: "The poorest man may in his cottage bid defiance to all the forces of the Crown. It may be frail; its roof may shake; the wind may blow through it; the storm may enter; but the King of England cannot enter—all his force dares not cross the threshold of the ruined tenement" (Hendrie, p. 25). In *United States v Dunn* (1987), the Court ruled:

> We believe that curtilage questions should be resolved with particular reference to four factors: the proximity of the area claimed to be curtilage to the home, whether the area is included within an enclosure surrounding the home, the nature of the uses to which the area is put, and the steps taken by the resident to protect the area from observation by people passing by.

Searches of trash may also extend to the local landfill. Jayre (1996, p. 139) notes:

> The modern sanitary landfill . . . has become a potential . . . bonanza for those in law enforcement hoping to unearth everything from missing bodies to incriminating documents.
>
> Today's highly regulated, state-of-the-art landfill can preserve buried material for decades, and its tracking system can pinpoint daily trash locations. . . . It's much like a pharoah's tomb waiting to be unsealed.

Jayre cautions, however, that such searches can be very expensive and a huge drain on personnel, further swamped by safety and environmental requirements.

Vehicle Searches

Cars, aircraft, boats, motorcycles, buses, trucks and vans can contain evidence of a crime. Again, the type of crime determines the area to be searched and the evidence to be sought. In a hit-and-run accident, the car's undercarriage can have hairs and fibers, or the interior may reveal a hidden liquor bottle. In narcotics arrests, various types of drugs are often found in cars, planes and boats. An ordinary vehicle has hundreds of places to hide drugs. In some cases, vehicles may have specially constructed compartments.

As with other types of searches, a vehicle search must be systematic and thorough. Evidence is more likely to be found if two officers conduct the search.

Remove occupants from the car. First search the area around the vehicle and then the exterior. Finally, search the interior along one side from front to back, and then return along the other side to the front.

Before entering a vehicle, search the area around it for evidence related to the crime. Next examine the vehicle's exterior for fingerprints, dents, scratches or hairs and fibers. Examine the grill, front bumper, fender areas and license plates. Open the hood and check the numerous recesses of the motor, radiator, battery, battery case, engine block, clutch and starter housings, ventilating ducts, air filter, body frame and supports. Open the trunk and examine any clothing, rags, containers, tools, the spare-tire well and the interior of the trunk lid.

An officer may search a vehicle without a warrant if he has probable cause to believe it contains evidence of a crime as established by the Carroll *decision.*

Finally, search the vehicle's interior, following the same procedures used in searching a room. Vacuum the car before getting into it. Package collections from different areas of the car separately. Then systematically examine ashtrays, the glove compartment, areas under the seats and the window areas. Remove the seats and vacuum the floor. Hairs and fibers or traces of soil may be discovered that will connect a suspect with soil samples from the crime scene.

Use a flashlight and a mirror to examine the area behind the dashboard. Feeling by hand is not effective because of the numerous wires located there. Look for fingerprints in the obvious places: window and door handles, underside of the steering wheel, radio buttons, ashtrays, distributor cap, jack, rearview mirror, hood latches and seat adjustment lever.

Figure 4.7 illustrates the areas of vehicles that should be searched. The vehicle is divided into specific search areas to ensure order and thoroughness. As in any other search, take precautions to prevent contaminating evidence.

The searcher must also be alert to what is an original part of the vehicle and what has been added. For example, compartments for concealing illegal drugs or other contraband are sometimes added. The systems and equipment of the vehicle should be validated. Is the exhaust real or phony? Check recesses and cup holders for sneaker flip panels that may contain contraband or weapons. Check the headliner. In convertibles, check the boot.

A new product, the Enspecta™, makes vehicle searches easier. Schmitt (1999, p. 88) reports:

> The Enspecta . . . utilizes dual periscopic mirrors and fluorescent lights mounted on a wheeled platform that easily rolls under a vehicle so you can view its underside.
>
> A companion, a hand-held version of the Enspecta, the Enspecta Jr.™, aids searches of vehicle interiors, engine compartments and even the tops of high-profile vehicles such as trucks and RVs. Best of all, this system of tools is completely legal, as it constitutes an "in full view" search.

Schmitt further notes the handheld model offers the benefit of increased officer safety because it can locate items such as needles between seats and other objects that may cause injury during a hand search.

Staying within the Law

Warrantless searches are often justified because of a vehicle's **mobility.** The precedent for a warrantless search of an automobile was established in *Carroll v United States* (1925).

- - - - - - - - -

The ***Carroll* decision** established that automobiles may be searched without a warrant if (1) there is probable cause for the search and (2) the vehicle would be gone before a search warrant could be obtained.

- - - - - - - - -

Regini (1999, p. 26) suggests: "The motor vehicle exception first recognized in *Carroll v United States* and often referred to as the *Carroll* doctrine, has evolved into

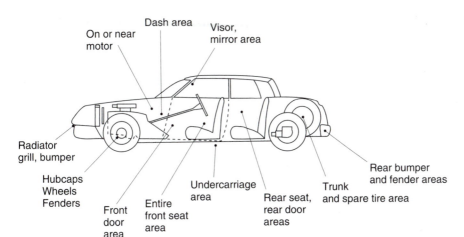

FIGURE 4.7 *Vehicle Areas That Should Be Searched*

On or near motor

Dash area

Visor, mirror area

Radiator grill, bumper

Hubcaps Wheels Fenders

Front door area

Entire front seat area

Undercarriage area

Rear seat, rear door areas

Trunk and spare tire area

Rear bumper and fender areas

an expansive search authority that effectively renders the need to obtain a warrant to search a vehicle unnecessary."

In *Maryland v Dyson* (1999), consistent with past cases, the Court ruled that police officers do not need to obtain a search warrant to search vehicles they believe to be carrying illegal narcotics ("U.S. Supreme Court News," 1999, p. 26).

When stopping moving vehicles, if officers have probable cause, they may search a vehicle and any closed containers in it. If probable cause does not exist, officers may be able to obtain voluntary consent to search, including any closed containers (*Florida v Jimeno,* 1990). The driver must be competent to give such consent, and silence is not consent. Further, if at any time the driver rescinds consent, the search must cease.

Officers must also know their state's laws regarding full searches of automobiles pursuant to the issuance of a traffic citation, which may often seem contradictory. Although several states have statutes that authorize searches of vehicles following the issuance of a traffic citation, the policy in most states is to allow searches only after a driver has been arrested and is in custody ("U.S. Supreme Court News," 1998, p. 6). In *Knowles v Iowa* (1998), the Supreme Court ruled that when an officer issues a citation instead of making an arrest, a full search of the driver's car violates the Fourth Amendment (Klobuchar, 1999, p. 1). As Ferrell (1999, p. 10) explains, Patrick Knowles was stopped by an Iowa police officer for speeding. He was issued a citation, and then, without Knowles's consent, the officer searched the car, finding a bag of marijuana and a pot pipe under the driver's seat. Knowles was arrested and charged with violating Iowa's controlled substances law and convicted. The U.S. Supreme Court, however, after granting **certiorari,** that is, agreeing to review a case, unanimously reversed the decision. Colbridge (1999, p. 31) notes:

The *Knowles* opinion had no impact upon the long recognized vehicle exception to the Fourth Amendment warrant requirement. The vehicle exception permits an officer to search a motor vehicle without a search warrant when he has probable cause to believe evidence or contraband will be found inside.

However, the Court has also ruled in *Wyoming v Houghton* that an officer may search the belongings of an automobile passenger simply because the officer suspects the driver has done something wrong ("U.S. Supreme Court News," 1999, p. 8). This "passenger property exception" ruling was intended to prevent drivers from claiming illegal drugs or other contraband belonged to passengers, not themselves ("Supreme Court Allows . . . ," 1998, p. 1).

Limitations on warrantless automobile searches were set in *United States v Henry* (1958). In this case the Court said: "Once these items [for which a search warrant would be sought] are located, the search must terminate. If, however, while legitimately looking for such articles, the officer unexpectedly discovers evidence of another crime, he can seize that evidence as well."

Unlike a search incidental to an arrest, a vehicle search need not be made immediately.

Chambers v Maroney (1970) established that a vehicle may be taken to headquarters to be searched.

When a motor vehicle is taken into custody, property within it is routinely inventoried to prevent claims by the vehicle owner that items were taken. Although inventory and search are technically two different processes, in practice they may take place simultaneously. If property found during such an inventory is evidence of a crime, it is admissible in court. It is advisable, however, where a vehicle is no longer mobile or is in the custody of the police, to obtain a search warrant so as not to jeopardize an otherwise perfectly valid case.

Inventory Searches

When police take custody of property, the courts have upheld their right to inventory such property for the following reasons:

■ To protect the owner's property. This obligation may be legal or moral, but the courts have supported the police's responsibility to protect property taken into custody from unauthorized interference.

■ To protect the police from disputes and claims that the property was stolen or damaged. Proper inventory at the time of custody provides an accurate record of the condition of the property at the time it was seized.

■ To protect the police and the public from danger. Custody of an automobile or a person subjects the police to conditions that require searching the person or the vehicle for objects such as bombs, chemicals, razor blades, weapons and so on that may harm the officers or the premises where the vehicle or person is taken.

■ To determine the owner's identity. Identifying the owner may be associated with identifying the person under arrest, or it may help the police know to whom the property should be released.

The courts have held that each of these factors outweighs the privacy interests of property and therefore justifies an inventory search. The search must be reasonable. To be correct in the inventory procedure, the police must show legal seizure and make an inventory according to approved procedures. Court cases related to automobile searches are listed in Table 4.1.

Table 4.1	**Summary of Major Court Rulings Regarding Vehicle Searches**
Case decision	*Holding*
Belton v New York (1981)	After a custodial arrest of an occupant of the vehicle, officers may conduct an immediate search of the vehicle, following the rule that the search is incident to arrest. The search must be limited to the passenger compartment and may be a general search without a specific object in mind. The search may include closed containers.
Florida v Jimeno (1991)	A warrantless search may be made when consent is obtained from the owner or person in possession of the vehicle. The entire vehicle may be searched, including closed containers, unless the consentor has expressed limitation.
Florida v Wells (1990)	The contents of a lawfully impounded vehicle may be inventoried for purposes of property accountability, public safety and protection against later claims of damage or loss of property.
Texas v Brown (1983)	Contraband or evidence in plain view may be confiscated. Two conditions must exist. The officer must be legally present and there must be probable cause to believe that the object in plain view is contraband or the instrumentality of a crime.
United States v Bowhay (1993)	Because a department policy required officers to search everything, the officers had no discretion. Therefore, the presence of an investigative motive did not prohibit the inventory search.
United States v Ibarra (1992)	If there is no statutory authority to impound, the vehicle cannot be taken into custody legally; therefore, an inventory search under these circumstances would be inadmissible.
United States v Ross (1982)	A search may be made when probable cause exists to believe that contraband or evidence is within the vehicle. This includes the trunk or closed containers in the vehicle.
United States v Williams (1991)	An on-site inventory of property is legally permissible, even though done in advance of impounding, if there is authority and circumstances to justify impound.

Suspect Searches

How a suspect should be searched depends on whether an arrest has been made. If you have probable cause to stop or arrest a person, be cautious. Many officers are injured or killed because they fail to search a suspect. If a suspect is in a car, have him or her step out of the car, being careful to protect yourself from a suddenly opened door.

If the suspect has not been arrested, confine your search to a patdown or frisk for weapons. If the suspect has been arrested, make a complete body search for weapons and evidence. In either event, always be on your guard.

Patdown or Frisk

One duty of police officers is to investigate suspicious circumstances, including stopping and questioning people who are acting suspiciously. The procedures for stopping and questioning suspects are regulated by the same justifications and limitations associated with lawful searches and seizures. If you suspect that a person you have stopped for questioning may be armed, conduct a through-the-clothes patdown for weapons. If you feel what may be a weapon, you may seize it.

Two situations require police officers to stop and question individuals: (1) to investigate suspicious circumstances and (2) to identify someone who looks like a suspect named in an arrest warrant or whose description has been broadcast in an all-points bulletin (APB). The landmark decision in *Terry v Ohio* (1968) established police officers' right to **pat down** or **frisk** a person they have stopped to question if they believe the person might be armed and dangerous. The prime requisite for stopping, questioning and possibly frisking someone is reasonable suspicion, a concept that is difficult to define.

The *Terry* decision established that a patdown or frisk is a "protective search for weapons" and as such must be "confined to a scope reasonably designed to discover guns, knives, clubs and other hidden instruments for the assault of a police officer or others."

The Court warned that such a search is "a serious intrusion upon the sanctity of the person which may inflict great indignity and arouse strong resentment, and it is not to be undertaken lightly."

The precedent established by *Terry* was strengthened four years later in *Adams v Williams* (1972) when the Court said:

The Fourth Amendment does not require a policeman who lacks the precise level of information necessary for probable cause to arrest to simply shrug his shoulders and allow a crime to occur or a criminal to escape. On the contrary, Terry recognizes that it may be the essence of good police work to adopt an intermediate response.

Terry has been further expanded in other cases. *Adams v Williams* (1972) established that officers may stop and question individuals based on information received from informants. In *Servis v Virginia*, the court ruled that a protective search incident to an investigatory stop may extend to a suspect's dwelling. *United States v Hensley* (1985) established that police officers may stop and question suspects when they believe they recognize them from "wanted" flyers issued by another police department.

Stop-and-frisk has been validated on the basis of (1) furtive movements; (2) inappropriate attire; (3) carrying suspicious objects such as a TV or pillowcase; (4) vague, nonspecific answers to routine questions; (5) refusal to identify oneself; and (6) appearing to be out of place. Milazzo (1998, p. 151) notes: "Most justifiable frisks stem from some combination of the following:

- A crime under investigation;

- Knowledge that the suspect was armed or dangerous;

- The behavior of the person being frisked;

- A bulge or the actual observation of an object; or

- The suspect's prior criminal record or history of violence."

Plain Feel/Touch "Pat-Down Searches" (1993, p. 7) notes: "The 'plain feel' exception is a legitimate extension of the 'plain view' exception." The article explains:

If a police officer lawfully pats down a suspect's outer clothing and feels an object that he immediately identifies as contraband, a warrantless seizure is justified because there is no invasion of the suspect's privacy beyond that already authorized by the officer's search for weapons (*Minnesota v Dickerson*).

In *Minnesota v Dickerson*, the Supreme Court ruled that officers may seize any contraband discovered during a legal patdown *if* it is immediately apparent to the officer that the object is an illegal substance. Kalk (1997, p. 45) explains:

Under the Plain Feel Doctrine, the police officer must be able to determine simultaneously that the item is not a weapon and that the item is contraband. If the police officer cannot determine that the item is contraband without additional probing or investigation, the Plain Feel Doctrine does not apply.

Thorough Search

If you arrest a suspect, conduct a complete body search for both weapons and evidence. Whether you use an against-the-wall spread-eagle search, a simple stand-up search or a search with all the suspect's clothes removed, follow a methodical, exact procedure. The complete body search often includes taking samples of hair and fingernail scrapings as well as testing for firearm residue when appropriate.

Regardless of whether an arrest has been made, respect the dignity of the suspect while you conduct the patdown or search, but do not let your guard down.

Strip searches may be conducted only after an arrest and when the prisoner is in a secure facility. Such searches should be conducted by individuals of the same gender as the suspect and in privacy and should follow written guidelines. Considerations in deciding when a strip search is necessary include the individual's past behavior, the possibility that the person is concealing dangerous drugs or weapons, whether the person will be alone or with others in a cell and how long the person will be in custody. Cavity searches go beyond the normal strip search and must follow very strict departmental guidelines. Normally such searches should be conducted by medical personnel.

Inhibitors to Thorough Search
A variety of factors may inhibit an officer's ability or desire to conduct a thorough search of a suspect. The presence of bodily fluids is one factor that may interfere with a complete search. Crotty (1998, p. 80) admits: "No officer wishes to make physical contact with a suspect's blood or other bodily fluids, due to the rising presence of HIV, Hepatitis A and B, Staph, and other diseases transmitted by such contact. It is doubtful that the search of a suspect wearing urine or blood soaked pants would be conducted in a thorough manner."

The threat of contracting AIDS or hepatitis infections in the line of duty has led police to consider using special equipment when searching suspects. Crotty (p. 81) notes: "One tactic which relieves some of the anxiety in searching such individuals is for officers to be equipped with readily available latex gloves. Patrol officers can carry a couple pairs on their duty belts." Gog-

gles or face masks are other pieces of equipment that reduce personal contact with blood and other body fluids, the main carriers of these viruses. Officers must also be alert to suspects who may spit on or bite them.

Another inhibitor to thorough searches is a fear of needles. When searching, officers should avoid putting their hands into suspects' pockets. They should use patting, rather than grabbing, motions to avoid being stuck by sharp objects such as hypodermic needles. Techniques for collecting evidence that might be contaminated with the AIDS virus are discussed in the next chapter.

Weather can be another factor that compromises the thoroughness of a search. Driving rains, freezing or sweltering temperatures, blowing snow—all may entice an officer to hurry through a search. Crotty (p. 82) identifies other situations and circumstances that may potentially inhibit a thorough search, including familiarity with the suspect, having previously arrested the suspect without incident, cross-gender searching and dealing with drunks.

Student Searches

The Fourth Amendment prohibition of unreasonable searches applies to public school officials because they represent the state. The Supreme Court has held that, although school children have a right to privacy, the school must maintain a climate of learning. Therefore, the Court eased restrictions on search by school officials. They do not need a search warrant if they have probable cause to believe the subject of the search has violated or is violating the law.

The key standard is *reasonableness under all circumstances,* meaning that if there is a reason to believe the search will yield evidence of a violation of the law or school rules and if the procedure followed is related to the purpose of the search and not excessively intrusive in view of the student's age and sex and the nature of the infraction, then the search is permissible (*New Jersey v T.L.O.,* 1985). Cases involving school and student searches have proliferated in recent years with the increased use of drugs. The majority of cases involve searches for drugs, explosives, explosive devices and guns.

Dead Body Searches

Searching a dead body is unpleasant, even when the person has died recently. It is extremely unpleasant if the person has been dead for a long period. In some such cases, the body can be searched only in the coroner's examination room, where effective exhaust ventilation is available.

--- --- --- --- --- --- ---

Search a dead body systematically and completely. Include the immediate area around and under the body.

--- --- --- --- --- --- ---

The search usually begins with the clothing, which is likely to reveal a wallet or personal identification papers as well as trace evidence. If the body is not fingerprinted at the scene, tie paper bags securely on the hands so that fingerprinting can be done at the coroner's laboratory. If possible, place the body in a body bag to ensure that no physical evidence is lost while it is being transported.

Search the area around and beneath the body immediately after it is removed. A bullet may have passed through part of the body and lodged in the floor or the dirt beneath it. Trace evidence may have fallen from the body or clothing as the body was removed. Inventory and describe all items removed from the deceased.

Department policy determines the extent of a search at the scene. Normally a complete examination is delayed until the body is received by the coroner's officer. The coroner may take fingernail scrapings, blood and semen samples and possibly some body organs to establish poisoning or the path of a bullet or knife.

Once the body is taken to a funeral home, its organs and fluids will be contaminated by burial preparation. Once the body is buried, it is a long, difficult legal process to exhume it for further examination. If the body is cremated, obviously no further examination is possible.

Use of Dogs in a Search

The use of police service dogs is at an all-time high in the United States (Wallentine, 1999, p. 35). Because of their acute sense of smell, dogs can be trained to track and locate suspects as well as detect certain evidence such as explosives and narcotics. Dogs are ideally suited to assist in searching large areas, areas with poor visibility, such as warehouses that may contain thousands of items or any area with numerous hiding places. Furthermore, using dogs for such purposes lessens the physical risk to investigating officers. Roen (1997, p. 48) states:

From protecting our nations' borders to detecting explosive devices before they blow, these seemingly fearless animals serve in the most dangerous of circumstances, providing tremendous results as well as protection for the men and women with whom they work. . . .

Traditionally used for patrol and apprehension, the police K-9s' job description covers an ever-widening range of incredible duties. Detection of drugs, explosives, firearms and even searching for drowning victims have enabled police departments to broaden their capabilities substantially.

--- --- --- --- --- --- ---

Dogs can be trained to locate suspects, narcotics and explosives.

--- --- --- --- --- --- ---

The use of dogs to sniff out narcotics has been widely publicized. Because narcotics can be concealed in so many different ways, using dogs to locate them has greatly assisted law enforcement officers. Attempts to mask drug odors from dogs trained to sniff out drugs are futile because dogs can smell more than one odor simultaneously.

Dogs have also been trained to detect explosives both before and after detonation. Their ability to detect explosives before detonation lessens the risk to officers and can help prevent crimes. A study by the Law Enforcement Assistance Administration and the Federal Aviation Authority demonstrated that dogs can locate explosives twice as often as a human can. In the case of detonated explosives, dogs have helped locate bomb fragments hidden under piles of debris and at considerable distances from the detonation point.

As agents of the police, dogs are subject to the same legal limitations on searches that officers are. Recent court rulings appear to highlight the benefits of using K-9s to build probable cause to seize and arrest. Wallentine (1999, p. 34) reports:

In *United States vs. Place*, the United States Supreme Court ruled that exposure of luggage located in a public place to a police K-9 sniff "did not constitute a search within the meaning of the Fourth Amendment. . . ."

The Supreme Court stated: "A canine sniff by a well-trained narcotics dog does not require opening the luggage."

In essence, such a ruling concedes that the use of dogs may lead to the same end via less intrusive means, thus sparing law enforcement other time-consuming steps required to effect a legal search.

Specially trained K-9s can be invaluable in searching for drugs. They are often used for inspections conducted at border checkpoints.

Wallentine (1999, p. 34) adds: "The most common deployment for a drug dog is a vehicle sniff, usually during a traffic stop. . . . Where government officials have lawfully detained a vehicle, a dog's sniff is not a search within the meaning of the Fourth Amendment." Further: "Courts routinely approve vehicle detentions of up to an hour . . . as long as officers are making reasonable efforts to get a drug dog to the scene." Trained K-9s are also used to detect drugs in students' school lockers, drugs in automobiles parked in public parking lots and contraband smuggling in correctional facilities (p. 35). Baratta (1995, p. 23) cites the following results of using K-9s:

■ Narcotics dogs were involved in more than 17,000 cases, helped confiscate or destroy over 54 million kilograms of dagga (cannabis) and assisted in more than 6,000 arrests.

■ Explosives dogs attended nearly 2,000 bomb threats and found explosives in 290 cases.

■ Handlers with tracker dogs made nearly 3,000 arrests and recovered lost or stolen property worth $3 million.

If a police department is not large enough to have or lacks sufficient need for a search dog and trained handler, learn where the nearest trained search dogs are and how they can be obtained if needed. Many major airports have dogs trained to locate explosives and may make these dogs available to police upon request.

Laws regulating how and when searches may be legally conducted are numerous and complex. It is critical, however, that officers who are responsible for criminal investigations know these laws and operate within them. The penalty for not doing so is extreme—

any evidence obtained during an illegal search will not be allowed at a trial, as established by the exclusionary rule.

The Exclusionary Rule

Through the exclusionary rule, the courts enforce the prohibition against unreasonable searches set forth in the Fourth Amendment. In the early 1900s the federal courts declared that "they would require that evidence be obtained in compliance with constitutional standards" contained in the Fourth Amendment.

The **exclusionary rule** established that courts may not accept evidence obtained by unreasonable search and seizure, regardless of its relevance to a case. *Weeks v United States* (1914) made the rule applicable at the federal level; *Mapp v Ohio* (1961) made it applicable to *all* courts.

Davis (1997, p. 104) explains that the exclusionary rule is not specifically required by the Fourth Amendment or any other constitutional provision but is instead a judicially created remedy designed to safeguard an individual's Fourth Amendment rights through its deterrent effect on the police.

The Fruit-of-the-Poisonous-Tree Doctrine

The exclusionary rule affects not only illegally seized evidence but also evidence obtained as a result of the illegally seized evidence, referred to as fruit of the poisonous tree. The fruit-of-the-poisonous-tree doctrine resulted from the case of *Silverthorne Lumber Co. v United States* (1920). In this case a U.S. marshal unlawfully entered and searched the Silverthorne Lumber Company's offices and seized several documents. When the company demanded the return of the documents, the government did so but only after making copies. A district court later impounded these copies, which became the basis of a grand jury indictment. When the company was subpoenaed to produce the original documents, it refused and was then found to be in contempt of court. The Supreme Court, however, reversed the decision, saying: "Once the primary source (the 'tree') is proven to have been obtained unlawfully, any secondary evidence derived from it (the 'fruit') is also inadmissible."

The **fruit-of-the-poisonous-tree doctrine** established that evidence obtained as a result of an earlier illegality must be excluded from trial.

The exclusionary rule may seem to favor criminals at the expense of law enforcement, but this was not the Court's intent. The Court recognized that important exceptions to this rule might occur. Two of the most important exceptions are the inevitable-discovery doctrine and the good-faith doctrine.

The Inevitable-Discovery Doctrine

In *Nix v Williams* (1984), a defendant's right to counsel under the Sixth Amendment was violated, resulting in his making incriminating statements and leading the police to the body of his murder victim. Searchers who had been conducting an extensive, systematic search of the area then terminated their search. If the search had continued, the search party would inevitably have discovered the victim's body.

The **inevitable-discovery doctrine** established that if illegally obtained evidence would in all likelihood eventually have been discovered legally, it may be used.

The intent of the exclusionary rule, the Court said, was to deter police from violating citizens' constitutional rights. In the majority opinion, Chief Justice Warren E. Burger wrote: "Exclusion of physical evidence that would inevitably have been discovered adds nothing to either the integrity or fairness of a criminal trial." Hendrie (1997, p. 27) adds:

> The Supreme Court consistently has recognized that the inflexible application of the exclusionary rule would generate disrespect for the law and impede the administration of justice. With that in mind, and because the exclusionary rule is not considered a constitutionally required remedy, courts have carved out a number of exceptions and limitations, where to otherwise apply the rule would go beyond the limited goal of simply deterring illegal police conduct.

The Good-Faith Doctrine

In *United States v Leon* (1984), police in Burbank, California, investigated a drug-trafficking operation, following up on a tip from an unreliable informant, applied for and were issued an apparently valid search warrant. Their searches revealed large quantities of drugs and other evidence at various locations. The defendants challenged the sufficiency of the warrant and moved to suppress the evidence seized on the basis of the search warrant. The district court held that the affidavit was insufficient to establish probable cause because of the informant's unreliability. The U.S. Court of Appeals affirmed the action of the district court. Then the U.S. Supreme Court reviewed whether the exclusionary rule should be modified to allow the admission of evidence seized in *reasonably good faith*. The Court noted that the exclusionary rule is a *judicially created remedy* intended to serve as a deterrent rather than a guaranteed constitutional right.

Massachusetts v Sheppard (1984) used the principles established in *United States v Leon* to decide a case in which the police relied on the assurances of a state judge and executed a search warrant based on an affidavit completed on the wrong form. The detective used a form that pertained to searches for controlled substances. He discussed this potential problem with the judge who advised that he would make the necessary changes so it could be considered a proper search warrant. The judge informed the detective that the warrant was sufficient in form and content to authorize the search.

The search revealed incriminating evidence, and Sheppard was indicted for first-degree murder. The defendant challenged the decision on the basis of an inadequate search warrant. The trial judge denied the motion, holding that the police had acted in good faith. On appeal, the Supreme Judicial Court of Massachusetts reversed the conviction. On review, the Supreme Court upheld the trial judge's ruling. The officers reasonably believed the search they were conducting was authorized by a valid warrant and had a reasonable basis for the mistaken belief.

- - - - - - - -

The **good-faith doctrine** established that illegally obtained evidence may be admissible if the police were truly not aware they were violating a suspect's Fourth Amendment rights.

- - - - - - - -

In applying the good-faith doctrine, the Court refused to rule that a police officer is required to disbelieve a judge who has advised the officer by word and action that the warrant authorizes the requested search.

These two cases involve search warrants. The Court has not ruled whether the same application would be made in warrantless searches. The officer must still be "objectively reasonable of good faith belief." The Court is still not interested in subjective, personal beliefs or opinions, and ignorance of the laws of search and seizure will still not be excused. Officers are required to have reasonable knowledge of what the law prohibits.

Summary

The Fourth Amendment to the Constitution forbids unreasonable searches and seizures. Therefore, investigators must know what constitutes a reasonable, legal search. To search effectively, know the legal requirements for searching, the items you are searching for and the elements of the crime. Be organized, systematic and thorough.

A search can be justified if (1) a search warrant has been issued, (2) consent is given, (3) the search is incidental to a lawful arrest or (4) an emergency exists. Each of these four situations has limitations. A search conducted with a warrant must be limited to the area and items specified in the warrant. A search conducted with consent requires that the consent be voluntary and that the search be limited to the area for which the consent was given. A search incidental to a lawful arrest must be made simultaneously with the arrest and be confined to the area within the suspect's immediate control *(Chimel)*. A warrantless search in the absence of a lawful arrest or consent is justified only in emergencies where probable cause exists and the search must be conducted immediately.

The most important limitation on any search is that the scope must be narrowed; general searches are unconstitutional. However, plain-view evidence—unconcealed evidence seen by an officer engaged in a lawful activity—maybe seized and is admissible in court.

A successful crime-scene search locates, identifies and preserves all evidence present. For maximum effectiveness, a search must be well organized. This entails dividing the duties, selecting a search pattern, assigning personnel and equipment and giving instructions. Knowing what to search for is indispensable to an effective search. Anything material and relevant to the crime might be evidence.

Search patterns have been developed that help to ensure a thorough search. Exterior search patterns divide an area into lanes, strips, concentric circles or zones. Interior searches go from the general to the specific, usually in a circular pattern that covers all surfaces of the area being searched. The floor is searched first.

In addition to crime scenes, investigators frequently search vehicles, suspects and dead bodies. When searching a vehicle, remove the occupants from the car. First search the area around the vehicle, then the vehicle's exterior. Finally, search the interior along one side from front to back and then return along the other side to the front. Vehicles may be searched without a warrant if there is probable cause and if the vehicle would be gone before a search warrant could be obtained *(Carroll). Chambers v Maroney* established that a vehicle may be taken to headquarters to be searched in certain circumstances.

When searching a suspect who has not been arrested, confine the search to a patdown for weapons *(Terry).* The *Terry* decision established that a patdown or frisk is a "protective search for weapons" and as such must be "confined to a scope reasonably designed to discover guns, knives, clubs, and other hidden instruments for the assault of a police officer or others." If the suspect has been arrested, conduct a complete body search for weapons and evidence. Always be on your guard.

Search a dead body systematically and completely; include the immediate area around and under the body. Specially trained dogs can be very helpful in locating suspects, narcotics or explosives.

If a search is not conducted legally, the evidence obtained is worthless. According to the exclusionary rule, evidence obtained in unreasonable search and seizure, regardless of how relevant the evidence may be, is inadmissible in court. *Weeks v United States* established the exclusionary rule at the federal level; *Mapp v Ohio* made it applicable to all courts.

The fruit-of-the-poisonous-tree doctrine established that evidence obtained as a result of an earlier illegality must be excluded from trial. Two important exceptions to the exclusionary rule are the inevitable-discovery doctrine and the good-faith doctrine. The inevitable-discovery doctrine states that if the illegally obtained evidence would in all likelihood eventually have been discovered anyway, it may be used. The good-faith doctrine states that illegally obtained evidence may be admitted into trial if the police were truly unaware that they were violating the suspect's Fourth Amendment rights.

Checklist

The Search

- Is the search legal?
- Was a pattern followed?
- Was all evidence photographed, recorded in the notes, identified and packaged properly?
- Was the search completed even if evidence was found early in the search?
- Were all suspects searched?
- Did more than one investigator search?
- Was plain-view evidence seized? If so, were the circumstances recorded?

Discussion Questions

1. What might the officers who arrested Ted Chimel have done differently to ensure that the evidence they obtained would be admissible in court?

2. What are the advantages of having several officers search a crime scene? What are the disadvantages?

3. What are the steps in obtaining a search warrant?

4. What procedure is best for searching a suspect?

5. Many court decisions regarding police involve the question of legal searches. What factors are considered in the legal search of a person, a private dwelling, abandoned property, a business building, a car, corporate offices?

6. What basic steps constitute a thorough search of a dwelling?

7. Should there be legal provisions for an officer to seize evidence without a warrant if the evidence may be destroyed or removed before a warrant can be obtained?

8. Under what circumstances are police authorized to conduct no-knock searches?

9. Imagine that you are assigned to search a tavern at 10 AM for illegal gambling devices. Twenty patrons plus the bartender are in the tavern, but the owner is not present. How would you execute the search warrant?

10. Police officers frequently stop vehicles for traffic violations. Under the plain-view doctrine, what

evidence may be taken during such a stop? May the officers search the vehicle? The driver? The occupants?

References

Baratta, Rick. "K-9s: Trained to Excel." *Law and Order,* April 1995, pp. 20–25.

Bourn, Kathryn. "Discovering Evidence without a Warrant." *Police,* December 1996, pp. 8–9, 24.

Bulzomi, Michael J. "Knock and Announce: A Fourth Amendment Standard." *FBI Law Enforcement Bulletin,* May 1997, pp. 27–32.

Colbridge, Thomas D. "Protective Sweeps." *FBI Law Enforcement Bulletin,* July 1998, pp. 25–32.

Colbridge, Thomas D. "Search Incident to Arrest: Another Look." *FBI Law Enforcement Bulletin,* May 1999, pp. 27–32.

Crawford, Kimberly A. "Crime Scene Searches: The Need for Fourth Amendment Compliance." *FBI Law Enforcement Bulletin,* January 1999, pp. 26–31.

Crotty, Jim. "Searching Suspects." *Law and Order,* February 1998, pp. 79–82.

Davis, Rebecca. "What Fourth Amendment? HR666 and the Satanic Expansion of the Good Faith Exception." *Policing: An International Journal of Police Strategy and Management,* Vol.20, No.1, 1997, pp. 101–112.

Ferrell, C. E. "U.S. Supreme Court: Don't Base Car Search Only on Traffic Violation." *The Police Chief,* Vol. LXVI, No. 5, May 1999, p. 10.

Hawley, Donna Lea. "Searching within Fourth Amendment Boundaries." *Police,* August 1996, pp. 24–26.

Hendrie, Edward M. "The Inevitable Discovery Exception to the Exclusionary Rule." *FBI Law Enforcement Bulletin,* September 1997, pp. 26–32.

Hendrie, Edward M. "Curtilage: The Expectation of Privacy in the Yard." *FBI Law Enforcement Bulletin,* April 1998, pp. 25–32.

Jayre, Walt. "Landfill Search." *Law and Order,* October 1996, pp. 139–145.

Kalk, Dan. "Stop-and-Frisk Limitations Exist." *Police,* December 1997, pp. 44–45.

Klobuchar, Amy. "Legal News You Can Use." (Minneapolis/St. Paul) *Star Tribune,* February 1, 1999, p. A1.

Milazzo, Carl. "Supreme Court Emphasizes Significance of Officer Safety." *The Police Chief,* October 1998, p. 151.

"Pat-Down Searches." *NCJA Justice Bulletin,* June 1993, p. 7.

Regini, L. A. "The Motor Vehicle Exception: When and Where to Search." *FBI Law Enforcement Bulletin* Vol. 68, No. 7, July 1999, pp. 26–32.

Roen, Sara. "Cross-Trained K-9s." *Police,* February 1997, pp. 48–51, 68.

Schmitt, Sheila. "Search Device." *Law and Order,* January 1999, p. 88.

"Supreme Court Allows Searches of Car Passengers' Belongings." *Criminal Justice Newsletter,* Vol.29, No.23, December 1, 1998, p. 1.

"U.S. Supreme Court News." *NCJA Justice Bulletin* Vol. 19, No. 6, June 1999, pp. 17–18.

"U.S. Supreme Court News: Search and Seizure." *NCJA Justice Bulletin,* December 1998, p. 6.

"U.S. Supreme Court News: Car Searches." *NCJA Justice Bulletin,* April 1999, p. 8.

Wallentine, Ken. "No-Knock and Nighttime Searches." *Police,* September 1998, pp. 37–39.

Wallentine, Ken. "K-9s: Making Scents." *Police,* January 1999, pp. 34–35.

Physical Evidence

Do You Know?

What is involved in processing physical evidence?

How to determine what is evidence?

What a standard of comparison is and how to use it?

What common errors in collecting evidence are?

How to identify evidence?

What to record in your notes?

How to package evidence?

How to convey evidence to a department or a laboratory?

What types of evidence are most commonly found in criminal investigations and how to collect, identify and package each?

What can and cannot be determined from fingerprints, bloodstains and hairs?

What constitutes "best evidence"?

What DNA profiling is?

How and where evidence is stored?

How to ensure admissibility of physical evidence in court?

How physical evidence is finally disposed of?

Introduction

"Modern forensic science dates back to 1910," says Wexler (1999, p. 22), "when Dr. Edmond Locard, a French criminologist devised his 'exchange principle.' The theory basically states that a criminal always removes something from the crime scene or leaves behind incriminating evidence." Wexler further notes: "Every crime scene tells a story. The key is to uncover the pieces that will conclusively reveal the beginning, the middle and the tragic end. No item, however small or innocuous, should ever be discounted."

Right: David Coffman of the Florida Department of Law Enforcement, demonstrates a DNA match on his computer screen.

Below: A laboratory technician prepares a blood sample for DNA analysis.

A primary purpose of an investigation is to locate, identify and preserve **evidence** for determining the facts in a case, for later laboratory examination and for direct presentation in court. Brecher (1999, p. 66) notes: "Recently, evidence handling has been in the spotlight due to its significance in highly publicized trials. This has raised public awareness concerning not only evidence handling, but also its storage and exmination."

This chapter begins with some basic definitions, followed by a discussion of investigative equipment. Next the chapter describes how to discover, recognize and examine evidence; how to collect, mark and identify it; and how to package, preserve and transport it. This is followed by a discussion of frequently examined evidence including fingerprints and bodily fluids, evidence handling and infectious disease. The chapter concludes with a discussion of protecting and storing evidence, presenting it in court and determining how to dispose of it when no longer needed. ■

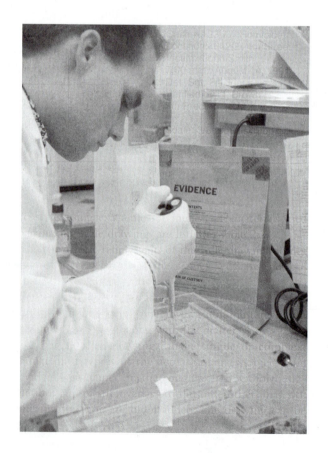

Definitions

Physical evidence is anything real—it has substance—that helps to establish the facts of a case. It can be seen, touched, smelled or tasted; solid, semisolid or liquid; large or tiny. It may be at an immediate crime scene or miles away; it may also be on a suspect or a victim.

Some evidence ties one crime to a similar crime or connects one suspect with another. Evidence can also provide new leads when a case appears to be unsolvable. Further, evidence corroborates statements from witnesses to or victims of a crime. Convictions are not achieved from statements, admissions or confessions alone. A crime must be proved by independent investigation and physical evidence.

For example, in a small western town, a six-year-old girl and her parents told police the girl had been sexually molested. The girl told police that a man had taken her to the desert, showed her some "naughty" pictures that he burned and then molested her. Because it was difficult for the police to rely on the girl's statement, they needed physical evidence to corroborate her story. Fortunately, the girl remembered where the man had taken her and led the police there. They found remains of the burned pictures and confiscated them as evidence. The remains of one picture, showing the suspect with a naked young girl on his lap, were sufficient to identify him by the rings on his fingers. This physical evidence supporting the girl's testimony resulted in a charge of lewdness with a minor.

Evidence can be classified in many ways. Extremely small items, such as hair or fibers, are called **trace evidence. Direct evidence** establishes proof of a fact without any other evidence. Evidence established by law is called **prima facie evidence.** For example, 0.1 percent ethanol in the blood is direct or prima facie evidence of intoxication in some states. Evidence that merely tends to incriminate a person, such as a suspect's footprints found near the crime scene, is called **circumstantial evidence.** A popular myth is that circumstantial evidence will not stand alone without other facts to support it, but many convictions have been obtained primarily on circumstantial evidence.

Also of extreme importance to the investigator is **exculpatory evidence,** that is, physical evidence that would clear one of blame, for example, having a blood type different from that of blood found at a murder scene. **Associative evidence** links a suspect with a crime. Associative evidence includes fingerprints, footprints, bloodstains, hairs and fibers. **Corpus delicti evidence** establishes that a crime has been committed. Contrary to popular belief, the **corpus delicti** in a murder case is not the body but the fact that death resulted from a criminal act. Corpus delicti evidence supports the elements of the crime. Pry marks on an entry door are corpus delicti evidence in a burglary. Physical evidence is not enough. To be of value, the evidence must be legally seized and properly and legally processed.

Processing physical evidence includes discovering, recognizing and examining it; collecting, recording and identifying it; packaging, conveying and storing it; exhibiting it in court; and disposing of it when the case is closed.

Before looking at processing a crime scene, consider the basic equipment that you may need.

Investigative Equipment

Frontline police personnel who conduct a preliminary investigation need specific equipment to accomplish their assigned tasks. Although not all crime scenes require all items of equipment, you cannot predict the nature of the next committed crime or the equipment that you will need. Therefore, you should have available at all times a crime-scene investigation kit containing basic equipment. Check the kit's equipment after each use, replacing items as required.

Investigations can be simple or complex and can reveal little or much physical evidence. Consequently, the equipment needs of each investigation are different. Table 5.1, alphabetized for easy reference, contains the investigative equipment most often used. The starred items have been discussed in earlier chapters.

Although the list may seem extensive, numerous other items are also often used in investigations: bags, binoculars, blankets, brushes, bullhorns, cable, capsules, chains, checklists, chemicals, chisels, coat hangers (to hang up wet or bloodstained clothing), combs, cotton, cutters, directories, drug kits, eyedroppers, files, fixatives, flares or fuses, floodlamps, forceps, forms, gas masks, generators, gloves, guns, hammers, hatchets, levels, lights, magnets, manuals, maps, matches, metal detectors, moulages (for making impressions or casts), nails, padlocks, pails, plastic sheets, punches,

Table 5.1 Equipment for Processing Evidence

Item	Uses
Cameras and film*	(Whatever type is available; perhaps several types) To photograph scene and evidence
Chalk and chalk line	To mark off search areas; to outline bodies or objects removed from the scene
Compass*	To obtain directions for report orientation and searches
Containers	(Boxes, bags of all sizes and shapes; lightweight; plastic or paper; telescoping or collapsible; glass bottles and new paint containers) To contain all types of evidence
Crayon or magic marker	To mark evidence
Envelopes, all sizes	To collect evidence
Fingerprint kit	(Various developing powders, fingerprint camera, fingerprint cards, ink pads, spoons, iodine fumer tube, lifting tape) To develop latent fingerprints
First-aid kit	To treat injured persons at the crime scene
Flashlight and batteries	To search dark areas, such as tunnels, holes, wells, windowless rooms; to search for latent fingerprints
Knife	To cut ropes, string, stakes, etc.
Labels, all sizes	(Evidence labels; labels such as "do not touch," "do not open," "handle with care," "fragile") To label evidence and to provide directions
Magnifier	To locate fingerprints and minute evidence
Measuring tape, steel	To measure long distances
Mirror with collapsible handle	To look in out-of-the-way locations for evidence
Money	To pay fares in case of vehicle failure, to tip, to purchase small amounts of needed supplies
Notebook*	To record information
Paper*	(Notebook, graph, scratch pads, wrapping) To take notes, sketch scene, wrap evidence
Pencils*	(At least two; sharpened) To make sketches
Pens*	(At least two; nonsmudge type) To take notes, make sketches
Picks	(Door lock picks and ice picks) To use as thumbtacks; to hold one end of a rope or tape
Plaster	To make casts of tire treads and footprints
Pliers	To pry and twist; to obtain evidence
Protractor	To measure angles
Rope	(Fluorescent, lightweight, approximately 300 feet) To protect the crime scene
Ruler, carpenter-type*	To measure short distances
Ruler, straightedge*	To measure small items/distances
Scissors	To cut tapes, reproduce size of objects in paper, cut first-aid gauze
Screwdrivers, standard and Phillips	To turn and pry
Scribe	To mark metal objects for evidence
Sketching supplies*	(Ruler, pencil, graph paper, etc.) To make sketches
Spatula	To dig; to stir
String	To tie objects and boxes containing evidence; to protect the crime scene; to mark off search areas
Tags	To attach to items of evidence
Templates	To aid in sketching
Tongue depressors, wooden	To stir; to add reinforcements to plaster casts; to make side forms for casting; to lift objects without touching them
Tubes, glass, with stoppers	To contain evidence
Tweezers	To pick up evidence without contamination
Wrecking bar	To pry open doors, windows, entryways or exits

*The use of these items has been discussed earlier in the text.

putty, rags, receipts, rubber, saws, scrapers, shovels, sidecutters, solvent, sponges, sprays, stamps, swabs, syringes, tape, tape recorders, thermometers, tin snips, towels, transceivers (to communicate in large buildings, warehouses, apartment complexes or open areas), vacuums, wax, wire and wrenches. The blood-test kits, gun-residue kits and other field-test kits described in Chapter 1 are also used.

Newer, more specialized equipment for investigation may also include pagers, cellular phones, latex gloves, goggles, electronic tracking systems, camcorders and much more, discussed throughout this section. Many departments are able to use forfeiture assets confiscated during drug busts to purchase specialized investigative equipment.

Additional heavy-duty, less-portable equipment such as large pry bars or long ladders are frequently found on fire and rescue vehicles and can be used jointly by the police and fire departments.

Considerations in Selecting Equipment

Survey the types of crimes and evidence most frequently found at crime scenes in your jurisdiction. Select equipment to process and preserve the evidence you are most likely to encounter. For example, because fingerprints are often found at crime scenes, fingerprint-processing equipment should be included in the basic kit. However, you would probably not need to take a shovel along to investigate a rape.

After the basic equipment needs are identified, select specific equipment. Select equipment that is frequently needed, lightweight, compact, high quality, versatile and reasonably priced. For example, boxes should either nest or be collapsible. Containers should be lightweight and plastic. The lighter and smaller the equipment, the more items can be carried in the kit. Consider miniaturized electronic equipment rather than heavier, battery-operated items. Select equipment that accomplishes more than one function, such as a knife with many features or other multipurpose tools.

Equipment Containers

The equipment can be put into one container or divided into several containers, based on frequency of use. This is an administrative decision determined by each department's needs. Dividing equipment results in a compact, lightweight kit suitable for most crime scenes while ensuring availability of other equipment needed to investigate less common cases.

This all-purpose investigation kit was designed for general crime investigation. It contains materials for lifting and developing fingerprints along with a variety of specialized tools for gathering and storing evidence.

Carriers or containers come in all shapes, sizes, colors and designs. Briefcases, attaché cases and transparent plastic bags are convenient to use. Some commercially produced kits include basic equipment. However, many departments prefer to design their own kits, adapted to their specific needs. The container should look professional, and a list of its contents should be attached to the outside or inside the cover.

Transporting the Equipment

Crime-scene investigative equipment is transported in a police vehicle, an investigator's vehicle or a crime van. The equipment can be transported in the trunk of a car, or a vehicle can be modified to carry it. For example, special racks can be put in the trunk, or the rear seat can be removed and special racks installed.

A mobile crime lab is usually a commercially customized van that provides compartments to hold equipment and countertops for processing evidence.

However, a van cannot go directly to some crime scenes, so the equipment must be transported from the van in other containers. The most frequently used equipment should be in the most accessible locations in the vehicle. Substances that freeze or change consistency in temperature extremes should be protected.

All selected vehicles should be equipped with radio communication and be capable of conveying equipment to disaster scenes as well as to crime scenes—to make them cost-effective. Cost-effectiveness can be further enhanced if the vehicles are available as command posts, for stakeouts and as personnel carriers.

Regardless of whether you work with a fully equipped mobile crime laboratory or a small, portable crime-scene investigation kit, your knowledge and skills as an investigator are indispensible to a successful investigation. The most sophisticated, expensive investigative equipment available is only as effective as you are in using it.

Training in Equipment Use

The largest failure in gathering evidence is not the equipment available but lack of training in using it effectively. Each officer should understand the use and operation of each item of equipment in the kit. Expertise comes with training and experience. Periodic refresher sessions should be held to update personnel on new techniques, equipment and administrative decisions.

Discovering, Recognizing and Examining Evidence

The importance of legal searches and seizures has been discussed, as has the fact that evidence must be **material, relevant** and **competent.** Specific procedures for presenting evidence and testifying in court are discussed in Chapter 8. Of importance at this point is recognizing evidence and then **processing evidence** properly.

During the search of a crime scene, it is often difficult to determine immediately what is or might be evidence. Numerous objects are present, and obviously not all are evidence.

> To determine what is evidence, first consider the apparent crime. Then look for any objects unrelated or foreign to the scene, unusual in location or number, damaged or broken or whose relation to other objects suggests a pattern that fits the crime.

The importance of physical evidence depends on its ability to establish that a crime was committed and to show how, when and by whom. Logic and experience help investigators determine the relative value of physical evidence. For example, evidence in its original state is more valuable than altered or damaged evidence.

Probabilities play a large role in determining the value of evidence. Fingerprints and DNA, for example, provide positive identification. In contrast, blood type does *not* provide positive identification, but it can help eliminate a person as a suspect.

An object's individuality is also important. For example, a heel mark's value is directly proportional to the number of its specific features, such as brand name, number of nails and individual wear patterns that can be identified. Some objects have identification marks on them. Other evidence requires a *comparison* to be of value—a tire impression matching a tire, a bullet matching a specific revolver, a torn piece of clothing matching a shirt.

> A **standard of comparison** is an object, measure or model with which evidence is compared to determine whether both came from the same source.

Fingerprints are the most familiar example of evidence requiring a standard of comparison. A fingerprint found at a crime scene must be matched with a known print to be of value. Likewise, a piece of glass found in a suspect's coat pocket can be compared with glass collected from a window pane broken during a burglary.

Sometimes, how an object fits with the surroundings determines whether it is likely to be evidence. For example, a man's handkerchief found in a women's locker room does not fit. The same handkerchief in a men's locker room is less likely to be evidence.

The value of evidence is affected by what happens to it after it is found. Make sure evidence does not lose its value—its integrity—because of improper handling or identification. **Integrity of evidence** refers to the requirement that any item introduced in court must be in the same condition as when it was found at the crime scene.

Forensic Light Sources

Forensic light sources such as UV lights and lasers have become popular. They can detect evidence not visible to

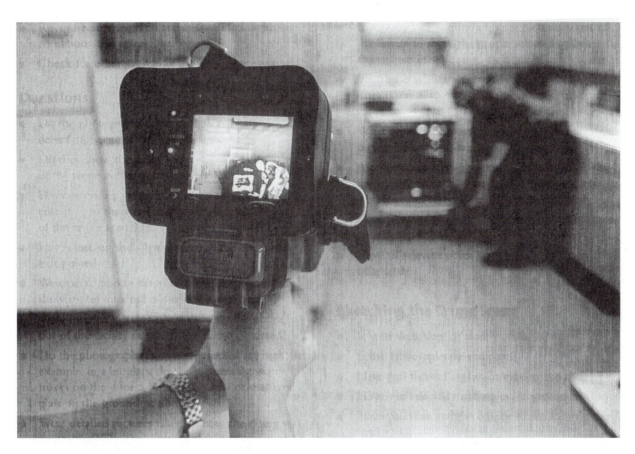

A hand-held thermal imaging camera displays heat generated by a stove and person in the background. These cameras can be used for search and rescue missions, fugitive searches and surveillance operations. They also can play an important role in crime scene investigations.

the naked eye, such as latent prints, bodily fluids and even altered signatures.

Evidence that fluoresces, or glows, is easier to see—sometimes thousands of times easier. For some kinds of hard-to-see evidence—small amounts of semen, for instance, or fibers—a forensic light source is the only practical way to make the invisible visible. A new, inexpensive tool for investigators projects a filtered light beam onto evidence dusted with fluorescent powder, and a luminescent print appears immediately. A portable longwave ultraviolet-light source can illuminate latent prints on several types of objects. Evidence is then exposed to superglue, then stained or dusted. After this it can be viewed under the UV light source.

Thermal imaging is another common forensic light technique. Paynter (1999, p. 22) states: "Statistics show that 47 percent of all violent crimes occur between the hours of 6 P.M. and 6 A.M. . . . Night

vision technology—light intensification and thermal imaging—turns night into day." He reports that the Law Enforcement Thermographers Association (LETA) has approved thermal imaging for search and rescue missions, fugitive searches, perimeter surveillance, vehicle pursuits, flight safety, marine and ground surveillance, structure profiles, disturbed surfaces and hidden compartments.

Paynter (p. 26) further notes: "Crime scene investigations are another emerging use. A thermal imager can assist officers in gathering evidence or pinpoint evidence tampering situations. Blood on a wall or floor that's been cleaned up still leaves thermal characteristics that can be viewed by a thermal imager." In one case a motorcyclist driving along a highway had shot a trucker. The crime scene was 1.5 miles long, and officers had 14 shell casings to locate. Using a thermal imager, they were able to recover all 14 casings.

Kash (1999, p. 43) states: "A thermal imager is often used by police to detect heat generated by indoor marijuana growing operations." He notes:

> Indoor growing operations require high intensity grow lamps that can generate temperatures up to 150 degrees Fahrenheit. . . . Police can take advantage of this necessity by using thermal imaging devices to detect the heat emissions and then use this information to establish probable cause in order to secure a search warrant.

The use of such techniques is not without legal challenge, however, as offenders claim such devices allow unreasonable searches of inherent privacy. Kash (p. 44) explains: "The seminal case which holds that the use of a thermal imager is not a search within the meaning of the Fourth Amendment is *U.S. vs. Penny-Feeney* (1991)." Kash concludes (p. 47):

> A review of the current case law on this issue confirms two schools of thought: the 9th and 10th federal circuits hold that utilizing a thermal imager requires a warrant since the device can see beyond walls, while the remaining circuits reason that since the device reads waste heat, a warrant is not required.
>
> The continual advancement of technology requires a perpetual interpretation of the Fourth Amendment.

Another advance in investigation is digital forensic imaging. Blitzer (1996, p. 14) notes:

> "Images are a crucial part of modern crime investigations, and imaging is growing in importance in the practice of law enforcement. . . . The technology has come a long way since the days of King Kong. However, it is still the integrity of the witness that is in question, not the technology in the lab."

Metal Detectors

Another device with applications in law enforcement is the metal detector. Nielsen (1999, p. 30) reports that: "A quality metal detector is an indispensable tool for effective crime scene management." Various types of specialized detectors are available, depending on the specifics of the

crime scene. For example, "two-box" metal detectors can locate very large objects buried deep beneath a surface, and underwater metal detectors are designed to ignore metals inherently found in sand and salt water (p. 32). Nielsen (p. 33) also states, however, that such tools are not intended as substitutes for standard evidence location methods: "It needs to be stressed that metal detectors don't replace traditional crime scene processing techniques—they only augment them. When properly employed, the role of metal detectors as a crime scene management tool doesn't begin until after the crime scene has been completely processed using standard methods."

Collecting, Marking and Identifying Evidence

How evidence is collected directly influences its later value. Remember to photograph and sketch before collecting evidence. Collect and identify all objects that are or may be evidence, leaving the final decision regarding relevance to the prosecutor.

Use small, versatile tools for collecting evidence. Ideally, each tool can be used to perform several tasks. Take extreme care to avoid **cross-contamination,** that is, allowing evidence to become mixed together. A claim of cross-contamination was a key defense in the O. J. Simpson trial. When using the same tool for several tasks, be certain it is thoroughly cleaned after each use.

Consider easy replacement and assembly as well as cost in selecting tools. Suggested collection equipment includes tape, knives, labels, containers, a flashlight, wrench, pick, hatchet and screwdriver. (Refer to Table 5.1.) The scene of a violent crime should be vacuumed with a machine that has a filter attachment. The vacuumed material can then be placed in an evidence bag and submitted to a crime laboratory.

Collecting evidence requires judgment and care. Put liquids in bottles. Protect cartridges and spent bullets with cotton, and put them in small containers. Put other items in appropriate containers to preserve them for later packaging and transporting.

- - - - - - - -

Common errors in collecting evidence are (1) not collecting enough of the sample, (2) not obtaining standards of comparison and (3) not maintaining the integrity of the evidence.

- - - - - - - -

To simplify testimony in court, one officer usually collects evidence, and another officer takes notes on the location, description and condition of each item. The officer collecting evidence enters this information in personal notes or witnesses and initials the notes of the officer assigned to record information. All evidence is identified by the officer who collects it and by any other officer who takes initial custody of it.

Mark or identify each item of evidence in a way that can be recognized later. Indicate the date and case number as well as your personal identifying mark or initials.

Make your marking easily recognizable and as small as possible—to reduce the possibility of destroying part of the evidence. Mark all evidence as it is collected or received. Do not alter, change or destroy evidence or reduce its value by the identification marking. Where and how to mark depends on the item. A pen is suitable for some objects. A stylus is used for those that require a more permanent mark that cannot be marked with pen, such as metal boxes, motor parts and furniture. Other objects can be tagged, labeled or placed in containers that are then marked and sealed.

Record in your notes the date and time of collection, where the evidence was found and by whom, the case number, a description of the item and who took custody.

Evidence descriptions can be computer-entered and cross-referenced to current cases in the local jurisdiction and the surrounding area.

Packaging and Preserving Evidence

Careful packaging maintains the evidence in its original state, preventing damage or contamination. Do not mix, or cross-contaminate, evidence. Each type of evidence has specific requirements. Some evidence is placed in sterile containers. Other types, such as firing-pin impressions or markings on a fatal bullet, are packed to prevent breakage or wrapped in cotton to prevent damage to individual characteristics. Hairs, fibers and other trace evidence are often placed in paper that is folded so that the evidence cannot fall out. This is called a *druggist fold* (see Figure 5.1).

Package each item separately in a durable container to maintain the integrity of evidence.

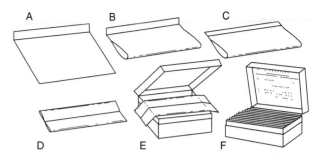

FIGURE 5.1 *The Druggist Fold*

Packaging is extremely important. Although some authorities use plastic bags, few large departments use plastic because it does not "breathe" and hence may cause condensation to form. This can impede a laboratory examination of the evidence. Many departments use new brown-paper grocery bags, especially for clothing. Although boxes might be better in some respects, they can be impractical to carry and difficult to find. You can usually find a supermarket open somewhere if you run out of bags. Be sure to provide a means of sealing whatever type of bag is used to maintain the integrity of the evidence.

Preserve evidence on immovable items at the scene. Often some reproduction of the evidence is made. Fingerprints are developed, photographed, lifted and later compared. Toolmarks are reproduced through photography, modeling clay, moulage, silicone and other impression-making materials. (These methods are acceptable in accordance with the best-evidence rule.) Specific requirements for the most frequently found evidence and best evidence are discussed later.

Submit movable items directly into evidence or send them to a laboratory for analysis. Sometimes an object is both evidence and a container of evidence. For example, a stolen radio found in a suspect's car is evidence of theft, and the fingerprints of a second suspect found on the radio are evidence that links that person to the theft.

Before packaging evidence for mailing to a laboratory, make sure it was legally obtained and has been properly identified and recorded in your notes. Submitting inadmissible evidence is costly and inefficient. Pack any bulky item in a sturdy box, seal the box with tape and mark it "evidence." If there is any latent evidence such as fingerprints on the surface of the object (see Figure 5.2), be sure to state this clearly.

Place a transmittal letter to the laboratory in an envelope attached to the outside of the box. This letter should contain the name of the suspect and the victim,

FIGURE 5.2
*Proper Sealing
of Evidence*

Source: Courtesy of the FBI.

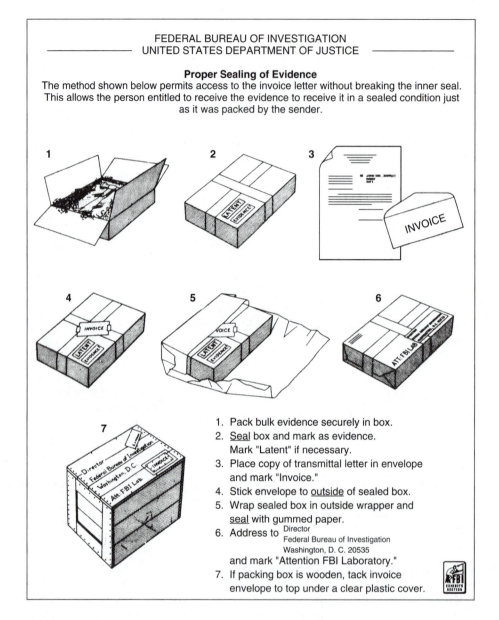

FEDERAL BUREAU OF INVESTIGATION
UNITED STATES DEPARTMENT OF JUSTICE

Proper Sealing of Evidence
The method shown below permits access to the invoice letter without breaking the inner seal.
This allows the person entitled to receive the evidence to receive it in a sealed condition just
as it was packed by the sender.

1. Pack bulk evidence securely in box.
2. Seal box and mark as evidence.
   Mark "Latent" if necessary.
3. Place copy of transmittal letter in envelope
   and mark "Invoice."
4. Stick envelope to outside of sealed box.
5. Wrap sealed box in outside wrapper and
   seal with gummed paper.
6. Address to Director
   Federal Bureau of Investigation
   Washington, D. C. 20535
   and mark "Attention FBI Laboratory."
7. If packing box is wooden, tack invoice
   envelope to top under a clear plastic cover.

if any; tell what examinations you desire and which tests, if any, have already been done; and refer to any other pertinent correspondence or reports. Include a copy of the letter with the evidence, and mail the original separately. Retain a copy for your files. Figure 5.3 shows a sample letter.

Transporting Evidence

If the crime laboratory is nearby, an officer can deliver the evidence personally. However, even if the evidence is personally delivered, include with it a letter on department letterhead or a department form.

— — — — — — —

Personal delivery, registered mail, insured parcel post, air express, Federal Express and United Parcel Service (UPS) are legal ways to transport evidence. Always specify that the person receiving the evidence is to sign for it.

— — — — — — —

How evidence should be transported depends on its size and type and the distance involved. Use the fastest method available. If the package is mailed, request a "return receipt."

```
┌─────────────────────────────────────────────────────────────┐
│              ┌──────────────────────────────┐                │
│              │    USE OFFICIAL LETTERHEAD    │                │
│              └──────────────────────────────┘                │
│                                                               │
│                              ⎛ Police Headquarters      ⎞     │
│                              ⎜ Right City, State zip code⎟     │
│                              ⎝ March 17, 20_ _           ⎠     │
│                                                               │
│  Director                                                     │
│  Federal Bureau of Investigation                              │
│  U. S. Department of Justice                                  │
│  Washington, D. C. 20535                                      │
│                       ATTENTION: FBI LABORATORY               │
│  Dear Director:                                               │
│                                                               │
│            RE:   GUY PIDGIN, SUSPECT                          │
│                  EMPALL MERCHANDISE MART                      │
│                  BURGLARY                                     │
└─────────────────────────────────────────────────────────────┘
```

FIGURE 5.3
Sample Letter to the FBI Lab
Source: Courtesy of the FBI.

Sometime during the early morning of March 16, 20_ _, someone entered the Empall Merchandise Mart through an unlocked side window and made an unsuccessful attempt to rip open the safe. The outer layer of metal on the safe door had been pried loose from the upper right corner and bent outward, ripping the metal along the top and down the side of the safe about 12" each way. The burglar may have been scared away because the job was not completed. Investigation led us to Guy Pidgin, who denies complicity. He voluntarily let us take his shoes and trousers and a crowbar that was under his bed in his rooming house.

I am sending by Federal Express a package containing the following evidence in this case:

1. One pair of shoes obtained from Guy Pidgin
2. A pair of grey flannel trousers obtained from Guy Pidgin
3. One 28" crowbar obtained from Guy Pidgin
4. Safe insulation taken from door of safe at Empall Merchandise Mart
5. Piece of bent metal approximately 12" x 12" taken from door of safe at Empall Merchandise Mart. In order to differentiate the two sides cut by us, we have placed adhesive tape on them.
6. Chips of paint taken from the side of safe
7. Fingerprint card for Guy Pidgin
8. Ten transparent lifts

Please examine the shoes and trousers for safe insulation or any paint chips that match the paint taken from the safe. Also, we would be interested to know if you can determine if the crowbar was used to open the safe. Examine items 5 and 8 to determine if latent fingerprints are present. If present, compare with item 7.

This evidence, which should be returned to us, has not been examined by any other expert.

Very truly yours,

James T. Wixling
Chief of Police

Frequently Examined Evidence

The laboratory analyzes the class and individual characteristics of evidence. **Class characteristics** are the features that place an item into a specific category. For example, the size and shape of a toolmark may indicate that the tool used was a screwdriver rather than a pry bar. **Individual characteristics** are the features that distinguish one item from another of the same type. For example, chips and wear patterns in the blade of a screwdriver may leave marks that are distinguishable from those of any other screwdriver.

Frequently examined physical evidence includes finger-prints, voiceprints, shoe and tire impressions, bite marks, tools and toolmarks, weapons and ammuni-tion, glass, soils and minerals, body fluids (including blood), hairs and fibers, safe insulation, rope and tape, drugs, documents and laundry and dry-cleaning marks.

Fingerprints

Fingerprints are a positive way to prove that a suspect was at a crime scene. The implications of finding identi-fiable prints at the scene vary with each case. For exam-ple, prints may not be important if the suspect had a legitimate reason for being there. Often, however, this is not the case.

Although many laypeople assume that identifiable fingerprints are almost always found at a crime scene, in many cases, none are found. Even when they are, it is often difficult to locate the person who matches the prints. If a person's prints are not on file and there are no suspects, fingerprints are virtually worthless. Other times, however, fingerprints are the most important physical evidence in a case. Finding fingerprints at a crime scene requires training and experience. Some sur-faces retain prints more easily than others.

Fingerprints are of various types:

- **Latent fingerprints** are impressions transferred to a surface, either by sweat on the ridges of the fin-gers or because the fingers carry residue of oil, dirt, blood or other substance. Latent fingerprints can be visible or invisible.

- **Visible fingerprints** are made when fingers are dirty or stained. They occur primarily on glossy or light-colored surfaces and can be dusted and lifted.

- **Plastic fingerprints,** one form of visible print, are impressions left in soft substances such as putty, grease, tar, butter or soft soap. These prints are pho-tographed, not dusted.

- **Invisible fingerprints** are not readily seen but can be developed through powders or chemicals. They are normally left on nonporous surfaces.

Any hard, smooth, nonporous surface can contain latent fingerprints.

Nonporous surfaces include light switches; window frames and moldings; enameled surfaces of walls, doors and objects that are painted or varnished; wood; lamps; polished silver surfaces; and glass. Fingerprints often occur on documents, glass, metals, tools and weapons used in a crime as well as on any objects picked up or touched by a suspect. Objects such as firearms, tools, small metal objects, bottles, glassware, documents and other transportable items are submitted to a laboratory, where the prints are developed by experts.

Some porous materials also produce latent prints. For example, paper and cloth surfaces have developed excel-lent prints. Passing a flashlight at an oblique angle over a surface helps to locate possible prints.

Latent prints have even been collected from human skin. According to Gulick (1998, p. 148): "Advancements in the recovery of latent fingerprints from both living and dead human skin have resulted in the identification and conviction of at least 39 perpetrators."

Begin the search for fingerprints by determining the entry and exit points and the route through a crime scene. Look in the obvious places as well as less obvi-ous places such as the underside of toilet seats and the back of car rearview mirrors. Examine objects that appear to have been moved. Consider the nature of the crime and how it was probably committed. Prints found on large, immovable objects are processed at the scene by photographing or dusting with powder or chemicals.

Dusting Latent Fingerprints Fingerprint dusting powders are available in various colors and chemical compositions to provide maximum development and contrasts. When dusting for fingerprints, use a powder that contrasts in color to the surface.

Do not powder a print unless it is necessary, and do not powder a visible print until after you photograph it.

To dust for fingerprints, follow these steps (see Fig-ure 5.4):

1. Make sure the brush is clean. Roll the handle of the brush between your palms to separate the bristles.

2. Shake the powder can to loosen the powder. Apply the powder *lightly* to the print, following the con-tour lines of the ridges to bring out details.

3. Remove all excess powder.

4. Photograph.

Apply the powder to the surface to discover the prints.

Clean up the print by gently brushing with the flow of the ridges. Do not brush the latent print too vigorously.

FIGURE 5.4 *Dusting for Fingerprints*

Use a camel-hair brush for most surfaces. Use an aspirator for dusting ceilings and slanted or difficult areas. If in doubt about which powder or brush to use, test them on a similar area first.

Learn to use the various materials by watching an experienced investigator demonstrate the correct powders, brushes and techniques. Then practice placing latent prints on various surfaces and using different colored powders to determine how well each adheres and how much color contrast it provides. Practice until you can recognize surfaces and select the appropriate powder. When photographing developed latent prints, record the color of the powder used, the color of the surface and the location of the prints. Place your identification, date and case number on the back of the photograph and submit it to the crime laboratory. The laboratory will determine whether it is an identifiable print and whether it matches a known suspect or other people whose prints were submitted for elimination.

Lifting Prints To lift fingerprints, use a commercially prepared lifter that has both a black-and-white background and a wide transparent lift tape. Use black lifters for light powders and light lifters for black powders. To lift prints on doorknobs or rounded surfaces, use trans-

parent tape so you can see any spots where the tape is not sticking. Put the tape over the dusted print. Do not use too much pressure. Work out any bubbles that appear under the tape by applying extra pressure. When you have lifted the print, transfer it to a fingerprint card. Figure 5.5 illustrates this procedure.

Common errors in lifting prints include removing too much or too little powder from the ridges, allowing bubbles to develop under the tape and failing to make two lifts when a second lift would be better than the first.

Chemical Development of Latent Fingerprints Although powders are used to develop latent fingerprints on many surfaces, they are not recommended for unpainted wood, paper, cardboard or other absorbent surfaces. Using powder on such surfaces will smudge any prints, destroying their value as evidence. For such surfaces, use special chemicals such as iodine, silver nitrate or ninhydrin.

Use gloves and a holding device to avoid contaminating the evidence by inadvertently adding your own fingerprints. The chemicals can all be applied to the same specimen because each reacts differently with various types of materials. However, if *all* are used, the order must be iodine first, then ninhydrin and finally silver nitrate.

The proper method of applying fingerprint tape.

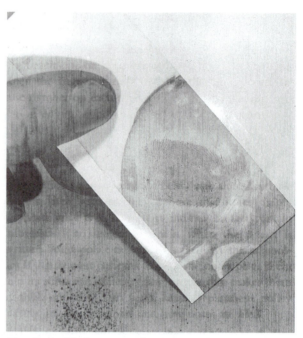

Transfer the lifted print to a fingerprint card.

FIGURE 5.5 *Lifting Prints*

In the *iodine method,* iodine crystals are placed in a fuming cabinet or a specially prepared fuming gun. The crystals are heated and vaporized, producing a violet fume that is absorbed by the oil in the fingerprints. The fingerprint ridges appear yellow-brown and must be photographed immediately because they fade quickly. Fuming cabinets and guns can be made or purchased from police supply houses.

The *ninhydrin method* develops amino acids. Ninhydrin (highly flammable) is available in spray cans or in a powder form from which a solution of the powder and acetone or ethyl alcohol is made. The evidence is then either sprayed, dipped in or brushed with the ninhydrin. Development of prints can be speeded by applying heat from a fan, pressing iron or oven. At room temperature, prints develop in a minimum of two hours; with a pressing iron, they develop almost immediately. Ninhydrin-developed prints do not fade immediately, but they eventually lose contrast. Therefore, photograph them soon after development.

The *silver nitrate method* develops sodium chloride in the fingerprint ridges into silver chloride that appears as a red-brown print. Because silver nitrate destroys oils and amino acids, it must be used *after* the iodine and ninhydrin methods. Immerse the specimen in a solution of 3–10 percent silver nitrate and distilled water. Remove it

immediately and hang it to dry. The prints can be developed more rapidly by applying light until they start to develop. They should be photographed immediately because they disappear after several hours.

Other Methods of Lifting Prints Fingerprints may also be located and developed by using Magnabrush techniques, laser technology, gelatin lifters and cyanoacrylate (superglue). Superglue fuming involves heating three or four drops of glue to generate fumes that adhere to fingerprints. The process can effectively develop prints on plastic, bank checks, counterfeit money, metal and skin.

Portable lasers are used to find and highlight fingerprints. They can detect fingerprints on the skin of a murder victim and trace a gunshot path.

Investigators can also use gelatin lifters to lift dusted prints or dust marks (footprints) from a wide variety of surfaces. Used in Europe for decades, the lifters are flexible and easily cut to suit specific needs. They can lift dust prints from any smooth surface, from tile floors to cardboard boxes. The high contrast of the black lifters allows investigators to see dust prints not visible to the naked eye, and the lifted prints photograph extremely well. In addition, the lifters can pick up particle samples such as hair or paint chips. In the laboratory, tweezers or a scalpel can remove the samples from the lifter without damaging the sampled material.

Inked Prints Most police departments have equipment for taking fingerprints. Standard procedure is to fingerprint all adults who have been arrested, either at the time of booking or the time of release. These fingerprint records help ensure that the person arrested is identified correctly. Some departments have portable fingerprint kits in patrol vehicles that allow them to take inked prints and develop latent prints at crime scenes.

To take inked prints, start by rolling the right thumb and fingers in the order stated on the card. Then roll the left thumb and fingers in order. Use a complete roll; that is, go from one side to the other. Next, *press* the fingers and then the thumb of each hand on the spaces provided on the card. The card also has spaces for information about the person and the classification made by the fingerprint examiner. Learn to take inked fingerprints by having someone demonstrate.

Electronic Fingerprinting Electronic fingerprinting is now replacing inked printing. Computers have greatly affected how fingerprints can be taken. An **automated fingerprint identification system (AFIS)** can digitize fingerprint information to produce **inkless fingerprints.** Latent fingerprints are scanned and converted into an electronic image that is stored in a database for rapid retrieval. In this method, a suspect's hand is placed onto a glass platen, where a laser optically scans the prints and transfers them onto a fingerprint card. Campbell (1998, p. 35) relates the value of this technology:

> AFIS technology first demonstrated its effectiveness in cracking the infamous "Night Stalker" serial killer case in 1985. "I was working at the Department of Justice at the time and the first AFIS system had just been installed," said Doonan. "We were . . . installing a database of about a half a million records." A partial print recovered from a victim's car was entered and a "hit" came up within three minutes. Richard Ramirez was arrested the same day. The LAPD estimated it would have taken a specialist 67 years to search the files manually.

AFIS technology is constantly being augmented with the introduction of new services and features. Smith (1998, p. 14) notes:

> The Integrated Automated Fingerprint Identification System (IAFIS) . . . will provide five major services to local, state and federal law enforcement and criminal justice agencies:

- Ten-Print-Based Identification Services
- Latent Fingerprint Services
- Subject Search and Criminal History Services
- Document and Image Services
- Remote Search Services

One major benefit of this technology is the ability to transmit the print image over telephone or cable lines from one AFIS system to another or to computerized criminal records centers. Pilant (1998b, p. 22) recounts an instance in which a local agency accessed the state's criminal history system: "In less than three minutes and without the intervention of a single human, the system sent the suspect's identification and history back to the arresting agency, a task that would once have taken days or even weeks in some cases." This feature also allows international sharing of databases to help capture criminals who move from one country to another. Lucchesi (1998, p. 32) notes: "Many countries are now adopting AFIS as a way to quickly compare fingerprints of an individual arrested or detained."

Other benefits of electronic fingerprinting systems are their increasing speed and accuracy. Pilant (1998a, p. 72) elaborates:

> Automatic Verification further automates and speeds the matching process by telling the computer to decide whether the candidate is a match. The computer compares the minutiae—the bifurcations and ending ridges that are unique to every fingerprint—and verifies a match with 99.9 percent accuracy. Anything less than that is considered a no-match.

An expert in the technology cited by Pilant further claims: "Automatic verification uses one-to-one matching. It will never give you a false positive" (1998a, p. 72).

Elimination Prints If fingerprint evidence is found, it is important to know whose prints "belong" at the scene.

------- -- --

Prints of persons with reason to be at the scene are taken and used as **elimination prints.**

------- -- --

For example, family members in a home where a crime has occurred or employees of a business that has been robbed should be fingerprinted so that their fingerprints at the scene can be eliminated from suspicion.

Fingerprint Files and Searches Computer searches are often conducted for fingerprints. Stored fingerprint information includes the sex, date of birth, classification formula and each finger's ridge count. When queried, the system selects the cards within the range limitations for the entered classification formula. Fingerprint experts then visually compare the prints (Figure 5.6).

If no match is found in local or state files, prints are submitted to the FBI Identification Division for a further search. This division has on file fingerprints of arrested people as well as nearly 100 million other people such as aliens and individuals in government services, including the military.

The automated fingerprint identification system uses computers to review and map fingerprints. It creates a spatial geometry of the minutiae of the print, which is changed into a binary code for the computer's searching algorithm. The capability of registering thousands of details makes it possible for the computer to complete a search in minutes that would take days manually. The search success rate has been up to 98 percent in some departments with files under one million.

Approximately 35–40 percent of crime scenes have latent prints. Considering that the FBI fingerprint files contain data on more than 100 million individuals, the AFIS is a tremendous advance in crime fighting.

Usefulness of Fingerprints
Fingerprints are of extreme evidentiary value in criminal investigations.

- - - - - - - - -

> Fingerprints are *positive* evidence of a person's identity. They cannot, however, indicate a person's age, sex or race.

- - - - - - - - -

Fingerprints can be sent via communications systems across the country and visually reproduced. Crime victims are identified by their prints to prove the corpus delicti. Courts, parole and probation officers and prosecutors use fingerprints to positively identify people with multiple criminal records.

Fingerprints also aid in noncriminal investigations by helping to identify victims of mass disasters, missing persons, amnesia victims and unconscious persons. Military agencies use fingerprints recorded at enlistment to identify those killed in combat. Hospitals use fingerprints or footprints to identify newborn babies. Furthermore, fingerprints are becoming widely used as identification for cashing checks and processing legal documents.

Other Types of Prints Suspects may also leave palm prints, footprints or even prints of lips & body pores. These impressions can be photographed and developed just as fingerprints are.

Palmprints contain up to 1,000 identifying landmarks compared to only about 60 to 100 in fingerprints, making them very valuable if found (Dees, 2000, p. 70).

In one interesting case a burglar shattered a restaurant's plate glass window. The police found no fingerprints around the window but did find footprints and a toe print on a piece of the broken glass. These were developed and lifted. Later a 17-year-old was arrested on vagrancy. Learning that he often went barefoot, police also took his footprints and forwarded them to the FBI. They were identical to those on the plate glass window fragment. It was learned that the youth had taken off his shoes and put his socks on his hands to avoid leaving fingerprints at the crime scene. He was found guilty.

In another case reported by Hoffman (1998, p. 31) a string of peeping-tom cases was solved because of three lip impressions left by the suspect on a windowpane. Hoffman also reported on a case in Illinois in which authorities matched lip prints on a piece of duct tape that the suspect had held in his mouth while binding a victim.

Admissibility in Court
Numerous court rulings have upheld the admissibility of fingerprints as evidence when supported by testimony of fingerprint experts.

Voiceprints

A **voiceprint** is a graphic record made by a sound spectrograph of the energy patterns emitted by speech. Like fingerprints, no two voiceprints are alike. Voiceprints can assist in identifying bomb hoaxers, obscene phone callers and others who use the telephone illegally. A voiceprint made during a telephone call can be retained until a suspect is in custody.

The use of voiceprints in criminal trials is controversial. In a number of cases, convictions obtained through voiceprints have been reversed because the voiceprints were not regarded as sufficiently reliable.

Biometrics

Biometrics is the statistical study of biological data such as fingerprints, which allows for positive identification of individuals.

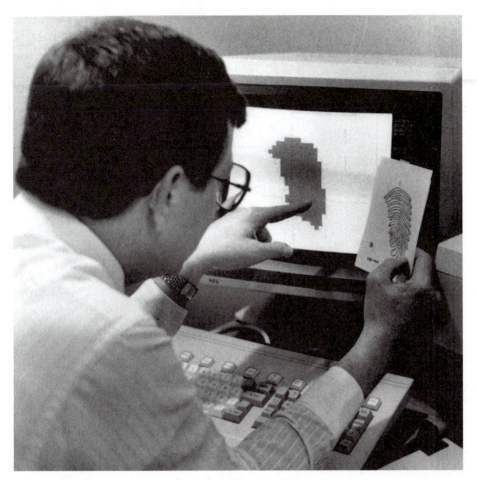

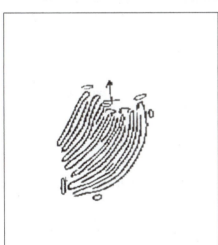

Search-print image   Candidate-print image

FIGURE 5.6 *Positive Identification of a Fingerprint*

The Automated Fingerprint Identification System used by the Illinois State Police matches fingerprints recovered at crime scenes with the 1.6 million prints in their files. Top photo: Fingerprint examiner edits a print for errors. Bottom photo: A search print (left) as it appears on the video screen and (right) a candidate's print image. The examiner holds a print image match as it would appear on the screen after a match-up (top).

According to Siuru (1998, p. 38):

> Biometric identification technology . . . developments range from the old standby, fingerprints, to techniques that recognize voices, hand geometry, facial characteristics, and even blood vessels. One of the most promising uses the eye's iris. The random patterns of the iris can be thought of as a complex human barcode that is created by a tangled meshwork of connective tissue and other visible features. . . .
>
> For all the people on the earth, no two have identical irises, not even among identical twins. Nor do they change during a person's life or can they be altered by medical procedures.

Siuru (p. 38) describes a biometric identification application called the IriScan System 2100, in which a "person looks into a camera lens and a video image of the iris is made. The image is digitized, processed into an IrisCode, and stored for future recognition. Both eyeglasses and contact lenses are accommodated easily and the whole process takes about 30 seconds." Such technology is being applied in detention centers and correctional facilities to provide absolute identification of inmates.

Even the IriScan director of technology applications recognizes that IriScan will never replace fingerprints for criminal forensics because the iris deteriorates shortly after death, and people do not leave an iris print when they commit a crime (Strandberg, 1999, p. 74).

Henry (1998, p. 16) describes another application of biometric technology that provides access control at universities—hand scanners. During the 1970s the University of Georgia's food service department was having problems with students using meal coupons they had not actually paid for themselves and decided to install biometric hand readers to positively identify each person entering the cafeteria. With the current biometric system in place, students have two choices when they go to eat (p. 18):

> They can take their student ID card, which has their student ID number encoded on the mag stripe, swipe it in the reader, then place their

hand and it recognizes their hand; or they can punch in their student ID number on the keypad and then place their hand to be scanned, so they don't have to carry their ID card with them.

In terms of relative error rates, fingerprints and iris recognition are considered most reliable, followed by facial and hand, with voice the least reliable (Dolan, 1999, p. 16).

Although biometrics is receiving much attention, disadvantages exist, including price, speed, difficulty in obtaining good data and biometric change in individuals (Pearson, 1999, p. 11).

Shoe and Tire Impressions

If shoe or tire prints are found on paper or cardboard, photograph them and then submit the originals for laboratory examination. Use latent fingerprint lifters to lift shoe and tire tread impressions from smooth surfaces. Photograph with and without a marker before lifting the impression. Do not attempt to fit your shoe into the suspect's shoe print to determine size. This can destroy the shoe print. Shoe and tire impressions may have unique wear patterns that should be cast when possible.

Cast shoe or tire tread impressions found in dirt, sand or snow.

Some departments use plaster, whereas others prefer dental casting material. The steps in making a plaster **cast** of an impression are these (see Figure 5.7):

1. Build a retaining frame around the impression about 2 inches from its edges.

2. Coat the impression with five or six layers of alcohol and shellac or inexpensive hairspray, allowing each coat to dry before applying the next. Apply talcum powder to the last layer so that the spray can easily be removed from the cast.

3. Rapidly mix the plaster following directions on the box.

4. Pour the plaster into the impression, using a spatula to cushion its fall and guide it into all areas of the impression. Fill the impression halfway.

5. Add wire or gauze to reinforce the impression.

6. Pour in more plaster until it overflows to the retaining frame.

FIGURE 5.7 *Making a Plaster Cast of a Shoe Impression*

7. Before the cast hardens, use a pencil or other pointed instrument to incise your initials, the case number and the date on the back of the impression.

8. After the cast hardens, remove it and the retaining frame. Do not wash the cast; the laboratory does this.

9. Carefully wrap the cast in protective material to avoid breakage, and place it in a strong box to ship to the laboratory.

The laboratory compares the cast with manufacturers' shoe and tire-tread files.

Value of Shoe and Tire Prints In addition to providing unique wear patterns that can be compared to a suspect's shoes, footprints can also indicate whether a person was walking or running, was carrying something heavy or was unfamiliar with the area or unsure of the terrain.

Tire marks can show the approximate speed and direction of travel, the manufacturer and year they were made. In the July 1999 slaying of a Yosemite Park naturalist, the killer "left behind footprints and the distinctive tracks of his baby blue International Scout, a vehicle that bore a different brand of tire on every wheel. It was those unique tracks, sources said, that allowed investigators to look for [the suspect]" ("Handyman Details Slayings . . . ," 1999, p. A4).

Bite Marks

Cast identifiable teeth impressions found in partially eaten food in the same way as shoe and tire-tread impressions. Dental impression material is preferred because of its fine texture. Take saliva samples using a swab before casting bite marks.

If the bite mark is not deep enough to cast, tape over it and trace it onto transparent plastic. A new type of drawing, called a *toneline,* is also available. This black photographic perimeter outline of a bite mark can be compared directly with models of an individual's teeth.

Tools and Toolmarks

Common tools such as hammers and screwdrivers are often used in crimes and cause little suspicion if found in someone's possession. Such tools are often found in a suspect's vehicle, on the person or at the residence. If a tool is found at a crime scene, determine if it belongs to the property owner. Broken tool pieces may be found at a crime scene, on a suspect or on a suspect's property (see Figure 5.8).

Identify each suspect tool with a string tag. Wrap it separately and pack it in a strong box for sending to the laboratory.

A **toolmark** is an impression left by a tool on a surface. For example, a screwdriver forced between a window and sill may leave a mark the same depth and width as the screwdriver. The resiliency of the surface may cause explainable differences in mark dimensions and tool dimensions. If the screwdriver has a chipped head or other imperfections, it will leave impressions for later comparison. Toolmarks are often found in burglaries, auto thefts and larcenies in which objects are forced open.

A toolmark provides leads as to the size and type of tool that made it. Examining a suspect tool determines, within limits, whether it could have made the mark in question. Even if you find a suspect tool, it is not always possible to match it to the toolmark, especially if the tool was damaged when the mark was made. However, residue from the forced surface may adhere to the tool, making a comparison possible.

Do not attempt to fit a suspected tool into a mark to see if it matches. This disturbs the mark, as well as any paint or other trace evidence on the suspect tool, making the tool inadmissible as evidence.

Photograph toolmarks and then either cast them or send the object on which they appear to a laboratory.

Photographing Toolmarks First photograph the location of the tool or toolmark within the general crime scene. Then take close-ups first without and then with a marker to show actual size and detail.

Casting Toolmarks Casting toolmarks presents special problems because they often are not on a horizontal surface. In such cases, construct a platform or bridge around the mark by taping tin or other pliable material to the surface. Plaster of Paris, plasticine and waxes do not provide the detail necessary for tool striation marks. Better results are obtained from moulage, silicone and other thermosetting materials.

Comparing Toolmarks Toolmarks are easy to compare if a suspect tool has not been altered or damaged since it made the mark. If the tool is found, send it to the laboratory for several comparison standards.

A toolmark is compared with a standard of comparison impression rather than with the tool itself.

The material used for the standard is as close as possible to the original material. Ideally, a portion of the original material is used.

The toolmark found at the scene and the standard of comparison are placed under a microscope to make the striation marks appear as light and dark lines. The lines are then adjusted to see whether they match. Variations of approximately 10 degrees in angle are permissible. Roughly 60 percent of the lines should match in the comparison (see Figure 5.9).

Value of Toolmarks A specific mark may be similar to or found in the same relative location as toolmarks found at other crimes. Evidence of the way a tool is applied—the angle, amount of pressure and general use—can tie one crime to another. A toolmark also makes it easier to look for a specific type of tool. Possession of, or fingerprints on, such a tool can implicate a suspect.

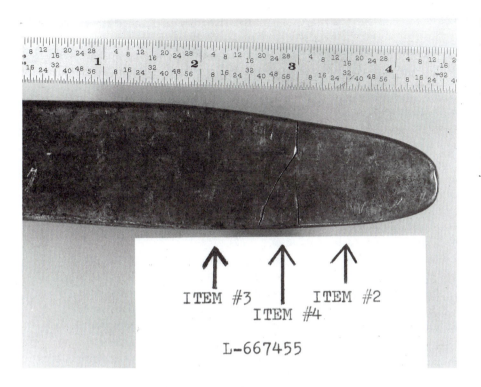

FIGURE 5.8

Broken Tool Comparison
Pry tool used to pry open the rear door of a hardware store. Items 2 and 4 were found at the scene of the burglary. Item 3 was found in a toolbox in the suspect's car. This evidence led to the suspect's conviction for burglary.

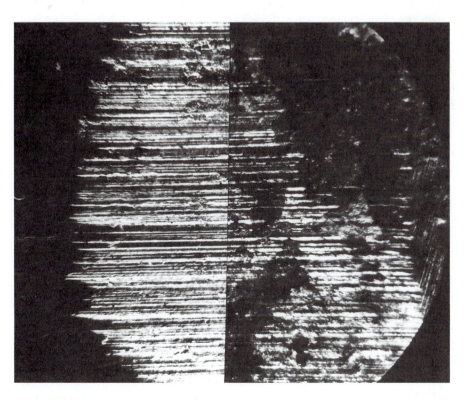

FIGURE 5.9

Comparison of Toolmarks
Striation pattern of a sledgehammer used to open a safe. The white marks are safe insulation. The left half of the photograph is evidence obtained at the scene of the crime; the right half shows the actual hammer seized from the suspect. The marks were matched up under a comparison microscope and magnified.

Weapons and Ammunition

The vast majority of violent crimes are committed with a firearm. Use extreme caution when handling firearms found at a crime scene. Tools used to manufacture weapons and defects in weapons acquired through use or neglect often permit positive identification. A bullet or cartridge case can often be linked with the weapon from which it was fired. When handling a weapon found at a crime scene, DePresca (1997, p. 77) cautions: "Contrary to television shows, do NOT put an object inside the barrel to pick it up. The object may scratch the inside of the barrel, affecting a ballistics test."

Include in your notes the weapon's make, caliber, model, type, serial number, finish and any unusual characteristics.

- - - - - - - - - -

> Examine weapons for latent fingerprints. Photograph weapons and then identify them with a string tag. Unload guns. Record the serial number on the string tag and in your notes. Label the packing container "Firearms." Identify bullets on the base, cartridges on the outside of the case near the bullet end and cartridge cases on the inside near the open end. Put ammunition in cotton or soft paper and ship to a laboratory. Never send live ammunition through the mail; use a common carrier.

- - - - - - - - - -

Gunpowder tests, shot pattern tests and functional tests of a weapon can be made and compared. The rifling of a gun barrel, the gun's ejection and extraction mechanisms and markings made by these mechanisms can also be compared.

Evidence bullets are compared to determine whether a specific bullet was fired from a specific comparison weapon. Shot patterns determine the distance from which the victim was shot and may disclose the type of choke on the gun and its barrel length. Gun parts found at a crime scene are compared with a weapon, and the trigger pull is tested and measured.

With proper collection techniques, forensic criminologists can use evidence smaller than a fingernail to build a case strong enough to put people in prison ("Crimes Solved with Science," 1997, p. 7B): "Each gun leaves a unique pattern of markings on the bullet. . . . Add that conclusion with metallurgic analysis of the fragments found in the body and the bullets found at the suspect's home," and the determination can be made that the same weapon was used in the crime.

The FBI laboratory and other laboratories have firearms reference collections, standard ammunition files and national unidentified ammunition files available to all law enforcement officers. Drugfire, a computer program distributed by the FBI laboratory, provides a method of storing ballistics information. It also enables comparison of the characteristic minutiae of various stored cartridge cases and the sharing of information among agencies. Such ballistics comparisons may be conducted online.

A computerized ballistics tracking system can now identify used cartridges and bullets much like the FBI identifies fingerprints. IBIS—the Integrated Ballastics Identification System—is "an automated image analysis system for analyzing the images of bullets and cartridge cases, and comparing them to other similar evidence" ("Technology and Teamwork . . . ," 1998, p. 43). The high-tech system can handle all types of ballistics evidence, including bullets, shell casings and guns (p. 43).

> Like a fingerprint, each fired bullet and discharged cartridge casing carries the firearm's unique bullet and cartridge casing markings, sometimes called the "ballistic signature." . . . IBIS can operate on bullets that are deformed or even on fragments, since its correlation algorithm can establish a match from markings on only a small part of one "land engraved area" (LEA) ("Technology and Teamwork," p. 45).

In one case a wealthy businessman had disappeared, and a farmer in a neighboring community found a gun in the weeds and turned it over to police. The weapon was, "run through" the tracing center and found to belong to an associate of the missing businessman. In another town the victim's body was discovered in a shallow grave. With IBIS, detectives were able to prove that bullets removed from the victim's body were fired from the associate's gun. The matching system is also useful in gang murders due to the randomness of the crimes and the lack of witnesses.

Several factors can affect a bullet's path. Intervening objects, especially the contents of pockets, can deflect bullets. A raised arm can produce the illusion that a bullet pierced the clothing and went sideways before entering the body. It may also suggest that the point of impact was lower than it actually was. This phenomenon gave rise to the controversy regarding the first bullet that struck President John F. Kennedy, which hit him in the neck. Because he had his arm raised to wave at the moment of impact, the hole in his jacket suggested that the bullet hit him between his shoulder blades when draped normally. Bullets can also veer within the body after striking a bone or upon leaving the body.

Glass

Glass can have great evidentiary value. Tiny pieces of glass can adhere to a suspect's shoes and clothing. Larger glass fragments are processed for fingerprints and can be fit back together to indicate the direction from which the glass was broken. The source of broken glass fragments also can often be determined.

> Label glass fragments using adhesive tape on each piece. Wrap each piece separately in cotton to avoid chipping and place in a strong box marked "fragile" to send to the laboratory.

Microscopic, spectrographic and physical comparisons are made of the glass fragments. Microscopic examination of the edges of two pieces of glass can prove they were one piece at one time. **Spectrographic analysis** can determine the elements of the glass, even extremely small fragments. Submit for comparison pieces of glass at least the size of a half-dollar.

The direction and angle of a bullet through glass can be determined by assembling the fragments. The resulting pattern of cracks indicates the bullet's direction. A bullet that does not shatter glass will leave a small, round entry hole and a larger, cone-shaped exit hole (see Figure 5.10).

The faster a bullet travels, the smaller the cracks and/or the tighter the entry point will be. The sequence of bullets fired through a piece of glass can also be determined from the pattern of cracks.

It is also possible to determine which side of a piece of glass has received a blow because a blow causes the glass to compress on that side and to stretch

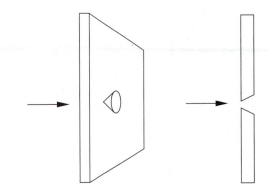

FIGURE 5.10 *Bullet Entry and Exit Holes*

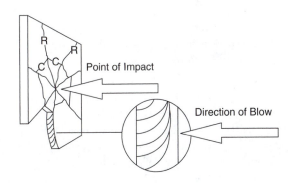

FIGURE 5.11 *Glass Cracks Caused by a Blow*

on the opposite side. As the blow is struck, circle cracks form around the point of impact. These circle cracks interconnect with radial cracks to form triangular pieces. The edge of each triangular piece has visible stress lines that tell the direction of the blow. The lines on the side that was struck have almost parallel stress lines that tend to curve downward on the side of the glass opposite the blow (see Figure 5.11). Such an examination can establish whether a burglar broke out of or into a building.

Because larger glass fragments can be matched by fitting the pieces together, a slight mark put on the side of the glass that was facing out helps to reconstruct stress lines. To protect glass as evidence, put sharp points in putty, modeling clay or some other soft substance.

Soils and Minerals

Forensic geologists examine soils and minerals—substances such as mud, cement, plaster, ceramics and insulation—found at a crime scene or on a victim, a suspect, clothing, vehicles or other items. This circumstantial evidence can place a suspect at a crime scene or destroy an alibi.

Although most soil evidence is found outdoors, suspects can bring soil into structures from the outside. Soils found inside a structure are most valuable if brought there on a suspect's shoes or clothing from his or her area of residence. Because soils found in the victim's residence may have been brought there by the victim or by other persons not suspected in the crime, collect elimination samples of soil from the area around the scene.

- - - - - - - - - -

Put one pound of comparison soil into a container identified on the outside. Collect evidence soil the same way. Seal both containers to prevent loss, wrap them and send them to a laboratory.

- - - - - - - - - -

Soils vary greatly in color, particle size, minerals and chemical composition. Some comparisons are visual; others are made through laboratory analysis. Both differences and similarities have value because soils separated by only a few inches can be very different. Therefore, take sufficient samples directly from and around the suspected area at perhaps 5–100-foot intervals, depending on the scene.

If soil evidence is in or on a suspect's clothing, send the entire article with the soil intact to the laboratory. If an object containing soil cannot be moved, use a spatula to gather the soil. Then place the soil in a can or paper bag, properly marked and identified.

Chemical analysis of soil is expensive and not always satisfactory. Soil is generally examined by density, by **X-ray diffraction** (to determine mineral content) and by microscope.

Because varied species of plants grow in different sections of the country, examination of dirt evidence that contains pollen and spores (palynology) is useful. It can refute the alibi of a suspect who is arrested at a distance from a crime scene and denies having been there. Electron microscope detection of pollen and spores found at the crime scene and on the suspect's clothing or vehicle will refute the alibi.

Safe Insulation

Most safes are fire-resistant, sheet-steel boxes with thick insulation. If safes are pried, ripped, punched, drilled or blown open, the insulation breaks apart and falls or disseminates into the room. Burglars often carry some of this insulation in their clothing. People with safe insulation in or on their clothing must be considered suspects because few people normally come into contact with safe insulation. Tools used to open a safe can also have insulation on them, as may the floor of a vehicle in which the tools were placed after a burglary.

- - - - - - - - - -

Put samples of safe insulation in paper containers identified on the outside.

- - - - - - - - - -

Safe insulation can be compared with particles found on a suspect or on the tools or vehicle used during a crime. Comparison tests can show what type of safe the insulation came from and whether it is the same insulation found at other burglaries. Insulation is also found on paint chips from safes. Always take standards of comparison if safe insulation is found at a crime scene.

The FBI and other laboratories maintain files on safe insulations used by major safe companies. Home and building insulation materials are also on file. This information is available to all law enforcement agencies.

Ropes, Strings and Tapes

Ropes, twines, strings and tapes are frequently used in crimes and can provide leads in identifying and linking suspects with a crime.

- - - - - - - - - -

Put labeled rope, twine and string into a container. Put tapes on waxed paper or cellophane and then place them in a container.

- - - - - - - - - -

Laboratories have various comparison standards for ropes, twines and tapes. If a suspect sample matches a known sample, the laboratory can determine the manufacturer of the item and its most common uses. Cordage can be compared for composition, construction, color and diameter. Rope ends can be matched if they are frayed. Likewise, pieces of torn tape can be compared to a suspect roll of tape.

Fingerprints can occur on either side of a tape. The smooth side is developed by the normal powder method or by using cyanoacrylate (superglue) if the surface is extremely slick. The sticky-side prints will be visible and are either photographed or retained intact.

Drugs

Drug-identification kits can be used to make a preliminary analysis of a suspicious substance, but a full analysis must be done at a laboratory.

Put liquid drugs in a bottle and attach a label. Put powdered and solid drugs in a pill or powder box and identify in the same way.

If a drug is a prescription drug, verify the contents with the issuing pharmacist. Determine how much of the original prescription has been consumed.

Documents

Typing, handwriting and printing can be examined. Typewriters and printers can be compared and paper identification attempted. Different types of writing instruments—pens, crayons and pencils—and various types of inks can also be compared. Indented writings, obliterated or altered writings, used carbon paper, burned or charred paper, shoeprint or tire-tread impressions made on paper surfaces—all can be examined in a laboratory. A document's age can also be determined.

Do not touch documents with your bare hands. Place documents in a cellophane envelope and then in a manila envelope identified on the outside.

Standards of comparison are required for many document examinations. To obtain handwriting standards from a suspect, take samples until you believe he or she is writing normally. The suspect should not see the original document or copy. Tell the suspect what to write and remove each sample from sight after it is completed. Provide no instructions on spelling, punctuation or wording. Use the same size and type of paper and writing materials as the original. Obtain right-handed and left-handed samples as well as samples written at different speeds. Samples of undictated writings, such as letters, are also helpful as standards. In forgery cases, include the genuine signatures as well as the forged ones.

As in other areas of evidence examination, computer programs have also been developed to analyze handwriting. Dusak (1997, p. 39) notes: "A

system now exists and has proved to be an excellent tool for use in handwriting comparisons of text writing." Dusak (pp. 40–41) explains:

> After the writing has been administratively entered, the desired features extracted and the mathematical computations performed, the new material is ready to be searched against writings previously recorded in the data base. . . .
>
> By merely pressing a key, the examiner can proceed down the list of possibilities, viewing the full document of the next-closest writing. Any of the writing that appears to be similar to the writing being searched can be saved on a list for more detailed viewing at a later date. . . .
>
> Even in cases that involve little written or printed correspondence, text writing appears on items such as videotape mailers and computer diskette labels.

Other document analysis techniques are also in use. The National Insurance Crime Bureau (NICB) helps law enforcement agencies combat insurance-related crime with the use of the VSC-1 document analyzer. Morrison (1999b, p. 72) relates: "The VSC-1 detects deception within minutes by reading through correction fluid, ink scribble and ink pen alterations on original documents. . . . [It also] detects and exposes alterations to original documents such as invoices, receipts or books of account. . . . The system is based on luminescence."

People often type anonymous or threatening letters, believing that typewritten materials are not as traceable as handwritten ones. However, some courts have held that typewriting can be compared more accurately than handwriting and almost as accurately as fingerprints. To collect typewriting standards, remove the ribbon from the suspected typewriter and send the ribbon to a laboratory. Use a different ribbon to take each sample. Take samples using light, medium and heavy pressure. Submit one carbon-copy sample with the typewriter on stencil position. Do not send the typewriter to a laboratory, but hold it as evidence.

Given enough typing samples, it is often possible to determine the make and model of a machine. Typewriter standard files are available for this purpose at the FBI laboratory. The information can greatly narrow the search for the actual machine. The most important comparison is between the suspect document and a specific typewriter. As word processing replaces typewriters, the word-processing software program and the printer used become important evidence.

Photographs frequently are also valuable evidence, whether taken by an officer or by someone outside the department. Some researchers are focusing their efforts on techniques to enhance grainy, blurred or poorly contrasted photographs by digitally converting them and subjecting them to software programs. Photographic images of injuries on human skin can be enhanced using reflective and fluorescent ultraviolet imaging.

The best-evidence rule stipulates that the original evidence is to be presented whenever possible.

For example, a photograph or photocopy of a forged check is not admissible in court; the check itself is required.

The FBI also maintains a national fraudulent check file, an anonymous letter file, a bank robbery note file, paper watermarks, safety paper and checkwriter standards. When submitting any document evidence to a laboratory, clearly indicate which documents are original and which are comparison standards. Also indicate whether latent fingerprints are requested. Although original documents are needed for laboratory examinations and court exhibits, copies can be used for file searches. A photograph is superior to a photocopy.

Laundry and Dry-Cleaning Marks

Many launderers and dry cleaners use specific marking systems. The Laundry and Dry Cleaning National Association has files on such marking systems. Many police laboratories also maintain a file of visible and invisible laundry marks used by local establishments. Military clothing is marked with the wearer's serial number, name and organization.

Use **ultraviolet light** to detect invisible laundry marks. Submit the entire garment to a laboratory, identified with a string tag or directly on the garment.

Laundry and dry-cleaning marks are used to identify the dead and injured in mass disasters such as airplane crashes, fires, floods and in other circumstances as well. For example, a dead baby was traced by the sheet's laundry marks. Clothing labels can also assist in locating the possible source of the clothing.

Blood and Other Body Fluids

Blood and other body fluids such as semen and urine can provide valuable information. Blood assists in establishing that a violent crime was committed, in re-creating the movements of a suspect or victim and in eliminating suspects. Body fluids can be found on a suspect's or victim's clothing, on the floor or walls, on furniture and on other objects.

If conditions are favorable, body fluids may yield important information years, even decades, after a crime is committed. In one case, a 22-year-old semen sample found on a victim's blood-soaked underwear was recovered as a possible means of identifying her killer ("22-Year-Old Semen Sample . . . ," 1999, p. 6A).

Blood is important as evidence in crimes of violence. Heelprints of shoes in blood splashes may be identifiable apart from the blood analysis. It is important to test the stain or sample to determine if it is in fact blood. In addition, because blood is so highly visible and recognizable, many individuals who commit violent crimes attempt to remove blood from items. A number of reagents—including Luminol, tetramethyl benzedrine and phenolphthalein—can identify blood at a crime scene. Because crime laboratories are swamped with evidence to examine, such preliminary on-scene testing is important.

Advances in the ways in which blood patterns can be assessed are also important to criminal investigators. Computer programs make bloodstain analysis faster, easier and more accurate. Some programs can calculate bloodstain measurements for point of origin. Bloodstain pattern analysis can assist in reconstructing specific spatial and sequential events that occurred before and during the act of bloodshed. Blood pattern analysis can help investigators determine where the blood originated, the distance from there to where the bloodstain came to rest, the type and direction of impact creating the bloodstains, the type of object producing them and the position of the victim, the assailant and items during and after the bloodshed. Blood-spatter patterns can help to determine a suspect's truthfulness. In many cases suspects have claimed a death was accidental, but the location and angle of blood-spatter patterns have refuted their statements.

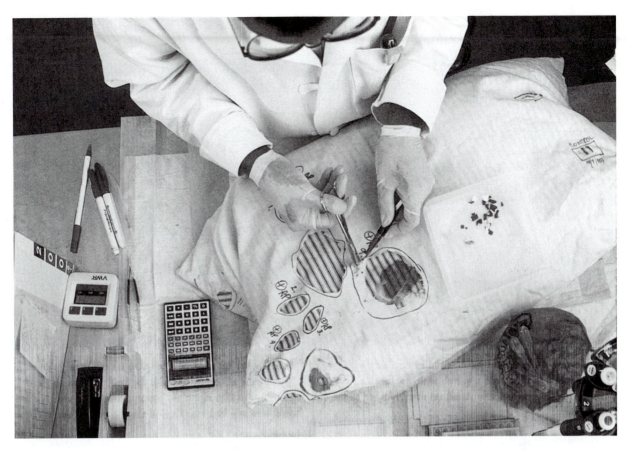

A laboratory technician recovers samples from a blood-stained pillow found at a crime scene. These samples can be used for DNA testing against blood drawn from a suspect. Good conservation of samples is the only condition required for DNA tests to be reliable, even after a long period of time.

Collect *liquid* blood with an eyedropper and put it in a test tube. Write the subject's name and other pertinent information on medical tape applied to the outside. Send by air express, priority mail or registered mail. Scrape *dry* blood flakes into a pillbox or envelope, identified in the same way. Mark bloodstained clothing with a string tag or directly on the clothing. If the bloodstain is moist, air-dry the clothing before packing.

Blood can be identified as animal or human and is most useful in eliminating suspects. Age, race or sex cannot be determined from blood samples, but DNA analysis can provide positive identification.

In some cases, blood can help to determine race; for example, sickle-shaped red blood cells occur primarily in African Americans.

DNA Profiling

Human cells contain discrete packs of information known as chromosomes, which are made of DNA. **DNA** is the abbreviation for *deoxyribonucleic acid,* an organic substance in the nucleus of all living cells that provides the genetic code determining a person's individual characteristics (see Figure 5.12). A human cell has 46 chromosomes whose arrangement is unique. Four building blocks, called *A, G, C* and *T,* make up a DNA chain. Burke and Van Patten (1998, p. 56) explain:

Much of human DNA has no known function, called noncoding DNA, or "junk" DNA. It is this noncoding DNA that is valuable in forensic analysis. . . . Noncoding DNA contains a number of repetitive sequences. . . . [that are] the source of what are called restriction fragment length polymorphisms (RFLP). RFLP is way of showing unique patterns when cut with restriction enzymes.

FIGURE 5.12

Method of Matching DNA Patterns Using STRs (Short Tandem Repeat)

STR (short tandem repeat) genetic markers run simultaneously on known and questioned DNA samples. Each person will have a maximum of two traits for each marker examined. The analyst identifies the traits for each of the three markers and determines whether the traits for the evidence match the traits from the samples of the suspects' DNA. In this case, the pattern of the evidence specimen matches that of suspect 2.

Source: Victor Walter Weedn and John W. Hicks. *The Unrealized Potential of DNA Testing.* National Institute of Justice Research in Action. June 1998, p. 4. (NCJ 170596)

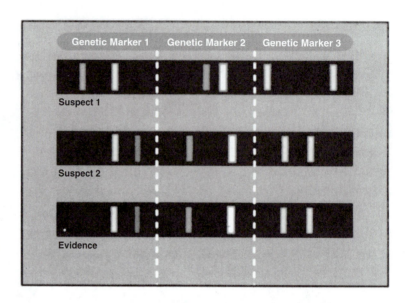

Because of the uniqueness of each individual's *genetic code,* DNA can be used to create a **genetic fingerprint** to positively identify a person. **DNA profiling** can be done on blood, hair, saliva, semen, indeed, cells from almost any part of the body (see Figure 5.13). Weedn and Hicks (1998, p. 3) state: "Recently researchers have reported that DNA can be recovered from fingerprints." Harman (1998, p. 91) adds: "Australian researchers have found that fingerprints and palm prints can provide enough DNA to provide a genetic profile of the person. . . . Genetic material from sweat or skin fragments could be obtained from such items as telephones, briefcases, car keys and gloves."

DNA profiling uses material from which chromosomes are made to identify individuals positively. Except for identical twins, no two individuals have the same DNA structure.

DNA can tell investigators the sample donor's gender, race, eye color and hair color. DNA technology is used in paternity testing, immigration disputes, missing persons and unidentified body cases, and criminal and assailant identification. DNA keeps its integrity in dried specimens for long periods and consequently can help unsolved cases.

The U.S. Department of Defense has established a military/naval DNA identification system to avoid any more "unknown soldiers." In addition, ("FBI Shifts Genetic . . . ," 1998, p. 1): "While Federal law authorizes all 50 states to take blood samples from some convicted felons to obtain their DNA 'fingerprints,' eight states . . . have not yet implemented the statute." Tischler (1998, p. 18) notes: "The FBI recently activated a database containing the DNA samples of approximately 600,000 offenders. The database, called National DNA Index System (NDIS), allows states to exchange DNA profiles and perform comparisons." Asplen (1999, p. 21) maintains:

CODIS (Combined DNA Index System) arguably is the most significant advance in criminal investigation of the 20th century. It is a computer database of DNA "profiles" of offenders convicted of serious crimes (such as rape, other sexual assault, and murder) and unknown suspects. . . .

So valuable is the technology that every State has enacted legislation establishing a CODIS database and requiring that DNA from offenders convicted of certain serious crimes be entered into the system. . . .

As of this writing, CODIS contains approximately 250,000 DNA profiles.

In June 1999 the FBI announced its first "cold hit" made through the NDIS. NDIS linked three sexual assault cases in Jacksonville, Florida, with six additional cases in Washington, DC, and connected all nine cases to one suspect ("FBI's DNA Profile Clearing House," 1999, p. 5).

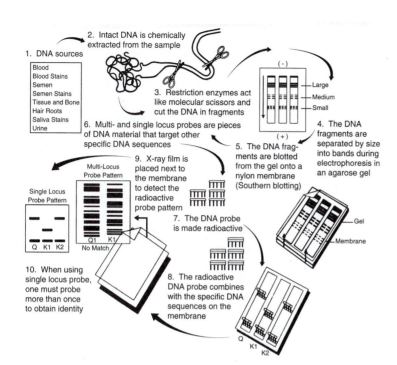

FIGURE 5.13 *DNA Profiling Process*

Source: Courtesy of the FBI.

DNA technology may soon be available to officers on the street. One source ("DNA Evidence Analysis . . . ," 1999, p. 7) states:

> The "Forensic DNA Chip" will enable police to use DNA information at the scene of a crime. . . . The chip will extract DNA from biological evidence placed into an attached well and sealed with tamper-proof evidence tape. It will identify the genetic codes and relay those markers to a computer screen in the investigator's car. A national data base linked to the computer will search for possible identification of an offender whose DNA is on file.

Another breakthrough in DNA analysis is the development of a portable electrophoresis system that can be run outside a laboratory and produce results in 35 minutes. Morrison (1999a, p. 88) explains that E-gels are a "self-contained bufferless precast agarose gel that makes DNA electrophoresis easier and more convenient." The procedure reduces the chance of error from contamination or time delays. When a power source is available, tests can be run anywhere, and they are relatively inexpensive. The E-Gel base and starter pack with nine E-gels costs less than $100.

However, as Strandberg (2000, p. 34) suggests: "DNA can be a boon to law enforcement, but it's not a panacea." One reason is the time usually involved in testing. Siuru (1999, p. 49) reports that the FBI has a huge backlog—about 400,000 samples awaiting analysis.

Because of the expense and time involved, three criteria must usually be met for a lab to accept DNA samples:

- Sufficient material must be submitted.
- Samples (exemplars) must be submitted from both the suspect and the victim.
- The evidence must be probative.

Probative evidence is evidence that is vital to investigate or prosecute a case, tending to prove or actually proving guilt or innocence.

Cases involving DNA are being decided by courts case by case. In the first appeal from a finding of guilty, the Virginia State Supreme Court upheld the conviction and death sentence of Timothy Spencer in the rapes and murder of two women, holding that DNA test results were reliable. In other cases, however, DNA analysis has been rendered worthless by the defense's successful attack on the methods used to collect and store the evidence on which DNA analysis was performed. Abshire (1998, p. 46) notes: "The O. J. Simpson trial is a good example. DNA matches were disregarded by jurors after questions were raised about how blood samples were collected, preserved and examined. And that's always been the best defense against DNA evidence."

Advancements continue to be made in DNA testing. The National Institute of Standards and Technology has developed a quality assurance standards kit for DNA typing that laboratories can use to assess the accuracy of their DNA testing procedures within a narrow margin of error. Suggestions for collecting and preserving DNA evidence are offered by Lifecodes Corporation in Table 5.2.

Hairs and Fibers

Hairs and fibers are often difficult to locate without a careful search and strong lighting. They are valuable evidence because they can place a suspect at a crime scene, especially in violent crimes in which interchange of hairs and fibers is likely to occur. Hairs and fibers can also be taken from the scene by the suspect.

Place hairs and fibers found at the crime scene in paper, using a druggist fold, or in a small box. Seal all edges and openings, and identify on the outside. If hairs and fibers are found on an object small enough to send to a laboratory, leave them on the object. Hairs and fiber often adhere to blood, flesh or other materials. If the hairs are visible but are not adhering firmly to the object, record their location in your notes. Then place them in a pillbox or glass vial to send to a laboratory. (Do not use plastic.)

If you suspect that hairs are on an object, carefully wrap the object and send it intact to a laboratory. Attempt to obtain 25 to 50 full hairs from the appropriate part of the suspect's body for comparison, using a forceps or comb.

Special filters, light sources and photomicrographs can reproduce the hair and fiber specimens in black-and-white or color.

Examining Hair
A hair shaft has a *cuticle* on the outside consisting of overlapping scales that always point toward the tip, a *cortex* consisting of elongated cells and the *medulla*—the center of the hair—consisting of variably shaped cells. Variations in these structures make comparisons and identifications possible.

- - - - - - - - -

Microscopic examination determines whether hair is animal or human. Many characteristics can be determined from human hair: the part of the body it came from; whether it was bleached or dyed, freshly cut, pulled out or burned; and whether there is blood or semen on it. Race, sex and age cannot be determined.

- - - - - - - - -

As with blood samples, it is extremely difficult to state that a hair came from a certain person, but it can usually be determined that a hair did *not* come from a certain person. DNA analysis can be done on hair for positive identification if the hair root is present.

Hair evidence is important because it does not deteriorate and is commonly left at a crime scene without a subject's knowledge. Laboratory examination does not destroy hair evidence as it does many other types of evidence. Hair evidence may be subjected to microscopic examination to determine type (e.g., facial or pubic), biological examination to determine blood-type group and toxicological examination to determine the presence of drugs or poisons.

Examining Fibers
Fibers fall into four general groups: mineral, vegetable, animal and synthetic. Mineral fibers most frequently submitted are glass and asbestos. Vegetable fibers include cotton, jute, manila, kapok, hemp and many others. Animal fibers are primarily wool and silk. Synthetics include rayons, polyesters, nylons and others. Each fiber has individual characteristics that can be analyzed chemically.

Fibers are actually more distinguishable than hairs. Fiber examination can determine a fiber's thickness, the number of fibers per strand and other characteristics that help identify clothing. Fibers can be tested for origin and color. Although often overlooked, fibers are the most frequently located microscopic evidence. They are often found in assaults, homicides and rapes, where personal contact results in an exchange of clothing fibers. Fibers can be found under a suspect's or victim's fingernails. Burglaries can yield fibers at narrow entrance or exit points where clothing gets snagged. Hit-and-run accidents often yield fibers adhering to vehicles' door handles, grills, fenders or undercarriages.

Other Types of Evidence

Paint
Police laboratories and the FBI maintain files of automobile paints. These standards can help identify the year, make and/or color of a motor vehicle from a chip of paint left at the scene.

Paints are complex and are individual in color, composition, texture and layer composition. In hit-and-run cases, collect paint samples from any area of the vehicle that had contact with the victim. Take paint samples down to the original metal to show the layer composition. Use small boxes for submitting paint samples to the crime lab, putting samples from different parts of the vehicle in separate small boxes. If paint chips are on the clothing of the victim or suspect, send the entire article of clothing in a paper bag to the laboratory, properly labeled and identified.

Table 5.2	Collecting Evidence for DNA Analysis

Types of evidence and minimal amounts to collect

Blood

Fresh liquid blood	3 drops
Stains	Quarter size
Drawn specimens (exemplars)	1 cc or 1 mL

Semen

Fresh liquid semen	3 drops
Stains	Dime size
Swabs	2 swabs

Other types

Tissues/Bones/Teeth: Although small amounts of evidence have provided enough DNA for analysis, the amount that will be needed is unpredictable and depends on many factors including age and concentration of sample.

How to collect biological evidence

Specimens should be collected and dried as soon as possible to avoid bacterial contamination.

Wet specimens

Quick-dry using a hair dryer on the cool setting.
For large amounts of material, use a large floor fan.
Absorb wet specimen onto sterile gauze, 100% cotton or Q-Tips and then dry.

Dry specimens

Scrape dried specimen from permanent surfaces.
Cut dried specimen out from large areas.
Package whole items if manageable.

Packaging specimens

Drying specimens isn't enough. They must be kept as free from moisture as possible. Therefore:

Small items

Place the collected specimen in a zip-lock bag.
Squeeze the air out of the bag.

Larger items

Use paper bags for large items and tape them closed.

Storing collected evidence

Heat can destroy DNA. Therefore, if the evidence is not sent for DNA analysis within a few days, store the packaged evidence as directed.

Short-term storage (less than 30 days)

Store in freezer.
If freezer is not available, refrigerate evidence.
Store at room temperature for only 1–2 days.

Extended storage (more than 30 days)

Call Lifecodes for recommendations. When it has been collected and stored properly, evidence as old as 10 years has been successfully analyzed.

Sending evidence for DNA analysis

Send evidence and exemplar samples, from the victim and suspect(s), properly labeled, together with a written description of the specimens. Include any other important or relevant facts concerning the case and origin of the sample(s) for the forensic scientist. Send samples via an overnight carrier. The sender is responsible for following the chain-of-custody.

Source: Lifecodes Corporation, Saw Mill River Road, Valhalla, NY 10595 © 1990. By permission.

Skeletal Remains Laboratory examination can determine whether skeletal remains are animal or human. If adequate human remains are available, the sex, race, approximate age at death, approximate height and approximate time since death can be determined. Dental comparisons and X-rays of old fractures are other important **identifying features.** In one case, sinus X-rays of a human skull found in an apartment building were determined to belong to a 40-year-old woman who had been missing for two years ("County Coroner IDs Skeletal Remains," 1999, p. 2B).

Wood Wood comparisons are made from items on a suspect, in a vehicle or in or on clothing found at a crime scene. The origin is determined by the size or the fit of the fracture with an original piece of wood or by matching the side or end of pieces of wood. The type of wood is determined from its cellular elements.

When handling wood evidence, if it is found wet, keep it wet; if it is dry, keep it dry. Chadbourne (1998, p. 29) notes: "Hands and fingernails and in crevices where shoes are stitched and on soft-material laces are excellent reservoirs for wood, chips and sawdust."

Other Prescription eyeglasses, broken buttons, glove prints and other personal evidence found at a crime scene can also be examined and compared. If there is a problem processing any evidence, a laboratory can provide specific collecting and packaging instructions.

Evidence Handling and Infectious Disease

Investigators are likely to encounter crimes of violence involving blood and other body fluids of persons with infectious diseases. Patrol officers are likely to encounter these infectious body fluids during routine activities. Edwards and Tewksbury (1996) note:

> Over a decade has passed since the medical and law enforcement communities first became aware of, and concerned about, the implications of HIV/AIDS for police officers. As a result of these concerns, a number of policies and standards have been implemented specifically addressing the training and employment issues relating to what the medical community has labeled the most serious public health threat today.

Heiskell (2000b, p. 14) provides assurance that AIDS is not spread through casual contact such as touching an infected person or sharing equipment. Nor is it spread through the air by coughing or sneezing.

Heiskell and Tang (1998, p. 34) stress that although law enforcement officers' chances of contracting a disease on the job are slim, almost daily policing personnel come in contact with victims and suspects infected with diseases without knowing it.

Chances are less than 1 percent that an officer will contract the AIDS virus on the job. Tuberculosis (TB), meningitis and hepatitis pose greater threats. *Tuberculosis* is transmitted through the air by coughing, hacking and wheezing. TB can also be transmitted through saliva, urine, blood and other body fluids. *Meningitis,* spread through the air, causes inflammation of the membranes that surround the brain. *Hepatitis B,* known today as HBV, is a bloodborne pathogen that can live outside the body longer than HIV. The hepatitis B virus is found in human blood, urine, semen, cerebrospinal fluid, vaginal secretions and saliva. A safe, effective vaccine to prevent HBV is available. According to Heiskell (2000a, p. 10): "Based on current medical knowledge the hepatitis vaccine provides protection against illness and development of the carrier state. The protection lasts nine years or perhaps longer."

Use precautions when collecting blood evidence and other body fluids. Consider all bodily secretions as potential health hazards. If there are body fluids at a crime scene, even if dried, wear latex gloves, goggles and a face mask. Secure evidence in glass, metal or plastic containers. Seal evidence bags with tape rather than staples. Do not allow hand-to-mouth or hand-to-face contact during collection. Do not eat, smoke, apply makeup, or drink at crime scenes because these activities may transfer contaminated body fluids to you. When finished, wash your hands with soap and water.

While processing the crime scene, constantly be alert for sharp objects, such as hypodermic needles and syringes. If practical, use disposable items where blood is present so the items can be incinerated. All nondisposable items, such as cameras, tools and notebooks must be decontaminated using a bleach solution or rubbing alcohol. Even evidence that has been properly dried and packaged is still potentially infectious. Therefore, place appropriate warnings on all items.

After processing, decontaminate the crime scene. If it is to be left for future decontamination, place biohazard warning signs and notify the cleaning team of possible contamination.

Further information on procedures for dealing with evidence with potential of transmitting an infectious disease can be obtained from the Centers for Disease Control, Office of Biosafety, 1600 Clifton Road N.E., Atlanta, GA 30333.

Protecting and Storing Evidence

Pilant (1996, p. 38) notes: "Headline after headline points out the lack of control in the property and evidence rooms of small and large agencies." She conducted a survey (pp. 38–39) of property and evidence rooms that obtained the following results:

- 74 percent had no alarm system.
- 70 percent had no regular inventory process in place.
- 65 percent never changed the locks when personnel changed and did not know how many keys had been issued to department personnel.
- 59 percent had no regular auditing system in place.
- Only 51 percent had written policies and procedures for the property and evidence room.

Such results are disturbing given the critical importance of evidence and the chain of custody. All too often defendants are found not guilty because evidence in the chain of custody is not documented and cannot be determined. Branscum (1998, p. 6) states: "Even the most convincing evidence can be tossed out of court if defendants can prove that access to the police department's evidence room isn't securely monitored." Morrison (1998, p. 66) stresses: "Make no mistake, [property and evidence] mismanagement can destroy a career, cause or allow criminal misconduct and ruin the reputation of the whole department."

Evidence is subject to chemical change, negligence, accident, intentional damage, theft and alteration during handling. Protecting and storing evidence is often the weakest link in the **chain of evidence.** Some evidence requires more care than others. Improperly sealed containers can allow liquid evidence to evaporate or moisture to enter. Envelopes can split open. Tags can fall off. Writing on labels can become smudged, blurred or faded to the point of illegibility.

Proper storage prevents theft, loss, tampering, contamination and deterioration. The storage area must be secure, well organized and free from pests, insects and excessive heat or moisture.

Package evidence properly to keep it in substantially the same condition in which it was found. Document custody of the evidence at every stage.

Evidence is stored in vaults, property rooms, evidence rooms, evidence lockers, garages, morgues or under special conditions such as refrigeration. At a crime scene, an officer's vehicle trunk can provide temporary storage. A proper storage area has ample space and is kept at 60–80 degrees Fahrenheit. A responsible person ensures that established procedures are followed and that the area is secure at all times.

All evidence received is recorded in a register, properly marked and put in an appropriate place. An evidence custodian checks each piece of evidence to ensure that all forms are properly completed and that the evidence is the same as described in the forms. Figure 5.14 shows a sample evidence card.

Strict checkout procedures ensure that the evidence is always accounted for. Everyone who takes evidence signs for it, giving the date, time, place it is to be taken and purpose. When the evidence is returned, it is again signed for, dated and examined to ensure it is in the same condition as when taken. Any change in condition is noted and explained.

Automated evidence storage can prevent many problems. Morrison (p. 64) reports: "Computer programs [are] available to aid in managing the property/evidence operations." The amount of property that must be tracked and stored in metropolitan departments is typically 100,000–400,000+ items. To account for so many items accurately and to maintain the chain of custody, each item should be categorized and described, including ownership (rightful, seized, found, etc.). Its location should be documented, as should its disposition (returned, auctioned, burned, etc.).

Many property control systems are using **barcodes,** which are extremely efficient and effective. At the time property is "booked," it is entered into a computer and given a barcode, which is affixed to the item. During any subsequent signing in/out of the property, the chain of custody is updated by scanning the item's evidence barcode into the log. Such a system provides an audit trail, helps with the inventory process, prints management and audit reports and prints disposition logs.

FIGURE 5.14
Evidence Card

Source: Courtesy of the
Boulder City Police
Department.

BOULDER CITY	EVIDENCE		POLICE DEPT.	
DATE 3-12-2000		DR. NUMBER #97-1640		
SUSPECT William Vellum			JUV ☐	ADULT ☒
CHARGE Rape				
LOCATION 1162 Maple Avenue, Boulder City, Nevada				
BOOKED BY (FINDING OFFICER'S SIGNATURE) Alfred Culp			DATE AND TIME	
INITIALS & P. NUMBER OF BOOKING OFFICER				

ARTICLES BOOKED

ITEM a pair of shorts		ITEM NO. 623
ITEM one womens slacks and panties		ITEM NO. 624
ITEM one bed sheet		ITEM NO. 625
INITIALS USED ON ITEMS BOOKED AC	THIS PACKAGE NO.	TOTAL NO. PACKAGES 3
CO-DEFENDANT none		JUV ☐ ADULT ☐
CO-DEFENDANT		JUV ☐ ADULT ☐

CHAIN OF CUSTODY

SIGNATURE	DATE 3-12-2000	TIME 1940
SIGNATURE	DATE	TIME
SIGNATURE	DATE	TIME
SIGNATURE	DATE	TIME
SIGNATURE	DATE	TIME
SIGNATURE	DATE	TIME

Presenting Evidence in Court

Be able to (1) identify the evidence as that found at the crime scene, (2) describe exactly where it was found, (3) establish its custody from discovery to the present and (4) voluntarily explain any changes that have occurred in the evidence.

Typically, the officer who will identify the evidence in court obtains it from the evidence custodian and delivers it to the prosecuting attorney, who takes it to the courtroom and introduces it at the proper time. The identifying officer uses the notes he or she made at the scene to lay the proper foundation for identifying the evidence.

When you are called to a witness stand to identify evidence with your personal mark, take time to examine the item thoroughly. Make sure that all marks are accounted for and that your mark has not been altered. A rapid identification may make a bad impression on the jury and may lead you into an erroneous identification.

Final Disposition of Evidence

The court or the prosecutor's office usually decides on the manner of disposition. No evidence is destroyed without permission of the prosecutor's office. Evidence must be legally disposed of to prevent major storage problems as well as pilferage or unauthorized conversion to personal use. State statutes and city ordinances specify how to dispose of evidence. The court may order disposition of some evidence such as pornography, narcotics or contraband.

Evidence is either returned to the owner, auctioned or destroyed.

Evidence is either disposed of continuously, annually or on a special date. Most evidence is disposed of annually. The status of items is reviewed, and items are then either returned to storage or disposed of.

Most evidence is held until the case is cleared. In cases in which prosecution is not anticipated, contraband items can be released at any time. Other items may be returned because the cases have exceeded the statute of limitations.

Witnessed affidavits of disposal list all items sold, destroyed or returned. The affidavits include the date, type of disposition, location and names of all witnesses to the disposition.

Summary

Criminal investigations rely heavily upon various types of evidence. To be of value, evidence must be legally and properly seized and processed. Processing physical evidence includes discovering, recognizing and examining it; collecting, recording and identifying it; packaging, conveying and storing it; exhibiting it in court; and disposing of it when the case is closed. The relative importance of physical evidence depends on its ability to establish that a crime was committed as well as how, when and by whom.

To determine what is evidence, first consider the apparent crime. Then look for any objects unrelated or foreign to the scene, unusual in their location or number, damaged or broken or whose relation to other objects suggests a pattern that fits the crime. The more individual the evidence, the greater its value.

Often standards of comparison are required. A standard of comparison is an object, measure or model with which evidence is compared to determine whether both came from the same source. Common errors in collecting evidence are (1) not collecting enough of the sample, (2) not obtaining standards of comparison and (3) not maintaining the integrity of the evidence.

Mark or identify each item of evidence in a way that can be recognized later. Include the date and case number as well as your identifying mark or initials. Record in your notes the date and time of collection, where it was found and by whom, case number, description of the item and who took custody of it. Package each item separately in durable containers to maintain the integrity of evidence. Personal delivery, registered mail, insured parcel post, air express, Federal Express and United Parcel Service (UPS) are legal ways to transport evidence. Always specify that the person who receives the evidence is to sign for it.

Frequently examined physical evidence includes fingerprints, voiceprints, shoe and tire impressions, bite marks, tools and toolmarks, weapons and ammunition, glass, soils and minerals, body fluids (including blood), hairs and fibers, safe insulation, rope and tape, drugs, documents and laundry and dry-cleaning marks.

Know how to locate, develop, photograph, lift and submit fingerprints for classification by experts. Any hard, smooth, nonporous surface can contain latent fingerprints. Do not powder a print unless it is necessary; do not powder a visible print until after photographing it. Prints of persons with reason to be at the scene are taken and used as elimination prints. Fingerprints are positive evidence of a person's identity. They cannot, however, indicate a person's age, sex or race.

Cast shoe or tire tread impressions found in dirt, sand or snow. Identify each suspected tool with a string tag, wrap it separately, and pack it in a strong box to send to a laboratory. Photograph toolmarks and then either cast them or send the object on which they appear to a laboratory. A toolmark is compared with a standard of comparison impression rather than with the tool itself.

Examine weapons for latent fingerprints. Photograph weapons and then identify them with a string tag. Unload guns, and record their serial number on a string tag and in your notes. Label the packing container "Firearms." Identify bullets on the base, cartridges on the outside of the case near the bullet end and cartridge cases on the inside near the open end. Put ammunition in cotton or soft paper and ship to a laboratory. Never send live ammunition through the mail; use a common carrier instead.

Label glass fragments using adhesive tape on each piece. Wrap each piece separately in cotton to avoid chipping and place in a strong box marked "fragile" to send to a laboratory. Put one pound of comparison soil into a container identified on the outside. Collect evidence soil the same way. Seal both containers to prevent loss, wrap them and send them to a laboratory.

Put samples of safe insulation in paper containers identified on the outside. Put labeled rope, twine and string in a container. Put tapes on waxed paper or cellophane and then place them in a container. Put liquid drugs in a bottle and attach a label. Put powdered and solid drugs in a pill or powder box and identify the same way.

Do not touch documents with your bare hands. Place them in a cellophane envelope and then in a manila envelope identified on the outside. Use ultraviolet light to detect invisible laundry marks. Submit the entire garment to a laboratory, identified with a string tag or directly on the garment.

Blood can be identified as animal or human and is very useful in eliminating suspects. Age, race or sex cannot be determined from blood samples. DNA analysis, however, can provide positive identification. DNA profiling uses material from which chromosomes are made to positively identify individuals. Except for identical twins, no two individuals have the same DNA structure.

Microscopic examination determines whether hair is animal or human. Many characteristics can be determined from human hair: the part of the body it came from; whether it was bleached or dyed, freshly cut, pulled out or burned; and whether there is blood or semen on it. Race, sex and age cannot be determined.

Package evidence properly to keep it in substantially the same condition in which it was found. Document custody of the evidence at every stage. The best-evidence rule stipulates that the original evidence is to be presented in court whenever possible.

When presenting evidence in court, be able to (1) identify the evidence as that found at the crime scene, (2) describe exactly where it was found, (3) establish its custody from discovery to the present and (4) voluntarily explain any changes that have occurred in the evidence.

After a case is closed, evidence is returned to the owner, auctioned or destroyed.

Checklist

Physical Evidence

- Was all physical evidence photographed before anything was moved?
- Was the physical evidence located in the crime-scene sketch?
- Were relevant facts recorded in your notebook?
- Was the evidence properly identified, including the date, case number, your initials or mark and a description of the evidence?
- Was the evidence properly packaged to avoid contamination or destruction?
- Were standards of comparison obtained if needed?
- Was the evidence sent in a way that kept it secure and provided a signed receipt, such as by registered mail?
- Was the evidence kept continuously secure until presented in court?

The following types of physical evidence are frequently found at a crime scene and should be searched for, depending on the type of crime committed:

- Blood
- Cigarettes, cigars, smoking materials
- Clothing and fragments
- Containers and boxes
- Documents and papers
- Dirt and dust particles
- Fibers, ropes and strings
- Fingernail scrapings
- Fingerprints, visible and latent
- Footprints
- Glass objects and fragments
- Greases, oils, salves, emulsions
- Hairs, human and animal
- Inorganic materials
- Insulation from safes, buildings and homes
- Metal objects and fragments
- Organic materials, plant and animal
- Paint and paint chips
- Palm prints
- Personal possessions
- Photographs
- Plastic impressions
- Soils
- Tires and tire tracks
- Tools and toolmarks
- Weapons
- Wood chips or fragments

Discussion Questions

1. What kind of physical evidence would you expect to find at a burglary scene?
2. What kind of physical evidence would you expect to find at the scene of an armed robbery? Why does this differ from your response to Question 1?
3. What is *material, relevant* and *competent* evidence?
4. What legal rule requires the submission of original evidence, and when is this rule followed? When is it permissible to substitute evidence that is not original?
5. What general procedures would you follow in finding and collecting evidence at a crime scene?

6. How would you mark for identification the following items of evidence: A broken window pane? A damaged bullet? Dried blood scraped from a wood floor? A shotgun shell casing? A piece of clothing with semen stains?

7. How would you locate, preserve, lift and identify a latent fingerprint on a wall in a house? How would you have the print examined?

8. What determines whether a government or private laboratory is used to examine evidence? What laboratory facilities are available to your police department?

9. *Continuity of evidence* is a legal term describing the chain of evidence necessary to make evidence legally admissible in court. Describe a chain of evidence from the time of discovery to introduction in court.

10. How does your police department dispose of evidence after it is no longer of value or has been released by the court?

References

Abshire, Richard. "DNA: Problems, Progress and Potential." *Law Enforcement Technology,* May 1998, p. 46.

Asplen, Christopher H. "Forensic DNA Evidence: National Commission Explores its Future." *National Institute of Justice Journal,* January 1999, pp. 17–24.

Blitzer, Herbert L. "Forensic Imaging Options: Worth a Thousand Words." *The Police Chief,* October 1996, p. 14.

Branscum, John. "Admissible Evidence." *Community Policing Exchange,* July/August 1998, pp. 6–7.

Brecher, Kim. "Protect Your Evidence and Protect Yourself." *Law Enforcement Technology,* March 1999, pp. 66–69.

Burke, Tod W. and Van Patten, Isaac. "Emerging Technology: Automated DNA Analysis." *Law Enforcement Technology,* March 1998, pp. 56–58.

Campbell, Frank. "Speed-Reading the Fine Prints." *Police,* December 1998, pp. 34–35.

Chadbourne, Robert. "The Science of Wood Evidence." *Law and Order,* November 1998, pp. 27–29.

"County Coroner IDs Skeletal Remains." *Las Vegas Review Journal,* February 23, 1999, p. 2B.

"Crimes Solved with Science." *Las Vegas Review Journal,* January 26, 1997, p. 7B.

Dees, Tim. "New Equipment at IACP '99." *Law and Order,* Vol. 48, No. 1, January 2000, pp. 69–73.

DePresca, John. "Handling Crime Scene Evidence." *Law and Order,* August 1997, pp. 75–79.

"DNA Evidence Analysis May Be as Close as Your Cruiser." *Law Enforcement News,* Vol. XXV, No. 514, June 30, 1999, p. 7.

Dolan, Thomas G. "Biometrics: Into the Mainstream or into the Gullies?" *Security Technology & Design,* Vol. 9, No. 7, July 1999, pp. 14–20.

Dusak, Richard A. "Automated Handwriting Technology a Boon to Police." *The Police Chief,* January 1997, pp. 39–41.

Edwards, Terry D. and Tewksbury, Richard. "HIV/AIDS: State Police Training Practices and Personnel Policies." *American Journal of Police,* Vol. XV, No. 1, 1996, pp. 45–62.

"FBI Shifts Genetic Investigation into High Gear." *Law Enforcement News,* Vol. XXIV, No. 498, October 31, 1998, pp. 1, 10.

"FBI's DNA Profile Clearing House Announces First 'Cold Hit.'" *Criminal Justice Newsletter,* Vol. 30, No. 6, 1999, pp. 5–6.

Gulick, Kristi. "Latent Prints from Human Skin." *Law and Order,* Vol. 46, No. 6, June 1998, pp. 148–149.

"Handyman Details Slayings of Yosemite Sightseers, Naturalist." (Minneapolis/St. Paul) *Star Tribune,* July 28, 1999, p. A4.

Harman, Alan. "Practical Applications in DNA Profiling." *Law and Order,* August 1998, pp. 91–93.

Heiskell, Lawrence. "Hepatitis B: What Are the On-Duty Risks?" *Police,* Vol. 24, No. 2, February 2000a, p. 10.

Heiskell, Lawrence. "HIV Disease: What Are the On-Duty Risks?" *Police,* Vol. 24, No. 1, January 2000b, p. 14.

Heiskell, Lawrence E. and Tang, David H. "AIDS and Hepatitis: What Are the Risks to Police Officers?" *Police,* January 1998, pp. 34–36.

Henry, Kate. "Biometric Program Provides Positive Identification at UGA." *Access Control and Security Systems Integration,* July 1998, pp. 16–18.

Hoffman, John. "Lip Prints." *Law and Order,* Vol. 46, No. 6, June 1998, pp. 31–32.

Kash, Douglas A. "Thermal Imaging Devices Heat Up 4th Amendment Issues." *Police,* July 1999, pp. 43–48.

Lucchesi, Carlo L. "Resolving AFIS Issues on an International Scale." *The Police Chief,* September 1998, pp. 30–33.

Morrison, Richard D. "Lock It Up! P & E Management." *Law Enforcement Technology,* April 1998, pp. 64–66.

Morrison, Richard D. "E-Gels Allow DNA Results in 35 Minutes." *Law Enforcement Technology,* Vol. 26, No. 8, August 1999a, pp. 88–90.

Morrison, Richard D. "NICB Offers Document Analysis and More." *Law Enforcement Technology,* May 1999b, pp. 72–73.

Nielsen, Eugene. "Get to the Mettle of High-Tech Crime Scene Investigations." *Police,* July 1999, pp. 30–33.

Paynter, Ronnie. "Images in the Night." *Law Enforcement Technology,* May 1999, pp. 22–26.

Pearson, Robert. "The Expanding Role of Biometrics." *Security Technology & Design,* Vol. 9, No. 7, July 1999, pp. 10–12.

Pilant, Lois. "Property & Evidence Management." *The Police Chief,* July 1996, pp. 37–44.

Pilant, Lois. "AFIS Automation and Accuracy." *Law and Order,* January 1998a, pp. 70–72.

Pilant, Lois. "The State of the Art in AFIS." *The Police Chief,* September 1998b, pp. 22–29.

Siuru, Bill. "Iris Recognition." *Law and Order,* November 1998, pp. 38–39.

Siuru, Bill. "Technology Promises Instant DNA Matching." *Law and Order,* Vol. 47, No. 11, November 1999, pp. 49–50.

Smith, Kimberley. "Integrated Automated Fingerprint Identification System: 21st Century Technology for Law Enforcement." *The Police Chief,* May 1998, p. 14.

Strandberg, Keith W. "The Present and Future of Biometrics." *Law Enforcement Technology,* Vol. 26, No. 8, August 1999, pp. 74–76.

Strandberg, Keith W. "The Truth Is in the DNA." *Law Enforcement Technology,* Vol. 27, No. 1, January 2000, pp. 34–38.

"Technology and Teamwork Go Ballistic." *Law and Order,* June 1998, pp. 43–47.

Tischler, Eric. "FBI's DNA Database." *Corrections Today,* December 1998, p. 18.

"22-Year-Old Semen Sample Found in Trial." *Las Vegas Review Journal,* February 7, 1999, p. 6A.

Weedn, Victor Walter and Hicks, John W. *The Unrealized Potential of DNA Testing.* Washington, DC: National Institute of Justice, Research in Action, June 1998. (NCJ-170596)

Wexler, Sanford. "Every Crime Scene Tells a Story." *Law Enforcement Technology,* Vol. 26, No. 8, August 1999, pp. 22–25.

Obtaining Information

Can You Define?

Do You Know?

What sources of information are available to investigators?

What a sources of information file is and what it contains?

What the goals of interviewing and interrogation are?

When and in what order individuals are interviewed?

What two requirements are needed to obtain information?

What the difference between direct and indirect questions is and when to use each?

What technique is likely to assist recall as well as uncover lies?

What basic approaches to use in questioning reluctant interviewees?

What the characteristics of an effective interviewer or interrogator are?

How to improve communication?

What the emotional barriers to communication are?

What the Miranda warning is and when to give it?

What the two requirements of a place for conducting interrogations are?

What techniques to use in an interrogation?

What third-degree tactics are and what their place in interrogation is?

What restrictions are placed on obtaining a confession?

What significance a confession has in an investigation?

What to consider when questioning a juvenile?

What a polygraph is and what its role in investigation and the acceptability of its results in court are?

Introduction

Knowledge obtained through both questioning and physical evidence are equally important. Most solved cases rely on both physical evidence and information obtained by interviewing and interrogating. Physical evidence can provide a basis for questioning people about a crime, and questioning can provide leads for finding physical evidence. Either or both provide the knowledge required to end an investigation successfully. Although physical evidence is important by itself, supporting oral testimony adds considerable value when presented in court. On the other hand, although a confession may appear conclusive, it cannot stand alone legally. It must be supported by physical evidence or other corroboration.

This chapter begins with a discussion of sources of information, followed by a discussion of how to enhance communication. Then, an in-depth look at interviews and interrogation is provided. Evaluating and corroborating information received during an interview or interrogation is the next area explored, followed by a discussion of how to question juveniles and young children. The chapter concludes with an explanation of scientific aids available for obtaining information. ■

Sources of Information

In addition to physical evidence, three primary sources of information are available.

Important sources of information include (1) reports and records, including those found on the Internet, (2) persons who are not suspects in a crime but who know something about the crime or those involved and (3) suspects in the crime.

Often these sources overlap. For example, information in a hotel's records may be supplemented by information supplied by the hotel manager or the doorkeeper.

Because so many informational sources exist in any given community, it is helpful to develop a **sources of information file.** Each time you locate someone who can provide important information on criminal activity in a community, make a card with information on this source or enter the information into a computer file. For example, if a hotel manager provides useful information, make a card with the manager's name, name of the hotel, address, telephone number, type of information provided and other relevant information. File the card under *hotel*.

A sources of information file contains the name and location of people, organizations and records that may assist in a criminal investigation.

We have progressed from the stone age to the agricultural age to the industrial age to the **information age.** Knowledge is doubling every two-and-one-half years. In no area have more advances been made than in that of moving information. The challenge is in how to keep abreast of it all.

Among the most important advances for law enforcement is the availability of computerized information. Such information has been in existence for several years but not in individual squad cars and easily accessible by the average "cop on the beat." Officers now receive information on stolen vehicles, individual arrest records and the like within minutes.

Reports and Records

An important information source is the records and reports of your police department, including all preliminary reports, follow-up investigative reports, offense and arrest records, modus operandi files, fingerprint files, missing persons reports, gun registrations and wanted bulletins. Closely examine the suspect's prior record and modus operandi. Examine all laboratory and coroner's reports associated with the case.

Also check records maintained by banks, loan and credit companies, delivery services, hospitals and clinics, hotels and motels, newspapers, telephone books, city directories, street cross directories, utility providers, departments of motor vehicles, pawnbrokers, storage companies, the Internal Revenue Service and taxi companies. Each time you locate a source whose records are helpful, add it to your sources of information file.

Optical-Disk Information-Storage Systems
Optical-disk information-storage systems allow law enforcement agencies to store information in a single location on a single disk and to index and recover it very rapidly. Such storage systems are essential in large agencies, which receive numerous requests for services and information from other agencies, insurance companies and the general public each day.

The Internet
The Internet is an endless and extremely valuable source of information. DeBeck (1997, p. 35) states:

In August 1999, the FBI arrested Cary Stayner, a handyman at a motel near Yosemite National Park, for the murder of naturalist Joie Armstrong. While confessing to Armstrong's killing, Stayner stunned investigators by further admitting to killing three park tourists—Carole Sund, Juli Sund and Silvina Pelosso—whose bodies were found the previous March. Until Stayner's confession, investigators had been focusing on a group of methamphetamine users as the persons responsible for the Sund-Pelosso murders. It turned out that investigators had actually questioned Stayner months earlier about the Sund-Pelosso killings, but let him go, ruling him out as a suspect—a tragic mistake that highlights the importance of the interviewing process in criminal investigations.

To continue to be effective in the 21st century, law enforcement must meet the challenge of cyberspace and learn to take advantage of the dedicated law enforcement resources and information available through the Internet. . . .

Intelligence information can be gathered on organized groups, such as militias, gangs, pedophiles, and Asian and West African crime rings. . . .

The CopNet–Police Resource List (*www.sas.ab.ca*) is dedicated to an international collection of works by and for law enforcement officers. This site provides links to official police sites, resource lists, "Cop Mall" and a restricted area requiring a password. A password can be obtained only after verification of actual law enforcement status. Other listings include crime prevention, canine search and rescue, forensics, computer crime, firearms, traffic, most wanted and training.

D'Arcy (1997, p. 16) adds:

Fast-breaking cases, such as a child's disappearance, can be assisted by law enforcement's ability to exploit the Internet's vast and growing network. Photographs and important details can be distributed much more efficiently and quickly from one central point. Complex criminal investigations involving multiple jurisdictions in many states also benefit from Internet use.

Dees (1999a, p. 14) reports: "The newest kid on the block is Law Enforcement Online (LEO), a project sponsored by the FBI." Membership is free but tightly restricted. Access is through a dedicated toll-free telephone line. LEO provides electronic mail, newsgroups, real-time chat sessions, links to national crime alerts, bul-letins on terrorist activity and training courses with multimedia features.

Complainants, Witnesses, Victims and Informants

Vast amounts of information come from people with direct or indirect knowledge of a crime. Although no one is legally required to provide information to the police except personal identification and accident information, citizens are responsible for cooperating with the police for their own and the community's best interests. Everyone is a potential crime victim and a potential source of information. Interview anyone other than a suspect who has information about a case. This includes complainants, witnesses, victims and informants.

A **complainant** is a person who requests that some action be taken. The complainant is especially important in the initial stages of a case. Listen carefully to all details and determine the extent of the investigative problems involved: the type of crime, who committed it, what witnesses were present, the severity of any injuries and any leads. Thank the complainant for contributing to the investigation.

A **witness** is a person who saw a crime or some part of it being committed. Good eyewitnesses are often the best source of information in a criminal investigation. Record the information a witness gives, including any details that can identify and locate a suspect or place the suspect at the crime scene. Although not always reliable, eyewitnesses' testimony remains a vital asset in investigating and prosecuting a case.

Sometimes a diligent search is needed to find witnesses. They may not want to get involved, or they may withhold or provide information for ulterior motives. Make every effort to locate all witnesses. Check the entire crime-scene area. Conduct a neighborhood canvass to determine whether anyone saw or heard anything when the crime occurred. Check with the victim's friends and associates. Make public appeals for information on radio and television.

Be aware that witness statements are not always reliable. A group of police officers attended a session on the reliability of witnesses' memory and were given a memory recall test. Every officer failed the test. Witnesses are often more confident in their knowledge of what happened than they are accurate. Many people see only a part of the commission of a crime but testify as though they witnessed the entire event.

A **victim** is a person injured by a crime. Frequently the victim is also the complainant and a witness. They are emotionally involved and may be experiencing anger, rage and fear. Such personal involvement can cause them to exaggerate or distort what occurred. Victims may also make a dying declaration that can provide valuable information to investigators. Bourne (1996, p. 8) notes: "A dying declaration may qualify as a hearsay exception and be admissible as evidence." Bourne (p. 8) continues:

> The Federal Rules of Evidence establish the criteria for determining whether a declaration qualifies as a "statement under belief of impending death." . . .
>
> 1. The declarant (the person who made the statement) believed his death was "imminent" when he spoke.
>
> 2. The statement concerned "the cause or circumstances of what the declarant believed to be his impending death."
>
> 3. And the declarant is "unavailable."

An **informant** is anyone who can provide information about a case but who is not a complainant, witness, victim or suspect. Informants may be interested citizens or individuals with criminal records. In noting the importance of informants, Hight (1998, p. 1) asserts: "The use of informants remains one of law enforcement's oldest and most essential investigative tools." Soto (1998, p. 94) states: "The right informant in the right scenario can speed up and make successful a failing police effort. The wrong informant in any scenario can result in failure, safety hazards and tragedy." Soto (p. 100) cautions: "Informants are a valuable source of information for police. However, they require control,

direction and management. Informants can be a double-edged sword and must be carefully monitored." Graves and Chanen (1999, p. B5) state: "They are a necessary evil of police work. In court records, they're called confidential and reliable informants. In cop lingo they're referred to as snitches. On the street, they're considered sellouts."

Such contacts are frequently given code names, and only the investigator knows their identity. Be extremely careful in using such contacts. Never make promises or deals you cannot legally fulfill. In some instances, however, informants may not remain anonymous, and their identity might have to be revealed.

Many jurisdictions have policies regarding the use of juveniles as informants. According to Hall (1998, p. 6), California "prohibits the use of children age 12 and under as informants in police investigations. Youths age 13 through 17 can be used as informants, but only after police get permission from a court." New York allows the use of juvenile informants, but only after receiving parental consent (p. 6).

Cellular Phones Cellular (or "cell") telephones are enhancing the safety of citizens and officers alike. Complainants, victims, witnesses and informants may be greatly aided by cellular phones in their possession. Many of the more than 16 million cellular phone owners in the United States own these phones for safety. However, they can also greatly speed reporting of information related to crimes. The cellular phone industry has contributed thousands of cell phones and free air time to citizen patrols and block watch groups across the country. Such phones are programmed to dial only local law enforcement or other emergency numbers designated by the local crime fighting groups ("Cellular Phone Industry . . . ," 1996).

Police should periodically publicize the importance of calling 911 if cellular phone owners see a crime being committed. Such immediate notification would substantially reduce police response time to calls for police service, increase arrests at the scene and provide for rapid protection of the crime scene to preserve evidence, increasing the chance for convicting a suspect.

The use of cellular telephones by police departments is also proliferating. Officers in leadership positions have used such phones for several years, but many departments are now issuing them to patrol officers, especially those involved in community policing. The transfer of calls from the police communications center to the officers allows officers to talk directly to victims and complainants. Schuiteman (1999, p. 53) explains: "CPs [cellular phones] allow [officers] to work in the field, yet maintain contact

and obtain help from headquarters." He suggests that surveillance, undercover and foot patrol officers believe their
CPs enabled them to call for backup, receive new information, request warrants and the like without ever leaving
their posts. Officers assigned to drug interdiction indicated
their CPs shortened their response to tips about packages
or suspects who might be carrying illegal drugs. Some
officers buy their own cellular phones and obtain permission from the department to use them on duty. In addition, the possession of cellular telephones by citizens
allows direct reporting of their information from the
scene. Although some questions of the security of information have arisen, cellular telephone calls are as secure as
radio transmissions, and security safeguards are becoming
available.

Cell phones and pagers have greatly enhanced the
capabilities of law enforcement, but the service
coverage of such devices has not always been
comprehensive. New technologies, however, have
been developed to "fill in the gaps." Morrison
(1997, pp. 47, 49) reports:

> The latest development is a satellite-based,
> wireless personal communications network
> designed to allow any type of telephone
> operation—voice, fax, data or paging—to reach
> any place on earth. The system has been
> dubbed the "Iridium." . . .
> The Iridium system will support millions of
> users worldwide which is a much greater
> capacity than current satellite systems. . . .
> As far as cops are concerned, Iridium will
> be a boon. Law enforcement activity can be
> enhanced by the global, secure [digital] satellite
> communications capability of the Iridium
> system. . . . The satellite service, coupled with
> the Iridium Cellular Roaming Service, will
> enable law enforcement agents to maintain
> contact with headquarters and other activity
> coordinations centers as well as with other
> agents in the field no matter where they are.

In the 1940s Dick Tracy communicated via a wrist
radio that at the time seemed highly unlikely. Now, however, a Swiss watch company, Swatch, has developed a cellular telephone built into a wristwatch (Dees, 1999b, p. 14).

Caller ID   Caller ID service records the number of the
telephone from which a call is placed, even if the call is
not answered. It also provides the date and time of the
call and can store numbers in its memory when more
than one call is received.

In some criminal investigations, evidence has been
obtained from telephones served by Caller ID. For
example, a person who committed a burglary first called
the business's office to see if anyone was there. The office
telephone recorded the number of the telephone the
burglar used, enabling the police to locate the suspect.

Caller ID could be helpful in cases involving telephoned threats, kidnappings and so on.

Another service provided by the telephone company
that can assist investigators is call tracing. Clede
(1997, p. 46) notes: "Call Trace is a new technology
that records where a call came from if it originated
in the same system. Some require subscription to
the service at a monthly fee; others offer it on a per-
call basis at about $1.50 per call."

Suspects

A **suspect** is a person considered to be directly or indirectly connected with a crime, either by overt act or by
planning or directing it.

Do not overlook the suspect as a chief source of
information. An individual can become a suspect either
through information provided by citizens or by his or
her own actions. Any suspicious individuals should be
questioned. Complete a field interview card for any suspicious person you stop. This card places a person or
vehicle in a specific place at a specific time and furnishes
data for future investigative needs. A sample field interview card is shown in Figure 6.1.

A person with a known modus operandi fitting a
crime may be spotted at or near the crime scene. The
person may be wanted for another crime or show an
exaggerated concern for the police's presence, or the
person may be in an illegal place at an illegal time—
often the case with juveniles.

When questioning occurs spontaneously on the
street (referred to as a **field interview**), it is especially
advantageous to officers to question someone suspected
of involvement in a crime right after the crime has
occurred.

FIGURE 6.1

Field Interview Card, Front and Back

Source: Courtesy of the Boulder City Police Department.

OP. LIC. NO.	STATE	NAME (Last name first)					
476-18-4681	NV	Pirino, John W.					

RESIDENCE ADDRESS	CITY	STATE	SEX	DESCENT	HAIR	EYES
7801 Dupoint	Las Vegas, Nv.		M	It	Bl	Br

HEIGHT	WEIGHT	BIRTHDATE	CLOTHING
5-11	187	5-14-40	Blue Jeans, Striped Shirt, Brown Jacket

PERSONAL ODDITIES	PHONE NO.
Limp-inj. left leg	421-1170

BUSINESS ADDRESS/SCHOOL/UNION AFFIL.	SOC. SEC. NO.
None	321-14-8645

MONIKER/ALIAS	GANG/CLUB
Jack	None

SUBJ. INFO. 1 LOITERER 3 SOLICITOR 5 GANG ACTIVITY 7 ON PAROLE [X] DRIVER
2 PROWLER 4 HITCHHIKER 6 HAS RECORD 8[X] ON PROBATION [ ] PASSENGER

	YEAR	MAKE	MODEL	TYPE	COLOR	VEH. LIC. NO.	STATE
V	1986	Chev St. Wagon		4 dr	beige	491-AMU	Nv

E	INSIDE COLOR	INT	1 BUCKET SEATS	EXT	1 CUST. WHEELS 3 LEVEL ALTER. 5 CUST. PAINT
H	Brown		2 DAMAGED INSIDE		2 PAINTED INSC 4 RUST/PRIMER 6 VINYL TOP

BODY [X] DAMAGE 3[X] STICKER 4 LEFT 6 FRONT **WIN-DOWS** [X] DAMAGE 3 CURTAINS 4 LEFT 6 FRONT
2 MODIFIED 5 RIGHT 7 REAR 2 CUST. TINT 5 RIGHT 7[X] REAR

Persons with subject:

LAST NAME	1st init.	SEX	LAST NAME	1st init.	SEX
Bixley, W C		M	Gurley, M S		F
Thoms, G A		M	Lecher, R L		F

ADDITIONAL INFO (ADDITIONAL PERSONS WITH SUBJECT, BKG. NOS., I.D. NOS., NARRATIVE, ETC.)

Vehicle going slow in alley, passengers in rear looking out rear window. No other persons or vehicles in alley, late at night.

DATE	TIME	LOCATION	Rept. Dist.
5-4-00	0130	Alley behind 602 Pine	

OFFICER'S NAME	SERIAL NO.	OFFICER'S NAME	SERIAL NO.
Wesley Jones	162	Thomas Begley	153

FIELD INTERVIEW BOULDER CITY POLICE DEPARTMENT	DIVISION	DETAIL	SUPERVISOR'S INITS.
	Patrol	Drug	HVM

Sometimes direct questioning of suspects is not the best way to obtain information. In cases in which direct contact would tip off the person, it is often better to use undercover or surveillance officers or various types of listening devices, as discussed in Chapter 7.

Interviewing and Interrogating

Information is obtained continuously throughout an investigation. Some is volunteered, and some the police officer must really work for; some is useful and some worthless or even misleading. Most of an officer's time is spent meeting people and obtaining information from them, a process commonly referred to by two terms, *interview* and *interrogation*.

An **interview** is questioning people who are not suspects in a crime but who know something about it or the people involved. An **interrogation** is questioning those suspected of direct or indirect involvement in a crime.

The ultimate goals of interviewing and interrogating are to identify those responsible for a crime and to eliminate the innocent from suspicion.

Investigators must obtain all the facts supporting the truth, whether they indicate a person's guilt or innocence. The best information either proves the elements of the crime (the corpus delicti) or provides leads.

The Interview

Interviewing is talking to people, questioning them, obtaining information and reading between the lines. The main sources of information at the crime scene are the complainant, the victim and witnesses. (These may be the same person.) Separate the witnesses and then obtain a complete account of the incident from each one. Listen, prompt if necessary and explore for new leads.

Interview witnesses separately if possible. Interview the victim or complainant first, then eyewitnesses and then people who did not actually see the crime but who have relevant information.

Finding, detaining and separating witnesses is a high priority. Witnesses who are not immediately detained can drift off into the crowd or decide not to become involved. Obtain the information as rapidly as possible. Identify all witnesses and check their names and addresses against their identification. Ask witnesses not to speak to one another or to compare stories until they have written down in their own words what happened.

If there are many witnesses, discuss the incident briefly with each. Then establish a priority for obtaining statements based on the witnesses' availability and the importance of their information.

In most cases interview complainants first because they can often provide enough information to determine whether a crime has been committed and, if so, what type of crime. If department policy requires it, have complainants read and initial or sign the information you record during the interview.

Anyone who saw what happened, how it happened or who made it happen is interviewed next. Such witnesses may be in a state of panic, frustration or anger. In the presence of such emotions, remain calm and detached, yet show sympathy and understanding—often a difficult feat.

After interviewing witnesses, interview people who can furnish facts about what happened before or immediately after the crime or who have information about the suspect or the victim.

Not all people with relevant information are at the crime scene. Some persons in the general area may have seen or heard something of value. Even people miles away from the scene may have information about the crime or the person committing it. Explain to such individuals why you are questioning them, check their identification and then proceed with your interview.

The main sources of immediate information away from the crime scene are neighbors, business associates, people in the general area such as motel and hotel personnel and longtime residents. Longer-term contacts may include informants, missing witnesses, friends and relatives. Appeals for public cooperation and reports from various agencies and organizations may also produce information.

Record both positive and negative information. The fact that a witness did *not* see anyone enter a building may be as important as seeing someone.

Conduct the interviews like a conversation, but with a purpose. Interviewing skills can be learned and perfected. After each interview, critique it and identify your mistakes and aspects that you want to improve. Then when you are planning your next interview, review what you have decided to do differently. Keep doing this with each new interview, and you will become an expert.

Advance Planning

Many interviews, at least initial ones, are conducted in the field and allow no time for planning. If time permits, plan carefully for interviews. Review reports about the case before questioning people. Learn as much as possible about the person you are going to question before you begin the interview.

Selecting the Time and Place

Sometimes there is no time to decide when and where to conduct an interview. Arriving at a crime scene, you may be confronted with a victim or witness who immediately begins to supply pertinent information. Recall that these *res gestae* statements are extremely valuable. Therefore, record them as close to verbatim as possible.

Determine as soon as possible who the complainant is, where and how many witnesses exist and whether the suspect has been apprehended. If more than one officer is present, the officer in charge decides who will be questioned and assigns personnel to do it.

Immediate contact with people who have information about a crime improves the chances of obtaining

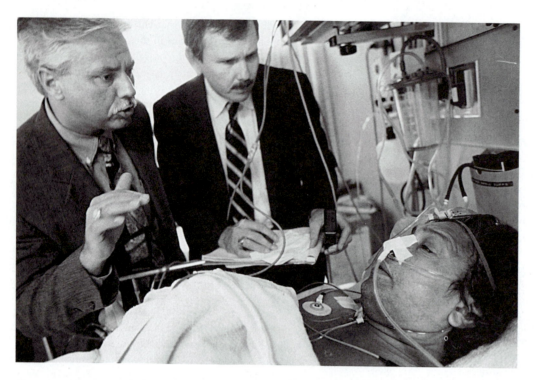

Some interviews are conducted under extremely difficult circumstances. Here investigators interview a hospitalized convenience store clerk in the intensive care unit of Ben Taub Hospital. The clerk was shot during a robbery of the convenience store.

information. Although emotions may be running high, witnesses are usually best able to recall details immediately after an incident. They are also less likely to embellish or exaggerate their stories because others present can be asked to verify the information. Moreover, witnesses can be separated so they will have no opportunity to compare information. Finally, the reluctance to give the police information is usually not so strong immediately after a crime. Given time to reflect, witnesses may fear that they will have to testify in court, that cooperation will take them away from work and cost them financially or that the criminal may retaliate.

Beginning the Interview

How an interview is started is extremely important. At this point the interviewee and the interviewer size each other up. Mistakes in beginning the interview can establish insurmountable barriers. Make your initial contact friendly but professional. Begin by identifying yourself and showing your credentials. Then ask a general question about the person's knowledge of the crime.

Establishing Rapport

Rapport is probably the most critical factor in any interview. **Rapport** is an understanding between individuals created by genuine interest and concern. People who are approached civilly may volunteer a surprising amount of useful information. Most people do not condone criminal behavior and will assist you. However, they often do not know what is important to a specific investigation. Provide every opportunity to establish rapport and to assist citizens in providing information.

Not everyone with information can provide it easily. People who are emotionally unstable, mentally deficient, have temporary loss of memory or fear police often cannot or will not be forthcoming. With them, establishing rapport is critical. If a person is deaf or speaks a foreign language, arrange for an interpreter. If a person appears unwilling to talk, find out why.

Give reluctant witnesses confidence by demonstrating self-assurance. Give indifferent witnesses a sense of importance by explaining how the information will help a victim. Remind them that someday they may be victims themselves and will then want others to cooperate.

Table 6.1   Interview Guidelines

- Ask one question at a time and keep your responses simple and direct.
- Avoid questions that can be answered "yes" or "no"; a narrative account provides more information and may reveal inconsistencies in the person's story.
- Be positive in your approach, but let the person save face if necessary so that you may obtain further information.
- Give the person time to answer. Do not be uncomfortable with pauses in the interview.
- Listen to answers, but at the same time anticipate your next question.
- Watch your body language and tone of voice.
- Start the conversation on neutral territory.
- Tape recorders can be frightening.
- React to what you hear.
- As you move into difficult territory, slow down.
- Don't rush to fill silences.
- Pose the toughest questions simply and directly.
- More room for resistance.
- No meltdowns. . . . You must establish professional distance. Keep your role clear.

Find a way to motivate every witness to talk with you and answer your questions.

Rapport is enhanced by careful listening. Do not indicate verbally or nonverbally that you consider a matter trivial or unimportant; people will sense if you are merely going through the motions. Take a personal interest. Discuss their family, their work or their hobbies. Offer them a handshake, a soft drink or coffee. Be sympathetic and assure them that everything possible will be done but that you need their help.

Networking an Interview

Most people are familiar with the concept of a business or professional **network**—a body of personal contacts that can further one's career. In reality, networks can extend much farther than this.

Networks also establish relationships between people and between people and their beliefs. They produce a context in which to understand a person. These networks may be social, ethnic, cultural, business, professional/occupational, religious or political. As American society becomes more diverse, officers will have to understand the networks in their jurisdictions.

Interviewing Techniques

Most cases are solved through good interviewing techniques. Investigators use questions and repetition effectively and also know how to interview reluctant interviewees. Many are also skilled at using cognitive interviews. No matter which technique or combination of techniques you select, you should follow two key requirements:

Two basic requirements to obtain information are to listen and to observe.

How people act during an interview can tell as much as or more than their words. Signs of unusual nervousness, odd expressions, rapid breathing, visible perspiration or a highly agitated state are cause to question the person's truthfulness. Table 6.1 summarizes the guidelines for a successful interview.

Direct vs. Indirect Questions   A subtle but important difference exists between direct and indirect questions. A **direct question** is to the point, allowing little possibility of misinterpretation. For example, "What time did you and your husband leave the restaurant?" In contrast, an **indirect question** is disguised. For example, a question such as, "How do you and your husband get along?" could elicit a variety of answers.

Ask direct questions, that is, questions that come right to the point. Use indirect questions—those that skirt the basic questions—sparingly.

The axiom that the shortest distance between two points is a straight line is generally true in obtaining information. Knowing the elements of the crime you are investigating lets you select pertinent questions.

Repetition

Anyone who watches detective shows has heard victims or suspects complain, "I've already told my story to the police." This is true to life. Individuals *are* asked to tell and retell their version of what happened and for very good reasons. Someone who is lying will usually tell a story exactly the same way several times. A truthful story, however, will contain the same facts but be phrased differently each time it is retold. After a person has told you what happened, guide the discussion to some other aspect of the case. Later, come back to the topic and ask the person to repeat the story.

Repetition is the best way to obtain recall and to uncover lies.

Often repeating what someone has told you helps the person provide additional information. Sometimes it also confuses the person being questioned, and if the original version was not true, another repetition will reveal this fact. If inconsistencies appear, go back over the information and attempt to account for them.

Reluctant Interviewees

Most people who are reluctant to be questioned respond to one of two approaches: logical or emotional.

Appeal to a reluctant interviewee's reason or emotions.

The *logical approach* is based on reason. Use logic to determine why the person refuses to cooperate. Explain the problems that result when people who know about a crime do not cooperate with investigators.

The *emotional approach* addresses such negative feelings as hate, anger, greed, revenge, pride and jealousy. You can increase these emotions or simply acknowledge them,

"Anyone in your situation would respond the same way." If such tactics do not work, warn the person of the serious consequences of withholding important information.

Whether to select a rational or an emotional approach depends on the person being interviewed, the type of investigation and your personal preference.

Cognitive Interview Technique Interview style has important implications for how much information is received from subjects. The interviewer tries to get the interviewee to recall the scene mentally by using simple mnemonic techniques aimed at encouraging focused retrieval. These techniques include allowing interviewees to do most of the talking; asking open-ended questions; allowing ample time for answers; avoiding interruptions; and encouraging the person to report all details, no matter how trivial.

This **cognitive interview** method calls for using a secluded, quiet place free of distractions and encouraging a subject to speak slowly. The interviewer first helps the interviewee *reconstruct the circumstances* by asking, "How did you feel . . . ?" Have the interviewee describe the weather, the surroundings, objects, people and smells. Interviewees are encouraged to *report everything,* even if they think something is unimportant. They might also be asked to *relate the events in a different order* or to *change perspectives.* What would another person present have seen?

Among the drawbacks of this method are the amount of time it takes and the need for a controlled environment. Nonetheless, the cognitive interview is especially effective for obtaining information from victims and witnesses who have difficulty remembering an event.

Characteristics of an Effective Interviewer/Interrogator

Many of the emotional and intellectual traits of an investigator (discussed in Chapter 1) are especially valuable in communicating with others. Presenting a favorable appearance and personality and establishing rapport are more important than physical attributes. Sometimes, however, it is an advantage to be of the same race or gender as the person being questioned. Under some circumstances it is better not to wear a uniform. Sometimes a suit or jeans and a sweater are more appropriate.

An effective interviewer/interrogator is adaptable, self-controlled, patient, confident, optimistic, objective, sensitive to individual rights and aware of the elements of crimes.

- *Adaptability*—Your cultural and educational background and experience affect your ability to understand people from all walks of life, to meet them on their own level on varied subjects and to adapt to their personalities and lifestyles.

- *Self-control and patience*—Use self-control and patience to motivate people to talk. Be sympathetic yet detached, waiting for responses while patiently leading the conversation and probing for facts. Remain professional, recognizing that some persons you interview may feel hostile toward you.

- *Confidence and optimism*—Do not assume that because the person you are questioning is a hardened criminal, has an attorney, is belligerent or is better educated than you that no opportunity exists to obtain information. Show that you are in command, that you already know many answers and that you want to corroborate what you know. If the conversation shifts away from the subject, steer the discussion back to the topic.

- *Objectivity*—Maintain your perspective on what is sought, avoiding preconceived ideas about the case. Be aware of any personal prejudices that can interfere with your questioning.

- *Sensitivity to individual rights*—Maintain a balance between the rights of others and those of society. Naturally, suspects do not want to give information that conflicts with their self-interests or threatens their freedom. Moreover, many citizens want to stay out of other people's business. Use reason and patience to overcome this resistance to becoming involved.

- *Knowledge of the elements of the crime*—Know what information you need to prove the elements of the crime you are investigating. Phrase questions to elicit information related to these elements.

Enhancing Communication

Successful questioning requires two-way communication between the investigator and the person being questioned. There are several ways to improve communication, whether interviewing or interrogating.

- - - - - - - -

To improve communication: prepare in advance, obtain the information as soon after the incident as possible, be considerate and friendly, use a private setting, eliminate physical barriers, sit rather than stand, encourage conversation, ask simple questions one at a time, listen and observe.

- - - - - - - -

Hess and Wrobleski (1996, pp. 43–44) maintain that these procedures improve communication with a witness, victim or suspect:

- *Prepare* for each interview in advance if time permits. Know what questions you need to have answered.

- Obtain your information as *soon after* the incident as possible. A delay may result in the subject's not remembering important details.

- *Be considerate* of the subject's feelings. If someone has just been robbed, seen an assault or been attacked, that person may be upset and emotional. Allow time for the person to calm down before asking many questions. Remember that when emotions increase, memory decreases.

- *Be friendly.* Try to establish rapport with the subject before asking questions. Use the person's name; look at the person as you ask questions; respond to the answers.

- *Use a private setting if possible.* Eliminate as many distractions as you can so that the subject can devote full attention to your questions.

- *Eliminate physical barriers.* Talking across a desk or counter or through a car window does not encourage conversation.

- *Sit* rather than stand. This will make the subject more comfortable and probably more willing to engage in conversation.

- *Encourage conversation.* Keep the subject talking by:

Keeping your own talking to a minimum.

Using open-ended questions, such as "Tell me what you saw."

Avoiding questions that call for only a "yes" or "no" answer.

Allowing long pauses. Pauses in the conversation should not be uncomfortable. Remember that subjects need time to think and organize their thoughts. Give them all the time they need.

- *Ask simple questions.* Do not use law enforcement terminology when you ask your questions. Keep your language simple and direct.

- *Ask one question at a time.* Allow the subject to answer one question completely before going to the next question.

- *Listen* to what is said and how it is said.

- *Watch* for indications of tension, nervousness, surprise, embarrassment, anger, fear or guilt.

Emotional Barriers to Communication

People often have reasons for not wanting to answer questions that police ask. Even though these reasons may have no logical basis, be aware of the common barriers to communication.

Emotional barriers to communication include ingrained attitudes and prejudices, fear, anger and self-preservation.

One important barrier to communication between police and the public is the ingrained attitude that telling the truth to the police is wrong. The criminal element, those closely associated with crime and even the police often use such terms as *fink* and *snitch,* which imply that giving information to the police is wrong, unsavory or illegal.

Prejudices concerning a person's race, beliefs, religion, size, amount of education, economic status or place of upbringing can be barriers to communication. You may encounter prejudice because you are a police officer or because of your race, your physical appearance or religious beliefs. Equally important, prejudices you hold can interfere with your communicating with some people and therefore with your investigation.

Fear is another barrier to communication. Some witnesses fear that criminals will harm them or their family if they testify, or they fear appearing in court or losing time and wages while testifying.

People actually involved in a crime can be reluctant to talk for many reasons, the most important of which is self-preservation. Although suspects naturally do not want to implicate themselves, other factors may also cause them to not answer questions. Severe guilt feelings can preclude telling anyone about a crime. Fear of consequences can be so great that nothing will induce them to tell the truth. They may fear that if they are sent to prison they will be sexually assaulted or beaten, or they may fear that any accomplices they implicate will seek revenge.

Language Barriers to Communication

English is not the only language spoken in this country. As ethnic diversity increases and other languages proliferate, language barriers become an increasing challenge to law enforcement. Allread (1999, p. 45) points out: "Recent statistics from the Census Bureau show Hispanics to be the fastest growing segment of the U.S. population. The Hispanic population is expected to contribute 35% of the nation's population growth from 1995 to 2000, 44% from 2000 to 2020, and 62% from 2020 to 2050." Siuru (1999, p. 43) states: "As the United States' population becomes more diverse, law enforcement officers are ever more likely to encounter criminals, victims, witnesses and just ordinary citizens who do not speak or understand English." Consequently, various technological devices have been developed to help bridge this language gap.

Siuru (p. 43) describes one advancement in language technology:

> The National Law Enforcement and Corrections Technology Center (NLECTC) is working with the Air Force Research Laboratory in Rome, New York, on Spoken Language Translation technology. . . .
>
> With [this] technology, a person speaks into a computer, the computer translates the input into another language and then "generates" the output in the desired language. The computer-generated spoken output could be produced either by text-to-speech or digital audio playback techniques.

Siuru (p. 44) further notes: "The current demonstration systems translate spoken English to computer-spoken Spanish, Korean or Mandarin Chinese, and spoken Spanish or Mandarin Chinese to computer-spoken English."

Another less sophisticated device is the Voice Response Translator (VRT). According to Siuru (p. 44):

> On voice command from an officer, the VRT sounds out pre-programmed phrases in various languages. . . .
>
> The prototype VRT allows an English-speaking officer to communicate with people in one of three languages—Spanish, Cantonese and Vietnamese. . . .
>
> The officer can select, in any order, phrases . . . using voice commands. For example, during a traffic stop, the officer would give the command, "Stay in your vehicle" which would be translated into the foreign language.

Other techniques are also routinely used to help officers communicate with non-English-speaking people. One of the more common methods is the Point Talk Translator, in which an officer locates the appropriate language either in a handbook or on a computer screen and then points to appropriate phrases to ask specific questions or elicit desired responses. Siuru (p. 45) notes the Point Talk Law Enforcement Translator is available on CD-ROM in 41 languages, from Arabic and Armenian to Ukrainian and Vietnamese. Allread (p. 47) lists several books available to help officers with perhaps the most commonly encountered foreign language—Spanish:

- *Spanish for Law Enforcement Personnel* (Barron's, 1996, $10.95) by William C. Harvey
- *The Complete Spanish Field Reference Manual for Public Safety Professionals* by Senior Trooper Robert Dent
- *Speedy Spanish,* a quick-reference guide for use in the field (Baja Books, $4.95)

Statements

If a person you interview has sufficient information to warrant being a witness in court, obtain a signed statement, defined by *Black's Law Dictionary* as "an allegation, a declaration of matters of fact." A **statement** is a legal narrative description of events related to a crime. It is a more or less formal, exact, detailed presentation. It begins with an introduction that gives the place, time, date and names of the people conducting and present at an interview. The name, address and age of the person questioned is stated before the main body of the statement. Figure 6.2 shows a sample statement.

The body of the statement is the person's account of the incident. A clause at the end states that the information was given voluntarily. The person making the statement reads each page, makes any needed corrections, initials each correction and then signs the statement.

FIGURE 6.2
Sample Voluntary Statement

POLICE DEPARTMENT
VOLUNTARY STATEMENT
DR# __943210__

DATE OCCURRED __12 Nov. 2000__ LOCATION OF

TIME OCCURRED __0315__ OCCURRENCE __Rear of bar and grill__

I, __Walter Wilson__ , am __28__ years of age, home phone: __444-4444__

and my address is __100 Main St., this city__ bus. phone: __444-4443__

1. __I left the bar and grill at about 0300 on the 12th of Nov. 2000. I went out the__
2. __back door, got in my car and drove home. I did not see anyone at the rear of the bar__
3. __and grill.__
4. _____
5. _____
6. _____
7. _____
8. _____
9. _____
10. _____
11. _____
12. _____
13. _____
14. _____
15. _____
16. _____

I have read this statement consisting of __1__ page (s) and I affirm to the truth and accuracy of the facts contained herein.

This statement was completed at (Location) __The Police Dept.__
on the __14th__ day of __Nov.__ at __1300__ , 20 __00__ .

WITNESS __(signature)__

WITNESS __(signature)__ __Walter Wilson__
                          Signature of person giving
                          voluntary statement.

Obtain statements in private, with no one other than police officers present, and allow no interruptions. However, other persons will need to be called in to witness the signing of the statement.

Statements can be taken in several ways: prepared in longhand by the person interviewed, dictated to a typist in question/answer format or tape-recorded for later typing and signing. As Sullivan (1998, p. 105) observes: "Courts nationwide accept the most common methods of recording statements: videotape, audiotape, written notes or a combination of those."

A combination of questions and answers, with the answers in narrative form, is often the most effective format. However, a question/answer format is often challenged in court on grounds that questions guide and control the response. Another alternative is for you to write down the words of the person and have the person read and sign your notes. Also record the ending time. Beginning and ending times may be of great value in court testimony.

Although a statement is not a confession, it may occasionally indicate that a witness or suspect is being deceptive. Strandberg (1998, p. 52) suggests that, when investigators suspect that a witness or suspect is hiding something, the investigators should "go back to the person's statement and re-examine it objectively, looking for clues and hints of deception among the words themselves. This is called statement analysis. . . . Special emphasis should be placed on parts of speech—nouns, pronouns and verbs." Strandberg elaborates (pp. 52–53):

> Truthful people routinely use the pronoun I in their sentences. . . . Not using I in a sentence that would normally call for it might mean that it's not completely the truth, or that it's a complete fabrication. . . .
>
> When a suspect switches from I to we in the middle of a statement, it would indicate an attempt to spread responsibility. . . .
>
> A shift from they to we is also a critical change, because it reveals personal involvement.

He (p. 54) concludes: "Changes in speech are warning signs, signals that the statements and the suspects are certainly worth taking a closer look."

Closing the Interview

End each interview by thanking the person for cooperating. If you have established good rapport with the interviewee, that person will probably cooperate with you later if needed.

The Interrogation

Questioning suspects is usually more difficult than questioning witnesses or victims. Once identified and located, a suspect who *is* involved in a crime may make a statement, admission or confession that, corroborated by independent evidence, can produce a guilty plea or obtain a conviction.

Many of the procedures used in interviewing are also used in interrogating, but you should note some important differences in how you question suspects. One of the most critical is ensuring that you do not violate suspects' constitutional rights so that the information you obtain will be admissible in court.

The Miranda Warning

Before interrogating any suspect, you must give the **Miranda warning,** as stipulated in *Miranda v Arizona* (1966). In this decision, the U.S. Supreme Court ruled that suspects must be informed of their right to remain silent, to have an attorney present and to have a state-appointed attorney if they cannot afford private counsel. Suspects must also be warned that anything they say may be used against them in court.

- - - - - - - - -

The Miranda warning informs suspects of their rights. Give the Miranda warning to every suspect you interrogate.

- - - - - - - - -

Many investigators carry a card, such as the one in Figure 6.3, on which the Miranda warning is printed, to guide them in this important consideration.

Thousands of words have been written for and against this decision. The general interpretation and application of the *Miranda* decision is that, once you have reasonable grounds to believe a person has committed a crime, that person's constitutional rights are in jeopardy unless the Miranda warning is given *before* any questioning.

Kelly (1999, p. 10) notes a common dilemma in deciding whether to apply *Miranda v Arizona* or *Terry v Ohio* (1968), the case ruling that officers may legally stop and "detain" an individual when lacking probable cause to arrest:

> There is no bright-line rule to determine whether a particular police-suspect encounter [is] a *Terry* stop or an arrest. . . . The current test employed by courts is the totality of the circumstances. . . . An accurate

FIGURE 6.3 *Miranda Warning*

Peace Officers
Constitutional Pre-Interrogation Requirements

The following warnings must be given prior to questioning a person who is in custody or is deprived of his freedom of action in any significant way:

THE CONSTITUTION REQUIRES I INFORM YOU THAT:
1) YOU HAVE THE RIGHT TO REMAIN SILENT.
2) ANYTHING YOU SAY CAN AND WILL BE USED AGAINST YOU IN COURT.
3) YOU HAVE THE RIGHT TO TALK TO A LAWYER NOW AND HAVE HIM PRESENT NOW OR AT ANY TIME DURING QUESTIONING.
4) IF YOU CANNOT AFFORD A LAWYER, ONE WILL BE APPOINTED FOR YOU WITHOUT COST.

Waiver of Rights
The suspect may waive his rights, but the burden is on the officer to show the waiver is made voluntarily, knowingly and intelligently.
He must affirmatively respond to the following questions:
1) DO YOU UNDERSTAND EACH OF THESE RIGHTS I HAVE EXPLAINED TO YOU?
2) DO YOU WISH TO TALK TO US AT THIS TIME?

Election of Rights
A subject can avail himself of his rights at any time and interrogation must then cease. If a subject will not waive his rights or during questioning elects to assert his rights, no testimony of that fact may ever be used against him at trial.

and detailed police report, explaining in detail how "intrusive" and "aggressive" the encounter was, is essential."

Walker (1999, p. 27) explains: "In most cases involving investigative detentions lasting only a few minutes, courts will not find the duration of the detention to be unreasonable." However, Walker (p. 28) also notes: "Courts faced with investigative detentions that have exceeded 90 minutes based on reasonable suspicion . . . generally have held such seizures to be unreasonable." An arrest and the accompanying Miranda warning would be more appropriate in such instances.

Many court cases illustrate the gray area that exists in determining when to give the warning. The terms most often used to describe when it should be given are **in custody** or **custodial arrest**. *In custody* generally refers to a point at which an officer has decided a suspect is not free to leave, there has been considerable deprivation of liberty or the officer has in fact arrested the suspect.

In *Oregon v Mathiason* (1977), the U.S. Supreme Court defined **custodial interrogation** as questioning initiated by law enforcement officers after a person has been taken into custody or otherwise significantly deprived of freedom.

The Miranda warning has never applied to voluntary or unsolicited statements, admissions or confessions. Someone can approach a police officer and say, "I want to confess that I killed Mark Jones. I took a gun from my car and shot him." If this remark was unsolicited and completely voluntary, police officers are under no obligation to interrupt the person giving the confession. In one instance, a person telephoned the police long distance to voluntarily confess to a felony. Kalk (1998, p. 52) adds: "Miranda warnings are not required to be given prior to fingerprinting and/or photographing as part of the arrest or booking process. Warnings are also not required prior to field sobriety testing or submission to a breathalyzer test."

If a suspect chooses to remain silent, ask no further questions. If the suspect requests counsel, ask no more questions until counsel is present.

A suspect can waive the rights granted by *Miranda* but must do so intelligently and knowingly. A **waiver** is accompanied by a written or witnessed oral statement that the waiver was voluntary (see Figure 6.4).

Silence, in itself, is *not* a waiver. A waiver of rights must be articulated by the suspect. Therefore, many officers read the Miranda warning aloud from a printed card and then have the suspect read and sign the card (see Figure 6.3). The date and time are also recorded. If no card is available, a summary of the Miranda warning can be written, read and signed. Police have the legal burden of proving that the suspect did waive his or her rights. The suspect retains the right to stop answering questions at any point, even when he or she originally waived the right to remain silent.

FIGURE 6.4
Miranda Waiver Form

ANYWHERE POLICE DEPARTMENT

DEFENDANT _____ Curtis Remke _____

INTERROGATION: ADVICE OF YOUR MIRANDA RIGHTS

Before we ask you any questions, you must understand your rights.

You have the right to remain silent . . . .   *CR*
                                                                          Initials

If you give up your right to remain silent, anything you say can
and will be used against you in a court of law. . . . .   *CR*
                                                                          Initials

You have the right to speak with an attorney for advice before we
ask you any questions and to have him with you during questioning . . .   *CR*
                                                                          Initials

If you cannot afford an attorney, one will be appointed for you
without charge before any questioning if you wish . . . .   *CR*
                                                                          Initials

If you decide to answer questions now without an attorney present,
you will still have the right to stop answering questions at any
time . . . .   *CR*
                                                                          Initials

Do you understand each of these rights I have read to you? . . . .   *CR*
                                                                          Initials

Are you willing to answer questions and make a statement, knowing
that you have these rights, and do you waive these rights freely and
voluntarily with no threats or promises of any kind having been
made to you ? . . . .   *CR*
                                                                          Initials

Charles Good   *Curtis Remke*

Witness's Signature   Signature of the defendant

_____

Witness's Signature

Date ___ 3-14-00 ___   TIME ___ 1330 hrs ___   D.R. # ___ 97-860 ___

The Miranda warning does not prevent suspects from talking. It simply requires that suspects be advised of and fully understand their constitutional rights. The basic intent of the *Miranda* decision is to guarantee the rights of the accused. The practical effect is to ensure that confessions are obtained without duress or coercion, thereby removing any inferences that third-degree tactics were used.

Several decisions in the past two decades relate to the Miranda warning. *Edwards v Arizona* (1981) estab-lished that once a suspect in custody states that he or she wants an attorney, police must halt all questioning and may not engage in further questioning unless the suspect requests it. The defendant in *Edwards v Arizona* interrupted a statement and said to FBI agents, "Maybe I should get a lawyer" but then resumed his story without prompting. The Court ruled that neither the Fourth nor the Fifth Amendment prohibits agents from merely listening to a defendant's voluntary statements and using them at a trial. Even if one inferred that the agents' silence amounted to "subtle compulsion," this would not necessarily vitiate the voluntariness of the defendant's statements.

In 1983 in *United States v Dockery,* the Court ruled that telling a suspect she was "free to leave at any time" and then asking her to wait in a reception area for further questioning was within the Miranda rule. In 1984 *Minnesota v Murphy* established that probation officers do not need to give the Miranda warning, and *Berkemer v McCarty* ruled that the Miranda warning is not required for traffic violations.

The U.S. Supreme Court ruled in *Illinois v Perkins* (1990) that jailed suspects need not be told of their right to remain silent when they provide information to undercover agents. Justice Anthony Kennedy wrote that the intent of the *Miranda* decision was to ensure that police questioning of suspects in custody is not sufficiently coercive to make confessions involuntary. Suspects must be told of their rights not to incriminate themselves. *Miranda* was *not* meant to protect suspects who boast about their criminal activities to individuals they believe to be cellmates.

The Miranda warning has recently come under attack. A February 1999 ruling by a three-judge panel of the Fourth Circuit Court of Appeals said "a long-ignored 1968 federal law trumped the Miranda decision and freed federal law enforcement officers from having to give the familiar warnings in every case" ("Supreme Court Will Back . . . ," 1999, p. 17A). In addition, "Congress said in the 1968 law that evidence obtained without the warning being given could be used at trial as long as federal judges were sure the statements were made voluntarily." Although it is likely the case will be referred to the full-Fourth Circuit court and then to the Supreme Court, many legal experts doubt the Supreme Court will let state and local police ignore its original decision in *Miranda*. To do so, legal scholars say, would require an unlikely decision by the Court to toss out more than 30 years of jurisprudence that has stemmed from Miranda (p. 17A).

Redlick (1999, p. 10) describes another instance in which the U.S. Supreme Court finds a "Miranda loophole." In this case a bank robber, Charles Dickerson, gave a statement to police that was repeated to a magistrate to establish probable cause to obtain a search warrant for Dickerson's apartment. Police found several highly incriminating items, including a "bait bill," dye-stained money and latex gloves. Dickerson then confessed without benefit of the Miranda warning. At his trial Dickerson filed a motion to suppress his statements, confession and the items found during the search. The trial judge ruled that Dickerson's statements could not be used as evidence because they were made in custody without his having received a Miranda warning. However, the judge allowed the items found during the search (with a warrant), saying that the statement had been given voluntarily. Therefore no Miranda warning was required and the search warrant was valid.

In some cases, even when the Miranda warning has been given, investigators may err in not following through on the warning. In a highly publicized case in Minnesota, Dale Jenson was on trial for the kidnapping and murder of his girlfriend's daughter, Jessica Swanson. The case was four years old when a highly trained investigator got Jenson to confess and to lead them to her body. The media praised the interrogation skills of this investigator (Doyle and Furst, 1999).

As the trial approached, however, Jenson's attorney said Jenson's confession should be thrown out because, although he had repeatedly asked for his lawyer, the questioning had continued without Jenson's lawyer present. A tape of the interrogation (required by law in Minnesota) contained the following dialog (Burcum, 1999, p. A11):

Jenson: "You're making me nervous because you want to know so bad, but you won't let me have an attorney."
Interrogator: "I will get you an attorney."
Jenson: "I don't understand why I can't have an attorney sitting here right now."
Interrogator: "What's that going to do for you?"

As this book goes to press, the trial has not concluded. One of the most important cases related to the *Miranda* decision is *New York v Quarles* (1984), which established the public safety exception.

The Public Safety Exception

On June 12, 1984, in *New York v Quarles,* the U.S. Supreme Court ruled on the **public safety exception** to the *Miranda* warning requirement. In 1980 two police officers were stopped by a young woman who told them she had been raped and gave them a description of her rapist, who, she stated, had just entered a nearby supermarket and was armed with a gun. The suspect, Benjamin Quarles, was located, and one of the officers ordered him to stop. Quarles ran, and the officer momentarily lost sight of him. When he was apprehended and frisked, he was found to be wearing an empty shoulder holster. The officer asked Quarles where the gun was, and he nodded toward some cartons and said, "The gun is over there."

The officer retrieved the gun, put Quarles under formal arrest and read him his rights. Quarles waived his rights to an attorney and answered questions.

At the trial the court ruled pursuant to *Miranda* that the statement "The gun is over there" and the subsequent discovery of the gun as a result of that statement were inadmissible.

After reviewing the case, the U.S. Supreme Court ruled that the procedural safeguards that both deter a suspect from responding and increase the possibility of fewer convictions were deemed acceptable in *Miranda* to protect the Fifth Amendment privilege against self-incrimination. However, if Miranda warnings had deterred the response to the officer's question, the cost would have been more than just the loss of evidence that might lead to a conviction. As long as the gun remained concealed in the store, it posed a danger to the public safety.

The Court ruled that in this case the need to have the suspect talk took precedence over the requirement that the defendant be read his rights. The Court ruled that the material factor in applying this "public safety" exception is whether a public threat could possibly be removed by the suspect making a statement. In this case, the officer asked the question only to ensure his and the public safety. He then gave the Miranda warning before continuing questioning.

Foreign Nationals and the Vienna Convention Treaty

In part because of concern that foreign nationals charged with crimes in the United States will not fully understand their rights within the complex U.S. legal system, the Vienna Convention Treaty gives such people the right to contact their consulate in the event of their arrest. The treaty was signed about three decades ago by the United States, Mexico and other countries and established a procedure for ensuring that consulates become aware of a foreign national's detention (Zack, 1999, p. B2).

When officers fail to inform foreign nationals of this right, any evidence or statements that result from a subsequent interview or interrogation may be ruled inadmissible by a court. Such is the situation in a Minnesota murder case involving suspect Rafael Mendoza, a Mexican. Following his arrest, Mendoza was read his rights in Spanish, and Spanish-speaking officers conducted the subsequent questioning, which ultimately revealed the location of the murder weapon and further details of the crime. Nonetheless, police neglected to tell Mendoza about his right under the Vienna Convention Treaty to contact the Mexican Consulate, an oversight that may lead the court to dismiss the murder charges and set Mendoza free (Zack, p. B1).

Selecting the Time and Place

Like interviews, interrogations are conducted as soon as possible after a crime. Selecting the right place to question suspects is critical because they are usually reluctant to talk to police. Most interrogations are conducted at police headquarters. However, if a suspect refuses to come to the station and evidence is insufficient for an arrest, the interrogation may take place at the crime scene, in a squad car or at the suspect's home or place of work. If possible, suspects should be interrogated in an unfamiliar place, away from their friends and family.

Conduct interrogations in a place that is private and free from interruptions.

Ideal conditions exist at the police department, where privacy and interruptions can be controlled. Visible movements or unusual noises distract a suspect undergoing questioning. Therefore, if possible, use a private room with little or no opportunity for interruptions.

Only the suspect, the suspect's attorney and the interrogator should be in the room. Having two officers conduct the interrogation helps deflect false allegations or other untrue claims by the suspect. Allow no telephone calls and no distracting noises; allow no one to enter the room. Under these conditions, communication is more readily established.

Opinions differ on how interrogation rooms should be furnished. An austere, sparsely furnished room is generally less distracting; pictures can reduce the effectiveness of questioning. Many interrogation rooms have only two chairs, one for the investigator and one for the suspect. Some include a small, bare table. Some officers feel it is better *not* to have a desk or table between the officer and the suspect because the desk serves as a psychological protection to the suspect. Without it, the suspect tends to feel much more uncomfortable and vulnerable. Keep all notebooks, pencils, pens and any objects of evidence to be used in the interrogation out of view, preferably in a drawer, until the appropriate time. An austere setting develops and maintains the suspect's absolute attention and allows total concentration on the conversation.

Other investigators, however, contend that such a setting is not conducive to good rapport. It may remind suspects of jail, and a fear of going to jail may keep them from talking. Instead, some investigators prefer a normally furnished room or office for interrogations. Doctors, lawyers, insurance investigators and others have shown that a relaxed atmosphere encourages conversation. Even background music can reduce anxiety and dispel fear, major steps in getting subjects to talk.

Allow Enough Time Vessel (1998, p. 5) notes the importance of patience and persistence in interrogations: "Generally, the chances of obtaining a confession increase 25 percent for every hour (up to 4 hours) of interrogation."

Starting the Interrogation

Conducting the interrogation at the police station allows many options in timing and approach. A suspect can be brought to the interrogation room and left alone temporarily. Often the suspect has not yet met the investigator and is apprehensive about what the investigator is like, what will be asked and what will happen. Provide time for the anxiety to increase, just as a football team sometimes takes a time-out before the opposing team attempts a critical field goal.

As you enter the room, show that you are in command, but do not display arrogance. The suspect is in an unfamiliar environment, alone, does not know you, has been waiting, is apprehensive and does not know what you will ask. At this point select your interrogation technique, deciding whether to increase or decrease the suspect's anxiety. Some investigators accomplish their goals by friendliness; others, by authoritarianism. Show your identification and introduce yourself to the suspect, state the purpose of the interrogation and then give the Miranda warning. Avoid violating the suspect's personal zone. Try to stay 2–6 feet away when questioning.

Do not become so wrapped up in yourself and your quest for information that you overlook body language that may indicate deception, anger or indifference. Most people exhibit body language, or **nonverbal communication.** Deception, for example, may be indicated by looking down, rolling the eyes up, placing the hands over the eyes or mouth or rubbing the hands around the mouth. Other possible indicators of deception include continual licking of the lips, twitching of the lips, intermittent coughs, rapid breathing, change in facial color, continued swallowing, pulsating of the carotid artery in the neck, face flushing, tapping the fingers and avoiding eye contact. Such nonverbal clues may:

Indicate a surfacing of emotions such as guilt, despair, embarrassment, distress, fear and "duping delight," in which a liar is exuberant over the deceit. Other clues may include shifts in pitch or pauses in speech; a discordant flash of anger across the face of someone who claims to be glad to cooperate in a police investigation; or the nearly imperceptible shaking of the head while telling a lie.

. . . Sometimes eye blinks that take a little longer can indicate a lie, suggesting that the person is taking more time thinking about an answer to an interrogator's question ("Spotting a Liar . . . ," 1999, p. 7).

Excessive protestations of innocence should also be suspect, for example, "I swear on my father's grave."

Establishing Rapport

As with interviewing, specific approaches during interrogating may either encourage cooperation or induce silence and noncooperation. The techniques for establishing rapport during an interview also apply in an interrogation. You might decide to instill the fear that there will be serious consequences if the suspect fails to cooperate. You might choose to appeal to the suspect's conscience, emphasizing the importance of getting out of the present situation and starting over with a clean slate. Try any approach that shows the person that cooperation is more desirable than having you find out about the crime another way.

It also helps to know why the crime was committed. Some crimes are committed out of uncontrollable passion, panic or fear without consideration of the consequences. Other crimes result from the demands of the moment; the presumed necessity of the crime appears to justify it. Some criminals' guilt becomes so overpowering that they turn themselves in to the police. Other criminals turn to drugs or alcohol or leave the area to start over somewhere else.

It takes skill to obtain information from those involved in crime, especially if they know that the consequences can be severe. Suspects who understand that there is no easy way out of a situation may become cooperative. At this point, offering alternatives may be successful. Because most people respond to hard evidence, show suspects the physical evidence against them. Acknowledge to the suspect that there is no totally agreeable solution, but point out that some alternatives may be more agreeable than others.

Make no promises, but remind the suspect that the court decides the sentence and is apt to be easier on those who cooperate. Also point out that family and friends are usually more understanding if people admit they are wrong and try to "go straight."

If the suspect will not provide the names of accomplices because they are friends, explain that such "friends" have put the suspect in the present predicament.

Approaches to Interrogation

As with interviews, interrogations can follow an emotional or a logical approach. An emotional approach is either sympathetic or authoritarian. After talking with the suspect, select the approach that seems to offer the best chance for obtaining information.

Interrogation techniques include inquiring directly or indirectly, forcing responses, deflating or inflating the ego, minimizing or maximizing the crime, projecting the blame, rationalizing and combining approaches.

Inquiring Indirectly or Directly Indirect inquiry draws out information without mentioning the main subject. For example, an indirect approach might be phrased, "Have you ever been in the vicinity of Elm Street? Grove Street? The intersection of Elm and Grove?" In contrast, a direct question would be, "Did you break into the house on the corner of Elm and Grove Streets on December 16th?"

Forcing Responses A forced response is elicited by asking a question that will implicate the suspect, regardless of the answer given. For example, the question, "What time did you arrive at the house?" implies that the suspect *did* arrive at the house at some time. Answering the question with a time forces the suspect to admit having been there. Of course, the suspect may simply state, "I never arrived there," or may refuse to answer at all.

Deflating or Inflating the Ego Belittling a suspect is often effective. For example, you might tell a suspect, "We know you couldn't be directly involved in the burglary because you aren't smart enough to pull off a job like that. We thought you might know who did though." Question the suspect's skill in committing a crime known to be his specialty. Suggest that the suspect's reputation is suffering because his latest burglaries have been bungled. The suspect may attempt—out of pride—to prove that it was a professional job.

The same results can be obtained by inflating suspects' egos, praising the skill shown in pulling off the job. Suspects may want to take the credit and admit their role in the crime.

Minimizing or Maximizing the Crime Concentrate your efforts on the crime itself, ignoring for the moment the person committing it. Instead of using the word *crime,* say "the thing that happened." Refer to stolen property as "the stuff that was taken." Do not use terms such as *robbery, homicide* or *arson.* Use other less threatening terms. For example, asking the suspect "to tell the truth" is much less threatening than asking someone "to confess."

Overstating the severity of an offense can be as effective as understating it. Mentioning that the amount of stolen money was $5,000 rather than the actual $500 puts the suspect on the spot. Is a partner holding out? Is the victim lying about the losses? Will the suspect be found guilty of a felony because of such lies? Making the offense more serious than it actually is can induce suspects to provide facts implicating them in lesser offenses.

Projecting the Blame Projecting blame onto others is another effective way to get suspects talking. Napier and Adams (1998, p. 13) note: "Projection excuses an act by placing the blame on something or someone else." When a suspect feels as if others are at fault, they may be more willing to share information that will ultimately incriminate themselves.

Rationalizing Rationalizing is another technique that shifts fault away from a suspect. Napier and Adams (p. 12) explain: "Rationalization offers plausible explanations for suspects' actions that reflect favorably on them by presenting their actions in a positive light." Even though the suspect committed the act, there was a good reason to justify it. Napier and Adams state: "Many individuals rationalize their actions to excuse errors of all kinds and degrees. Competent investigators comprehend this psychological process and convey empathy by indicating that they understand suspects' frames of reference."

Combining Approaches Having the suspect tell the story using different methods can reveal discrepancies. If an oral statement has been given, have the suspect put this information in writing and compare the two versions. Then give the story to two different investigators and have them compare the versions.

Using Persuasion during Interrogation

Sometimes investigators may obtain much better results using persuasive techniques: making sure the suspect is comfortable and has basic needs taken care of, such as being allowed to go to the bathroom and to get a drink of water. Once the suspect has been made comfortable, begin by acknowledging that a problem exists but that before they can talk about it, the suspect needs to be informed of his rights. Then suggest that the suspect probably already knows all about these rights, and ask the suspect to tell what he does know. Usually the suspect can paraphrase the Miranda warning, and you can then compliment him on his knowledge. This helps establish rapport. Next, encourage the suspect to tell his side of the story in detail, intervening only to give encouragement to continue talking. When the suspect has finished, review the account step by step.

Following this, begin a "virtual monologue about robbery" and how some people's desperate financial circumstances lead them into such a crime. The monologue describes how no one starts out planning a life of crime, but some, like an addict, fall into a criminal pattern that leads either to getting shot and killed or to spending a lifetime in prison. End the monologue by "emphasizing that the inevitable result of this pattern of crime is life in prison or death."

Next, suggest that the suspect can avoid this fate only by breaking this pattern and that the first step is to admit that it exists. Add that a person's life should not be judged by one mistake, nor should that person's life be wasted by a refusal to admit that mistake. Following this monolog, begin to talk about the suspect's accomplices and how they are still free, enjoying the "fruits of the crime."

Finally, talk about the suspect's previous encounters with the criminal justice system and how fairly it has treated the suspect. In the past the suspect has probably always claimed to be not guilty. Judges are likely to go easier on suspects who indicate remorse for what they have done. This cannot happen unless the suspect first admits the crime. Point out that "intelligent people recognize when it is in their own best interest to admit a mistake."

Ethics and the Use of Deception

Police officers are supposed to be honest, but what happens when they are lied to? Unfortunately, criminal interrogations do not follow a set of rules that mandates everyone to tell the truth. The fact is, criminals lie as a matter of course. Faced with scant evidence, yet a positive belief that a suspect has committed a particular crime, what might an investigator do? Dillingham (1996, p. 105) suggests:

> We lie to them, using deception as a tool. We lie to make it appear that there is evidence against the criminal, and that we know that this particular criminal committed this particular crime. We lie to suspects because the Supreme Court tells us that not only is it necessary to do so in order to get a confession in most cases, but because it is legal do to so.

Dillingham (pp. 105–6) cites the following cases that support the use of deception:

- *U.S. ex rel. Caminito v Murphy* (1955). It is permissible to tell a suspect that he has been identified by witnesses even though that is untrue.
- *Moore v Hopper* (1975). It is permissible to tell a suspect that material evidence, such as a weapon used to perpetrate a crime, has been found.
- *Frazier v Cupp* (1978). It is permissible to tell a suspect that an accomplice has already confessed when this is actually untrue.
- *Roe v State of New York* (1973). It is permissible to tell a suspect that his fingerprints (or other physical evidence linking him to the offense) were located at the scene of the crime, when this is in fact untrue.

Dillingham (p. 108) concludes: "While it may not be public knowledge that police can legally lie to suspects, that does not negate the value of deception as a tool. Wisely used, deception can be a great asset in obtaining confessions." Interrogatory deception may include fabricating evidence, making promises, using the "good cop/bad cop" routine, misrepresenting the seriousness of the offense or misrepresenting identity, for example, pretending to be a cellmate.

The use of deception in interrogation and the determination of ethical, professional behavior remain important issues.

Third-Degree Tactics

Considerable literature deals with the use of the third degree in police interrogations. It is not known how widely these methods are used and how much of what is claimed is exaggeration.

Third degree is the use of physical force, the threat of force or other physical, mental or psychological abuse to induce a suspect to confess to a crime. Third-degree tactics, which are illegal, include striking or hitting a suspect, denying food or water or sleep for abnormal time periods, not allowing a suspect to go to the toilet, having a number of officers ask questions in shifts for prolonged time periods and refusing normal privileges. Obtaining information by these methods is inexcusable.

Third-degree tactics—physical force, threats of force or other physical, mental or psychological abuse—are illegal. Any information so obtained, including confessions, is inadmissible in court.

The image of police brutality is difficult to offset when third-degree tactics are used. Such tactics create a loss of respect not only for the officer involved but also for the entire department and the police profession.

Although physical force is not permitted, this does not rule out physical contact. Placing a hand on a shoulder or touching a suspect's hand can help to establish rapport. Looking directly at a suspect while talking and continuing to do so during the conversation is not using physical force, even though it usually makes the suspect extremely uncomfortable.

If you give a suspect all the privileges you take, there is no cause for a charge of third-degree tactics. Allow the suspect the same breaks for meals, rest and going to the toilet that you take. Law enforcement officers are obligated to protect both the public interest and individual rights. No situation excuses a deliberate violation of these rights.

Television and movies often depict the "good cop/bad cop" method of interrogation, portraying one officer as very hostile and another one as trying to protect a suspect from the hostile officer. Routines such as this could be considered illegal if carried to an extreme. Some interrogation techniques, even if not illegal, may be unethical.

Admissions and Confessions

When a suspect has become cooperative, you can increase the amount of conversation. Once rapport is established, listen for words indicating that the suspect is in some way connected with the crime, such as "I didn't do it, but I know who did." If the suspect is not implicated in the crime but has relevant information, attempt to obtain a statement. If the suspect is implicated, try to obtain an admission or confession. Zulawski and Wicklander (1998, p. 90) note:

> Research has attempted to quantify the reasons for a confession. . . . External factors, the fear of being arrested, threats or other issues contributed to a confession less than 20% of the time. Internal factors proved to be a much stronger reason to confess. Suspects, 42%, indicated that they experienced relief after talking and explaining their side of the story. . . . Some 55% of the suspects in the study said that they confessed because they believed that the police could prove their involvement.

The format for obtaining admissions and confessions from suspects in criminal cases is fairly standard. However, state laws, rules and procedures for taking admissions and confessions vary, so you need to know the rules and requirements of your jurisdiction.

An **admission** contains some information concerning the elements of a crime but falls short of a full confession (see Figure 6.5). A **confession** is information supporting the elements of a crime given by a person involved in committing it. It can be oral or written and must be voluntary and not given in response to threats, promises or rewards. It can be taken in question/answer form or in a narrative handwritten by the suspect or the interrogator (see Figure 6.6).

A confession, oral or handwritten, must be given of the suspect's free will and without fear or in response to threats, promises or rewards.

The voluntary nature of the confession is essential. For example, Ernesto Miranda had an arrest record and was familiar with his rights; yet his confession was ruled inadmissible because these rights had not been clearly stated to him. Although formal education is not required for making a confession, a suspect must be intelligent enough to understand fully everything stated.

In most states, oral confessions are admissible in court, but written confessions usually carry more weight. Put an oral confession into writing as soon as possible, even if the suspect refuses to sign it. Have the suspect repeat the confession in the presence of other witnesses to corroborate its content and voluntariness. In extremely important cases, the prosecutor often obtains the confession to ensure that it meets all legal requirements. Many departments are now videotaping statements and confessions.

FIGURE 6.5 *Sample Admission*

POLICE DEPARTMENT

ADMISSION   DR# __933210__

DATE OCCURRED __12 Nov. 2000__   LOCATION OF

TIME OCCURRED __0315__   OCCURRENCE __Rear of bar and grill__

I, __Walter Wilson__ , am __28__ years of age,

home phone: __444-4444__

and my address is __100 Main St.,this city__   bus. phone: __444-4443__

1. __I came out of the bar and grill at approx. 0300 on 12 Nov. 2000 and saw__

2. __Mr. Victim standing there. He spoke to me and we had an argument. We__

3. __argued a little while and I left. He was alive when I saw him last.__

4. _____

5. _____

6. _____

7. _____

8. _____

9. _____

10. _____

11. _____

12. _____

13. _____

14. _____

15. _____

16. _____

17. _____

18. _____

I have read this statement consisting of __1__ page (s) and I affirm to the truth and accuracy of the facts contained herein.

This statement was completed at (Location) __The Police Dept.__
on the __14th__ day of __Nov.__ at __1300__ , 20 __00__ .

WITNESS _William Bennett_

WITNESS _John H. Scott_   _Walter Wilson_
Signature of person giving
voluntary statement.

After obtaining a confession, you may also go with the suspect to the crime scene and reenact the crime before witnesses. Take pictures or films of this reenactment. Go over the confession and the pictures with the suspect to verify their accuracy. (Such confessions and reenactments can also be used for police training.)

Even though a confession is highly desirable, it may not be true, it may later be denied, or there may be claims that it was involuntary.

- - - - - - - -

A confession is only one part of an investigation. Corroborate it by independent evidence.

- - - - - - - -

Your investigation will proceed in much the same way with or without a confession. However, a confession often provides additional leads. Although it cannot stand alone, it is an important part of the case.

FIGURE 6.6

Sample Confession

POLICE DEPARTMENT

CONFESSION

DATE __14 Nov. 2000__ TIME __1300__ PLACE __Police Dept.__

I, __Walter Wilson__, am __28__ years of age,

and my address is __100 Main St., this city__,

I have been duly warned by __police officer name__, who has identified

himself as __a police officer__

that I do not have to make any statement at all, and that any statement I make may be used in evidence against me on the trial for the offense concerning which this statement is herein made. Without promise of hope or reward, without fear or threat of physical harm, I freely volunteer the following statement to the aforesaid person:

____I left the bar and grill at about 0300 on 12 Nov. 2000. I went out the back

door and I met Mr. Victim coming in. He bumped into me and we got in an argument.

He picked up a rock to hit me with, so I took out my knife and stabbed him. I

think he was dead when I left.

I have read the __1__ pages of this statement and the facts contained therein are true and correct.

WITNESS: *Wm Bennett*

WITNESS: *Jehu H Scott*

Walter Wilson

Signed by the arrested party.

Page __1__ of __1__ pages.

Questioning Juveniles

Special considerations exist when you question juveniles. You must obtain parental permission before questioning a juvenile, unless the situation warrants immediate questioning at the scene. Parents usually permit their child to be questioned separately if the purpose is explained and you have valid reasons for doing so. Overprotective parents can distract and interfere with an interview or interrogation. Often, however, parents can assist if the youth is uncooperative. They can ask questions and bring pressures to bear that you cannot. They know and understand the child and can probably sense when the child is lying. Decide whether to question a juvenile in front of the parents or separately after you determine their attitudes when you explain to them the reasons for the inquiry.

Obtain parental permission before questioning a youth. Do not use a youth as an informant unless the parents know the situation.

Your attitude toward youths will greatly influence how well you can communicate with them. Ask yourself whether you consider the youth a person who has a problem or a youth who *is* a problem.

Many juveniles put on airs in front of their friends. For example, in one case a juvenile and some other youths were brought into a room for observation by wit-

Police officers should be skilled at communicating with people of all ages and from other cultures. Cultural diversity within the department can be of great benefit.

nesses. The suspect youth knew he was being watched and challenged his school principal by stating that he had a right to know who was looking at him and why. This ten-year-old boy wanted to impress his friends. A few days later the boy's parents brought him to the police station at the officer's request. It took two questions to determine that he had set a fire that resulted in an $80,000 loss. After a third question, the youth admitted his guilt. Although he had acted like a "big shot" in front of his friends, his action weighed heavily on his conscience. The presence of the police and the knowledge that his parents were waiting in another room motivated him to cooperate.

Many youths also have very active imaginations, tend to exaggerate and may have periods of fantasy. They may describe suspects as bigger than they really are or may view an event as more serious or important than it is.

Finally, juveniles may have definite opinions about the police. Some dislike adults in general and the police in particular. Like adults, however, most of them do not dislike the police and will cooperate with them. Put yourself in their shoes; learn their attitudes and the reasons for them. Time and patience are your greatest allies when questioning juveniles. Explain why you are questioning them, and you will probably gain their confidence.

Do not underrate the intelligence or cleverness of young people. They are often excellent observers with good memories. Talk to them as you would to an adult. Praise them and impress on them their importance to the investigation.

If a juvenile confesses to a crime, bring in the parents and have the youth repeat the confession to them. The parents will see that the information is voluntary and not the police's account of what happened. Parents often provide additional information once they know the truth. For example, they may be alerted to stolen items at home and report them.

Evaluating and Corroborating Information

Do not accept information obtained from interviews and interrogations at face value. Verify all information. You cannot know the motives of all those who provide information. Do not assume that all information, even though volunteered, is truthful. Corroborate or disprove statements made during questioning.

To cross-check a story, review the report and the details of the offense. Determine the past record, family status, hobbies and special interests of the persons questioned. If a person has a criminal record, determine his or her prior modus operandi. With such information, you will be able to ask questions in a way that indicates you know what you are talking about and that deceptive answers will be found out.

A person who resorts to half-truths or lies usually ends up on the defensive and becomes entangled in deceit. Knowing the facts of a case allows you to neutralize deliberate lies. If discrepancies in statements occur, question the suspect again or use polygraph or psychological tests. Compare the replies of people questioned and assess whether they are consistent with the known facts.

Breaking a "Pat" Story

A person who is telling the truth can usually repeat the story the same way many times, although he or she may use different words and a different sequence in retelling it. Times and dates may be approximate, and the person may simply not be able to remember some things. In contrast, a person who is telling a fabricated story can usually repeat it word for word innumerable times. Dates and times are usually precise, and all details are remembered. However, it is difficult to repeat lies consistently; each one sounds better than the other, and the story becomes distorted with mistakes and exaggerations.

To break a pat story, ask questions that require slightly different answers and serve to alter memorized responses.

Scientific Aids to Obtaining and Evaluating Information

Many attempts have been made to determine the truth through scientific instruments. Even before instruments were developed, however, trials by ordeal and other tests relied on psychological and physiological principles. For example, it was common knowledge for centuries that when a person was lying or nervous, visible or measurable physiological changes in the body occurred. These include dryness of the mouth, shaking or trembling, perspiration, increased heartbeat, faster pulse and rapid breathing. The ancient Chinese capitalized on the symptom of mouth dryness when they made a suspect chew rice. If the rice remained dry after being chewed, the suspect was assumed to be lying.

Science and technology have provided aids to help determine the reliability of information. Among them are the polygraph, CVSA, hypnosis and truth serums.

The Polygraph and CVSA

As implied by the name, a **polygraph** (literally, "many writings") records several measurements on a visible graph.

- - - - - - - - -

The polygraph scientifically measures respiration and depth of breathing, changes in the skin's electrical resistance and blood pressure and pulse.

- - - - - - - - -

A person does not actually have to respond verbally for a polygraph to work because the machine measures the mental and emotional responses regardless of whether the person answers questions.

The same factors measured by the polygraph may be visible to a trained observer through such signs as flushing of the face, slight pulsing of the neck arteries, beads of perspiration, rapid breathing and other signs of nervousness such as licking the lips.

Measurements taken by the polygraph can be interpreted at the time the test is administered or later. The results can be shown to the subject to demonstrate which responses were shown to be truthful and which were not.

Many law enforcement agencies use polygraphs in their investigations; however, the effectiveness of the polygraph has been questioned by many. Among supporters of the polygraph, opinions differ as to its accuracy. Although not infallible, it can detect physiological changes indicating deception anywhere from 75 to 96 percent of the time. Its accuracy depends on the subject, the equipment and the operator's training and experience. In some cases, the machine may fail to detect lies because the subject is on drugs, makes deliberate muscular contractions or has a psychopathic personality.

The subject must be physically, mentally and emotionally fit for the examination. The examination must be voluntary and completed under conditions conducive to cooperation. A clear, concise summary of the test results is furnished only to authorized personnel.

Despite advances in technology, improved training of polygraph operators and claims of 95% accuracy, polygraph results are not now accepted by the courts as absolute evidence, except when stipulated by all parties. The Supreme Court has said "there is simply no consensus that polygraph evidence is reliable. To this day, the scientific community remains extremely polarized about the reliability of polygraph techniques. . . . There is simply no way to know in a particular case whether a polygraph examiner's conclusion is accurate, because certain doubts and uncertainties plague even the best polygraph exams" ("Supreme Court Finds . . .," 1998, p. 3). Some authorities claim that the results violate hearsay rules because it is impossible to cross-examine a machine.

- - - - - - - -

The polygraph is an instrument used to verify the truth, not a substitute for investigating and questioning. Although the results are not presently admissible in court, any confession obtained as a result of a polygraph test is admissible.

- - - - - - - -

Many polygraph inaccuracies have been failures to detect lies, not failures to indicate truthful statements. Thus the polygraph is sometimes useful to develop leads, verify statements and cross-check information. Moreover, it provides the police with a psychological advantage that may lead to a confession. Such confessions are admissible in court even though the test results are not. Even in jurisdictions in which the polygraph is not admissible in court, prosecuting attorneys often give weight to the findings of a polygraph examination in deciding whether to prosecute a case.

Competent questioning is as important as the instrument used. As in an interrogation, the right questions must be asked in the right sequence. Although examiners are trained to give the test and interpret the graphs, they rely heavily on background information that the investigator provides.

All but nine states have licensing or limitation laws that establish minimum requirements for polygraph examiners. The normal procedure for setting up a polygraph test is for the police agency to request in writing that a polygraph test be conducted. The examiner should review the complete case in question, including any statements made by the subject before the test is conducted. A pretest interview with the subject should cover the information to be included in the test, a review of the questions to be asked and an advisement of the suspect's constitutional rights.

The polygraph examiner will want the following information before the test:

- The case facts—the precise criminal offense involved, the complete case file and a summary of the evidence.

- Information about the subject—complete name, date of birth, physical, mental, emotional and psychological data if known and criminal history.

The proper tests are then decided on and the questions prepared and reviewed with the subject. The test itself may include mixed questions, yes-or-no questions, a card test or a guilt-complex test.

After the test is completed, the subject and the police are advised of the results in person or by letter. If the test indicates deception, an individual interrogation may follow. Any confessions that follow from such tests are almost universally accepted by the courts. The examiner's testimony is not conclusive evidence but rather opinion evidence regarding either guilt or innocence.

A recent innovation is computerized polygraphy. This eliminates most of the mechanical equipment, replacing it with a virtual graph on a computer monitor. The graph can be printed, if desired. In computerized polygraph systems, the software analyzes physiological changes and reports the probability that the person has answered the question truthfully. Clede (1998, p. 91) reports: "Computerized models use the POLYSCORE mathematical algorithm developed at Johns Hopkins University by the Applied Physics Lab (APL). Making statistics comparisons of the signals recorded during an examination, APL claims an interpretation accuracy of over 95%."

In the 1970s the Psychological Stress Evaluator (PSE) was introduced. The PSE measured stress in the microtremors of the human voice. A more recent version of this technology is the Computer Voice Stress Analyzer (CVSA).

CVSA is popular in many law enforcement agencies. Morrison (1999, p. 67) claims:

The theory of voice stress analyzers revolves around two basic components of speech: Amplitude Modulation (AM) and Frequency Modulation (FM). AM sound is audible, while FM is not. When people lie, the FM part of their speech diminishes or disappears altogether. The Computer Voice Stress Analyzer (CVSA) from the National Institute for Truth Verification (NITV) in West Palm Beach, Florida, measures this FM loss to note any deception.

NITV claims its CVSA has a 98 percent accuracy rate. . . .

The CVSA does not require only "yes" or "no" answers from the person being tested. The unit can analyze any spoken word.

Both the polygraph and CVSA reduce investigative costs, focus on specific suspects, increase conviction rates (because many tests are followed by confessions) and eliminate suspects. Police agencies should not go on a "fishing expedition," however. The suspects should be narrowed to not more than two persons through normal investigative practices before a polygraph examination or CVSA is used. Table 6.2 compares the polygraph and CVSA.

Brain Fingerprinting

Technology has taken the polygraph one step further and brings investigators one step closer to being able to read people's minds. Burke (1999, p. 28) explains:

Brain fingerprinting is the latest in computer-based technology that allows investigators to identify or exonerate subjects based upon measuring brain-wave responses to crime related pictures or words presented on a computer screen. . . .

To determine if a subject was present or has specific knowledge concerning a crime, words or pictures relevant (and irrelevant) to that crime are flashed on a computer screen. . . . If the subject recognizes the pictures, words or phrases (target or probe), a MERMER (Memory and Encoding Related Multifaceted Electroencephalographic Response) will occur. . . .

A MERMER will not occur in an innocent subject or someone who has no knowledge of the crime. . . . A computer then analyzes the brain responses to these MERMERS (or lack of MERMERS) to scientifically determine if a subject has specific information related to the crime stored in his/her brain.

Hypnosis and Truth Serums

Like the polygraph, hypnosis and truth serums are supplementary tools to investigation. They are not used as short-cuts but rather in specific cases where the criteria for their use have been determined by thorough review. Criteria cases are normally crimes of violence or cases where loss of memory or ability to recall is involved and where all other standard investigative efforts have been

exhausted. Because of the restricted criteria, these techniques are used in a comparatively small number of cases.

Hypnosis **Hypnosis** is used with crime victims and witnesses to crimes, not with suspects. It should be used only after careful consultation with the person to be hypnotized and after a detailed review of the case as well as of the subject's mental, physical and emotional condition. DePresca (1996, p. 82) advises:

Check with your District Attorney's office. . . . They are the people who will have to convince a judge, at a suppression hearing, or a jury, beyond a reasonable doubt, that hypnotically refreshed testimony was obtained according to your state's rules of evidence.

Most forensic hypnotists will be able to provide to prosecutor's offices a series of questions and answers that will satisfy judicial requirements at trial. . . .

You can contact a local FBI office, state police headquarters or a larger law enforcement agency in your area as to the availability of a forensic hypnotist.

You must obtain written consent from the subject and permission from the prosecutor's office. It is advisable to have an attorney present as well.

A professional should carefully analyze the subject and the case before hypnosis is conducted. The actual act of hypnotism and interrogation should be performed only by a psychiatrist, psychologist or physician specifically trained in the techniques.

Courts have established guidelines for using testimony gained from hypnosis. The guidelines require that a trained professional perform it and that the professional be independent of, rather than responsible to, the prosecution. The number of persons present should be restricted to the hypnotist and the coordinator from the police agency who has knowledge of the case and perhaps an artist who can draw a sketch based on any descriptions of suspects. And although forensic hypnosis has finally been accepted as a valuable crime-fighting tool, many states remain reluctant to allow into court testimony elicited from hypnosis. Hall (1999, p. 42) reports: "Currently, the laws surrounding hypnosis vary greatly from state to state. Some do not recognize it at all while others have severe restrictions. Nevada has broken the mold by allowing 'hypnotically refreshed' testimony admissible in court in both civil and criminal cases." Hall (p. 44) further notes:

Hypnosis can be an invaluable tool to the criminal investigator. The use of a hypnoinvestigator can bring forth crucial information regarding a crime by

---

Table 6.2	Comparison of the Polygraph and CVSA

	Polygraph	*CVSA*
Initial cost:	About $12,000 including machine, room, furniture, training and certification of examiners.	About $7,000 for machine and examiner certification.
Accuracy:	70–95% proven in extensive studies by various sources over many years.	98% claimed, but shortage of accepted studies based on empirical data.
Flexibility:	Normally limited to testing room environment.	Portable, plus flexibility of field recordings.
Inputs measured:	Heartbeat, blood pressure, pulse wave, breathing and skin resistance.	Audible voice microtremors.
Admissibility:	By stipulation.	By stipulation.
Exam time:	2 hours.	2 hours.

Source: A.W. Whitworth. "Polygraph or CVSA: What's the Truth about Truth Deception Analysis?" *Law and Order,* November 1993, p. 31. Reprinted by permission of the publisher.

eliciting heretofore unknown information (to the investigator) from a victim or witness.

The session should be recorded and videotaped, if possible. Questions should relate only to what the witness states under hypnosis. The witness should not be prompted or induced in any way.

Truth Serums **Truth serums** are fast-acting barbiturates of the type used to produce sleep at the approximate level of surgical anesthesia. Alcohol produces somewhat the same effects to a much lesser degree. The theory is that the drug removes a person's inhibitions so the person is more likely to tell the truth. In the past, scopolamine and hyascine were the most used drugs, but sodium amytol and sodium pentathol are more commonly used today.

Truth serums are not used extensively by the police because the accuracy of the information obtained with them is questionable. Truth serum is administered by a physician, preferably a psychiatrist, who remains to monitor the person's condition while the questions are asked. The drugs can cause serious consequences, so the subject must be monitored continually. Some patients also become violently excited. Moreover, individuals vary greatly in their response to truth serums. Some can with-

hold information even under the influence of a large dose of the serum.

The courts do not officially recognize truth serums or their reliability, nor do they admit the results as evidence.

Use of Psychics

Use of psychics in criminal investigations has been popularized by television shows and, to many, the incidents depicted are entirely believable. Although use of psychics in criminal investigations is controversial, some agencies are willing to consider any possible lead or source of information, including psychics. According to O'Brien (1996): "For the most part, law enforcement authorities concede that when all else fails, they welcome help from any source. . . .Whatever success comes from a psychic source, it usually involves the discovery or identification of a body."

An FBI spokesman states: "We really make no determination as to the quality of psychic phenomenon," a sentiment echoed by many others in law enforcement, who add: "Anyone with information is always encouraged to come forward" (O'Brien).

Summary

Most solved cases rely on both physical evidence and information obtained from a variety of sources. Important sources of information include (1) reports and records, including those found on the Internet, (2) persons who are not suspects in the crime but who know something about the crime or those involved and (3) suspects in the crime. A sources-of-information file contains the name and location of people, organizations and records that may assist in a criminal investigation.

The ultimate goals of interviewing and interrogating are to identify those responsible for a crime and to eliminate the innocent from suspicion. Interview anyone other than a suspect who has information about the case. This includes complainants, witnesses, victims and informants.

Interview witnesses separately if possible. Interview the victim or complainant first, then eyewitnesses and then those who did not actually see the crime but who have relevant information.

Two basic requirements to obtain information are to listen and to observe. Ask direct questions that come right to the point. Use indirect questions—those that skirt the basic question—sparingly. Repetition is the best way to obtain recall and to uncover lies. Appeal to a reluctant interviewee's reason or emotions.

The effective interviewer/interrogator is adaptable, self-controlled, patient, confident, optimistic, objective, sensitive to individual rights and knowledgeable about the elements of the crime. Regardless of whether you are interviewing or interrogating, there are several ways to improve communication: prepare in advance and obtain the information as soon after the incident as possible; be considerate and friendly; use a private setting and eliminate physical barriers; sit rather than stand; encourage conversation; ask simple questions one at a time; listen and observe. Emotional barriers to communication include ingrained attitudes and prejudices, fear, anger or hostility and self-preservation.

Although many of the same principles apply to interrogating and interviewing, interrogating involves some special considerations. One important consideration is when to give the Miranda warning, which informs suspects of their rights and must be given to any suspect who is interrogated. It is also important to conduct interrogations in a place that is private and free from interruptions. Interrogation techniques include inquiring directly or indirectly, forcing responses, deflating or inflating the ego, minimizing or maximizing the crime, projecting the blame, rationalizing and combining approaches. Third-degree tactics—physical force, threats of force or other physical, mental or psychological abuse—are illegal. Any information so obtained, including confessions, is inadmissible in court. Any confession, oral or handwritten, must be given of the suspect's free will and not in response to fear, threats, promises or rewards. A confession is only one part of the investigation. It must be corroborated by independent evidence.

Special considerations are also observed when questioning youths. Obtain parental permission before questioning a juvenile. Do not use a juvenile as an informant unless the parents know the situation.

In addition to skills in interviewing and interrogating, you can sometimes use scientific aids to obtain information and determine its truthfulness. The polygraph scientifically measures respiration and depth of breathing, changes in the skin's electrical resistance and blood pressure and pulse rate. It is an instrument used to verify the truth, not a substitute for investigating and questioning. Although the results are not presently admissible in court, any confession obtained as a result of a polygraph test is admissible. Other scientific aids include hypnosis and truth serums, but such aids must be monitored closely, and the results are seldom admissible in court.

Checklist
Obtaining Information

- Were the complainant, witnesses, victim and informants questioned?
- Were all witnesses found?
- Was all information recorded accurately?
- Was the questioning conducted in an appropriate place? At an appropriate time?
- Was the Miranda warning given to all suspects before questioning?
- Were the type of offense and offender considered in selecting the interviewing or interrogating techniques?
- Were answers obtained to the questions of who, what, where, when, why and how?
- Were all available reports and records checked? Sources of information file? Field identification cards? The National Crime Information Center?

Other police agencies? Public and private agencies at the local, county, state and national levels?

■ Were confidential informants sought?

■ Was a request for public assistance or an offer of a reward published?

■ Is there a private number to call or a private post office box to write to for persons who have information about a crime?

■ Was a polygraph used to check the validity of information given?

■ Were all statements, admissions and confessions rechecked against other verbal statements and against existing physical evidence?

■ Were those providing information thanked for their help?

■ Were all statements, admissions and confessions properly and legally obtained? Recorded? Witnessed? Filed?

Discussion Questions

1. What do you consider to be the essential steps in developing information about a crime?

2. What advantages do you see in the concept of *interroview?* What disadvantages?

3. Emphasis is often placed on obtaining a confession, or at least an admission, from a suspect in a criminal inquiry. Under what conditions is a confession of greatest value? Of no value?

4. The Miranda warning is now accepted by law enforcement agencies as a necessary requirement of interrogation under specific circumstances. What circumstances make it mandatory? What circumstances do not require its use?

5. Do you believe use of the Miranda warning has increased or decreased the number of confessions obtained in criminal cases?

6. How could polygraph results be used in plea bargaining?

7. What categories are included in your police department's sources of information file?

8. Should informants be protected by law from having to testify in court about information they have furnished police? What are the effects on

investigative procedures and the frequency of cases cleared if informants are not protected?

9. Criminals or others who give the police information about a crime that eventually leads to an arrest or a conviction are sometimes paid for the information. Is this a legitimate use of tax funds, or should private donations be used?

10. How accurate is the typical television portrayal of an informant?

References

Allread, Walter. "Language Skills Important." *Law and Order,* January 1999, pp. 44–47.

Bourne, Kathryn. "Preserving a Victim's Deathbed Declaration." *Police,* September 1996, pp. 8–9.

Burcum, Jill. "Jenson's Attorney Says His Confession Should Be Thrown Out." (Minneapolis/St. Paul) *Star Tribune,* September 2, 1999, pp. A1, A11.

Burke, Tod W. "Brain 'Fingerprinting': Latest Tool for Law Enforcement." *Law and Order,* June 1999, pp. 28–31.

"Cellular Phone Industry Enlisted to Help Fight Neighborhood Crime." (Minneapolis/St. Paul) *Star Tribune,* July 18, 1996.

Clede, Bill. "How Phone Companies Can Assist in Investigations." *Law and Order,* February 1997, pp. 43–46.

Clede, Bill. "Technology: It Helps Find the Truth." *Law and Order,* July 1998, pp. 91–93.

D'Arcy, Stephen. "Plugging into the Net." *The Police Chief,* February 1997, p. 16.

DeBeck, Michael. "Taking Advantage of the Internet." *The Police Chief,* January 1997, pp. 35–38.

Dees, Tim. "Law Enforcement Websites and the Machineless Fax." *Law and Order,* Vol. 47, No. 4, April 1999a, pp. 14–16.

Dees, Tim. "Notes-Based Software for Smaller Agencies." *Law and Order,* Vol. 47, No. 9, September 1999b, pp. 13–14.

DePresca, John. "Forensic Hypnosis." *Law and Order,* September 1996, pp. 79–82.

Dillingham, Christopher. "Deception in Law Enforcement Interrogations." *Law and Order,* October 1996, pp. 105–108.

Doyle, Pat and Furst, Randy. "Man Held in Tot's Death." (Minneapolis/St. Paul) *Star Tribune,* August 26, 1999, pp. A1, A16–A17.

Graves, Chris and Chanen, David. "Risk Comes with the Turf when Cooperating with Police." (Minneapolis/St. Paul) *Star Tribune,* February 28, 1999, p. B5.

Hall, Dennis. "California Law on Youth Informants Not Needed." *Police,* November 1998, p. 6.

Hall, E. Gene. "Watch Carefully Now: Solving Crime in the 21st Century." *Police,* June 1999, pp. 42–45.

Hess, Kären M. and Wrobleski, Henry M. *For the Record: Report Writing in Law Enforcement,* 4th ed., Bloomington, MN: Innovative Systems—Publishers, Inc., 1996.

Hight, James E. "Avoiding the Informant Trap: A Blueprint for Control." *FBI Law Enforcement Bulletin,* November 1998, pp. 1–5.

Kalk, Dan. "The Rights Stuff: Reviewing the Miranda Warnings." *Police,* October 1998, pp. 50–52.

Kelly, J.C. "The Officer's Dilemma: *Terry* 'Detention' or *Miranda* 'Custody.' " *The Police Chief,* January 1999, p. 10.

Morrison, Richard D. "Iridium—New Way to Communicate?" *Law Enforcement Technology,* July 1997, pp. 47–49.

Morrison, Richard D. "The 'Truth' About Truth Verification." *Law Enforcement Technology,* May 1999, pp. 66–69.

Napier, Michael R. and Adams, Susan H. "Magic Words to Obtain Confessions." *FBI Law Enforcement Bulletin,* October 1998, pp. 11–15.

O'Brien, John. "Psychics Try to Solve Crimes." *Las Vegas Review Journal,* November 7, 1996.

Redlick, James. "Old Law Learns New Tricks; Court Finds Miranda Loophole." *The Police Chief,* Vol. LXVI, No. 6, June 1999, p. 10.

Schuiteman, John. "Cellular Phones and Pagers for Police." *Law and Order,* Vol. 47, No. 6, June 1999, pp. 51–53.

Siuru, Bill. "Technology Aids Translators." *Law and Order,* June 1999, pp. 43–45.

Soto, Javier. "Informant Operations." *Law and Order,* October 1998, pp. 94–100.

"Spotting a Liar Is No Easy Task for Police." *Law Enforcement News,* Vol. XV, Nos. 511, 512, May 15/31, 1999, p. 7.

Strandberg, Keith W. "Guilty . . . In Their Own Words: Statement Analysis." *Law Enforcement Technology,* March 1998, pp. 52–54.

Sullivan, Michael J. "Obtaining and Recording Out of Court Statements." *Law and Order,* May 1998, pp. 105–108.

"Supreme Court Finds No Violation in Ban on Polygraph Evidence." *Criminal Justice Newsletter,* Vol. 29, No. 5, March 3, 1998, pp. 3–4.

"Supreme Court Will Back 1966 Miranda Ruling." *Las Vegas Review Journal,* February 12, 1999, p. 17A.

Vessel, David. "Conducting Successful Interrogations." *FBI Law Enforcement Bulletin,* October 1998, pp. 1–6.

Walker, Jayme. "Investigative Detentions: How Long Is Too Long?" *FBI Law Enforcement Bulletin,* Vol. 68, No. 8, August 1999, pp. 26–32.

Zack, Margaret. "Oversight May Free Mexican Held in Killing." (Minneapolis/St. Paul) *Star Tribune,* August 9, 1999, pp. B1–B2.

Zulawski, David E. and Wicklander, Douglas E. "Interrogations: Understanding the Process." *Law and Order,* July 1998, pp. 82–90.

Chapter 7

Identifying and Arresting Suspects

Can You Define?

arrest
"bugging"
close tail
cover
criminal profiling
electronic surveillance
entrapment
exceptional force
field identification
fixed surveillance
geographic profiling
lineup identification
loose tail
moving surveillance
National Crime Information
Center (NCIC-2000)
nightcap provision
photographic identification
plant
psychological profiling
raid
reasonable force
rough tail
solvability factors
stakeout
stationary surveillance
subject
surveillance
surveillant
tail
tight tail
undercover
wiretapping

Do You Know?

What field identification is and when it is used?

What rights a suspect has during field identification and what case established these rights?

How a suspect is developed?

How to help witnesses describe a suspect and/or a vehicle?

When mug shots are used?

What the NCIC is and how it assists in criminal investigations?

What the four basic means of identifying a suspect are?

What photographic identification requires and when it is used?

What a lineup requires and when it is used?

What rights suspects have regarding participation in a lineup and which cases established these rights?

When surveillance is used? What its objectives are?

What the types of surveillance are?

When wiretapping is legal and what the precedent case is?

What the objectives of undercover assignments are? What precautions you should take?

What the objectives of a raid are?

When raids are legal?

What precautions you should take when conducting a raid?

When you can make a lawful arrest?

When probable cause must exist for believing that a suspect has committed a crime?

What constitutes an arrest?

When force is justified in making an arrest? How much force is justified?

Introduction

The classic question in detective stories is "whodunit?" This question is also critical in criminal investigations. In some cases the suspect is obvious. Chanen (1999, p. B1) recounts:

> In between neighborhood visits during National Night Out . . . , Minneapolis Police Chief Robert Olson . . . heard [on the police scanner] an officer ask for a squad car to drive by the car she had pulled over.
>
> "She saw that the men in the car were acting funny and moving their feet like they were kicking something under the seat."
>
> Olson didn't hear any other squad cars responding, so he decided to cruise by the area. Before he arrived the officer got back on her portable radio and called dispatch for help.
>
> Two of the men stayed put, but the third took off running. The race was on.
>
> While her partner stayed behind, the officer chased the suspect down [the street], where a citizen attempted to help, Olson said. He grabbed the suspect by the shorts, which was all he was wearing. The man slipped away, but his white shorts stayed behind.
>
> "I heard the officer get on the radio and say 'He's naked.' " . . .
>
> The officer lost sight of the man . . . , but Olson saw him pop out from behind some brush. "I had no problem identifying the suspect," he said.

In most cases, there is no suspect initially. Although many crimes are witnessed, victims and witnesses may not recognize or be able to describe the suspect. Further, many crimes are not witnessed.

Factors crucial to resolving criminal investigations are called **solvability factors.** These are factors you should consider when deciding whether to investigate a crime. Among the most important are the existence of one or more witnesses and whether a suspect can be named or at least described and located.

Even if a suspect is known or has confessed, you must prove the elements of the crime and establish evidence connecting the suspect with the criminal act. Some cases require that suspects be developed, located, identified and then arrested. Others begin with an arrest and proceed to identification. No set sequence exists. Regardless of whether an arrest begins or ends an investigation, the arrest must be legal.

This chapter explains the most immediate form of suspect identification, field identification, and follows with a discussion of how to develop, locate and identify suspects, including photographic identification and lineup identification. Next is a description of three specialized areas of suspect development and identification: surveillances, undercover assignments and raids. The chapter concludes with a discussion of what constitutes a legal arrest and how much force is allowed when making an arrest. ■

Field Identification

If a suspect is apprehended while committing a crime, you can have witnesses identify the suspect. The same is generally true if the suspect is apprehended at or near the crime scene.

Field identification is on-the-scene identification of a suspect by a victim of or witness to a crime. Field identification must be made within minutes after the crime.

The critical element in field identification is *time.* Identification must occur very soon after the crime was committed (usually 15–20 minutes). If the suspect has fled but is apprehended within minutes, you can either return the suspect to the scene or take the witness to where the suspect was apprehended. It is usually preferable to take the witness to the suspect than to return the suspect to the crime scene.

Whether the identification is made at or away from the scene, the victim or witness must identify the suspect as soon after the crime as possible so that details are still clear. However, a reasonable basis must exist for believing that immediate identification is required before using field identification.

United States v Ash, Jr. (1973) established that a suspect does *not* have the right to have counsel present at a field identification.

Read suspects the Miranda warning before questioning them. Suspects may refuse to answer questions and may demand a lawyer before any questioning occurs, but they do not have the right to have a lawyer present before field identification is made. Suspects may not even know such identification is occurring. Victims or witnesses may be positioned so they can see the suspect while the suspect cannot see them.

Field identifications have been attacked on the basis that the victim or witness is too emotionally upset at the time to make an accurate identification, but such objections are seldom upheld. Mistaken identification is less likely if the person committing the crime is apprehended at the scene and is identified immediately. Have the victim or witnesses put their positive identification in writing, sign and date it and then have it witnessed.

Developing a Suspect

If a suspect is not at the scene and not apprehended nearby, you must develop a suspect.

Suspects are developed through the following means:

- Information provided by victims, witnesses and other persons likely to know about the crime or the suspect
- Physical evidence left at the crime scene
- Psychological profiling
- Information in police files
- Information in the files of other agencies
- Informants

Many sources are sometimes needed to develop a suspect. At other times the victim or witnesses provide the required information. Then your task is to corroborate the identification through associative evidence such as fingerprints or DNA analysis, shoe prints, personal belongings left at the scene, tools used, weapons, stolen property in the possession of the suspect, injuries sustained, soil in shoes, safe insulation and other such evidence described in Chapter 5. Police agencies also have automated fingerprint identification systems and computerized imaging systems to assist in identifying suspects.

Victims and Witnesses

Developing a suspect is much easier if the victim or witnesses can describe and identify the person who committed the crime. Witnesses may not have observed the actual crime but may have seen a vehicle leaving the scene and can describe the vehicle and its occupants. Obtain a complete description of the suspect and any vehicles involved.

Ask very specific questions and use an identification diagram to assist witnesses in describing suspects and vehicles.

Rather than simply asking a witness to describe a suspect, ask specific questions about each item in Table 7.1. A description sheet with a diagram also helps people to describe suspects (see Figure 7.1).

Obtain information about how the suspect left the scene—on foot or in a vehicle. If in a vehicle, obtain a complete description of it. Identifying the car may lead to identifying the suspect.

Victims can provide information about who has a motive for the crime, who has the knowledge required to commit it and who is not a likely suspect. For example, in an "inside" burglary, the employer may be able to provide important information about which employees might or might not be suspects.

Victim or eyewitness identification of a suspect should be corroborated by as much physical and circumstantial evidence as possible.

Mug Shots

If the victim or witness does not know the suspect but saw him or her clearly, mug shots may be used.

Have victims and witnesses view mug shots in an attempt to identify a suspect you believe has a record.

This procedure, frequently depicted in television detective shows, is very time consuming and is of value only if the suspect has a police record and has been photographed.

Table 7.1	Key Items in Suspect Identification

- Gender
- Height
- Weight
- Build—stout, average, slim, stooped, square-shouldered
- Age
- Nationality
- Face—long, round, square, fat, thin; pimples, acne, scars
- Complexion—flushed, sallow, pale, fair, dark
- Hair—color; thick, thin, partly bald, completely bald; straight, curly, wavy; long, short
- Forehead—high, low; sloping, straight, bulging
- Eyebrows—bushy, thin, average
- Eyes—color; close together or wide-set; large, small; glasses or sunglasses
- Nose—small, large; broad, narrow; crooked, straight; long, short
- Ears—small, large; close to head or protruding; pierced
- Mustache—color; short, long; thick, thin; pointed ends
- Mouth—large; small; drooping, upturned
- Lips—thick, thin
- Teeth—missing, broken, prominent, gold, conspicuous dental work
- Beard—color; straight, rounded; bushy, thin; long, short
- Chin—square, round, broad; long, narrow; double, sagging
- Neck—long, short; thick, thin
- Distinctive marks—scars, moles, amputations, tattoos
- Peculiarities—peculiar walk or talk, twitch, stutter, foreign accent, distinctive voice or dialect
- Clothing—shabby or well-dressed, monograms, association with an occupation or hobby, general description
- Weapon—(if any) specific type, how carried, how displayed and when
- Jewelry—any obvious rings, bracelets, necklaces, earrings, watches

Composite Drawings and Sketches

If witnesses can provide adequate information, a composite image can be made of the person who committed the crime. Composite drawings are most commonly used to draw human faces or full bodies, but they can also be used for any inanimate object described by a witness—for example, vehicles, unusual marks or symbols, tattoos or clothing. Such composite sketches are usually created with the help of a police artist or an identification kit such as Identi-Kit, although some training is required to use these computerized kits.

DESCRIPTION SHEET

Complete the form below as soon after a crime as you can, then give it to the FBI, Police or Sheriff
IN THE EVENT OF A CRIME, THE FIRST QUESTION THE FBI, POLICE OR SHERIFF WILL ASK IS "WHAT DID THE INDIVIDUAL LOOK LIKE?"

HAT(color, style, condition) __none__

HAIR (color, thick, thin, straight, curly, hair part, style of combing)
__brown - straight back__

EYES (close or far set, color, small or large)
__blue__

EARS (small or large, close to head or extended)
__normal__

NOSE (small, large, broad, narrow, long, short)
__large - pimply__

CHIN (square, broad, long, narrow)
__normal__

COMPLEXION (light, dark, ruddy, pale, etc.)
__dark - tanned__

SHIRT __plaid - blue__

TIE or SCARF __none__

COAT or JACKET __none__

GLOVES __cotton work__

TROUSERS __corduroy__

SOCKS __didn't notice__

SHOES __cowboy boots__

RACE __White__

SEX __Male__

AGE __30-35__

HEIGHT __6-0 to 6-1__

WEIGHT __185-195__

PHYSICAL CHARACTERISTICS (describe whether slight or heavy build, scars, marks, manner of walking, tattoos, mustache, nervous, calm, etc.)
WEAPONS AND EQUIPMENT (note whether pistol, revolver, rifle, shotgun, knife, etc., were used by robber)
REMARKS (note here anything that the robber may have said, his accent, whether he used any names, his movements, etc.)

SUBMITTED BY __Majorie Stills__

TIME & DATE OF CRIME __1140 4-6-00__

YOUR ADDRESS __115 Stilling Ct.__

YOUR PHONE NUMBER __702-284-5674__

FIGURE 7.1
Witness Identification Diagram

Identi-Kit 2000 is a computerized version of the original Identi-Kit that was developed in the late 1950s. The process starts with a police officer asking a series of initial questions which creates a general composite, or likeness, of a suspect based on a victim's or witness's description. After creating a general composite, officers can fine tune the image of the criminal. Identi-Kit 2000 provides the opportunity to look at the entire face as opposed to looking at partial facial features. The product is currently used by over 1,700 police departments throughout the country ("Identi-Kit 2000 . . . ," 1998, pp. 33–35).

Florida A&M University bombing suspect Lawrence Michael Lombardi, right, is lead out of the federal courthouse in Tallahassee, Florida, by a U.S. Marshal in October 1999. Lombardi was arrested in connection with two racist bombings at the predominantly black university after he was recognized on a hardware store surveillance tape buying the pipe used in the blasts, the FBI said.

Other software such as CompuSketch or Visatex is also becoming more popular for drafting computer-generated composites. Police officers may also be trained to sketch freehand while interviewing a victim or witness. Sketching courses may be available at local colleges or through the FBI Academy.

Psychological or Criminal Profiling

One method of suspect identification is **psychological** or **criminal profiling,** which attempts to identify an individual's mental, emotional and psychological characteristics. Cook and Hinman (1999, p. 230) state: "Criminal profiling is a useful investigative technique that combines art and science." Abnormal, criminal behavior patterns and the characteristics of criminals who have committed specific types of crimes have been studied for many years. This research provides the basis for psychological profiling.

Profiles are developed primarily for crimes of violence such as homicides, sadistic crimes, sex crimes, arson without apparent motive and crimes of serial or ritual sequence. Davis (1999, p. 291) asserts: "The manner in which a violent crime is performed expresses the psychological pattern, makeup, and expression of the individual performing it." The profile provides investigators with corroborative information about a known suspect or possible leads to an unknown suspect. Barrientos (1996, p. 29A) states:

> Profilers jump in when a case is baffling or particularly gruesome, or when local detectives need help narrowing down their suspects. . . .
>
> Basically . . . a profiler's job is to answer the one question that hangs over any terrible crime scene: "What sort of person could do this?" . . .
>
> When profilers are trying to find a killer, they pore over photos of crime scenes as if they were children searching for Waldo, scavenging for the smallest clues, for what they call the offender's "signature."
>
> Each offender's signature is different, like a fingerprint.

Although profilers contend their work is not glamorous, Cook and Hinman (p. 230) note: "Criminal profiling of serial killers has captured the public's fancy more than any other law enforcement investigative technique."

The psychological profile is determined by examining all data and evidence from a specific crime scene, including, but not limited to, crime-scene photographs, detailed photos of bodily injuries to victims, photos of any mutilation evidence, information related to the condition of the victim's clothing or absence thereof, information regarding whether the crime scene was altered or unaltered, photos of the area beyond the immediate crime scene, available maps of the area, the medical examiner's report and opinion and any other relevant information concerning the crime, particularly abnormalities such as multiple slashings, disembowelment, drinking of the victim's blood, beheading or dismembering the body.

Specific information is then categorized to produce predictive information regarding the suspect's likely age, sex, race, weight, height; physical, mental and psychological condition; area of residence; whether known to the victim; whether the suspect has a criminal record; and other details.

The psychological profile produced by experts in criminal behavior analysis can provide excellent leads for investigators. Investigators who desire such assistance may provide a complete crime report to the local office of the FBI, Domestic Cooperative Services. If the report

is accepted, it is then forwarded to the FBI Behavioral Science Unit.

Egger (1999, pp. 256–257) elaborates:

> As with many processes . . . the computer is playing a greater role [in profiling]. Attempts have been made to computerize the process of offender profiling in the last few years; however, few have been successful . . . . Possibly the program with the greatest success in computerizing the profiling process has been the Surrey Police Behavioral Science Section's development of the Behavioral Analysis Data Management Auto-indexing Networking System (BADMAN). This system application, although initially aimed at sexual assaultive crimes, will deal with a full range of crimes when it becomes fully operational. BADMAN currently provides support in four areas:
>
> ■ The identification of possible suspects
> ■ Case linking by behavior
> ■ Preparation of similar fact evidence
> ■ Criminal profiling

In one criminal investigation, the FBI's Behavioral Science Unit advised a police department that the serial rapist they were seeking was probably a 25–35-year-old, divorced or separated white male, with a high-school education who worked as a laborer, lived in the area of the rapes and engaged in voyeurism. Based on this information, the agency developed a list of 40 suspects with these characteristics. Using other information in the profile, they narrowed their investigation to one suspect and focused on him. Within a week they had enough information to arrest him.

Another case involved the rape/murder of a 25-year-old white married woman. The criminal profiler told a very surprised detective that he had probably already interviewed the killer. The profiler gave the detective a scenario based on color photographs, physical evidence and interviews.

Interestingly, William Tafoya of the FBI developed a psychological profile of the Unibomber that many rejected. However, after the arrest of Theodore Kaczynski, Tafoya's assessment was observed to be much more accurate than many in the FBI had believed.

Psychological profiling is most often used in crimes against people in which a motive is unknown. The profile seeks to disclose a possible motive. Continued use of the technique has shown that the more information the police furnish to the FBI, the greater the possibility of obtaining accurate leads. Reporting the unusual is extremely important. Psychological profiling can help to both eliminate and develop suspects, thereby saving investigative time. Davis (p. 291) notes that, although profiling is not intended to replace conventional, traditional investigative police work, "law enforcement agencies are beginning to realize the benefits of this technique as a viable investigative tool."

Since 1991 the International Criminal Investigative Analysis Fellowship (ICIAF) has been training law enforcement officers in criminal profiling, including the behavioural approach to investigating homicides, sexual assaults, arsons, bombing and child abductions (Lines, 1999, p. 49).

Geographic Profiling

As Pilant (1999, p. 38) explains: "**Geographic profiling** takes conventional crime mapping techniques and turns them inside out. Instead of predicting the date or the site of the next crime, it takes the locations of past crimes and using a complex mathematical algorithm, calculates probabilities of the suspect's residence." According to MacKay (1999, p. 51): "Geographic profiling can help investigators:

■ Prioritize suspect lists.
■ Direct patrol saturation and static stakeouts.
■ Conduct neighborhood canvases.
■ Limit the sample size for forensic testing."

Racial Profiling

Racial profiling occurs when an officer focuses on an individual as a suspect based solely on that person's race. Strandberg (1999, p. 62) asks:

If a bulletin states a suspect in a robbery is an Arab, 5-foot 10-inches tall and driving a late-model tan car, and the officer stops people fitting this description, is it racial profiling?

If . . . statistics say the majority of drug arrests in one particular neighborhood have been Jamaican males, ages 18 to 24, and you spot a Jamaican male acting strangely, and . . . stop him and ask some questions, is that racial profiling?

If you're searching for a gunman, . . . described as a white male, 6 foot 2 inches tall, and you stop the first white man that's about that height, is that racial profiling?

The examples above, from a law enforcement perspective, are considered standard police work. That's what the general public doesn't understand.

The problem occurs when officers single out people based on their race alone, not in combination with other identifying features. Indeed, the IACP recommends zero tolerance for officers who commit racial profiling and advocates they "be weeded out of the force" (Strandberg, p. 65). Kennedy (1998, p. 29) observes: "The great majority of police officers, lawyers, and judges would agree that acting *solely* on the basis of race would be wrong and is illegal. The controversial issue is whether police ought to be allowed to use race *at all* in determining suspicion." Strandberg, however, notes (p. 66): "The 'catch 22' of it all is that race is part of the general description."

Kennedy (p. 30) recounts the case of *United States v Weaver* (1992), in which a DEA agent stopped and questioned Arthur Weaver at a Kansas City airport "because he was 'roughly dressed,' young, black, and on a direct flight from Los Angeles, a source city for drugs." Kennedy (pp. 30–31) further notes:

Although the young man, as it turned out, was carrying illicit drugs, he challenged the legality of the officer's intervention. The Eighth Circuit Court of Appeals upheld the officer's conduct and . . . explained its position in this way:

Facts are not to be ignored simply because they may be unpleasant—and the unpleasant fact in this case is that the [DEA agent] had knowledge, based upon his own experience and upon the intelligence reports he had received from Los Angeles authorities, that young, male members of the African-American Los Angeles gangs were flooding the Kansas City area with cocaine. To that extent then, race, when coupled with the other factors [the agent] relied upon, was a factor in the decision to approach and ultimately detain [the suspect]. We wish it were otherwise, but we take the facts as they are presented to us, not as we would wish them to be.

What may, in fact, appear to be discriminatory might simply be the result of a community's ethnic and racial composition. A sergeant in San Diego explains (Strandberg, p. 63): "In our city, in certain sections of certain communities, for example, a higher percentage of all of our stops are going to be Latino. On the west side, it's mostly white, so more whites are going to be stopped. In the African-American communities, more stops are going to be African-American."

Strandberg (p. 65) notes that officers need to be extra conscious of their reasons for stopping people, as if they had to defend every action in court. "Almost any case can be perceived as racially motivated if there is a person of color involved, so it makes sense for law enforcement to go out of its way to explain the reasoning and procedures behind every stop, every detainment, every arrest."

Tracking

Sometimes a knowledge of tracking is helpful. Hanratty (1998, p. 39) notes: "Forensic tracking can be described as the science of locating, retaining and interpreting footprint impressions for the purpose of solving criminal cases. This type of tracking consists of three parts: man tracking, footprint interpretation and footwear impression evidence recovery." Lee (1998, p. 26) mentions: "In the world of wildlife law enforcement, man tracking is still frequently used. Given these opportunities to practice and improve, most wildlife officers have extensive skills in this area."

The length of stride and depth of impression of footprints can help to determine the size or height of the person or whether the person was carrying a heavy load. Yet tracking skill can be developed for impressions other than footprints, which can provide many investigative leads. For example, the direction of vehicle travel from a crime scene can be determined by tire-tread marks. People hiding in outside areas may leave foot, knee, hand, heel or body impressions. Broken tree branches provide evidence of when the branch was broken; the lighter the color of the break, the more recent it is. Recent overturning of a stone may be indicated by the dirt or by the moist side being on top.

Other Identification Aids

Visual aids such as newspaper photos or video and news films disseminated to the public may provide rapid identification of suspects. Canon (1997, p. 21A) notes: "In many precincts around the country, detectives routinely gather yearbooks to show to victims and witnesses when a student might be involved in a crime." Fingerprints and footprints are other commonly used means of positive identification, and voiceprints and DNA profiling are becoming more frequently used.

If a suspect or victim is deceased and the identity is unknown, dental and orthopedic records may help. Facial reconstruction is also used in many areas to identify unknown victims or suspects if sufficient skull and facial parts are available. Amazing likenesses can be achieved to assist in identifying unknown deceased persons.

Developing a Suspect through Modus Operandi Information

A series of crimes often creates a recognizable modus operandi, such as forgers who use the same or a very similar name on each forgery or burglars who take the same type of property. If a series of burglaries occurs at the same time of day, this may be the suspect's time away from a regular job. Such MOs furnish important investigative leads.

Check the details of a specific crime against your department's MO files. If no similar MO is listed, a new criminal may be starting activity in your area, or this may be the only crime the suspect intends to commit. In such cases, the suspect must be developed through sources other than modus operandi information.

Information in Police Files and Files of Other Agencies

Police records on solved crimes and on suspects involved in certain types of crimes often suggest leads. For example, in the "Son of Sam" case in New York City, one lead was provided by a woman who saw an illegally parked car that fit the description of the car reported as being used in the crimes. Police then checked all parking tickets issued on that date for that time and location. This information, combined with other information, eventually led to the suspect.

Police files contain considerable information about people who commit or are suspected of committing crimes. The files contain such information as the person's physical characteristics, date of birth, age, race, general build, kind of clothing usually worn, height, weight, hair color and style, facial features and unusual marks, tattoos, deformities, abnormalities, alcohol or drug use, MO and other information.

Field-interview cards that patrol officers file when they stop people under suspicious circumstances can also provide leads. An officer may not know of an actual crime committed at the time of a stop but may later learn that a business or residence in the area of the stop was burglarized at about the same time. Descriptions of vehicles in a high-crime area that do not fit the neighborhood also help to identify suspects.

If the MO is discernible or if you have a good description of the suspect, check with other police departments in the area. Review all reports on the case and any cases that seem similar. Many other official sources of information at all levels of government as well as private agencies can also provide leads in developing and locating a suspect.

Although police files contain a wealth of information, unfortunately, the information often is not shared because of "serious information gaps . . . caused by the multiple, often incompatible computer systems" used within a state as well as from state to state (Klobuchar, 1999, p. D4).

Community Level Almost every department of community government can provide some type of information during a criminal investigation. These sources include the city clerk, city attorney's office, municipal court, finance office, public utilities, building inspectors, public works departments, voter registration records, school files, welfare files and civil service files. Local agencies can often furnish names, birthdates, addresses, changes of address, occupations, places of birth, parents' names, family names, property ownership, legal descriptions of property, proposed businesses and business ownership, prior employment, past criminal offenses and many other details. Banks and credit unions are another excellent source of information.

County Level Sources of information at the county level include the treasury department, the health department, engineering departments, license bureaus, the assessor's office, courts, probate courts, the welfare department, the coroner's office, civil service, the building inspector, the register of deeds, the sheriff's office and the fire marshal. Such sources can furnish information on the payroll of county employees, names, addresses, changes of address, employment and building inspections. County agencies are also a source for birth and death certificates showing parents' names, maps, legal descriptions and values of property, deeds, mortgages, court records, marriage license and divorce records, handwriting specimens, criminal records, business listings, diagrams of buildings and similar information.

Some counties are developing ways to link these sources of information to make investigations more efficient and effective. For example, Paynter (1999a, p. 45) describes Los Angeles County's new Consolidated Criminal History Reporting System (CCHRS):

> CCHRS uses an Oracle data server to provide almost real-time data from multiple source systems, including the L.A. County court system, the L.A. County Sheriff's Department criminal history information system and jail system, the district attorney's information system, the juvenile automated index, the state Department of Justice system, the state Department of Motor Vehicles system, and county, state and FBI warrant systems.

> Furthermore (p. 45): "The system is also fingerprint-based to ensure greater accuracy of the data. . . . [So] it doesn't matter whether a suspect comes in and tells us his name is 'John Doe' or 'Jim Smith.' We have his fingerprints and the information listed with them belongs to him."

State Level State agencies from which information is available include the liquor control board, secretary of state, highway department, highway patrol, bureau of investigation, bureau of narcotics and drug abuse, fish and game agency, insurance department, motor vehicles department, personnel department, state supreme court, state board of probation and parole, state prisons and juvenile detention facilities. These agencies provide access to criminal records within the restrictions of the Privacy and Security Act, vehicle registrations, real estate sales records, licensing information, names, present and past addresses, business associates, civil suits, election information, birth and death records and other personal information.

Federal Level The federal government has many agencies, not only in Washington, DC, but also in regional offices throughout the United States, that provide information valuable in developing and locating suspects. The investigative agencies of the U.S. Navy, Army, Marines, Coast Guard, Merchant Marine and Air Force can provide much information. Other federal sources include the Civil Service Commission; Department of Health, Education and Welfare; Internal Revenue Service; Department of Commerce; Federal Bureau of Investigation; Central Intelligence Agency; Secret Service; State Department; Immigration and Naturalization Service; Federal Communications Commission; Postal Service; Interstate Commerce Commission; Department of Labor; Federal Aviation Administration; Veterans Administration; Department of the Interior; and task forces on organized crime activities. Such agencies provide information on military service, military criminal records, census data, drug abuse and narcotics involvement, aliens, firearms registration, plane registration and licensing, as well as information on security investigations.

One of the most important federal-level information sources is the FBI's National Crime Information Center (NCIC):

> On July 11, 1999, the 30-year-old NCIC was replaced by NCIC-2000, a $183 million system serving more than 80,000 criminal justice agencies throughout the country. The new system can process more than 2.4 million transactions a day and provides access to over 39 million records. The records include information on stolen vehicles, articles and securities and guns; wanted persons; gangs, gang members and terrorists ("NCIC-2000 Goes Online," 1999, p. 8).

- - - - - - - -

The FBI's **National Crime Information Center (NCIC-2000)** contains criminal fingerprint records and information on wanted criminals and stolen property, including vehicles and guns.

- - - - - - - -

The new capabilities associated with NCIC-2000 include the addition of image processing (i.e., mugshot, signature, identifying marks), the addition of automated single-finger fingerprint matching, the automation of some NCIC functions that are currently manually performed (e.g., validation, collection of benefits data), access to new databases (e.g., Convicted Persons on Supervised Release), the addition of linkage fields, which will provide the ability to associate multiple records with the same criminal or the same crime, access to external databases (e.g., the Federal Bureau of Prisons' "SENTRY" database) and the automatic collection of statistics for system evaluation ("NCIC-2000," p. 8).

Image transmission to and from officers in the field is one goal of NCIC-2000. The ability to have photographs and fingerprints sent within seconds to and from a patrol car provides officers with information about whether an individual temporarily detained is a wanted person on file at a local, state or national level.

Another federal information source is the FBI's Uniform Crime Reports (UCR) and its evolving National Incident Based Reporting System (NIBRS). The advantage of the NIBRS is that it reports every crime that occurs instead of just the most serious crime or event. As Hoffmann (2000, p. 31) explains: "Under the UCR/Summary requirements if two holdup men rob 18 customers in a restaurant and then shoot and kill the manager on the way out, you report just one murder. Under NIBRS you report one murder and 18 armed-robberies."

The Internet As with other aspects of police investigation, the Internet is a valuable resource in suspect location and identification. One article ("CertiFINDER Uses . . . ," 1999, p. 88) states: "There's a whole wide world of suspect information online."

> LEXIS-NEXIS offers a Web-based report service to help law enforcement . . . find suspects quicker . . . CertiFINDER searches public records and newspapers nationwide. . . . LEXIS-NEXIS has compiled more than 2.3 billion documents online in nearly 9,876 databases. Its warehouse is larger than the World Wide Web, and grows . . . about 30 percent each year . . . .
>
> CertiFINDER searches corporate and limited partnership registrations, doing-business-as and fictitious name registrations, obituaries and death notices, professional licenses, aircraft registrations, boat registrations, deed transfers and tax assessor records, bankruptcy filings, liens and judgment filings, crime indices and Social Security Administration death benefits lists. . . .
>
> Plans for CertiFINDER include additional sources such as marriage records, divorce decrees, driver's licenses and motor vehicle registrations.

Alvaro (2000, p. 44) also notes: "Tomorrow's criminal bounty hunters might well turn out to be surfers who find that they can profit from online access to a plethora of crime-fighting tools and information." Alvaro (p. 47) further suggests: "Use of websites to fight crime is likely to gain greater acceptance as a useful and important tool as more and more law enforcement agencies and citizens become connected, awareness of crimefighter sites increases, and, ultimately, search engines develop the ability to help locate missing persons."

INTERPOL The International Criminal Police Organization (INTERPOL) is a network of national central bureaus (NCBs) in 177 member-countries. Originated in 1914 and headquartered in Lyon, France, INTERPOL compiles and dispenses information on criminals and cases that cross national boundaries. Imhoff and Cutler (1998, p. 11) state: "INTERPOL connects its worldwide offices through a secure communications network that enables confidential and instantaneous handling of messages and leads for international criminal investigations."

The main U.S. office is in Washington, DC, and INTERPOL has operations in all the states. Available 24 hours a day to public law enforcement, INTERPOL's telecommunications network links it with nearly all U.S. investigative agencies such as the DEA, FBI, CIA and the Treasury Department. Imhoff and Cutler (1999, p. 33) point out that: "A law enforcement investigator does not need to 'join' INTERPOL. There are no dues or user fees. A police agency is welcome to utilize INTERPOL services by virtue of its country's membership."

INTERPOL can provide information on the location of suspects, fugitives and witnesses; criminal history checks; terrorists; stolen artworks, weapons and motor vehicles; and license plate traces. Lorenson (1998, pp. 32–33) notes the USNCB office in Washington, DC, has five investigative divisions:

- The Investigative Services Division
- The Alien/Fugitive Investigative Division
- The Financial Fraud Investigative Division
- The Drug Investigative Division
- The Criminal Investigative Division

Law enforcement officers may contact the USNCB online at usdoj.gov/usncb/interpol.htm.

Private Agencies Many private agencies also assist in developing and locating suspects. These include gas and electric companies, credit bureaus, financial institutions, educational facilities, the National Auto Theft Bureau, telephone companies, moving companies, Better Business Bureaus, taxi companies, real estate sales and rental agencies, laundry and dry-cleaning associations and insurance underwriters. Check your local city directory for possible additional private sources of information.

Informants

Informants have been a source of police information for centuries, as discussed in Chapter 6. Informants may work in a position that places them in frequent contact with criminals, or they may have committed crimes themselves or be associates of active criminals.

Most informants closely associated with the criminal world insist on remaining anonymous. This is usually to law enforcement's advantage because much information would no longer be available to informants if their cooperation with the police were known. Assign a code name to such informants and keep records of their information in a confidential file to help preserve their anonymity. Be aware of circumstances under which anonymity cannot be preserved and make informants aware of these circumstances.

One disadvantage of using anonymous informants is that information they provide is not accepted as evidence in court. It must be independently corroborated. However, such information can save much investigative time and lead to the recovery of valuable property or the arrest of suspects.

The information that some informants provide is of such value in solving or preventing crimes that the informants are paid. Many police agencies, at all levels of government, have informant-payment funds. Care must be used in paying informants because the payment motivates some of them to give contrived, false information. Cross-checking for truthfulness is required, and informants' reliability should be documented for future reference.

Departments that use community-oriented policing may develop informants more easily because officers are closer to the people in their patrol area. Because of the negative connotations of the word *informant,* many agencies refer to these individuals as *citizens who assist the police with information.*

Locating Suspects

Many information sources used to develop a suspect can also help to locate the suspect. If the suspect is local and frequents public places, the victim may see the suspect and call the police. In one instance, a rape victim saw the alleged rapist in a shopping center and remembered that she had seen him there just before her rape occurred. The investigator accompanied the victim to the shopping center for several evenings until the victim saw the suspect and identified him.

Telephone calls to other investigative agencies, neighborhood inquiries at the suspect's last known address, questioning relatives, checking the address on a prison release form, utility checks and numerous other contacts can help locate suspects.

Identifying Suspects

- - - - - - - - -

Suspects can be identified through field identification, mug shots, photographic identification or lineups.

- - - - - - - - -

Field identification and mug shots have been discussed previously.

Photographic Identification

Often the victim or witnesses get a good look at the suspect and are able to make a positive identification.

- - - - - - - - -

Use **photographic identification** when you have a good idea of who committed the crime but the suspect is not in custody or when a fair lineup cannot be conducted. Tell witnesses they need not identify anyone from the photographs.

- - - - - - - - -

Photographs can be obtained through surveillance or from files. Select pictures of at least five people of comparable race, height, weight and general appearance. The photographs can be kept separate or mounted on a composite board. Write a number or code on the back of each photograph to identify the individual, but do not include any other information, especially information that the person has a criminal record. Tell witnesses that they need not identify anyone from among the photographs and that it is as important to eliminate innocent people from suspicion as it is to identify the guilty.

If there are several witnesses, have each one view a separate set of pictures independently—preferably in a different room if other witnesses are viewing the photographs at the same time. If witnesses recognize a photograph, have them indicate that by placing their initials and the date on the front side. Then have them initial and date the back side of each remaining picture. This procedure establishes the fairness of the identification.

It is unwise to show a single photograph to a victim or witness to obtain identification. Such identification is almost always inadmissible as evidence because it allows little chance of mistaken identity. The Supreme Court decision in *Manson v Brathwaite* (1977), however, did approve the showing of a single picture in specific circumstances.

After identification is made, review with the witness the conditions under which the suspect was seen, including lighting at the time and distance from the suspect.

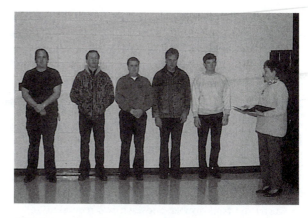

This lineup shows five suspects of comparable race, height, weight, age and general appearance in accordance with lineup standards set by the U.S. Supreme Court.

- - - - - - - - -

A suspect does not have the right to a lawyer if a photographic lineup is used (*United States v Ash, Jr.,* 1973).

- - - - - - - - -

Lineup Identification

Lineup identification is commonly used when the suspect is in custody and there were witnesses to the crime. Police have adopted lineup procedures to ensure accurate, fair identifications and to meet the standards established by Supreme Court decisions. Basically, a lineup has the same requirements as photographic identification.

- - - - - - - - -

Use lineup identification when the suspect is in custody. Use at least five individuals of comparable race, height, weight, age and general appearance. Ask all to perform the same actions or speak the same words. Instruct those viewing the lineup that they need not make an identification.

- - - - - - - - -

Lineups may have from five to ten people. The suspect must not be of a different race, exceptionally taller or shorter, have longer or shorter hair or be dressed very differently from the others in the lineup. The suspect must not be handcuffed unless everyone in the lineup is handcuffed. Nor may the suspect be asked to step forward, turn a certain direction or speak certain words unless everyone in the lineup is asked to do the same.

- - - - - - - - -

Suspects may refuse to participate in a lineup, but such refusals can be used against them in court (*Schmerber v California*). Suspects have a right to have an attorney present during a lineup (*United States v Wade*).

- - - - - - - - -

In *United States v Wade* (1967) on September 21, 1964, a robber forced a cashier and a bank official to place money in a pillowcase. The robber had a piece of tape on each side of his face. After obtaining the money, he left the bank and drove away with an accomplice who had been waiting outside in a car.

In March 1965, an indictment was returned against Wade and an accomplice for the bank robbery. He was arrested April 2, 1965. Approximately two weeks later, an FBI agent put Wade in a lineup to be observed by bank employees. Wade's counsel was not notified of the lineup. Each person in the lineup had strips of tape similar to those worn by the bank robber, and each was requested to say words allegedly spoken at the robbery. Both bank employees picked Wade out of the lineup as being the robber, and both employees again identified Wade in the courtroom.

The defense objected that the bank officials' courtroom identifications should be stricken because the original lineup had been conducted without the presence of Wade's counsel. The motion was denied, and Wade was found guilty. Counsel held that this violated his Fifth Amendment right against self-incrimination and his Sixth Amendment right to counsel being present at the lineup.

The *Wade* decision ruled that: "Prior to having a suspect participate in a lineup, the officer must advise the suspect of his constitutional right to have his lawyer present during the lineup." Recall that this right to a lawyer does not apply to field identification or photographic identification. If suspects waive their right to counsel, get the waiver in writing. A waiver such as the one in Figure 7.2 can be used.

The Court held that a suspect has the right to have counsel present at the lineup because a lineup is held for identification by eyewitnesses and may involve vagaries leading to mistaken identification. The Court cited the many cases of mistaken identification and the improper manner in which the suspect may have been presented. The Court commented that neither the lineup nor anything that Wade was required to do in the lineup violated his privilege against self-incrimination.

The Court stated in *Schmerber v California* (1966) that protection against self-incrimination involved disclosure of knowledge by the suspect. Both state and federal courts have held that compulsion to submit to photographs, writing, speaking, fingerprints, measurements or blood analysis is not self-incrimination under the Fifth Amendment.

If the suspect refuses to participate in the lineup or a lineup cannot be conducted for some reason, simply photograph the suspect and each individual in the lineup separately and use photographic identification.

- - - - - - - -

Avoid having the same person make both photographic and lineup identification. If you do so, do not conduct both within a short time period.

- - - - - - - -

If suspects choose to have a lawyer, they may either select their own or ask you to obtain one. The lawyer may confer with the suspect in private before the lineup and may talk with witnesses observing the lineup, but witnesses are not obligated to talk with the lawyer. Witnesses may wear face covers to avoid recognition by the suspect. Usually the lineup room ensures viewers' anonymity.

Give witnesses clear instructions before the lineup. Tell them that they need not identify anyone in the lineup, that they are not to confer with any other witnesses viewing the lineup and that they are not to indicate an identification in any way. Tape-record or videotape the proceedings and take a color photograph of the lineup to nullify any allegations by the defense counsel of an unfair lineup. The form in Figure 7.3 provides additional evidence of the fairness and reliability of a lineup identification.

Photo Identification Lineup Paynter

(1999b, p. 98) describes a new imaging technology that facilitates the recognition and identification of suspects, missing people, parolees and convicted criminals:

> InSpeck-3D is a computer-aided non-contact optical 3D digitizer that measures the 3D form and texture of a given surface. The 3D models . . . later can be imported into popular 3D-modeling and animated software for skull reconstructions, age progressions and photo lineups.

Furthermore (p. 100):

> The information . . . also could be used to generate a 3D police lineup. . . . You could generate images of [a suspect] from different angles and different lighting conditions.

WAIVER OF RIGHT TO LEGAL COUNSEL AT LINEUP

Your Rights Are: The police are requesting you to personally appear in a lineup. There will be a number of other persons similiar in physical characteristics with you. The purpose of the lineup is to permit witnesses to observe all persons in the lineup, to make an identification. You may be asked to perform certain actions such as speaking, walking or moving in a certain manner or to put on articles of clothing. You must appear in the lineup, but you have a right to have legal cousel of your choice present. If you do not have an attorney, one can be appointed for you by the court, and the lineup will not be held until your legal counsel is present. An attorney can help you defend against an identification made by witnesses at the lineup.

You have the right to waive legal counsel being present at the lineup.

WAIVER

I have read, or have had read to me, this statement of my rights and I understand these rights. I am willing to participate in a lineup in the absence of legal counsel. I fully understand and give my consent to what I am being asked to do. No promises or threats have been made to me, and no pressure of coercion has been used against me. I understand that I must appear in the lineup, but this consent is to the waiver of legal counsel being present at the lineup.

Signed   Place

Witness   Date

Witness   Time

FIGURE 7.2 *Sample Waiver*

Surveillances, Undercover Assignments and Raids

"Follow that car!" "I think we're being tailed!" "I lost him!" "My cover's blown!" "We've been made!" "It's a raid!" Police officers, criminals and the public are very aware of investigative practices such as observing suspects, their houses or apartments; tailing suspects; staking out locations; and conducting raids. Television shows and movies, however, usually depict the glamorous, danger-ous sides of this facet of investigation. We seldom see the long hours of preparation or the days—even weeks—of tedious watchfulness frequently required.

> Surveillance, undercover assignments and raids are used only when normal methods of continuing the investigation fail to produce results.

These techniques are expensive and potentially danger-ous and are not routinely used.

POLICE REPORT OF LINEUP

Boulder City Police
Police Department

Name of suspect ___John Vance___ Birth date ___2-14-1964___

Address ___1424 Colten Street, Boulder City___

Case Number ___6432___ Complainant or victim ___Thelma Crump___

Name of legal counsel ___John Simmons___ Present: Yes _X_ No _____

Was waiver signed: Yes _X_ No _____

Place of lineup ___Las Vegas, Nevada, Police Dept.___

Date of lineup ___5-12-00___ Time of lineup ___1640___

Names of persons in lineup (left to right, facing the lineup)

	Name	Height	Weight	Birth date	Other
1.	Charles Upright	5-11	184	4-10-1966	
2.	Gary Starrick	5-10	178	2-14-1965	
3.	Jerry Stilter	5-11	190	10-11-1967	
4.	Ralph Barrett	5-10	185	12-24-1968	
5.	John Vance	5-10	183	2-14-1964	
6.	Christian Dolph	5-11	190	6-12-1964	
7.					
8.					
9.					
10.					

Subject identified by witness: Number ___5___ Name ___John Vance___

Recording taken of lineup: Yes _X_ No ___ Photos taken of lineup: Yes _X_ No ___

Persons present at lineup ___Thelma Crump   Alfred Nener___

___John Simmons   Emmanuel Sorstick___

Person conducting lineup ___Sgt. Lloyd Brenner, LVPD___

FIGURE 7.3 *Police Report of Lineup*

Surveillance

Surveillance (literally, "to watch over") is the covert, discreet observation of people or places.

- - - - - - - -

The objective of surveillance is to obtain information about people, their associates and their activities that may help to solve a criminal case or to protect witnesses.

- - - - - - - -

Surveillance can help do the following:

- Gain information required for building a criminal complaint.
- Determine an informant's loyalty.
- Verify a witness's statement about a crime.
- Gain information required for obtaining a search or arrest warrant.
- Gain information necessary for interrogating a suspect.

- Identify a suspect's associates.
- Observe members of terrorist organizations.
- Find a person wanted for a crime.
- Observe criminal activities in progress.
- Make a legal arrest.
- Apprehend a criminal in the act of committing a crime.
- Prevent a crime.
- Recover stolen property.
- Protect witnesses.

Because surveillance is a time-consuming, expensive operation that can raise questions of invasion of privacy, first exhaust all alternatives. Balance the rights of the individual against the need for public safety.

The Surveillant

The **surveillant** is the plainclothes investigator who makes the observation. Surveillants must be prepared for tedium. No other assignment requires as much patience and perseverance while simultaneously demanding alertness and readiness to respond instantly. Surveillants must display ingenuity in devising a cover for the operation. Lack of resourcefulness in providing adequate answers at a moment's notice can jeopardize the entire case. The most successful surveillants do not attract attention but blend into the general populace.

Multiple surveillants may also compose a surveillance team (ST). An effective ST requires everyone to be "on the same page," which calls for communication and briefings. According to Otto (1998, p. 39):

> The familiarization or "fam" briefing for an ST should answer:
>
> 1. What information are we supposed to collect?
> 2. Why is that information required?
> 3. How are we going to report the information?
>
> If you go into the field unable to answer these three questions then you have not been adequately briefed and your ST is handicapped. It's as simple as that.

The Subject

The **subject** is who or what is observed. It can be a person, place, property, vehicle, group of people, an organization or object. People under surveillance are usually suspects in a crime or their associates. Surveil-lance of places generally involves a location where a crime is expected to be committed: the residence of a known criminal; a place suspected of harboring criminal activities such as illegal drug transactions, gambling, prostitution, purchase of stolen goods or fencing operations; or the suspected headquarters of a terrorist organization.

Surveillance Equipment

Surveillance equipment includes binoculars, telescopes, night-vision equipment, body wires and video systems. Surveillance systems have become extremely sophisticated. One system, for example, conceals a periscope in what looks like a standard air vent in the roof of a van. The periscope rotates 360 degrees and is undetectable. Remote motion detectors activate the system to videotape the area under surveillance.

Many systems have night-vision and/or telephoto lenses as well as time-and-date generators. Many also have hard-copy printers that produce black-and-white or color photographic copies on site.

Siuru (1997, p. 38) describes a new addition—laser radar—to the "increasing menu of techniques to see the bad guys in the dark." The Advanced Ranging Imaging Sensor (ARIS) is "a scannerless laser radar imaging system that simultaneously generates both two-dimensional reflectance images and three-dimensional radar images." Siuru explains: "ARIS uses diffused, infrared energy from a scannerless laser transmitter to floodlight the entire surveillance scene to produce instantaneous three-dimensional images."

The laser range-finding binoculars that Morrison (1997, p. 35) describes are another surveillance innovation: "The Leica binoculars offer high-quality optics giving bright, sharp images in a wide range of conditions, and are ideal for surveillance and sniper work." Such binoculars can eliminate distance-judging errors.

Types of Surveillance

The type of surveillance used depends on the subject and the objective of the surveillance. In general, surveillance is either stationary or moving.

- - - - - - - -

The types of surveillance include stationary (fixed, plant or stakeout) and moving (tight or close, loose, rough, foot or vehicle).

- - - - - - - -

Stationary Surveillance

Stationary, or **fixed, surveillance,** also called a **plant** or **stakeout,** is used when you know or suspect that a person is at or will come to a known location, when you suspect that stolen goods are to be dropped or when informants have told you that a crime is going to be committed. Such assignments are comparatively short. An outside surveillance simplifies planning. The observation may be from a car, van or truck or by posting an officer in an inconspicuous place with a view of the location. A "dummy" van or a borrowed business van and a disguise as a painter, carpenter or service technician are often used. Take photographs and notes throughout the surveillance.

In longer surveillances, it is often necessary to photograph people who frequent a specific location such as a store suspected of being a cover for a bookmaking operation or a hotel or motel that allows prostitution or gambling. If the subject of surveillance is a place rather than a person, obtain a copy of the building plan and personally visit the building in advance if possible. Know all entrances and exits, especially rear doors and fire escapes. To properly record what is observed, use closed-circuit camera equipment, movie or video cameras, binoculars with a camera attached, telephoto lenses or infrared equipment for night viewing and photographing.

Lengthy fixed surveillance is often conducted from a room with an unobstructed view of the location, such as an apartment house opposite the location being watched. Naturally, the surveillant must not be noticed entering the observation post.

Whether the stationary surveillance is short or long, have adequate communications such as radio, horn signals or hand signals. Use simple hand signals such as pulling up the collar, buttoning the shirt, pulling down the brim on a hat, tying a shoelace, running the hand through the hair or checking a wristwatch. If you use radio communications, find out whether the subject might be monitoring police radio frequencies and, if likely, establish a code.

Select the surveillance team to fit the case and area, and have enough surveillants to cover the assignment. Scout the area in person or by studying maps. Sketch the immediate area to determine possible ways the subject could avoid observation or apprehension. Be aware of alleys, abnormal street conditions, one-way streets, barricades, parking ramps and all other details. This is especially critical when the objective of the surveillance is to apprehend people committing a crime. In such cases, all members of the stakeout must know the signal for action and their specific assignments.

Moving Surveillance

The subjects of **moving surveillance** are almost always people. The surveillant may be referred to as a **tail.** The first step in planning such a surveillance is to obtain as much information about the subject as you can. View photographs and, if possible, personally observe the subjects. Memorize their physical descriptions and form a mental image of them. Concentrate on their appearance from behind, as this is the view you normally have while "tailing" them. Although subjects may alter their physical appearance, this usually presents no problem. The major problem is keeping subjects under constant surveillance for the desired time. Know the subjects' habits, where they are likely to go and whether they walk or drive. If they drive, find out what kind of vehicles they use. Also find out who their associates are and whether they are likely to suspect that they are being observed.

Other problems of moving surveillance are losing the subject and having the subject recognize you as a surveillant. Sometimes it is not important if the subject knows of the surveillance. This is often true of material witnesses the police are protecting. It is also true of organized-crime figures, who know they are under constant surveillance and take this into account. In such instances, a **rough tail** is used. You need not take extraordinary means to remain undetected. The major problem of a rough tail is the charge of police harassment or invasion of privacy.

At other times it is more important to remain undetected than to keep the subject under constant observation. In such cases, a **loose tail** is used. Maintain a safe distance. If the subject is lost during surveillance, you can easily relocate the subject and resume the surveillance. A loose tail is often used when you need general information about the subject's activities or associates.

Often, however, it is extremely important not to lose the subject, and a very **close (tight) tail** is maintained. On a crowded street this means staying within a few steps of the subject; on a less crowded street, it means keeping the subject in sight. A close tail is most commonly used when you know the subject is going to commit a crime, when you must know the subject's exact habits or when knowledge of the subject's activities is important to another critical operation.

When tailing a subject on foot, you can use numerous delaying tactics. You can cross to the other side of the street, talk to a person standing nearby, increase your distance from the subject, read a magazine or newspaper, buy a soda, fix the engine in your car, tie your shoe, look in windows or in parked cars or stall in any other way.

If the subject turns a corner, do not follow closely. When you do turn the corner, if you find the subject waiting in a doorway, pass by without paying attention. Then try to resume the tail by guessing the subject's next move. This is often possible when you have advance information on the subject's habits.

If the subject enters a restaurant, you can either enter and take a seat on the side of the room opposite from the subject, making sure you are near the door so you can see the subject leave, or you can wait outside.

If a subject enters a building that has numerous exits, follow at a safe distance, noticing all potential exits. If the subject takes an elevator, wait at the first floor until the subject returns, noticing the floors at which the elevator stops. If there is a stairway near the elevator, stand near the door so you can hear if the subject has gotten off the elevator and taken the stairs. Such stairs are seldom used, and when someone is going up or down, their footsteps echo and can easily be heard.

When tailing a subject on the street, do not hesitate to pass the subject and enter a store yourself. The less obvious you are, the more successful you will be.

Use the glass in doors and storefront windows to see behind you.

Subjects who suspect they are being followed use many tricks. They may turn corners suddenly and stand in a nearby doorway, go into a store and duck into a restroom, enter a dressing room, hide behind objects or suddenly jump on a bus or into a taxi. They may do such things to determine *whether* they are being followed or to lose someone they *know* is following them.

It is usually better to lose subjects than to alert them to your presence or to allow them to identify you.

Surveillants often believe they have been recognized when in fact they have not. However, if you are certain the subject knows you are following, stop the surveillance, but do not return to the police department right away because the subject may decide to tail you.

If it is critical not to lose the subject, use more than one surveillant, preferably three. Surveillant A keeps a very close tail immediately behind the subject. Surveillant B follows behind Surveillant A and the subject. Surveillant C observes from across the street parallel with the other two. If the subject turns the corner, Surveillant A continues in the previous direction for a while, and Surveillant B or C picks up the tail. Surveillant A then takes the position previously held by the surveillant who picked up the close tail.

When tailing by vehicle, have descriptions of all vehicles the subject drives or rides in. The subject's vehicle can be marked in advance by an electronic device or beeper monitored by a receiver in your car, or you can place the beeper in an object the subject will be carrying. A small amount of fluorescent paint can be applied to the rear bumper of the vehicle to make it easily identifiable day or night.

Your own vehicle should be inconspicuous. Obtain unregistered ("dead") plates for it from the motor vehicle authorities and change them frequently, or change your vehicle daily, perhaps using rental cars. Changing the number of occupants tends to confuse a suspicious subject. If surveillance is to be primarily at night, install a multiple contact switch to allow you to turn off one of your headlights at will.

Like subjects being tailed on foot, subjects being tailed by vehicle often use tricks to determine whether they are being tailed or to lose an identified tail. They may turn in the middle of the block, go through a red light, suddenly pull into a parking stall, change traffic lanes rapidly, go down alleys or go the wrong way down a one-way street. In such cases, if temporarily losing the subject causes no problem, stop the surveillance.

If it is critical not to lose the subject, use more than one vehicle for the surveillance. The ideal system uses four vehicles. Vehicle A drives ahead of the subject and observes through the rearview mirror. (This vehicle is not used if only three vehicles are available). Vehicle B follows right behind the subject. Vehicles C and D follow on left and right parallel streets to pick up the tail if the subject turns in either direction.

Avoiding Detection

Criminals are often suspicious of stakeouts or of being followed and may send someone to scout the area to see whether anybody has staked out their residence or their vehicle. This person may stand on the corner near the residence or drive around the block several times to see if everything is clear. Criminals often watch the windows or roofs of buildings across the street for movements. When they leave their residences, they may have an accomplice trail behind to see if anyone is following. Anticipate and plan for such activities. Sometimes a counter-countersurveillance is used if personnel is available.

Not every surveillance is successful. In some instances the subject is lost or the surveillant is recognized, despite the best efforts to avoid either. Like any other investigative technique, failure results from unforeseen circumstances such as vehicle malfunction, illness of the surveillant, unexpected absence of the subject due to illness or emergency, abnormal weather conditions or terrain and other factors beyond control. Usually, however, information and evidence obtained through surveillance are well worth the time and effort invested. In all instances a form such as the one shown in Figure 7.4 should be completed after a surveillance assignment.

Aerial Surveillance

Aerial surveillance may provide information about areas inaccessible to foot or vehicle surveillance. Communica-

FIGURE 7.4
Surveillance Intelligence Form

Surveillance Report

Date __4-16-00__ Time started __1130__ Time finished __1330__ Case No. __6432__

Address, location or name of subject __116 7th St-Ralph Burns__

Purpose of surveillance __Sales of controlled substance__

Weather conditions __Fair__ Equipment used __binoculars__

Conversations with subject __None__

Telephone calls made __None__

Persons contacted by subject __None__

Record of observations during surveillance _____

Time __Female adult entered garage 1142__

Time __Male, adult subject met Burns on step 1154__

Time __2 males in 1974 brown car stopped at above address 1232__

Time __Burns left residence in car 1315 NV; 134-MMN__

Time _____

Signature of surveillant _____

tion between air surveillance and ground vehicles facilitates the operational movement in and around the target area. The aerial pilot should either be a police officer or be carefully selected by the police. The pilot should be familiar with the landmarks of the area because many such surveillances involve moving suspect-vehicles.

Photographs taken from navigable air space, usually 1,000 feet, do not violate privacy regulations.

In one aerial surveillance, officers viewed a partially covered greenhouse within the residential curtilage from a helicopter 400 feet above the greenhouse. The greenhouse, which contained marijuana plants, was located 10–20 feet behind the residence, a mobile home. A wire fence surrounded the entire property, and "Do Not Enter" signs were posted. Nonetheless, *Florida v Riley* (1989) approved the warrantless aerial surveillance, noting there should be no reasonable expectation of privacy from the skies above.

Audio Surveillance

In special instances electronic devices are used in surveillance. Such **electronic surveillance** techniques include wiring a person who is going to be talking with a subject or entering a suspicious business establishment, **"bugging"** a subject's room or vehicle or **wiretapping** a telephone. The exclusionary rule requires that all evidence against a suspect be acquired according to the standards set forth in the Fourth Amendment.

- - - - - - - -

Electronic surveillance and wiretapping are considered forms of search and are therefore permitted only with probable cause and court order *(Katz v United States)*.

- - - - - - - -

In a landmark case, *Katz v United States* (1967), the U.S. Supreme Court considered an appeal by Charles Katz, who had been convicted in California of violating gambling laws. Investigators had observed Katz for several days as he made telephone calls from a particular phone booth at the same time each day. Suspecting he was placing horseracing bets, the investigators attached an electronic listening/recording device to the telephone booth and recorded Katz's illegal activities. The evidence was used in convicting Katz. The Supreme Court reversed the California decision, saying: "The Fourth Amendment protects people not places. . . . Wherever a man may be, he is entitled to know that he will remain free from unreasonable searches and seizures." The investigators did have probable cause, but they erred in not presenting their information to a judge and obtaining prior approval for their actions.

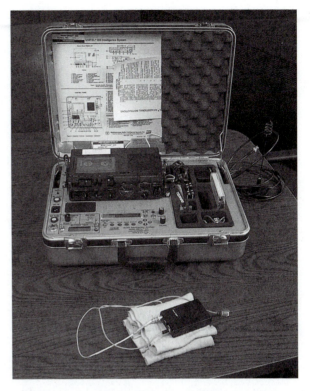

This photograph depicts a wire and recorder used in police surveillance work. The case, which is typically carried in a police van, includes a tape recorder. A sensitive remote recording device is worn by the investigator.

The importance of electronic surveillance is recognized, however, in the introduction to Title III of the Omnibus Crime Control and Safe Streets Act of 1968, which authorized court-ordered electronic surveillance of organized-crime figures. The U.S. Congress stated:

> Organized criminals make extensive use of wire and oral communications in their criminal activities. The interception of such communications to obtain evidence of the commission of crimes or to prevent their commission is an indispensible aid to law enforcement and the administration of justice.

Federal and state laws allow electronic surveillance (eavesdropping), provided it is authorized by a federal or state judge and specified procedures are followed. Advertisements in police magazines describe state-of-the-art surveillance systems that make undercover work more efficient and effective. Laser technology can direct a beam at the glass in a window with another beam modulated by sonic vibrations inside the room, bouncing the sound back to a receiver so officers can hear what is being said. Eavesdropping with "bugs" is now easier than ever. Criminals are using high-tech electronic counter-measures to detect such devices in a room before they hold a meeting or conversation there.

The courts have thus far upheld the right of officers to tape conversations that occur inside their squad cars. Kash (1998, p. 35) explains:

> Indeed, one of the most atypical aspects of this profession is that an officer's patrol car *is* his office. It is this seemingly subtle distinction that leads courts through the legal analysis and to the conclusion that taping conversations in a patrol car is a constitutionally acceptable investigative technique.

Kash (p. 36) notes that in *U.S. v McKinnon* (1993): "Two subjects were stopped for a traffic violation and asked to sit in the patrol car while the officer conducted a consent search in the vehicle for drugs. . . . The subjects engaged in incriminating conversations, which unbeknownst to them, were recorded." Although one of the defendants argued the recording violated his right to privacy, the court disagreed, ruling "no reasonable expectation of privacy exists in the back seat of a patrol car" (p. 36). Kash (p. 37) concludes: "In light of these decisions, a recording device should be a standard weapon in a police officer's investigative arsenal."

Traditionally, the equipment used to wiretap phone lines relied on analog-based networks that are linked with "twisted pair copper wire" telephone systems (Dees, 1999, p. 15). However, the development and proliferation of digital switches, fiber-optic cable and cellular technology rendered the old-fashioned wiretap devices useless. Consequently, as Dees (p. 15) noted: "In 1994, Congress enacted the Communications Assistance for Law Enforcement Act [CALEA], encouraging telecommunications providers to develop and implement standards to make legally authorized electronic surveillance more accessible." Muscoplat (1999, p. 36) predicts that: "If CALEA garners the kind of publicity it deserves, the message will quickly spread that criminals should not feel safe conducting their business on any phone lines, wireless or not."

Unfortunately, the telecommunications industry opposes several aspects of the law that preserve law enforcement's ability to use lawfully authorized electronic surveillance. Although Congress authorized $500 million to reimburse telecommunications carriers for reasonable costs associated with carrying out CALEA's mandates, the industry contends that the costs could result in a billion-dollar-plus electronic surveillance tax that they would pass on to the ratepayer.

Because of the disagreements, the deadline to implement the mandates has been extended to June 30, 2000 (Szwajkowski, 1999, pp. 40–42).

Strandberg (1997, p. 40) observes that: "Over the past decade the use of court-ordered wiretaps has resulted in the arrest of over thirty thousand felons, and the conviction of over twenty thousand." Strandberg suggests that wiretaps played a significant role in the World Trade Center bombing investigation.

Undercover Assignments

The nonuniformed or plainclothes investigator is in a good position to observe illegal activities and obtain evidence. For example, a male plainclothes officer may appear to accept the solicitations of a prostitute, or any plainclothes police officer may attempt to buy stolen goods or drugs or to place illegal bets. Many such activities require little more than simply "not smelling like the law." Unlike other forms of surveillance in which a prime objective is not to be observed, **undercover** surveillants make personal contact with the subject using an assumed identity or **cover**.

The objective of an undercover assignment may be to gain a person's confidence or to infiltrate an organization or group by using an assumed identity and to thereby obtain information or evidence connecting the subject with criminal activity.

Band and Sheehan (1999, p. 1) state: "Law enforcement agencies frequently rely on undercover employees (UCEs). By infiltrating criminal organizations, UCEs gather the critical evidence needed to dismantle them." Undercover assignments can be designed to:

■ Obtain evidence for prosecution.

■ Obtain leads into criminal activities.

■ Check the reliability of witnesses or informants.

■ Gain information about premises for use in later conducting a raid or an arrest.

■ Check the security of a person in a highly sensitive position.

■ Obtain information on or evidence against subversive groups.

Undercover assignments are frequently made when criminal activity is greatly suspected or even known, but

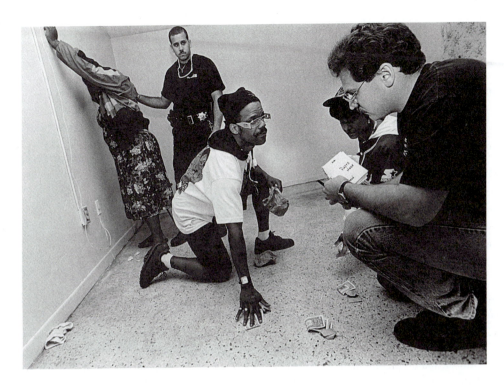

Undercover officers posing as small-time street dealers, sorting out who bought what. This operation, known as a "reverse sting," has been held as legal in the courts; however, a defense of entrapment is often used.

no legal evidence of it exists. Such assignments can be extremely dangerous and require careful planning and preparation. As Strandberg (1998, p. 82) notes: "Sometimes the psychological dangers can outweigh the physical dangers for undercover cops."

The undercover agent selected must fit the assignment. Age, sex, race, general appearance, language facility, health, energy level, emotional stability and intelligence are all important selection considerations. Undercover agents must be good actors—able to assume their role totally. They must be intelligent and able to deal with any problems that arise, make quick decisions, improvise plans and actions and work with the person or within the group or organization without arousing suspicion. Strandberg (p. 82) asserts: "Undercover operations are the ultimate method acting. The undercover officer has to look and act whatever part he or she is playing, but the stakes are much higher. The consequence of a bad performance isn't a bad review, it could be a matter of life or death."

A good cover is essential. Rookies are often used because they are not yet known and because they have not been in law enforcement long enough to acquire expressions or mannerisms that hardened criminals recognize as "the law."

In addition to devising a good cover, the undercover agent learns everything possible about the subject,

regardless of whether it is a person or an organization. If you are going to be working undercover, make plans for communicating with headquarters. Make telephone calls from public pay phones, or mail letters to a fictitious friend's post office box. Have a plan for communicating emergency messages, and know what to do if the authorities move in on the subject when you are there. Have a plan for leaving the subject when you have acquired the desired information or evidence.

It is vital that undercover investigators keep accurate notes during their investigation, yet they must not allow the subject to be aware of such documentation. Soto (1999, p. 55) asserts: "No matter the effort put forward, the case may fail if the documentation is poor." He continues:

> In preparing reports related to undercover efforts, investigators need to . . . [minimize] reports and [coordinate] information. . . .
>
> Much of the information collected . . . may not be fact, but be based on guesses, theories and personal opinion. Care must be exercised to ensure reports show facts only. . . .
>
> A vital record for court is the document describing transactions or meetings leading to evidence. A Memorandum of Contact (MOC) documented the undercover agent's (UCA) activities and observations during a transaction that yielded evidence or major leads.

Soto (p. 57) concludes: "Unlike television where undercover cops buy drugs and never fill out reports, officers are liable and responsible for their actions, time and efforts. . . . In documenting investigative efforts, records should provide more than ample ammunition to make the case stick in court."

Precautions for undercover agents:

- Write no notes the subject can read.

- Carry no identification other than the cover ID.

- Ensure that any communication with headquarters is covert.

- Do not suggest, plan, initiate or participate in criminal activity.

The fourth precaution is important because, if you ignore it, the defense can argue that entrapment occurred. The Supreme Court has defined **entrapment** in *Sorrells v United States* (1932) as: "the conception and planning of an offense by an officer, and his procurement of its commission by one who would not have perpetrated it except for the trickery, persuasion or fraud of the officer." *Sorrells* also explained the need for trickery in obtaining evidence: "Society is at war with the criminal classes, and the courts have uniformly held that in waging this warfare the forces of prevention and detection may use traps, decoys and deception to obtain evidence of the commission of a crime."

Sorrells concludes: "The fact that government agents merely afford opportunities or facilities for the commission of the offense does not constitute entrapment." These Court rulings still stand. In *Sherman v United States* (1950) the Court explained:

Entrapment occurs only when the criminal conduct was "the product of the creative activity" of law-enforcement officials. To determine whether entrapment has been established, a line must be drawn between the trap for the unwary innocent and the trap for the unwary criminal.

Hawley (1996, p. 8) notes: "Suspects caught red-handed may escape conviction if entrapment is involved." Hawley (p. 9) describes police conduct that might be considered entrapment: "appeals to sympathy, illness, pity or friendship; inducements making the crime unusually attractive to a law-abiding person; guarantees that the act is legal; or an offer of exhorbitant sums of money."

Because it is possible that you may be arrested if the subject is arrested, learn ahead of time whether you are to "blow your cover" or submit to arrest. In some instances outside sources may interfere with the lawful arrest, posing great danger for an undercover agent whose identity has become known during the arrest.

When the assignment is successfully completed, give the subject a plausible explanation for leaving because it may be necessary to reestablish the undercover contact later.

It is often better to use undercover agents than informants because the testimony of a reliable, trained investigator is less subject to a defense attorney's attack than that of an informant.

The legality of placing an undercover officer in a high school to investigate student drug use was decided in *Gordon v Warren Consolidated Board of Education* (1983). High-school officials had put an undercover officer into classes. The claimants alleged deprivation of their civil rights, but the case was dismissed by the federal district court for failure to state a cause of action. On appeal, the Supreme Court affirmed the prior judgment, stating that the presence of the undercover police officer did not constitute any more than a "chilling" effect on the First Amendment right because it did not disrupt classroom activities or education and had no tangible effect on inhibiting expression of particular views in the classroom.

Raids

A police **raid** is a planned, organized operation based on the element of surprise. Lonsdale (1996, p. 56) states: "A raid could be defined as 'the invasion of a building or locality for lawful purposes.'" Consider all other alternatives before executing a raid.

The objectives of a raid are to recover stolen property, seize evidence or arrest a suspect.

Sometimes all three objectives are accomplished in a single raid.

The first consideration is whether there are alternatives to a raid. A second consideration is the legality of the raid.

A raid must be the result of a hot pursuit or be under the authority of a no-knock arrest or search warrant.

If you are in hot pursuit of a known felon and have no time to plan a raid, make sure enough personnel and

Minneapolis police officers raiding a suspected crackhouse. Surprise, swiftness and sufficient personnel are required for a successful raid.

weapons are available to reduce danger. Call for backup before starting the raid. If time permits, however, careful planning and preparation will enhance the likely success of the raid.

Planning, organizing and executing a raid are somewhat similar to undertaking a small military attack on a specific target. Lonsdale (p. 56) explains: "In addition to training and safety factors, the primary components of a raid are planning, preparation, intelligence, coordination and execution."

Planning a Raid

Lonsdale (p. 59) states: "Raids are not single-step activities, but rather carefully choreographed productions that must be well organized and orchestrated." Begin planning a raid by gathering information on the premises to be raided, including the exact address and points of entry and exit for both the raiding party and the suspect. Obtain a picture or sketch of the building and study the room arrangement. Lonsdale (p. 57) suggests obtaining additional location information from aerial photographs, drive-bys, surveillance photos, walking the neighborhood, bogus utility visits and the city planning department.

Next, study the suspect's background. What crimes has the suspect committed? What difficulties were encountered in making past arrests? Is the suspect a narcotics addict? An alcoholic? Likely to be armed? If so, what type of weapon is the suspect likely to wield?

Obtain the appropriate warrants. Most raids are planned and result from an arrest warrant. In such cases the subject is usually living under circumstances that necessitate a raid to make an arrest. In addition, if the raid is conducted to obtain evidence or property, obtain not only an exact description of the property sought and its likely location on the premises but also a legal search warrant. Specify that you require a no-knock warrant to conduct the raid and also perhaps a nighttime warrant to enhance the element of surprise.

Throughout the entire planning process, keep the raid plan as simple as possible. Because the subject may be extremely dangerous, intend to use adequate firepower and personnel. Determine the required weapons and equipment. Plan for enough personnel to minimize violence, overcome opposition through superiority of forces and prevent the suspect's escape or destruction of evidence. Make sure all entrances and exits will be covered and that a communication system is established. Decide how to transport the raiding party to the scene and how to take the suspect or evidence and property away. Determine which one person will be in command during the raid.

It is important to remember that other people may be in the vicinity of the raid. If possible, evacuate everyone from the area of the raid without making the suspect suspicious. It is not always possible to do this without losing the element of surprise vital to the success of the raid.

Finally, before the raid goes into action, keep in mind Lonsdale's five "S" factors in executing a successful raid:

■ Speed—movement by the raid team must be swift; otherwise, suspects will have time to arm themselves, evidence will disappear, agents will face increased resistance, and the raid may fail.

■ Surprise—this may come from the use of undercover vehicles, disguises, ruses, "buy-bust" operations or no-knock warrants.

■ Shock action—this is a by-product of speed, surprise and a dynamic entry at the least expected time and place.

■ Simplicity—individual duties must be kept simple and described in a clear and concise manner.

■ Safety—get everyone "on the same sheet of paper" and moving and shooting as part of a coordinated team effort.

Executing a Raid

The raid should occur only after a careful briefing of all members of the raiding party. Each participant must know the objective, who the suspect is or what evidence or property is sought and the exact plan of the raid itself. Give each participant proper equipment such as body armor, weapons, radios, whistles, megaphones and signal lights. Give each participant a specific assignment, and answer all questions about the raid before leaving the briefing. The raid commander directs the raid, giving the signal to begin and coordinating all assignments.

Decisions about the initial entry and control phase of a raid must be made rapidly because control is usually established within the first 15–30 seconds of a successful raid. No two raids are executed in precisely the same manner. The immediate circumstances and events dictate what decisions and actions are made. Spaulding (1998) recommends that raid teams use the "immediate threat concept" upon entering the raid site:

> The first officer through the door takes on the most serious threat he sees. The following officers must

"read" what the officer in front of them does and take the next most serious threat.

Threats are rated as people first, doors second, and places where people can hide as third.

Handguns are still the most versatile weapon during a raid, but shotguns and other assault-type weapons are useful in the perimeter operations and to control arrested individuals. If guard animals are known to be inside the raid area, provide for their control. Special equipment such as sledgehammers or rams may help in breaking down fortified entrances. An ambulance should be on standby, or raid personnel should at least know the fastest route to the nearest hospital.

Because raids are highly visible, the public and the news media often take interest. Therefore, raids are likely to be the object of community praise or criticism. They are also often vital to prosecuting a case successfully.

Precautions in conducting raids:

■ Ensure the raid is legal.
■ Plan carefully.
■ Assign adequate personnel and equipment.
■ Thoroughly brief every member of the raiding party.
■ Be aware of the possibility of surreptitious surveillance devices at the raid site.

It is becoming increasingly common for suspects to rig alarm systems at one location so a breach in security alerts those in other locations. Such systems can also monitor the actions and words of officers who have arrived at the scene. As O'Neal (1998, p. 10) relates:

> Imagine the perfect textbook execution of a search warrant at the primary location used by a major drug ring. The police have taken all of the necessary precautions, including instructing the alarm company to disregard any signals it receives from the site. However, upon entering, the officers unknowingly trigger a second alarm system installed by the suspects themselves using parts ordered by mail and instructions from the Internet. . . . Arrest teams are dispatched to the various locations [of high-profile drug distributors] in the city; however, all report the same unusual event—the suspects apparently had fled minutes before the teams had arrived.

What had happened? . . . Is it possible that the suspects had used computers to surreptitiously eavesdrop on the officers during the execution of the warrant? It is not only possible but also extremely likely.

Amazingly powerful, low-cost computer systems that only a few short years ago would have been unthinkable now are readily available . . . [and] can be used as effective, remote-controlled surreptitious audio surveillance devices.

Drugs busts and raids on crackhouses have become increasingly common. In some instances police have used front-end loaders and other tanklike vehicles to break through the walls of suspected crackhouses. They have unfortunately sometimes had the wrong address.

Sometimes a raid is unsuccessful and results in a standoff or a hostage situation as in the ATF raid on the Branch Davidian cult in Waco, Texas, in February 1993.

SWAT Teams

Many police agencies have developed tactical squads, sometimes called *Special Weapons and Tactics (SWAT) teams,* to execute raids. Hawkins (1999, p. 53) notes: "Over the last two decades, law enforcement has made great strides in the development of Special Weapons and Tactics/Special Operations Teams." These units, also called paramilitary police units (PPUs), are thoroughly trained to search areas for criminals, handle sniper incidents and hostage situations, execute arrest and search warrants and apprehend militants who have barricaded themselves inside a building or other location.

In the last 20 years police have made many advances in the development, training and negotiation skills of SWAT teams. Since cross training of SWAT and negotiation teams, use of lethal force has lessened. In one study 96 percent of the incidents involving these specially trained units were resolved without shots being fired. Seventeen percent of departments having such teams used the same personnel in proactive patrol assignments.

Efforts are currently being made to cross-train crisis team members in a variety of skills. Strentz (1998, p. 13) states: "There is a growing, basically healthy trend in this country for agencies to train the SWAT team members as negotiators, and provide negotiators with SWAT training. The goal of this cross training is to help each person understand the role of other crisis team members."

A recent survey of police departments across the country revealed the following data regarding PPUs ("Militarizing Mayberry," 1998, p. 117):

- Over 65% of smaller police departments have a SWAT team; only 20% had such a unit in 1980.

- The total number of deployments has risen from 200 in 1980 to almost 4,000 in 1995.

- Small-town SWAT units are taking an increasingly offensive posture.

- About 17% of the departments use their SWAT teams for "proactive patrol work."

Results of another survey (Stevens, 1999, p. 48) revealed that "tactical units enhance the likelihood of a safer resolution to critical incidents."[1] Stevens (p. 49) notes that of the 186 critical incidents examined from July 1996 to June 1997: "Ninety-six percent (179) of those incidents were resolved without shots fired after SWAT's arrival. Fifty-seven percent (106) of those involved firearms, and only five resulted in the death of the suspect by SWAT." He (p. 51) concludes: "It is clear that agencies with police tactical units resolve critical incidents far safer than agencies without tactical units (71% versus 44% of the time)."

Legal Arrests

Once a suspect has been located and identified, the next step is generally an arrest. Police powers to arrest (or search) are restricted by the Fourth Amendment, which forbids unreasonable searches or seizures without probable cause. Just as state laws define and establish the elements of crimes, they also define arrest and establish who may make an arrest, for what offenses and when. Most state laws define an **arrest** in general terms as "the taking

---

[1]Defined as any high-risk encounter with police-civilian contacts when officers reasonably believe they are legally justified in using deadly force.

of a person into custody in the manner authorized by law for the purpose of presenting that person before a magistrate to answer for the commission of a crime." An arrest may be made by a police officer or a private person. It may be made with or without a warrant, although a warrant is generally preferred because this places the burden of proving that the arrest was illegal on the defense.

Police officers are authorized to make an arrest:

- For any crime committed in their presence.

- For a felony not committed in their presence if they have probable cause to believe the person committed the crime.

- Under the authority of an arrest warrant.

Most arrests are for misdemeanors such as disorderly conduct, drunkenness, traffic violations, minor larceny, minor drug offenses, minor assaults, minor sex offenses, nuisances and other offenses of lesser severity. In most states you must see such offenses to make an arrest without a warrant. In many states an arrest may also be made by a private citizen who witnesses a misdemeanor and then turns the suspect over to law enforcement authorities. Figure 7.5 shows a sample citizen's arrest form.

If you have probable cause to believe a suspect has committed a felony and there is no time to obtain an arrest warrant, you can make an arrest without the warrant. Facts gathered *after* the arrest to justify probable cause are *not* legally admissible as evidence of probable cause. They can however strengthen the case if probable cause was established *before* the arrest.

Probable cause for believing the suspect committed a crime must be established before a lawful arrest can be made.

An arrest for a felony or gross misdemeanor can usually be made any time if there is an arrest warrant or if the arresting officer witnessed the crime. An arrest may be made only in the daytime if it is by warrant, unless a magistrate has endorsed the warrant with a written statement that the arrest may be made at night. This is commonly referred to as a **nightcap provision.**

Officers are allowed to break an inner or outer door to make an arrest after identifying themselves, stating the purpose for entry and demanding admittance. This is often necessary when officers are in plain clothes and hence not recognized as police. The courts have

CERTIFICATE AND DECLARATION OF ARREST BY PRIVATE PERSON
AND DELIVERY OF PERSON SO ARRESTED TO PEACE OFFICER

DATE ___5-3-00___

TIME ___1440___

PLACE ___Boulder City___
1115 Bolt st.

I, ___Joyce Mayberry___ , hereby declare and certify that I have arrested

(NAME) ___John Mayberry___

(ADDRESS) ___1115 Bolt St. Boulder City, Nevada___

for the following reasons: _____

John arrived home about fifteen minutes ago and we had

an argument about his drinking and spending all the

money. He struck me twice on the side of my face and

twice in the stomach. He told me that next time he

would kill me.

and I do hereby request and demand that you ___Officer James McGraw___ ,
a peace officer, take and conduct this person whom I have arrested to the nearest
magistrate to be dealt with according to law; and if no magistrate can be contacted before
tomorrow morning, then to conduct this person to jail for safekeeping until the required
appearance can be arranged before such magistrate, at which time I shall be present, and
I will then and there sign, under oath, the appropriate complaint against this person for the
offense which this person has committed and for which I made this arrest; and I will then
and there, or thereafter as soon as this criminal action or cause can be heard, testify
under oath of and concerning the facts and circumstances involved herein. I will save
said officer harmless from any and all claim for damage of any kind, nature and
description arising out of his acts at my direction.

Signature of private person
making this arrest ___Joyce J Mayberry___

Peace Officer Witnesses to this statement

___James McGraw___

___C S Steiner___

FIGURE 7.5   *Certificate of Citizen's Arrest*

approved no-knock entries in cases in which the evidence would be immediately destroyed if police announced their intention to enter. Officers may break a window or door to leave a building if they are illegally detained inside. They may break a door or window to arrest a suspect who has escaped from custody. Finally, officers may break an automobile window if a suspect rolls up the windows and locks the doors to prevent an arrest. You should give proper notification of the reason for the arrest and the intent to break the window if the suspect does not voluntarily comply.

You can accomplish the physical act of arrest by taking hold of or controlling the person and stating, "You are under arrest for. . . ." In most jurisdictions the arresting officer's authority must be stated, and the suspect must be told for what offense the arrest is being made. If you are going to question the suspect, read the Miranda warning first.

- - - - - - - -

If your intent is to make an arrest and you inform the suspect of this intent and then restrict the suspect's right to go free, you have made an arrest.

- - - - - - - -

Use of Force

Physical force is not a necessary part of an arrest; in fact, most arrests are made without physical force. The amount of resistance to arrest varies, and this determines how much force you should use.

- - - - - - - -

When making an arrest, use only as much force as is necessary to overcome any resistance. If no resistance occurs, you may not use any force.

- - - - - - - -

Deciding how much force to use in making an arrest requires logic and good judgment. However, in the heat of the moment, police officers may use more force than intended. Courts and juries have usually excused force that is not blatantly unreasonable, recognizing that many factors are involved in such split-second decisions.

Reasonable force is the amount of force a prudent person would use in similar circumstances. **Exceptional force** means more than ordinary force. Use of exceptional force (such as striking with a nightstick) is justified only when exceptional resistance occurs and there is no other way to make the arrest. Use handcuffs on suspects you believe will harm you, someone else or themselves or who will attempt to escape.

McEwen (1996, p. 46) draws an important distinction between "use of excessive force" and "excessive use of force": "*Use of excessive force* means that police applied too much force in a given incident, while *excessive use of force* means that police apply force legally in too many incidents." Neubauer (1999, p. 6) notes:

The IACP has developed a quantifiable definition for the term "excessive use of force"—the application of an amount and/or frequency of force greater than what is required to compel compliance from a willing or unwilling subject.

An IACP report on the use-of-force rates revealed a total of 654 incidents of excessive use of force per every 10,000 incidents between 1996 and 1998. Neubauer states: "Expressed another way, excessive force was used in 0.45 percent of all reported incidents, and was not applied in 99.54 percent of all reported cases."

In *Graham v Connor* (1989) the Supreme Court ruled: "Our Fourth Amendment jurisprudence has long recognized that the right to make an arrest or investigatory stop necessarily carries with it the right to use some degree of physical coercion or threat thereof to effect it." In *Graham,* the Court explained: "The reasonableness of a particular use of force must be judged from the perspective of a reasonable officer on the scene, rather than with the 20/20 vision of hindsight" (McGuinness, 2000, p. 58). Ross (1999, p. 5) notes another result of the *Graham* case:

The U.S. Supreme Court established five important factors to evaluate the facts in alleged cases of excessive force.

1) What is the severity of the crime at issue?
2) Was the suspect an immediate threat to the officer or others?
3) Were the circumstances tense, uncertain, and rapidly evolving?
4) Was the suspect attempting to evade arrest by flight?
5) Was the suspect actively resisting arrest?

Graham v Connor (1989) further held that plaintiffs alleging excessive use of force need show only that the officer's actions were unreasonable under the standards of the Fourth Amendment.

In the aftermath of the Rodney King case in Los Angeles and the alleged use of excessive force in other cities since then, much national attention has focused on the question of the definition of excessive force. Sometimes the force used is obviously excessive and outrageous. In one instance ("Cop Pleads Guilty . . . ," 1999, p. A4), New York City police officer Justin Volpe admitted assaulting and sodomizing Abner Louima with a broomstick in an attempt to humiliate and intimidate the handcuffed Haitian immigrant. Volpe also threatened to kill Louima if he told anyone about the torture. Volpe was not the only officer charged in the incident: "Officer Charles Schwartz was convicted of holding down Louima while fellow officer Justin Volpe rammed a stick into [Louima's] rectum in August 1997. U.S. Attorney Zachary Carter called it 'the most depraved act that's ever been reported or committed by a police officer or police officers against another human being' " ("Mixed Verdict . . . ," 1999, p. A4).

The public is very aware of and sensitive to police use of force. The instantaneous decisions and actions by police officers at the scene are subject to long-term review by the public and the courts. Police departments must review their policies on the use of force to ensure that they are clear and in accordance with court decisions as well as effective in ensuring officer safety. Officers should know their department's policies regarding use of force. Further, uses of force in making arrests should be critiqued, and complaints of excessive force should be thoroughly reviewed.

Most police departments know of officers who tend to become involved in resistance or violent situations more frequently than others. In some instances these officers' approach seems to trigger resistance. However, in any situation that is *not* out of control when you arrive, give a friendly greeting and state who you are and your authority if you are not in uniform. Speak calmly and convey the impression that you are in control. Show your badge or identification and give your reason for the questioning. Ask for identification and listen to their side of the story. Then decide on the appropriate action: warn, release, issue a citation or make an arrest.

Although voluntary compliance is the "best" arrest, there are always situations that are not peaceful. In such cases use only as much force as is necessary to overcome the resistance, progressing from control by empty-hand methods (defensive tactics), to the use of control agents (such as mace or tear gas), to the use of a police baton or—in the case of life-threatening resistance—to deadly force.

Nonlethal Weapons

Several nonlethal weapons are available, including sticky foam, pepper spray, rubber bullets, stun guns and robots. Fairburn (1996, p. 78) describes a Taser electronic device, which fires high-voltage electrical currents to subdue resistant subjects, and the Net Gun, which, once it makes contact with a suspect, entangles the person in a net, preventing further resistance. Fairburn (p. 103) notes:

> These less-lethal weapons offer police agencies the means to defend [their] officers from attack, disperse unruly individuals or crowds, and control dangerous subjects to make apprehension easier. In the future, we may see chemical munitions that will render a subject quickly unconscious.
>
> As much as we might like to have one of Captain Kirk's phasers that could be "set to stun," such weaponry remains in the realm of science fiction. But for now, these very capable less-lethal alternatives will help us control dangerous situations without gunfire.

Entanglement systems are a new method for subduing suspects with nonlethal tactics:

> The Webshot is a nonlethal round that combines speed and positive capture effectiveness in a compact, lightweight, standard weapons package. The nets come in two forms: Snare-Net, a plain entanglement system, or Sting-Net, an enhanced net with a remotely controlled high voltage pulse (HVP) system. These nets are the only response that can capture without pain compliance, restrict movement, neutralize threatening animals, minimize injury and collateral damage, work indoors, outdoors and in all types of weather and fit a standard weapon ("Entanglement Systems," 1999, p. 70).

In discussing the benefits of pepper spray, Scott (1998, pp. 40–41) explains: "Oleoresin capsicum, or OC for short, is a non-carcinogenic, biodegradable, organic substance, and therefore is safe and effective when properly used. . . . Effects [may] include temporary incapacitation of vision due to contact with the eyes." It must be noted, however, that some people are relatively unaffected by pepper spray. Flynn (1996b, p. 48) states:

> The greatest need for pepper spray is when the subject is extremely violent. But unfortunately, the violent subject is the least likely to be slowed down by pepper spray. It does not always work, especially if your subject is high on drugs or mentally ill. People with high tolerances for pain or violent goals can work through the spray.

Use of aerosol weapons (often referred to as aerosol subject restraints or ASRs) is not without problems. Ashley (1996, p. 35) points out: "Three issues which consistently raise significant concerns are aerosol training, placement of aerosols on a force continuum, and in-custody death." As far as the third issue is concerned, Ashley (p. 37) contends: "There is far less likelihood of suspect injury with an aerosol weapon than with a baton or firearm, and far less likelihood of officer injury with empty hand control techniques."

Figure 7.6` shows a use-of-force continuum, in which each level represents a "step up" in the degree of force applied. Such continuums are very common in

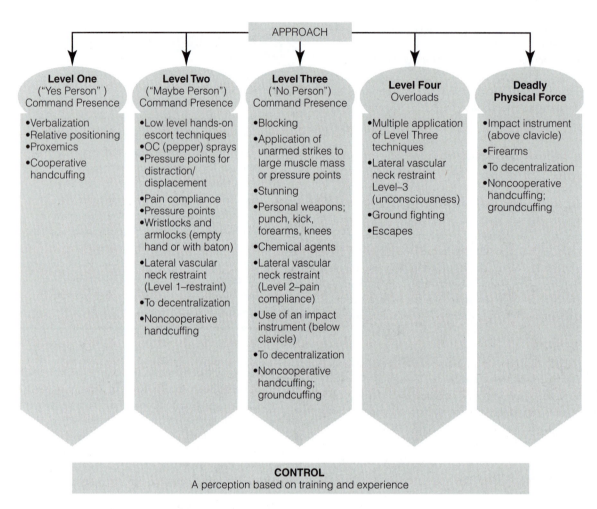

FIGURE 7.6   *Use of Force Continuum*

Source: *Police.* November 1995, p. 263. Reprinted by permission of Bobit Publishing, Redondo Beach, CA.

training. Warren and Rose (1999), however, feel a ladder-type view is misleading. They suggest, instead, a force wheel (see Figure 7.7), explaining (p. 107):

> In this suggested Force Wheel policy, the officer is placed at the center of the force wheel and is expected to move along a "spoke" toward the edge of the wheel. The officer responds with the "reasonable" amount of force to control the situation. If the situation changes to the point where the option is to escalate or de-escalate, the officers' force level travels around the "tire" of the wheel or straight across to reach the appropriate level to meet the "tense, uncertain and rapidly evolving" situation the officer faces. The Supreme Court intends to surround police with a fairly wide zone of protection in close cases that are "tense, uncertain and rapidly evolving" *(Roy v Lewiston)*.

Use of Deadly Force

Olson (1998, p. 1) states: "As one of the most liability-prone activities in law enforcement, deadly force decision making tops the list of training priorities for many agencies." Whether to use deadly force is a major and difficult decision for police officers. When it should be used is generally defined in state statutes, but three elements should always be present:

1. The suspect is threatening the officer or another person with a weapon.

2. The officer has probable cause to believe the suspect has committed a crime involving the inflicting or threatened inflicting of serious bodily harm.

3. The person is fleeing after committing an inherently violent crime, and the officer has given a warning.

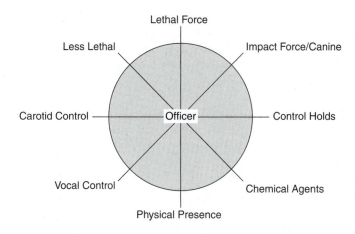

FIGURE 7.7 *Force Wheel*

Source: Rocky Warren and Dave Rose. "A New View on Police Use-of-Force." *Law and Order,* Vol. 47, No. 4, April 1999, p. 105. Reprinted by permission.

The use of deadly force is sometimes unavoidable. This officer, using his car as a shield, waits for a bank robber to emerge from the bank.

Officers should be aware of and mentally review these elements before making a decision. Justification of deadly force is based primarily on the facts and circumstances that caused the officer to believe the person to be dangerous.

Everyone understands that force should be used as a last resort. Use other nonlethal means when you have opportunity and time. Millions of arrests—many with the potential for use of deadly force—have been made without such force. Yet, even when officers try every possible means to avoid using such force, the actions of the subject or suspect may demand a response with deadly force. For example, "Seven police officers opened fire on a pickup and killed a 66-year-old dentist after a high-speed chase and standoff that ended when the driver tried to run down officers" ("Police Defend Killing . . .," 1999, p. 10B). Although the driver was unarmed, he tried several times to run over officers with his vehicle. When the brief chase ended in front of the driver's home, a police supervisor tried unsuccessfully to verbally coax the driver from the truck. Attempts to subdue the driver with a nonlethal beanbag fired from a shotgun also failed. When the driver finally revved the engine and threw the truck into reverse toward the police, officers opened fire. The driver was killed. According to the police chief, "The officers made every attempt to try to resolve the situation without injury to the suspect, but the actions of the suspect took those options away."

Dealing with mentally ill or otherwise emotionally disturbed people can also present a use-of-force challenge. Flynn (1996a, p. 45) notes: "The mentally ill may show an unreasonable fear of persons, places or things. They may become introverted or violent without provocation. . . . The mentally ill sometimes exhibit signs of panic—showing extreme fright or depression—for unapparent reasons." Furthermore (p. 46): "Mentally ill persons tend to exhibit greater strength than normal individuals." The dilemma, according to Flynn (p. 44), is: "Some officers have used too little force in these situations and were injured or killed. Others used too much force and lost their careers or went to jail." "Suicide by police" is a phenomenon in which someone intentionally acts so threatening toward officers as to force them to fire, accomplishing the subject's ultimate goal of dying, albeit not by their own hand.

In making an arrest, the officers' judgment regarding the degree of force is subject to the review and criticism of others who will have ample time to consider all the facts of a situation. Such hindsight is far different from the necessity of making a life-and-death decision within seconds. Numerous Supreme Court rulings have supported the need for officers to make split-second decisions involving deadly force, rulings grounded in several provisions set forth in the U.S. Constitution. Hall (1999, pp. 28, 32) explains:

> Because the Fourth Amendment governs the use of deadly force relating to arrests or other seizures of persons, and the Eighth Amendment governs the use of deadly force against convicted prisoners, it may be stated as a general principle that due process governs deprivations of life, liberty or property that fall outside the boundaries of those two amendments. . . .
>
> Just as with the Fourth and Eighth Amendment standards, the due process standard gives considerable deference to an officer's judgment in high-stress and fast-moving situations.

Police officers carry guns and are trained in using them. They also have department policy on deadly force as a guide. Unfortunately, the point of last resort may be immediate because many police situations rapidly deteriorate to the point of "deadly force decision making." When such situations occur, they must be viewed in the light of both the department policies and the individual situation.

Department policies on deadly force should be reviewed periodically in the light of the most recent Supreme Court decisions. They must be restrictive enough to limit unreasonable use of deadly force but not so restrictive that they fail to protect the lives of officers and members of the community.

Use of a deadly weapon is carefully defined by state laws and department policy. Such policies usually permit use of a gun or other weapon only in self-defense or if others are endangered by the suspect. Some policies also permit use of a deadly weapon to arrest a felony suspect, to prevent an escape or to recapture a felon when all other means have failed. Warning shots are not usually recommended because they can ricochet, harming others.

One technological advance in firearms has shown promise in reducing deadly force incidents. As Wollander (1998, p. 80) states: "In order to reduce the potential for use of deadly force, many agencies across the country have begun to authorize and issue Crimson Trace laser sights as standard equipment." He further explains:

> In moments of tension and high stress, an officer's verbal commands to a suspect at gunpoint often go unanswered. These are critical moments when the officer must make split second, life or death decisions. The visual impact of the red laser dot has assisted officers in gaining compliance quickly.

Increased officer safety is another benefit of this device. Wollander notes (p. 81):

> The ability to gain target acquisition without lining up your eye to the weapon's fixed sights can reduce [officers'] head exposure by as much as 25 percent. . . . When dealing with a multiple suspect apprehension, officers arriving on the scene can quickly determine which suspects are covered by other officers and which are not. During the subsequent arrest and cuffing of the suspects, awareness of the laser helps officers stay out of each others' line of fire.

An important Supreme Court ruling, *Tennessee v Garner* (1985), bans law enforcement officers from shooting to kill fleeing felons unless an imminent danger to life exists. This ruling invalidates laws in almost half the states, allowing police officers to use deadly force to prevent the escape of a suspected felon. In this case police shot and killed an unarmed 15-year-old boy who had stolen $10 and some jewelry from an unoccupied house. The Court ruled: "A police officer may not seize an unarmed, nondangerous suspect by shooting him dead."

The *Garner* decision did not take away police officers' right to use deadly force. The Court acknowledged legitimate situations in which deadly force is not only acceptable, but necessary:

> Where the officer has probable cause to believe that the suspect poses a threat of serious physical harm, either to the officer or to others, it is not constitutionally unreasonable to prevent escape by using deadly force. Thus, if the suspect threatened the officer with a weapon or there is probable cause to believe that he had committed a crime involving the infliction or threatened infliction of serious physical harm, deadly force may be used if necessary to prevent escape and if—where feasible—some warning has been given.

In situations that involve a fleeing felon, officers must assess the situation rapidly, considering the law, department policy and the specific existing conditions. An officer need not wait to see a flash from a suspect's gun muzzle before taking action. On the other hand, the *Garner* decision effected policy changes in many departments that had previously approved shooting fleeing felons under all circumstances, including unarmed fleeing felons.

Off-Duty Arrests

Every department needs a policy that allows off-duty officers to make arrests. A suggested policy for off-duty arrests requires officers to:

- Be within the legal jurisdiction of their agency.
- Not be personally involved.
- Perceive an immediate need for preventing a crime or arresting a suspect.
- Possess the proper identification.

Unless all these conditions exist, officers should not make an arrest but should report the incident to their department for disposition. Garner (1997, pp. 34–35)

offers other suggestions for off-duty intervention, including these:

- Gather data and assess.
- Seek assistance immediately.
- Do not aggravate the situation.
- Find cover promptly.
- Do not get too close too soon.
- Never pose a threat to on-duty officers.

Garner (p. 35) concludes: "Do nothing that might contribute to a misidentification tragedy. Have your credentials in hand, and hold them up toward the arriving help."

False Arrest

Police officers always face the possibility of false arrest. Some officers carry insurance to protect themselves against such lawsuits. Most are idle threats, however.

A false-arrest suit is a civil tort action that attempts to establish that an officer who claimed to have authority to make an arrest did not have probable cause at the time of arrest. The best protection is to be certain that probable cause to arrest does exist, to have an arrest warrant or to obtain a conviction in court.

Even when the defendant is found not guilty of the particular offense, a basis for a false-arrest suit is not automatically established. A court will consider the totality of the circumstances at the time of the arrest and will decide whether they would lead an ordinarily prudent person to perceive probable cause and take the same action.

Police officers reduce the probability of valid false-arrest actions by understanding the laws they enforce, the elements of each offense and what probable cause is needed to prove each element. Police officers who honestly believe they have probable cause for an arrest can use the "good faith" defense, as established in *Pierson v Ray* (1967):

> A policeman's lot is not so unhappy that he must choose between being charged with dereliction of duty if he does not arrest when he has probable cause, and being mulcted [penalized] in damages if he does. Although the matter is not entirely free from doubt, the same consideration would seem to require excusing him from liability for acting under a statute that he reasonably believed to be valid but that was later held unconstitutional on its face or as applied.

Summary

Developing, locating, identifying and arresting suspects are primary responsibilities of investigators.

Field identification is on-the-scene identification of a suspect by a victim of or witness to a crime. Field identification must be made within minutes (usually 15–20 minutes) after a crime to be admissible. Suspects do *not* have the right to counsel at a field identification *(United States v Ash, Jr.)*.

If the suspect is not immediately identified, you must develop a suspect through information provided by victims, witnesses and other people likely to know about the crime or the suspect; through physical evidence at the crime scene; through psychological profiling; through information in police files; through information in other agencies' files; or through informants. Help witnesses describe suspects and vehicles by asking very specific questions and using an identification diagram.

Use the FBI's National Crime Information Center (NCIC-2000) to assist in developing or identifying suspects. The NCIC contains criminal fingerprint records and information on wanted criminals as well as on stolen property and vehicles.

Suspects can be identified through field identification, mug shots, photographic identification or lineups. Use field identification when the suspect is arrested at or near the scene. Use mug-shot identification if you believe the suspect has a police record. Use photographic identification when you are reasonably sure who committed the crime but the suspect is not in custody or a fair lineup cannot be conducted. The pictures should portray at least five people of comparable race, height, weight and general appearance. Tell witnesses they need not identify anyone from the photographs. A suspect does *not* have the right to a lawyer if a photographic lineup is used *(United States v Ash, Jr.)*.

Use lineup identification when the suspect is in custody. Have at least five people of comparable race, height, weight, age and general appearance. Ask them all to perform the same actions or speak the same words. Instruct those viewing the lineup that they need not make an identification. Suspects may refuse to participate in a lineup, but such refusal may be used against them in court *(Schmerber v California)*. Suspects have a right to have an attorney present during a lineup *(United States v Wade)*. Avoid having the same person make both photographic and lineup identification. If you do so, do not conduct both within a short time period.

Some investigations reach a point after which no further progress can be made without using surveillance, undercover agents or a raid. Before taking any of these measures, you should exhaust all alternatives.

The objective of surveillance is to obtain information about people or their associates and activities that may help solve a criminal case or protect witnesses. Surveillance can be stationary (fixed, plant or stakeout) or moving (tail or shadow). Moving surveillance can be rough, loose or close (tight) and done on foot or by vehicle. Electronic surveillance and wiretapping are considered forms of search and therefore are permitted only with probable cause and by direct court order *(Katz v United States)*.

The objective of an undercover assignment may be to gain a person's confidence or to infiltrate an organization or group by using an assumed identity and to thereby obtain information or evidence connecting the subject with criminal activity. If you are working undercover, write no notes the subject can read, carry no identification other than the cover ID, make sure any communication with headquarters is covert and do not suggest, plan, initiate or participate in any criminal activity.

The objectives of a raid are to recover stolen property, seize evidence or arrest a suspect. To be legal, a raid must be the result of a hot pursuit or under authority of a no-knock arrest warrant or a search warrant. Precautions in conducting raids include ensuring the raid is legal, planning carefully, assigning adequate personnel and equipment, thoroughly briefing every member of the raiding party and being aware of the possibility of surreptitious surveillance devices at the raid site.

An arrest may occur at any point during an investigation. Police officers are authorized to make an arrest (1) for any crime committed in their presence, (2) for a felony not committed in their presence if they have probable cause to believe the person committed the crime or (3) under the authority of an arrest warrant. A lawful arrest requires that probable cause for believing the suspect committed a crime be established *before* the arrest.

If your intent is to make an arrest and you inform the suspect of this intent and then restrict the suspect's right to go free, you have made an arrest. When making an arrest, use only as much force as is necessary to overcome any resistance. If no resistance occurs, you may not use any force.

Checklist

Identifying and Arresting Suspects

- Was a suspect observed by police on arrival at the scene?
- Was a suspect arrested at the scene?
- Was anyone observed at the scene by any other person?
- Was a neighborhood check made to determine suspicious people, vehicles or noises?
- Was the complainant interviewed?
- Were statements taken from witnesses or people having information about the crime?
- Was a description of the suspect obtained?
- Was the description disseminated to other members of the local police force? To neighboring police departments?
- Was any associative evidence found at the scene or in the suspect's possession?
- Were informants checked?
- Were similar crimes committed in the area? The community? Neighboring communities?
- Were field identification cards checked to determine who was in the area?
- Were modus operandi files reviewed to determine who commits the type of crime? Are the suspects in or out of prison?
- Were traffic tickets checked to see whether any person or vehicle was in the area at the time of the crime? Does the vehicle or crime compare with the suspect vehicle or person?
- Have other agencies been checked? Municipal? County? State? Federal?
- How was the person identified? Field identification? Mug shots? Photographic identification? Lineup identification? Was it legal?
- Was the arrest legal?

Surveillance

- Is there any alternative to surveillance?
- What information is needed from the surveillance?
- What type of surveillance is needed?
- Have equipment and personnel needs for the surveillance area been determined?
- Are the required equipment and personnel available?
- Are proper forms available for recording necessary information during the surveillance?
- Are all signals preestablished?

Undercover Assignments

- Is there any alternative to undercover work?
- What information is needed from the assignment?
- Is adequate information about the subject available?
- Have you established a good cover?
- How will you communicate with headquarters?
- What are you to do if you are arrested?
- Do you have an alternative plan if the initial plan fails?
- Do you have a plausible explanation for leaving once the assignment is completed?

Raids

- Is there any alternative to a raid?
- Have appropriate warrants been obtained?
- Have the objectives of the raid been clearly specified?
- Has a presurveillance of the raid location been conducted?
- Are adequate personnel and equipment available?
- Has a briefing been held?

Discussion Questions

1. Imagine that a burglary has occurred each of the last four nights in a 10-block residential area in a city of 200,000 people. How might an investigator start to determine who is committing these crimes? What sources of information and techniques can be used in developing a suspect?

2. Suppose you have obtained information concerning a suspect in a rape case. Two witnesses saw someone near the rape scene at about the time of the offense, and the victim was able to describe her assailant. How should identification be made?

3. How do cooperation of the public and of other police agencies each help in identifying and arresting suspects? Which is more important, public cooperation or the cooperation of other police agencies?

4. How are people selected for a lineup? How should a lineup be conducted—what are the legal requirements? What is done if the suspect refuses to participate?

5. What balance must be maintained between an individual's right to privacy and the public interest when using surveillance?

6. Under what conditions should a police raid be considered?

7. In what types of crimes would the use of an undercover agent be justified?

8. What type of "tail" would you use for each of the following: Checking the loyalty of an informant? A suspected bank robber planning to "case" a bank? A burglar known to meet frequently with another burglar? Someone suspected of being an organized-crime leader?

9. How much risk is involved in undercover assignments and raids? How can you minimize this risk?

10. When do outside agencies participate in surveillances, undercover assignments and raids?

References

Alvaro, Mardee. "Online 'Substations' Enhance Public Safety Efforts." *Police,* Vol. 24, No. 2, February 2000, pp. 44–47.

Ashley, Steven D. "Managing Aerosol Issues." *Law and Order,* March 1996, pp. 35–37.

Band, Stephen R. and Sheehan, Donald C. "Managing Undercover Stress: The Supervisor's Role." *FBI Law Enforcement Bulletin,* Vol. 68, No. 2, February 1999, pp. 1–6.

Barrientos, Tanya. "FBI Profiler Says Work not Glamorous." *Las Vegas Review Journal,* November 24, 1996, p. 29A.

Canon, Angie. "Critics Give Failing Grade to Police Use of High School Yearbooks." *Las Vegas Review Journal,* April 27, 1997, p. 21A.

"CertiFINDER Uses News, Public Records to Help Locate Suspects." *Law Enforcement Technology,* Vol. 26, No. 7, July 1999, pp. 88–92.

Chanen, David. "First Arrest as City's Chief Comes *Au Naturel* to Olson." (Minneapolis/St. Paul) *Star Tribune,* August 5, 1999, pp. B1, B3.

Cook, Patrick E. and Hinman, Dayle L. "Criminal Profiling: Science and Art." *Journal of Contemporary Criminal Justice,* Vol. 15, No. 3, August 1999, pp. 230–241.

"Cop Pleads Guilty to Torturing Immigrant." (Minneapolis/St. Paul) *Star Tribune,* May 26, 1999, p. A4.

Davis, Joseph A. "Criminal Personality Profiling and Crime Scene Assessment." *Journal of Contemporary Criminal Justice,* Vol. 15, No. 3, August 1999, pp. 291–301.

Dees, Tim. "New Wiretap Laws and Technology." *Law and Order,* June 1999, pp. 15–16.

Egger, Steven A. "Psychological Profiling." *Journal of Contemporary Criminal Justice,* Vol. 15, No. 3, August 1999, pp. 242–261.

"Entanglement Systems." *Law and Order,* January 1999, p. 70.

Fairburn, Dick. "To Kill . . . Or Not To Kill." *Police,* August 1996, pp. 78–103.

Flynn, Michael. "Mentally Ill." *Police,* November 1996a, pp. 44–46.

Flynn, Michael. *Police,* November 1996b, pp. 46–49.

Garner, Gerald. "Smart Approaches to Off Duty Intervention." *Police,* January 1997, pp. 34–35.

Hall, John C. "Due Process and Deadly Force." *FBI Law Enforcement Bulletin,* Vol. 68, No. 2, February 1999, pp. 27–32.

Hanratty, Thomas F. "Forensic Tracking." *Law and Order,* June 1998, pp. 39–41.

Hawkins, Jeff. "Violent Confrontations Are Escalating." *Law and Order,* March 1999, pp. 53–55.

Hawley, Donna Lea. "Undercover Officers Walk a Fine Legal Line." *Police,* November 1996, pp. 8–9.

Hoffman, John. "National Incident Based Reporting System: Still Far from 'National.' " *Law and Order,* Vol. 48, No. 1, January 2000, pp. 31–34.

"Identi-Kit 2000 and the Electronic Booking System." *Law and Order,* November 1998, pp. 33–35.

Imhoff, John J. and Cutler, Stephen P. "INTERPOL: Extending Law Enforcement's Reach Around the World." *FBI Law Enforcement Bulletin,* December 1998, pp. 10–16.

Imhoff, John J. and Cutler, Stephen P. "INTERPOL: Helping Police Around the World." *Law and Order,* March 1999, pp. 33–36.

Kash, Douglas A. "Tale of the Tape Is Most Often Legal." *Police,* July 1998, pp. 35–37.

Kennedy, Randall. "Race, the Police, and 'Reasonable Suspicion.' " In *Perspectives on Crime and Justice: 1997–1998 Lecture Series.* National Institute of Justice, November 1998. (NCJ-172851)

Klobuchar, Amy. "Closing This Gap Could Save Lives." (Minneapolis/St. Paul) *Star Tribune,* September 24, 1999, p. D4.

Lee, Bob. "He's Often on the Right Track." *Police,* September 1998, pp. 26–30.

Lines, Kate. "Police Profilers: A Behavioural Approach to Criminal Investigations." *The Police Chief,* Vol. LXVI, No. 9, September 1999, p. 49.

Lonsdale, Mark. "Raids." *Police,* January 1996, pp. 56–59.

Lorenson, Stacey. "INTERPOL: 'The World Is Our Beat.' " *Police,* September 1998, pp. 32–33.

MacKay, Ron. "Geographic Profiling: A New Tool for Law Enforcement." *The Police Chief,* Vol. LXVI, No. 12, December 1999, pp. 51–59.

McEwen, Tom. *National Data Collection on Police Use of Force.* Washington, DC: Bureau of Justice Statistics and the National Institute of Justice, April 1996.

McGuinness, J. Michael. "Judging Split-Second Decisions." *Police,* Vol. 24, No. 1, January 2000, pp. 58–59.

"Militarizing Mayberry." *Law and Order,* March 1998, p. 117.

"Mixed Verdict in Louima Torture Case." (Minneapolis/St. Paul) *Star Tribune,* June 9, 1999, p. A4.

Morrison, Richard. "Target Control: Laser Range-Finding Binoculars." *Law Enforcement Technology,* January 1997, pp. 35–36.

Muscoplat, Rick. "Keeping a Lid on Wiretap Costs." *Law and Order,* Vol. 45, No. 5, May 1999, pp. 35–37.

"NCIC-2000 Goes Online." *Law Enforcement Technology,* Vol. 26, No. 8, August 1999, p. 8.

"NCIC-2000: More Than Images." *NCJA Justice Bulletin,* March 1998, pp. 8–11.

Neubauer, Ronald S. "Police Use of Force in America: An IACP Update." *The Police Chief,* August 1999, p. 6.

Olson, Dean T. "Improving Deadly Force Decision Making." *FBI Law Enforcement Bulletin,* February 1998, pp. 1–9.

O'Neal, Charles W. "Surreptitious Audio Surveillance: The Unknown Danger to Law Enforcement." *FBI Law Enforcement Bulletin,* June 1998, pp. 10–13.

Otto, James P. "Sharpening Your Surveillance Skills." *Police,* June 1998, pp. 38–40.

Paynter, Ronnie L. "Imaging Technology: 3D I.D.s." *Law Enforcement Technology,* Vol. 26, No. 6, June 1999a, pp. 98–100.

Paynter, Ronnie L. "It Isn't Easy." *Law Enforcement Technology,* January 1999b, pp. 44–48.

Pilant, Lois. "Crime Mapping and Analysis." *The Police Chief,* Vol. LXVI, No. 12, December 1999, pp. 38–49.

"Police Defend Killing of Dentist after Chase." *Las Vegas Review Journal,* February 11, 1999, p. 10B.

Ross, Darrell L. "Assessing the Patterns of Citizen Resistance during Arrests." *FBI Law Enforcement Bulletin,* Vol. 68, No. 6, June 1999, pp. 5–11.

Scott, Brian. "Heat: Deploying OC Pepper Spray." *Police,* March 1998, pp. 40–41.

Siuru, William D., Jr. "Seeing in the Dark." *Law Enforcement Technology,* January 1997, p. 38.

Soto, Javier. "Documenting Undercover Investigations." *Law and Order,* Vol. 47, No. 5, May 1999, pp. 55–57.

Spaulding, Dave. "Plan and Train before Executing Search Warrant." *Law and Order,* December 1998, pp. 31–39.

Stevens, Dennis J. "Police Tactical Units and Community Response." *Law and Order,* March 1999, pp. 48–52.

Strandberg, Keith W. "Wiretapping." *Law Enforcement Technology,* January 1997, pp. 40–44.

Strandberg, Keith W. "Walking in a Criminal's Shoes." *Law Enforcement Technology,* October 1998, pp. 82–84.

Strandberg, Keith W. "Racial Profiling." *Law Enforcement Technology,* Vol. 26, No. 6, June 1999, pp. 62–66.

Strentz, Thomas. "Cross-Trained Versus Cross-Qualified." *Law and Order,* October 1998, pp. 113–114.

Szwajkowski, Leslie M. "Preserving Lawful Electronic Surveillance." *The Police Chief,* Vol. LXVI, No. 9, September 1999, pp. 40–42.

Warren, Rocky and Rose, Dave. "A New View on Police Use-of-force." *Law and Order,* April 1999, pp. 105–107.

Wollander, Adam. "Tactical Technology for the Next Millennium." *Law Enforcement Technology,* April 1998, pp. 80–81.

Preparing for and Presenting Cases in Court

Do You Know?

Why some cases are not prosecuted?

How to prepare a case for court?

How to review a case?

What to include in the final report?

What occurs during the pretrial conference?

What the usual sequence in a criminal trial is?

What direct examination is? What cross–examination is?

What kinds of statements are inadmissible in court?

How to testify most effectively?

When to use notes while testifying?

What nonverbal elements can influence courtroom testimony positively and negatively?

What strategies can make testifying in court more effective?

What defense attorney tactics to anticipate?

How to avoid objections to your testimony?

Introduction

For many possible reasons, most criminal cases are resolved without a trial. An excellent investigation may cause the defendant to plead guilty, the defendant may desire to plead guilty without going through a trial, or the plea-bargaining process may bring about a satisfactory resolution. Police training seldom devotes enough time to the subject of trial testimony. Most officers receive on-the-job experience with all its anxieties and frustrations.

Law enforcement is beginning to use some technology currently used in corporate presentations. As Strandberg (1996, p. 34) suggests:

> Justice may be blind, but she doesn't have to be technologically impaired. . . . Lawyers, judges and law enforcement alike will have to alter the way their jobs are done in . . . a virtual courtroom, but the task of the jury may be made easier by the advantage of reviewing exactly what happened in any given case. Justice may prevail, even better than it did before.

This chapter discusses the reasons some cases do not go to court and ways that a case might be closed by arrest and prosecution. Then it explains how to prepare a case for prosecution. Next the chapter describes the typical sequence of events in a criminal trial. Then suggestions are provided for testifying under direct examination, strategies for excelling as a witness and testifying under cross-examination. The chapter ends with a discussion on concluding your testimony. ■

Nonprosecution

A criminal case can be closed without prosecution for several valid reasons.

- - - - - - - -

Cases are not prosecuted if:

■ The complaint is invalid.

■ The prosecutor declines after reviewing the case.

■ The complainant refuses to prosecute.

■ The offender dies.

■ The offender is in prison or out of the country and cannot be returned.

■ No evidence or leads exist.

- - - - - - - -

Invalid Complaints

Some complaints turn out to be unfounded. For example, investigation may reveal that property that was claimed stolen was actually lost or misplaced and later found. Damage may have been caused by other than a criminal act. The complainant may be senile, habitually intoxicated, mentally incapacitated or for some other reason incapable of providing a valid crime report.

Exceptional Clearance

Some cases cannot be prosecuted because of circumstances beyond the investigating officer's control. Despite ample evidence, prosecution may be impossible because the complainant refuses to prosecute and withdraws the complaint, the suspect dies or the offender is identified but is in prison or out of the state or country and cannot be returned for prosecution.

Lack of Evidence or Leads

Administrative policy sometimes closes cases to further investigation. Specific criteria are established for these decisions. The caseload of investigative personnel has grown so large that cases with little probability of successful prosecution must be closed as a matter of maintaining priorities.

Many police departments have incorporated such criteria into their crime report forms. If enough criteria are met, the department closes the case to further investigation and notifies the complainant. This often happens when the complainant files a report "only because my insurance company requires me to report the loss to the police." The loss may have occurred many days before the report, or there may be no leads. In some cases there are insufficient facts to support the complaint, but the victim insists on filing a complaint and has the right to do so.

In other cases, there is a valid report, but investigation reveals that witnesses have left the area or that no physical evidence remains at the crime scene. Without physical evidence, witnesses, identifiable leads or information to follow up, it is unwise to pursue the case when more pressing cases abound. Such cases are placed in an inactive file and are reopened only if time is available or new information is received. Occasionally such cases are cleared by the admission or confession of a suspect arrested for another crime. The case is then reopened and cleared by exceptional clearance.

Closing a Case by Arrest and Prosecution

If sufficient evidence exists to continue an investigation or if a person is already in custody for an offense, pursue the case for all possible evidence to prove innocence or guilt. If no arrest has been made, consider all information to determine whether a crime was committed, whether evidence is sufficient to prosecute and whether to arrest the suspect. Make such decisions after consulting with the prosecuting attorney's office.

The prosecutor is your legal adviser throughout the process—during the investigation, the pretrial conference and the court presentation. Follow the prosecutor's advice even if you disagree, for it is best to work out the issues of the case together. Jealousy and animosity must not impede the objective: justice. Tell the prosecutor the facts of the case, and then listen to and learn from the prosecutor.

The decision to charge or to arrest is made by the investigator alone or jointly with the prosecuting attorney's office. If the suspect was at the scene of the crime, you probably made an immediate arrest. Otherwise, consult the prosecuting attorney's office to obtain an arrest warrant.

The prosecutor's office may have its own investigator. As Stone (1999, p. 24) explains: "A district attorney's investigator's . . . assignments can range from basic trial preparation to specialty investigations, such as officer-involved shootings and organized crime." Stone adds that such investigators are typically sworn police or peace officers, are armed and have full arrest powers (p. 24).

Preparing a Case for Prosecution

Once the decision is made to prosecute a case, more than "probable cause" is required. The prosecution must prove the case *beyond a reasonable doubt*—the degree of proof necessary to obtain a conviction. To do so, the prosecution must know what evidence they can introduce, what witnesses will testify, the strengths and weaknesses of the case and the type of testimony police investigators can supply.

To prepare a case for court:

- Review and evaluate all evidence, positive and negative.
- Review all reports on the case.
- Prepare witnesses.

- Write the final report.
- Hold a pretrial conference with the prosecutor.

Review and Evaluate Evidence

Each crime consists of one or more elements that must be proven. The statutes and ordinances of the particular jurisdiction define these elements.

Concentrate on proving the elements of the crime and establishing the offender's identity.

Review physical evidence to ensure that it has been properly gathered, identified, transported and safeguarded between the time it was obtained and the time of the trial. Make sure the evidence is available for the trial and that it is taken to the courtroom and turned over to the prosecuting attorney. Arrange for trained laboratory technicians' testimony if necessary. Select evidence that is material, relevant and competent and that helps to establish the corpus delicti: what happened and who was responsible.

Review and evaluate witnesses' statements for credibility. If a witness claims to have seen a specific act, determine whether the light was sufficient and whether the witness has good eyesight and was in a position to see the act clearly. Also assess the witness's relationship to the suspect and the victim.

Establish the identity of the suspect by eyewitness testimony, transfer evidence and supporting evidence such as motive, prior knowledge, opportunity and known modus operandi.

Videotapes are being used increasingly in court, especially in child abuse and sex crimes. Expert witnesses with heavy time commitments may be allowed to testify by videotape, saving the time and expense of a trip to the city where the trial is taking place. Videotapes have also been made of witnesses who are severely injured and cannot appear in court. In addition, videotapes of suspects' confessions and of crime scenes are invaluable.

Reviewing every aspect of the case before entering the courtroom is excellent preparation for testifying. Do not memorize answers to imagined questions, but be prepared.

Review Reports

Review written reports of everything done during the investigation. This includes the preliminary report, mem-

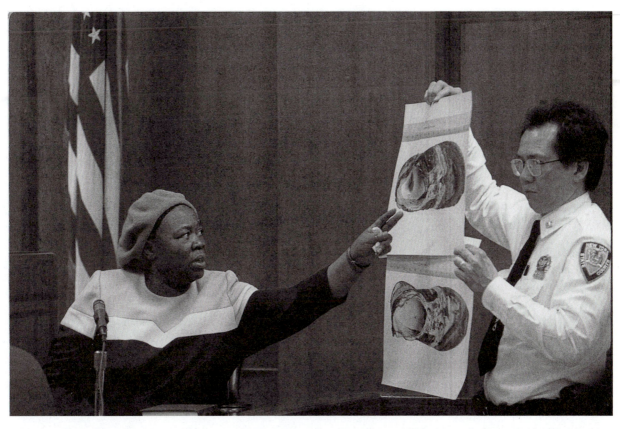

A witness at the 1996 trial of accused subway firebomber Edward Leary points to photographs of his burned shoes as she testifies that when Leary took a subway seat next to her, she began "to smell gasoline." Leary, an unemployed computer programmer, was charged with 45 counts of attempted murder for two 1994 subway firebombings.

orandums, summary reports, progress reports, evidence records and receipts, photographs and sketches, medical examiner's reports, emergency squad records, laboratory test reports on evidence, statements of witnesses (positive and negative) and any other reports on actions taken during the investigation.

Prepare Witnesses

Reinterview witnesses to refresh their memories. Read their previous statements to them and ask if this is the evidence they will present in court. Such a review also helps allay any fears witnesses have about testifying in court. Describe trial procedures to the witnesses so they understand what will occur. Explain that they can testify only to facts from their own personal knowledge or from common knowledge. Emphasize that they must tell the truth and present the facts as they know them. Explain the importance of remaining calm, having a neat, clean appearance and remaining impartial.

By experience, police officers know of the many delays in court proceedings and of the waits in the courtroom or in the hall outside before they can testify. This should also be explained to witnesses who may be testifying for the first time so they can make flexible arrangements for the day. In addition, the complainants should be prepared for the possible delays and continuances that may be part of the defense's strategy to wear them down so they will drop the charges.

Prepare the Final Report

The final, or prosecution, report contains all essential information for prosecution. Submit the entire case file along with the prosecution report. The final decision about what evidence to use is made by the prosecutor who will try the case in court.

The report presents the facts of the case, a criminal history of the person charged, the types of evidence available and the names of those who can support such evidence by testimony in court, names of people the prosecutor can talk to for further information and a chronological account of the crime and subsequent investigation.

The final report contains (1) the complaint; (2) the preliminary investigation report; (3) all follow-up reports; (4) statements, admissions and confessions; (5) laboratory reports; (6) photographs, sketches and drawings; and (7) a summary of all negative evidence.

Prepare the report after a careful review of all information. Organize the facts logically.

The Complaint Include a copy of the original complaint received by the police dispatcher and complaint desk. This should include the date and time of the complaint, location of the incident, brief details, times when officers were dispatched and the names of the officers assigned to the initial call.

The Preliminary Investigation Report The report of the officer's initial investigation at the crime scene provides essential information on the time of arrival, lighting and weather conditions, observations at the scene and immediate and subsequent actions taken by officers responding to the call.

Follow-Up Reports Assemble each contact and follow-up report in chronological order, presenting the sequence of the investigation and the pattern used to follow leads. These reports contain the essential information gathered in proving the elements of the crime and in linking the crime to the suspect. The reports can be in the form of progress notes.

Statements, Admissions and Confessions Include the statements of all witnesses interviewed during the investigation. If written statements were not obtained, report the results of oral interviews with witnesses. Assemble all statements, admissions or confessions by suspects in a separate part of the report. Include the reports of all polygraphs or other examinations used to determine the truth of statements, admissions or confessions.

Laboratory Reports Assemble laboratory results in one segment of the final report. Make recommendations on how these results relate to other areas of the report.

Photographs, Sketches and Drawings Include photographs, sketches and drawings of the crime scene to show conditions when officers arrived and the available evidence.

Summary of Negative Evidence Include a summary of all negative evidence developed during the investigation. Statements of witnesses who claim the suspect was elsewhere at the time of the crime are sometimes proved false, but the prosecution must consider such statements and develop a defense. If information exists that the suspect committed the crime but did so in self-defense or accidentally, state this in the report. Include all recognizable weaknesses in proving the corpus delicti or the offender's identity.

Write the report clearly and accurately, following the guidelines presented in Chapter 3. The quality of the final report influences its credibility.

Arrange the material in a logical sequence and a convenient format. A binder or loose-leaf notebook works well for this because it allows the various units of information to be separated, with a labeled, tabbed divider for each unit.

Pretrial Conference

Before testifying in court and after you have made the final case preparation and final report, arrange for a pretrial conference with the prosecuting attorney. Organize the facts and evidence and prepare a summary of the investigation. Include in this summary the focal points and main issues of the case, an envelope containing copies of all reports and all other relevant documents.

At the pretrial conference with the prosecutor:

■ Review all the evidence.

■ Discuss the strengths and weaknesses of the case.

■ Discuss the probable line of questioning by the prosecutor and the defense.

Discuss complicated or detailed information fully to avoid misunderstanding. Discuss any legal questions concerning admissibility of evidence or testimony.

Sometimes witnesses are included in the pretrial conference. If so, listen carefully to what each witness says to the prosecuting attorney and to the prosecuting attorney's responses. During the trial, the judge may exclude all witnesses from the courtroom except the person testifying. Therefore, you may have no opportunity to hear the testimony of other witnesses or the approach used by the prosecuting attorney.

It is also a good idea to review the case with other officers who are going to testify. You may not hear their actual testimony, and it will help you if you know in advance what they are going to say.

Final Preparations

Shortly before the trial, again review your notes and your final report. Take with you only those notes you want to use in testifying. Be certain that the physical evidence is being taken to the courtroom and will be available for the prosecuting attorney when needed. Also make sure that laboratory technicians are available to appear when necessary.

Find out which courtroom you will be testifying in and look it over before the trial.

Dress appropriately. Most police departments have regulations regarding attire when officers appear in court. Usually these specify that officers should appear in uniform. A weapon may not be worn into the courtroom without special permission. If one is worn, it should not be visible. Do not wear dark or deeply tinted glasses. If you wear street clothes, dress conservatively. Avoid bright colors and large plaids. Do not overdo on accessories, and avoid bizarre haircuts. Your personal appearance reflects your attitude and your professionalism and will have a definite effect on the jury.

Finally, be on time.

The Trial

The main participants in a trial are the judge, jury, attorneys, the defendant and witnesses. The *judge,* or **magistrate,** presides over the trial, rules on the admissibility of the evidence and procedures, keeps order, interprets the law for the jurors and passes sentence if the defendant is found guilty.

The *jurors* hear and evaluate the testimony of all witnesses. Jurors consider many factors other than the words spoken. The attitude and behavior of witnesses, suspects and attorneys are constantly under the jury's scrutiny. Jurors notice how witnesses respond to questions and their attitudes toward the prosecution and the defense. They reach their verdict based on what they see, hear and feel during the trial. Typical jurors will have had limited or no experience with the criminal justice system outside of what they have read in the newspaper and seen on television.

Legal counsel presents the prosecution and defense evidence before the court and jury. Lawyers act as checks against each other and present the case as required by court procedure and the rulings of the presiding judge.

Defendants may or may not take the witness stand. If they do so, they must answer all questions put to them. They may not use the Fifth Amendment, which protects a person from self-incrimination, as a reason for not answering. However, some believe it is time to force defendants to tell their side of the story. Kaul (1997, p. 13B) asserts: "The crucial difference in the two O. J. [Simpson] trials was that he wasn't forced to testify in the first (criminal) and was in the second." Indeed, as Kalk (1997, p. 54) states: "Today, if the defendant does not take the stand, he can enhance his chances of successfully defending against a criminal prosecution by attempting to destroy the credibility of the police officer testifying against him."

Witnesses present the facts as they know them. Police officers are witnesses for the prosecution. Law enforcement witnesses present a challenge to the prosecution's case because the prosecuting attorney must establish the burden of proof beyond a reasonable doubt.

Sequence of a Criminal Trial

A trial begins with a case being called from the court docket. If both the prosecution and the defense are ready, the case is presented before the court.

The sequence in a criminal trial is as follows:

- Jury selection
- Opening statements by the prosecution and the defense
- Presentation of the prosecution's case
- Presentation of the defense's case
- Closing statements by the prosecution and the defense
- Instructions to the jury
- Jury deliberation to reach a verdict
- Reading of the verdict
- Acquittal or passing of sentence

If the trial is before a judge *without a jury,* the prosecution and the defense make their opening statements directly to the court. The opening statements are brief summaries of both the prosecution and the defense attorneys' plans. In a *jury trial,* the jury is selected and then both counsels make their opening statements before the judge and jury.

The prosecution presents its case first. Witnesses for the prosecution are sworn in, and the prosecuting attorney asks them questions. Then the defense attorney may cross-examine the witnesses. After this cross-examination the prosecuting attorney may redirect examine, and then the defense attorney may re-cross-examine.

Direct examination is the initial questioning of a witness or defendant by the lawyer who is using the person's testimony to further his or her case. **Cross-examination** is questioning by the opposing side for the purpose of assessing the validity of the testimony.

After the prosecutor has completed direct examination of all prosecution witnesses, the defense presents its case. After the direct examination of each defense witness, the prosecutor may cross-examine, the defense counsel may redirect examine and the prosecutor may re-cross-examine.

After each side has presented its regular witnesses, both sides may present *rebuttal* and *surrebuttal* witnesses. When the entire case has been presented, prosecution and defense counsel present their closing arguments. In these arguments the lawyers review the trial evidence of both sides and tell the jury why the defendant should be convicted or acquitted. Sometimes the lawyers also make recommendations for penalty.

The judge instructs the jury on the laws applicable to the case and on how they are to arrive at a decision. The jury then retires to the jury room to deliberate and arrive at a verdict. When the jury reaches a verdict, court is reconvened and the verdict is read. If the verdict is for acquittal, the defendant is released. If the verdict is guilty, the judge passes sentence or sets a time and date for sentencing.

Testifying under Direct Examination

You are on trial, too—your credibility, your professionalism, your knowledge, your competence, your judgment, your conduct in the field, your use of force, your adherence to official policies, your observance of the defendant's rights—they're all on trial.

—Devallis Rutledge

First impressions are critical. Know what you are doing when you enter the courtroom. When your name is called, answer "Here" or "Present" and move directly to the front of the courtroom. Do not walk between the prosecutor and the judge; go behind the attorneys. Walk confidently; the jurors are there to hear the facts from you. If your investigation has been thorough and properly conducted, the jury will give a great deal of weight to your testimony.

If you have notes or a report, carry them in a clean manila file folder in your left hand so your right hand is free for taking the oath. Taking the oath in court is basically the same as taking your oath of office. Stand straight and face the clerk of court, holding the palm of your hand toward the clerk. Use a clear, firm voice to answer "I do" to the question: "Do you promise to tell the truth, the whole truth and nothing but the truth, so help you God?" Do not look at the judge, either legal counsel or the jury.

Sit with your back straight but in a comfortable position, usually with your hands folded in your lap or held on the arms of the chair. Do not move the chair around or fidget because this is distracting. The witness chair in all courtrooms is positioned so you can face the judge, legal counsel, jury or the audience, depending on to whom your answers are directed. Hold notes and other reports in your lap.

The prosecutor will ask you to state your name, department and position. As you respond, keep in mind the types of statements that are not admissible.

Inadmissible statements include:

■ Opinions and conclusions (unless the witness is qualified as an expert).

■ Hearsay.

■ Privileged communication.

■ Statements about character and reputation, including the defendant's criminal record.

Testify only to what you actually saw, heard or did, not what you believe, heard from others or were told about. You can testify to what a defendant told you directly, but any other statements must be testified to by the person making them.

Preparation is the key to being a good witness. After a review of your personal notes and all relevant reports, you will be familiar with the case and can "tell it like it is." This will come across well to the jury and establish your credibility.

- - - - - - - - -

Guidelines for effective testimony:

- Speak clearly, firmly and with expression.
- Answer questions directly. Do *not* volunteer information.
- Pause briefly before answering.
- Refer to your notes if you do not recall exact details.
- Admit calmly when you do not know an answer.
- Admit any mistakes you make in testifying.
- Avoid police jargon, sarcasm and humor.
- Tell the complete truth as you know it.

- - - - - - - - -

How you speak is often as important as what you say. Talk slowly, deliberately and loudly enough to be heard by everyone. Never use obscenity or vulgarity unless the court requests a suspect's or victim's exact words and they include it. In such cases, inform the court before you answer that the answer requested includes obscenity or vulgarity.

Ignore the courtroom's atmosphere. Devote your entire attention to giving truthful answers to questions. Answer all questions directly and politely with "Yes" or "No" unless asked to relate an action taken, an observation made or information told to you directly by the defendant. Refer to the judge as "your honor" and to the defendant as "the defendant." Do not volunteer information. Instead, let the prosecution decide whether to pursue a particular line of questioning.

Take a few seconds after hearing the question to form your answer. If the counsel or the court objects to a question, wait until instructed to proceed. If it takes some time for the judge to rule on an objection, ask to have the question repeated.

- - - - - - - - -

Refer to your notes if you are uncertain of specific facts, but do not rely on them excessively.

- - - - - - - - -

Reviewing the case thoroughly before your courtroom appearance does not mean you should memorize specific dates, addresses or spellings of names and places. Memorization can lead to confusion. Instead use notes to help avoid contradictions and inconsistencies. An extemporaneous answer is better received by the judge and jury than one that sounds rehearsed.

Using notes too much detracts from your testimony, weakens your presentation and gives the impression you have not adequately prepared for the case. It can also lead to having your notes introduced into the record. If, as you refer to your notes, you discover you have given erro-

neous testimony such as an incorrect date or time, notify the court immediately. Do not try to cover up the discrepancy. Everyone makes mistakes. If you admit them in a professional manner, little harm results. Do not hesitate to admit that you do not know the answer to a question or that you do not understand a question. Never bluff or attempt to fake your way through an answer.

In addition, be aware of certain phrases that may leave a negative impression on the jury. Phrases such as "I believe" or "to the best of my recollection" will not impress a jury. Do not argue or use sarcasm, witticisms or "smart" answers. Be direct, firm and positive. Be courteous whether the question is from the prosecutor or an objection from the defense or the judge. Do not hesitate to give information favorable to the defendant. Your primary responsibility is to state what you know about the case.

Nonverbal Factors

Do not underestimate the power of nonverbal factors as you testify.

- - - - - - - - -

Important nonverbal elements include dress, eye contact, posture, gestures, mannerisms, rate of speech and tone of voice.

- - - - - - - - -

Avoid actions associated with deception such as putting a hand over your mouth, rubbing your nose, preening, straightening your hair, buttoning up your coat, picking lint off your clothing or tugging at your shirt or a pant leg.

Strategies for Excelling as a Witness

Kalk (p. 55) stresses: "In order to do battle in the courtroom, a police officer must remain in top mental condition, be alert and be prepared." He suggests 13 ways to increase your chances of success in the courtroom:

- Do your homework.
- Educate the prosecuting attorney.
- Be truthful and professional.
- Look professional.
- Establish your credentials.
- Communicate to the jury.
- Use demonstrative evidence.

Las Vegas police officer Bruce Gentner stands before a Clark County coroner's inquest jury and demonstrates how Las Vegan John Perrin was reaching into his waistband during the pair's deadly confrontation in April 1999.

- Keep the jury interested.
- Enhance your credibility.
- Force the defense attorney to prove the defendant's case.
- Control your testimony.
- Maintain your professional composure.
- Testify in a professional manner.

The quotation at the beginning of the previous section is by Devallis Rutledge, a former police officer, presently a prosecutor. His book *Courtroom Survival: The Officer's Guide to Better Testimony* (1987) contains more than 180 pages of practical, commonsense, vital advice for courtroom testimony and many examples of courtroom dialogue.

Rutledge's strategies for testifying in court include the following: (1) set yourself up, (2) provoke the defense into giving you a chance to explain, (3) be unconditional and (4) do not stall.

- Get into the habit of thinking ahead to the trial while you are still out in the field. Ask yourself, "What if they ask me this in court?"
- The rules of court severely restrict your answers to questions. No competent defense attorney is ever going to give you a chance to explain anything. So, you need to know how to provoke the defense attorney into giving you a chance to explain. Some of these provokers are: *definitely; certainly; certainly not; naturally; naturally not;* and one that always works: *Yes . . . and no.*
- Be unconditional. Some police officers seem to like the sound of the conditional word *would*. When I am prosecuting a case, I cringe at the sound of it because it is too indefinite.

Example:
Q: Who was your partner?
A: That would be Officer Hill.

- Do not stall. Do not repeat the attorney's question.

Example:
Q: Were you holding a flashlight?
A: Was I holding a flashlight? Yes, I was.

Expert Testimony

Officers who qualify as experts in an area are allowed to give opinions and conclusions, but the prosecution must qualify the officer as an expert on the stand. The prosecution must establish that the person has special knowledge that others of moderate education or experience in the same field do not possess. To qualify as an **expert witness,** one must have as many of the following as possible:

- Present or prior employment in the specific field
- Active membership in a professional group in the field
- Research work in the field
- An educational degree directly related to the field
- Direct experience with the subject if not employed in the field
- Papers, treatises or books published on the subject or teaching experience in it

Police officers can become experts on sounds, firearms, distances, lengths of time, visibility problems and so on simply by years of experience in police work. Other areas, such as firearms identification, fingerprint classification and handwriting analysis, require specialized training.

Just who qualifies as an expert is not always clear, and different qualifications may exist for scientific and non-scientific evidence. In 1993 the U.S. Supreme Court adopted rules for judging when scientific expert testimony should be allowed in civil cases ("Justices Debate Use . . . ," 1998, p. 7A). However, some justices have expressed doubts about courts' abilities to draw rigid lines between the black-and-white rules for scientific and nonscientific testimony. As Supreme Court Justice Ginsburg states: "The world is not that simple; there are shades."

Testifying under Cross-Examination

Stutler (1997, p. 1) notes:

> Courtroom dramas portrayed in the movies or on television often pit crafty defense attorneys against law enforcement officers who seem to have spent their entire careers on the witness stand. Their unimpeachable testimony stands up to grueling cross-examination, and the suspect goes to prison for life.
>
> In reality, over the course of their careers, most law enforcement officers rarely testify during actual trials. Still, when they do, they are considered expert witnesses whose credibility can make, or break, a case. Knowing this, defense attorneys attempt to undermine their credibility by challenging everything from their investigative techniques to their personal belief systems.

No contemporary case demonstrated these cross-examination attacks on police credibility more effectively than the O. J. Simpson murder trial. The defense was successful in shifting the focus away from the issue of the defendant's guilt and putting it directly on the incompetence of the police investigators. Robert Philibosian, former Los Angeles County District Attorney, states ("After the O. J. Verdict . . . ," 1996, p. 44): "Lawyers have always put the police department on the defensive. What this case [the O. J. Simpson murder

trial] has done has exposed some flaws in the way that this investigation was conducted that allowed defense attorneys to point to this as a horrible example and exaggerated the flaws that were present in this particular case."

Vail (1995, p. 23) notes: "It might be a bit upsetting to know that attorneys are willing to spend $375-plus to learn professional acting techniques in order to defend criminals in court—while making you, a professional police officer, look as inept and stupid as possible."

Cross-examination is usually the most difficult part of testifying. The defense attorney will attempt to cast doubt on your direct testimony in an effort to win an acquittal for the defendant. Know the methods of attack for cross-examination to avoid being trapped.

- - - - - - - - - -

During cross-examination the defense attorney might:

- Be disarmingly friendly or intimidatingly rude.
- Attack your credibility and impartiality.
- Attack your investigative skill.
- Attempt to force contradictions or inconsistencies.
- Ask leading questions or deliberately misquote you.
- Ask for a simple answer to a complex question.
- Use rapid-fire questioning.
- Use the silent treatment.

- - - - - - - - - -

The defense attorney can be extremely friendly, hoping to put you off guard by making the questioning appear to be just a friendly chat. The attorney might praise your skill in investigation and lead you into boasting or a show of self-glorification that will leave a very bad impression on the jury. The "friendly" defense attorney might also try to lead you into testifying about evidence of which you have no personal knowledge. This error will be immediately exposed and your testimony tainted, if not completely discredited.

At the opposite extreme is the defense attorney who appears outraged by statements you make and goes on the attack immediately. This kind of attorney appears very excited and outraged, as though the trial is a travesty of justice. A natural reaction to such an approach is to exaggerate your testimony or lose your temper, which is exactly what the defense attorney wants. If you show anger, the jury might believe you are more interested in obtaining a conviction than determining the truth. It is often hard for a jury to believe that the well-dressed, meek-appearing defendant in court is the person who was armed with a gun and robbed a store. Maintain your dignity and impartiality, and show concern for only the facts.

The credibility of your testimony can be undermined in many ways. The defense may attempt to show that you are prejudiced, have poor character or are interested only in seeing your arrest "stick." If asked, "Do you want to see the defendant convicted?" reply that you are there to present the facts you know and that you will abide by the court's decision.

The defense may also try to show that your testimony itself is erroneous because you are incompetent, lack information, are confused, have forgotten facts or could not have had personal knowledge of the facts you have testified to. Do not respond to such criticism. Let your testimony speak for itself. If the defense criticizes your reference to notes, state that you simply want to be completely accurate. Be patient. If the defense counsel becomes excessively offensive, the prosecutor will intervene. Alternatively, the prosecutor may see that the defense is hurting its own case by such behavior and will allow the defense attorney to continue.

The defense attorney may further try to force contradictions or inconsistencies by incessantly repeating questions using slightly different wording. Repeat your previous answer. If the defense claims that your testimony does not agree with that of other officers, do not change your testimony. Whether your testimony is like theirs or different is irrelevant. The defense will attack it either way. If it is exactly alike, the defense will allege collusion. If it is slightly different, the defense will exaggerate this to convince the jury the differences are so great that the officers are not even testifying about the same circumstances.

The defense counsel may use an accusatory tone in asking whether you talked with others about the case and what they told you about how to testify. Such accusations may make inexperienced officers feel guilty because they know they have talked about the case with many people. Because the accusing tone implies this was legally incorrect, the officers may reply that they talked to no one. Such a response is a mistake because you may certainly discuss the case before testifying. Simply state that you have discussed the case with several people in an official capacity, but that none of them told you how to testify.

If defense counsel asks whether you have refreshed your memory before testifying, do not hesitate to say "yes." You would be a poor witness if you had not done so. Discussions with the prosecution, officers and witnesses and a review of notes and reports are entirely proper. They assist you in telling the truth, the main purpose of testimony.

Leading questions are another defense tactic. For example, defense counsel may ask, "When did you first strike the defendant?" This implies you did in fact strike the defendant. Defense attorneys also like to ask questions that presume you have already testified to something when in fact you may not have done so. If you are misquoted, call it to the counsel's attention and then repeat the facts you testified to. If you do not remember your exact testimony, have it read from the court record.

In addition, defense counsel may ask complicated questions and then say, "Please answer 'yes' or 'no.'" Obviously, some questions cannot be answered that simply. Ask to have the question broken down. No rule requires a specific answer. If the court does not grant your request, answer the question as directed and let the prosecutor bring out the information through redirect examination.

Rapid-fire questioning is yet another tactic that defense attorneys use to provoke unconsidered answers. Do not let the attorney's pace rush you. Take time to consider your responses.

Do not be taken in by the "silent treatment." The defense attorney may remain silent for what seems like many seconds after you answer a question. If you have given a complete answer, wait patiently. Do *not* attempt to fill the silence by saying things such as, "At least that's how I remember it," or "It was something very close to that."

Another tactic frequently used by defense attorneys is to mispronounce officers' names intentionally or address them by the wrong rank. This is an attempt to distract the officer.

Regardless of how your testimony is attacked, treat the defense counsel as respectfully as you do the prosecutor. Do not regard the defense counsel as your enemy. You are in court to state the facts and tell the truth. Your testimony should exhibit no personal prejudice or animosity, and you should not become excited or provoked at the defense counsel. Be professional.

Few officers are prepared for the rigor of testifying in court, even if they have received training in this area. Until officers have actually testified in court, they cannot understand how difficult it is. Because police officers are usually the primary and most damaging witnesses in a criminal case, defense attorneys know they must attempt to confuse, discredit or destroy the officers' testimony.

The best testimony is accurate, truthful and in accordance with the facts. Every word an officer says is recorded and may be played back or used by the defense.

Handling Objections

Rutledge (pp. 99–115) gives the following suggestions for handling objections (reprinted by permission of the publisher):

> There are at least 44 standard trial objections in most states. We're only going to talk about the two that account for upwards of 90 percent of the problems a testifying officer will have: that your answer is a conclusion, or that it is non-responsive.
>
> ■ How to avoid conclusions. One way is to listen to the form of the question. You know the attorney is asking you to speculate when he starts his questions with these loaded phrases:
>
> Would you assume . . . ?
>
> Do you suppose . . . ?
>
> Don't you think that . . . ?
>
> Couldn't it be that . . . ?
>
> Do you imagine . . . ?
>
> Wouldn't it be fair to presume . . . ?
>
> Isn't it strange that . . . ?
>
> And the one you're likely to hear most often:
>
> Isn't it possible that . . . ?
>
> ■ Another major area of conclusionary testimony is what I call mindreading. You can't get inside someone else's brain. That means you don't know for a fact—so you can't testify—as to what someone else sees, hears, feels, thinks or wants; and you don't know for a fact what somebody is trying to do, or is able to do, or whether he is nervous, excited, angry, scared, happy, upset, disturbed, or in any of the other emotional states that can only be labeled with a conclusion.
>
> ■ How to give "responsive" answers. You have to answer just the question you're asked—no more, no less. That means you have to pay attention to

how the question is framed. You answer a yes-or-no question with a "yes" or "no."

> Q: Did he perform the alphabet test?
>
> A: Yes, twice—but he only went to "G."

Everything after the "yes" is non-responsive. The officer anticipated the next three questions and volunteered the answers. He should have limited each answer to one question:

> Q: Did he perform the alphabet test?
>
> A: Yes.
>
> Q: How many times?
>
> A: Twice.
>
> Q: How far did he go correctly the first time?
>
> A: To the letter "G."

-- -- -- -- -- --

To avoid objections to your testimony, avoid conclusions and nonresponsive answers. Answer yes-or-no questions with "yes" or "no."

-- -- -- -- -- --

The defense lawyer's most important task is to destroy your credibility—to make you look like you're either an incompetent bungler, a liar, or both. How does he do that? He attacks you. He tricks you. He outsmarts you. He confuses you. He frustrates you. He annoys you. He probes for your most vulnerable characteristics (Rutledge, p. 118).

Concluding Your Testimony

Do not leave the stand until instructed to do so by the counsel or the court. As you leave the stand, do not pay special attention to the prosecution, defense counsel, defendant or jury. Return immediately to your seat in the courtroom or leave the room if you have been sequestered. If you are told you may be needed for further testimony, remain available. If told you are no longer needed, leave the courtroom and resume your normal activities. To remain gives the impression you have a special interest in the case.

If you are in the courtroom at the time of the verdict, show neither approval nor disapproval at the outcome. The complainant should be notified of the disposition of the case. A form such as the one shown in Figure 8.1 is frequently used.

FIGURE 8.1

Case Disposition Notice

CASE DISPOSITION REPORT

Date Disposition Made: __4-25-99__   D.R. #: __97-1002__
Date of Incident: __2-10-97__   Type of Incident: __Burglary__

DISPOSITION:
(X) Case Clearance
(X) Property Recovered
( ) Disposition of Property: (X) Owner ( ) Police Evidence
( ) Other
If <u>Other</u>, specify type: _____

VICTIM: (If Runaway Juvenile or Missing Adult, disregard this section)
Name __Jerome Slater__ Address __3041 Harding, Edina, Minnesota__

SUSPECT(S):
NO. 1: __John Toben__ Arrested? __Yes__ BCPD I.D. # __20146__
NO. 2: __William Moss__ Arrested? __Yes__ BCPD I.D. # __20147__
NO. 3: _____ Arrested? _____ BCPD I.D. # _____

PROPERTY RECOVERED:
Item No. 1: __One Car Radio, Sears__ Value __$87.00__
Item No. 2: __One car battery, Sears__ Value __60.00__
Item No. 3: __Micro Wave Oven-GE__ Value __250.00__
Item No. 4: __One 17" TV-Sears Solid State__ Value __350.00__
Recovering Agency: __Edina Police Department__ Total Value Recovered Property: __$747.00__

CANCELLATIONS: (Specify date, time, agency and officer receiving cancellation and officer making cancellation)

NCIC: _____
Other Agencies: __Hennepin County Sheriffs Office__
Other Agencies: _____

OFFICER MAKING DISPOSITION: _____
SUPERVISOR APPROVING: _____
DETAILS: __Full recovery of property__

Summary

To prosecute or not to prosecute is often a question. Some cases are never prosecuted because the complaint is invalid, it is exceptionally cleared, or no evidence or leads exist. If the decision is made to prosecute, thorough preparation is required. To prepare a case for court: (1) review and evaluate all evidence, positive and negative; (2) review all reports on the case; (3) prepare witnesses; (4) write the final report; and (5) hold a pretrial conference with the prosecutor. Concentrate on proving the elements of the crime and establishing the offender's identity.

The final report contains (1) the complaint; (2) the preliminary investigation report; (3) all follow-up and progress reports; (4) statements, admissions and confessions; (5) laboratory reports; (6) photographs, sketches and drawings; and (7) a summary of all negative evidence. The quality of the content and writing of the report influences its credibility.

Before the trial, hold a conference with the prosecutor to review all the evidence, to discuss the strengths and weaknesses of the case and to discuss the probable line of the prosecutor's and defense attorney's questioning.

A criminal trial begins with the jury selection. When court convenes, prosecution and defense make their opening statements. The prosecution then presents its case, followed by presentation of the defense's case. After closing statements by the prosecution and the defense, the judge instructs the jury, which then retires to deliberate its verdict. When a verdict is reached, court is reconvened and the verdict read. If the defendant is found guilty, the judge passes sentence or sets a sentencing date.

Direct examination is the initial questioning of a witness or defendant by the lawyer who is using the person's testimony to further that lawyer's case. Cross-examination is questioning by the opposing side with the intent of assessing the validity of the testimony.

Certain types of statements are inadmissible in court, including opinions, conclusions, hearsay, privileged communications and statements about the defendant's character and reputation. To present testimony effectively, speak clearly, firmly and with expression; answer questions directly, and do *not* volunteer information; pause briefly before answering; refer to your notes if you do not recall exact details; admit calmly when you do not know an answer; admit any mistakes you make in testifying; avoid police jargon, sarcasm and humor; and above all, tell the complete truth as you know it. Refer to your notes if you are uncertain of specific facts, but do not rely on them excessively; this would give the impression that you are not prepared for the case and thus weaken your testimony. Important nonverbal elements include dress, eye contact, posture, gestures, mannerisms, rate of speech and tone of voice.

Strategies for testifying in court include (1) setting yourself up, (2) provoking the defense into giving you a chance to explain, (3) being unconditional and (4) not stalling. Anticipate the tactics commonly used by defense attorneys during cross-examination. They may be disarmingly friendly or intimidatingly rude; attack your credibility and impartiality; attack your investigative skill; attempt to force contradictions or inconsistencies; ask leading questions or deliberately misquote you; request a "yes" or "no" answer to complex questions; use rapid-fire questioning; or use the "silent treatment." To avoid objections to your testimony, avoid conclusions and nonresponsive answers. Answer yes-or-no questions with "yes" or "no."

If you are well prepared, know the facts and present them truthfully and professionally, you have done your part in furthering the cause of justice. The disposition of a case should be made known to the complainant.

Checklist
Presenting the Case in Court

■ Have all reports been reviewed?

■ Have all reports been organized for presentation to the prosecutor?

■ Has all evidence been located and made available for court presentation?

■ Has all evidence been examined by competent laboratories and the results obtained? Are copies of the reports available?

■ Have all known leads been developed?

■ Have both negative and positive information been submitted to the prosecuting attorney?

■ Has all arrest information been submitted?

■ Has a list of witnesses been prepared? Addresses? Telephone numbers?

■ Has the final report been assembled? Does it contain copies of investigators' reports? Photographs? Sketches? Evidence? Lab reports? Medical examiner's reports? Statements? Confessions? Maps? All other pertinent information?

■ Has a pretrial conference been held with the prosecutor's office?

■ Have all witnesses been reinterviewed? Notified of the date and time of the trial?

■ Have all expert witnesses been notified of the date and time of the trial?

■ Has someone been designated to take the evidence to court?

■ Have notes needed for testimony been removed from your notebook?

■ Is your personal appearance professional?

Discussion Questions

1. Plea bargaining has become very controversial in many states, and some states have eliminated it as a part of the prosecution process. Is plea bargaining good or bad?

2. The news media can affect jury and court decisions by publicizing information about a criminal case before it goes to trial. May police refuse to give information to the press if doing so might jeopardize the case in court? How significantly does such publicity affect the trial?

3. Are you familiar with cases in which outside judges have had to be brought in to try a case or in which the trial has had to be moved to another jurisdiction because of advance publicity?

4. Should criminal trials be televised? What are the advantages and disadvantages?

5. What is the investigator's role in preparing a case for court? How does the investigator cooperate with the prosecutor to enhance the courtroom presentation?

6. What are the necessary steps in preparing to testify in a criminal trial? What materials may be brought into the courtroom?

7. Imagine that you are preparing a final report for the prosecutor. What materials should you include? How should you organize them to show the continuity of your investigation and the way you gathered evidence related to the elements of the offense charged?

8. If you were accused of a crime, would you prefer a trial with or without a jury?

9. Is there a better system than the jury system?

10. Does an acquittal mean the investigator failed?

References

"After the O. J. Verdict: Looking for Clues." *Law Enforcement Technology,* March 1996, pp. 31–33, 44–45.

"Justices Debate Use of Experts in Court." *Las Vegas Review Journal,* December 8, 1998, p. 7A.

Kalk, Dan. "Witness or Suspect?" *Police,* July 1997, pp. 54–55.

Kaul, Donald. "The Fifth Amendment." *Las Vegas Review Journal,* February 19, 1997, p. 13B.

Rutledge, Devallis. *Courtroom Survival: The Officer's Guide to Better Testimony.* Incline Village, NV: Copperhouse Publishing Company, 1987.

Stone, Rebecca. "Investigators for the Prosecution Consider All the Angles." *Police,* May 1999, pp. 24–28.

Strandberg, Keith W. "The Courtroom of the Future." *Law Enforcement Technology,* June 1996, pp. 34–39.

Stutler, Thomas R. "Stand and Deliver: Cross-Examination Strategies for Law Enforcement." *FBI Law Enforcement Bulletin,* September 1997, pp. 1–5.

Vail, Christopher. "Combating Courtroom Butterflies." *Law and Order,* September 1995, pp. 23–26.

Investigating Crimes against Persons

Part One of the FBI's *Uniform Crime Reports* (UCR) contains statistics on eight types of serious crimes: murder, aggravated assault, forcible rape, robbery, burglary, larceny/theft, motor vehicle theft and arson. According to recent UCR statistics, 1998 showed the seventh consecutive annual drop in crime ("FBI's UCR Shows . . . ," 1999, p. 3):

> Both violent crimes and property crimes decreased in 1998 compared to the year before. . . . The greatest decrease in the violent crime category was for robbery, which dropped 11 percent in one year. The number of murders dropped 8 percent. Rape and aggravated assault figures declined 5 percent.

Caution must be used in looking at such figures. A National Crime Survey conducted by the United States Census Bureau found that about half of all crimes are *not* reported to police.

According to the *Uniform Crime Reports* for *1998,* a violent crime occurred nationally every 19 seconds:

- 1 robbery every 1 minute
- 1 aggravated assault every 32 seconds
- 1 forcible rape every 6 minutes
- 1 murder every 31 minutes

Investigating crimes against persons is made more difficult by the emotionalism usually encountered not only from the victim but also from the public.

Generally, however, investigating crimes against persons results in more and better information and evidence than investigating crimes against property, discussed in Section Four.

In crimes against persons, the victim is often an eyewitness, an important source of information and a key to identifying the suspect. The victim and other witnesses are often able to provide important information on the type of crime, the person attacked, how and by what means the attack was made, what the attacker's intent or motive was and what words may have been spoken.

Weapons may provide physical evidence, as may any injuries the victim suffered. Typically, crimes against persons yield much physical evidence, with the type of evidence to anticipate directly related to the type of crime committed. Normally you can expect to find such evidence as a weapon, blood, hair, fibers, fingerprints, footprints and so on, depending on the specific crime. Consequently the arrest rate is high.

In recent years, violent-crime investigations have been enhanced by the establishment of the Violent Crime Apprehension Program (VICAP) at the FBI National Police Academy in Quantico, Virginia. The goal of this program is to coordinate major violent-crime cases, regardless of their location, in the United States. Information considered viable is published in the FBI's *Law Enforcement Bulletin*. If the case merits interagency cooperation, a major case investigation team of investigators from all involved agencies may be formed.

Viability is determined by specialists at VICAP who review the information submitted and compare it with information received from other departments about similar cases and their modus operandi. This is especially important in serial killings and other major violent crimes in which the suspects have moved to other areas and committed similar crimes.

The chapters in this section of the book discuss specific considerations in investigating robbery (Chapter 9), assault (Chapter 10), rape and other sex offenses (Chapter 11), child abuse (Chapter 12) and homicide (Chapter 13). In actuality, more than one offense can occur in a given case. For example, what begins as a robbery can progress to an assault, then a forcible rape and finally a homicide. Each offense must be proven separately. Section Four discusses the remaining Index Crimes. The frequency of occurrence of the eight Index Crimes is shown in the following FBI Crime Clock.

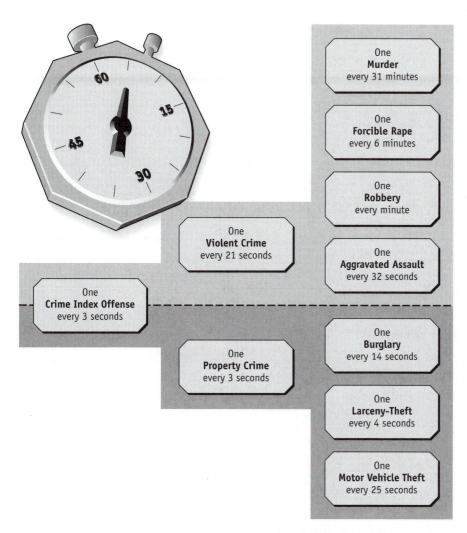

One
Murder
every 31 minutes

One
Forcible Rape
every 6 minutes

One
Robbery
every minute

One
Violent Crime
every 21 seconds

One
Aggravated Assault
every 32 seconds

One
Crime Index Offense
every 3 seconds

One
Burglary
every 14 seconds

One
Property Crime
every 3 seconds

One
Larceny-Theft
every 4 seconds

One
Motor Vehicle Theft
every 25 seconds

The Crime Clock should be viewed with care. Being the most aggregate representation of UCR data, it is designed to convey the annual reported crime experience by showing the relative frequency of occurrence of the Index Offenses. This mode of display should not be taken to imply a regularity in the commission of the Part I Offenses; rather, it represents the annual ratio of crime to fixed time intervals.

The 1998 Crime Clock

Source: The FBI's *Uniform Crime Reports*, October, 1999.

Robbery

Do You Know?

How robbery is defined?

How robberies are classified?

What home invaders are?

In what types of robbery the FBI and state officials become involved?

What relatively new category of robbery has become a national concern?

What the elements of the crime of robbery are?

What special challenges are posed by a robbery investigation?

What factors to consider in responding to a robbery-in-progress call?

How to prove each element of robbery?

What descriptive information is needed to identify suspects and vehicles?

What modus operandi information to obtain in a robbery case?

What physical evidence can link a suspect with a robbery?

Introduction

Robbery has plagued the human race throughout our history. During the 1930s John Dillinger, America's number-one desperado, captured the attention of citizens and law enforcement officers alike. This notorious bank robber's tools of the trade were a Thompson submachine gun and a revolver. Although admired by many for his daring and cast as a folk hero, Dillinger gunned down 10 men. "Pretty Boy" Floyd began his criminal career by robbing a local post office of $350 in pennies. Like Dillinger, he also killed 10 people. Who can forget the murder and robbery spree of Bonnie Parker and Clyde Barrow through Missouri, Texas and Oklahoma? A more recent case is the following (Meyer, 1997, p. 27):

> When LAPD Officers Loren Farell and Martin Perello drove by the Bank of America while on routine patrol in North Hollywood, Calif., on Feb. 28, 1997, they just happened to see armed robbers dressed like Ninja Turtles enter the bank.

The officers called for assistance. . . . Five minutes later, LAPD had the bank surrounded. . . .

The ensuing gunbattle ended in the deaths of both suspects and injuries to 11 officers and seven civilians.

According to Meyer (p. 32), the two bank robbers had five fully-automatic rifles, a semiautomatic pistol and a Molotov cocktail during the bank robbery. Zingo (1997, p. 23) states: "This gunbattle will be one of the classics that is talked about and viewed in survival tactics training classes for decades to come."

The preceding are vivid examples of the violent nature of many robberies. Robbery is one of the three most violent crimes against the person. Only homicide and rape are considered more traumatic to a victim.

This chapter begins with an overview of robbery and a description of how robberies might be classified. This is followed by an explanation of the elements of the crime of robbery. Next is a discussion of special challenges in investigating robberies, the preliminary investigation, proving the elements of the offense and conducting the complete investigation. The chapter concludes with a look at the problem of false robbery reports. ■

Robbery: An Overview

--- --- --- --- --- ---

Robbery is the felonious taking of another's property, either directly from the person or in that person's presence, through force or intimidation.

--- --- --- --- --- --- ---

Robbery takes many forms, from the daring exploits of criminals such as Dillinger to purse snatching and muggings. Whatever the form, the potential for violence exists.

Most robbers carry a weapon or other threatening item or indicate to the victim that they are armed. Therefore, little direct personal contact occurs between the robber and the victim, which reduces the probability of physical evidence remaining at the crime scene. Despite the inherent danger to the victim during a robbery, most robberies do not result in personal injury. Sometimes, however, a violent physical act is performed against the victim early in the robbery, either by original intent or

because of unexpected circumstances or resistance. Such cases involve additional charges of aggravated assault or, in the case of death, murder.

According to the FBI's *Uniform Crime Reports,* the use of violence during robberies has increased during the past 10 years, but such violence is not nearly as frequent as the public might expect. One theory about the low rates of injury and death during robberies is that threats of force, use of force or the presence of a weapon reduce the likelihood of the victim resisting. Confronted with threatening statements, a threatening note or a visible weapon, most robbery victims obey the robber's demands.

However, the behavior of an armed robber is unpredictable. In some cases when the victim resists, the robber may flee without completing the robbery. In one case, a man armed with a shotgun demanded and obtained $10,000 from a bank teller. Instead of leaving, he talked to the teller for 15 minutes, telling her that he was drunk and considering suicide. Then he handed the money back to the teller and walked out of the bank. In another case, a robber handed a bank teller a note that said, "Please put the money in this bag and no one will get hurt. Thank you very much." The teller called a bank guard and handed him the note. The guard read the note and told the robber, "Get out, you bum, or I'll blow your brains out." The robber quickly left the bank. In other instances, however, resisting victims have been injured or killed.

Violence against the victim also occurs in muggings and purse snatchings in which the victim is struck with a weapon, club or the fists or is knocked down. Older people are often injured by the fall resulting from such violent acts. Any such violent contact increases the probability of hair, fibers, scratches or other evidence being found on the victim or the suspect.

Most robbers are visibly armed with a weapon or dangerous device and make an *oral demand* for the desired money or property. For example, a robber uses a gun to obtain money from an attendant inside a service station. The gun is either visible, or the robber's hands are in a coat or jacket pocket in such a way as to indicate possession of a weapon.

Some robbers present a *note* rather than speaking. Figure 9.1 shows the actual wording of a note used in a robbery in Los Angeles. The robber may or may not ask for the note to be returned. It is important evidence if left behind.

Hostages are held in some robberies. In one case a bank's head cashier, his wife and their child were held captive by a robber for five hours one Saturday. The cashier was ordered to go to the bank and get money.

New York City Police Sgt. Gerard Rosato stands in the doorway of the Central Park Precinct station house on Oct. 13, 1999. Central Park, one of the city's most popular tourist attractions, is also the site of a recent string of fake robberies staged by foreign visitors to claim insurance money back in their home countries.

THIS IS A HOLD UP
I MEAN IT!
GIVE ME ALL YOUR
MONEY

FIGURE 9.1 *Bank Robbery Note*

The wife and child were tied up but left unharmed. In another case a woman was taken from her home and forced to drive two men to a bank in her car. They forced her to accompany them into the bank, robbed it, left her there and used her car for their getaway. Bank robberies and hostage situations are discussed later in this chapter.

Robbers use various ruses to get themselves into position for the crime. They may loiter, pose as salespeople or feign business, watching for an opportune moment to make their demands. Once the opportunity presents itself, robbers act quickly and decisively. Sometimes, however, their actions before the robbery give them away. One such case involved a robber who was captured by two FBI agents just as the teller was handing over the money. The robber was unaware that the FBI agents had been watching him since he entered the bank. His nervous actions had attracted their attention even though they were in the bank on other business at the time.

Stolen jewelry or cash usually cannot be recovered unless an arrest is made immediately after the crime. Stolen purses and wallets are usually discarded within minutes of the robbery.

The vast majority (91 percent) of robberies are committed by males. Robbers are usually serial criminals and may commit 15–25 robberies before being apprehended. People who commit robberies are often egotistical braggarts, prone to boasting of their crimes. Because of this, informants can provide excellent leads in robbery cases.

The most frequent victims of robberies are drug houses, liquor stores, fast-food places, jewelry stores, convenience stores, motels, gambling houses and private residences. The elderly are frequently robbery victims. Most such robberies are snatches of purses or packages committed by amateurs or juveniles.

Other characteristics of robberies include the following:

- They are committed with the use of stolen cars, stolen motor-vehicle license plates or both.
- They are committed by two or more people working together.
- The offender lives within 100 miles of the robbery.
- Robberies committed by a lone robber tend to involve lone victims and are apt to be crimes of opportunity (on the spur of the moment).
- Youths committing robberies tend to operate in groups and to use strong-arm tactics more frequently than adults.
- Less physical evidence is normally found after robberies than in other violent crimes.
- They take much less time than other crimes.
- Middle-aged and older people tend to be the victims.

In confrontational robberies, regardless of the offender's weapon, victims who defend themselves in some way are less likely to lose property than victims who take no actions. However, victims who defend themselves against armed offenders are more likely to be injured than are those who take no actions during the crime.

Classification

Robberies are classified into four categories, each committed by different types of people using different techniques.

Robberies are classified as residential, commercial, street and vehicle driver.

Residential Robberies

Residential robberies include those that occur in hotel and motel rooms, garages, elevators and private homes. These robberies are less frequent than the other types but are dangerous and traumatic because they tend to involve entire families.

Entrance is frequently gained by knocking on the door and then forcing entrance when the occupant appears. Most residential robberies occur in the early evening when people are apt to be home. Victims are frequently bound and gagged or even tortured as the robber attempts to learn the location of valuables. In some cases, people are robbed because they arrive home to discover a burglary in progress. The burglar is thus "forced" to become a robber.

Hotel, motel, garage or elevator robberies are carried out rapidly and frequently involve injury. Information from employees that a person has a large amount of jewelry or money determines the victim for some robberies.

A relatively new type of residential robber that is challenging police departments across the country has been dubbed the *home invader*. Home invaders usually target a resident, not a residence, often women, senior citizens or drug dealers.

Commercial Robberies

Convenience stores, loan companies, jewelry stores, liquor stores, gasoline or service stations and bars are especially susceptible to robbery. Drugstores are apt to be targets of robberies to obtain narcotics as well as cash.

Commercial robberies occur most frequently toward the end of the week between 6 P.M. and 4 A.M. Stores

Robberies involving motel rooms, garages, elevators and private homes are all classified as residential robberies. Though infrequent, compared to other robbery classifications, they are considered dangerous as they pose a threat to entire families.

with poor visibility from the street and few employees on duty are the most likely targets. Many stores now keep only a limited amount of cash on hand during high-risk times. Stores also attempt to deter robbers by using surveillance cameras, alarm systems, guards and guard dogs.

Many commercial robberies are committed by individuals with criminal records; therefore, their MOs should be compared with those of past robberies. Because of the offenders' experience, commercial robberies are usually better planned than street or vehicle-driver robberies.

Many robbers of convenience stores are on drugs or rob to pay for drugs. Convenience stores that are robbed once are likely to be robbed again. In fact, about 8 percent of convenience stores account for more than 50 percent of the robberies.

The National Association of Convenience Stores' *Robbery Deterrence Manual* lists these deterrents:

■ Keep the cash-register cash balance low.

■ Provide good lighting outside and inside the store.

■ Elevate the cash-register area so the clerk has better viewing ability and is in sight of passersby.

■ Remove outdoor pay phones from the premises.

Yarbrough and Meyer (1996, p. 33) describe the robbery of a major computer chip manufacturer having normal physical security. A heavily armed Asian gang took hostage an employee having a cigarette break outside the plant. The robbers used this employee's proximity access card to gain entrance and then tied and blindfolded the few employees working the night shift. They then unloaded a pallet of packaged computer chips valued at a half-million dollars, loaded them into their car and drove off.

Manufacturers should anticipate this type of robbery and take preventive measures. Computer chips are an easy target: They are small, impossible to identify and extremely valuable. They are often seen as worth the risk of a strong-arm robbery.

Bank Robbery " 'Bank robbery!' The call could mean a possible shootout or a hostage situation. It is not a nice thought, but you are on your way to whatever fate awaits you" (Morrison, 1996, p. 159). Morrison (p. 160) stresses: "It is paramount that the first officer on the scene, the investigator and all members of the department know and understand the bank's policies and procedures for a robbery call. Knowing how the employees are trained to respond will make the job easier and safer."

Bank robbery is both a federal and a state offense. U.S. Code Title 18, Section 2113, defines the elements of the federal crime of bank robbery. This statute applies to robbery, burglary or larceny from any member bank of the Federal Reserve system, any bank insured by the Federal Deposit Insurance Corporation (FDIC), any bank organized and operated under the laws of the United States, any federal savings and loan association or any federal credit union.

-- -- -- -- -- -- --

Bank robberies are within the jurisdictions of the FBI, the state and the community in which the crime occurred and are jointly investigated.

-- -- -- -- -- -- --

Because of the large sums of money involved, bank robberies are committed by rank amateurs as well as by habitual criminals. Amateurs are usually more dangerous because they are not as familiar with weapons and often are nervous and fearful. A study involving interviews with convicted bank robbers (Carroll and Loch, 1997, pp. 11–12) revealed all of the offenders had "graduated" to bank robbery from other types of commercial robbery in an effort to obtain larger amounts of money.

Bank robbers often act alone inside the bank, but most have a getaway car with lookouts posted nearby. These individuals pose additional problems for the approaching police. The robbery car often has stolen plates or is itself stolen. Robbers use this "hot" car to leave the robbery scene and to transport them and their loot to a "cold" car left a distance from the robbery. Morrison (p. 160) suggests: "A cardinal rule is that even if only one robber has been reported at the scene, an armed accomplice may be nearby."

The number of bank robberies has increased with the number of branch banks, many of which are housed in storefront offices and outlying shopping centers and thus provide quick entrance to and exit from the robbery scene. Bank robberies in rural communities are also on the rise ("Hard-Boiled Yeggs . . . ," 1997, p. 8):

They were called "yeggs" in the early part of the century—robbers who specialized in rural bank heists. And now, with greater security measures in place at urban and suburban banks . . . , more and more bank robbers are becoming "yeggs" and pulling takeover jobs at small-town branches.

ATM robberies are also on the rise, as brazen robbers wait nearby for people either on foot or in their vehicles to approach the ATM for a withdrawal. These types of "bank" robberies tend to occur after dark in poorly lit areas but can occur any time of the day. Carroll and Loch (p. 11) note: "The prime time for bank robberies is from 10 a.m. to 3 p.m. Friday remains the day of choice for most bank robbers."

Adding clerks is not necessarily a deterrent because a person with a gun has the advantage regardless of the number of clerks. Furthermore, interviews with convicted bank robbers revealed (Carroll and Loch, p. 13): "Each of the offenders interviewed believed that bank tellers were trained not to resist during a robbery but to surrender money without hesitation." The same study also showed: "The offenders unanimously stated that the presence of a uniformed security guard would have deterred them from targeting a particular financial institution."

The association reports that adding bulletproof glass around the cashier increased the incidence of hostage taking. This problem was reduced in some banks by enclosing and securing the bank's administrative areas.

Other deterrents to bank robberies involve the use of **bait money** and dye packs. Carroll and Loch (p. 11) explain:

Federal banking regulations require that federally insured financial institutions maintain bait money—U.S. currency with recorded serial numbers—at each teller position. Dye packs consist of bundles of currency that contain a colored dye and tear gas. Given out during a robbery, they are activated when the subject crosses an electromagnetic field at the facility's exit. Upon activation, the pack stains the money with a brightly colored dye and emits a cloud of colored smoke.

Rehder (2000, p. 16) reports that from 1992 to 1998 the number of bank robberies was reduced by 75 percent, the lowest number in 30 years. According to Rehder: "The most important factor in reducing bank robberies involved establishing an effective working relationship between law enforcement agencies and financial institutions."

Street Robberies

Street robberies are most frequently committed on public streets and sidewalks and in alleys and parking lots. Most are committed with a weapon, but some are strong-arm robberies, in which physical force is the weapon. Both victim and robber are usually on foot.

Speed and surprise typify street robberies, which are often crimes of opportunity with little or no advance planning. Because such robberies happen so fast, the victim is often unable to identify the robber. Sometimes the victim is approached from behind and never sees the attacker.

Nearly half of street-robbery victims are injured by being struck or shoved to the ground. Women and older men are the most frequent victims. Because most street robberies yield little money, the robber often commits several robberies in one night.

In areas with large influxes of diverse groups of immigrants, especially undocumented ones, special problems occur. In Yonkers, New York, for example, great numbers of illegal immigrants from Mexico, Central America and South America are preyed upon by robbers. Because of their illegal status, few of these immigrants have social security numbers. Without one, they are unable to open a bank account or get paid by check. Therefore, they tend to carry large amounts of cash, sometimes their entire savings. Compounding the problem are the language barrier, fear and mistrust of police, fear of deportation and lack of understanding of the justice system.

Vehicle-Driver Robberies

Drivers of taxis, buses, trucks, milk trucks, delivery and messenger vehicles, armored trucks and personal cars are frequent targets of robbers. Taxi drivers are vulnerable because they are often alone while cruising for fares or are dispatched to addresses in vulnerable locations. Some taxi companies have taken preventive steps such as placing protective shields between the passenger and driver and reducing the amount of cash drivers carry. To reduce the amount of cash in the driver's possession, buses in many cities require passengers to have the exact change. Delivery vehicle drivers may be robbed of their merchandise as they arrive for a delivery, or the robbers may wait until after the delivery and take the cash.

Somerville, Massachusetts, police and federal authorities gather at the scene of a fatal armored car robbery outside a Star Market at the Twin City Mall, where three masked men attempted to rob the vehicle, fatally shot a guard at the scene and escaped in a van.

Armored-car robberies are of special concern because they are usually well planned by professional, well-armed robbers and involve large amounts of money. One approach to this problem is to develop an intelligence network between the police department and the armored car industry.

Drivers of personal cars are often approached in parking lots or while stopped at red lights in less-traveled areas. These robberies are generally committed by teenagers. Drivers who pick up hitchhikers leave themselves open not only to robbery but also to assault and auto theft. Some robbers force people off roads or set up fake accidents or injuries to lure motorists into stopping. A combination of street and vehicle-driver robberies that has increased drastically over the past few years is carjacking.

Carjacking

A relatively new category of robbery appeared late in 1990 and has increased substantially.

Carjacking, a category of robbery, is the taking of a motor vehicle by force or threat of force. It may be investigated by the FBI.

The force may consist of use of a handgun, simulated handgun, club, machete, axe, knife or fists.

The federal carjacking statute provides that a person possessing a firearm who "takes a motor vehicle . . . from the person or presence of another by force and violence or by intimidation . . . shall—(1) be . . . imprisoned not more than 15 years . . . , (2) if serious bodily injury . . . results, be . . . imprisoned not more than 25 years . . . , and (3) if death results, be . . . imprisoned for any number of years up to life" ("U.S. Supreme Court News," 1999, p. 8). Furthermore, the *Criminal Justice Newsletter* ("Carjackings Resulting in Injury," 1998, p. 3) reports: "Sentences of 25 years or life in prison for carjackings are not mere 'sentencing enhancements' that can be imposed if a judge determines that a carjacker injured or killed a victim. . . . Rather, they are separate sentences for separate crimes that must be proved beyond a reasonable doubt."

Nearly every major city has experienced armed carjacking offenses in sufficiently substantial numbers that *Uniform Crime Reports* may soon be required to use this as a designation rather than being reported without uniformity as armed robbery, auto theft or some other offense. Klaus (1999, p. 1) notes: "About 49,000 completed or attempted nonfatal carjackings took place each year in the United States between 1992 and 1996. . . . In addition, . . . about 27 homicides by strangers each year involved automobile theft. Some of these may have been carjackings."

A weapon was used in 83 percent of all carjackings. Of the completed carjackings, approximately 23 percent resulted in injuries to the victims, as did 10 percent of the attempted carjackings ("49,000 Non Fatal Carjackings Annually," 1999, p. 6).

Carjackings have resulted in car thefts, injuries and deaths. Initially, the more expensive vehicles were involved, but this trend now covers all types of motor vehicles. The stolen vehicle is then used as in the conventional crime of vehicle theft: for resale, resale of parts, joyriding or use in committing another crime.

Parking lots are the favorite location for carjacking, followed by city streets, private residence driveways, sporting events, car dealerships, gas stations and bank teller machines. Handguns are the most frequently used weapon.

The motivation for carjacking is not clear because the vehicles are taken under so many different circumstances and for so many different reasons. One theory for the sudden increase is that the increased use of alarms and protective devices on vehicles, especially on more expensive ones, makes it more difficult to steal a vehicle by traditional means. Car operators are easy prey compared to convenience stores or other commercial establishments that may have surveillance cameras and other security measures in effect. Another theory suggests that status is involved: A criminal who carjacks a vehicle achieves higher status in the criminal subculture than one who steals it in the conventional manner. In addition, some police officers believe the crime is becoming a fad among certain groups of young people as a way to enhance their image with their cohorts.

Carjackers employ many ruses to engage a victim. Some stage accidents. Others wait for their victims at workplace parking lots or residential driveways. Other likely locations include commercial parking lots, stoplights, service stations, automatic teller machines, drive-up bank windows and pay telephones.

Carjackings have become a serious problem for police, who investigate them in the same way as other armed robberies. Publication of prevention techniques has become standard policy for police agencies in an effort to prevent losses of property, injuries and deaths. Some agencies use decoys in an effort to apprehend carjackers.

In October 1992, Congress passed, and President Bush signed, the Anti-Car Theft Act of 1992, making armed carjacking a federal offense. Under this law, automakers must engrave a 17-digit vehicle identification number on 24 parts of every new car.

Federal agencies are becoming active in investigating carjacking. The FBI includes it with gang activity and drug-related violence as crimes investigated by a 300-member team of former foreign counterintelligence agents. The FBI uses undercover officers, decoys and informants to pursue carjackers.

In addition to knowing how robberies are generally classified, investigators must be familiar with the elements of the crime of robbery in their particular jurisdictions.

Elements of the Crime: Robbery

State laws define *robbery* precisely. Although the general public tends to use the term *robbery* interchangeably with *burglary, larceny* and *theft,* the specific elements of robbery clearly distinguish it from these offenses. A businessman might say that his store was robbed when, in fact, it was burglarized. A woman may have money taken from her purse at work while she is busy waiting on customers and say that she was robbed when, legally, the crime was larceny. Such thefts are not robbery because the necessary elements are not present.

Some states have only one degree of robbery. Others have both simple and aggravated robbery. Still others have robbery in the first, second and third degree. However, in most state laws common elements exist.

- - - - - - - - -

The elements of the crime of robbery are:

■ The wrongful taking of personal property,

■ From the person or in the person's presence,

■ Against the person's will by force or threat of force.

- - - - - - - - -

Wrongful Taking of Personal Property

Various statutes use phrases such as *unlawful taking, felonious taking* or *knowing he is not entitled thereto.* Intent is an element of the crime in some, but not all, states. To take "wrongfully," the robber must have no legal right to the prop-

erty. Moreover, property must be *personal property,* as distinguished from real property.

From the Person or in the Presence of the Person

In most cases, *in the presence of a person* means that the victim sees the robber take the property. This is not always the case, however, because the victim may be locked in a separate room. For example, robbers often take victims to a separate room such as a restroom or a bank vault while they search for the desired items or cash. Such actions do not remove the crime "from the presence of the person" as long as the separation from the property is the direct result of force or threats of force used by the robber.

Against the Person's Will by Use of Force or Threat of Force

This essential element clearly separates robbery from burglary and larceny. As noted, most robberies are committed with a weapon or other dangerous device or by indicating that one is present. The force or threat is generally sufficient to deter resistance. It can be immediate or threatened in the future. It can be directed at the victim, the victim's family or another person with the victim.

Special Challenges in Investigation

As a violent crime, robbery introduces challenges that require special attention from the dispatcher, patrol officers, investigators and police administrators. Three major problems occur in dealing with robberies: (1) they are usually not reported until the offenders have left the scene; (2) it is difficult to obtain good descriptions or positive identification from victims; (3) the items taken, usually currency, are difficult to identify.

- - - - - - - - -

The speed of a robbery, its potential for violence and the taking of hostages and the usual lack of evidence at the scene pose special challenges for investigators.

- - - - - - - - -

Police response time can be reduced if the robbed business or residence has an alarm system connected to the police department or a private alarm agency. Silent alarms can provide an early response, and audible alarms sometimes prevent a robbery. The lag time—that is, the elapsed time between the commission of a robbery and the time the police are notified—is usually much longer than the actual police response time.

A robbery-in-progress call involves an all-units response, with units close to the scene going there directly while other units cover the area near the scene, looking for a possible getaway vehicle. Other cars go to checkpoints such as bridges, converging highways, freeway entry and exit ramps, dead-end streets and alleys. Observe all vehicles as you approach a robbery scene. Whether to use red lights and sirens depends on the information received from the dispatcher. It is often best to arrive quietly to prevent the taking of hostages. If shooting is occurring, using lights and siren may cause the robber to leave before you arrive.

When responding to a robbery-in-progress call:

- Proceed as rapidly as possible, but use extreme caution.
- Assume the robber is at the scene unless otherwise advised.
- Be prepared for gunfire.
- Look for and immobilize any getaway vehicle you discover.
- Avoid a hostage situation if possible.
- Make an immediate arrest if the suspect is at the scene.

Upon arrival, attempt to locate any vehicle that the suspects might use, even if you have no description of it. It will probably be within a block of the crime scene, and its engine may be running. It generally has a person in it (the "wheelman" or lookout) waiting for the robber to return. If the vehicle is identified through prior information and is empty, immobilize it by removing the distributor cap or letting the air out of a tire. If a cohort is waiting in the car, arrest the person and then immobilize the vehicle.

Decide whether to enter the robbery location immediately or to wait until sufficient personnel are in position. Department policy determines whether it is an immediate or a timed response. Too early an entry increases the chances of a hostage situation or of having to use weapons. The general rule is to avoid a confrontation if it will create a worse situation than the robbery itself.

If you arrive at the robbery scene and find a suspect there with the victim, surround the building and order the suspect to come out. Get other people in the area to

leave because of possible gunfire. Know the operational limitations imposed by the number of officers and the amount of equipment available at the scene. Take advantage of vehicles and buildings in the area for cover.

Because the robber is committing a violent crime and is usually armed, expect that the robber may use a weapon against the police and that a hostage may be taken.

Hostage Situations Pearson (1996, p. 48) stresses: "The actions of the first officer on the scene of a hostage situation can mean the difference between life and death." The priorities in a hostage situation are to (1) preserve life, (2) apprehend the hostage taker and (3) recover or protect property. To accomplish these priorities requires specialized training in hostage situations.

In general, consider a direct assault only if there has already been a killing or if further negotiations would be useless. Hostage situations may last from less than an hour to more than 40 hours; the average length is approximately 12 hours. Strandberg (1999, p. 68) reports: "The more time passes, the better our chances are. Between 15 minutes and 45 minutes is the highest chance of something bad happening." He further observes:

> There are four types of approaches to hostage situations: contain, isolate and negotiate with a hostage taker; contain and demand a surrender; use chemical agents to force a surrender; and, finally, the use of tactical teams. Most experts agree that the use of tactical force is the last option, provided that none of the hostages has been hurt. The longer a situation goes on, the more people may press to move up the force continuum.

The need for negotiation is based on the principle that preserving life—that of the hostages or the hostage takers, as well as police or innocent bystanders—is the main priority. SWAT teams or expert sharpshooters are often at or near the scene but do not participate in negotiations and in some cases are not visible except as a last resort. Figure 9.2 illustrates the typical emotions hostage takers experience during negotiations.

Usually you do not need to rush into the scene immediately and proceed with direct contact. In a few cases it may be better not to do anything but to let the hostage taker resolve the situation. Passage of time can accomplish the following:

- Provide the opportunity for face-to-face contact with the hostage taker.
- Allow the negotiator to attempt to establish a trustful rapport.

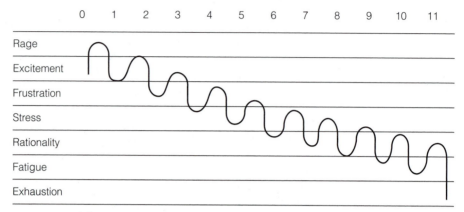

FIGURE 9.2　*Time Line Pattern for Emotions of Hostage Takers during Negotiation*

Source: Thomas Strentz. "The Cyclic Crisis Negotiations Time Line." *Law and Order,* March 1995. p. 73. Reprinted by permission of the publisher.

- Permit mental, emotional and physical fatigue to operate against the hostage taker.

- Increase the hostage taker's needs for food, water, sleep and elimination.

- Increase the possibility of reducing demands to reasonable compliance levels.

- Allow hostage-escape possibilities to occur.

- Provide for more rational thinking, in contrast to the emotionalism usually present during the initial stage of the crime.

- Lessen the hostage taker's anxiety and reduce his or her adrenalin flow, allowing more rational negotiations.

- Allow for important intelligence gathering concerning the hostage taker, hostages, layout, protection barriers and needed police reinforcement.

- Possibly foster the "Stockholm Syndrome," by which hostages begin to identify with their captors and sympathize with them.

Fuselier (1999, p. 22) explains the "Stockholm Syndrome":

On an August morning in 1973, an escaped convict took four bank employees hostage in Stockholm, Sweden. For 131 hours, the hostages shared a bank vault with another convicted criminal, the former cellmate of the hostage taker, who had demanded his release from a nearby penitentiary. Despite their ordeal, the hostages reported that they had no ill feelings toward the hostage takers and, further, that they feared the police more than [they feared] their captors. Psychologists called this newly discovered phenomenon the **Stockholm Syndrome** [boldface added].

The negotiator should have street knowledge and experience with hostage incidents. Sometimes the first officers at the scene have established rapport with the hostage taker, and the negotiator only advises. In some cases a trained clinical psychologist may be called to the scene, not as a negotiator but as a consultant regarding possible behavioral deviations of the hostage taker. Wexler (1998, p. 42) contends: "Not only must he be a good listener, but the ideal negotiator needs to think quickly on his feet while he is talking." Garner (1998, p. 26) offers the following advice for first responders awaiting the arrival of a trained negotiator: "Follow a time-tested formula of time, tactics and talk to gain control of a situation and up the odds for success in your favor."

Face-to-face negotiations are ideal because they provide the best opportunity for gathering knowledge about and personally observing the reactions of the hostage taker. Such contact should be undertaken only if circumstances indicate the negotiator will not be in danger. An alternative is telephone contact, allowing for personal conversation and establishing rapport without the dangers of face-to-face contact. Use of bullhorns is not the personal type of communication desired. Nonetheless, it may be the only available method of communication.

Moore (1999, p. 42) describes the use of robots in hostage negotiations to enhance officer safety: "The San Diego Sheriff's Department's Special Enforcement Detail (SED) and Hostage Negotiations Team (HNT) have access to 'Lonny the Robot.' . . . Lonny can be remotely driven to a suspect location . . . and a negotiator can talk to (and see via TV camera) the suspect from a position of safety." Moore (pp. 44–45) discusses the advantages and disadvantages of the robots:

> The overriding "pro" of using robots in hostage situations is officer safety. . . .
>
> As with anything, there are some "cons" to using robots. Cost is one factor. Robots . . . can easily cost over $100,000. . . .
>
> [Also,] people fear the unknown. The reaction of suspects upon seeing and hearing Lonny is to run and hide. . . . Small children are especially frightened by the robot.

Moore concludes (p. 45): "Regardless of potential drawbacks, the age of robotics is here and available as a tool for law enforcement."

Negotiable items may include food and drink (but not liquor unless it is known that liquor would lessen the hostage taker's anxieties rather than increase them); money; media access and reduced penalties. Transportation is generally not negotiable because of the difficulty in monitoring and controlling the situation. Police departments should establish policies regarding hostage negotiations in advance. In general, nothing should be granted to a hostage taker unless something is received in return.

To help negotiators determine whether their efforts are being successful, Noesner (1999, p. 12) offers this advice:

The following indicators signify progress and generally mean that current negotiation initiatives should continue. Specifically, since negotiations have begun:

- no additional deaths or injuries have resulted,
- the subject has reduced threats and is using less violent language,
- the subject's emotions have lowered,
- the subject has exhibited increased rationality in speech and action,
- deadlines have passed,
- the subject has become increasingly willing to bargain,
- the subject has lowered demands,
- the subject has released a hostage,
- the negotiator has built a rapport with the subject,
- the subject has made positive statements about the welfare of the hostage/victim, and/or
- the subject has asked about the consequences of surrendering.

Table 9.1 presents information about hostage takers, their characteristics and possible motives and guidelines for possible actions. FBI reports concerning hostage taking indicate that the majority of these incidents involve mentally disturbed people; therefore, the first four categories in the table are especially important.

In the several instances in which the author has been a negotiator, each incident both lent itself to the general guidelines but was also unique. Decisions had to be made based on the immediate factors involved. In the vast majority of cases, effectively handled negotiations can resolve the situation without injury or death.

If the robber emerges on request or is already outside the building, arrest him or her immediately. Have the victim and any witnesses make a field identification, and then remove the suspect from the scene.

A wounded suspect presents an especially dangerous situation. Be alert to the possibility that a suspect is feigning more serious injury than exists to draw you off guard and get you close enough to shoot. Keep the suspect covered at all times. Immobilize him or her with handcuffs as soon as possible. If the suspect is seriously injured, arrange for an armed escort in the ambulance and for taking a dying declaration if necessary. If the suspect is killed, notify the coroner or medical examiner.

Table 9.1	Hostage Takers		
Type	*Characteristics*	*Motives*	*Guidelines for Action*
Paranoid schizophrenic	Out of touch with reality Hallucinations, delusions Above-average intelligence	Needs to carry out plans Imagines perceived wrongs Feels he or she is right	Do not lie or attempt to trick Do not argue about beliefs Accept statements May negotiate
Manic depressive	Out of touch with reality Feels unworthy Suicidal Slow speech	To remove hostages from "this horrible life"	Needs understanding and support Try to induce subject to talk about something positive
Inadequate personality	Homicidal Loser complex In touch with reality Fired from many jobs	To get attention To prove him- or herself High point of life	Needs understanding and acceptance Can be negotiated with Make only promises that can be kept Do not bring parents to scene
Antisocial personality— sociopath or psychopath	Absence of conscience or guilt; no moral values Con man; snow jobs Impulsive Self-centered Street- and police-wise	Manipulates people for own gain	Do not use tricks Do not make unrealistic promises Stimulate ego
Prisoners	Usually not mentally disturbed Guards likely to be hostages and likely to be killed	Improve prison conditions Bargaining power	Requires rapid police action Do not allow a leader to develop
Criminals	Know what to expect from police Usually a spontaneous reaction to being cornered	Media attention To escape safely from a crime Demand additional money	Accept physical safety of criminal in return for release of hostage Obtain all facts
Terrorists	Much planning Hostages are in serious jeopardy Local police may not be able to meet demands May need state or federal assistance	Media attention Fast, intense media attention Further a cause Martyr complex Demand money Hope government will overreact, so blame is on government, not terrorists	Admit points are well made Let it be known demands are understood and action is being considered Impress that killing hostages will only discredit cause Activate SWAT teams

The Preliminary Investigation

Rice (1998, p. 38) asserts: "It takes a combination of skills and know-how to ensure the successful outcome of a robbery investigation." He adds (p. 41): "Proper approach, awareness of robbery strategies, scene mainte-nance, information gathering, and suspect encounter techniques are skills and tasks that place the primary responding officer at the pivotal position in a robbery investigation."

Frequently, officers arriving at the scene of a robbery find that the robber has just fled. After taking care of emergencies, broadcast initial information about the suspect, the getaway vehicle and the direction of travel.

Follow-up vehicles dispatched to the general area of the robbery can then attempt to apprehend the escaping robbers. Early information helps determine how far the suspect may have traveled and the most likely escape routes.

Robbery usually leaves victims and witnesses feeling vulnerable and fearful, making it difficult for them to give accurate descriptions and details of what occurred. Be patient.

Witnesses to a robbery suffer varying degrees of trauma even though they have not lost any property. They may have had to lie on the floor or been placed in a locked room or a bank vault, possibly fearing that the robber would return and kill them. Their ability to recall precise details is further impaired by the suddenness of the crime. Victims and witnesses may be asked to complete a form such as the one in Figures 9.3A and 9.3B.

ROBBER IDENTIFICATION FORM

DO NOT DISCUSS DETAILS OF THE CRIME OR ROBBER DESCRIPTIONS WITH ANYONE EXCEPT OFFICER IN CHARGE OR LAW ENFORCEMENT OFFICIALS.

RECORD YOUR OWN OBSERVATIONS, NOT WHAT SOMEONE TELLS YOU.

Use separate form for each robber.

Time of Robbery _____ A.M. _____ P.M.   No. of robbers involved _____   This form describes Robber No._____

Race   White ☐   Black ☐   Am. Indian ☐

Mexican Am. ☐ Puerto Rican ☐ Cuban ☐

Asian ☐   Other _____

Sex: Male ☐   Female ☐

Age _____ **Height** _____ **Weight** _____

Build: Small ☐ Medium ☐ Large ☐

Stature: Thin ☐ Medium ☐ Heavy ☐

Complexion: Light ☐ Medium ☐ Dark ☐

Ruddy ☐ Fair ☐ Wrinkled ☐

Hair: Bald ☐ Partially Bald ☐

Color _____ Very Short (close cropped) ☐

Short ☐ Medium ☐

Long ☐ Very Long ☐

Beard: No ☐ Yes ☐   **Mustache:** No ☐ Yes ☐

Sideburns: No ☐ Yes ☐

If Yes — Short ☐ Medium ☐ Long ☐

Glasses: No ☐ Yes ☐

If Yes — Regular ☐ Sunglasses ☐

Size of Frame: Small ☐ Medium ☐ Large ☐

Type of Frame: Wire ☐ Plastic ☐ Color _____

Shape of Frame: Regular ☐ Round ☐

Square ☐ Rectangular ☐

Hat: No ☐ Yes ☐ If Yes — Color _____

Type _____

Tie: No ☐ Yes ☐ If Yes — Color _____

Shirt or Blouse: Color _____

Type: Work ☐ Sport ☐ Dress ☐ T-Shirt ☐

Sweatshirt ☐ Other Data _____

Sweater: No ☐ Yes ☐ If Yes — Color _____

Type: Button ☐ Pullover ☐

Other Data _____

Pants: Color _____

Type: Work ☐ Jeans ☐ Dress ☐

Shoes: Color _____

Style: Work ☐ Sport ☐ Dress ☐

Type of Heel _____

Coat: No ☐ Yes ☐ If Yes — Color _____

Type: Business Suit ☐ Sport Suit ☐

Jacket ☐ Overcoat ☐ Raincoat ☐

Style: Button ☐ Zipper ☐ Other _____

Length: Hip Level ☐ Knee Level ☐

Thigh Level ☐ Other _____

Gloves: No ☐ Yes ☐ If Yes — Color _____

Type _____

Mask or Disguise: No ☐ Yes ☐

If Yes — Describe _____

_____

_____

_____

Continued other side

FIGURE 9.3A   *Robber Identification Form, Front*

```
Weapon:  None Seen ☐   Gun ☐    Knife ☐     Motor Vehicle:      Colors:

         Other (describe)_____                        Top _____

         If gun,    Rifle ☐    Shotgun ☐                        Bottom _____

         Pistol ☐  Revolver ☐  Automatic ☐        Make: _____

Color of Gun:   Black ☐  Chrome ☐  Blue ☐        Model: _____

Speech:  Coarse ☐  Refined ☐  High ☐  Low ☐      2 Dr. ☐  4 Dr. ☐  Sedan ☐  Wagon ☐

         Accent ☐  Drawl ☐  Stutter ☐            Van ☐  Other_____

         Lisp ☐   Normal ☐                       License Plate No.: _____

Manner:  Polite ☐   Gruff ☐   Nervous ☐          State_____

         Calm ☐  Alcoholic ☐                     Color of Plate: _____

Direction of Escape: _____      Color of numbers _____

_____           Number of people in vehicle _____

Scars, marks or moles _____

Does subject resemble any acquaintance?_____

Subject first observed:  Remarks_____

_____

Actions of subject:  Remarks _____

_____

Words spoken by subject:  _____

Was the money placed in a container?    No ☐   Yes ☐   If Yes — Describe _____

_____

Other remarks; peculiarities; jewelry, etc. _____

_____

Other Details_____

_____

_____

_____

Location of Employee/Customer in relation to subject(s) _____

_____

Name of Witness (Print)_____ Tele. Home _____ Business _____

Address _____ City _____ State _____ Zip _____

Signature_____ Date_____
```

FIGURE 9.3B *Robber Identification Form, Back*

Proving the Elements of the Offense

Know the elements of robbery in your jurisdiction so you can determine whether a robbery has in fact been committed. Each element must be proven separately. Proving some of the elements is not sufficient.

The Elements of Robbery

Was Personal Property Wrongfully Taken?

Taking of property necessitates proving that it was carried away from the lawful owner or possessor to permanently deprive the owner of the property. Prove that the robber had no legal right to the property taken.

> Determine the legal owner of the property taken.
> Describe completely the property and its value.

Who is the legal owner? Take statements from the victim to show legal possession and control of the property before and during the robbery.

Was property taken or intended to be taken? Obtain a complete description of the property and its value, including marks, serial numbers, operation identification number (if available), color, size and any other identifying characteristics.

Obtain proof of what was lost and its value. In a bank robbery, the bank manager or auditor can give an accurate accounting of the money taken. In a store robbery, any responsible employee can help determine the loss. Cash register receipts, sales receipts, retail and wholesale prices, reasonable estimates by people in the same business or the estimate of an independent appraiser can help determine the amount of the loss. In robberies of the person, the victim determines the loss. Some robbery victims claim to have lost more or less than was actually taken, thus complicating the case.

Was Property Taken from the Person or in the Person's Presence? *From the person or in the presence of the person* necessitates proving that the property was under the victim's control before the robbery and was removed from the victim's control by the robber's direct actions.

> Record the exact words, gestures, motions or actions the robber used to gain control of the property.

Answer such questions as:

■ Where was the property before it was taken?

■ Where was the victim?

■ How was the property taken?

■ Was the removal against the victim's will by force or the threat of force?

> Obtain a complete description of the robber's words, actions and any weapon used or threatened to be used.

If nothing was said, find out what gestures, motions or other actions compelled the victim to give up the property.

The force need not be directly against the robbery victim. For example, a woman may receive a call at work, telling her that her husband is a hostage and will be killed unless she brings money to a certain location, or the robber may grab a friend of the victim or a customer in a store and direct the victim to hand over money to protect the person being held from harm.

Describe any injuries to the victim or witnesses. Photograph them, if possible, and have them examined by a doctor, emergency room personnel or ambulance paramedics.

The Complete Investigation

Most robberies are solved through prompt actions by the victim, witnesses and the police patrolling the immediate area or by police at checkpoints. In many cases, however, a robbery investigation takes weeks or even months. Begin your investigation with an immediate canvass of the neighborhood because the suspect may be hiding in a parked car, in a gas station restroom or on the roof of a building. Check motels and hotels in the area. If another city is nearby, check the motels there. Look for discarded property such as the weapon, a wallet, money bag or other item taken from victims. Check car rental agencies if no vehicle was reported stolen. Check airports, bus and train stations and taxi companies for possible links.

Recheck all information and physical descriptions. Have a sketch of the suspect prepared and circulate it. Alert your informants to listen for word of the robbery. Check known "fences." Check modus operandi files. Where applicable, check police field interview/contact forms and communications records relating to recent citizen calls complaining about suspicious people or vehicles in the area of the robbery.

Prepare your report carefully and thoroughly and circulate it to any officers who might assist. Even if you do not apprehend your suspect, the suspect may be apprehended during a future robbery, and his or her MO and other evidence may implicate him or her in the robbery you investigated.

Identifying the Suspect

The various techniques used in suspect identification (discussed in Chapter 7) are relevant at this point.

> Obtain information about the suspect's general appearance, clothing, disguises, weapon and vehicle.

If the suspect is apprehended within a short time (20 minutes or so), he or she may be taken back to the scene for identification by the victim. Alternatively, the victim may be taken to where the suspect is being held. Several people should be in the area of the suspect to witness that the victim makes any identification without assistance from the police. Photo lineups may be used if no suspect is arrested at or near the scene of the crime. Photo lineups should include five other people in addition to the suspect. A person who has been arrested does not have the right to refuse to have a photo taken.

Eyewitness identification is affected by many factors: the distance between the witness and the suspect at the time of the robbery, the time of day and lighting conditions, the amount of violence involved, whether the witness had ever seen or knew the suspect and the time it took for the crime to be committed.

Disguises Many robbers use face masks such as ski masks, nylon stockings pulled over the head and paper sacks with eye holes. Other disguises include wigs, dyed hair, sideburns, scarves, various types of false noses or ears and makeup to alter appearance. Gauze is sometimes used to distort the shape of the cheeks or mouth and tape to simulate cuts or to cover scars.

Clothing also can serve as a disguise. Collars can be pulled up and hats pulled down. False heels and soles can increase height. Various types of uniforms that fit in with the area of the robbery scene, such as delivery uniforms or work clothes, have been used.

Clothing and disguises may be discarded by the robber upon leaving the scene and are valuable evidence if discovered because they may provide DNA evidence.

Weapons Pistols, revolvers and automatic weapons are frequently used in robberies. Sawed-off shotguns, rifles, airguns, various types of imitation guns, knives, razors and other cutting and stabbing instruments, explosives, tear gas and various acids have also been used. Such weapons and devices are often found on or near the suspect when arrested, but many are hidden in the vehicle used or are thrown away during the escape.

Vehicles Most vehicles used in robberies are inconspicuous, popular makes that attract no attention and are stolen just before the robbery. Some robbers leave the scene on foot and then take buses or taxis or commandeer vehicles, sometimes at gunpoint.

Establishing the Modus Operandi

Even if the suspect is apprehended at the scene, the MO can help link the suspect with other robberies.

- - - - - - - -

Important modus operandi information includes:

- Type of robbery.
- Time (day and hour).
- Method of attack (real or threatened).
- Weapon.
- Number of robbers.
- Voice and words.
- Vehicle used.
- Peculiarities.
- Object sought.

- - - - - - - -

Finding that an MO matches a previous robbery does not necessarily mean that the same robber committed the crime. For example, in one instance three masked gunmen robbed a midwestern bank of more than $45,000 and escaped in a stolen car. The MO matched a similar robbery in the same town a few weeks earlier in which $30,000 was obtained. The three gunmen were identified and arrested the next day and more than $41,000 of the loot recovered. One gunman told the FBI agent that he planned the robbery after reading about the successful bank robbery three other masked gunmen had pulled off. The FBI agent smiled and informed the robber that the perpetrators had been arrested shortly after the robbery. Aghast, the copycat robber bemoaned the fact that he had seen no publicity on the arrest.

Physical Evidence

Physical evidence at a robbery scene is usually minimal. Sometimes, however, the robbery occurs where a surveillance camera is operating. The film can be processed immediately and used as evidence.

- - - - - - - -

Physical evidence that can connect a suspect with a robbery includes fingerprints, shoe prints, tire prints, restraining devices, discarded garments, fibers and hairs, a note or the stolen property.

- - - - - - - -

Fingerprints may be found at the scene if the suspect handled any objects, on the holdup note if one was left

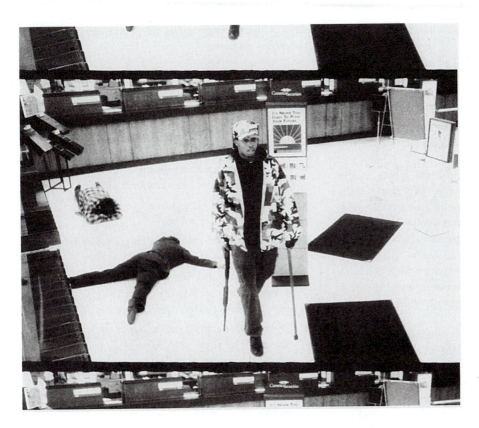

As seen from the bank's surveillance camera, a gunman carries a shotgun into a branch of the Commercial Bank in northeast Detroit as two customers lay on the floor during the robbery attempt. The gunman killed two bank employees and wounded another before taking the life of a hostage outside the bank. He was later killed by police.

behind, on the getaway car or on recovered property. They might also be found on pieces of tape used as restraints, which, in themselves, are valuable as evidence.

In one residential robbery, the criminal forced entrance into a home, bound and gagged the residents, stole several items of value and then left. As he backed up to turn his car around, he inadvertently left the impression of the vehicle's license plate clearly imprinted on a snowbank. He was apprehended within hours of the robbery.

Recovering stolen property is a major problem. Jewelry and cash are particularly difficult to identify and are easily disposed of or hidden. The federal Bank Protection Act (1968) requires that banks and establishments with a high risk of robbery keep bait money on hand. This is currency whose serial numbers are recorded and that is kept accessible so that it can be added to any robbery loot. In one bank robbed, bait money had been placed in each teller's case so that it would trip the alarm system when it was moved. Unfortunately, the teller forgot about the bait money, and the robber made off with $5,000.

Robbery Information Clearinghouses

Because robbery is inherently serial, robbery information clearinghouse programs have proven successful.

Officers from the Miami-Dade Police Department in Florida note: "The mission of the clearinghouse is not to directly solve investigations, but rather to provide a foundation of intelligence and assistance to investigators, prosecutors and law enforcement agencies country-wide, thus expanding multi-jurisdictional awareness of robbery trends" (Ronczkowski and Jose, 1999, p. 28).

False Robbery Reports

Investigators need to rule out the probability that the robbery report is false. Among the indicators of a false robbery report are the following:

- Unusual delay in reporting the offense
- Amount of the loss not fitting the victim's apparent financial status
- Lack of correspondence with the physical evidence
- Improbable events
- Exceptionally detailed or exceptionally vague description of offender
- Lack of cooperation

Summary

Robbery is the felonious taking of another's property from his or her person or in his or her presence through force or intimidation. Robberies are classified as either residential, commercial, street or vehicle-driver robberies. One relatively new category is carjacking—the taking of a motor vehicle by force or threat of force. The FBI may investigate carjacking.

A relatively new type of residential robber is the home invader. Home invaders are usually young Asian gang members who travel across the country robbing Asian families, especially Asian business owners. The FBI, state and local law enforcement personnel jointly investigate bank robberies.

The elements of robbery are (1) the wrongful taking of personal property, (2) from the person or in the person's presence, (3) against the person's will by force or threat of force.

The rapidity of a robbery, its potential for violence and the taking of hostages and the usual lack of evidence at the scene pose special challenges. When responding to a robbery-in-progress call, proceed as rapidly as possible but use extreme caution. Assume the robber is at the scene unless otherwise advised, and be prepared for gunfire. Look for and immobilize any getaway vehicle you discover. Avoid a hostage situation if possible, and make an immediate arrest if the situation warrants.

Prove each element of robbery separately. To prove that personal property was wrongfully taken, determine the legal owner of the property and describe the property and its value completely. To prove that it was taken from the person or in the person's presence, record the exact words, gestures, motions or actions the robber used to gain control of the property. To prove the removal was against the victim's will by force or threat of force, obtain a complete description of the robber's words, actions and any weapon the robber used or threatened to use.

Obtain information about the suspect's general appearance, clothing, disguises, weapon and vehicle. Important modus operandi information includes type of robbery, time (day and hour), method of attack (threatened or real), weapon, object sought, number of robbers, voice and words, vehicle and any peculiarities. Physical evidence that can connect the suspect with the robbery includes fingerprints, shoe prints, tire prints, restraining devices, discarded garments, fibers and hairs, a note and the stolen property.

Checklist
Robbery

- Are maps and pictures on file of banks and other places that handle large amounts of cash?
- Are there plans for police response in the event these facilities are robbed?
- Was the place that was robbed protected by an alarm? Was the alarm working?
- Was the place that was robbed protected by a surveillance camera? Was the camera working? Was the film immediately removed and processed?
- What procedure did police use in responding to the call? Did they enter directly? To avoid a hostage situation, did they wait until the robber had left?
- Did police interview separately everyone in the robbed place? Did they obtain written statements from each?
- Are all elements of the crime of robbery present?
- How was the robber dressed? Was a disguise used?
- What were the robber's exact words and actions?
- What type of weapon or threat did the robber use?
- Was anybody injured or killed?
- Was there a getaway car? Description? Direction of travel? A second person in the car?
- Was a general description of people and vehicles involved quickly broadcast to other police agencies?
- Did police secure and photograph the scene?
- What property was taken in the robbery? What was its value?
- Who is the legal owner?
- If a bank was robbed, were the FBI and state officials notified?
- If the suspect was arrested, how was identification made?
- If money or property was recovered, was it properly processed?

Application*

Read the following account of an actual robbery investigation. As you read, list the steps the investigators took. Review the list and determine whether they took all necessary steps.

On December 16, close to midnight, a woman looked in the window of the grocery store owned by Efimy Romanow at 187 Ashmun Street, New Haven, Connecticut, and saw Romanow lying behind the counter with the telephone receiver clutched in his right hand. Thinking Romanow was sick, the woman notified a neighbor, Thomas Kelly, who went to the store and then called an ambulance. Romanow was pronounced dead on arrival at the hospital.

Autopsy revealed he had been shot near the heart. The bullet was removed and turned over to detectives, who immediately began an investigation. Officers protected the crime scene and made a thorough search for possible prints and other evidence. They found a small amount of money in the cash register. At the hospital, $15.50 was found in Romanow's pockets, and $313 in bills was found in his right shoe. A thorough check of neighborhood homes was made without result. One report received was that two white men were seen leaving the store before Romanow's body was discovered.

About 1 A.M., December 17, Mrs. Marion Lang, who lived directly opposite the store but was not home when the officers first went there, was contacted. She stated that at about 11:10 P.M. she had heard loud talking in the street, including the remark, "Damn it, he is shot, let's get out of here." She did not look out the window, so she was unable to describe the persons she heard talking.

The investigation continued without any tangible clues until 9:25 P.M., December 17, when a phone call was received from George M. Proctor, owner of a drugstore on a street parallel to Ashmun Street and one block away. He had just overheard a woman talking in the telephone booth in his store say, "I will not stand for her taking my fellow away. I know who shot the storekeeper on Ashmun. It was Scotty and Almeda at 17 Dixwell." Mr. Proctor did not know the woman whom he had overheard.

Two detectives were assigned to this lead, and they began a search. A few hours later they learned that Scotty and Almeda were in a room at 55 Dixwell Avenue. Arriving with several uniformed officers, they entered and found Francis Scott and Henry Almeda in bed with their clothes on. Both had previous records and were well known to the local police. The detectives took the two men to headquarters for questioning and then returned to the room. Their search revealed five .32 caliber bullets at the top of a window casing where plaster had been broken up.

They also received information that Almeda and Scott had earlier visited Julia Redmond, who had a room in the same house. They asked Ms. Redmond if Almeda and Scott had left anything there. She responded, "They put something under the mattress." Turning over the mattress, the detectives found a .32 caliber Harrington and Richardson revolver, serial number 430-087. Ms. Redmond said, "That belongs to Almeda and Scott."

The detectives returned to headquarters and searched the stolen gun files. They discovered that this gun had been reported stolen in a burglary at the home of Geoffrey Harrell, 46 Webster Street, in November. Both suspects were questioned during the night and denied any part in the shooting.

The questioning resumed on the morning of December 18 at 9:00 A.M. At 3:45 P.M. that day, Almeda broke and made a confession in which he involved Scott. Almeda's statement was read to Scott with Almeda present. When Almeda identified the confession and stated it was true, Scott also admitted his part in the shooting.

When Almeda was shown the .32 caliber H & R revolver, he identified it as the gun used in shooting Romanow. He explained that they had to shoot Romanow because he refused to give up his money and placed himself between them and the door. In order to get out, he shot Romanow. Both stated that they had no car and that no one else was involved.

A preliminary examination of the bullet taken from Romanow's body did not satisfy the detectives that the bullet had been fired from the gun in their possession, even though it had been identified by both Almeda and Scott as the one used.

A detective took the gun and bullet to the FBI Technical Laboratory in Washington, DC, where a ballistics comparison established that the gun furnished for examination was not the gun that fired the death bullet. A search of the Technical Laboratory

---

*Adapted from a report by Captain Raymond J. Eagan, New Haven, Connecticut.

files revealed that the gun matched a bullet furnished by the same department as evidence in a holdup of Levine's Liquor Store on December 1 of that year. One shot had been fired, striking a chair and deflecting into a pile of rubbish in the rear of the store. The bullet had been recovered by detectives after sifting through the rubbish.

When confronted with this information, Scott and Almeda admitted that they had committed this holdup and shooting while masked. They also admitted they had stolen an automobile to use that night and that they had burglarized Harrell's home in November when they took the gun.

The detectives conducted an extensive search for the gun used in killing Romanow. They cut a hole in the bottom of the flue leading from the room occupied by Almeda and Scott and even had the sewer department clean out 15 sewer-catch basins in the area of the crime, but no weapon was discovered.

Both Almeda and Scott were indicted by the grand jury for first-degree murder. They were scheduled for trial February 13. The night before the trial was to begin, they told their lawyers that a third man had furnished the gun and driven the getaway car. In a conference with the state's attorney and detectives, the lawyers identified the third man as William Sutton. Within half an hour, Sutton was apprehended and brought to the state attorney's office where, in the presence of Scott and Almeda, their statements were read to Sutton. He admitted participating in the crime.

This new turn in the case also revealed that the gun used in the killing was loaned to Sutton by John Foy. The morning after the shooting, Sutton brought the gun back to Foy and left it with him. A short time later Sutton returned and asked for the gun. He had decided he should get rid of it because it was hot. Sutton then took the cylinder from the gun while Foy broke the rest of it into small parts, which he threw in various places. Foy, who admitted he knew the gun was to be used in a holdup, was charged with conspiracy.

Sutton, Almeda and Scott pled guilty to second-degree murder and received life sentences in the Connecticut State Prison. Foy received a one-year jail sentence.

Questions

1. List the steps the investigators followed.
2. Did they omit any necessary steps?
3. What comparison evidence was helpful in the case?

4. How did law enforcement agencies cooperate?
5. What interrogation techniques did they use?
6. How important was citizen information?

Discussion Questions

1. In a robbery of a neighborhood grocery store, how important is citizen information? Should a neighborhood check be made if the incident occurred at 3 A.M.? How would you attempt to locate two witnesses who saw the robber enter the store if the owner does not know their names? How else could you develop information on the robber's description, vehicle and the like?

2. Imagine that you are a police officer responding to the scene of a bank robbery. Should you enter the bank immediately? Should you close the bank to business during the investigation? Can the drive-up window be used for business if it was not involved in the robbery? What should be done with the bank employees after the robbery? With customers in the bank at the time of the robbery? What agencies should work jointly on this type of crime?

3. How important is an immediate response to a robbery call? What vehicles should respond to the scene? To the area surrounding the scene? What types of locations near the scene are most advantageous to apprehending the suspect?

4. If a robber takes a hostage inside a building, what are immediate considerations? If the hostage situation is not resolved in the first 15 minutes, what must be considered? Should a police officer offer to take the hostage's place? What might you say to the robber to induce him or her to release the hostage? To surrender after releasing the hostage?

5. Why is a robbery in progress dangerous for the police? For the victim? What can the police do to reduce the potential danger while responding? To reduce the danger to the hostage?

6. Which takes priority: taking the robber at all risks (to remove him or her from the street and prevent future robberies) or ensuring the safety of the victim and witnesses?

7. What other crimes often occur along with a robbery?

8. What types of establishments are most susceptible to robbery? What types of establishments are most often robbed in your community?

9. What measures can a police department take to prevent robbery? What preventive measures does your department take?

10. What measures can citizens take to help prevent robberies? How can the police assist citizens in these measures?

References

"Carjackings Resulting in Injury." *Criminal Justice Newsletter,* Vol. 29, No. 23, December 1, 1998, pp. 2–3.

Carroll, Paul and Loch, Ronald John. "The Chicago Bank Robbery Initiative." *FBI Law Enforcement Bulletin,* April 1997, pp. 9–14.

"FBI's UCR Shows Lower Crime for Seventh Consecutive Year." *Criminal Justice Newsletter,* Vol. 30, No. 2, January 19, 1999, p. 3.

"49,000 Non Fatal Carjackings Annually." *Law and Order,* Vol. 47, No. 4, April 1999, p. 6.

Fuselier, G. Dwayne. "Placing the Stockholm Syndrome in Perspective." *FBI Law Enforcement Bulletin,* July 1999, pp. 22–25.

Garner, Gerald W. "Before SWAT Arrives: Negotiation Skills for First Responders." *Police,* April 1998, pp. 26–31.

"Hard-Boiled Yeggs Turn Their Focus to Softer Bank Targets." *Law Enforcement News,* June 15, 1997, p. 8.

Klaus, Patsy. *Carjackings in the United States, 1992–96.* Bureau of Justice Statistics, Special Report, March 1999. (NCJ-171145)

Meyer, Greg. "40 Minutes in North Hollywood." *Police,* June 1997, pp. 27–37.

Moore, Russ. "Consider 'RoboCops' for the 21st Century." *Police,* August 1999, pp. 42–45.

Morrison, Richard D. "Bank Robbery." *Law and Order,* October 1996, pp. 159–160.

Noesner, Gary W. "Negotiation Concepts for Commanders." *FBI Law Enforcement Bulletin,* January 1999, pp. 6–14.

Pearson, Cecil. "No Nonsense Negotiations." *Police,* April 1996, pp. 48–51.

Rehder, William J. "Reducing Violent Bank Robberies in Los Angeles." *FBI Law Enforcement Bulletin,* Vol. 69, No. 1, January 2000, pp. 13–17.

Rice, Thomas. "When You're First at a Robbery Scene." *Police,* May 1998, pp. 38–41.

Ronczkowski, Michael and Jose, Maria. "Successful Real-Time Intelligence Analysis." *The Police Chief,* Vol. LXVI, No. 9, September 1999, pp. 28–30.

Strandberg, Keith W. "Hostage Negotiations." *Law Enforcement Technology,* January 1999, pp. 64–70.

"U.S. Supreme Court News: Carjacking." *NCJA Justice Bulletin,* Vol.19, No.4, April 1999, p. 8.

Wexler, Sanford. "Crisis Negotiators." *Law Enforcement Technology,* March 1998, pp. 42–47.

Yarbrough, Kenneth R. and Meyer, Ted. "Investigating High-Tech Robbery and Theft." *The Police Chief,* July 1996, pp. 33–35.

Zingo, Nick. "LAPD Urban Warfare in North Hollywood Bank Shoot Out." *Police,* April 1997, pp. 20–23.

Assault

Do You Know?

What constitutes assault?

How simple assault differs from aggravated assault?

When force is legal?

What the elements of the crime of simple assault are? Of aggravated (felonious) assault? Of attempted assault?

What special challenges are posed in an assault investigation?

How to prove the elements of both simple and aggravated assault?

What evidence is likely to be at the scene of an assault?

What offenses might be categorized as separate crimes rather than simply as assault?

What constitutes domestic violence?

What constitutes stalking?

What constitutes elder abuse?

Introduction

Two people have a violent argument and hurl insults at each other. A "bouncer" physically ejects a belligerent drunk from a bar; an "enforcer" breaks all the fingers of a man who is past due on a gambling debt. An angry wife hurls a frying pan, striking her husband in the back. A teacher slaps a disrespectful student. A group of teenagers mugs an old man. A jealous lover stabs a rival with a knife. Each of these scenarios has one thing in common—each is an assault.

This chapter begins with a discussion of the classification of assault. This is followed by an explanation of the elements of the crime and special challenges involved in investigating assaults. Next the chapter discusses the investigation and how to prove the elements of the crime. The chapter concludes with a close-up look at domestic violence, stalking and elder abuse. ∎

Assault: An Overview

Assault is "an intentional, unlawful act of injury to another by force, or force directed toward another person, under circumstances that create fear of imminent peril, coupled with apparent state of ability to execute attempt, if not prevented. The intention to harm is of the essence. Mere words, although provoking or insulting, are not sufficient" (*Naler v State,* 1933).

Assault is unlawfully threatening to harm another person, actually harming another person or attempting unsuccessfully to do so.

Assaults range from violent threats to brutal gangland beatings, from a shove to a stabbing. Many assaults arise from domestic conflicts, often during periods of heavy drinking by one or both parties. Some result from long-developing ill feelings that suddenly erupt into open violence. Some result from an argument such as a barroom dispute that ends in a brawl. They often are connected with robberies. In fact, 50 percent of all robberies include an assault of some form.

Formerly, in many states the term *assault* referred to threats of or attempts to cause bodily harm, whereas **battery** referred to the actual carrying out of such threats. Actual physical contact is not required for assault. The threat or fear of an assault along with ability to commit the act is sufficient.

In most revised state statutes, the term *assault* is synonymous with *battery,* or the two terms have been joined in a single crime termed *assault.* Some states, however, still have separate statutory offenses of assault and battery. Where one statute remains, battery includes the lesser crime of assault.

Classification

Assaults are classified as either simple or aggravated (felonious).

Simple assault is intentionally causing another person to fear immediate bodily harm or death or intentionally inflicting or attempting to inflict bodily harm on the person. **Aggravated (felonious) assault** is an unlawful attack by one person on another to inflict severe bodily injury.

Nicole Barret, 27, sustained severe head injuries after being struck in the back of the head with a brick as she was walking in midtown Manhattan on November 16, 1999. A homeless man was later charged in the assault, which spurred a crackdown on the city's transients.

Simple assault is usually a misdemeanor. It does not involve a deadly weapon, and the injuries sustained, if any, are neither severe nor permanent. Aggravated assault, on the other hand, is a felony. Nationally, it is the most frequent of the crimes against a person. Aggravated or felonious assault is sometimes further classified as assault with a deadly weapon or assault with intent to commit murder.

Legal Force

Physical force may be used legally in certain instances.

In specified instances, teachers, people operating public conveyances and law enforcement officers can legally use reasonable physical force.

Teachers have the authority of **in loco parentis** ("to take the place of the parent") in many states and are allowed to use minimum force to maintain discipline, stop fights on school property or prevent destruction of school property. Bus drivers, train conductors, airplane pilots and ship captains have authority to use force to stop misconduct by passengers. Law enforcement officers may use as much force as needed to overcome resistance to a lawful arrest. Force used in self-defense is also justifiable.

Elements of the Crime

Simple Assault

Most state statutes have common elements.

- - - - - - - - -

The elements of the crime of simple assault are:

- Intent to do bodily harm to another.
- Present ability to commit the act.
- Commission of an overt act toward carrying out the intention.

- - - - - - - - -

Intent to Do Bodily Harm to Another Evidence of specific *intent* to commit bodily injury must be present. Injury that is caused accidentally is not assault. A suspect's words and actions or any injuries inflicted on a victim imply this intent. The injury must be to another person; injury to property or self-inflicted injury—no matter how serious—is not assault.

The bodily harm or injury in simple assault need not cause severe physical pain or disability. The degree of force necessary in simple assault ranges from a shove or a slap to slightly less than that required for the great bodily harm that distinguishes aggravated assault.

Present Ability to Commit the Act The suspect must have been physically able to commit the act at the time. A suspect who hurled a knife at a victim who was obviously out of range would not have had the ability to hit the target.

Commission of an Overt Act An overt act, more than a threat or gesture, must have been completed. If the suspect was in range to strike the victim, even if someone intervened, an assault can be proven. Intentionally pushing, shoving or physically preventing someone from entering or leaving property is often determined to be simple assault.

Aggravated Assault

Aggravated assault includes the three elements of simple assault plus an element relating to the severity of the attack. Aggravated assault is usually committed with a weapon or by some means likely to produce great bodily harm or death.

- - - - - - - - -

An additional element of aggravated assault is that the intentionally inflicted bodily injury must have resulted in one of the following:

- A high probability of death
- Serious, permanent disfigurement
- Permanent or protracted loss or impairment of the function of any body member or organ or other severe bodily harm

- - - - - - - - -

As with simple assault, the act must be intentional—not accidental.

High Probability of Death An assault is considered aggravated if it is committed by any means so severe that a reasonable person feels it would result in a high probability of death. Examples include a blow sufficient to cause unconsciousness or coma, a gunshot or knife wound that causes heavy bleeding or burns inflicted over most of a person's body.

Serious, Permanent Disfigurement Permanent disfigurement includes such things as losing an ear, eye or part of the nose or permanent scarring of the face or other parts of the body that are normally visible. It cannot be a temporary injury that will eventually heal and not be evident.

Loss or Impairment of Body Members or Organs Regardless of the part of the body affected, a charge of aggravated assault is supported by the loss or permanent impairment of body members or organs, or maiming. "Maiming signifies to cripple or mutilate in any way which deprives of the use of any limb or member of the body, to seriously wound or disfigure or disable" (*Schackelford v Commonwealth,* 1945).

Only one of these additional elements is needed to show aggravated assault, although two or all three are sometimes present. Some states do not require permanent or protracted injury or loss if the weapon used in the assault is a dangerous weapon that causes fear of immediate harm or death.

Attempted Assault

Attempted aggravated assault is also a crime in many states. If the suspect intended to assault someone but was prevented from doing so for some reason, it is still a punishable offense categorized as "unlawful attempt to commit assault."

Attempted assault requires proof of intent along with some overt act toward committing the crime.

Intent or preparation is not enough to prove attempted assault. For example, a suspect must have done more than obtain a weapon or make a plan or even arrange to go to the scene. Rather, the suspect must actually have gone there and have had the weapon in possession when the effort was aborted.

A person who intends to rob a grocery store and whose gun accidentally discharges while the person is in the store has indeed committed an overt act. However, if the gun discharges while the person is driving to the store, there is no overt act to support an attempted assault charge. Likewise, if a potential rapist approaches a woman and has raised his arm to strike her when he is apprehended, an overt act toward an assault has been committed. But if the man is apprehended while still lurking behind a bush, reasonable doubt exists.

Special Challenges in Investigation

Special challenges in assault investigations include distinguishing the victim from the suspect, determining whether the matter is civil or criminal and determining whether the act was intentional or accidental. Obtaining a complaint against a simple assault also is sometimes difficult. Moreover, such calls may be dangerous for responding officers.

Sometimes it is difficult to know who started a fight. Both parties may claim the other person struck the first blow. In such cases, both may be charged with disturbing the peace until officers can obtain more information.

It is also necessary to determine whether the altercation is a civil or a criminal matter. A person who accidentally injures someone is not guilty of a criminal offense but may be sued in a civil court by the victim.

It is sometimes difficult, especially in cases of wife and child beating, to obtain a complaint from the victim. If it is simple assault, which is a misdemeanor, you must see the offense committed or obtain a complaint and arrest warrant or have the victim make a citizen's arrest.

Patrol officers usually make the first contact with the complainant or assault victim. Police on regular patrol sometimes observe an assault occurring. Usually, however, they are sent to the assault scene by the dispatcher. Assault calls are potentially dangerous for the police. In fact, according to the FBI's *Uniform Crime Reports,* more police officers are injured and killed in response to domestic and assault calls than in response to robbery and burglary complaints.

You may arrive at the point of most heated emotions and in the middle of a situation that stems from a deep-rooted problem entirely unknown to you. Your first act is to stop any assaultive action by disarming, separating or arresting the people involved. This reduces the possibility of further conflict.

Be on your guard, and do not take sides in any dispute. If people are injured, administer first aid or summon emergency personnel to the scene. Determine whether more help is needed and whether a description of the suspect must be broadcast.

In most assault cases, arriving police officers find the assault has been completed. However, verbal abuse and considerable confusion may still exist. The victim is normally conscious and, even if severely injured, can provide information about the assailant. Interview the victim as soon as possible to obtain details about the injury, the degree of pain, medical assistance rendered and other facts related to the severity of the attack. The extent and nature of the injury determines the degree of assault to be charged. Further facts supporting the severity of the attack are obtained by noting what treatment the victim requires and by talking to medical personnel.

The victim frequently knows who committed the assault, either by name or by an association that can be checked. Determine the reason for the assault. Find out what actions the victim and assailant took before, during and after the assault. If the victim of an aggravated assault is severely injured and indicates by words, gestures or appearance that death may be imminent, obtain a "dying declaration."

If the suspect is at the scene, make an arrest if the situation warrants, or have the victim make a citizen's arrest. If the suspect is known but is not at the scene, broadcast the suspect's description and begin your investigation.

The Preliminary Investigation

At a minimum, an officer arriving on the scene of an assault should:

■ Control and disarm those involved in the altercation.

■ Provide medical aid to injured people.

■ Separate suspects.

■ Protect the crime scene.

■ Give the Miranda warning if applicable.

■ Obtain preliminary statements.

■ Photograph evidence.

■ Collect and preserve evidence.

■ Reconstruct the crime.

Proving the Elements of Assault

An assault that involves no dangerous weapon and results in no serious injury is a relatively minor crime. In contrast, aggravated assault is an extremely serious crime.

> To prove the elements of assault, establish the intent to cause injury, the severity of the injury inflicted and whether a dangerous weapon was used.

You can establish intent by determining the events that led up to the assault. Record the suspect's exact words and actions and take statements from the victim and any witnesses.

Establish the severity of the assault by taking photographs and describing all injuries in your notes. Describe the size, location, number, color, depth and amount of bleeding of any injuries. Some bruises do not become visible for several hours or even a day or two. Assault victims should be advised of this and told that additional photographs should be taken. Obtain an oral or written statement from a qualified medical person as to the sever-

ity and permanence of the injuries and any impairment of bodily functioning.

Determine the means of attack and the exact weapon used. Was it hands, fists, feet, a gun or a knife?

Evidence in Assault Investigations

Corroborate the victim's information with physical evidence.

> Physical evidence in an assault includes photographs of injuries, clothing of the victim or suspect, weapons, broken objects, bloodstains, hairs, fibers and other signs of an altercation.

Two important pieces of evidence are photographs of injuries and the weapon used in the assault. If the hands, fists or feet were used, examine them for cuts and bruises, and photograph any injuries. Obtain fingernail scrapings from both the victim and the suspect.

Take as evidence any weapons found at the scene. The victim's clothing may contain evidence such as bullet holes or tears made by a knife or other cutting instrument. If you suspect alcohol or drug use may have contributed to the assault, arrange for the appropriate urine, blood and saliva tests. Photograph and make notes regarding evidence that indicates the intensity of the assault, for example, overturned furniture, broken objects, torn up sod and bent shrubs.

Reflective ultraviolet photography can allow investigators to document injuries on flesh up to nine months after they have visibly healed. Reflective ultraviolet photography can reveal pattern injuries—that is, injuries that have a recognizable shape—including cigarette burns, whip or belt marks, bruising, contusions, abrasions, injury margins from immersion burns, bite marks and scratches.

> To aid in data collection, three special categories of assault are domestic violence, stalking and elder abuse.

Investigating Domestic Violence

Thistlethwaite et al. (1998, p. 388) report that: "Domestic assault is the most common form of violence encountered by the police."

> **Domestic violence (DV)** is defined as a pattern of behaviors involving physical, sexual, economic and emotional abuse, alone or in combination, by an intimate partner often for the purpose of establishing and maintaining power and control over the other partner (Geberth, 1998, p. 51).

Healey and Smith (1998, p. 2) state:

> Although the legal definition of battering varies from State to State, many intervention providers explain it as a constellation of physical, sexual, and psychological abuses that may include physical violence, intimidation, threats, emotional abuse, isolation, sexual abuse, manipulation, using the children as pawns, economic coercion, and the assertion of male privilege.

As Magnotti (1999, p. 48) asserts: "A DV victim is dependent on the abuser, socially, emotionally and financially." He suggests: "Any threat to the liberty and financial power of the abuser is viewed by the victim as an equally serious threat to themselves. This is the area which is the principal cause of frustration for police officers." Officers may not understand that although it appears the victim can change the circumstances, the victim does not believe she has this capability.

History of Domestic Violence and the Police Response

Litaker (1996, p. 87) explains the historic acceptance of wife beating:

> Historically, English common law gave husbands the right to chastise their wives. There once existed a "rule of thumb" which held that a husband had the right to beat his wife with a stick, but the stick must not be any thicker than his thumb.

Although wife beating is not accepted in the twenty-first century, the law-enforcement approach to it has varied with time. Schmitt (1997, p. 83) acknowledges: "Until recently domestic violence was often shrugged aside or given little attention by police because of cultural conditioning." Martin (1998, p. 55) notes: "Before 1970, . . . domestic violence was a family dilemma, usually ignored, unspoken of and kept secret within the walls of the home. . . . By the 1980s social standards were metamorphosing to more intense enforcement policies." As a result, during the 1980s many police departments developed mandatory arrest policies in response to criticism of prior practices of noninvolvement. Recent research, however, has called into question the effectiveness of mandatory arrest.

The Cycle of Violence

Jarret (1996, p. 16) explains that abuse generally occurs in a three-stage cycle:

- Tension building
- The acute battering episode
- The honeymoon

Jarret believes that this cycle typically increases both in frequency and severity. This pattern of abuse is also a vicious cycle because children who have witnessed abuse or have been abused themselves are 1,000 times more likely to abuse a spouse or child when they become adults.

Prevalence of Domestic Violence and Its Victims

Strandberg (1998, p. 32) states: "Some experts estimate that family violence accounts for more than 40 percent of all violent crime calls." Yet, Martin (p. 57) reports: "Domestic violence is the most under reported crime in America. The FBI reports that in the United States a woman is murdered by a boyfriend or husband every six hours. A woman is physically abused every nine seconds by a husband or boyfriend." One out of six murders is a domestic crime, most of which are the murder of a spouse or lover. Four out of five murders by females are reported to be responses to present or continuing domestic violence.

Tjaden and Thoennes (1998a, p. 20) report: "Physical assault is widespread among American women: 52 percent of surveyed women said they were physically assaulted as a child by an adult caretaker and/or as an adult by any type of perpetrator." Meizner (1998) adds: "As many as four million women in this country suffer some kind of violence at the hands of their husbands or boyfriends each year." Furthermore, another one to two million men are battered by their wives or girlfriends each year. Getz (1998, p. 45) claims: "In all, domestic violence affects the lives of 8 to 15 million people in America when its impact on families is included in the equation."

Table 10.1 shows the prevalence of *reported* domestic violence for both male and female victims. According to Feder (1998, p. 335):

> FBI reports indicate that more than one quarter of all female victims of murders were slain by their husbands

Table 10.1	Percentage of Persons Physically Assaulted by an Intimate Partner in Lifetime by Type of Assault and Sex of Victim[a]	
Type of Assault	Women (n = 8,000)	Men (n = 8,000)
Total physical assault by intimate partner[b]	22.1	7.4
Threw something[b]	8.1	4.4
Pushed, grabbed, shoved[b]	18.1	5.4
Pulled hair[b]	9.1	2.3
Slapped, hit[b]	16.0	5.5
Kicked, bit[b]	5.5	2.6
Choked, tried to drown[b]	6.1	0.5
Hit with object[b]	5.0	3.2
Beat up[b]	8.5	0.6
Threatened with gun[b]	3.5	0.4
Threatened with knife[b]	2.8	1.6
Used gun[b]	0.7	0.1
Used knife	0.9	0.8

[a]Intimate partner includes current or former spouses, opposite-sex cohabiting partners, same-sex cohabiting partners, dates, and boyfriends/girlfriends.
[b]Differences between women and men are statistically significant: p-values ≤ .001.

Source: Patricia Tjaden and Nancy Thoennes. *Prevalence, Incidence, and Consequences of Violence against Women: Findings from the National Violence Against Women Survey.* National Institute of Justice, Centers for Disease Control and Prevention Research in Brief. November 1998, p. 7. (NCJ-172837)

or boyfriends. Furthermore, approximately 2.1 million women are beaten each year. However, these numbers greatly undercount the true extent of spousal violence in that they rely only on incidents that come to police attention.

Sadly, many who are involved in domestic violence, either as victims or abusers, still believe it to be a private family matter.

Fear is another reason such crimes go unreported. Many women do not report domestic assaults because of threats such as "I'll take the kids and you'll never see them again" or "I'll kill you if you call the police." In many instances the wife fails to report the abuse (and to leave the relationship) because she has no work skills and no independent income, because of the stigma and embarrassment associated with the offense or because she has one or more children to support.

Domestic violence is found at all income levels and in all races. However, Healey and Smith (p. 2) note: "African-American women are more likely than women of other races to be victimized [by domestic violence], as are women who live in urban areas." They further note (p. 2): "Domestic violence is also associated with low marriage rates, high unemployment, and social problems." It may or may not involve alcohol or drugs. The crime occurs with heterosexual and homosexual partners and with married, divorced, separated and living-together couples. It can involve male or female aggression, although most instances of heterosexual domestic violence involve male suspects. The offense may be a misdemeanor, a gross misdemeanor or a felony, depending on the severity of the assault.

The Police Response

Responding to domestic violence calls is one of the most disagreeable duties of police officers. In some instances, officers who are not trained for this type of duty may have preconceptions or prejudices that it is a "family mat-

Domestic abuse situations can prove dangerous for police. Here, officers have separated the victim from the perpetrator in order to diffuse the potential for further violence.

ter." Additionally, domestic assault calls are dangerous for the police. Jackson (1996, p. 33) explains: "The highly emotional atmosphere accompanying domestic abuse situations, the raw violence often displayed, the family lives destroyed and the victim's frequent hesitancy to prosecute or seek shelter all place a heavy burden on the officers sent to these disturbances." Nonetheless, an appropriate and effective police response to domestic violence calls is necessary.

Response to such calls may be initiated by the dispatcher, who can save hours of legwork by exploring with the victim her frame of mind and that of the potential attacker. From that point on, responding officers' actions are critical, notes Pentelei-Molnar (1996, p. 32):

> The most important ingredient to an effective domestic violence policy is properly addressing the initial response and procedure of the responding officer. What you do as the primary officer will often determine what happens in court—whether an effective arrest will be conducted and whether or not proper evidence will be collected. . . .
>
> When responding to a domestic violence call, remember that the situation can involve . . . simple battery, assault, kidnapping, trespassing, murder, stalking,

terrorist threats, spousal rape and many others. . . . Never assume that the people . . . are merely involved in the types of squabbles that mom and dad used to get in over the television remote. . . .

> Upon arrival, don't park your patrol car within view of the location you are responding to. This may allow the suspect to see you, become even more enraged at the thought of going to jail, inflict more injury on the victim or have time to gather weapons to assault you with.

The increasing availability of laptop computers in patrol vehicles and the use of real-time response software enable a premise and individual records checks as part of the preliminary investigation. This may include previous calls for service from the complainant's residence, complaints of illegal activities at this address, open warrants for involved parties and background information on the victim or alleged assailant. This information enhances the safety of the officers and helps them better assess the situation upon arrival at the scene. Pentelei-Molnar (p. 34) suggests how to proceed when you arrive at the scene:

> The first rule, of course, is to interview the suspect and victim separately. When initially contacting a suspect, do not immediately Mirandize him or her. At this point,

until you have determined both the nature of the crime and relationship between the suspect and victim, the suspect is not under arrest for domestic violence. They are simply under detention for investigation, since you have reasonable suspicion to detain them.

This is critical because many domestic violence suspects, based on their agitated emotional state, will make admissible, spontaneous statements that can be used against them later in court. Let them make all the spontaneous statements they want.

Police officers must listen to the facts and determine who the offender is if the assault is not continuing when they arrive. Officers need to reduce the level of tension at the scene by separating and talking to the participants. Officers must consider the safety of the participants and any children present.

Basically, any evidence that would lead an officer to make an arrest in any other situation also applies to spousal situations. Most states permit an arrest based on probable cause. Zorza (1998, p. 56) advocates: "With probable cause, police should arrest all abusers not acting in self-defense and issue an arrest warrant even if the offender is absent. A final [note]: The length of time an arrested abuser is held should be no shorter than that of other offenders."

Twenty states now mandate police to make an arrest in domestic violence incidents if there is a protective or restraining order against the attacker. Furthermore, 13 states require an arrest even though no such order exists ("Creative and Innovative . . . ," 1999). A number of states make it mandatory for the officer to make an arrest if there is probable cause, even without a signed complaint by the victim. In Nevada, for example, if the police have sufficient reason to believe that a person, within the preceding four hours, committed an act of domestic violence or spousal battery, the officer is required to arrest that person if there are no mitigating circumstances.

Officers must *not* base their decisions regarding arrest on their perception of the willingness of the victim or witnesses to testify. The victim need not sign a complaint. If the battery was a mutual battery, that is, committed by both people involved, officers must try to determine who the primary physical aggressor was and then arrest that person. Factors to consider in making this determination include:

- Prior domestic violence involving either person
- The relative seriousness of the injuries inflicted upon each person involved

- The potential for future injury
- Whether one of the alleged batteries was committed in self-defense
- Any other factor that helps the officer decide which person was the primary physical aggressor

Obtain all evidence, including photographs of injuries, victim's statements, prior police reports, doctor or hospital reports, weapons used, damaged clothing or other property and statements from neighbors or other witnesses. Explain to the victim that an "order of protection" may be obtained from a court to help prevent future assaults.

Bourn (1996, pp. 37–38) suggests that department policies and protocols address the following:

- Medical attention. Have the victim sign a release for medical records.
- Victim's statements. Also include the victim's demeanor.
- Degree of pain
- Victim's written statement
- Defendant's statements
- Photographs
- Follow-up investigation. Check back a few days later because bruises typically do not appear until a day or two after an assault.

Pentelei-Molnar (p. 35) stresses the importance of the incident report:

As with any crime report, the better your report, the better chance you have of obtaining a conviction in court. When writing your report, remain objective in the documentation of the crime. . . .

Be sure to include all elements of the crime, the relationship and background of the suspect and victim—and whether . . . the victim was advised of a private person's arrest during evaluation. Of course, describe in detail the origin of the call, the investigation and any evidence and drawing you may want to provide of the scene. . . .

Also, be sure to accurately label and describe each photograph that you've taken of injuries and the victim's physical condition. Some departments have a supplement report form to document evidence in domestic violence cases [see Figure 10.1 A, B].

PAGE ____ OF ____

SAN DIEGO POLICE DEPARTMENT   DOMESTIC VIOLENCE SUPPLEMENTAL   137000 P.C.

VICTIM'S NAME (L, M, F)   DATE OF BIRTH   SDPD CASE NUMBER

I responded to a call of   at   (SDPD Dispatch Center #   )

I found the victim   The victim displayed the following emotional and physical conditions:

VICTIM   DESCRIBE ALL CONDITIONS OBSERVED; PHYSICAL, EMOTIONAL AND CRIME SCENE

☐ ANGRY   ☐ COMP. OF PAIN
☐ APOLOGETIC   ☐ BRUISE (S)
☐ CRYING   ☐ ABRASION (S)
☐ FEARFUL   ☐ MINOR CUT (S)
☐ HYSTERICAL   ☐ LACERATION (S)
☐ CALM   ☐ FRACTURE (S)
☐ AFRAID   ☐ CONCUSSION (S)
☐ IRRATIONAL   ☐ OTHER: EXPLAIN
☐ NERVOUS
☐ THREATENING   ALWAYS explain
☐ OTHER: EXPLAIN   OPPOSITES in narrative.

SUSPECT

☐ ANGRY   ☐ COMP. OF PAIN
☐ APOLOGETIC   ☐ BRUISE (S)
☐ CRYING   ☐ ABRASION (S)
☐ FEARFUL   ☐ MINOR CUT (S)
☐ HYSTERICAL   ☐ LACERATION (S)
☐ CALM   ☐ FRACTURE (S)
☐ AFRAID   ☐ CONCUSSION (S)
☐ IRRATIONAL   ☐ OTHER: EXPLAIN
☐ NERVOUS
☐ THREATENING   ALWAYS explain
☐ OTHER: EXPLAIN   OPPOSITES in narrative.

RELATIONSHIP BETWEEN VICTIM AND SUSPECT
MARK ALL THAT APPLY
☐ SPOUSE   LENGTH OF RELATIONSHIP   PRIOR HISTORY OF DOMESTIC VIOLENCE?   ☐ YES   ☐ NO
☐ FORMER SPOUSE   PRIOR HISTORY OF VIOLENCE DOCUMENTED?   ☐ YES   ☐ NO
☐ COHABITANTS
☐ FORMER COHABITANTS   ____ YEAR(s) ____ MONTH(s)   NUMBER OF PRIOR INCIDENTS [   ]   ☐ MINOR   ☐ SERIOUS
☐ DATING/ENGAGED
☐ FORMER DATING   IF APPLICABLE,   CASE NUMBER(S) _____
☐ SAME SEX   DATE RELATIONSHIP ENDED:
☐ EMANCIPATED MINOR   INVESTIGATING AGENCY _____
☐ PARENT OF CHILD FROM
   RELATIONSHIP

MEDICAL TREATMENT   PARAMEDICS AT SCENE ☐ YES ☐ NO   HOSPITAL: _____

☐ NONE
☐ WILL SEEK OWN DOCTOR   UNIT NUMBER: _____   ATTENDING PHYSICIAN(S): _____
☐ FIRST AID   NAME(S) ID#:
☐ PARAMEDICS
☐ HOSPITAL   _____
☐ REFUSED MEDICAL AID

EVIDENCE COLLECTED   DESCRIBE ALL EVIDENCE AND DISPOSITION

FROM: ☐ Crime Scene ☐ Hospital ☐ Other; Explain
PHOTOS: ☐ Yes ☐ No   Number _____
TYPE: ☐ 35mm   ☐ Polaroid

TAKEN BY: _____
DESCRIBE ALL PHOTOGRAPHS
Photos of victim's injuries: ☐ Yes   ☐ No
Photos of suspect's injuries: ☐ Yes   ☐ No
Weapon used during incident: ☐ Yes   ☐ No

Type of weapon used: _____
Weapon impounded: ☐ Yes   ☐ No
Firearm(s) impounded for safety: ☐ Yes   ☐ No

PROPERTY TAG NUMBER: _____   ☐ CONTINUED

REPORTING OFFICER   ID NUMBER   DIV. WATCH   DATE & TIME   APPROVED BY: NAME & ID

PD-965-FDS (Rev. 10/94)   This information is available in alternate formats upon request.

continued

FIGURE 10.1A   *Sample Report Form to Document Evidence in Domestic Violence Cases, Front*

Source: Kathryn Bourn. "Battles on the Homefront." *Police,* March 1996, p. 62. Reprinted by permission of Bobit Publishing, Redondo Beach, CA.

FIGURE 10.1B *Sample Report Form to Document Evidence in Domestic Violence Cases, Back*

Source: Kathryn Bourn. "Battles of the Homefront." *Police,* March 1996, p. 62. Reprinted by permission of Bobit Publishing, Redondo Beach, CA.

		PAGE ____ OF ____

WITNESS

WITNESSES PRESENT DURING DOMESTIC VIOLENCE? ☐ YES ☐ NO
STATEMENT TAKEN? ☐ YES ☐ NO
CHILDREN PRESENT DURING DOMESTIC VIOLENCE? ☐ YES ☐ NO   NUMBER PRESENT?____ AGE(S)____
STATEMENT TAKEN? ☐ YES ☐ NO
WITNESS INFO LISTED ON ARJIS FORMS? ☐ YES ☐ NO

RESTRAINING ORDERS: ☐ YES ☐ NO
☐ CURRENT ☐ EXPIRED
TYPE: ☐ EMERGENCY ☐ TEMPORARY ☐ PERMANENT

ISSUING COURT: _____
ORDER OR DOCKET NUMBER: _____

VICTIM GIVEN:
☐ DOMESTIC VIOLENCE INFORMATION SHEET (PD-964)
☐ SDPD CRIME CASE NUMBER
☐ DOMESTIC VIOLENCE UNIT PHONE NUMBER

VICTIM WILL BE AT A TEMPORARY ADDRESS? ☐ *YES, INTEROFFICE MEMO ATTACHED.* ☐ *NO*

V.   S.?

HT. ____
WT. ____

PLEASE DRAW ON DIAGRAM(S) THE LOCATION OF ANY INJURIES.

V.   S.?

HT. ____
WT. ____

☐ CONTINUED ON ARJIS # FORM

As with other aspects of investigation, technology is enhancing the processing of domestic violence cases. Getz (p. 47) explains how the Largo (Florida) Police Department's Internet Project is helping law enforcement fight domestic violence:

No matter how good the evidence is, if it's not in front of a prosecutor and a judge in time for the first appearance, the perpetrator often walks free. What the Internet accomplishes is to bring the crime scene to the prosecutor's office and the courtroom by the very next morning—something the department was never able to do before. The judge can see the bruises on the victim's face, hear the victim recounting her experience and listen to the screaming in the background. It is convincing evidence.

The department is able to scan photos onto its Home Page and run video and 911 tapes through the computer, turning sound and film into digitized images for the Internet, accessible from any online computer.

Technological advances have also helped decrease the potential for domestic abusers to commit another assault. Domash (1998, p. 46) explains:

> Officials in Nassau County [New York] have produced a first-generation electronic device designed to deter offenders in domestic violence cases. . . .
>
> The system modifies and combines the technology of the alarm system called Criminal Apprehension Provided by Electronic Response . . . and the electronic cuff that is presently used throughout the country for "house arrest" situations. . . .
>
> The victim could wear a small pendant transmitter that she could set off if she felt herself in danger. . . .
>
> An ankle cuff will be put on the offender. If the offender comes within 500 feet of his victim, the alarm will automatically be triggered and immediately notify the police department's communications bureau. . . .
>
> The victim is called and kept on the line until the patrol car arrives. The alarm also sets off an audible sound, notifying the victim that she is in danger.

Police Nonresponse One reason officers are criticized for not responding to domestic violence incidents is that they commonly receive calls from uninvolved third parties. For example, an apartment tenant calls to say the couple across the hall is shouting at each other and it sounds like things are being thrown and glass is breaking. When officers arrive, the couple may be embarrassed or angry because this is how they argue. They see no reason to involve the law and are irritated at the interference of neighbors and police. In other cases, a spouse may report a false domestic violence incident just to see the other party punished or the threat of punishment inflicted.

Several studies have examined whether the police response to domestic violence calls does in fact receive a lower priority than other crime calls. The results generally show an increasingly high priority being placed on such calls. Jones and Belknap (1999, p. 249) state: "Overall the findings suggest a far more serious police response

to batterers than found in prior studies." They add (p. 268): "A serious police response is more likely in jurisdictions where pro-arrest policies and progressive governmental agencies overseeing systematic reactions to battering have been in place for a number of years." Feder (p. 335) compared police handling of domestic and nondomestic assaults in one south Florida jurisdiction and "found evidence that police are not responding less vigorously to domestic assault calls." In fact, Feder notes (p. 346): "The . . . police were almost twice as likely to arrest when answering a domestic call than a nondomestic call." At least in this one jurisdiction, police are treating domestic violence as the serious crime it is.

Domestic Violence as a Crime

Bourn (p. 36) maintains that: "Domestic violence is a silent epidemic, often leaving its victims fearful, voiceless and uncooperative. To increase the likelihood of a conviction, police should treat the call and investigation as they would a homicide." Statistics document that many batterers eventually kill their intimate. Some victims chose to stay with their batterers for fear that leaving would further enrage their partner. In fact, Schmitt (p. 85) points out: "Women who leave their batterers face a 75% greater risk of being killed by their batterers than those who stay."

In some instances the batterer becomes the victim of homicide. In such cases the defense often attributes the murder to the "battered-woman syndrome," which is based on the concept of duress and results from a cycle of violence.

Several departments throughout the United States have adopted a "zero tolerance" approach to domestic violence, including the Tampa Police Department (Holder, 1996, p. 35) and the Hillsborough County Sheriff's Office, Tampa, Florida (Henderson and Reder, 1996, p. 54). This approach appears to be highly successful. Holder (p. 54) states: "Domestic violence is a serious social problem that is said to be at the root of all other social ills. It is also a criminal problem—a crime that can be prevented." O'Dell (1996, p. 21) stresses:

> The research in this area is conclusive. In every community across the country where domestic violence is viewed as the crime that it is and steps are taken to change the criminal justice system, lives are saved.

O'Dell cites as an example San Diego, California, where the domestic violence homicide rate was reduced by 59 percent in two years.

Restraining Orders Domestic violence victims themselves are also taking a more active role in preventing recurring assaults, notes Feltgen (1996, p. 46):

> The sensationalism surrounding the O. J. Simpson trial has [cast] a spotlight on the problem of domestic violence, and started a domino effect with regard to the number of reported incidents. Victims of domestic violence increasingly are seeking the courts' protection in the form of both temporary and permanent restraining orders/injunctions against their spouses in an attempt to stop the violence.

Although abuse victims are certainly encouraged to protect themselves, they cannot rely solely on a piece of paper for security. Keilitz et al. (1998, p. 48) suggest that criminal justice practitioners "stress the importance of safety planning to victims seeking protection orders, particularly those whose abusers have a history of violent crime." Klein (1998, p. 53) cautions: "Civil restraining orders do not adequately protect women from further abuse, and a primary reliance on such orders must be seriously questioned. Any effectiveness that they have in preventing reabuse comes from their issuance, rather than their maintenance." In fact, some studies have found that women who seek restraining orders are well aware of their potential ineffectiveness. Harrell and Smith (1998, p. 49) state: "Many women thought the temporary restraining order was helpful in documenting that the abuse had occurred, but fewer than half thought the man believed he had to obey the order."

Legislation Jarret (p. 16) notes: "In response to public pressure, state legislatures across the United States have enacted legislation that makes domestic violence investigations and prosecutions a law enforcement priority." He concludes (p. 19): "The current state of affairs in domestic violence policy is emotionally charged, politically sensitive and highly visible."

Many departments have a mandatory arrest policy. In fact, some states have legislated that police must have and implement such a policy. This was due in large part to the "Minneapolis Experiment" conducted by Sherman and Berk in the early 1980s that concluded that arrest was a more effective deterrent to repeat offenses than advising or sending the suspect away. This report, sometimes summarized as "arrest works best," had helped create a nationwide pro-arrest sentiment in domestic violence situations. However, since that time Sherman and others have stated that alternatives to arrest might be better in specific circumstances.

Results of various studies are contradictory regarding the deterrent effect of arrest and prosecution on batterers. Thistlethwaite et al. (p. 388) found: "Qualitatively, more severe sentences (e.g., jail combined with probation versus either probation or jail) corresponded with lower recidivism likelihoods. Also, these sentences appeared most effective for persons with greater stakes in conformity (i.e., those less transient in terms of residence and employment and those living in neighborhoods with higher socioeconomic status)." However, Davis et al. (1998, p. 441) assert: "We found no evidence that prosecution outcomes affected the likelihood of recidivism in domestic violence misdemeanor cases. . . . Our findings are consistent with those from other studies in the field, none of which has demonstrated a deterrent effect of prosecution."

Schmidt and Sherman (1998, p. 55) examined official records in six cities to evaluate the deterrent effects of various police responses, including arrest, to domestic violence. Among their findings were the following:

- Arrests reduced violence by some abusers (e.g., employed abusers; those whose victims were white and Hispanic) and increased it for others (e.g., unemployed abusers, those whose victims were black).

- Arrests may reduce domestic violence in the short run but may increase it in the long run.

- None of the innovative treatments—namely, counseling or protective orders—produced any improvement over arrest versus no arrest.

- Citations to appear in court caused more violence than arrests [in one city].

- [In one city] offenders who had left the scene before police arrived and against whom warrants were issued were responsible for less repeat violence than absent offenders against whom warrants were not issued.

In addition to mandatory arrest laws, other laws address issues concerning convicted domestic abusers. One such statute is the Lautenberg Amendment to the Crime Control Bill of 1968, which enforces an aspect of gun control in supporting domestic violence victims. Magaw (1997, p. 4) notes: "Section 658 of H.R. 4278, signed September 30, 1996, prohibits individuals convicted of misdemeanor crimes involving domestic violence from owning or possessing a firearm."

Despite the many laws devoted to reducing or eliminating domestic violence, Davis et al. warn that criminal justice should not expect too much from such legislation. They contend (p. 442) that domestic assault recidivism perhaps is not so much a true failure on the part of criminal justice as it is a simple incapacity to have any significant impact on this crime:

> There may well be limitations on the ability of the criminal justice system to deter domestic violence. . . . Domestic violence cases are messy: The people involved often have strong reasons (children in common, economic interdependency, emotional bonds) for remaining in close proximity. Furthermore, habitual behavior that occurs in the privacy of people's homes and out of the public eye is likely to be highly resistant to change in many instances. The criminal justice system has an important role to play in protecting victims from abuse by more powerful persons, but we should not be surprised if criminal justice intervention is not always the controlling factor in interpersonal relationships governed by complex forces.

When the Abuser Is a Police Officer

When the abuser is a police officer, special challenges may exist. In a number of cases, abusive police officers have injured or killed their spouses with their service weapons. One source ("IACP Releases Model Policy . . . ," 1998, p. 62) reports: "While difficult to document on any national level, acts of domestic violence perpetrated by police officers are assumed to be at least as prevalent as acts of domestic violence committed by the general population." Feltgen (p. 42) describes this problem:

> When officers were dispatched to suspected calls of domestic violence involving one of their co-workers, any policy or law regarding the enforcement of domestic violence procedures was quickly abandoned. Responding officers would often speak only briefly with the "off-duty officer" and, predictably, dismiss the call without any further investigation, written report or—most importantly—a check on the spouse's welfare and safety.
>
> In case after case, victims of domestic violence at the hands of a police officer had made emergency requests for law enforcement intervention, only to have their calls fall on deaf ears. . . .
>
> Abused spouses of police officers become even more traumatized by a system assumed to protect "all" victims of domestic violence as they become tragically lost in a system that fails even to record them as statistics.

Strandberg (1998, p. 36) adds: "The specter of police family violence hangs like a cloud over every single police force investigating these crimes in the commu-

nity." He continues (1999b, p. 41): "The first step toward solving the problem of domestic abuse within police departments is to acknowledge the problem exists, then meet it head on." Strandberg (1999b, p. 38) reports:

> The International Association of Chiefs of Police has studied the issue of domestic violence by police officers and has issued a "Model Policy on Police Officer Domestic Violence" for departments to follow. Victims, advocates and police met five times [from 1997 to 1999] to examine the issue and develop a pro-active response. The ultimate goal of the policy is zero-tolerance for domestic violence among police officers.

Recall the legislation prohibiting people convicted of domestic violence misdemeanors from owning or possessing firearms. This statute obviously presents a dilemma for law enforcement officers for, as Strandberg (1999b, p. 38) observes: "If cops are caught and convicted, they are going to lose their jobs." Stravelle (1997, p. 32) reports: "Data collected from newspapers, personal interviews, and Internet surveys of 65 police departments of varied sizes from 32 different states reveals that about 300 officers out of the 59,000 surveyed have been affected by the statute." Despite this seemingly minimal impact, that statute is haunting some police careers. Stravelle (p. 33) notes:

> The statute is retroactive, which means that individuals convicted of domestic violence misdemeanors anytime in their lives will be required to turn in their weapons or be subject to arrest under federal law.

Interestingly, the Ninth Circuit Court of Appeals recently ruled that the portion of the law denying possession of firearms to police officers convicted of spouse abuse is unconstitutional.

Cooperative Efforts to Deal with Domestic Violence

Geberth (p. 52) asserts: "Law enforcement agencies alone cannot eliminate domestic violence." They must cooperate with community social service agencies, as Hamilton (1996, p. 32) says: "Departments need to establish networks in the community to address the needs of domestic violence victims and their families." Such networks should involve schools, the clergy and neighbors, friends and co-workers of domestic violence victims.

Strandberg (1998, p. 32) adds: "Law enforcement . . . [has] to have the support of the community, the courts and the prosecutors. They have to work hand-in-hand to battle victim reluctance." Lyons (1996, p. 34) claims: "The key to working together is to eliminate turf boundaries, rethink past practices and work as a community team to tackle the problem." For example, as Mullen (1996, p. 35) says:

> If an abuser violates his probation, we enlist the aid of the entire community in an effort to secure his quick arrest and incarceration. Photographs are displayed in local newspapers with a description of his criminal history. Thanks to public tips, our apprehension rate is over 85 percent, with most violators arrested before they commit any new crime or abuse.

Kramer and Black (1996, p. 5), of the Colorado Springs Police Department, describe another example of cooperative efforts. This department collaborates with multiple rural law-enforcement agencies to provide them assistance through equipment, training and support of community volunteer advocates. They also collaborate with Pikes Peak Legal Services to provide legal aid, advocacy and advice to domestic violence victims who have limited financial resources.

Although batterer intervention programs play an important part in the fight to break the cycle of domestic abuse, Healey and Smith (p. 2) assert: "[These] programs cannot deter domestic violence unless they are supported by the criminal justice system." They advocate an integrated criminal justice response that includes:

> . . . coordination among agencies; use of victim advocates throughout the system; designation of special, designated batterer intervention units; and provision of training for agency personnel. Probation officers have a key role as the critical link between the justice system and batterer interventions.

Avoiding Lawsuits

Failure to respond appropriately to domestic violence can result in serious financial liability to local governments. More and more, victims of domestic violence are suing local governments for failure to protect them. Perhaps the most well-known case is that of Tracy Thurman in Torrington, Connecticut. The police department was ordered to pay almost a million dollars because they failed to protect Tracy from her husband, who had a history of battering her (*Thurman v City of Torrington,* 1984).

To reduce lawsuits, departments should have a pro-arrest policy if officers have probable cause to believe a domestic assault has occurred. They should train officers in this pro-arrest policy and require officers to document why an arrest is or is not made.

Investigating Stalking

A **stalker** is someone who intentionally and repeatedly follows, tries to contact, harasses and/or intimidates another person.

Stalking generally refers to repeated harassing or threatening behavior.

The Violence Against Women Grants Office (1998, p. 5) also notes:

> Legal definitions of stalking vary widely from State to State. Though most States define stalking as the willful, malicious, and repeated following and harassing of another person, some States include in their definition such activities as lying-in-wait, surveillance, nonconsensual communication, telephone harassment, and vandalism.

Wexler (1998, p. 34) explains: "While statutes vary from state to state, most define stalking as a 'course of conduct that would place a reasonable person in fear for his or her safety, and that the stalker intended and did, in fact, place the victim in fear.' " A more comprehensive definition is provided by the National Violence Against Women (NVAW) Survey, co-sponsored by the National Institute of Justice (NIJ) and the Centers for Disease Control (CDC) (Violence Against Women, p. 6), which defines stalking as:

> A course of conduct directed at a specific person that involves repeated visual or physical proximity, nonconsensual communication, or verbal, written or implied threats, or a combination thereof, that would cause a reasonable person fear.

In the preceding definitions, "repeated" means two or more incidents.

Types of Stalking

Three broad categories of stalking have been defined, based on the relationship between the stalker and the victim: intimate or former intimate, acquaintance and stranger stalking.

In *intimate or former intimate stalking,* the stalker and victim "may be married or divorced, current or former cohabitants, serious or casual sexual partners, or former sexual partners" (Violence Against Women, p. 2). Wexler (p. 35) notes 70 to 80 percent of stalking cases fall into this category.

Guy Paul Dukes, a 32-year-old security guard, pleaded guilty in October 1999 to charges of stalking and criminal impersonation after masquerading as a police officer to gain access to actress Ashley Judd's home. Unlike most victims of stalkers, Judd was not injured during the encounter. Dukes was sentenced to a year of probation, the primary condition of which was that he stay away from Judd and her family.

In *acquaintance stalking,* the stalker and victim know each other casually. They may be neighbors or co-workers. They may have even dated once or twice but were not sexual partners.

In *stranger stalking,* the stalker and victim do not know each other at all. According to Wexler (p. 35): "This behavior is characterized by stalkers who develop a love obsession or fixation on another person with whom they have no personal relationship." Cases involving public figures and celebrities fall into this category.

Brody (1998, p. E5) notes that the growth of e-mail and use of the Internet has spawned a psychiatric legal term: **cyberstalking.** This refers to preying on a victim via computer.

The Justice Department ("Justice Depart. Urges Police," 1999, p. 5) notes that all 50 states and the District of Columbia have general stalking laws, some of which can be applied to cyberstalking offenses, and that 16 states have added laws specifically targeting cyberstalking. The Department speculates that there may be potentially tens or even hundreds of thousands of victims of recent cyberstalking incidents in the United States. The Department illustrates the serious nature of cyberstalking by describing the first case prosecuted under California's new cyberstalking law. In this case a 50-year-old former security guard pleaded guilty to stalking and other charges for soliciting the rape of a 28-year-old woman who had rejected him. The man impersonated her in Internet chat rooms, giving her phone number and address and the message that she had fantasies of being raped. On at least six occasions men knocked on her door saying they wanted to rape her.

The Department notes: "Computers and the Internet are becoming indispensable parts of America's culture, and cyberstalking is a growing threat. Responding to a victim's complaint by saying 'just turn off your computer' is not acceptable."

Prevalence of Stalking and Its Victims

Tjaden and Thoennes (1998b, p. 5) report: "Women are the primary victims of stalking and men are the primary perpetrators." They note (1998a, p. 2): "Stalking is more prevalent than previously thought: 8 percent of surveyed women and 2 percent of surveyed men said they were stalked at some time in their life." They continue (1998a, p. 2): "One million women and 371,000 men are stalked annually in the United States." According to the Department of Justice: "Sixty percent of women are stalked by spouses, former spouses, live-in partners or dates, while 70 percent of men are stalked by 'acquaintances' or strangers" (Wexler, p. 35).

The seriousness of this problem is reflected by the fact that almost one-third of the women killed in the United States are murdered by their husbands or boyfriends and as many as 90 percent are stalked before the murder (Wexler, p. 34).

The Police Response

The traditional law enforcement response to stalkers has been to issue restraining orders. Unfortunately, such orders are often ineffective, as demonstrated when one offender dramatically stabbed his wife to death and "knifed" the court order to her chest. Tjaden and Thoennes (1998b, p. 2) report: "Of all victims with restraining orders, 69 percent of the women and 81 percent of the men said their stalkers violated the order."

Because of this proven ineffectiveness of restraining orders, the perceived inability of criminal justice to effectively handle stalkers and victims' fear of antagonizing and angering their stalkers, many stalking incidents go unreported. Tjaden and Thoennes (1998b, p. 2) report: "About half of all stalking victims report their stalking cases to the police . . . and about 12 percent of all stalking cases result in criminal prosecution." Of offenders convicted for stalking, most were sentenced "for violations of protection orders that had been issued by the court in domestic violence cases" (Violence Against Women, p. 40).

When dealing with stalkers, investigators should encourage victims to make police reports of the incidents and document the harassment. Such records can serve as the basis for action against the stalker. Wells (1997, p. 9) states: "The crime of stalking requires the victim actually suffer 'substantial emotional distress' because of the stalker's conduct." Investigators may demonstrate such victim distress through documentation of the victim's response to the harassment (Wells, p. 9). Such documentation might include answers to the following questions:

Has the victim:

- Moved to a new location?
- Obtained a new phone number?
- Put a trap on the phone?
- Told friends, co-workers, family of the harassment?
- Given photos of the defendant to security?
- Asked to be escorted to the parking lot and work site?
- Changed work schedule or route to work?
- Stopped visiting places previously frequented?
- Taken self-defense courses?
- Bought pepper spray?
- Purchased a gun?
- Put in an alarm system?

These are just some indicators the victim's state of mind to prove that element of the crime.

Legislation

According to Wexler (p. 34) the nation's first antistalking law was passed in California in 1990: "Since then, all 50 states have passed laws that criminalize stalking behavior. In 1996, a federal law prohibiting interstate stalking was also enacted." Such legislation makes stalking a specific crime and empowers law enforcement to combat the stalking problem. Antistalking laws describe specific threatening conduct and hold the suspect responsible for proving that his or her actions were not intended to frighten or intimidate the victim.

Jarrett (p. 18), after reviewing various stalking laws, found two types of stalking—misdemeanor and felony:

> Misdemeanor stalking, in which the offender willfully, maliciously and repeatedly follows or harasses another, is most frequently punishable by up to one year in jail. Felony, or aggravated, stalking—most commonly punishable by up to five years in jail—is defined as willfully, maliciously and repeatedly following or harassing another person and making a credible threat with the intent to place that person in reasonable fear of death or bodily injury.

Investigating Elder Abuse

As the average lifespan in developed countries increases, our nation's population is, as a whole, getting older. Older Americans will double their ranks in the next 20 years. By 2020 there will be seven million of the "oldest old," many living in nursing homes or requiring care from children who themselves are elderly ("Baby Boomers Creating Elderly Boom," 1996, p. A4).

As the U.S. population ages, a growing concern in law enforcement is elder abuse. Strandberg (1999a, p. 22) states: "Elder abuse is the third wave of abuse in domestic situations: child abuse, spouse abuse and then elder abuse." Like carjacking, elder abuse is not a specific crime category in many states, which makes its frequency data difficult to obtain. It is typically included in the assault, battery or murder category.

Elder abuse is the physical and emotional abuse, financial exploitation and general neglect of the elderly. The extent of elder abuse is currently unknown (Miller and Hess, 1998, p. 259).

Prevalence of Elder Abuse

In addition to the difficulty of determining the extensiveness of the problem due to the lack of data, investigators also recognize a reluctance to report the crime—similar to the situation with domestic assault. Elder abuse has been called a "hidden" or "silent" crime because a large percentage of cases are not reported.

Some elderly individuals are physically incapable of providing information or may be suffering from conditions such as senility or Alzheimer's disease that might cause others not to believe their statements. In other cases, victims may fear further abuse or loss of the care of the only provider they have, or they may be embarrassed that their child could mistreat them. Strandberg (1999a, p. 22) observes: "In the United States, about 450,000 different elders experienced abuse and neglect in domestic settings [each year]. . . . In almost nine out of 10 incidents of domestic elder abuse and neglect the perpetrator is a family member." Elder abuse is perpetuated not only by those of a younger generation; elderly spouses may also abuse each other. Getz (p. 46) notes: "The Older Women's League (OWL) estimates that 1 million women over 65 years old are abused by their husbands or partners."

Signs of Physical Abuse of the Elderly

Signs of physical abuse of the elderly that investigators should be aware of include the following:

■ Injury incompatible with the given explanation

■ Burns (possibly caused by cigarettes, acids or friction from ropes)

■ Cuts, pinch marks, scratches, lacerations or puncture wounds

■ Bruises, welts or discolorations

■ Dehydration and/or other malnourishment without illness-related causes; unexplained loss of weight

■ Pallor; sunken eyes or cheeks

■ Eye injury

■ Soiled clothing or bedding

■ Lack of bandages on injuries or stitches where needed, or evidence of unset bone fractures

■ Injuries hidden under the breasts or on other areas of the body normally covered by clothing

■ Frequent use of the emergency room and/or clinic

The American Medical Association provided doctors with the following questions, which are equally applicable to law enforcement officers:

■ Has anyone at home ever hurt you?

■ Has anyone ever scolded or threatened you?

■ Have you ever signed any documents that you didn't understand?

■ Are you often alone?

■ Are you afraid of anyone at home?

■ Has anyone ever touched you without your consent?

■ Has anyone ever made you do things you didn't want to?

The Police Response

Controversy exists about the role of law enforcement in dealing with elder abuse, especially in identifying "hard to detect" cases. Some departments believe this is the responsibility of social services, not law enforcement. Other departments feel they are in an ideal position to learn from and to assist social services in dealing with cases of elder abuse. Stiegel (1998, p. 34) contends:

Criminal court involvement in elder abuse cases is appropriate when:

■ The case involves criminal intent, criminal neglect, or a crime committed in a nursing home that would be prosecuted if committed on the street.

■ The alleged offender is a public guardian, a person with a history of abusive behavior, a caregiver, or someone who violated protective orders.

■ The abused elder is mentally ill or mentally impaired.

■ The abuse involved severe physical harm or injury or sexual abuse.

Reducing Elder Abuse

One approach to reducing elderly victimization is TRIAD, a cooperative effort of the International Association of Chiefs of Police (IACP), the American Association of Retired Persons (AARP) and the National Sheriffs' Association (NSA). These three organizations are working together to design programs to reduce victimization of the elderly, to assist those who have been victimized and to generally enhance law enforcement services to older adults and the community at large.

Summary

Assault is unlawfully threatening to harm another person, actually harming another person or attempting unsuccessfully to do so. Simple assault is intentionally causing another to fear immediate bodily harm or death or intentionally inflicting or attempting to inflict bodily harm on another. It is usually a misdemeanor. Aggravated assault is an unlawful attack by one person on another to inflict *severe* bodily injury. It often involves use of a dangerous weapon and is a felony. In specified instances, teachers, persons operating public conveyances and law enforcement officers use physical force legally.

The elements of the crime of simple assault are (1) intent to do bodily harm to another, (2) present ability to commit the act and (3) commission of an overt act toward carrying out the intent. An additional element in the crime of aggravated assault is that the intentionally inflicted bodily injury results in (1) a high probability of death, (2) serious, permanent disfigurement or (3) permanent or protracted loss or impairment of the function of any body member or organ or other severe bodily harm. Attempted assault requires proof of intent and an overt act toward committing the crime.

Special challenges in investigating assaults include distinguishing the victim from the suspect, determining whether the matter is civil or criminal and whether the act was intentional or accidental. Obtaining a complaint against simple assault is also sometimes difficult.

To prove the elements of the offense of assault, establish the intent to cause injury, the severity of the injury inflicted and determine whether a dangerous weapon was used. Physical evidence in an assault includes photographs of injuries, clothing of the victim or suspect, weapons, broken objects, bloodstains, hairs, fibers and other signs of an altercation.

Domestic assault, stalking and elder abuse are candidates for categorization as separate crimes rather than being lumped in the general category of assault for reporting and research purposes. Domestic violence is defined as a pattern of behaviors involving physical, sexual, economic and emotional abuse, alone or in combination, by an intimate partner often for the purpose of establishing and maintaining power and control over the other partner. Stalking generally refers to repeated harassing or threatening behavior. Elder abuse is the physical and emotional abuse, financial exploitation and general neglect of the elderly. The extent of elder abuse is currently unknown.

Checklist
Assault

- Is the assault legal or justifiable?
- Are the elements of the crime of assault present?
- Who committed the assault?
- Is the suspect still at the scene?
- Who signed the complaint? Who made the arrest?
- Has the victim made a written statement? Have witnesses?
- Are injuries visible?
- Have photographs been taken of injuries? In color?
- If injuries are not visible, has the victim received medical attention?
- If medical attention was received, has a report on the nature of the injuries been received? Did the victim grant permission?
- What words did the assailant use to show intent to do bodily harm?
- Was a dangerous weapon involved?
- Has a complete report been made?
- If the assault is severe enough to be aggravated assault, what injuries or weapons support such a charge?
- If the victim died as a result of the attack, was a dying declaration taken?
- Was it necessary and legal to make an arrest at the scene? Away from the scene?
- How was the suspect identified?

Application

Read the following and then answer the questions:

Mike S. was drinking beer with friends in a local park about 9:00 P.M. It was dark. He knew Tom C. was at the other end of the park and that Tom had been seeing Mike's girlfriend, Susy H. Susy was with Mike, trying to talk him out of doing anything to Tom. Mike said he was going to find Tom and "pound him into the ground. When I get through with him, they'll have to take him to the hospital."

Mike left the group and Susy then, telling them to wait for him. Tom C. was found later that night two blocks from the park, lying unconscious on a boulevard next to the curb. His clothes were torn and his left arm was cut. When he regained consciousness, he told police he was walking home from the park when someone jumped out from some bushes, grabbed him from behind, beat him with fists and then hit him over the head with something. He did not see his assailant.

Mike S. was arrested because a person at the park overheard his threats.

Questions

1. What is the probability that Mike committed the assault?
2. Did he have the intent? The present ability to commit the act?
3. Did he commit the act? Should he have been arrested?

Discussion Questions

1. If a police officer wearing a concealed armored vest confronts a man burglarizing a store and the burglar fires a gun at the officer, striking him in the chest, is this assault? If so, what type? Which elements of the offense are and are not present?

2. What if the same situation existed except that, as the burglar fired, he slipped and the bullet struck a tree at some distance from the officer?

3. Under what circumstances is a person justified in using force against another person? When is a police officer justified in using force?

4. Imagine that Mrs. Jones has reported to the police department that she and her husband were arguing over his drinking and that Mr. Jones had just beaten her. She wants the police to come to their home and arrest her husband. How would you proceed with this complaint? What precautions would you take?

5. Do your state's laws differentiate between the crimes of assault and battery?

6. Suppose a teacher is having a serious discipline problem with a five-year-old student and sends the student to the principal's office. The principal spanks the student. Under the *in loco parentis* doctrine, is this action legal? Do you agree with this doctrine? Does your state have such a law?

7. Does a sniper firing on a crowd commit assault?

8. In what crimes is assault often an additional crime?

9. If two people become involved in a violent struggle that seriously injures one or both of them, and if both claim the other started the fight, what do you do?

10. Can police officers be sued for making verbal threats to a suspect?

References

"Baby Boomers Creating Elderly Boom." (Minneapolis/St. Paul) *Star Tribune,* May 21, 1996, p. A4.

Bourn, Kathryn. "Battles on the Homefront." *Police,* Vol. 20, No. 3, March 1996, pp. 36–38, 62–63.

Brody, James. "Deep Disorders Drive Stalkers, Experts Say." (Minneapolis/St. Paul) *Star Tribune,* August 30, 1998, p. E5.

"Creative and Innovative Domestic Abuse Programs." 1998–1999.

Davis, Robert C.; Smith, Barbara E.; and Nickles, Laura B. "The Deterrent Effect of Prosecuting Domestic Violence Misdemeanors." *Crime and Delinquency,* Vol. 44, No. 3, July 1998, pp. 434–442.

Domash, Shelly Feuer. "Putting the Cuffs on Domestic Abusers." *Police,* Vol. 22, No. 1, January 1998, pp. 46–47.

Feder, Lynette. "Police Handling of Domestic and Nondomestic Assault Calls: Is There a Case for Discrimination?" *Crime and Delinquency,* Vol. 44, No. 2, April 1998, pp. 335–349.

Feltgen, John. "Domestic Violence: When the Abuser Is a Police Officer." *The Police Chief,* Vol. LXIII, No. 10, October 1996, pp. 42–49.

Geberth, Vernon. "Domestic Violence Homicides." *Law and Order,* Vol. 46, No. 11, November 1998, pp. 51–54.

Getz, Ronald J. "Largo Police Attack Domestic Violence." *Law and Order,* Vol. 46, No. 11, November 1998, pp. 44–50.

Hamilton, Douglas. "Domestic Violence: Challenges for Law Enforcement." *The Police Chief,* Vol. LXIII, No. 2, February 1996, p. 32.

Harrell, Adele and Smith, Barbara. "Effects of Restraining Orders on Domestic Violence Victims." In *Legal Interventions in Family Violence: Research Findings and Policy Implications.* Washington, DC: National Institute of Justice, July 1998, pp. 49–51. (NCJ-171666)

Healey, Kerry Murphy and Smith, Christine. *Batterer Programs: What Criminal Justice Agencies Need to Know.* National Institute of Justice Research in Brief, July 1998. (NCJ-171683)

Henderson, Cal and Reder, R. D. " 'Zero-Tolerance' Policy in Hillsborough County." *The Police Chief,* Vol. LXIII, No. 2, February 1996, pp. 54–55.

Holder, Bennie R. "A Three-Pronged Strategy." *The Police Chief,* Vol. LXIII, No. 2, February 1996, pp. 35–36.

"IACP Releases Model Policy on Police Officer-Involved Domestic Violence." *The Police Chief,* Vol. LXV, No. 6, June 1998, p. 62.

Jackson, James G. "Ending the Cycle." *The Police Chief,* Vol. LXIII, No. 2, February 1996, pp. 33–34.

Jarret, Joseph G. "Domestic Violence: Developing Policies and Procedures Poses Challenge for Law Enforcement." *The Police Chief,* Vol. LXIII, No. 2, February 1996, pp. 16–19.

Jones, Dana A. and Belknap, Joanne. "Police Responses to Battering in a Progressive Pro-Arrest Jurisdiction." *Justice Quarterly,* Vol. 16, No. 2, June 1999, pp. 249–273.

"Justice Depart. Urges Police to Recognize 'Cyberstalking.' " *Criminal Justice Newsletter,* Vol. 30, No. 9, May 3, 1999, pp. 5–6.

Keilitz, Susan; Hannaford, Paula; and Efkemen, Hillery S. "The Effectiveness of Civil Protection Orders." In *Legal Interventions in Family Violence: Research Findings and Policy Implications.* Washington, DC: National Institute of Justice, July 1998, pp. 47–48. (NCJ-171666)

Klein, Andrew R. "Re-abuse in a Population of Court-Restrained Male Batterers: Why Restraining Orders Don't Work." In *Legal Interventions in Family Violence: Research Findings and Policy Implications.* Washington, DC: National Institute of Justice, July 1998, pp. 52–53. (NCJ-171666)

Kramer, Lorne and Black, Howard. "Taking Domestic Violence Investigation to the Next Level." *Subject to Debate,* Vol. 10, Nos. 11/12, November/December 1996, pp. 5–6.

Litaker, G. Ed. "Dealing with Domestic Violence." *Law and Order,* Vol. 44, No. 6, June 1996, pp. 87–89.

Lyons, Scott. "Cooperative Efforts." *The Police Chief,* Vol. LXIII, No. 2, February 1996, p. 34.

Magaw, John. "Clarifying the Domestic Violence Provision of the Omnibus Consolidated Appropriations Act." *The Police Chief,* Vol. LXIV, No. 2, February 1997, p. 4.

Magnotti, Mike. "Understand Relationships as the Key to Handling Domestic Violence Calls." *Police,* Vol. 23, No. 10, October 1999, pp. 42–48.

Martin, Monica. "Evaluating Domestic Violence." *Law and Order,* Vol. 46, No. 11, November 1998, pp. 55–57.

Meizner, Julie. "Domestic Violence, The Hidden Crime." Eden Prairie, MN: *Neighborhood News Letter,* 1998.

Miller, Linda S. and Hess, Kären M. *The Police in the Community: Strategies for the 21st Century,* 2nd ed. Belmont, CA: West/Wadsworth Publishing Company, 1998.

Mullen, Francis E. "Long-Term Effectiveness." *The Police Chief,* Vol. LXIII, No. 2, February 1996, pp. 34–35.

O'Dell, Anne. "Domestic Violence Homicides." *The Police Chief,* Vol. LXIII, No. 2, February 1996, pp. 21–23.

Pentelei-Molnar, John. "Putting Out the Fire." *Police,* Vol. 20, No. 3, March 1996, pp. 32–35.

Schmidt, Janell D. and Sherman, Lawrence W. "Does Arrest Deter Domestic Violence?" In *Legal Interventions in Family Violence: Research Findings and Policy Implications.* Washington, DC: National Institute of Justice, July 1998, pp. 54–55. (NCJ-171666)

Schmitt, Sheila. "Combating Domestic Violence." *Law and Order,* Vol. 45, No. 4, April 1997, pp. 83–85.

Stiegel, Lori A. "Recommended Guidelines for State Courts Handling Cases Involving Elder Abuse." In *Legal Interventions in Family Violence: Research Findings and Policy Implications.* Washington, DC: National Institute of Justice, July 1998, pp. 34–35. (NCJ-171666)

Strandberg, Keith W. "Reducing Family Violence." *Law Enforcement Technology,* Vol. 25, No. 1, January 1998, pp. 32–36.

Strandberg, Keith W. "Child and Elder Abuse." *Law Enforcement Technology,* Vol. 26, No. 6, June 1999a, pp. 20–22.

Strandberg, Keith W. "Domestic Abuse among Cops." *Law Enforcement Technology*, Vol. 26, No. 6, June 1999b, pp. 38–41.

Stravelle, Charles. "Domestic Abuse Convictions Haunting Some Police Careers." *Police*, Vol. LXIV, No. 7, July 1997, pp. 32–33.

Thistlethwaite, Amy; Wooldredge, John; and Gibbs, David. "Severity of Dispositions and Domestic Violence Recidivism." *Crime and Delinquency*, Vol. 44, No. 3, July 1998, pp. 388–398.

Tjaden, Patricia and Thoennes, Nancy. *Prevalence, Incidence, and Consequences of Violence against Women: Findings from the National Violence Against Women Survey*. National Institute of Justice, Centers for Disease Control and Prevention Research in Brief, November 1998a. (NCJ-172837)

Tjaden, Patricia and Thoennes, Nancy. *Stalking in America: Findings from the National Violence against Women Survey*. National Institute of Justice, Centers for Disease Control and Prevention Research in Brief, April 1998b. (NCJ-169592)

Violence Against Women Grants Office. *Stalking and Domestic Violence: The Third Annual Report to Congress under the Violence against Women Act*. Washington, DC: U.S. Department of Justice, July 1998. (NCJ-172204)

Wells, Kerry. "Stalker Interviews Are Crucial." *Law Enforcement Quarterly*, November 1996–January 1997, pp. 9–12, 31.

Wexler, Sanford. "The Crime of Stalking." *Law Enforcement Technology*, Vol. 25, No. 6, June 1998, pp. 34–37.

Zorza, Joan. "Must We Stop Arresting Batterers? Analysis and Policy Implications of New Police Domestic Violence Studies." In *Legal Interventions in Family Violence: Research Findings and Policy Implications*. Washington, DC: National Institute of Justice, July 1998, pp. 55–57. (NCJ-171666)

Sex Offenses

Do You Know?

How sex offenses are classified?

How rape is defined and classified?

What the elements of sexual assault are?

What modus operandi factors are important in investigating a sexual assault?

What special challenges exist in investigating sex offenses?

What blind reporting is and what its advantages are?

What evidence is often obtained in sex offense investigations?

What evidence to seek in date rape cases?

What agencies can assist in a sexual assault investigation?

What is generally required to obtain a conviction in sexual assault cases?

Whether recent laws have reduced or increased the penalties for sexual assault and why?

Which three federal statutes form the basis for sex offender registries?

Introduction

Tjaden and Thoennes (1998, p. 2) report:

> Rape is a crime committed primarily against youth: 18 percent of women surveyed said they experienced a completed or attempted rape at some time in their life and 0.3 percent said they experienced a completed or attempted rape in the previous 12 months. Of the women who reported being raped at some time in their lives, 22 percent were under 12 years old and 32 percent were 12 to 17 years old when they were first raped.

Figure 11.1 shows the percentages of women victims' ages at the time of their first rape.

Physically attractive or unattractive people of any age—from very young children to senior citizens—may be victims of sexual assault. Sex offenses range from **voyeurism** (the Peeping Tom) to rape and murder. Sex offenses can be difficult

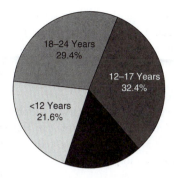

FIGURE 11.1   *Women Victims' Ages at Time of First Rape* (*n*=1,323 women victims)

Source: Patricia Tjaden and Nancy Thoennes. *Prevalence, Incidence, and Consequences of Violence against Women: Findings from the National Violence against Women Survey.* National Institute of Justice, Centers for Disease Control and Prevention Research in Brief, November 1998, p. 6. (NCJ-172837)

In 1993, 21-year-old Brandon Teena was raped and murdered in Falls City, Nebraska, after he was revealed to be a woman. Brandon (born Teena Brandon and shown here in a high school photo) had successfully passed as a man since moving to Falls City earlier that year, dating women and even befriending the two men who later became his assailants. One of the men is serving a life sentence; the other remains on death row.

to investigate because the victim is often emotionally distraught. Moreover, investigating officers may be uncomfortable because they lack special training in interviewing sex offense victims or offenders.

Some sex offenders are emotionally disturbed and feel no remorse for their actions. For example, a 38-year-old man with a 20-year history of sex offenses admitted to a prison psychiatrist that even he could not remember how many rapes and sexual assaults he had committed. The suspect also talked freely about his sexual exploits with children and showed no emotion at all. A **pedophile**—a person who is sexually attracted to young children—can be extremely dangerous, as can a **sadist,** a person who derives sexual gratification from causing pain to others, often through mutilation.

Although some sex offenders are emotionally disturbed, the fact remains that most victims know their attacker and that most attacks occur not in dark alleys but in living rooms and bedrooms.

This chapter begins with a discussion of the classification of sex offenses and the investigation of obscene phone calls. Next the chapter discusses the definition of rape/sexual assault, the elements of the crime, an explanation of sex offense terminology, a description of sex offenders, the special challenges in

investigating sex crimes and the benefits of blind reporting. Other topics covered are the police response, an explanation of relevant physical evidence, factors to consider when investigating date rape, the importance of the victim's medical examination and procedures for taking a suspect into custody. Next is a discussion of victim and witness interviews, ways to interrogate sex offenders, the importance of behavioral profiling in sex offense cases, methods of conducting the follow-up investigation and clearance and the importance of coordinating efforts with other agencies. The chapter concludes with a look at the prosecution of rape cases and statutory changes affecting sexual assault cases, including the civil commitment of sex offenders following release from prison and the establishment of sex offender registries and notification laws. Please note that this chapter assumes that the victim is female and the suspect male. ■

Classification

- - - - - - - -

Sex offenses include bigamy, child molestation, incest, indecent exposure, prostitution, rape *(sexual assault)* and sodomy.

- - - - - - - -

Sex crimes are sometimes classified according to whether they involve physical aggression and a victim—for example, rape—or are victimless acts between consenting adults, such as sodomy. The former are most frequently reported to police and investigated. The latter are often simply offensive to others and are seldom reported or investigated.

Bigamy is marrying another person when one or both parties are already married.

Child molestation is usually a felony and includes lewd and lascivious acts, indecent exposure, incest or statutory rape involving a child, male or female, under age 14. This is a difficult charge to prove because children frequently are not believed. Moreover, parents are often reluctant to bring charges in such cases. (This offense is discussed in depth in the next chapter.)

Incest is sexual intercourse with another person nearer of kin than first cousin when the relationship is known. In some states incest extends beyond blood lines to include people who are related by adoption.

Indecent exposure is revealing one's genitals to another person to such an extent as to shock the other's sense of decency. It is not necessary to prove intent. The offense is a misdemeanor, although repeated offenses can be charged as a felony in many states. Ordinarily, **exhibitionists**—those who expose themselves—are not dangerous but may become so if they are humiliated or abused.

Prostitution—soliciting sexual intercourse for pay—not only contributes to the spread of venereal disease, but profits from it often go to organized crime. Of special concern to law enforcement officers is the practice of enticing very young girls into prostitution. Legislation, for example, the Mann Act attempts to prevent such actions. Section 2423 of the act prohibits "coercion or enticement of minor females and the taking of male or female persons across the state line for immoral purposes."

Another concern regarding prostitution is the spread of deadly, sometimes fatal, diseases. Pilkington and Tolbert (1997, p. 165) point out: "Let's consider whether or not prostitution really is a victimless crime. . . . The current estimates of street prostitutes with HIV or AIDS range from 12. 9 to 50 percent. Tragically, estimates put the proportion of prostitutes unaware of their positive HIV or AIDS status at 72 percent."

Rape—or sexual assault—is sexual intercourse with a person against his or her will. Rape is usually considered the most serious crime except murder and carries a heavy penalty in most states. It is now viewed as a violent assault rather than a type of deviance.

Sodomy is any form of anal or oral copulation. Although commonly thought of as being performed by homosexual males, sodomy can occur between a male and female, between two females or between a human and an animal (bestiality). Oral or anal penetration must be proven. Both parties are guilty if the act is voluntary. Because sodomy is usually a private act between consenting adults, it is difficult to obtain sufficient evidence for prosecution. In some states sodomy between consenting adults is no longer a crime. Such acts between adults and juveniles remain crimes, however.

Sex offenses may include a wide range of forbidden sexual activity, including the following:

- **Cunnilingus**—sexual activity involving oral contact with the female genitals
- **Fellatio**—sexual activity involving oral contact with the male genitals
- **Oral copulation**—the same as cunnilingus and fellatio; the act of joining the mouth of one person with the sexual organ of another person
- **Penetration**—any intrusion, however slight, of any part of a person's body or any object manipulated or inserted by a person into the genital or anal openings of another's body, including sexual intercourse in its ordinary meaning
- **Sadomasochistic abuse**—fettering, binding or otherwise physically restraining, whipping or torturing for sexual gratification
- **Sexually explicit conduct**—any type of sexual intercourse between persons of the same or opposite sex, bestiality, sadomasochistic abuse, lewd exhibition or mutual masturbation

Investigating Obscene Telephone Calls

Making obscene telephone calls is a crime. Police departments receive complaints of many types of harassment calls that are not of a sexual nature and have established procedures for investigating such calls. The same procedures apply to telephone calls with sexual implications.

In most obscene phone calls, the callers want to remain anonymous, using the telephone as a barrier between themselves and their victims. The callers receive sexual or psychological gratification from making contact with victims, even from a distance. Calls involving sexual connotations are threatening to the victims because they have no way of knowing the caller's true intent. Although such calls may be made randomly, in many cases the caller knows the victim.

If the victim wants to prosecute, the first contact may be the telephone company. The information section at the front of most telephone directories provides information about what constitutes a violation of telephone company regulations and the law and provides instructions on what to do if a person receives obscene or harassing calls (stay calm, do not respond and quietly hang up the phone; if the calls persist, call the telephone company). The company will assist the victim in contacting the police for further investigation. Caller ID may discourage obscene calls because the caller's phone number may be provided to the victim, who can then give it to the police. The police may also use traps and traces if they are given a signed affidavit from the victim stating the facts related to the obscene calls.

Rape/Sexual Assault

Rape is often classified as either forcible or statutory.

Forcible rape is sexual intercourse against a person's will by the use or threat of force. **Statutory rape** is sexual intercourse with a minor, with or without consent.

Forcible rape is the only sex offense that is an Index Crime, and most of the remainder of the chapter addresses this offense. According to the *Uniform Crime Reports,* forcible rape, like robbery and assault, has doubled in frequency in the past 10 years even though it is the least reported of the Index Crimes. Rape is underreported for a variety of reasons. Many victims feel worthless or guilty afterward. Some fear the social stigma associated with rape. Others have a close relationship with their rapist and fear that a charge of rape would damage the relationship. Many victims appear to be intimidated by the criminal justice system in general or by the way the system appears to have dealt with rape cases in the past.

When investigating cases of sexual assault, officers should be aware of several assumptions that are not based on fact (Table 11.1).

Table 11.1	**Assumptions versus Facts about Sexual Assault**
Assumption	*Fact*
Most rapes are impulsive acts.	Most rapes are planned.
Victims are attacked suddenly, without conversation.	The attack is usually preceded by conversation.
Men rape because they lack sexual outlets.	Many rapists have access to sex; they want to express power, dominance and control.
Rape is a sex crime.	Rape is a crime of violence. Sex is often not the goal.

Source: Minnesota P.O.S.T., *Learning Objectives*

By 1993 at least 22 states had substituted the term *sexual assault* for *rape,* and the number of states adopting this definition has been growing steadily. In this chapter the words *rape* and *sexual assault* are used synonymously and interchangeably. In some states statutory rape is classified as "illegal intercourse." In other states it is classified as "assault with intent to commit rape" or as "attempted rape" when the suspect is prevented from completing the act. Some states, including Minnesota and Illinois, have broadened their definition to provide that the victim *and* the perpetrator may be of either sex. In addition, several states provide greater penalties for attacks on the very young and the very old.

Elements of the Crime of Rape

Rape is defined in various ways by state laws, but certain elements of the offense are fairly universal.

The elements of the crime of rape or sexual assault commonly include:

■ An act of sexual intercourse.

■ With a female other than the wife.

■ Committed without the victim's consent.

■ Against the victim's will and by force.

An Act of Sexual Intercourse The element of sexual intercourse does not require establishing that a complete sex act accompanied by ejaculation occurred. Any degree of penetration of the vagina by the penis is sufficient to constitute sexual intercourse. An emission of semen is not required.

With a Female Other than the Wife This element precludes the possibility of a man being raped, either by a male or female. Some states, as noted, are revising their laws to include as rape forcible sex acts committed by an adult male against another male.

Although most states require that the victim not be the man's wife, a husband can be charged with assault. Moreover, some states include as rape an act of forced sexual intercourse with the wife during a legal separation if the act fulfills the other requirements of rape. Other states are considering laws that would include as rape a husband's forced sexual intercourse accompanied by serious assault threats against the wife's life. Oregon has such a law and has tried (and acquitted) a husband.

Committed without the Consent of the Victim Consent that is given because of fear, panic, emotional disturbance, mental illness or retardation; while on drugs or unconscious; or by a child is *not* considered true consent.

Against the Victim's Will and by Force This element has traditionally been the most difficult to prove and the most subject to attack by the defense. Although laws require the woman to use the utmost resistance possible, such resistance can result in additional violence and even death. A man who is willing to rape is often willing to injure. Therefore, legislation in many states emphasizes the words, actions and intent of the rapist rather than the degree of resistance by the victim.

Police officers are often asked if it is better for a woman to resist or to submit to a sexual attack. Does resistance increase the attacker's violence? It is a difficult question to answer because researchers have arrived at different conclusions. Some results indicate that resisting reduces the likelihood of continued assault; others, that it makes the attacker more violent. Some people who have been sexually assaulted report that they fought back only after they had already been harmed, which would appear to preclude that resisting caused increased violence. It has been found that people who have been attacked previously are more apt to resist.

One study pointed out that in no other crime are victims expected to resist or not to resist their assailants. Certainly everyone has a right to defend themselves, but whether it is more harmful to the victim to choose to defend is not possible to state. This must be an individual decision. Some police departments do not give advice on this question because of the possibility of lawsuits.

What works in one instance may not in another. It is an individual decision that must be based on individual circumstances. More emphasis should be placed on the behavior of the attacker than on that of the victim. Increasing the penalty where the attacker uses extreme violence may help reduce the severity of the attacks, although this is problematic because of the emotional status and possible mental instability of this type of criminal.

Sex Offense Terminology

Intimate parts usually refers to the primary genital areas, groin, inner thighs, buttocks and breasts.

Sexual contact usually includes any act committed without the complainant's consent for the suspect's sexual or aggressive satisfaction. This includes touching the complainant's intimate parts, forcing another person to touch one's intimate parts or forcing another person to touch the complainant's intimate parts. In any of these cases, the body area may be clothed or unclothed.

Sexual penetration includes sexual intercourse, cunnilingus, fellatio, anal intercourse or any other intrusion, no matter how slight, into the victim's genital, oral or anal openings by the suspect's body or by an object. An emission of semen is not required. Any act of sexual penetration by the suspect without the affirmative, freely given permission of the victim to the specific act of penetration constitutes the crime of sexual assault.

Sex Offenders

Some sexual assault offenders are sadistic and commit physical abuses in such hostile, vicious manners that they result in injury or even death to the victim. Others seek to control their victims through threats and physical strength but do not cause permanent physical injuries. Still others act out aggression and hatred in short attacks on women selected as random targets. Rapists may be categorized as motivated by either power or anger. Each category is further divided into two subcategories (see Table 11.2).

Table 11.2	**Profiles of Rapists**			
	Power Rapists		**Anger Rapists**	
	Manhood reassurance	*Manhood assertive*	*Retaliatory/punishing*	*Excitation/sadistic*
Purpose	Confirm manhood to self	Express manhood to victim	Punish women for real or imagined wrongs	Obtain pleasure from inflicting pain
Preassault behavior	Fantasizes about successful sexual relationships Plans attack	Seldom pre-planned Crime of opportunity	Spontaneous act in response to a significant stressor	Violent fantasies Careful planning
Victim selection	Observes (prowler, window peeker)	By chance	Spontaneous	Cruises
Victim characteristics	Same race Meek, nonassertive	Same age and race	Resembles female in his life	Same age and race
Location of approach	Inside victim's residence	Singles bars	Near his residence or job	Any location
Type of approach	Stealth Hand over mouth	Smooth talker Con	Blitz Immediate excessive use of force	Brandish a weapon
Weapon	Of opportunity if used	Of opportunity if used	Of opportunity if used	Of choice or planned
Time of day	Nighttime	Nighttime	Anytime	Anytime
Sexual acts	Normal	Self-satisfying Vaginal/penile intercourse Vaginal/anal intercourse Fellatio Spends long time	Violent, painful sex acts Degrading, humiliating acts Spends short time	Experimental sex Inserts objects into body cavities Spends long time
Sexual dysfunction	Erection problems Premature ejaculation	Retarded ejaculation	—	—
Other behaviors	Relatively nonviolent	Tears clothing off	Profanity Injury-provoking, assaultive	Excessive, brutal force; bondage; torture; cuts clothing off Protects identity (mask, gloves) Most likely to kill
Postassault behavior	Likely to apologize Takes personal items Keeps a diary	Likely to threaten Takes items as trophies Boasts of conquests	Leaves abruptly May or may not threaten	Straightens scene Shows no remorse

Source: William C. Bradway. "Stages of a Sexual Assault." *Law and Order,* September 1990, pp. 119–124. Reprinted by permission of the publisher.

No personality or physical type can be automatically eliminated as a sex offender. Sex offenders include those who are married, have families and good jobs, are college educated and are active churchgoers.

Suspects fall into two general classifications: those who know the victim and those who are known sex offenders. In the first category are friends of the victim, persons who have daily contact with the victim's relatives, those who make deliveries to the victim's residence or business and neighbors. In the second category are those on file in police records as having committed prior sex offenses. Known offenders with prior arrests are prime suspects because rehabilitation is often unsuccessful.

If a suspect is arrested at or near the scene, conduct a field identification. If much time has elapsed between the offense and the report, use other means of identification. If the victim knows the assailant, obtain his name, address, complete description and the nature of their relationship. Then obtain arrest and search warrants. If the suspect is unknown to the victim, check modus operandi files and have the victim look at photo files on sex offenders.

Modus operandi factors important in investigating sex offenses include type of offense, words spoken, use of a weapon, actual method of attack, time of day, type of location and age of the victim.

These modus operandi factors are manifested in the offender's behavior and should be asked about when interviewing victims, as discussed shortly.

Challenges to Investigation

The initial call concerning a rape (or other sexual offense) is normally taken by the dispatcher, communications officer or complaint clerk. The person taking the call immediately dispatches a patrol unit, not only because rape is a felony but also because it is a crime in which the offender may be known or close to the scene. The person taking the call then tells the victim to wait for the police to arrive if she is at a safe location and not to alter her physical appearance or touch anything at the scene. The victim is asked whether she can identify or describe the suspect, whether she has sustained serious injuries and whether she needs immediate medical assistance. The victim should also be advised not to wash, shower or douche before having a medical exam. As

with any crime against the person, early response is critical not only in apprehending the suspect but also in reducing the victim's anxiety.

Special challenges to investigating rape include the sensitive nature of the offense, social attitudes and the victim's horror and/or embarrassment. A rape investigation requires great sensitivity.

To help investigators overcome some of these challenges, many departments are implementing a procedure for victims of sexual assault known as *blind reporting*.

Blind Reporting

Garcia and Henderson (1999, p. 12) report: "Up to 84 percent of all sexual assaults go unreported" because the victim feels foolish, hurt, ashamed, vulnerable and frightened. Furthermore, the prospect of reliving the entire experience by having the police ask detailed and personal questions is more than many victims can bear, particularly immediately after the incident. However, given time, victims may come to trust others enough to recount the attack, even hoping to prevent the same assailant from attacking others.

Blind reporting allows sexual assault victims to retain their anonymity and confidentiality while sharing critical information with law enforcement. It also permits victims to gather legal information from law enforcement without having to commit immediately to an investigation.

Garcia and Henderson (p. 13) assert:

Law enforcement benefits from accepting blind reports because investigators have a clearer picture of sexual violence in their communities. Moreover, when investigators can pinpoint dangerous scenarios, they can better educate the public. . . .

Blind reporting also provides other benefits. . . . [It] lets victims take the investigative process one step at a time, allowing time to build trust between the investigator and the victim and making the whole process feel more manageable.

Blind reporting procedures also provide for the collection of crucial medical-legal evidence from sexual assault victims, as discussed shortly. However, for the 16 percent of sexual assault victims who do report the attack immediately, law enforcement personnel must be prepared for a swift yet sensitive response.

The Police Response

The first officers to arrive can make or break a rape case depending on how they approach the victim. All police officers should have special training in handling sexual assault victims. Whenever possible, an officer without such training should not be assigned to this kind of case.

As soon as you arrive at the scene, announce yourself clearly to allay fears the victim may have that the suspect is returning. Explain to the victim what is being done for her safety. If the rape has just occurred, if there are serious injuries or if it appears the victim is in shock, call for an ambulance.

Protect the crime scene and broadcast a description of the assailant, means and direction of flight and the time and exact location of the assault. The victim may be unable to describe the suspect because of stress or darkness or because the perpetrator wore a mask or other identity-concealing clothing. A time lapse before reporting the offense can occur because of the victim's embarrassment, confusion or shock or because the victim was taken to a remote area, giving the suspect time to escape.

Establish a command post away from the scene to divert attention from the address of the victim and also to preserve the scene. Conduct the preliminary investigation as described in Chapter 1. Ascertain the background of both the accuser and, if possible, the accused. At a minimum, officers on the scene should do the following:

- Record their arrival time.
- Determine the victim's location and condition. Request an ambulance if needed. Obtain identification of the suspect if possible.
- Determine whether the suspect is at the scene.
- Protect the crime scene.
- Identify and separate witnesses. Obtain valid identification from them and then obtain preliminary statements.
- Initiate crime broadcast if applicable.

Sometimes it is difficult to determine whether an assault or homicide is a sex-related crime. Geberth (1996, p. 77) lists the following evidence of sexual activity observable at the crime scene or upon the victim's body:

- The type of, or lack of, attire on the victim
- Evidence of seminal fluid on, near or in the body
- Evidence of sexual injury and/or sexual mutilation
- Sexualized positioning of the body

- Evidence of substitute sexual activity, that is, fantasy, ritualism, symbolism and/or masturbation
- Multiple stabbing or cutting to the body, including slicing wounds across the abdomen of the victim, throat slashing and overkill-type injuries that are considered suggestive of a sexual motivation

Physical Evidence

Morrison (1997, p. 48) states: "In sexual assault cases, the evidence has to be protected from destruction by the victim and/or EMS personnel. Of course, the victim's injuries are given priority, but evidence preservation steps have to be taken to maximize the chances of identifying and prosecuting the perpetrator."

Evidence in a rape case shows the amount of force that occurred, establishes that a sexual act was performed and links the act with the suspect.

- - - - - - - - -

Evidence in a rape case consists of stained or torn clothing; scratches, bruises or cuts; evidence of a struggle and semen and bloodstains.

- - - - - - - - -

Because such evidence deteriorates rapidly, obtain it as soon as possible. Some police departments have a rape kit that contains the equipment needed to collect, label and preserve evidence.

Photograph all injuries to the victim, and take as evidence any torn or stained clothing. Examine the scene for other physical evidence such as fingerprints, footprints, a weapon, stains or personal objects the suspect may have left behind. Examine washcloths or towels the suspect may have used. Photograph any signs of a struggle such as broken objects, overturned furniture or, if outdoors, disturbed vegetation.

If the assault occurred outdoors, take soil and vegetation samples for comparison. If the assault occurred in a vehicle, vacuum the car seats and interior to obtain soil, hairs and other fibers. Examine the seats for blood and semen stains. DNA analysis has become increasingly important in sexual assault cases.

If a suspect is apprehended, photograph any injuries, marks or scratches on the suspect's body. Obtain blood and hair samples, and give the appropriate tests to determine whether he is intoxicated or on drugs. Obtain any clothing or possessions of the suspect that might connect him with the rape. If necessary, obtain a warrant to search his vehicle, home or office. Such searches may reveal items associated with perversion or weapons of the type used in the assault.

Sex crimes evidence collection kits are designed to assist in the uniform collection of evidentiary specimens in sexual assaults. Most kits include instructions for handling trace evidence, clothing and underwear, debris, dried secretions, fingernail scrapings, head and pubic hairs, saliva, blood, vaginal/penile smears and anal smears.

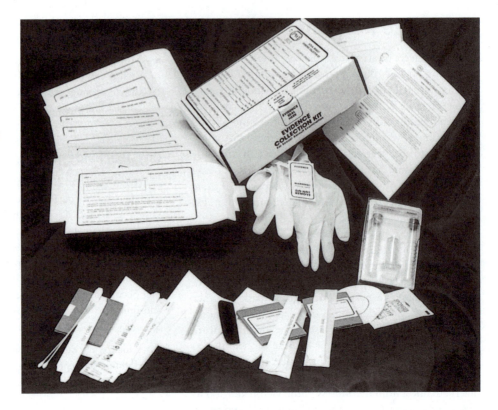

Investigating Date Rape

A particularly difficult type of sexual assault is **date rape,** in which the victim knows the suspect. Morrison (pp. 48–49) explains:

> Whether or not the sex was consensual is the pivotal question. Often the suspect will admit the act, but give a statement denying the victim was forced, drugged or intimidated. . . .
>
> Incidentally, physical evidence is especially critical in proving a date rape because the testimony of the victim is often viewed with skepticism by the defense attorney, the jury and sometimes even the judge because of the blame-the-victim mentality many have acquired.

— — — — — — — —

Additional evidence in date rape cases may include the presence of drugs in the victim's system.

— — — — — — — —

Such evidence may take the form of drugs found in the victim's body. Gardiner (1998, p. 37) describes the attributes of one such drug, an odorless and tasteless sedative, illegal in the United States and dubbed the "New Stealth Weapon":

Rohypnol, or the "date rape drug," dissolves rapidly when placed in a carbonated drink, making it virtually impossible for unsuspecting victims to detect. Once in the victim's system, it quickly produces physical as well as mental incapacitation. . . . Rohypnol's sedative effect occurs 20 to 30 minutes after ingestion. The main side effect is amnesia, but it also produces an intoxicated appearance, impaired judgement, impaired motor skills, drowsiness, dizziness and confusion. . . .

When confronted with an incident whose circumstances suggest that Rohypnol might be involved, investigators should treat it as both a sex and drug case. . . .

The most challenging evidence to find and secure is the Rohypnol in the victim's body. Although detection can be made through a urine screen, the drug dissipates rapidly. . . .

To neutralize the "New Stealth Weapon," if you believe Rohypnol might be involved in your case, be meticulous, work quickly to secure urine analysis and be methodical on the scene to gather physical evidence.

Rohypnol, also called "roofies," seems to be the most popular "date rape" drug, but other drugs can produce even more devastating effects for victims. Morrison (p. 49) explains: "If you grind up Zanax, Valium or some other form of depressant so it can be easily mixed with alcohol, you've created a doubly potent mix which can cause someone to go into a coma and never return." Acknowledging the severe and dangerous nature of such drug-assisted sexual assaults, the Drug-Induced Rape Prevention and Punishment Act was signed in 1996, allowing courts to impose prison sentences up to 20 years for anyone intending to use illicit drugs to aid in the commission of sexual assault.

The Victim's Medical Examination

The rape victim should have a medical examination as soon as possible to establish injuries, to determine whether intercourse occurred and to protect against venereal disease and pregnancy. Some hospitals provide drugs at the initial examination to lessen the possibility of pregnancy. Further examination for venereal disease is also conducted.

Although each hospital has its own procedures, emergency room doctors and nurses are trained to observe and treat trauma; therefore, they can provide counseling and support services to the victim during this initial critical phase. Good examination-stage care promotes later cooperation from the victim.

The hospital obtains medical–legal evidence that includes a detailed report of an examination of the victim for trauma, injuries and intercourse. The report contains precise descriptions of all bruises, scratches, cuts or other injuries. The physician's report contains descriptions of the physician's findings and treatment, the victim's statements, a report of a social worker's interview with the victim or the history of the sexual assault taken by the doctor, documentation of the presence or absence of semen, documentation of the presence of drugs in the victim's system, the specific diagnosis of trauma and any other specific medical facts concerning the victim's conditions. The report should contain no conclusions as to whether the woman was raped because this is a legal matter for the court to decide. However, in some states, hospitals are required by law to report suspected rape cases to the police.

Most hospitals have a sexual assault and vaginal kit in the examination room with the proper forms and tests for sperm and semen. Tests can be made of the vagina, anus or mouth, depending on the type of assault. After the examination, these kits are given to the police at the victim's request and sent to a crime laboratory for analysis.

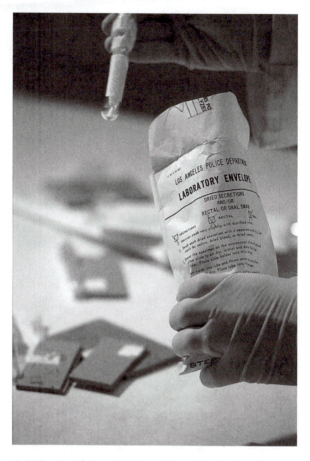

LAPD scientific investigation staff examine evidence from a sexual assault case.

The victim should be asked to sign a release form that authorizes the medical facility to provide a copy of the examination record to the police. Hospital reports may be introduced as evidence even if a police officer was not present during the examination. Also ask the hospital and the victim for the clothing the victim was wearing at the time of the assault if it was not obtained earlier.

The victim is reimbursed for medical examination costs in jurisdictions that have victim compensation laws. In other states, local or state health agencies may cover the costs. Rape crisis center personnel can assist in these arrangements. Such information is important to many victims.

As mentioned, many rape victims choose not to go to the police immediately following their attack. Such victims, however, must be encouraged to seek prompt medical attention and to allow for the collection of evidence at a medical examination in case they later decide to proceed with an investigation. Given these victims' overwhelming need for privacy and confidentiality at this critical time, the availability of blind reporting is extremely beneficial in motivating sexual assault victims to proceed with the collection and processing of medical evidence. Garcia and Henderson (p. 13) explain:

> In some states, victims who file blind reports can receive rape victim's assistance, which provides compensation for the costs associated with an emergency rape examination or other related expenses. Some victims may be reluctant to have medical evidence collected because they cannot afford the $600–850 expense for the emergency room or because they do not want the treatment to show up on insurance and billing records.

Taking a Suspect into Custody

If a suspect is apprehended at the scene, record any spontaneous statements made by the suspect and photograph him. If more than one suspect is present, separate the suspects. Do not allow communication between suspects, the victim and witnesses. Remove the suspects from the scene as soon as possible.

After emergency matters have been taken care of, interview the victim separately from any witnesses and in private.

Interviewing the Victim

Rape is typically a horrifying, violent experience of violation to the victim. Reporting it to the police is frequently a courageous act because the victim knows she will be forced to relive the experience through numerous retellings and that her word may be doubted. In addition, rape is humiliating and can involve numerous undesirable repercussions such as ostracism by friends and family, hospitalization, pregnancy, venereal disease and even AIDS. At the time of the interview, the rape victim may be hysterical or unusually calm. Remember: Rape is a crime of aggression and hostility and is usually conducted violently. Attempt to establish rapport by using sympathetic body language and explaining the necessity for asking sensitive questions.

Attempt to reinforce the victim's emotional well-being, but also obtain the facts. The pressure and stress caused by rape can make victims uncooperative. Insensitive actions by a male investigator may reinforce the female victim's image of male aggressiveness and result in refusal to answer questions.

Rape victims sometimes complain that investigative personnel question the validity of the complaint even before hearing the facts, are rude and overly aggressive, fail to explain the procedures used in the investigation, ask highly personal questions too early in the interview, have unsympathetic attitudes or express negative attitudes about the victim's personal appearance, clothing or actions, implying that the victim may be partly responsible for the crime.

Both uniformed and investigative personnel, male and female, can help the victim cooperate if they are sympathetic, understanding and supportive. Such an approach not only contributes to the victim's psychological well-being but also helps obtain information and evidence required to apprehend and prosecute the offender. Some departments require two investigators or a victim's advocate be present when interviewing a rape victim.

Although some police feel professional medical personnel should obtain the personal details of a sex attack, this is shirking responsibility. Deal with the emotional and psychological needs of the sex offense victim while making a complete investigation of the case and preserving evidence.

Whether the gender of the investigator affects the cooperation of the victim is debatable. Some believe a female investigator should interview the female victim. Others feel a male can better show the victim that men can be understanding and nonaggressive. How much the victim cooperates usually depends less on the gender of the interviewer than on the interviewer's attitude, patience, understanding, competence and ability to establish rapport. Treat the victim with care, concern and understanding. Assume that the sexual assault is real unless facts should ultimately prove it otherwise.

The location of the interview is also important. The police station may be unsatisfactory. The victim's home may be ideal—if the rape did not occur there. Tell the victim you must ask questions about the incident and ask where she would be most comfortable talking about it. If the victim is hospitalized, consult with the medical staff as to when you can question her.

No matter where the interview is conducted, do it privately. Although the victim should be allowed to have a relative or friend near by to talk to, it is better to be alone when specific questions are asked. If the victim insists on having someone with her, discuss with this person the procedure to be followed. Explain that the person's presence is important to the victim for reassurance and security but that the person must allow the victim to talk freely and not interrupt.

The victim's family and friends can considerably influence whether the victim relates the entire story. A wide range of emotions can occur from mothers, fathers, husbands or other family members. They may be silent, hysterical or angry to the point that they are "going to kill him if I find him." Sometimes such anger is turned against the victim.

Make a complete report of the victim's appearance and behavior: presence of liquor or drugs; bruises, scratches or marks; manner of speech; emotional condition; appearance of clothes or hair; color of face; smeared makeup; torn clothes; and stains. Take photographs to supplement your notes.

The needed initial information includes the victim's name, age, home address, work address, telephone numbers and any prior relationship with the offender, if the offender is known. At a *later* interview, investigators should obtain additional information about the victim, including the following:

- Children and their ages
- Victim's educational level
- Family and parents and the nature of the victim's relationship with them
- Fears
- Financial status, past and present
- Friends and enemies
- Hobbies
- Marital status
- Medical history, physical and mental
- Occupation, past and present
- Personal habits
- Physical description, including attire at the time of the incident
- Recent court actions
- Recent changes in lifestyle
- Reputation on the job and in the neighborhood
- Residence, past and present
- Social habits
- Use of alcohol and drugs

Obtain a detailed account of the crime, including the suspect's actions and statements, special characteristics or oddities and any unusual sexual behaviors. Determine exactly where and how the attack occurred, what hap-

pened before and after the attack and whether the victim can give any motive for the attack. Explain what you need to know and why, the procedures that you will follow and how important the victim's cooperation is. Use open-ended questions such as, "Take your time and tell me exactly what happened."

Determine the exact details of resistance, even if these are not required by law. Was there any unconsciousness, paralysis or fainting? Was there penetration? Who did the victim first talk to after the assault? How soon was the report made, and if there was a delay, what was the reason?

Establish lack of consent. Obtain the names of any witnesses. Determine where the victim was before the attack and whether someone might have seen her and followed her. The suspect's description can then be used at that location to see whether anyone there can identify him. Obtain as much information as possible about the suspect: voice, mannerisms, clothing, actions and general appearance.

It is important to obtain as many details as possible even though they may appear insignificant at the time. How the initial contact was made; attempts at concealment; the suspect's voice, appearance and exact words; unusual behavior, including unusual sexual acts performed—all these things can be helpful.

While obtaining all the detailed information to investigate the crime, investigators should keep in mind the guidelines established by the National Center for Women and Policing (NCWP) described by Lonsway and Welch (1999, pp. 31–35):

- Develop positive rapport.
- Communicate empathy (and objectivity).
- Provide information about the police role and the investigation.
- Help the victim regain control.
- Address concerns about prosecution.
- Recognize the victim's reaction. (May respond in ways that seem inappropriate.)
- Allow the presence of others when possible.
- Allow the victim to set the pace/tone.
- Understand disorganized thinking. (Common for initial statement to contain inconsistent or missing information.)
- Closing the interview. (Reaffirm her strength by complimenting her on her ability to survive the attack. Explain the next steps and provide information on her rights. Provide the case number and phone number of the police department, and make sure she knows of the availability of social service agencies such as rape crisis centers.)

Ending the Victim Interview

End the interview with an explanation of available victim assistance programs, such as Sexual Offense Services (S.O.S.). Arrange for relatives, friends or personnel from a rape crisis center to help the victim. If the victim refuses to be questioned, is incapable of answering questions because of shock or injuries or begins the interview but then breaks down emotionally, terminate the interview for the time being, but return later.

Following the interview of the victim, officers should determine whether the crime scene or evidence has been altered or contaminated. Investigators should also interview all possible witnesses to the offense.

Interviewing Witnesses

Locate witnesses as soon as possible, and obtain their names, addresses and phone numbers. Canvass the neighborhood for possible witnesses. Even though witnesses may not have seen the incident, they may be able to describe the suspect or his vehicle. They may have heard screams or statements made by the victim or the offender.

Determine whether a relationship exists between the witness and the victim or offender. Determine exactly what they saw and heard. Did they see the victim before, during or after the assault? Did they see the victim with the suspect? How did they happen to be in the vicinity where the offense occurred? Interview acquaintances and individuals known to the victim because many victims know their rapists. In fact, the incidence of date rape has been increasing. In such cases it is a matter of proving lack of consent.

Interrogating Sex Offenders

When interrogating sex offenders, obtain as much information as possible and yet remain nonjudgmental. The suspect should be the last person interviewed. This allows the interviewer to have all information possible by the time of the suspect interview: facts about the victim, the type of offense and the location of the crime; statements from witnesses, neighbors and informants; and information about the suspect's background.

As in most interrogation situations, building rapport is the first step. Suggest to the suspect that you understand what he is going through. Ask about his family, his job and his interests. Assess the suspect's character. After rapport is established, ask the suspect to tell his side of the story from beginning to end, and do not interrupt him. Show interest in what he is saying and keep him talking. The interrogator's approach should be one of "you tell me what happened and I will understand," even though that may not be the investigator's actual feelings.

The objective of the interview is to obtain the truth and the information necessary for proving guilt or innocence. To help accomplish this goal, attempt to gain the suspect's confidence. Many suspects feel they can justify their actions by putting some blame on the victim, for example, "She came on to me."

During the interrogation, remember that the seriousness of the charge to be brought will be based on the information you obtain. All elements of the charged offense must be proven, so keep the possible charges in mind and prepare questions to elicit supporting information.

Mann (1996, p. 117) describes "fantasy-based interviewing" as an investigations approach for predatory sex offenders. He suggests that although everyone has fantasies, "the fantasies of sex offenders are mental rehearsals for actual, hands-on acts." Therefore, investigators should "assertively go after this type of information." The fantasy-based interview consists of six steps (Mann, pp. 118–119):

1. Create a comfortable, relaxed environment.

2. Establish a common ground for discussion (human fantasy). Emphasize that all humans fantasize.

3. Speak in the language and tone a therapist would use, for example, *disclosure, deviant thoughts, urges.*

4. Make the suspect feel safe enough to disclose his fantasies.

5. Get the suspect to discuss his fantasies openly. The details can provide a blueprint for past criminal acts or future planned acts.

6. Match the fantasies to criminal behavior.

Mann (p. 119) concludes:

> Do not ignore fantasy behavior! Look for it in all forms (verbal and nonverbal). . . . As distasteful as the fantasy-based interview might be, it works. The benefits are worth the discomfort. You just might be instrumental in preventing a crime from occurring.

The Behavioral Profile in Sex Offense Cases

Because rapists are generally recidivists (about 70 percent of them commit more than one rape), it is possible that the details and MOs of offenses in another area of the same city or another community may be identical to the present case. For this reason, the usefulness of behavioral profiling becomes apparent, and interviews with victims of sex offenders should focus on the offender's behavior.

Several specific areas should be covered in the behavior-oriented interview of rape victims, including three essential basic steps: (1) carefully interview the victim about the rapist's behavior, (2) analyze that behavior to ascertain the motivation underlying the assault and (3) compile a profile of the individual likely to have committed the crime.

The three types of rapist behavior of concern to investigators are physical (use of force), verbal and sexual. First, ascertain the method of approach. Three common approaches are the "con" approach, in which the offender is initially friendly, even charming, and dupes the victim; the "blitz" approach, in which the offender directly physically assaults the victim, frequently gagging, binding or blindfolding the victim; and the "surprise" approach, in which the offender hides in the back seat of a car, in shrubbery or behind a wall or waits until the victim is sleeping.

After determining the approach, you should determine how the perpetrator maintained control. Four common methods of control are (1) mere presence, (2) verbal threats, (3) display of a weapon and (4) use of physical force.

If the rapist used physical force, it is important to determine the amount of force, as this gives insight into the offender's motivations. Four levels of physical force may be used: (1) *minimal,* perhaps slapping; (2) *moderate,* repeated hitting; (3) *excessive,* beating resulting in bruises and cuts; and (4) *brutal,* sadistic torture. This offender is typically extremely profane, abusive and aggressive, and the victim may require hospitalization or may die.

Sexual sadists become more sexually excited the more the victim suffers. The pleasure of complete domination over another person is the essence of the sadistic drive. Most sadists are cunning and deceitful and feel no remorse or compassion. They feel superior to society, especially the law. They often use pliers, electric cattle prods, whips, fire, bondage, amputation and objects inserted into the vagina. They may keep diaries, tape recorders, sexual devices, photographs of victims, devices to torture victims and other incriminating evidence—all items to be included in a search warrant.

In addition to the offender's sexual behavior, investigators should inquire about the offender's verbal behavior. Themes in rapists' conversation include threats, orders, personal inquiries of the victim, personal revelations, obscene names, racial epithets and inquiries about the victim's sexual "enjoyment."

Also ask about the verbal behavior of the victim. Did the offender demand that the victim say certain words or demand that she beg or plead or scream? Such demands also shed insight into the offender's motivation.

Specifically ask victims about any change in the offender's behavior, either verbal, physical or sexual. Such changes can indicate weakness or fear if the offender lessens his efforts, or anger and hostility if he suddenly increases his efforts.

A further area of inquiry relates to the offender's experience level. Did he take actions to protect his identity, to destroy or remove evidence or to make certain he had an escape route? The novice rapist may take minimal or obvious actions to protect his identity, for example, wearing a ski mask and gloves, changing his voice tone, affecting an accent, ordering the victim not to look at him or blindfolding and binding the victim. These are common precautions a person not knowledgeable of phosphotate tests of hair and fiber evidence would be expected to take. In contrast, the experienced rapist may walk through the residence or prepare an escape route, disable the telephone, order the victim to shower or douche, bring bindings or gags, wear surgical gloves or take or force the victim to wash items the rapist touched or ejaculated on, such as bedding and the victim's clothing.

Investigators should also determine whether any items other than those of evidentiary value were taken by the offender. Of interest are not only items of value but also items of a personal nature. It is important to determine not only whether items were taken but also why. Again, such information may provide insight into the offender's motivation.

Follow-Up Investigation and Clearance

After the preliminary investigation and medical examination are completed, conduct a follow-up investigation. Interview the victim again in two to five days to obtain further information and to compare the statements made after time has elapsed.

Some victims decide not to prosecute because of pressure from family or friends, fear of reprisal, shame, fear of going to court or emotional or mental disturbance. Sometimes the prosecuting attorney refuses to take the case to court because the case is weak and thus has little chance of conviction. For example, there may not be enough physical evidence to corroborate the victim's complaint, or the victim may be a known prostitute or a girlfriend of the rapist or she may be pregnant because of prior sexual relations with the assailant.

At other times the report is unfounded and unsubstantiated by the evidence.

False Reports

Women make false reports of sexual assault for a number of reasons including getting revenge on a lover who has jilted her, covering up a pregnancy or getting attention. Such circumstances need to be ruled out when investigating a reported sexual assault. The credibility of rape reports is probably questioned more frequently than that of any other felony report. A polygraph can help to determine the truth of the complainant's statements. If the evidence of a false report is overwhelming, include all the facts in your close-out report.

If the victim admits orally or in writing that her story was false, close the case. When the victim's credibility is in serious doubt because of contradictory evidence, the investigating officer's superior or the prosecutor can close the case.

Coordination with Other Agencies

A number of other agencies and individuals assist in handling rape cases.

- - - - - - - -

A rape case often involves cooperation with medical personnel, social workers, rape crisis-center personnel and news media.

- - - - - - - -

The public and the news media can greatly influence the prosecution of a rape case. Medical and hospital personnel influence the victim's attitude and her cooperation in obtaining facts for medical reports and the necessary evidence for use in court. Rape crisis centers can provide various kinds of support to the victim and encourage her to sign a complaint.

Prosecution of Rape and Statutory Changes

Few criminal cases are as difficult to prosecute as rape is, at least under older laws. Despite changes in the law, it is virtually impossible to obtain a conviction on the victim's testimony alone.

- - - - - - - -

Conviction in sexual assault cases requires medical evidence, physical evidence such as torn clothing, evidence of injuries and a complaint that is reported reasonably close to the time of the assault.

- - - - - - - -

Defendants usually want a jury trial because of present laws and attitudes regarding rape. The defendant is not required to testify, but the victim not only must relate a very difficult ordeal but also is subjected to cross-examination that can make her appear to be on trial.

Juries tend to be unsympathetic with a victim who was drinking heavily, hitchhiking or using drugs or who left a bar with a stranger or engaged in other socially "unacceptable" actions. Many newer laws make it very explicit that such conditions are not to be considered during the trial. Newer laws also state that the victim's testimony need not be corroborated and that testimony about the degree of resistance—although it may be admitted—is not required. Moreover, testimony about the victim's previous sexual conduct is not admissible unless (1) the woman has had prior sexual relations with the defendant, (2) there is evidence of venereal disease or pregnancy resulting from the assault, (3) circumstances suggest that consent occurred within the calendar year or (4) the victim has not told the truth or has filed a false report.

Juries must not be instructed that a victim who consented to sexual intercourse with other persons would be likely to have consented with the defendant, that the victim's prior sexual conduct may be used to determine her credibility or that the victim's testimony should be subjected to any greater test of credibility than in any other crime.

Some have argued, however, that victims' characters are being judged even before a case has a chance to go to trial. These critics contend that victim characteristics and credibility issues frequently prevent sexual assault cases from ever reaching court by negatively impacting prosecutors' charging decisions in sexual assault cases. Spears and Spohn (1997, p. 501) maintain:

> Feminists contend that legally irrelevant victim characteristics determine the outcome of sexual assault cases. . . . [One] empirical study . . . confirms this [with findings] that the *only* significant predictors of charging were victim characteristics. . . . Overall the results of this study suggest . . . that prosecutors attempt to avoid uncertainty by screening out sexual assault cases unlikely to result in a conviction because of questions

about the victim's character, the victim's behavior at the time of the incident, and the victim's credibility.

In contrast, others have found little or no evidence of such screening practices. In examining the roles of prior relationship and "negative" victim characteristics in sexual assault case processing, Kingsnorth et al. (1999, p. 275) observe:

> Neither of these variables played a role in either the decision to prosecute, the decision to go to trial rather than resolve by guilty plea, trial outcomes, or punishment severity as indicated by a prison (versus nonprison) term. Both variables were, however, significant in determining sentence length. When selection bias and relevant legal factors were controlled, the existence of a prior relationship reduced sentence length by 35 months; each additional negative victim characteristic reduced the period of incarceration by 17 months.

Some states have made it illegal to publish the names or addresses of sex crime victims and have required that the county where the crime occurred pay the medical examination expenses.

Many recent laws have reduced the penalties for sexual assault, which should lead to more convictions.

Former penalties were so severe that many juries hesitated to convict. More recent laws usually include both oral and anal sexual conduct, and many classify sexual offenses by degrees.

Civil Commitment of Sex Offenders after Sentences Served

Because of the high recidivism rate of sex offenders following their release from jail or prison, many are advocating legislation that allows the civil commitment of sex offenders upon completion of their sentence. Such legislation acknowledges that, although sex offenders may have paid a debt to society by spending time behind bars, often little if anything is accomplished during this period of incarceration to address and treat the disorders that lead offenders to commit sexual assault. For example:

> In the first case of its kind in Florida, a convicted sex offender will be held at a secure psychiatric hospital under the newly enacted Jimmy Ryce Act rather than be released at the end of his prison sentence.
>
> A six-member civil jury . . . determined that Stanley Ridgeway is still a threat to society and should not be freed until he is successfully treated to stem his sexual urges. . . .
>
> The act . . . is named after a 9-year-old Miami-Dade County boy who was abducted, raped, murdered and dismembered in 1995 ("Florida Sex Offender . . . ," 1999, p. 19A).

Although many contend these acts violate offenders' civil rights, the Supreme Court has upheld the constitutionality of at least one state's civil commitment law:

> In *Kansas v. Hendricks*, the High Court upheld Kansas' Sexually Violent Predator Act, which establishes procedures by which that state may civilly commit to a mental hospital persons who are likely to commit predatory acts of sexual violence due to a mental abnormality or personality disorder. . . .
>
> Justice Clarence Thomas reasoned that the act does not violate due process because it requires a finding of future dangerousness and links that finding to the existence of a mental abnormality or personality disorder that makes it difficult for the person to control his behavior ("Civil Commitment of . . . ," 1997, pp. 13–14).

Sex Offender Registry and Notification

With the realization that many convicted sex offenders have committed one or more such crimes prior to the current act for which they are serving time has come a flurry of legislation designed to notify the public of such predators living in their communities and to assist law enforcement in keeping track of these recidivism-prone individuals. Wilson (1999, p. 60) explains: "The justification for public notification is public safety. Notifications are a proactive procedure that attempts to prevent crime before it occurs." However, because of the highly mobile nature of today's society, it is increasingly difficult to keep tabs on these offenders as they move from jurisdiction to jurisdiction, changing their names and appearances along the way. Nonetheless, state and national sex offender registries have proliferated in recent years, as mandated by law.

The evolution of sex offender registries can be traced to a trilogy of federal statutes: the Jacob Wetterling Act, Megan's Law and the Pam Lychner Act.

The first act was named for an 11-year-old boy who was abducted in October 1989 near his home in rural Minnesota. It is noted (*Sex Offender Community Notification,* 1997, p. 5): "Similarities between Jacob's abduction and a case involving a boy from a neighboring town who was abducted and sexually assaulted earlier that year prompted police to believe that the two cases were linked. Jacob Wetterling has never been found." Sorkin (1998, p. 16) notes:

> The Jacob Wetterling Crimes Against Children and Sexually Violent Offender Registration Act . . . was enacted as part of President Clinton's 1994 Crime Act. It requires States to establish effective registration systems for convicted child molesters and other sexually violent offenders. It also requires the establishment of a more stringent set of registration requirements for a subclass of the most highly dangerous offenders, who are designated under the Act as "sexually violent predators."

The second act was named after 7-year-old Megan Kanka, allegedly raped and murdered by a convicted sex offender who lived across the street from Megan's family with two other released sex offenders:

> Megan's Law, which was signed by President Clinton on May 17, 1996, amends the Jacob Wetterling Act in two ways. Megan's Law requires States to release any relevant information about registered sex offenders necessary to maintain and protect public safety. Under the original Jacob Wetterling Act provisions, States could release information on registered offenders, however, they were not required to do so. . . . Megan's Law also allows disclosure of information collected under a State registration program for any purpose permitted under the laws of the State (*Sex Offender Community Notification,* p. 8).

The third law in the federal trilogy was named for a victims' rights advocate killed in a plane crash in July 1996. Officially called the Pam Lychner Sexual Offender Tracking and Identification Act, it "amends the Jacob Wetterling Act by directing the FBI to establish a national sex offender database and makes more stringent the registration requirements set forth in [that act]" (*Sex Offender Community Notification,* p. 8). According to the U.S. Department of Justice (*National Sex Offender . . . ,* 1998, p. 1):

> The permanent National Sex Offender Registry File will be developed as part of the FBI's NCIC-2000 project and will include a fingerprint and photo (mugshot) image of the registered offender. The file will be a "hot file" and be accessible to authorized users without submitting fingerprints.

Some states, however, were considering the importance of sex offender notification laws well before the passage of federal legislation. The first such law was passed in Washington State in 1990, as a component of its Community Protection Act. Years later, in response to Megan's Law, Paynter (1999, p. 76) notes: "Congress passed the Community Notification Act of 1997 decreeing that each state maintain a sex offender registry and take steps to make the public aware of who was listed on it."

Besides creating individual state registries, efforts are under way to link registries to allow states to share information, as well as to compile a national sex offender registry. Chaiken (1998, p. 8) reports: "National sex offender registries are the outgrowth of increased technical capability and evolving public awareness of the new uses that can be made of offender information recorded at each step in the criminal justice system."

Internet access is quickly revolutionizing the way the public keeps informed of the whereabouts of convicted sex offenders. In many jurisdictions residents are now able to access a registry online, enter their zip codes and obtain information on sex offenders living in their area. Paynter (p. 78) notes:

> The Virginia State Police found posting violent sex offenders on its Web site to be the most cost-effective solution. "An Internet-based program allowed us to do this with the minimum amount of money and manpower," [the captain of the State Police said]. "In other communities officers go out to the community and call everyone together to tell them. That takes up a lot of resources to accomplish little more than what we're doing."

> Fourteen states currently post sex offender registries on Web sites, including Alaska, Alabama, Connecticut, Delaware, Florida, Georgia, Indiana, Kansas, Michigan, South Carolina, Texas, Utah, Virginia and West Virginia ("Megan's Law Registries . . . ," 1999, p. 6).

Many arguments exist both for and against sex offender registries and notification laws. Tucker (1999, p. 39) notes: "Designed to protect children from manipulative and violent sex offenders, these laws have become involved in a controversy concerning possible constitutional rights violations." Pearson (1998, pp. 45–46) elaborates:

> People who . . . advocate for sex offender registration and notification cite the following reasons for doing so:
>
> ■ The significant number of sex offenders under community supervision
>
> ■ Fear of recidivism
>
> ■ Tools for law enforcement to assist in investigations, and grounds for holding those who do not comply with registration laws
>
> ■ Deterring sex offenders
>
> ■ Offering citizens information to protect their children and their families

Tucker (p. 39) adds: "Proponents of community notification base their stand on the high recidivism rates and low rehabilitation successes for sexual offenders." Furthermore, advocates of community notification claim the prevention of even one assault justifies the process. In examining the public safety potential of Megan's Law in preventing sex offenses in Massachusetts, Petrosino and Petrosino (1999, p. 140) found: "Assuming a registration and notification system of complete integrity, proactive police warnings could have potentially reached subsequent victims in 6 of the 12 stranger-predatory cases."

Nonetheless, many vigorously oppose such legislation. Pearson (p. 46) notes:

> Those who oppose registration and notification laws cite the following reasons:
>
> ■ False sense of security
>
> ■ Vigilantism, harassment
>
> ■ Offenders avoid treatment
>
> ■ No data on effectiveness
>
> ■ Migration

Sacco (1998, pp. 50–51) contends the three basic objections to notification laws center around punishment, privacy and due process issues. Some offenders claim that registering subjects them to additional punishment. However, in April 1998, the Supreme Court rejected constitutional challenges that claimed that the laws' notification requirements represented an unconstitutional added punishment ("Court OK's Sex-Offender Notification Laws," 1998, p. 9). Regarding due process violations, at least one state's notification law has been found partially unconstitutional and in need of revision:

The Pennsylvania Supreme Court has struck down a major part of the state's "Megan's Law," saying it is a violation of federal due process to create a presumption that persons convicted of certain sexual offenses are "sexually violent predators" subject to stricter penalties ("Pennsylvania Court Strikes . . . ," 1999, p. 5).

Another concern of opponents is that notification will lead to harassment of offenders and increased acts of vigilantism. As reported recently ("Is Megan's Law Showing . . . ," 1998, p. 5): "Opponents of community-notification laws say two recent incidents involving paroled sex offenders—the suicide of a California parolee and a shooting at the home of a convicted New Jersey rapist—are evidence that fears about such laws spawning vigilantism are coming true." Presser and Gunnison (1999) criticize sex offender notification as being inconsistent with the principles of community justice (p. 311):

> Sex offender notification is a flawed strategy for controlling sex crime. It reflects a skewed view of sex offenders and, lacking a plan for problem solving, it encourages citizen action in the form of vigilantism. Notification relies on stigma, such that offenders are likely to retreat into denial and eventually to recidivate.

Sometimes the stigma placed on sex offenders is too great a burden to handle: "A convicted child molester in Maine shot himself to death on New Year's Eve, saying in a tape-recorded message he left behind that he feared living in a world with no forgiveness" ("Megan's Legacy Continues . . . ," 1998, p. 9).

In the end, however, it appears sex offender registration and notification have more supporters than opponents. Tucker (p. 40) explains: "The trend [today] is to value the rights of citizens, especially children, more than the rights of 'sexually violent predators.' "

Summary

Sex offenses include bigamy, child molestation, incest, indecent exposure, prostitution, rape (sexual assault) and sodomy. The most serious of these is rape—sexual intercourse with a person against the person's will. Rape is classified as forcible (by use or threats of force) or statutory (with a minor, with or without consent).

Most states include the following elements in defining the crime of rape or sexual assault: (1) an act of sexual intercourse, (2) with a female other than the wife, (3) committed without the victim's consent, (4) against the victim's will and by force.

Modus operandi factors important in investigating sex offenses include type of offense, words spoken, use of a weapon, method of attack, time of day, type of location and age of the victim. Special challenges in investigating rape include the sensitive nature of the offense, social attitudes and the victim's embarrassment. A rape investigation requires great tact. To help overcome some of these challenges, many departments are implementing a procedure known as blind reporting, which allows sexual assault victims to retain their anonymity and confidentiality while sharing critical information with law enforcement. It also permits victims to gather legal information from law enforcement without having to commit immediately to an investigation.

Physical evidence commonly found in rape cases includes stained or torn clothing; scratches, bruises and cuts; evidence of a struggle and semen and bloodstains. Additional evidence in date rape cases may include the presence of drugs in the victim's system.

A rape case often involves cooperation with medical personnel, social workers, rape crisis-center personnel and news media. Conviction in sexual assault cases requires medical evidence, physical evidence such as torn clothing, evidence of injuries and a complaint that is reported reasonably close to the time of the assault. Many recent laws have reduced the penalties for sexual assault, which should lead to more convictions.

The evolution of sex offender registries can be traced to a trilogy of federal statutes: the Jacob Wetterling Act, Megan's Law and the Pam Lychner Act.

Checklist

Sexual Assault

- What specific sex offense was committed?
- Are all the elements of the crime present?
- Who is the victim? Were there any injuries? Were they described and photographed?
- Were there any witnesses?
- Was the surrounding area canvassed to locate possible leads?
- Is there a suspect? A description of a suspect?
- Has there been a relationship between the suspect and the victim?
- What evidence was obtained at the scene?
- Was evidence submitted to the crime laboratory? Were reports received?

- Was the victim taken to the hospital for a medical examination?
- What evidence was obtained at the hospital? Is a medical report available?
- Was the victim interviewed? Will she sign a complaint?
- Was the victim reinterviewed four to five days after the assault?
- Was a background check made of the victim?
- Were other police agencies in the area notified and queried?
- Were field interrogation cards, MO files and other intelligence files checked?
- Have patrol divisions been checked for leads on cars or persons in the area?
- Has a sexual assault or rape crisis center been contacted for help?

Application

Several young people in a car wave down a police car and tell the officers that screams are coming from the south end of a nearby park. At about the same time, the police dispatcher receives a call from a resident who says she hears screams and cries for help but cannot tell exactly what part of the park they are coming from. The officers talk to the juveniles, get their names and a description of the area and then head for the park without red lights and siren to avoid warning the attacker. Arriving at the south end of the park, the officers see a man running from some bushes. He is wearing a dark jacket and is bareheaded. One officer goes to find the victim; the other attempts to follow the fleeing man. At the scene the officer observes a woman with torn clothing and a cut on the side of her head. She is unable to speak coherently, but she has obviously been assaulted. The juveniles have followed the squad car to the scene and crowd around the victim to offer help. The officer chasing the suspect has lost him and has returned to the scene. Both officers help the victim into the squad car and leave the scene with red lights and sirens, heading for the hospital. After leaving the victim at the hospital, they return to the scene. They find that branches are broken from some of the bushes. They also find an article of clothing from the victim and a switchblade knife on the ground. They secure the scene by posting several of the juveniles around the area until further help arrives.

Questions

1. Should red lights and siren have been used in going to the scene?
2. Was it correct for the officers to split up as they did?
3. Evaluate the effectiveness of the officers' actions after arriving at the scene.

Discussion Questions

1. What myths and prejudices have you heard about prosecuting rape cases? Are rape cases more difficult to prosecute than other crimes?

2. What are the penalties for rape in your state? Are these penalties adequate, or should they be more or less severe?

3. Past rape laws have required the utmost resistance on the part of the victim. Present laws have reduced this requirement. Do you support this change?

4. What persons or agencies can assist the police in rape investigations? What functions or services can they provide? What resources are available in your community? Your state?

5. Should the rape victim be interviewed by male or female investigators?

6. Rape victims often complain about the attitudes of police and medical personnel during a rape investigation. Do you believe this is justified, or is it due to the victim's emotional stress?

7. In the late 1970s, a case in Oregon received wide publicity because a husband was charged with raping his wife during a temporary separation and was acquitted. Do you agree with this verdict? Are there circumstances under which such a charge should be supported?

8. What environment is best for interviewing the victim of a rape or sexual assault? How would you start the interview? How supportive of the victim would you be? What questions would you ask? Who would you allow to be present? How would you close the interview?

9. How vigorously should sex offenses such as sodomy, indecent exposure and prostitution be investigated? Should unnatural sexual acts between consenting adults be considered criminal acts?

10. Why is semen, rather than sperm, the evidence sought in a rape case?

References

Chaiken, Jan M. "Sex Offenders and Offending: Learning More from National Data Collection Programs." In *National Conference on Sex Offender Registries.* Washington, DC: U.S. Department of Justice, May 1998, pp. 8–12. (NCJ-168965)

"Civil Commitment of Sex Offenders." *NCJA Justice Bulletin,* July 1997, pp. 13–14.

"Court OK's Sex-Offender Notification Laws." *Law Enforcement News,* May 15, 1998, p. 9.

"Florida Sex Offender Held at Mental Hospital after Jail Release." *Las Vegas Review Journal,* February 6, 1999, p. 19A.

Garcia, Sabrina and Henderson, Margaret. "Blind Reporting of Sexual Violence." *FBI Law Enforcement Bulletin,* Vol. 68, No. 6, June 1999, pp. 12–16.

Gardiner, A. G. "Rohypnol: The New 'Stealth' Weapon." *The Police Chief,* Vol. LXV, No. 4, April 1998, p. 37.

Geberth, Vernon J. "Sex-Related Crimes." *Law and Order,* Vol. 44, No. 8, August 1996, pp. 78–81.

"Is Megan's Law Showing Its Darker Side?" *Law Enforcement News,* July/August 1998, p. 5.

Kingsnorth, Rodney F.; MacIntosh, Randall C.; and Wentworth, Jennifer. "Sexual Assault: The Role of Prior Relationship and Victim Characteristics in Case Processing." *Justice Quarterly,* Vol. 16, No. 2, June 1999, pp. 275–302.

Lonsway, Kimberly A. and Welch, Sue. "Sexual Assault Response: Innovative Research and Training Initiatives." *The Police Chief,* Vol. LXVI, No. 9, September 1999, pp. 31–38.

Mann, Mark. "Fantasy-Based Interviewing." *Law and Order,* Vol. 44, No. 5, May 1996, pp. 117–119.

"Megan's Law Registries Are an Internet Sensation." *Law Enforcement News,* Vol. XXV, No. 505, February 14, 1999, p. 6.

"Megan's Legacy Continues to Spread." *Law Enforcement News,* May 15, 1998, p. 9.

Morrison, Richard D. "The Victim's Viewpoint." *Police,* Vol. 21, No. 1, January 1997, pp. 48–51.

National Sex Offender Registry: Fiscal Year 1998 Program Announcement. Washington, DC: U.S. Department of Justice, March 1998. (NCJ-169273)

Paynter, Ronnie L. "Getting the Word Out." *Law Enforcement Technology,* Vol. 26, No. 6, June 1999, pp. 76–80.

Pearson, Elizabeth A. "Status and Latest Developments in Sex Offender Registration and Notification Laws." In *National Conference on Sex Offender Registries.* Washington, DC: U.S. Department of Justice, May 1998, pp. 45–49. (NCJ-168965)

"Pennsylvania Court Strikes Down Major Part of State Megan's Law." *Criminal Justice Newsletter,* Vol. 30, No. 4, February 16, 1999, pp. 5–6.

Petrosino, Anthony J. and Petrosino, Carolyn. "The Public Safety Potential of Megan's Law in Massachusetts: An Assessment from a Sample of Criminal Sexual Psychopaths." *Crime and Delinquency,* Vol. 45, No. 1, January 1999, pp. 140–158.

Pilkington, Cyndra and Tolbert, Juliette. "Cleaning the Streets: Savannah's Prostitution Task Force." *The Police Chief,* Vol. LXIV, No. 4, April 1997, pp. 165–167.

Presser, Lois and Gunnison, Elaine. "Strange Bedfellows: Is Sex Offender Notification a Form of Community Justice?" *Crime and Delinquency,* Vol. 45, No. 3, July 1999, pp. 299–315.

Sacco, Dena T. "Arguments Used to Challenge Notification Laws—and the Government's Response." In *National Conference on Sex Offender Registries.* Washington, DC: U.S. Department of Justice, May 1998, pp. 50–53. (NCJ-168965)

Sex Offender Community Notification. Washington, DC: National Criminal Justice Association, October 1997.

Sorkin, Lisa Gursky. "The Trilogy of Federal Statutes." In *National Conference on Sex Offender Registries.* Washington, DC: U.S. Department of Justice, May 1998, pp. 16–18. (NCJ-168965)

Spears, Jeffrey W. and Spohn, Cassia C. "The Effect of Evidence Factors and Victim Characteristics on Prosecutors' Charging Decisions in Sexual Assault Cases." *Justice Quarterly,* Vol. 14, No. 3, September 1997, pp. 501–524.

Tjaden, Patricia and Thoennes, Nancy. *Prevalence, Incidence, and Consequences of Violence Against Women: Findings from the National Violence Against Women Survey.* National Institute of Justice, Centers for Disease Control and Prevention Research in Brief, November 1998. (NCJ-172837)

Tucker, Jane M. "Protecting the Innocent." *Police,* Vol. 23, No. 2, February 1999, pp. 39–40.

Wilson, Craig R. "Megan's Law: Public Notification of Sex Offender Information." *Law and Order,* Vol. 47, No. 4, April 1999, pp. 59–62.

Crimes against Children

Do You Know?

What crimes against children are frequently committed?

What the Child Protection Act involves?

What effects child abuse can have?

What challenges are involved in investigating crimes against children?

When a child should be taken into protective custody?

What factors to consider in interviewing child victims?

Whether children are generally truthful when talking about abuse?

What a multidisciplinary team is?

Who usually reports crimes against children?

What types of evidence are important in child neglect or abuse cases?

What things can indicate child neglect or abuse?

What a pedophile is?

What types of sex rings exist in the United States?

How a pedophile might typically react to being discovered?

How crimes against children can be prevented?

Introduction

A man admitted to a law enforcement investigator that he had molested 5,000 boys in his lifetime; a 42-year-old man admitted more than 1,000; and a 62-year-old oil executive stated he had molested a boy a day for 30 years. Child molestation is but one type of crime against children. Other crimes against children may occur repeatedly with the same victim, as in most instances of child abuse, whether physical, emotional or sexual abuse. Drowns and Hess (2000, p. 141) state:

> Throughout history children have been subjected to physical violence. Infants have been killed as a form of birth control, to avoid the dishonor of illegitimacy, as a means of power, as a method of disposing of retarded or deformed children and as a way of protecting financial security.
>
> In ancient Greece a child was the absolute property of the father, and property was divided among the male children. The father would raise the first son and expose subsequent children to the elements. Under Roman law the father had the power of life and death *(patria potestas)* over his children and could kill, mutilate, sell or offer them as a sacrifice.

Bilchik (1997, p. 1) states: "The victimization of the weak by the strong—in this case, of children by adults—is one of the most shameful constants in human history. Unfortunately, contemporary American society is not immune from this repugnant behavior." It is estimated that a child is physically or sexually abused every 10 seconds in the United States (Quill and Yahner, 1999, p. 8). Studies show that as many as 20 percent of all boys and between 25 and 35 percent of all girls are sexually abused ("Study Says Sexual Abuse . . . ," 1998, p. 9A) and that 29 percent of rape victims are under age 11 (Allen, 1998, p. 17). According to the Justice Department, more children die in the United States as the result of child abuse than are killed by accidental falls, drowning, choking on food, home fires or suffocation combined (Quill and Yahner, p. 8). Kelley et al. (1997, p. 2) state: "The majority of [abuse] victims (85%) are under age 5, and nearly half (45%) of the victims never reach their first birthday."

The underreporting of such abuse is of major concern. It is estimated that for every report of abuse the police and child protective services receive, there are 10 unreported cases. Allen (p. 18) reports: "The typical sex offender against children molests an average of 117 youngsters, most of whom do not report the offense."

Another concern involves the frequency with which children are abused by people they know. Although

Six-year-old JonBenet Ramsey's highly publicized murder investigation came to a halt on Oct. 13, 1999, when a grand jury dismissed the case, citing insufficient evidence to charge anyone in her 1996 death.

many parents stress to their children the importance of staying away from strangers, the sad truth is that: "The overwhelming majority of sexual abuse is committed by men and by persons known to the child. Family members represent one-third to one-half of the perpetrators against girls and 10 percent to 20 percent of the perpetrators against boys" (Quill and Yahner, p. 8). According to Allen (p. 18), one study of child sexual abuse found: "In 71 percent of the cases, the offender and victim knew each other at least casually, and in 14 percent of the cases, the offender was a member of the child's immediate family."

A third concern is the cycle of abuse being documented. One study notes: "Forty percent of sexual offenders and 76 percent of serial rapists report they were sexually abused as youngsters" ("Study Says Sexual Abuse . . . ," p. 9A).

A final complicating factor is the perceived ambiguity of what constitutes child abuse. As Johnson (1998, p. 77) states: "Child abuse means different things to different people; some believe that spanking a child is abuse, while others do not. Some believe child abuse only involves physical acts and that psychological torment is not a form of abuse."

This chapter begins with a classification of crimes against children, including some clinical definitions, important terminology and the effects of child abuse. It also discusses challenges in investigating crimes against children. Next the chapter describes the initial report and the police response and provides guidelines for interviewing abused children, a sample protocol, examples of the evidence to collect and possible suspects. The chapter concludes with a description of child sexual rings, an examination of children as witnesses in court and a discussion of preventing crimes against children. ■

Classification

Law enforcement agencies are charged with investigating all crimes, but their responsibility is especially great where crimes against children are involved. Children need the protection of the law to a greater degree than other members of society because they are so vulnerable, especially if the offense is committed by one or both parents. Even after the offense is committed, the child may still be in danger of further victimization.

- - - - - - - - -

Crimes against children include kidnapping, abandonment, neglect, exploitation, physical abuse, emotional abuse, incest and sexual assault.

- - - - - - - - -

Kidnapping is taking someone away by force, often for ransom. Child kidnapping is especially traumatic for the parents and for those called upon to investigate. A highly publicized child kidnapping case in 1989 involved the abduction of 11-year-old Jacob Wetterling, who was taken at gunpoint from near his home by a masked man. No ransom was demanded, and despite national publicity and a nationwide search, Jacob remains missing.

Some child kidnappings are committed by a parent who has lost custody of the child in divorce proceedings. In such cases, ransom is not demanded. Rather, the parent committing the kidnapping may take on a new identity and move to another part of the country. Childless couples have also been known to kidnap babies or young children to raise as their own.

Abandonment refers to a parent's desertion of a child. This may occur not because the parents no longer love the child but because they feel the child would have a better life without them. It sometimes occurs when a young girl has a child and does not want anyone to know about it.

Neglect refers to failure to care for a child properly and can include not providing humane living quarters, adequate food or adequate love and attention. According to Johnson (p. 77), the clinical definition of child neglect is quite broad: "The inattention to the basic needs of a child: one that suffers neglect lacks proper supervision, adequate clothing, and proper nutrition."

An example of physical abuse or neglect is a couple who raped, drugged and fed fried rats and boiled cockroaches to their four children over a period of at least four years ("Chicago Couple . . . ," 1996, p. A8). These children were fed "as a regular diet, skinned and boiled rats rolled in flour and deep-fried and boiled cockroaches served with hot sauce."

Exploitation refers to taking unfair advantage of children or using them illegally. This includes using children in pornography and prostitution. It can also involve forcing children to perform physical labor beyond what could be reasonably expected of a child.

Physical abuse refers to beating, whipping, burning or otherwise inflicting physical harm upon a child. Johnson (p. 77) notes the clinical definition of child physical abuse is "the non-accidental physical injury of a child caused by the child's caretaker." Child abuse has been identified as the biggest single cause of death of young children. One study found that between three and four million children have at some time been kicked, beaten or hit with a fist by their parents; and between 900,000 and 1.8 million have been assaulted with a knife or gun.

Emotional abuse refers to causing fear or feelings of unworthiness in children by such means as locking them in closets, ignoring them or constantly belittling them. Johnson (p. 78) states: "Emotional maltreatment is the chronic failure of the child's caretaker to provide the child with support and affection." He adds: "As an example, Charles Manson was raised by an uncle who subjected him to severe emotional maltreatment by constantly calling him derogatory names and sending him to school dressed in girl's clothes."

Child sexual abuse includes sexually molesting a child, performing sexual acts with a child and statutory rape and seduction. "[It] involves contact or interaction between a child and an adult in which the child is used for the sexual gratification of the perpetrator" (Johnson, p. 78). Sexual assault victims may number in the millions, and perhaps some 90 percent of child molestations are not reported.

Some cultures sanction sexual relationships between adults and children, despite the fact that such acts are illegal in this country. Cart (1998, p. A3) tells the story of one teen in Utah:

The bedraggled girl walked 6 dusty miles to a gas station pay phone and punched 911. Then she did what she was taught never to do: She told. Help me, she said to the sheriff. My father beat me when I ran away from an arranged marriage with my uncle. I was his 15th wife.

With one phone call to an outside world she scarcely knew, the battered 16-year-old gave voice to silent women who live within the secretive constraints of polygamy. . . .

Critics say the practice of polygamy leads to pregnant women with no prenatal care, children who never see doctors and huge families with no health or dental insurance. Girls as young as 10 are forced into arranged marriages, they say. . . .

Former polygamy wives say they've seen rampant incest and child abuse. The uncle of the girl who called authorities was charged with unlawful sexual conduct, and her father with felony child abuse.

Terminology

State statutes differ in their definitions of *minor,* with the most common specifying under the age of 16 and under the age of 18.

When classifying crimes against children, several state statutes are applicable, including offenses of physical assault, sexual assault, incest, sexual seduction, indecent exposure, lewdness and molestation. Physical and sexual assault and incest have been previously defined. **Sexual seduction** means ordinary sexual intercourse, anal intercourse, cunnilingus or fellatio committed by a nonminor with a consenting minor. **Lewdness** means touching a minor to arouse, appeal to or gratify the perpetrator's sexual desires. The touching may be done by the perpetrator or by the minor under the perpetrator's direction. **Molestation** is a broader term, referring to any act motivated by unnatural or abnormal sexual interest in minors that would reasonably be expected to disturb, irritate or offend the victim. Molestation may or may not involve touching of the victim.

Legislatures in a number of states are attempting to broaden penalties to make them match the severity of the offense, especially if the victim is very young. There is also a concerted effort to expand the offenses to make genders equal, recognizing that victims and offenders may be male or female. The age of the offender as well as the type of the crime are both taken into account. Illinois, for example, has consolidated nine sex offenses into four but provides for twenty-four combinations of charges.

At the federal level, child abuse statutes pertain mainly to exploitation, but they also set forth important definitions that apply to any type of child abuse. Public Law 95–225 (1978) defines **sexual exploitation** as follows:

Any person who employs, uses, persuades, induces, entices, or coerces any minor to engage or assist in engaging in any sexually explicit conduct for the purpose of producing any visual or print medium, knowing that such visual or print medium will be transported interstate or in foreign commerce or mailed, is guilty of sexual exploitation. Further, any parent or legal guardian who knowingly permits such conduct, having control and custody of the child, is also subject to prosecution.

Visual print or **medium** means any film, photograph, negative, slide, book, magazine or other visual print or medium. **Commercial exploitation** means having as a direct or indirect goal monetary or other material gain.

The Child Protection Act (1984) prohibits child pornography and greatly increases the penalties for adults who engage in it.

The law describes child pornography as being highly developed into an organized, multimillion-dollar industry operating on a national level, exploiting thousands of children including runaways and homeless youth, producing and distributing pornographic materials. It states that such exploitation is harmful to the physiological, emotional and mental health of the individual and to society.

Many states have passed similarly worded statutes and have also increased penalties for sexual abuse and the production and distribution of child-pornographic materials. Although adult pornography has always been objectionable to many people, it has not resulted in the aggressive public and legislative action that child pornography has received. In 1977 Congress passed the Protection of Children Against Sexual Exploitation Act. This and other federal and state laws have prohibited commercial and noncommercial distribution of pornographic materials and more recently have made it a violation of law to *possess* such materials. The basis for these laws has been the acceptance of a relationship between child-pornographic materials and child sexual abuse offenders and offenses.

Indeed, in many cases, arrested pedophiles have had in their possession child-pornographic literature used to lower their selected victims' inhibitions. It is often necessary to obtain search warrants for the suspect's premises to obtain these materials. It is necessary in the investigation to gain as much evidence as possible because the problems of child testimony in court are well established.

The Effects of Child Abuse

The effects of child abuse can be devastating.

- - - - - - - - -

Child abuse can result in permanent and serious physical, mental and emotional damage.

- - - - - - - - -

Physical damage may involve the brain, vital organs, eyes, ears, arms or legs. Severe abuse may also cause mental retardation, restricted language ability, restricted perceptual and motor-skill development, arrested physical development, blindness, deafness, loss of limbs or even death.

Emotional damage may include impaired self-concept as well as increased levels of aggression, anxiety and tendency toward self-destructiveness. These self-destructive tendencies can cause children to act out antisocial behavior in the family, the school and the community at large. Such self-destructiveness can also manifest itself in risky behavior that endangers youths' health and safety. For example, one study ("Studies Identify Risks . . . ," 1997, p. 7) examined the dynamics of teen pregnancy and found: "Among the girls who reported having been pregnant at least once, 48 percent reported that they had been sexually abused and 60 percent reported that they had been both physically and sexually abused." Furthermore (pp. 7–8):

> Victims of sexual abuse more often than nonvictims reported a lack of parental supervision and a history of physical abuse. They also reported higher levels of school absenteeism, less involvement in extra-curricular activities, and lower grades. . . .
>
> The findings also indicated associations between a history of sexual abuse and substance use, thoughts or attempts of suicide, and risky sexual behaviors, such as having sex without birth control and having multiple sexual partners.

Another study, by Kelley et al. (p. 11) reports: "Subjects with a history of maltreatment were more likely to engage in serious and violent delinquency, use drugs, perform poorly in school, display symptoms of mental illness, and (for girls) become pregnant." A further complicating factor in examining child abuse and teen pregnancy is noted by Maynard and Garry (1997, p. 2): "Children born to adolescent mothers were found to be twice as likely to be victims of abuse and neglect than children born to 20- or 21-year-old mothers."

As mentioned, another likely effect of child abuse is that, as an adult, the former victim very frequently becomes a perpetrator of child abuse, thereby creating a vicious circle sometimes called the intergenerational transmission of violence. Research shows that a child's history of physical abuse predisposes that child to violence in later years. Victims of neglect are also likely to engage in later violent criminal behavior:

> A survey of convicted male felons in a New York State prison has found that two-thirds of the inmates suffered physical abuse, sexual abuse, and/or neglect as children, according to the National Institute of Justice (NIJ).
>
> The most common type of victimization was physical abuse, with 35 percent of the inmates reporting severe abuse. . . .
>
> About 14 percent reported some type of sexual abuse . . . ; 26 percent of sex offenders reported sexual abuse as a child. . . .
>
> Childhood neglect was reported by 20 percent of the inmates convicted of violent crimes ("Two-Thirds of Prisoners . . . ," 1998, p. 7).

Wolfe et al. (1998, p. 25) report: "Children from violent families had a rate of behavior and social competency problems 2.5 times higher than those from nonviolent families." A study by Lemmon (1999) found neglect and maltreatment to be important contributors to delinquency, particularly to violent crime (pp. 372–373):

> Maltreated youths were referred to the juvenile justice system more often than their nonabused and nonneglected counterparts. . . . They were also significantly younger at the time of their initial referral. . . . Their delinquency also was more chronic and more severe. In regard to substantiated serious offenses, the maltreatment group accounted for 78 percent of all aggravated assaults, 88 percent of all felony-level sex offenses, 83 percent of all robberies, 86 percent of all weapons offenses, and 66 percent of all felony-level drug offenses. The findings show that the boys with the maltreatment characteristic were persistent and violent offenders, while those who did not suffer maltreatment were infrequent, routine offenders, comparable to low-risk offenders under any conditions.

Challenges to Investigation

Many prosecutors at all levels of the judiciary perceive crimes against children as among the most difficult to prosecute and obtain convictions. Therefore, officers interviewing child witnesses and victims should have specialized training not only to convict the guilty but also to protect the innocent. Regardless of whether crimes against children are handled by generalists or specialists within the department, certain challenges are unique to these investigations.

Challenges in investigating crimes against children include the need to protect the child from further harm, the possibility of parental involvement, the difficulty of interviewing children, credibility concerns and the need to collaborate with other agencies.

Protecting the Child

When child abuse is reported, investigators may initiate an investigation on their own, or they may investigate jointly with the welfare department. Regardless of the source of the report and regardless of whether the investigation is a single or joint effort, the primary responsibility of the investigator assigned to the case is the immediate protection of the child.

If the possibility of present or continued danger to the child exists, the child must be removed into protective custody.

Under welfare regulations and codes, an officer may take a child into temporary custody without a warrant if there is an emergency or if the officer has reason to believe that leaving the child in the present situation would subject the child to further abuse or harm. **Temporary custody without hearing** usually means for 48 hours. Conditions that would justify placing a child in protective custody include the following:

- The child's age or physical or mental condition makes the child incapable of self-protection.
- The home's physical environment poses an immediate threat to the child.
- The child needs immediate medical or psychiatric care, and the parents refuse to get it.

- The parents cannot or will not provide for the child's basic needs.
- Maltreatment in the home could permanently damage the child physically or emotionally.
- The parents may abandon the child.

Consultation with local welfare authorities is sometimes needed before asking the court for a hearing to remove a child from the parents' custody or for protective custody in an authorized facility because police rarely have such facilities. As soon as possible the child should be taken to the nearest welfare facility or to a foster home, as stipulated by the juvenile court. The parents or legal guardians of the child must be notified as soon as possible.

Difficulty in Interviewing Children

When children are very young, a limited vocabulary can pose a severe challenge to investigators. Unfortunately, by the time children are old enough to possess the words or other skills needed to communicate and describe their abusive experiences, they have also developed the ability to feel such shame, embarrassment and fear over these events as to resist talking about them.

Interviewing a child abuse victim takes special understanding, skill and practice. Children often have difficulty talking about abuse, and often they have been instructed not to tell anyone about it. They may have been threatened by the abuser, or they may have a close relationship with the abuser and not want anything bad to happen to that person.

When interviewing children, officers should consider the child's age, ability to describe what happened and the potential for retaliation by the suspect against a child who "tells."

Another difficulty in interviewing children is their short attention spans. Questions should be short and understandable, a skill that often proves difficult and requires training and practice. Interviewers who are excellent with adults may not be so successful with children.

Investigators may consider inviting a social service professional to help conduct the interview because they often have more formal training and experience in interviewing children at their level and may therefore be better able to establish rapport.

More specific guidelines for interviewing abused children are discussed in detail shortly.

Credibility Concerns

Assessing the credibility of persons reporting child abuse is a constant challenge for investigators. As repulsive as society finds child abuse, particularly sexual abuse, investigators must exercise great care to protect the innocent and falsely accused. No other crime is so fraught with stigma. Consequently, accusations of this type can be difficult to dispel even if they are false.

Because of the "loaded" nature of child sexual abuse allegations, parents who are divorcing may be tempted to use such claims as ammunition against their soon-to-be ex-spouse. For investigators, sorting through details of such allegations to determine their credibility can be extremely challenging. Goldstein and Tyler (1998, p. 2) note: "Child abuse investigations can be the most difficult cases to prove. In divorce and custody cases, added credibility concerns make abuse allegations even more likely to be unsubstantiated or unfounded." They also report (p. 1):

> A study of 9,000 families embroiled in contested divorce proceedings found that 1 to 8 percent involved allegations of child sexual abuse. Unfortunately, the warlike atmosphere inherent in divorce often discredits valid claims. Though rare, false allegations of abuse do occur. Another study revealed that out of 169 cases of alleged child sexual abuse arising in marital relations courts, only 14 percent were deliberate, false allegations.

Occasionally the credibility of the child victim is called into question. However, investigators must approach each case and each victim with an open mind. As Laws (1999, p. 37) asserts: "The first thing investigators need to do is be mentally prepared to believe the child themselves. It is very difficult for a child to talk to anyone about being abused—much less a strange adult, even a police officer whom they should be able to trust."

- - - - - - - -

In the vast majority of child abuse cases, children tell the truth to the best of their ability.

- - - - - - - -

People who work with child abuse cases point out that children will frequently lie to get out of trouble, but they seldom lie to get into trouble. Although most child abuse reports are valid, investigators must use caution to weed out those cases reported by a habitual liar or by a child who is telling a story to offset other misdeeds he

or she has committed. A child's motivation for lying may be revenge, efforts to avoid school or parental disapproval, efforts to cover up for other disapproved behavior or, in the case of sexual abuse, an attempt to explain a pregnancy or to obtain an abortion at state expense.

The Need to Involve Other Agencies: The Multidisciplinary Team Approach

Another challenge facing law enforcement is the need to collaborate with various social service, child welfare and health agencies to more effectively handle child abuse cases. Traditionally, law enforcement and social service agencies have worked fairly independently on child abuse cases, with each conducting their own separate interviews and investigations. In fact, many police departments have seen no need to collaborate with social services unless their investigation determines a need to remove the child from parental custody. However, it is increasingly evident that this lack of communication and coordination among these agencies has led to numerous cases "falling through the cracks" of the disjointed system, sometimes with devastating results. Ells (1998, p. 1) relates one tragic case:

> Two months before her seventh birthday in 1995, Elisa Izquierdo was killed. Over a period of months, she had been physically and emotionally abused, repeatedly violated with a toothbrush and a hairbrush, and finally beaten to death by her mother. Elisa's mother told police that before she smashed Elisa's head against a cement wall, she made Elisa eat her own feces and used her head to mop the floor. The police told reporters that there was no part of the 6-year-old's body that had not been cut or bruised. Thirty marks initially thought to be cigarette burns turned out be the imprints of a stone in someone's ring.
>
> An investigation after her death revealed that Elisa had been the subject of at least eight reports of abuse and that several government agencies had investigated the reports. Nonetheless, Elisa Izquierdo was left with her abuser and eventual killer.

Ells (p. 3) notes: "Over the past two decades, the number of reports of child abuse and neglect has greatly increased, straining resources to investigate allegations effectively." To overcome these strains and promote well-coordinated child abuse investigations, Ells advocates the formation of multidisciplinary teams (MDT) comprising "government agencies and private practitioners responsible for investigating crimes against children and protecting and treating children in a particular community" (p. 2).

------- -------

"A multidisciplinary team (MDT) is a group of professionals who work together in a coordinated and collaborative manner to ensure an effective response to reports of child abuse and neglect" (p. 2).

------- -------

Ells (p. 4) continues:

No single profession or State agency has the ability to respond adequately to any allegation of child maltreatment. . . .

It is now well accepted that the best response to the challenge of child abuse and neglect investigations is the formation of an MDT. In fact, formation of such teams is authorized, and often required, in more than three-quarters of the States and at the Federal level. . . .

The MDT approach often extends beyond joint investigations and interagency coordination into team decisionmaking.

Ells (p. 4) states: "Some of the recognized benefits of a proficient MDT include:

- Less 'system inflicted' trauma to children and families.

- Better agency decisions, including more accurate investigations and more appropriate interventions.

- More efficient use of limited agency resources.

- Better trained, more capable professionals.

- More respect in the community and less burnout among child abuse professionals."

The importance of a coordinated response to crimes against children is supported by numerous studies. Strandberg (1999, p. 20) notes:

The state-of-the-art or best practice is to use specially trained law enforcement officers in teams with child welfare workers from the start, when children are brought into custody to minimize the trauma, to protect evidence and to minimize the number of times a child has to tell his/her story.

Coordinated responses can also minimize the likelihood of conflicts among agencies with different philosophies and mandates. In describing how working together makes child abuse investigations safer and more effective, Ennis (1999, p. 55) notes: "Police spend more time in noninvestigative activities, child protection workers spend more time as investigators, and their spheres of influence overlap in many areas. Both have shifted emphasis from reactive to proactive response when possible."

Joint investigations often result in more victim corroborations and perpetrator confessions than independent investigations. In addition, referral agencies provide support and assistance to families and victims experiencing child abuse or neglect. A collaborative, community-based approach to problems associated with children and youth should result in identifying, developing and implementing more effective, multiagency solutions.

The U.S. Department of Justice's Office of Juvenile Justice and Delinquency Prevention (OJJDP) is supporting a new program involving such teamwork ("Young People Exposed. . . ," 1999, p. 14):

A pilot initiative, the Child-Development-Community-Policing (CD-CP) model, emphasizes the importance of developing collaborative relationships between the law enforcement and mental health communities in ensuring that youth who are exposed to violence have access to a wide array of services offered to them by their communities.

A Child Protection Center (CPC) can be of great assistance in child abuse cases. Ideally it would be connected to a regional hospital whose medical staff is specially trained in examining abused children. They should know how to conduct the exam, collect evidence for prosecution and maintain the chain of custody. Quill and Yahner (p. 8) describe one such center in Arizona that is proving beneficial to all parties involved:

The partnership between the group Childhelp USA and the Phoenix Police Department . . . led to the creation of the Childhelp Children's Center of Arizona. This integrated, multiagency facility allows all aspects of handling crimes against children—including criminal investigations and interviews, medical examinations, counseling, foster placement of children and victim/family assistance programs—to be completed at a single location. The primary goals of the center are really quite simple: create a victim-friendly environment, reduce secondary trauma, and enhance investigative efficiency.

Another community involvement program that can assist in the investigation of abused, abandoned or abducted children is the National Fingerprint for Children Identification project, which provides information to law enforcement agencies about the identification of children who have been fingerprinted and are listed in their files. These confidential files contain some 40,000 children. The prints are submitted by parents, police and sometimes civic organizations as a community project.

Other technological developments allow police to communicate more effectively with organizations such as the media in cases involving child abductions—cases where speed of information dissemination is critical.

Bradford (1998, p. 3) describes a new tool used by the Houston Police Department and other regional agencies to help search for missing children:

> Technology to Recover Abducted Kids (TRAK) is a computer system that slashes delays by allowing police to distribute photos and information about a missing child almost immediately. . . .
>
> Recently a law enforcement support group that frequently assists Houston area law enforcement purchased 33 TRAK units for police departments, television stations and newspapers. With these additional resources, we now have a regional communications system that can be used the moment we learn that a child is missing.

The Initial Report

Most reports of child neglect or abuse are made by third parties such as teachers, neighbors, siblings or parents. Seldom does the victim report the offense.

In most states certain individuals who work with or treat children are required by law to report cases of suspected neglect or abuse. This includes teachers, school authorities, child-care personnel, camp personnel, clergy, physicians, dentists, chiropractors, nurses, psychologists, medical assistants, attorneys and social workers. Such a report may be made to the welfare department, the juvenile court or the local police or sheriff's department. It may be made verbally, but it should also be put into writing as soon as possible after the initial verbal report is made. Some states have special forms for child abuse cases. These forms are sent to a central location in the state, thereby helping to prevent child abusers from taking the child to different doctors or hospitals for treatment and thus avoiding the suspicion that would accompany multiple incidents involving the same child.

Child neglect/abuse reports should contain the name, age and address of the child victim; the name and address of the child's parents or other persons responsible for the child's care; the name and address of the person suspected of the abuse; the nature and extent of the neglect or abuse and any evidence of this or previous neglect or abuse. These reports are confidential.

In most states, action must be taken on a report within a specified time, frequently three days. If in the judgment of the person receiving the report it is neces-

sary to remove the child from present custody, this is discussed with the responsible agency, such as the welfare department or the juvenile court. If the situation is deemed life threatening, the police may temporarily remove the child. No matter who receives the report or whether the child must be removed from the situation, it is the responsibility of the law enforcement agency to investigate the charge.

The Police Response

Traditionally, as with domestic violence, child abuse/neglect was viewed as a family matter—a social issue regulated by child protection agencies. It was not a crime. Currently, child abuse is viewed as a crime and within jurisdiction of the criminal justice system. Therefore it needs to be investigated by trained criminal investigators.

The investigator must talk with people who know the child and obtain background information on the child. For example, does the child have behavior problems? Is the child generally truthful?

If interviews are conducted with the parents, every attempt should be made to conduct the interviews in private. Explain why the interview is necessary. Be direct, honest, sympathetic, understanding and professional in your approach. Do not accuse, demand, give personal opinions about the situation, request information from the parents unrelated to the matter under discussion, make judgments, place blame or reveal the source of your information. If the parents are suspects, provide them the due process rights granted by the Fourth and Fifth Amendments, including the Miranda warning.

Interviewing Abused Children

Before the interview, obtain relevant background information from the parents or guardian and anyone else involved in the case, including caseworkers, counselors and physicians. Also review the assault report.

Often several interviews are necessary to get a complete statement without overwhelming the child. The initial interview should be brief, merely to establish the facts supporting probable cause, with a second interview later. Explain to the child that it is important to tell the truth.

Generally it is best to conduct the interview in private in the child's or a friend's home or in a small room at a hospital or the police station. An interview room in a police station can be converted into a friendly environment for youngsters with the addition of some simple toys or coloring books. If the interview is to take place at the child's home, it might be best not to wear a uniform, especially if the child thinks he or she is to blame. The uniform could be too intimidating and frighten the child into thinking he or she is going to be arrested. Plainclothes, casual and comfortable, are usually best.

Regardless of whether the interview is conducted at the child's home or at the police station, it is usually not advisable to have a family member present—but if the child so desires, the wish should be respected. The family member should be seated out of the child's view so as not to influence the interview. However, if a parent is suspected of being the offender, neither parent should be present. The investigator should record the time the interview begins and ends. (A note: Because taking written statements from children is difficult, it is sometimes better to videotape the interview. Videotapes may be used by other officers, prosecutors and the courts, which eliminates having to requestion the victim.)

When conducting an interview with a child, investigators must establish rapport. The gender of the interviewer generally does not matter—the ability to elicit accurate information is the key quality. The interviewer should sit next to the child and speak in a friendly voice, without talking down to the child. It may help to play a game with the child or to get down on the floor at the child's level to get attention and to encourage the child to talk naturally. Allow the child freedom to do other things during the interview, such as moving around the room or playing with toys, but do not allow distractions from the outside. Learn about the child's abilities and interests by asking questions about everyday activities, such as school and household chores. Ask about the child's siblings, pets, friends, favorite games or TV shows. It may help to share personal information when appropriate, such as children or pets. Evaluate the child's cognitive level by asking if he or she can read, write, count or tell time. Do they know their birthdate? Can they recount past events (yesterday, holidays)? Do they know about various body parts and their functions? Assess their maturity level by asking about their responsibilities—making their own breakfast, walking the dog, and so on. Do they enjoy any privileges (staying home alone, going places on their own)?

Make the child feel comfortable, and keep in mind that questioning children is apt to be more of a sharing experience than a formal interview. Because young children have a short attention span, fact-finding interviews should last no more than 15 or 20 minutes. Questions should pertain to what happened, who did it, when it happened, where it happened and whether force, threats or enticements were involved. Ask simple, direct, open-ended questions. Avoid asking "why" questions because they tend to sound accusatory. To alleviate the anxiety, fear or reluctance found in children who have been instructed or threatened not to tell by the offender (*especially* if a parent), try statements such as, "It's not bad to tell what happened," "You won't get in trouble," "You can help your dad/mom/friend by telling what happened," and "It wasn't your fault." Never threaten or try to force a reluctant child to talk because such pressure will likely lead a child to "clam up" and may cause further trauma.

Whitcomb (1998, p. 5) notes children often do not organize their thoughts logically and have a limited understanding of space, distance and time, tending to confuse or mix separate incidents. Therefore, determining when the events occurred may require creative questioning such as "Was it before your birthday?" "After Halloween?" "Did it happen after dinner?" "After your brother's bedtime?" "Was it nighttime or daytime?"

To obtain the most thorough and accurate account of the abuse possible, investigators should be proficient in cognitive interview techniques. According to Saywitz et al. (1998, p. 8): "Cognitive interviewing with practice was superior to cognitive interviewing without practice and both were superior to standard police interview techniques." In evaluating children's recall performance during various types of interviews, these authors found (p. 8): "Practice with these novel interviewing techniques prior to the interview produced a significantly greater number of correct pieces of information recalled."

It is extremely important not to put words into a child's mouth. When the child answers your questions, be certain you understand the meaning of his or her words. A child may think "sex" is kissing or hugging or touching. If the child uses a word, learn what the word really means to the child to get to the truth and avoid later embarrassment in court.

In the case of sexual abuse of young children, it may be helpful to use drawings or anatomical dolls to assist the child in describing exactly what happened and the positions of the child and the abuser when the offense took place. Controversy exists, however, in whether such anatomically detailed dolls help or hinder interview progress. According to Whitcomb (p. 5): "Critics suggested that the use of dolls places unnatu-

Anatomical dolls are sometimes used to diagnose and treat sexual abuse victims. The dolls enable victims (generally children) to better express thoughts and actions by "acting out" their trauma. Each doll features a male or female sex organ, breasts, jointed legs, ears, navel and individual fingers.

ral and increased attention on body parts, so that abused children might display sexually explicit behavior. . . . Others point out that research does not support that claim and suggest that there is no evidence that the dolls disturb children in any way."

To assess the credibility and competence of children in sexual abuse cases, consider the following (Sexual Assault Center, Seattle, WA):

- Does the child describe acts or experiences to which a child of his or her age would not normally have been exposed? The average child is not familiar with erection or ejaculation until adolescence at the earliest.

- Does the child describe circumstances and characteristics typical of a sexual assault situation? "He told me that it was our secret"; "He said I couldn't go out if I didn't do it"; "She told me it was sex education."

- How and under what circumstances did the child tell? What were the child's exact words?

- How many times has the child given the history, and how consistent is it regarding the basic facts of the assault (times, dates, circumstances, sequence of events, etc.)?

- How much spontaneous information does the child provide? How much prompting is required?

- Can the child define the difference between the truth and a lie? (This question is not actually very useful with young children because they learn this by rote and may not truly understand the concepts.)

During the interview do not try to extract promises from the child regarding testifying in court because an undue emphasis on a trial will have little meaning and may frighten the child, causing nightmares and apprehension.

After the interview is completed, give the parents "simple, straightforward information about what will happen next in the criminal justice system and approximately when, the likelihood of trial and so on. Enlist their cooperation. Let them know who to contact for status reports or in an emergency; express appreciation and understanding for the efforts they are making by reporting and following through on the process. Answer any questions the parents or child have."

One final note: Exact notes are critical in interviews of child sexual abuse victims because such cases are an exception to the hearsay rule, meaning an officer *may* testify in court about the victim's statements. Therefore, officers should be meticulous in recording all statements verbatim. The child may not be able to repeat the statements due to fear or anxiety. For this reason, as well as others mentioned earlier, interviews should be videotaped whenever possible.

Sample Protocol

The following excerpt from the Boulder City (Nevada) Police Department's protocol for investigating reports of sexual and physical abuse of children is typical. (Reprinted by permission.)

It is the policy to *team* investigate all abuse allegations.

When a report comes in, a juvenile officer is immediately assigned all abuse cases. This officer is responsible for maintaining a 72-hour time frame. Contact is made as soon as possible.

The investigative process includes the following:

A. The investigator contacts Nevada Welfare, and together they contact the victim at a location where the victim can be interviewed briefly, and not in the presence of the alleged perpetrator of the crime.

B. During the initial interview the juvenile officer tries to determine if the report is a substantiated abuse, unsubstantiated or unfounded.

C. If the report is substantiated, the juvenile officer or Nevada State Welfare remove the child from the home and book the child into protective custody. If the juvenile officer and Nevada State Welfare investigator determine the child is not in danger of *any* abuse, the child can be allowed to remain in his/her home environment.

D. If the report is unsubstantiated, the child is left in the home.

E. If the report is unfounded, the reason for the false report is also investigated to identify other problems. . . .

F. If the case is substantiated abuse, the victim is housed at Child Haven, and there is a detention hearing at 9:00 A.M. the following working day.

An in-depth interview is conducted with the victim by the juvenile officer and the Nevada State Welfare investigator. Several aids are used, depending on the child's age and mental abilities: structured and unstructured play therapy, picture drawings and use of anatomical dolls.

The juvenile officer also contacts the accused person and interviews him/her about the specific allegations, makes a report or statement relevant to the interview and makes these reports available to Nevada State Welfare and/or Clark County Juvenile Court. Nevada State Welfare is encouraged to attend these interviews, and a team approach is used during this phase of the investigation also.

The juvenile officer also interviews other people, including witnesses or victims—anyone who might have information about the case. The officer prepares an affidavit and presents the case to the district attorney's office to determine whether the case is suitable for prosecution. If so, a complaint is issued, and a warrant or summons is issued for the accused. Once a warrant is obtained, the investigating officer locates and arrests or causes the accused person to be arrested.

Evidence

All the investigator's observations pertaining to the physical and emotional condition of the victim must be recorded in detail.

— — — — — — — —

Evidence in child neglect or abuse cases includes the surroundings, the home conditions, clothing, bruises or other body injuries, the medical examination report and other observations.

— — — — — — — —

Photographs may be the best way to document child abuse and neglect where it is necessary to show injury to the child or the conditions of the home environment. Pictures should be taken immediately because children's injuries heal quickly and home conditions can be changed rapidly. Pictures in both color and black-and-white should be taken, showing bruises, burns, cuts or any injury requiring medical treatment. These photographs should be witnessed by people who can later testify about the location and extent of the injuries, including medical personnel who examined the child.

Explain the need for the pictures to the child to avoid further fear or excitement. All procedures for photography at a crime scene (discussed in Chapter 2) should be followed. Stephenson (1996, p. 9) stresses:

Photos are a powerful reinforcement to the information contained in the police report. Broken glass, exposed electrical wiring, matches, explosives, knives, squalid and foul living quarters—when photos of these conditions are taken and attached to the report, I don't have to rely on the narrative for documentation. I can see it. It's one thing to read about a roach infested house; it's another to see photos of the roaches crawling all over the kitchen counter.

Laws (p. 38) notes:

When a sexual abuse allegation is made, one of the first steps is to arrange for the child to have a medical examination, preferably at a children's hospital with personnel trained in this area. This exam will document any physical injury that may not be readily visible. . . . According to some experts, physical injury occurs only in about 50 percent of sexual abuse cases; the possibility must not be overlooked as this medical evidence may be all there is to give the victim's report added credibility.

Additional types of evidence that may be obtained in sexual assault cases include photographs, torn clothing, ropes or tapes and trace evidence such as the hair of the offender and the victim and, in some instances, semen.

Indicators of Child Neglect and Abuse

Indicators of neglect or abuse may be physical or behavioral or both.

Caution: The lists of indicators in this section are not exhaustive; many other indicators exist. In addition, the presence of one or more of these indicators does not prove that neglect or abuse exists. All factors and conditions of each specific case must be considered before you make a decision.

Neglect Indicators The *physical* indicators of child neglect may include frequent hunger, poor hygiene, inappropriate dress, consistent lack of supervision (especially in dangerous activities or for long time periods), unattended physical problems or medical needs and abandonment.

The *behavioral* indicators may include begging, stealing food, extending school days by arriving early and/or leaving late, constant fatigue, listlessness or falling asleep in school, alcohol or drug abuse, delinquency, stealing and stating that no one is at home to care for them.

Emotional Abuse Indicators *Physical* indicators of emotional abuse may include speech disorders, lags in physical development and general failure to thrive.

Behavioral indicators may include habit disorders such as sucking, biting and rocking back and forth and conduct disorders such as antisocial, destructive behavior. Other possible symptoms are sleep disorders, inhibitions in play, obsessions, compulsions, phobias, hypochondria, behavioral extremes and attempted suicide.

Physical Abuse Indicators *Physical* indicators of physical abuse include unexplained bruises or welts, burns, fractures, lacerations and abrasions. These may be in various stages of healing.

Behavioral indicators include being wary of adults, being apprehensive when other children cry, extreme aggressiveness or extreme withdrawal, being frightened of parents and being afraid to go home.

Parental indicators may include contradictory explanations for a child's injury; attempts to conceal a child's injury or to protect the identity of the person responsible; routine use of harsh, unreasonable discipline inappropriate to the child's age or transgressions and poor impulse control.

Sexual Abuse Indicators *Physical* indicators of sexual abuse are rarely observed. Venereal disease or pregnancy, especially in preteens, are two indicators.

Behavioral indicators of sexual abuse may include unwillingness to change clothes for or to participate in physical education classes; withdrawal, fantasy or infantile behavior; bizarre sexual behavior, sexual sophistication beyond the child's age or unusual behavior or knowledge of sex; poor peer relationships; delinquent or runaway; reports of being sexually assaulted.

Parental indicators may include jealousy and overprotectiveness of a child. Incest incidents are insidious, commonly beginning with the parent fondling and caressing the child between the ages of three and six months and then progressing over a long time period, increasing in intensity of contact until the child is capable of full participation, usually between the ages of eight and ten. A parent may hesitate to report a spouse who is sexually abusing their child for fear of destroying the marriage or for fear of retaliation. Interfamily sex may be viewed as preferable to extramarital sex.

The Suspect

In most instances of child neglect and physical or emotional abuse, the suspect is one of the parents. In instances of sexual abuse, however, the suspect may be a close family member or a complete stranger.

People who have normal behavior patterns in all other areas of life may have very abnormal sexual behavior patterns. Child sexual abusers may commit only one offense in their lifetime, or they may commit hundreds. Surveys indicate that 35 to 50 percent of the offenders know their victims. Some studies indicate an even higher percentage. Therefore, the investigator of a child sexual crime may not be looking for an unknown suspect or stranger.

The Parent as Suspect

Sexual abuse of one or more children in a family is one of the most common child sexual-abuse problems, but it is not often reported. Because of the difficulties in detecting it, it is the least known to the public. The harm to the child from continued, close sexual relationships with a family member may be accompanied by shame, fear or even guilt. Additional conflict may be created by admonitions of secrecy.

Although girls are more frequently victims, keep in mind that if a girl is sexually abused by a family member, a boy in the same family may also be a victim.

Incest usually involves children under 11 and becomes a repeated activity, both in severity and frequency. Courts have ruled that the spousal immunity rules do not apply to child sexual abuse cases. One spouse may be forced to testify against the other in court.

Münchausen Syndrome and Münchausen Syndrome by Proxy (MSBP) Münchausen Syndrome involves self-induced or self-inflicted injuries. If a child's injuries appear to be self-induced or self-inflicted, the child may be seeking attention, sympathy or avoidance of something. Parents—usually the mother—may inflict injuries on their children for basically the same reasons. **Münchausen Syndrome by Proxy (MSBP)** is a form of child abuse in which a parent or adult caregiver deliberately provides false medical histories, manufactures evidence and causes medical distress in a child. MSBP is usually done so that the child will be treated by a physician and the abuser may gain the attention or sympathy of family, friends and others. Birge (1996, p. 96) relates:

> In cases of MSBP, which are cases of child abuse, often the greatest harm to the child is not committed by the parent, but by the medical staff while they attempt to pinpoint the cause of a child's illness and plan the appropriate treatment. Many patients, often at the request of their mothers, endure routine X-rays, urine and stool tests, as well as invasive diagnostic procedures—which can include blood tests, catheterization and even surgery.
>
> All of these are usually based on the history provided by the mother. Although medical personnel are performing the often life-saving procedures, the mother is still the perpetrator of the abuse.

Birge (p. 96) advocates a multidisciplinary approach in MSBP cases to stop abusers and protect children from future abuse: "This protection may have to include permanent removal from the mother's care in order to save the child's life, as about 10% of MSBP victims die." MSBP should be considered as a possible motive in any questionable or unexplained death of a child.

The following checklist might be used by investigators who suspect MSBP (*FBI Law Enforcement Bulletin,* June 1992, reprinted by permission):

Investigators' Checklist

Investigators assigned to work child abuse cases should investigate cases of MSBP as they do similar cases of

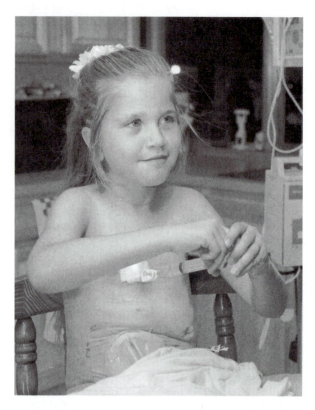

At her Coral Springs, Florida, home, Jennifer Bush applies medicine from a syringe as treatment for a rare disease. She has been hospitalized more than 200 times, undergone 40 operations and accumulated $3 million in medical expenses. Jennifer has been placed under state care and her mother jailed for allegedly causing her illnesses, known as Münchausen Syndrome by Proxy, a rare form of child abuse in which an adult intentionally makes a child ill to get attention.

abuse. In general, however, when confronted with possible cases of MSBP, investigators should:

■ Review the victim's medical records to determine condition and illness.

■ Determine from contact with medical personnel the reporting parent's concerns and reactions to the child's medical treatment.

■ Compile a complete history of the family to determine previous involvement with law enforcement agencies, medical facilities, and social and child protection services.

■ Compile a detailed social history of the family, including deaths, injuries, and illnesses.

■ Interview family members, neighbors, and babysitters.

- Use video surveillance in the hospital in accordance with state law.
- Use a search warrant for the family's residence when collecting evidence of the assaults.

Whereas MSBP is a disorder that clearly results in a form of child abuse, another disorder whose symptoms closely resemble child abuse, and for which parents are often mistakenly accused of abuse, is Osteogenesis Imperfecta.

Osteogenesis Imperfecta (OI) Osteogenesis Imperfecta (OI), or brittle bone disease, is a genetic disorder characterized by bones that break easily, often from little or no apparent cause. The United Kingdom Osteogenesis Imperfecta Foundation notes: "There are striking similarities between the symptoms of O.I. and the symptoms of abuse." The foundation further notes: "It has been estimated that as many as 20% of the parents of children with O.I. have been wrongly accused of child abuse at some time or another."

The United States Osteogenesis Imperfecta Foundation (OIF) states: "A minor accident may result in a fracture; some fractures may occur while a child is being diapered, lifted, or dressed." The most routine child-care activities, performed by the most careful and loving parents, can easily and spontaneously break the bones of a child with OI, and in some severe cases, the condition may be lethal. The OIF reports:

> False accusations of child abuse may occur in families with children who have milder forms of OI and/or in whom OI has not previously been diagnosed. Types of fractures that are typically observed in both child abuse and OI include fractures in multiple stages of healing, rib fractures, spiral fractures and fractures for which there is no adequate explanation of trauma.

The similarities between OI and child abuse symptoms can easily confuse investigators and anger parents wrongly accused of abuse. The UK OIF notes:

> Unexplained injuries and multiple fractures in various stages of healing are considered tell tale signs of abuse. At the same time these are also symptoms of O.I. The same collagen mutation (the main protein found in bones) that causes brittle bones can weaken the skin or cause unusually thin skin, resulting in easily bruised children, yet another indication of child abuse. O.I. children tend to be small for their age, thus they are often thought to have symptoms that are indicative of neglect.

When these symptoms are detected, how do investigators determine whether the suspected abuse case is actually OI? First, a medical professional experienced in diagnosing OI should evaluate the child. Genetic coun-seling may also reveal a previously unrecognized family history of mild OI. Investigators should also look for inconsistencies between the explanation for the injury given by the child or parent and the diagnosis provided by the treating physicians and other medical personnel. Parents may also try to conceal child abuse by frequently changing doctors or hospitals, thus avoiding a build-up of incriminating records at any one office or facility. Keep in mind also that the presence of OI does not automatically preclude the existence of child abuse.

Sudden Infant Death Syndrome (SIDS) Another tragic condition that takes the lives of young victims and for which parents may become suspected of child abuse is **Sudden Infant Death Syndrome,** or **SIDS.** Esposito et al. (1998, p. 2) note that SIDS claims the lives of 3,000 to 4,000 infants every year in the United States and is defined as "the sudden death of an infant under 1 year of age that remains unexplained after a thorough case investigation, including performance of a complete autopsy, examination of the death scene and review of the clinical history." They also note that SIDS may occur in children as old as 24 months. Furthermore (p. 2):

> Although the cause of SIDS remains uncertain, it is known that suffocation, pneumonia, choking, or the result of a neglected illness does not cause SIDS. SIDS is not contagious; it is not caused by the diptheria, pertussis, tetanus (DPT) vaccine or other immunizations; and it is not child abuse.

Because examination of the death scene is a critical factor in determining SIDS, officers responding to a call of an "infant not breathing" must be observant of several elements. Esposito et al. (p. 3) state:

> Officers should note such observations as the position of the infant when found, the condition of the crib and surrounding area, the presence of objects in the crib, any unusual or dangerous items in the room, and any medications being given to the baby, along with room temperature and air quality.

Officers may also observe certain bodily appearances in the victim that typically occur in SIDS cases resulting from the death process. According to Esposito et al. (p. 2), officers may detect: "Discoloration of the skin; settling of the blood (most evident in the arms and legs); frothy drainage from the nose or mouth, which may be blood tinged; small marks that look severe; and cooling rigor mortis, which takes place quickly in infants, usually in about 3 hours depending upon environmental conditions."

Table 12.1 compares the characteristic features of SIDS to child abuse, and Table 12.2 summarizes the characteristics of MSBP, OI and SIDS.

Table 12.1 **Comparison of SIDS and Child Abuse Characteristics**

Characteristic/feature	SIDS	Child abuse/neglect
Age typically affected	May occur from birth to 24 months, but most common from 2 to 4 months of age	May occur at any time, but most abused children are 1 to 3 years in age
External signs of injury?	Not usually	Yes—distinguishable and visible signs
Signs of malnourishment?	Not usually; appears well developed	Common
Do siblings show any symptoms?	Not usually; siblings appear normal and healthy	May show patterns of injuries
Parents' account of investigated event	Placed healthy baby to sleep in the crib and later found infant lifeless	May sound suspicious or may not account for all injuries to the child
Annual number of deaths in the United States	3,000–4,000 infants	1,000–4,000 children; 300 are infants

Source: Adapted from Linda Esposito, Larry Minda and Claire Forman. "Sudden Infant Death Syndrome." *FBI Law Enforcement Bulletin,* September 1998, pp. 1–5.

Table 12.2 **Comparison of the Characteristics of MSBP, OI and SIDS**

Characteristic/feature	Münchausen Syndrome by Proxy (MSBP)[1]	Osteogenesis Imperfecta (OI)[2]	Sudden Infant Death Syndrome (SIDS)[3]
Age of child typically afflicted		any age	occurs in newborn to 24 months, but is most frequent from 2–4 months
Number of children who die every year in the United States due to it			3,000–4,000
External signs of injury	Occasionally (parent-inflicted)	Not usually	Not usually
Is it child abuse?	Yes	No	No

Source: [1,3]Adapted from Linda Esposito, Larry Minda and Claire Forman. "Sudden Infant Death Syndrome." *FBI Law Enforcement Bulletin,* September 1998, pp. 1–5.
[2]U.K. Osteogenesis Imperfecta Foundation: http://www.ukoifoundation.org/fs2.htm and U.S. Osteogenesis Imperfecta Foundation: http://www.oif.org/tier2/childabuse.htm

The Nonparent Suspect

Habitual child sex abusers, whether they operate as loners or as part of a sex ring, have been classified into three types. First is the **misoped,** the person who hates children, who has sex with them and then brutally destroys them. The second type is the **hebephile,** a person who selects high-school-age youth as his or her sex victims.

The Pedophile The pedophile is the third and most common habitual child sex abuser.

The pedophile is an adult who has either heterosexual or homosexual preferences for young boys or girls of a specific, limited age range.

Although pedophiles are typically male, this is not always the case. Women are also involved in the sexual abuse of children.

Rarely deviating from the preferred age range, the pedophile is an expert in selecting and enticing young people. The pedophile frequently selects children who stand apart from other children, who are runaways or who crave attention and love. Although some pedophiles are child rapists, the majority rarely use force, relying instead on befriending the victims and gaining their confidence and friendship. They may become involved in activities or programs that interest the type of victims they want to attract and that provide them with easy access to these children. They may also use drugs or alcohol as a means of seduction, reducing the child's inhibitions.

Pedophiles may obtain, collect and maintain photographs of the children with whom they are or have been involved with. Many pedophiles maintain diaries of their sexual encounters with children. They may collect books, magazines, newspapers and other writings on the subject of sexual activities with children. They may also collect addresses, phone numbers or lists of people who have similar sexual interests.

A relatively new way for pedophiles to locate and attract victims is through the computer. Bilchik (1999) asserts: "The Internet has become a cyberplayground for those who prey on children." Armagh et al. (1999, p. 5) add: "Offenders can use the computer to troll for and communicate with potential victims with minimal risk of being identified." The OJJDP has predicted that by 2002 some 45 million children will be surfing the "net" (Paynter, 1999, p. 52), and as Kopelev (1999, p. 47) cautions: "The very same offenders that once combed the playgrounds seeking victims now lurk in cyberspace." According to McCauley (1996, p. 33):

> One of the more repulsive crimes of the computer age is the proliferation of child pornography on the Internet. Low-cost technology has proved a boon to those who sexually victimize children. Readily available scanning equipment converts photos into computer graphics, while electronic mail transmits digital images anywhere in the world. Data encryption and anonymous e-mail services make enforcement more difficult.

The proliferation of online child pornography is heightened by the "deceptively anonymous lure of the Internet" and perpetuated by "people who think they're indulging in forbidden fantasies in the solitude of their homes" (Fritz, 1998, p. 1A). Lesce (1999, p. 76) observes:

"Pedophile organizations . . . have web sites devoted to justifying sexual contacts with minors and exchanging information among pedophiles." One international online child porn organization under investigation was the Wonderland Club, "to which prospective members were required to supply 10,000 images of child pornography to join" (Fritz, p. 1A).

A **chicken hawk** is an online pedophile who uses chat lines and member profiles to locate potential victims, sometimes posing as another youth to establish a bond. Armagh et al. (p. 7) describe two other broad categories of computer sex offenders:

- Dabbler—usually a typical adolescent searching for pornography, a curious adult with a newly found access to pornography, or a profit-motivated criminal
- Preferential offender—usually a sexually indiscriminate individual with a wide variety of deviant sexual interests or a pedophile with a definite preference for children

Detecting online child pornography can be challenging, but as McCauley (p. 34) notes: "Fortunately for law enforcement, many of the areas that are accessible to online perverts can be monitored by police as well. These include public chat rooms where pedophiles have been known to recruit young victims" (p. 34). However, Lesce (p. 78) points out:

> Pedophiles have always been ahead of the power curve, and law enforcement has trailed, sometimes far behind, in apprehending them. The Internet is merely the latest area in which pedophiles have captured a huge lead because of their networking and technical expertise.

Lesce (p. 76) also notes: "Some [online pedophile organizations] post bulletins exposing law enforcement stings, frustrating these efforts." Another challenge to monitoring child pornography sites is that they are constantly moving because many Internet Service Providers (ISPs) expel them once they become aware of the nature of the site.

Lesce notes (p. 77) that to catch pedophiles, officers (usually U.S. Customs and U.S. Postal Inspectors) may organize a "sting," in which an online advertisement is placed offering child pornography for sale. Those who order the "porn" are subject to arrest if they accept delivery. In the Wonderland Club case, U.S. Customs Service agents, police in 22 states and authorities in 13 other countries used wiretaps, a seized list of user names and search warrants to conduct raids that resulted in approximately 60 arrests worldwide (Fritz, p. 1A). Armagh et al. (pp. 8–9) advise:

> The investigation of the use of computers in child sexual exploitation is complex and may exceed the resources available to your jurisdiction. When initiating an investigation, you should take the following issues into consideration:
>
> - *Jurisdiction.* Will your investigation remain local or extend to Federal or State jurisdiction?
> - *Expertise.* Does your organization have the technical expertise to deal with this investigation?
> - *Equipment.* Does your organization have the equipment needed or the resources to obtain the necessary equipment to conduct this investigation?
> - *Time/Personnel.* Does your organization have the time and personnel to devote to this type of investigation? Is it willing to do so?
> - *Followup.* Can your organization perform the necessary followup on additional suspects and victims that may arise from the investigation?

Many pedophiles are members of sex rings.

Child Sexual Abuse Rings

Adults (at least 10 to 15 years older than the victims) are usually the dominant leaders, organizers and operators of sex rings. The adult leader selectively gathers young people together for sexual purposes. The involvement varies, with the longest periods occurring when prepubescent children are involved. Most cases involve male ringleaders, but some involve a female as well, usually a husband/wife pair.

Many ringleaders use their *occupation* as the major access route to the child victims. The adult has a legitimate role as an authority figure in the lives of the children selected for the ring or is able to survey vulnerable children through access to family records or history.

Sometimes rings are formed by an adult targeting a *child,* who then uses his or her connections and peer pressure to bring other children into the group. The initial child may be a relative or a previously unknown child. One common technique is to post a notice on a store bulletin board requesting girls to help with housework.

The adult's status in the *neighborhood* sometimes helps to legitimize his presence with the children and their parents and to permit unquestioned movement of young people into his home. Such an offender often is well liked by his neighbors.

Types of Sex Rings

Investigators should be aware of three types of sex rings: solo, transition and syndicated. Certain cults are also involved in the sexual abuse of children.

Solo Sex Rings The organization of solo sex rings is primarily by the age of the child—for example, toddlers (ages two to five), prepubescent (six to twelve), or pubescent (thirteen to seventeen). This type of offender prefers to have multiple children as sex objects, in contrast to the offender who seeks out one child at a time.

Transition Sex Rings Although pedophilia is a sex offense in all states, pedophiles have a strong need to communicate with others about their interest in children. In transition rings, experiences are exchanged, whereas in solo rings, the pedophile keeps his or her activities and photographs totally secret. Photographs of children as well as sexual services may be traded and sold.

The trading of pornography appears to be the first move of the victim into the "possession" of other pedophiles. The photographs are traded, and victims may be tested by other offenders and eventually traded for their sexual services.

Syndicated Sex Rings The third type of ring is the syndicated ring, a well-structured organization that recruits children, produces pornography, delivers direct sexual services and establishes an extensive network of customers. Syndicated rings have involved a Boy Scout troop, a boys' farm operated by a minister and a national boy prostitution ring.

Cults Cults are groups that use rituals or ceremonial acts to draw their members together into a certain belief system. According to Wrobleski and Hess (2000, p. 96): "When the rituals of a group involve crimes, . . . [including] child sexual abuse . . ., they become a problem for law enforcement." Crimes associated with cults are discussed in Chapter 19.

Sex Crimes by Other Children

Although seldom discussed, an increasing number of child sex crimes are being committed by other children. Many people think that such crimes do not occur because they often view children as not being sexually capable. However, arrests of 12- to 14-year-olds for sexual offenses increased 70 percent during the 1980s. Some child sexual abusers were molested themselves. When investigators receive reports of children committing sex crimes against other children, they must not automatically dismiss them as fantasy and must thoroughly investigate all such reports.

Victimology

People involved in the intervention, investigation or prosecution of child pornography and sex ring cases must recognize that a bond often develops between the offender and the victims. Many victims find themselves willing to trade sex for attention, affection and other benefits. Pedophile ring operators are, by definition, skilled at gaining the continued cooperation and control of their victims through well-planned seduction. They are skilled at recognizing and then *temporarily* filling the emotional and physical needs of children. They know how to listen to children—an ability many parents lack. They are willing to spend all the time it takes to seduce a child.

This positive offender/victim bond must not be misinterpreted as consent, complicity or guilt. In one case a prosecutor announced to television reporters that the victims were as guilty as—if not more guilty than—the offenders. Police investigators, in particular, must be sensitive to this problem.

Offender Reactions

When a child pornography and sex ring is discovered, certain reactions by the pedophile offenders are fairly predictable. The intensity of these reactions may depend on how much the offenders have to lose by their identification and conviction.

Usually a pedophile's first reaction to discovery is complete denial. The offenders may act shocked, surprised or even indignant about an allegation of sexual activity with children. This denial frequently is aided by their friends, neighbors, relatives and co-workers, who insist that such wonderful people could not have done what is alleged.

If the evidence rules out total denial, offenders may switch to a slightly different tactic, attempting to minimize what they have done in both quantity and quality. Pedophiles are often knowledgeable about the law and might admit to acts that are lesser offenses or misdemeanors.

Either as part of the effort to minimize or as a separate reaction, pedophiles typically attempt to justify their behavior. They might claim that they care for these children more than their parents do and that what they do is beneficial to the children. They may claim to have been under tremendous stress, have a drinking problem or not to have known how young a certain victim was. The efforts to justify their behavior often center around blaming the victim. Offenders may claim that they were seduced by the victims, that the victims initiated the sexual activity or that the victims were promiscuous or even prostitutes.

When various reactions do not result in termination of the investigation or prosecution, pedophiles may claim to be sick and unable to control themselves. Pedophile manuals advocate this tactic when all else fails.

Pedophiles' reactions to being discovered usually begin with complete denial and then progress to minimizing the acts, justifying the acts and blaming the victims. If all else fails, they may claim to be sick.

Difficulty in Prosecuting

According to Lesce (1997, p. 104):

> There are problems prosecuting pedophile rings because organized child molesters employ sophisticated communications, exchange information regarding counter-measures to police efforts, and freely cross multiple jurisdictions in their search for victims.

Furthermore (Lesce, p. 104): "Multiple jurisdictions hamper prosecution because the definition of child molestation varies."

Another complicating factor in prosecuting pedophiles is that the stigma of such arrests can lead suspects to commit suicide. Citing the decision of 49-year-old retired Air Force pilot Kenneth Nighbert to take his own life, Fritz (p. 1A) states:

> Nighbert is notable not just because U.S. Customs Service agents had filed a lawsuit to seize possession of

his home—a weapon they say they will increasingly deploy against Internet-cruising pedophiles—or because he was suspected of being a member of a multinational club of men who swapped child pornography and commiserated inside a secret, exclusive chat room known as Wonderland. Or that he was swept up last month in the biggest Internet porn sting in history.

What makes his case unusual is the fact that his death was not: Nighbert is the fourth person to commit suicide from the 34 Americans either charged or somehow suspected in the case. Authorities say such deaths have become common, and in most instances the suicide victims are seemingly upstanding people. . . .

These people, experts say, are most likely to find suicide the only escape—not only from a possible prison sentence, but from humiliation and social censure on a scale beyond comprehension.

Children as Witnesses in Court

With the increase in criminal cases involving physical and sexual abuse of children, the problems associated with children providing testimony in court have increased proportionately. Court procedures and legal practices that benefit the child witness may not be balanced with the rights of the accused, and vice versa. To resolve some of these problems, the courts have changed a number of rules and procedures, such as the following:

- Some courts give preference to these cases by placing them ahead of other cases on the docket.

- Some courts permit videotaping child interviews and then providing access to the tapes to numerous individuals to spare the child the added trauma of multiple interviews.

- Courts are limiting privileges for repeated medical and psychological examinations of children.

- To reduce the number of times the child must face the accused, the courts are allowing testimony concerning observations of the child by another person who is not a witness, allowing the child to remain in another room during the trial and/or using a videotape of the child's testimony as evidence.

- Some courts remove the accused from the courtroom during the child's testimony.

Many of these changes in rules and procedures are being challenged, however. For example: "The Pennsylvania Supreme Court has struck down a state constitutional amendment that allowed children to testify as victims or witnesses to a crime via videotaped depositions or closed-circuit television, in order to spare them further trauma" ("Closed-Circuit Testimony . . .," 1999, p. 6). In this case, the court ruled the amendment "violated a provision of the state constitution giving defendants the right to meet the witnesses face to face." Future court decisions will establish precedents to be followed in child abuse and neglect cases.

Despite some courts' stance that children should be made to testify in court as any other victim or witness, some studies have provided evidence that courtroom testimony is not always the best way to elicit accurate information from children. Regarding two groups of children, one of which was interviewed at their school and one of which was interviewed in the courtroom, Saywitz and Nathanson (1998, p. 11) report:

- Children interviewed at school recalled significantly more correct items than children interviewed at court on the free recall part of the questioning.

- For probed questions, children interviewed at court gave significantly more incorrect responses to probed questions than children interviewed at school.

- Children interviewed at school made significantly fewer errors on misleading questions than did children interviewed at court.

- Children interviewed at court perceived their experience as significantly more stressful on some of the measures than children interviewed at school.

- The more stressful children perceived their court experience to be, the fewer correct items they reported in free recall.

If children will be testifying in court, several courtroom preparation techniques are recommended by Whitcomb (p. 6) to improve their testimony and place them more at ease, including:

- Tours of courtrooms and introductions to key court personnel

- Coloring or activity books

- Miniature-sized courtrooms with moveable figures and furniture
- Videotapes explaining the court process

Preventing Crimes against Children

Crimes against children may be prevented by educating them about potential danger and by keeping the channels of communication open.

Child abusers can be of any race, age or occupation; they can be someone close or a complete stranger. When given adequate information, children can avoid dangerous situations and better protect themselves against such predators.

The following specific suggestions should assist in preventing crimes against children. Although the suggestions refer to parents, they apply equally to guardians or other individuals who care for children.

- Parents should teach their children about sexual abuse, what forms it might take and what to do about it. Children should learn to discuss sex questions with their parents. They should know what sexual abuse is, including anyone touching their anus, penis, vagina or breasts. They should learn to tell their parents if they encounter any abnormal sexual behavior from adults.

- Parents should listen to their children. Children may drop subtle hints such as "Uncle Charlie was not very nice to me today." An appropriate response might be "Oh? How was he not nice?" Such a response might elicit a statement such as "He asked me to take down my pants when I was in the car."

- Children should be instructed to tell their parents when someone tells them, "Don't tell anyone." Usually if someone says not to tell, it is about something that is wrong.

- Parents should understand that children do not usually tell tales about sexual abuse. Experience has taught parents and police that the vast majority of sexual abuse incidents that children tell are true. Therefore, if a child tells a parent about being sexually abused, the parents should report it to the police immediately.

- Older children should be taught to tell their parents where they are going, with whom and approximately when they expect to return. They should learn to call home if plans change.

- Children should be taught to stay with the group when they are on picnics or at events away from home and that if they become lost, they are to go to an area where people are present and seek help.

- Children should be taught that when they are home alone they should lock the doors and windows and never let strangers in. Parents should see that doors and windows are locked before they leave the child alone. They should also give proper instructions for leaving the home in case of fire.

- Children should be taught that sometimes it is all right to tell a lie. For example, if a child is home alone and receives a phone call for one of the parents, it is all right to say the parents are home but cannot come to the phone because they are resting or in the shower or some other excuse.

- Parents should help children plan safe routes to and from school and their friends' homes. Children should then travel these routes. "Block parent" programs can provide places where children can stop if in danger, or the parents should tell their children what houses they can stop at where friends of the family live. Children should be taught to play in groups; to avoid vacant buildings, alleys and restrooms; and to walk with friends when possible.

- Baby sitters should be selected carefully. Parents should always request and check references.

Digital technology is allowing police to become more effective in preventing and handling crimes against children. For example, some law enforcement departments are teaming up with schools and the community to create digital files of local children in a step toward discouraging child abduction. Such files contain digitized photographs, fingerprints and other personal information of area students and, because of their digital nature, can be dispatched within minutes to any law enforcement agency, business or other organization involved in the search for a missing child.

Summary

Crimes against children include kidnapping, abandonment, neglect, exploitation, physical abuse, emotional abuse, incest and sexual assault. Such crimes can result in permanent and serious damage physically, mentally and emotionally. The Child Protection Act prohibits child pornography and greatly increases the penalties for adults who engage in it.

Challenges in investigating crimes against children include the need to protect the child from further harm, the possibility of parental involvement, the difficulty in interviewing children, credibility concerns and the need to collaborate with other agencies.

The primary responsibility of the responding officer is the safety of the child, and if the possibility of present or continued danger to the child exists, the child must be placed in protective custody. When interviewing children, officers should consider the child's age, ability to describe what happened and the potential for retaliation by the suspect against a child who "tells." In the vast majority of child abuse cases, children tell the truth to the best of their ability. The current trend in investigating crimes against children is to use a multidisciplinary team (MDT), a group of professionals who work together in a coordinated and collaborative manner to ensure an effective response to reports of child abuse and neglect.

Most reports of child neglect or abuse are made by third parties such as teachers, neighbors, siblings and parents. Seldom does the victim report the offense. When such reports are received, investigators must look for evidence of the crime, including the surroundings, the home conditions, clothing, bruises or other body injuries, the medical examination report and other observations. Investigators should also listen carefully to children and should look for indicators of neglect or abuse. These indicators may be physical or behavioral or both.

Investigators should also be aware of pedophiles—adults who have either heterosexual or homosexual preferences for young boys or girls of a specific, limited age range. Many pedophiles are members of sex rings, three types of which have been identified: solo, transition and syndicated. Certain cults also practice sexual abuse of children. Pedophiles' reactions to being discovered usually begin with complete denial and progress through minimizing the acts, justifying the acts and blaming the victims. If all else fails, they may claim to be sick.

Crimes against children can be prevented by educating them about potential dangers and by keeping the channels of communication with them open.

Checklist

Crimes against Children

- What statute has been violated, if any?
- What are the elements of the offense charged?
- Who initiated the crime?
- Are there witnesses to the offense?
- What evidence is needed to prove the elements of the offense charged?
- Is there physical evidence?
- Has physical evidence been submitted for laboratory examination?
- Who has been interviewed?
- Are written statements available?
- Would a polygraph be of any assistance in examining the victim? The suspect?
- Is there probable cause to obtain a search warrant?
- What items should you include in the search?
- Is the victim able to provide specific dates and times?
- Is the victim able to provide details of what happened?
- What physical and behavorial indicators are present in this case?
- Were photographs taken of the victim's injuries?
- Is the victim in danger of continued abuse?
- Is it necessary to remove the victim into protective custody?
- Has the local welfare agency been notified? Was there a joint investigation to avoid duplication of effort?
- Is there a file on known sexual offenders in the community?
- Is a child sexual abuse ring involved in the offense?
- Could the offense have been prevented? How?

Application

A. A police officer receives an anonymous call reporting sexual abuse of a 10-year-old white female. The caller states that the abusers are the father and brother of the girl and provides all three names and their address. When the officer requests more details, the caller hangs up. You are assigned the case and initiate the investigation by contacting the alleged victim at school. She is reluctant to talk to you at first but eventually admits that both her father and brother have been having sex with her for almost a year. You then question the suspects and obtain written statements in which they admit the sexual abuse.

Questions

1. Should the investigation have been initiated on the basis of the anonymous caller?
2. What type of crime has been committed?
3. Was it appropriate to make the initial contact with the victim at her school?
4. Who should be present at the victim's initial interview?
5. What should be done with the victim after obtaining the facts?
6. What would be the basis for an affidavit for an arrest warrant?

B. A police officer receives an anonymous phone call stating that a child is being sexually assaulted at a specific address. The officer goes to the address—an apartment—and through an open door sees a child lying on the floor, apparently unconscious. The officer enters the apartment and, while checking the child for injuries, notices blood on the child's face and clothing. The child regains consciousness, and the officer asks, "Did your dad do this?" The child answers, "Yes." The officer then goes into another room and finds the father in bed, intoxicated. He rouses him and places him under arrest.

Questions

1. Was the officer authorized to enter the apartment on the basis of the initial information?
2. Was the officer authorized to enter without a warrant?
3. Should the officer have asked whether the father had injured the child? If not, how should the question have been phrased?
4. Was an arrest of the father justified without a warrant?
5. What should be done with the victim?

C. A woman living in another state telephones the police department and identifies herself as the ex-wife of a man she believes is performing illegal sexual acts with the daughter of his present lover. The man resides in the police department's jurisdiction. The woman says the acts have been witnessed by her sons who have been in the area visiting their father. The sons told her that the father goes into the bathroom and bedroom with his lover's eight-year-old daughter and closes the door. They also have seen the father making suggestive advances to the girl and taking her into the shower with him. The girl has told her sons that the father does "naughty" things to her. Her sons are currently at home with her, but she is worried about the little girl.

Questions

1. Should an investigation be initiated based on this third-hand information?
2. If the report is founded, what type of crime is being committed?
3. Who has jurisdiction to investigate?
4. What actions would be necessary in the noninitiating state?
5. Where should the initial contact with the alleged victim be made?

D. A reliable informant has told the police that a man has been molesting children in his garage. Police establish a surveillance of the suspect and see him invite a juvenile into his car. They follow the car and see it pull into the driveway of the man's residence. The man and the boy then go into the house. The officers follow and knock on the front door but receive no answer. They knock again and loudly state their purpose. Continuing to receive no answer, they enter the house through the unlocked front door, talk to the boy and based on what he says, they arrest the suspect.

Questions

1. Did the officers violate the suspect's right to privacy and domestic security?
2. Does the emergency doctrine apply?
3. What should be done with the victim?
4. Was the arrest legal?
    Note: In each of the preceding cases, the information is initially received not from the victim but from third parties. This is usually the case in child abuse offenses.

Discussion Questions

1. At what age does a child cease to be a minor in your state?

2. What is the child sexual-abuse problem in your community? How many offenses were charged during the past year? Is there any method of estimating how many unreported offenses occurred?

3. What are some common physical and behavioral abuse indicators?

4. What evidence is commonly found in child sexual-abuse cases?

5. What types of evidence are needed for establishing probable cause for a search warrant?

6. Who are suspects in child sexual-abuse cases?

7. What statutes in your state or community are applicable to prosecuting child sexual-abuse cases?

8. What are some special difficulties in interviewing children? In having children testify in court?

9. What is being done in your community to prevent crimes against children?

10. Have any sex rings been exposed in your community? Your state?

References

Allen, Earnest E. "Keeping Children Safe: Rhetoric and Reality." *Juvenile Justice,* Vol. V, No. 1, May 1998, pp. 16–23.

Armagh, Daniel S.; Battaglia, Nick L.; and Lanning, Kenneth V. *Use of Computers in the Sexual Exploitation of Children.* Washington, DC: Office of Juvenile Justice and Delinquency Prevention, June 1999. (NCJ-170021)

Bilchik, Shay. "From the Administrator." In *In the Wake of Childhood Maltreatment* by Barbara Tatem Kelley, Terence P. Thornberry and Carolyn A. Smith. Washington, DC: Office of Juvenile Justice and Delinquency Prevention, Juvenile Justice Bulletin, August 1997, p. 1. (NCJ-165257)

Bilchik, Shay. "Foreword." In *Use of Computers in the Sexual Exploitation of Children* by Daniel S. Armagh, Nick L. Battaglia and Kenneth V. Lanning. Washington, DC: Office of Juvenile Justice and Delinquency Prevention, June 1999. (NCJ-170021)

Birge, Anne C. "Münchausen Syndrome by Proxy." *Law and Order,* March 1996, pp. 91–96.

Bradford, C. O. "TRAKing Abducted Kids." *Community Policing Exchange,* July/August 1998, p. 3.

Cart, Julie. " 'Utah's Dirty Little Secret.' " (Minneapolis/ St. Paul) *Star Tribune,* August 24, 1998, p. A3.

"Chicago Couple Face Multiple Charges of Long-Term Abuse of Four Children." (Minneapolis/ St. Paul) *Star Tribune,* February 7, 1996, p. A8.

"Closed-Circuit Testimony by Children Struck Down." *Criminal Justice Newsletter,* Vol. 30, No. 4, February 16, 1999, p. 6.

Drowns, Robert W. and Hess, Kären M. *Juvenile Justice,* 3rd ed. Belmont, CA: Wadsworth Publishing Company, 2000.

Ells, Mark. *Forming a Multidisciplinary Team to Investigate Child Abuse.* Washington, DC: Office of Juvenile Justice and Delinquency Prevention, November 1998. (NCJ-170020)

Ennis, Charles. "Child Protection Teamwork." *Law and Order,* Vol. 47, No. 4, April 1999, pp. 55–58.

Esposito, Linda; Minda, Larry; and Forman, Claire. "Sudden Infant Death Syndrome." *FBI Law Enforcement Bulletin,* Vol. 67, No. 9, September 1998, pp. 1–5.

Fritz, Mark. "Child Porn Arrests Can Lead to Suicides." *Las Vegas Review Journal,* October 25, 1998, pp. 1A, 24A.

Goldstein, Seth L. and Tyler, R. P. "Frustrations of Inquiry: Child Sexual Abuse Allegations in Divorce and Custody Cases." *FBI Law Enforcement Bulletin,* Vol. 67, No. 7, July 1998, pp. 1–6.

Johnson, Richard R. "A Patrol Officer's Guide to Identifying Child Abuse." *Law and Order,* Vol. 46, No. 4, April 1998, pp. 77–79.

Kelley, Barbara Tatem; Thornberry, Terence P.; and Smith, Carolyn A. *In the Wake of Childhood Maltreatment.* Washington, DC: Office of Juvenile Justice and Delinquency Prevention, Juvenile Justice Bulletin, August 1997. (NCJ-165257)

Kopelev, Sergio D. "Cyber Sex Offenders: How to Proactively Investigate Internet Crimes against Children." *Law Enforcement Technology,* Vol. 26, No. 11, November 1999, pp. 46–50.

Laws, Michael E. "Substantiating Children's Statements in Sexual Abuse Cases." *The Police Chief,* Vol. LXVI, No. 9, September 1999, pp. 37–38.

Lemmon, John H. "How Child Maltreatment Affects Dimensions of Juvenile Delinquency in a Cohort of

Low-Income Urban Youths." *Justice Quarterly,* Vol. 16, No. 2, June 1999, pp. 357–376.

Lesce, Tony. "Albuquerque Pedophile Unit." *Law and Order,* Vol. 45, No. 3, March 1997, pp. 103–107.

Lesce, Tony. "Pedophiles on the Internet: Law Enforcement Investigates Abuse." *Law and Order,* Vol. 47, No. 5, May 1999, pp. 74–78.

Maynard, Rebecca A. and Garry, Eillen M. *Adolescent Motherhood: Implications for the Juvenile Justice System.* Fact Sheet #50. Washington, DC: Office of Juvenile Justice and Delinquency Prevention, January 1997. (FS-9750)

McCauley, Dennis. "Hi-Tech Crooks." *Police,* Vol. 20, No. 12, December 1996, pp. 32–49.

Paynter, Ronnie L. "Riding the Cyber Wave." *Law Enforcement Technology,* Vol. 26, No. 11, November 1999, pp. 52–55.

Quill, Emmett H. and Yahner, Joseph. "A Partnership that Works, for Kids' Sake." *Law Enforcement News,* Vol. XXV, No. 506, February 28, 1999, pp. 8, 10.

Saywitz, Karen J.; Geiselman, R. Edward; and Bornstein, Gail K. "Effects of Cognitive Interviewing and Practice on Children's Recall Performance." In *Legal Interventions in Family Violence: Research Findings and Policy Implications.* Washington, DC: National Institute of Justice, July 1998, pp. 7–8. (NCJ-171666)

Saywitz, Karen J. and Nathanson, Rebecca. "Children's Testimony and Their Perceptions of Stress in and out of the Courtroom." In *Legal Interventions in Family Violence: Research Findings and Policy Implications.* Washington, DC: National Institute of Justice, July 1998, pp. 10–11. (NCJ-171666)

Stephenson. "When Adults Hurt Kids." *Instant Evidence,* Summer 1996, pp. 8–9.

Strandberg, Keith W. "Child and Elder Abuse." *Law Enforcement Technology,* Vol. 26, No. 6, June 1999, pp. 20–22.

"Studies Identify Risks to Adolescents' Safety, Health." *NCJA Justice Bulletin,* October 1997, pp. 7–12.

"Study Says Sexual Abuse of Boys Underreported, Little Treated." *Las Vegas Review Journal,* December 2, 1998, p. 9A.

"Two-Thirds of Prisoners Were Abused as Children, Study Finds." *Criminal Justice Newsletter,* April 15, 1998, pp. 7–8.

U.K. Osteogenesis Imperfecta Foundation: http://www.ukoifoundation.org/fs2.htm

U.S. Osteogenesis Imperfecta Foundation: http://www.oif.org/tier2/childabuse.htm

Whitcomb, Debra. "Techniques for Improving Children's Testimony." In *Legal Interventions in Family Violence: Research Findings and Policy Implications.* Washington, DC: National Institute of Justice, July 1998, pp. 4–6. (NCJ-171666)

Wolfe, David A.; Jaffe, Peter; Wilson, Susan Kaye; and Zak, Lydia. "Impact of Domestic Violence on Children's Behavior." In *Legal Interventions in Family Violence: Research Findings and Policy Implications.* Washington, DC: National Institute of Justice, July 1998, pp. 25–26. (NCJ-171666)

Wrobleski, Henry M. and Hess, Kären M. *Introduction to Law Enforcement and Criminal Justice,* 6th ed. Belmont, CA: Wadsworth Publishing Company, 2000.

"Young People Exposed to Violence More Likely to Experience Stress Disorder." *NCJA Justice Bulletin,* Vol. 19, No. 7, July 1999, pp. 14–17.

Homicide

Do You Know?

What a basic requirement in a homicide investigation is?

What the four categories of death are?

How to define and classify homicide, murder and manslaughter?

What degrees of murder are frequently specified?

How criminal and noncriminal homicide differ?

How excusable and justifiable homicide differ?

What the elements of each category of murder and manslaughter are?

What special challenges are encountered in a homicide investigation?

What the first priority in a homicide investigation is?

How to establish that death has occurred?

How to identify an unknown homicide victim?

What factors help in estimating the time of death?

What cadaveric spasm is and why it is important?

What effect water has on a dead body?

What the most frequent causes of unnatural death are and what indicates whether a death is a suicide or a homicide?

What information and evidence are obtained from a victim?

Why determining a motive is important in homicide investigations?

What physical evidence is usually found in homicides?

What information is provided by the medical examiner or coroner?

Introduction

You arrive at the scene of a death in response to an emergency call and find the body of a 55-year-old white male crumpled at the bottom of a steep staircase—obviously dead. Did the victim trip and fall (accidental death)? Did he suffer a fatal heart attack at the top of the stairs and then fall (natural death)? Did he throw himself down the stairs to end some intense physical or mental suffering (suicide)? Or was he pushed (homicide)?

Only the fourth explanation involves a criminal action meriting an official police investigation. However, because the police must determine whether it actually was homicide, the other three possible explanations must be investigated.

A basic requirement in a homicide investigation is to establish whether death was caused by a criminal action.

Statistically, murder is the least significant of the Index Crimes. However, deaths reported as accidents or suicides may actually have been murder, and vice versa. It may be necessary to determine whether a death was a murder made to appear as a suicide to eliminate further investigation or a murder made to appear as an accident to collect life insurance.

Because homicides have received increasingly extensive media attention, it may appear as if these crimes are occurring more frequently. However, according to Fox and Zawitz (1999, p. 1): "With the largest cities leading the way, the Nation's murder rate in 1997 fell to its lowest level in three decades." They also note: "Homicide is of interest not only because of its severity but also because it is a fairly reliable barometer of all violent crime. At a national level, no other crime is measured as accurately and precisely." The most recent homicide statistics (Fox and Zawitz, pp. 2–3) show the following:

Males are most often the victims and the perpetrators in homicides: males were more than 9 times more likely than females to commit murder, and male and female offenders were more likely to target male than female victims. . . .

Blacks were seven times more likely than whites to be homicide victims and eight times more likely than whites to commit homicides.

Eighty-five percent of white murder victims were killed by whites, and 94% of black victims were killed by blacks. . . .

The number of homicides cleared by arrest of the perpetrator has been declining: 66% of all homicides were cleared in 1997 compared to 79% in 1976.

Confronted with rising debts and a failing marriage, Mark Barton went on a shooting spree in two downtown Atlanta office buildings in June 1999, killing nine people and wounding 13 others before committing suicide. It was later learned that Barton had also bludgeoned his wife and two children to death prior to the office shooting.

Homicides continue to receive the most attention by police, not only because they are considered the most serious crime but also because they are complex cases to investigate.

This chapter begins with a classification of homicide and descriptions of criminal homicide, noncriminal homicide and suicide. It then discusses the elements of the crime, special problems in investigating homicides and the preliminary investigation. Next the chapter focuses on identifying the victim and estimating the time of death. Then it presents a discussion of unnatural causes of death and the method used, as well as drug-related homicides. Then follows an examination of victims, witnesses and suspects and a look at the physical evidence often found in homicide investigations. The chapter concludes with a description of the role of the medical examination, the importance of collaborative efforts in investigating homicides and the unpleasant task of death notification. ■

Classification

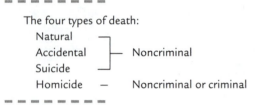

The four types of death:
Natural
Accidental ⎤
Suicide ⎦—— Noncriminal
Homicide —— Noncriminal or criminal

Natural Causes

Natural causes of death include heart attacks, strokes, fatal diseases, pneumonia, sudden crib deaths and old age. Frequently, a person who dies of natural causes has been under a physician's care, and a death from natural causes is easily established.

Sometimes, however, a death is made to look as though it resulted from natural causes. For example, drugs that simulate the effects of a heart attack might be used in a suicide or homicide.

Accidental Deaths

Among the causes of accidental death are falling, drowning, unintentionally taking too many pills or ingesting a poisonous substance, entanglement in industrial or farm machinery or involvement in an automobile, boat, train, bus or plane crash.

Some are advocating that certain accidental deaths be investigated as criminal homicide. For example, Kinchin (1999, p. 41) notes that some police forces in England are treating fatal road accidents as murders:

> When a dead body is found lying in an alleyway, it is investigated as a major incident. But, if the same body is discovered in a car after a road smash, the incident is treated as a fatal road accident that does not involve the same level of investigation. . . .
>
> A murder investigation can routinely involve 30 officers. A fatal road accident (fatacc) investigation is usually completed by just one officer.
>
> Essex Police believe this is wrong and now approach fatalities in the same way as they might approach a murder.

As with natural deaths, an apparently accidental death can actually be a suicide or a homicide. For example, a person can jump or be pushed from a roof or in front of a vehicle or can voluntarily or involuntarily take an overdose of pills.

Suicide

Suicide—the intentional taking of one's own life—can be committed by shooting, stabbing, poison, burns, asphyxiation or ingesting drugs or poisons. However, homicides are often made to look like suicides, and many suicides are made to look like accidents, usually for insurance purposes or to ease the family's suffering. In most states it is not a crime to commit suicide, but aiding and abetting or assisting suicides is controversial. Is such assistance a crime or not?

Although suicide is not a criminal offense, in most states it is a crime to attempt to commit suicide. This allows the state to take legal custody of such individuals for hospitalization or treatment. It may be a crime to help someone commit or attempt to commit suicide either by intentionally advising, encouraging or actually assisting the victim in the act, as previously noted.

At the center of this controversy are the actions of Jack Kevorkian, "Dr. Death," an assisted-suicide crusader who has assisted in more than 130 suicides since 1990. After being tried four times on assisted suicide charges, with three acquittals and one mistrial, Kevorkian was eventually tried for murder, found guilty and sent to prison. In defending his actions, Kevorkian stated: "To have a crime, you need a vicious will and a vicious act. . . .What I was trying to prove here was that I didn't have the intent to kill, just as the executioner doesn't. But he's forced to do it by his position" ("Kevorkian Says He . . . ," 1999, p. A4).

Homicide

If another individual is the direct or indirect cause of the death, the death is classified as homicide.

Homicide is the killing of one person by another.

Homicide includes the taking of life by another human or by an agency, such as a government. It is either criminal or noncriminal, that is, felonious or nonfelonious. **Criminal homicide** is subdivided into murder and manslaughter, both of which are further subdivided. **Noncriminal homicide** is subdivided into excusable and justifiable homicide.

```
- - - - - - -
    Classification of homicides:
       Criminal (felonious)
          Murder (first, second and third degree)
          Manslaughter (voluntary and involuntary)
       Noncriminal (nonfelonious)
          Excusable homicide
          Justifiable homicide
- - - - - - - -
```

Thus, *murder* and *homicide* are not synonymous. All murders are homicides (and criminal), but not all homicides are murders (or criminal).

Criminal Homicide

The two classes of criminal homicide—murder and manslaughter—have several similarities but also important differences.

Murder

Murder is the most severe statutory crime, one of the few for which the penalty can be life imprisonment or death. (In some states treason and ransom kidnapping carry a similarly severe penalty.) Some laws classify murder as first, second or third degree. **First-degree murder** requires premeditation (advanced planning) and the intent to cause death. Some statutes include in this classification any death that results while committing or attempting to commit a felony such as rape or robbery. **Second-degree murder** includes the intent to cause death but not premeditation. An example is a violent argument that ends in one person spontaneously killing the other. **Third-degree murder** involves neither premeditation nor intent. It results from an act that is imminently dangerous to others and shows a disregard for human life, such as shooting into a room where people are likely to be present or playing a practical joke that might result in someone's death.

Manslaughter

Manslaughter is the unlawful killing of another person with no prior malice. It may be voluntary or involuntary.

Voluntary manslaughter is intentionally causing the death of another person in the heat of passion, caused by words or acts that provide adequate provocation. For example, the law generally recognizes such acts as adultery, seduction of a child or rape of a close female relative as outrageous enough to constitute adequate provocation. This provocation must result in intense passion that replaces reason and leads to the immediate act. The provocation, passion and fatal act must occur in rapid succession and be directly, sequentially related; that is, the provocation must cause the passion that causes the fatal act.

Involuntary manslaughter is accidental homicide that results from extreme (culpable) negligence. Examples of involuntary manslaughter include handling a firearm negligently, leaving poison where children might take it or operating an automobile, boat or aircraft in a criminally negligent manner. Some states, such as California, have a third category of manslaughter: manslaughter with a motor vehicle.

Other acts that can be classified as involuntary manslaughter include shooting another person with a firearm or other dangerous weapon while mistakenly believing that person to be an animal; setting a spring gun, pitfall, deadfall, snare or other dangerous device designed to trap animals but capable of harming humans; and negligently and intentionally allowing a known vicious animal to roam free.

```
- - - - - - - -
Murder
   First degree      Premeditated and intentional, or
                     while committing or attempting to
                     commit a felony
   Second degree     Intentional but not premeditated
   Third degree      Neither intentional nor premedi-
                     tated, but the result of an immi-
                     nently dangerous act
Manslaughter
   Voluntary         Intentional homicide caused by
                     intense passion resulting from ade-
                     quate provocation
   Involuntary       Unintentional homicide caused by
                     criminal (culpable) negligence
- - - - - - - -
```

Noncriminal Homicide

Although the term *homicide* is usually associated with crime, not all homicides are crimes.

```
- - - - - - - -
```

Excusable homicide is the unintentional, truly accidental killing of another person. **Justifiable homicide** is killing another person under authorization of the law.

```
- - - - - - - -
```

Excusable homicide results from an act that normally would not cause death or from an act committed with ordinary caution that, because of the *victim's* negligence, results in death, as when a person runs in front of a moving car.

Justifiable homicide includes killing in self-defense or in the defense of another person if the victim's actions and capability present imminent danger of serious injury or death. Killing an enemy during wartime is also classified as justifiable homicide. This classification further includes capital punishment, death caused by a public officer while carrying out a court order and deaths caused by police officers while attempting to prevent a dangerous felon's escape or to recapture a dangerous felon who has escaped or is resisting arrest.

Some research suggests that police use of deadly force is strongly influenced by the dangerousness of the particular time periods in which officers are working. A study by MacDonald et al. (1999, p. 162) found that:

> Robbery-related and justifiable citizen homicides represent clear patterns of violence which affect the police and publics [sic] perception of the dangers of police work. Therefore, police are more likely to use deadly force during time periods when the frequency of these incidents is at their highest level, and the perceived threat to themselves and the general public is particularly high.

Elements of the Crime

Laws on criminal homicide vary significantly from state to state, but certain common elements are usually found in each, as summarized in Table 13.1. The degree eventually charged is decided by the prosecuting attorney based on the available evidence. For example, the only difference between first- and second-degree murder is the element of premeditation. If thorough investigation does not yield proof of premeditation, a charge of second-degree murder is made.

Causing the Death of Another Human Usually the death of a human is not difficult to prove; a death certificate completed by a physician, coroner or medical examiner suffices. If a death certificate is not available, the investigator must locate witnesses to testify that they saw the body of the person allegedly killed by the suspect. When insufficient remains exist to identify the body positively, death is proven by circumstantial evidence such as examination by a qualified pathologist or by other experts and their expert testimony regarding dental work, bone structure and the like.

A more difficult portion of the element to prove is the cause of death. To show that the suspect's act caused the death: (1) prove the cause of death and (2) prove that the suspect, through direct action, inflicted injury sufficient to cause the death with some weapon or device. For example, if the cause of death was a fatal wound from a .22-caliber weapon, it is necessary to show that the suspect produced the cause of death. Did the suspect own such a weapon? Can witnesses testify that the suspect had such a weapon immediately before the fatal injury? Was the suspect seen actually committing the offense? Did the suspect admit the act by statement or confession?

Premeditation **Premeditation** is considering, planning or preparing for an act, no matter how briefly, before committing it. Laws use such terms as *premeditated design to kill* or *malice of forethought*. Whatever the law's wording, it is necessary to prove some intention and plan to commit the crime before it was actually committed.

-- -- -- -- -- --

Premeditation is the element of first-degree murder that sets it apart from all other classifications.

-- -- -- -- -- --

Were oral statements or threats made during a heated argument? Did the suspect buy or have a gun just before the crime was committed or travel a long distance to wait for the victim? Premeditation can be proved in many ways. Sometimes the time interval between thought and action is only a minute; other times it may be hours, days, weeks, months or even years.

Determine at what time before the killing the suspect considered, planned, threatened or made some overt act to prepare to commit the murder. This might be established by statements from witnesses or from the victim before death, from evidence at the crime scene or through a review of the suspect's criminal history and past statements.

Intent to Effect the Death of Another Person Intent is a required element of most categories of criminal homicide. Evidence must show that the crime was intentional, not accidental. **Malicious intent,** an element of first- and second-degree murder, implies ill will, wickedness or cruelty. How the act was committed shows the degree of intent. The type of weapon used, how and when it was acquired and how the suspect and victim came together helps prove the intent as well as the act that caused the death.

Table 13.1 **Degrees of Homicide**

Element	Murder			Manslaughter	
	First Degree	Second Degree	Third Degree	Voluntary	Involuntary
Causing the death of another human	**	**	**	**	**
Premeditation	*				
Malicious intent	*	*			
Adequately provoked intent resulting in the heat of passion				*	
†While committing or attempting to commit a felony	*				
†While committing or attempting to commit a crime not a felony			*	*	
When forced or threatened				*	
Culpable negligence or depravity			*		
Negligence					*

†Indicates that the other single-starred elements need not be proven.

Intent and premeditation are not the same. Premeditation is not a requirement of intent. Most crimes of passion involve intent but not premeditation or malicious intent.

This element also applies to a death caused to someone other than the intended victim. For example, in one case a woman intended to kill her husband by placing poison in a bottle of whiskey he kept under the seat of the family car. Unknowingly, the husband offered a drink from the bottle to a friend, who died as a result. The wife was charged with first-degree murder and convicted even though the person who died was not her intended victim. It was a reasonable consequence of her act. An explosive set for one person may detonate prematurely and kill someone else. A person shooting at an intended victim may miss and kill an innocent bystander. Both of these would constitute first-degree murder.

Adequately Provoked Intent Resulting from Heat of Passion

This element is the alternative to premeditation. It assumes that the act was committed when the suspect suddenly became extremely emotional, thus precluding premeditation. **Heat of passion** results from extremely volatile arguments between two people, from seeing a wife or family member raped, from a sudden discovery of adultery or from seeing a brutal assault being committed against a close friend or family member.

While Committing or Attempting to Commit a Felony

In some states a charge of first-degree murder does not require that the murder was committed with premeditation if the victim died as a result of acts committed while the suspect was engaged in a felony such as rape, robbery or arson. Proof of the elements of the felony must of course be established.

While Committing or Attempting to Commit a Crime Not a Felony

If a death results from an act committed by a suspect engaged in a nonfelonious crime such as purse-snatching or petty theft, it can be charged as either third-degree murder or voluntary manslaughter, depending on the state in which the offense occurs.

Culpable Negligence or Depravity

The act and the way it is committed establish this element. The act must be so dangerous that any prudent person would see death of a person as a possible consequence. A person causing a death while depraved and committing acts evident of such depravity is guilty of third-degree murder.

Negligence

A fine line separates this element from the preceding element. Some laws make no distinction, classifying both in a separate category of **criminal negligence.** Where separate categories exist, this lesser degree of negligence involves creating a situation that results in an unreasonable risk of death or great bodily harm.

Challenges in Investigation

Police have an obligation to act on behalf of the deceased and their families. They are expected to conduct a professional investigation to identify, arrest and prosecute suspects. One apparent injustice in the criminal justice system is that, to an outsider, it appears that the police are constantly trying to protect the rights of the perpetrator and pay slight attention to the rights of the deceased or the family.

Challenges in homicide investigations include pressure by the media and the public, the difficulty of establishing that a crime has been committed, identifying the victim and establishing the cause and time of death.

Homicides create high interest in the community, as evidenced by increased sales of newspapers and higher ratings for the news media. Indeed, the media have a special interest in police investigations of deaths—accidental or otherwise. Police officers who have dealt with the news media understand the important relationship between law enforcement and the media, as discussed in Chapter 1.

Police policies and guidelines should specify what information is to be released: the deceased's name, accused's name and general identifying information, any details regarding formal charges and general facts about the investigation that are not harmful to the continuing investigation of the case.

Do not pose the accused for photographs, and do not permit the accused to talk to the press. If investigators have details known only to them and the accused, that information must not be released. Exercising good sense, getting to know the reporters personally and refraining from giving "off the record" comments will prevent many problems. Reporters have a right to be at the scene, and cooperation is the best policy—within the policies and guidelines of the department.

From time to time, public outrage over particular crimes places increased pressure on the police to solve murders. A more serious problem is the difficulty of establishing that a crime has, in fact, been committed. Search warrants can be issued if proof of a crime exists; however, such proof may not be legally available without a warrant. In addition, many perpetrators attempt to make the crime scene look as if a robbery or burglary has taken place. It can also be difficult to determine whether the death was homicide or suicide.

Suicide

Statistics about suicide are sobering (Marcotty and Smith 1999, p. B7):

- More Americans die by suicide than by homicide.
- Fifteen percent of people with major depression take their own lives.
- Fifteen percent of people who suffer from schizophrenia take their own lives.
- Research studies have shown that 85 percent of suicides are premeditated and that 90 percent of those who take their lives communicate their intentions to someone they know.

These statistics are important to investigators, who should try to determine whether a suicide victim was suffering from depression or schizophrenia or whether the victim had talked to anyone about committing suicide.

The reason for an apparent suicide must be determined. An act that appears to be too violent for suicide and is therefore a suspected homicide might actually be a natural death. Never exclude the possibility of death from natural causes in the initial phase of an investigation because of the presence of obvious marks of violence. The abnormal activity of a person suffering from an acutely painful attack can create the appearance of a struggle. The onset of more than 70 diseases can produce sudden death. People who experience such an attack may disarrange their clothing and sustain severe injury by falling. In one case a man shot himself to relieve excruciating pain, and the autopsy showed that a ruptured aorta caused his death, not the gunshot. What appeared to be suicide was declared to be death by natural causes.

Check for weapons on or near the body. Were there any prior suicide attempts, a history of mental illness or recent traumatic incidents? Were there any recent changes or conflicts in the victim's personal relationships? Was the victim being treated for a medical condition? Were any prescription drugs found at the scene? What was the cause of death?

When investigating suspected suicides, attempt to find a note or letter. However, lack of a note does not eliminate the possibility of suicide—a suicide note is left in only a fourth of the cases investigated. If you do find a note, have it compared with the deceased's handwriting. Preserve all evidence until the medical examiner or coroner's office rules whether the death is a suicide.

Also look for videos or cassettes describing the actions taken. Examine any pads of paper near the body for the presence of indented writing remaining from sheets of paper torn from the pad and destroyed. Look for manuals on how to commit suicide. Check on prior arrangements with an undertaker or other evidence of putting one's affairs in order.

Learn whether the victim was left- or right-handed and see whether this fits with the method of committing suicide. Note lividity conditions and the body's location to determine how long the person has been dead and whether the body has been moved. Note the condition of rigor mortis. Are there "hesitation marks" indicating indecision before the final act? Do not assume that any blood on the victim is the victim's; it may be from a murderer. (These issues are discussed later in the chapter.)

When smaller-calibre weapons are fired, blood may not appear on the hands of the person firing the gun. In fact, in most suicide cases blood does not appear on the hands. In more than 75 percent of suicide cases in which a gun is used, the gun is not found in the victim's hand but is near the body. In a number of suicides the victims have had multiple wounds. If evidence surfaces after the initial investigation that proves a suicide was actually a homicide, do not hesitate to reopen the case.

What appears to be a double suicide can also present problems. It may be a murder–suicide. Determine who died first or who inflicted the fatal wounds. Attempt to determine the motive. Search for a note. Look for signs of a violent struggle before death. Sometimes suicide is obvious, as when suspects kill themselves to avoid being captured by the police.

Geberth (1998c, p. 163) notes the psychology of suicide is rooted in depression and suggests investigators be aware of three basic considerations to establish if a death might be a suicide:

- The presence of the weapon or means of death at the scene

- Injuries or wounds that are obviously self-inflicted or that could have been inflicted by the deceased

- The existence of a motive or intent on the part of the victim to take his or her own life

Geberth (1998c, p. 165) further asserts: "The investigation should focus on any prior mental disease or defect. Was the deceased under any professional treatment? Consider obtaining this information via subpoena if necessary. The therapist-client relationship is terminated with the death of the client." To gain a better understanding of the victim's frame of mind when the suicide occurred or to reveal that the act was perhaps not suicide at all, it is vital for investigators to study the per-

sonality traits, character and life style of the victim, reconstructing as accurately as possible the days and hours preceding the victim's death.

Suicide by Police

Suicide by police refers to a situation in which a person decides he or she wants to die but does not want to pull the trigger. The person may view suicide as socially or religiously unacceptable but believes that, if killed by police, the stigma of suicide will be averted and society may see him or her as a victim. Consequently, the individual creates a situation in which police are forced to shoot. Parent (1998, p. 113) explains:

> It is well known through television, movies and literature that police officers are trained to—and typically will—deploy deadly force upon being confronted by a life-threatening situation. As a result, an individual predisposed to suicide may confront the police with a knife or other weapon, advancing upon and forcing the officer to use lethal force. An extreme individual may even confront the police with a loaded firearm or discharge his weapon at the police in the hope of being killed. These situations would provide few, if any, options for the attending officers except to respond with deadly force.

Many such cases involve a "man-with-a-gun" call. Arriving police are confronted with a person acting bizarrely and threatening to shoot himself/herself, a hostage or the responding officers. In many instances, the gun is not loaded, is a fake or is inoperative, but if it is pointed at the police, the police are forced to shoot.

Kennedy et al. (1998, p. 23) note: "Police may confront shootings motivated by suicidal subjects more often than reports indicate." In fact, a study examining shootings by the Los Angeles County Sheriff's Department found that suicide-by-cop incidents composed 25 percent of all fatal and nonfatal officer-involved shootings in 1997 ("Ending Your Own . . . ," 1999, p. 1). Burke and Rigsby (1999, p. 98) report that some estimates place the proportion of police shootings involving suicide by police as high as 50 percent.

Parent (p. 112) notes that discovering suicide-by-cop cases is usually difficult because little or no documentation exists of the victim's intent. In one rare case, however, officers were made acutely aware of their role in ending a young man's life: A 19-year-old was shot and killed after pulling a revolver from his waistband, advancing on officers and ignoring repeated commands to drop his weapon. After officers fired on the young man, they discovered the "weapon" was actually a toy. A search of the man's car produced the following note, addressed to the officer who would eventually take the man's life: "Officer, I'm sorry to get you involved. I just needed to die. Please let my family know I had to do this. This was all my doing. You had no way of knowing" (Burke and Rigsby, p. 97).

Scoville (1998, p. 38) reports on a study to reveal commonalities in various suicide-by-police cases:

> In almost all instances, the victims were male; an overwhelming majority were whites or Latino. There were also high incidences of prior domestic violence, alcohol or chemical abuse, and prior suicide attempts.
>
> The most easily recognized catalyst was the dissolution of a relationship.

Suicide-by-cop offender profiles indicate that such subjects often have a poor self-image, feel a sense of guilt for great harm they have caused, talk about death and express a desire to be with deceased loved ones, speak often of a higher being, are aggressively confrontational with police and possess an unloaded or nonfunctioning (toy) gun. Burke and Rigsby (p. 99) list additional indicators that may help officers recognize suicide-by-cop situations. The subject may do any of the following:

- Refuse to negotiate with authorities during a barricade situation.
- Have just killed a "significant other."
- Have learned or perceive he has a terminal illness.
- Have had a traumatic experience in his life affecting family, self or career.
- Have given away personal possessions that he deems valuable.
- Have a previous criminal record involving assaultive behavior.
- Not be concerned about escape—no demands or plans of escape.
- Surrender only to the officer in charge (e.g., chief of police).
- Have taken steps to plan his death.
- Wish to die like a "hero."
- Desire to "go out in a big way."
- Express feelings of hopelessness.
- Provide authorities with a will.
- Demand to be killed by others.
- Set a deadline for authorities to kill him.

Keeping this list of factors in mind may help officers identify and avoid potential suicide-by-cop cases. Burke and Rigsby (p. 102) state: "If force must be used to subdue the offender, officers should attempt non-lethal means if possible. This would include pepper spray, Tasers, rubber bullets, bean bag rounds, glue guns, net guns, etc." Kennedy et al. (p. 27) add: "Properly trained officers who understand the motivations of subjects with suicidal impulses and know how to deal with them will be better prepared to avert these tragedies."

Suicide of Police Officers

There is no question—police work is stressful. And it can take its toll in tragic ways. Strandberg (1997, p. 38) states: "Police officers commit suicide more than any other professional group, and the incidence is increasing." Zamora (1997, p. A9) notes: "Several studies indicate police officers . . . are more than twice as likely to kill themselves as the general population." The Centers for Disease Control report a national suicide rate of 12 per 100,000, yet the NYPD's suicide rate is 15.5 per 100,000—nearly 30 percent higher than that of the general population. A study by the National Fraternal Order of Police found a rate of 22 self-inflicted deaths per 100,000 officers in 1995 ("PDs Grope for . . . ," 1999, p. 5).

Although many consider police work to be a dangerous profession primarily because of the risk of encountering violent and armed individuals, Quinnett (1998, p. 21) notes: "More officers lose their lives to suicide than to homicide." A study of the nation's largest police agencies found that, whereas 36 NYPD officers have been killed in the line of duty since 1985, 87 have committed suicide during the same period; the Chicago Police Department had 12 officers killed in the line of duty and 22 who committed suicide from 1990 to 1998; the FBI lost 18 agents to suicide and only 4 to line-of-duty deaths between 1993 and 1998 ("PDs Grope for . . . ," p. 5). Zamora (p. A9) reports that a study of officers in Buffalo, New York, found they were eight times more likely to kill themselves than to be killed by criminals. Furthermore, notes Zamora: "About 95 percent do it with their own service revolver."

As with other victims of suicide, "alcohol, family issues and the breakup of relationships all contribute to the rate of police suicides." ("PDs Grope for . . . ," p. 5). But why should law enforcement officers suffer significantly higher suicide rates than those in other professions or in the general population? Various theories exist. Some attribute it to "a distorted but culturally correct sense of invincibility and independence" (Zamora, p. A9). Quinnett (p. 20) claims: "Law enforcement personnel present an elevated suicide risk to themselves based on the often-cited reluctance of officers to seek help voluntarily or in a timely fashion." The public's image of the police, and indeed officers' image of themselves, is that of the strong protector of society. Yet police work forces officers to confront daily the dark side of human nature and may eventually cause officers to lose their faith in the goodness of humanity or in their abilities to make a positive impact on the lives of others. This sense of weakness and failure is so contradictory to the image of the police that some officers may simply see no other choice than to "take themselves out of the game."

The Preliminary Investigation

The initial investigation of a homicide is basically the same as for any other crime, although it may require more flexibility, logic and perseverance. The primary goals of the investigation are (1) to establish whether a human death was caused by the criminal act or omission of another and (2) to determine who caused the death.

The homicide case normally begins with a report of a missing person or the discovery of a body. The officer in the field seldom makes the initial discovery. The first notification is received by the police communications center or a dispatcher who records the date, time and exact wording used. Because the original call is sometimes made anonymously by a suspect, a voice recording is made for comparison with later suspects.

When responding to a call, be sure to protect yourself. Garner (1997, p. 27) states: "You don't want to find yourself added to the casualty list on the death scene. Be prepared for surprise threats even before you arrive. Watch out for the suspicious or out of place. . . . You should be aware, of course, that things as well as people can hurt you." While exercising caution of your surroundings, the next step is to secure the scene. Garner (p. 26) advises: "Be cautious in your approach to the death location. Whether your scene is inside or outdoors, try to ensure that all personnel enter and exit by the same route, avoiding stepping in or kicking around potential evidence, like blood splatters."

As you enter the scene, it is important to introduce yourself, identify key personnel, establish rapport and assess the safety of the scene. Clark (1997, p. 15) advises:

> Introductions at the scene allow the investigator to establish formal contact with the other official agency representatives. The investigator must identify the first

responder to ascertain if any artifacts or contamination may have been introduced to the death scene. The investigator must work with all key people to ensure scene safety prior to his/her entrance into the scene.

Clark's *National Guidelines for Death Investigation* is a valuable resource for homicide investigators because it details not only the steps to take when arriving at the scene but also important investigative tools and equipment, documenting and evaluating both the scene and the body, establishing and recording decedent profile information and completing the scene investigation.

Of course, if you discover upon arrival the victim is still alive, the first priority is to render emergency aid and make sure an ambulance is en route.

> The first priority is to give emergency aid to the victim if he or she is still alive or to determine that death has occurred.

As noted before, if the suspect is still at the scene, priorities may differ drastically. Normally, however, the suspect is not at the scene, and the victim is the first priority. If the victim is obviously dying, take a dying declaration. The live victim is taken to a hospital as rapidly as possible.

The first officer on the scene determines the path to the victim that will least disturb evidence. If the victim is obviously dead, the body remains at the scene until the preliminary investigation is complete. It is then taken to the morgue by the medical examiner or coroner for postmortem examination or autopsy.

Following the assessment of the victim, investigators must document everything they can about the scene. This includes detaining and identifying all persons present, obtaining brief statements from each one, maintaining control of the scene and everyone present, listing all officers present upon the investigator's arrival and throughout the investigation and recording all other personnel present (medical personnel, coroner and family members).

A death scene checklist developed by the FBI can help ensure a thorough preliminary investigation. This checklist is reprinted in Appendix A.

Determining That Death Has Occurred

Medically, death is determined by the cessation of three vital functions: heartbeat, respiration and brain activity. The first two signs are observable.

Signs of death include lack of breathing, lack of heartbeat, lack of flushing of the fingernail bed when pressure is applied to the nail and then released and failure of the eyelids to close after being gently lifted.

Cessation of respiration is generally the first visible sign of death. However, in cases such as barbiturate overdoses, breathing can be so shallow that it is undetectable. Therefore, always check for a heartbeat and pulse. Except in some drug overdoses and with certain types of blindness, failure of the pupils to dilate in reaction to light is also a sign of death.

If the victim appears to have just died, attempt resuscitation with the standard cardiopulmonary resuscitation methods.

The Focus of the Homicide Investigation

As with any other criminal investigation, the homicide scene must be secured, photographed and sketched, and all evidence must be obtained, identified and properly preserved. Videotaping the crime scene can produce excellent results and is becoming more frequently used.

After priority matters are completed, the focus of the homicide investigation is to:

■ Identify the victim.

■ Establish the time of death.

■ Establish the cause of and the method used to produce death.

■ Develop a suspect.

The preliminary investigation either accomplishes these things or provides leads that investigators can follow up.

Discovering and Identifying the Victim

In some cases no body is present. It may have been burned, cut up beyond recognition or dissolved in a vat of acid. Some states allow the use of circumstantial evidence to prove the corpus delicti when no body can be found. In other cases, there is a body, but locating it is a challenge. It may have been weighted and sunk in a body of water or buried underground.

Various technologies can help investigators search for human remains, including ground-penetrating radar, magnetometers, metal detectors and specially trained dogs. One relatively new technique for searching both small and large areas with 100 percent coverage is infrared thermography: "This unusual technology was able to distinguish between new and old grave sites. . . . Among its attributes was the fact that it was faster and more discerning than any of the other techniques when used on an actual demonstration site containing hidden grave sites" ("Infrared Thermography. . . ," 1998, p. 42).

In most homicides, a body does exist. The problem sometimes is to identify the victim.

Homicide victims are identified by family, relatives or acquaintances; personal effects, fingerprints, DNA analysis, dental and skeletal studies; clothing and laundry marks; or through missing-persons files.

In many cases identifying the deceased is no problem. The parents, a close friend or a relative makes the identification. If possible, have several people identify the body because people under stress make mistakes. In a number of cases, a homicide victim has been identified only to turn up later alive. Although personal identification by viewing the deceased is ideal, corroborate it by other evidence.

Personal effects found on the victim assist in identification. However, such personal effects may not necessarily belong to the deceased. Therefore, check them carefully.

If identification cannot be made by relatives or acquaintances or by personal effects, the most positive identification is by fingerprint or DNA analysis. Comparative fingerprints are not always available, however, and blood type does not provide a positive identification, although it can prove that a body is *not* a specific person.

For an unknown victim, record a complete description and take photographs if possible. Check these against missing-persons files. Circulate the description and photograph in the surrounding area. Check the victim's clothing for possible laundry marks or for labels that might indicate where the clothes were purchased.

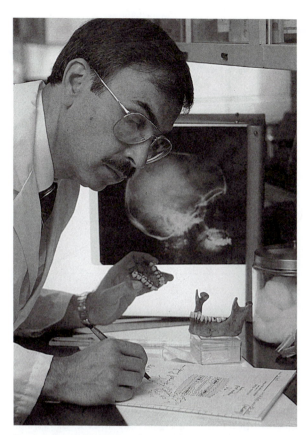

Bones often assist in identification of victims through comparison with health and dental records.

If the body is badly decomposed, the bones provide a basis for estimating height, sex and approximate age as well as proof that the deceased was a human. If there are leads as to who the victim might be, you can attempt identification by comparing dental charts and X-rays of prior fractures and by examining signs of prior surgical procedures, such as scars or other abnormalities.

Estimating the Time of Death

The time of death relates directly to whether the suspect could have been at the scene and to the sequence of multiple deaths. It is also important to the victim's family in settling insurance claims and social security and pension payments.

Both the investigator and the medical examiner or coroner are responsible for estimating the time of death. Knowing how the professional examiner estimates time of death helps investigators to understand better what circumstances are important at the crime scene and alerts them to observe and record specific factors that aid in estimating the time of death. Some of these factors are available only to the first officers at the scene.

Without eyewitnesses, the time of death is seldom completely accurate. Normally, however, the time of the death—if it has occurred within the past four days—can be determined to within four hours, depending on the examiner's expertise and the factors available for examination. Figure 13.1 shows the timing of various body changes after death.

Factors that help in estimating the time of death are body temperature, rigor mortis, postmortem lividity (livor), appearance of eyes, stomach contents, stage of decomposition and evidence suggesting a change in the victim's normal routine.

Recent Death

A time of death that is less than a half-hour before examination is normally the easiest determination to make. The body is still warm; mucous membranes are still moist but drying; blood is still moist but drying; the pupils have begun to dilate; and the skin is becoming pale white in Caucasians.

Death That Occurred One-Half Hour to Four Days Prior

Generally, if the death occurred within the past four days but more than one-half hour ago, the mucous membranes and any blood from the wounds are dry, there are skin blisters and skin slippage, the body is slightly pink, body temperature has dropped, rigor mortis and postmortem lividity are present and the pupils are restricted and cloudy.

Body Temperature Although not an accurate measure of time of death, body temperature is helpful in conjunction with other factors. After death, the body tends to assume the temperature of its environment. Record the temperature of the surroundings and the amount of clothing on the body. Reach under the clothing to

FIGURE 13.1

Timing of Postmortem Body Cooling, Livor and Rigor Mortis and Putrefactive Changes

Source: Irwin M. Sopher. "The Law Enforcement Officer and the Determination of the Time of Death." *FBI Law Enforcement Bulletin,* October 1973. Reprinted with permission.

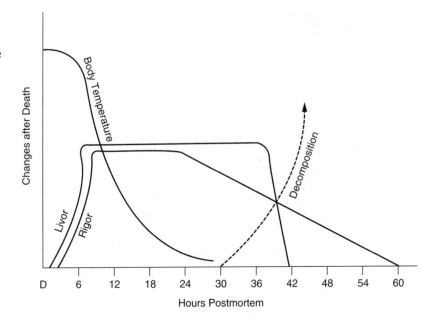

determine the warmth or coldness of the body. Compare this with exposed parts of the body to determine whether body heat is being retained by the clothing.

Body temperature drops 2 to 3 degrees in the first hour after death and 1 to 1½ degrees for each subsequent hour up to 18 hours.

These amounts vary in abnormally hot or cold environments. Also, body temperature drops more slowly in large or obese people, if a high fever was present before death, if humidity prevents evaporation and if strenuous physical activity occurred immediately before death.

Rigor Mortis The body is limp after death until rigor mortis sets in. **Rigor mortis** is a stiffening of parts of the body after death, presumably because of enzyme breakdown. It begins in the jaw and head 5 to 6 hours after death and then moves downward through the entire body. The body remains rigid from 18 to 26 hours. However, within about 36 hours, rigor mortis normally disappears in the same sequence as it appeared.

Rigor mortis:

Appears in head	5 to 6 hours
Appears in upper body	12 hours
Appears in entire body	18 hours
Disappears in same order	36 hours

The degree of rigor mortis as an indicator of time of death is usually accurate to within four hours when used along with other factors. Excitement, vigorous activity, heavy clothing and abnormally high temperatures increase the rapidity of rigor; cold slows it. Babies and the aged have little rigor.

Closely associated with rigor mortis is **cadaveric spasm,** a condition that occurs in specific muscle groups rather than the entire body. It occurs most often when the victim is holding something in the hand at the time of death. The hand closes tightly around the object because of the stress and tension of death occurring. The condition does not disappear as rigor mortis does, and it cannot be induced by another person. Cadaveric spasm does not always occur, but when it does, it helps to establish whether death was homicide or a suicide. If a dead person is found with a gun or knife tightly clutched in the hand and this is the only area of the body showing this condition, the victim was holding the weapon at the moment of death.

A weapon tightly clutched in the victim's hand as the result of cadaveric spasm indicates suicide.

Ensure that the weapon clutched *was* the murder weapon. It might be that both the victim and an assailant were armed and that the death was not suicide. Likewise, absence of cadaveric spasm does not preclude suicide because it does not always occur.

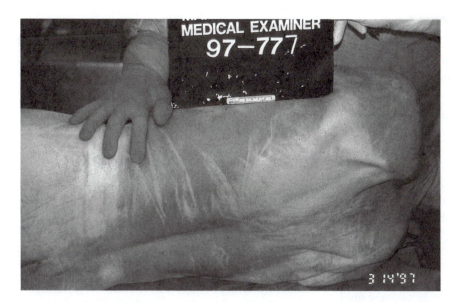

Postmortem lividity pattern. After death, blood coagulates down to the underside of the body. Such patterns can indicate if a body has been moved after death.

Postmortem Lividity When the heart stops beating at death, the blood no longer circulates, and gravity drains the blood to the body's lowest levels. This causes a dark blue or purple discoloration of the body called **postmortem lividity,** or livor mortis. Lividity is cherry red or a strong pink if death is caused by carbon monoxide poisoning, and various other poisons give lividity other colors.

If a body is on its back, lividity appears in the lower portion of the back and legs. If on the front, it appears on the face, chest, stomach and legs. If on the side, lividity appears on the side on which the body is resting, and if the body is upright, it appears in the buttocks and lower legs.

- - - - - - - - -

Postmortem lividity starts one-half to three hours after death and is congealed in the capillaries in four to five hours. Maximum lividity occurs within ten to twelve hours.

- - - - - - - - -

Any part of the body pressing directly on a hard surface does not show lividity because the pressure of the body's weight prevents blood from entering the blood vessels in that area. If there are large wounds from which blood has been released, very little if any lividity occurs.

Postmortem lividity and bruises appear similar, but they are easy to distinguish. When bruises are pressed with the thumb or fingers, they remain the same, whereas lividity turns white, or blanches, when pressure is applied. If the blood has already congealed, an incision

reveals whether the blood is still in the vessels (lividity) or outside them (bruise). In addition, the color of a bruise varies, whereas the color of lividity is uniform.

- - - - - - - - -

The location of lividity can indicate whether a body was moved after death.

- - - - - - - - -

Besides helping to establish time of death and sometimes the cause, lividity helps determine whether the body was moved after death occurred. Postmortem lividity in a body moved immediately after death would provide no clues. However, if the body was moved to a different position after lividity had set in, lividity will occur in unlikely areas, indicating that the body was moved.

Examination of the Eyes The appearance of the eyes also assists in estimating the time of death. After death, eye muscle tone lessens and tends to disappear. The pupils tend to dilate.

- - - - - - - - -

A partial restriction of the pupil occurs in about seven hours. In twelve hours the cornea appears cloudy.

- - - - - - - - -

The cornea clouds more rapidly if the eyes are open after death.

During the medical examination, fluid can be withdrawn from the eyeball (or the spine) to determine the level of potassium, which tends to rise at a predictable rate after death.

Examination of Stomach Contents Although the stomach contents must be examined during the medical examination, the investigator can provide important information for the examiner.

Determine when and what the victim last ate. If any vomit is present, preserve it as evidence and submit it for examination.

Attempt to find out when the victim last ate. The medical examiner can often determine how long the victim lived after eating because digestion is a fairly constant process, measurable in hours. Food remains in the stomach one to two hours after eating and then empties into the small intestine, where it takes two to four hours to pass into the large intestine. If the stomach is full, death occurred within one to two hours after eating. If the small intestine is full, death occurred four to six hours after eating. If the large intestine is empty, twelve or more hours passed after the victim ate and before death occurred.

Digestive time is affected by many factors, however. Mental and emotional upsets, poor health, fatigue and constipation all decrease digestive time; diarrhea increases it.

If the victim has vomited, the stomach is empty and will distort the estimate of time of death; therefore, report the presence of any vomit near the body. Preserve such vomit as evidence as it may provide information on drugs or poisons related to the cause of death.

Many Days after Death

It is more difficult to estimate the time of death if death occurred several days before discovery of the body. The cadaver is bloated, lividity is darkened, the abdomen is greenish, blisters are filled with gas and a distinct odor is present.

Decomposition The medical examiner makes a rough estimate of time of death based on the body's state of decomposition. Decomposition is first observed as an extended stomach and abdomen, the result of internal gases developing. In general, decomposition is increased by higher temperatures and decreased by lower temperatures.

If the body is in a hot, moist location, a soapy appearance called **adipocere** develops. This takes up to three months to develop fully. Attacks by insects, bacteria, animals and birds also increase the decomposition rate.

The presence on the body of insect eggs, their stage of development and the life cycle of the species, as well as various stages of vegetation on or near the body, also provide information on the time of death. A forensic entomologist (FE) can examine various types of insects to assist in estimating the time of death. According to Wells (1998, p. 6A), an expert on flesh-eating insects: "It's like a ticking clock. If you understand the biology of the creature and you know the conditions of the crime scene, you can come up with a useful estimate." Wells notes that investigators can use such estimates when assessing suspects' alibis:

Firefighters once found a woman's body in a burning house in Oakland, Calif. They suspected her female roommate in the death, but couldn't prove it.

[A forensic entomologist] showed that, based on the age of the maggots found on her body, the woman died days before the fire.

Examination of insects is especially helpful when death occurred more than a week before. Insects can detect newly dead body odors two miles away. Because particular insects work or rest during the day or the night, the types of insects at the scene provide clues as to the timing of the body's deterioration. Furthermore, it is possible to tie a suspect to the area in which a body is found by comparing evidence on the body with insect parts smashed on the suspect's windshield, grill or other vehicle parts. Expert entomologists examine this type of evidence at the Forensic Science Research and Training Center at Quantico, Virginia.

Complete dehydration of all body tissues results in **mummification.** A cadaver left in an extremely dry, hot area will mummify in about a year and will remain in this condition for several years if undisturbed by animals or insects.

Effects of Water

Bodies immersed in water for a period of time undergo changes that help to determine time of death. A body immersed in water may decompose rapidly, depending on the water temperature and the effects of fish and other marine life.

A dead body usually sinks in water and remains immersed for eight to ten days in warm water or two to three weeks in cold water. It then rises to the surface unless restricted. The outer skin loosens in five to six days, and the nails separate in two to three weeks.

The medical examination also determines whether the person was alive or dead at the time the body was immersed in water. This provides evidence to support homicide, suicide or accidental death.

Factors Suggesting a Change in the Victim's Routine

Check telephone calls made to and by the victim. Check dates on mail, newspapers and food in the refrigerator. Determine who normally provides services to the victim, such as dentists, doctors, barbers, hairdressers and clerks. Find out if any appointments were not kept. Were any routines discontinued, such as playing cards or tennis, going to work on schedule or riding a particular bus? Was there food on the stove or the table? Was the stove on? Were the lights, television, radio or stereo on or off? Were pets fed? Were dirty dishes on the counters or in the sink? Was this normal for the victim? Was a fire burning in the fireplace? Was the damper left open? All such facts help to estimate the time of death and can corroborate the estimate based on physical findings.

Unnatural Causes of Death and Method Used

In all cases of violent death, industrial/accidental death or suicide, the medical examiner determines the cause of death. A number of deaths involve circumstances that are investigated by police and the medical examiner, even though many are not criminal homicides.

> Among the most common causes of unnatural death are gunshot wounds; stabbing and cutting wounds; blows from blunt instruments; asphyxia induced by choking, drowning, hanging, smothering, strangulation, gases or poisons; poisoning and drug overdose; burning; explosions, electric shock, and lightning.

Table 13.2 indicates the probability of a specific cause of death being the result of an accident, suicide or homicide.

Gunshot Wounds

Most deaths due to gunshot wounds result from handguns, rifles or shotguns. Knowing the type of weapon is important for making comparison tests and locating unknown weapons. The major cause of death from gunshot wounds is internal hemorrhaging and shock. The size, number and velocity of the ammunition used and the type of weapon determine the effect on the body.

Shots fired from a distance produce little or no powder tattooing or carbons on the skin around where the

---

Table 13.2 **Causes of Death**

Cause of Death	Accident	Suicide	Homicide
Gunshot wound	*	*	*
Stabbing and cutting wounds	rare	*	*
Blow from blunt instruments			
Fall	*	*	*
Hit-and-run vehicle			*
Asphyxia			
Choking	*		
Drowning	*	*	*
Hanging	autoerotic	*	rare
Smothering	*		rare
Strangulation	autoerotic	rare	*
Poisoning and overdose	*	*	*
Burning	*		
Explosion	*		
Electric shock	*	rare	
Lightning	*		

*means reasonable to suspect as the cause of death.

This photo shows a clean, close-range (1–6 inches) gunshot wound resulted from an accidental shooting.

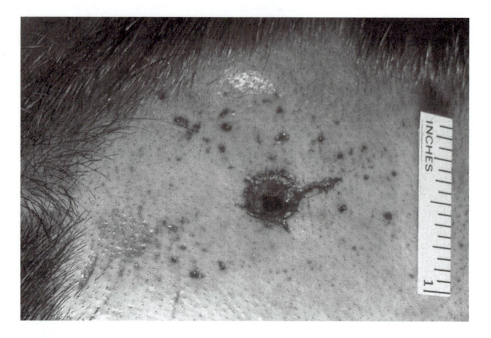

bullet entered the body, and it is difficult to determine the exact distance—even though the angle of trajectory can be determined from the bullet's path through the body. In the middle-distance range, tattooing appears on the clothing or the body when handguns are fired from up to approximately two feet away. Powder tattooing results from both burned and unburned powder. By using test-firing pattern comparisons with the same weapon and ammunition, the actual firing distance can be determined.

If the muzzle of the weapon was in direct contact with the body, contact wounds will be evident. You may notice a muzzle impression on the skin and soot or powder fragments in the entrance area or around the wound. At the entry point, the hole is smaller than the bullet because the skin's elasticity closes the entry point slightly. Entrance wounds are normally round or oval with little bleeding. As the bullet passes through the skin, it leaves a gray to black abrasion collar around the edges of the entry wound.

The exit wound is larger, bleeds more profusely and has no abrasion collar. It is larger because gases build up in the body, especially from shots at close range, and tissues bunch up ahead of the bullet until reaching the outer skin. Elasticity then forces the skin outward until it breaks, permitting the bullet and the gases to pass through. The exit wound is generally jagged and torn. The difference between entry and exit wounds is observable.

Shotgun wounds are distinctly different because numerous pellets penetrate the body. At close range these leave a much larger hole than does a bullet, and at farther range they produce a discernible pellet pattern. Both the entry and exit wounds are larger than those produced by single bullets.

Shotgun-wound patterns and the appearance of entrance and exit wounds from handguns and rifles help determine the distance from which the gun was fired. Contact wounds (fired at point-blank range) cause a large entry wound with smudging around the edges. The principal damage is due to the blasting and flame of the powder. Smudging around a wound can be wiped off, but the tattooing pattern cannot be eliminated. If the gun is more than 18 inches from the body when fired, no tattooing or smudging occurs.

In addition, a bullet or pellets from any weapon produce a track through the body that follows the angle between the weapon and the victim at the time of firing. The bullet's path or angle helps to determine the angle at which the weapon was fired and therefore the suspect's possible location at the time of firing. This angle also helps differentiate between suicide and murder.

When investigating gunshot deaths, determine whether the death was due to the wound or to some other injury. Was the wound impossible for the victim to have produced? What is the approximate distance from which the weapon was fired? Were there one or more wounds? Examine the victim's hands to determine whether he or she fired the gun. What was the position of the body when found?

- - - - - - - -

Suicide Indicators:

Gun held against skin

Wound in mouth or in right temple if victim is right-handed and left temple if left-handed

Not shot through clothing, unless shot in the chest

Weapon present, especially if tightly held in hand

Murder Indicators:

Gun fired from more than a few inches away

Angle or location that rules out self-infliction

Shot through clothing

No weapon present

- - - - - - - -

Stabbing and Cutting Wounds

Stabbing and cutting wounds differ in shape, size and extent of external and internal bleeding. A knife is the most frequently used weapon. The weapon and wound can be different sizes, depending on the depth and severity of the wound and whether it is into or across the tissues and fibers.

Stabbing Wounds Stab wounds are caused by thrusting actions. They vary in size in different areas of the body but are usually smaller than cutting wounds. A stab wound in a soft part of the body produces a larger hole than one in the head or a bony area. Ice-pick wounds in a skull covered by a substantial amount of hair can easily be missed on initial examination.

The major damage in stab wounds is to internal tissues, followed by bleeding, primarily internal. The extent and rapidity of internal bleeding depends on the size of the blood vessels affected. In most cases, the cause of death is bleeding rather than damage to a vital organ. A stab wound can be deeper than the length of the weapon used because the force of the thrust on the softer tissues can compress the body's surface inward.

Even if a weapon is found, it can rarely be designated as the murder weapon unless part of it separates and remains in the body or it contains blood, tissue and fibers from the deceased.

Most stabbing deaths are murders. In murders, stab wounds can be single or multiple and can be in several areas of the body if the victim attempted self-defense. **Defense wounds**—cuts on the hands, arms and legs—result when the victim attempts to ward off the attacker.

Cutting Wounds With cutting wounds, external bleeding is generally the cause of death. Cutting wounds are frequently the result of suicide. It is common in such cases to observe **hesitation wounds** in areas where the main wound occurs. These less severe cutting marks are caused by attempts to build up courage to make the fatal wound.

Suicidal cutting wounds are made at an angle related to the hand that held the weapon, generally in a downward direction because of the natural pull of the arm as it is brought across the body.

- - - - - - - -

Suicide Indicators:

Hesitation wounds

Wounds under clothing

Weapon present, especially if tightly clutched

Usually wounds at throat, wrists or ankles

Seldom disfigurement

Body not moved

Murder Indicators:

Defense wounds

Wounds through clothing

No weapon present

Usually injuries to vital organs

Disfigurement

Body moved

- - - - - - - -

Blows from Blunt Objects

Fatal injuries can result from hands and feet and blows with various blunt objects, including hammers, clubs, heavy objects and rocks. It is often impossible to determine the specific type of weapon involved. The injuries can occur to any part of the body and can result in visible external bruises. The size of the bruise may not correspond to the size of the weapon because blood escapes into a larger area. Severe bruises are not often found in suicides.

In a battered-child investigation, death rarely results from a single blow or a single series of blows but rather from physical abuse over an extended period. An autopsy reveals prior broken bones or injuries. Death may also have been caused by starvation or other forms of neglect.

Falls can cause death or can be used to conceal the real cause of death. In some cases the victim is taken to a staircase and pushed down after being severely beaten. Intoxication is often given as the reason for the fall, but this can easily be checked through blood tests.

Asphyxia

Asphyxiation results when the body tissues and the brain receive insufficient oxygen to support the red blood cells. An examination of blood cells shows this lack of oxygen.

Discoloration occurs in all dead bodies, but in asphyxia deaths, it is usually more pronounced and varied due to the lack of oxygen—especially in the blood vessels closest to the skin surface. It is most noticeable as a blue or purple color around the lips, fingernails and toenails. Although you need not know the varied coloration produced by different causes and chemicals, be certain to record precise descriptions of coloration that can be interpreted by the medical examiner and related to probable cause of death.

Asphyxia deaths result from many causes, including choking, drowning, smothering, strangulation, hanging, swallowing of certain chemicals, poisoning and overdosing on sleeping pills.

Choking Foreign bodies in the throat cause choking, as do burial in grain or sand slides or rapid pneumonia in infants in cribs. Such deaths are almost always accidental.

Drowning The majority of drownings are accidental. Murder is rarely proven unless witnesses are present. If a dead body is placed in water to make it appear as though death was caused by drowning, a medical examination can determine whether the person was dead when immersed.

Smothering Smothering is an uncommon means of murder, despite many fictional depictions of this method. Intoxicated persons, the elderly and infants are most likely to be victims of smothering, usually by the hands or a pillow. Often, however, such deaths are accidental. For example, an infant weak from disease may turn over, face downward, or become tangled in bedclothes and accidentally suffocate.

Hanging Hangings are normally suicides, but murders have been made to appear as hanging suicides. Some hangings result from experimentation to achieve sexual satisfaction, as discussed later. In suicides the pressure on the neck is usually generated by standing on a chair or stool and kicking the support away, jumping off or simply letting the body hang against the noose. (A body need not be completely suspended to result in death by hanging.) Although it is commonly thought that death results from a broken neck, it is usually the result of a broken trachea or a complete constriction of the air supply.

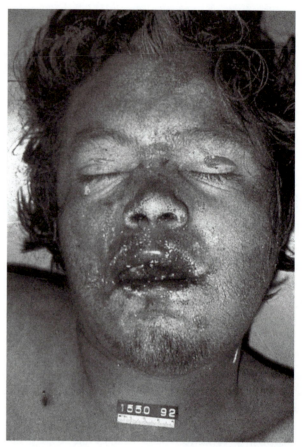

A victim of asphyxiation, as is evident form the characteristic skin discoloration.

In hangings the ligature marks start from the area of the neck below the chin and travel upward to the point just below the ears. Observe the condition and angle of these marks, and save the entire rope, including the knot, as evidence.

Strangulation Strangulation by rope, hands, wire or scarves produces the same effect as hanging. In both, the cause of death is total restriction of air. In contrast to hangings, however, the ligature marks caused by strangulation are normally evenly grooved and are horizontal around the neck. In cases of manual strangulation, marks often remain from the hand pressure.

Poisons, Chemicals and Overdoses of Sleeping Pills
Asphyxiating chemicals, including ammonia and chloroform, can cause irritation severe enough to totally constrict the breathing passages. Examination of the air passages indicates paralysis.

- - - - - - - -

Asphyxiation deaths: Most cases of choking, drowning and smothering are accidental; most cases of hanging are suicides; most cases of strangulation are murder.

- - - - - - - -

Autoerotic Asphyxiation In **autoerotic asphyxiation,** sexual gratification has been sought by placing a rope around the neck and causing just enough restriction to result in semiconsciousness. Such experimentation may be successful a number of times but then result in total unconsciousness rather than semiconsciousness. In such a case, the body goes limp in the noose, and the weight of the body causes the noose to tighten, causing death. Although not common, autoerotic asphyxiation should be recognized by police officers. In these instances suicides are in fact tragic accidents that occurred during dangerous autoerotic acts. Such deaths are classified into three categories: suffocation, strangulation and chemical asphyxia—the most common of which is strangulation resulting from suspension of the body. In such cases the body is usually touching the ground, and the victim is often bound. Analysis will show, however, that the binding could have been done by the victim.

Indicators of accidental death during autoerotic practices include:

- Nude or sexually exposed victim.
- Evidence of solo sexual activity.
- Mirrors placed to observe the ritual.
- Evidence of masturbation and presence of such items as tissues or towels for clean-up.
- Presence of sexual fantasy aids or sexually stimulating paraphernalia (vibrators, dildos, sex aids and pornographic magazines).
- Presence of bondage.

Poisoning

Poisoning, one of the oldest methods of murder, can occur from an overwhelming dose that causes immediate death or from small doses that accumulate over time and cause death. Poisons can be injected into the blood or muscles, inhaled as gases, absorbed through the skin surface, taken in foods or liquids or inserted into the rectum or vagina.

Toxicology (the study of poisons) experts can determine the type of poison, the amount ingested, the approximate time ingested and the effect on the body.

An overdose death is not necessarily a suicide. It might have been accidental—a result of the person's not knowing when medication was last taken or being in a semistupor and taking more pills than intended. If a prescription bottle is found, determine from family members how many pills were in the bottle before the death. Check with the issuing pharmacist to determine whether it was a legal prescription, how many pills were prescribed and the date the prescription was last filled. Preserve all evidence until the coroner's office rules the death accidental or a suicide. Other important evidence includes the contents of the medicine cabinet, any excretions or vomit at the scene and any food the victim recently ate.

If a child is poisoned by accidentally ingesting cleaning fluid, detergents, pills or other such substances, the parents are sometimes charged with manslaughter or negligent homicide.

Burning

Most deaths by burning are accidental. However, a death resulting from burns received in a fire caused by arson is classified as murder. Moreover, people sometimes try to disguise murder by burning the victim's body. Even in the most destructive fires, however, considerable information is available from an autopsy because bones are not easily burned. Even in extreme heat, enough blood usually remains to enable a carbon monoxide analysis to determine whether the victim was alive at the time of the fire. However, in extremely hot fires the heat may cause the skin to break open on the surface, and the resulting wounds may appear to be knife or other wounds inflicted by an assailant prior to the fire.

Explosions, Electrocution and Lightning

Death due to explosives can result from the direct tearing force of the blast, from a shock wave or from the victim's being blown off the top of a structure or against an object with enough force to cause death. Such deaths are usually accidental.

Electrocution paralyzes the heart muscle, causing rapid death. Nearly all electrocution deaths are accidental (except, of course, in capital punishment cases). High-voltage lines and lightning are the main causes. Lightning leaves linear stripes on the body, turns the skin blue and burns the skin, especially at the lightning bolt's entry and exit points.

- - - - - - - - -

Poisoning deaths can be accidental, suicide or murder. Most deaths caused by burning, explosions, electrocution and lightning are accidental, although burning is sometimes used in an attempt to disguise murder.

- - - - - - - - -

Drug-Related Homicides

The same techniques used in death investigations also apply to drug-related death investigations. Look for evidence of alcohol use and/or consumption of drugs (pill bottles or paraphernalia). Alcohol mixed with certain drugs can pose a particularly lethal combination. Keep in mind that prescription drugs are the leading cause of drug-related deaths in the United States.

Different categories of drug-related homicides include deadly disputes involving individuals high on drugs (no organized drug/gang affiliation); drug hits on traffickers, dealers or buyers (may be gang-related); drug assassinations against law enforcement or others fighting drug trafficking; and the killing of innocent bystanders in drug-related disputes. Each category presents specific investigative options, summarized in Table 13.3. Most of these investigative options are discussed in detail in Chapter 20.

The Victim

In most crimes the victim provides verbal details of what occurred. In homicides the victim may be able to provide such information if witnesses or the police are present before death occurs. However, the information

- -

Table 13.3	Drug-Related Homicides and Investigative Options
Category	*Investigative Options*
Drug hit	Intelligence information Narcotics buy operation Buy and bust operation Informant information
Interpersonal drug disputes	Buy and bust operation Informant information Narcotics buy operation
Murder of innocent bystanders	Reward money Crime Stoppers program Use of news media Community activists Buy and bust operation Informant information
Drug assassinations	Intelligence operations Electronic eavesdropping Narcotics buy operations Reward money Crime Stoppers program Use of news media

Source: Vernon J. Geberth. "Investigation of Drug-Related Homicides." *Law and Order,* November 1990, p. 76. Reprinted by permission.

usually comes from the crime scene, witnesses, physical and circumstantial evidence and the suspect.

Victims often know the person who killed them, so information about the deceased can furnish leads to the suspect. Obtain the victim's name, address, age, sex, nationality and type and place of work. Also find out the names of family members, close friends and known enemies and learn about the victim's habits. Ask about any religious, political or business actions or remarks that might have enraged someone. Take the victim's fingerprints and determine whether any criminal history might lead to a suspect.

Interview personal contacts such as doctors, pastors or counselors to learn about the victim's physical and emotional condition, especially if it has not yet been determined whether the death was an accident, suicide or homicide. The person's medical background may provide information about an extremely painful or terminal disease that could motivate suicide. Inquire about the victim's mental stability. Most suicide victims attempt to avoid inflicting severe pain on themselves when they take their lives, but this is not always true. One woman cut off both her feet before fatally stabbing herself in the chest. Some people set themselves on fire to commit suicide.

The victim's background provides information about whether the death was an accident, suicide or homicide. If a homicide, the background often provides leads to a suspect. Evidence on the victim's body can also provide important leads.

In violent murders the victim may grab the suspect's hair, buttons or clothing or scratch or claw the suspect. A victim may leave injuries on the suspect, and traces of the suspect's flesh may be found under the victim's fingernails. Identify and preserve all belongings and evidence on or near the deceased. Carefully examine the location where the body was found if it is not where death occurred.

After the entire scene and the evidence have been photographed and sketched, move the body carefully. Lift it a few inches off the surface and slide a sheet under it to catch any evidence that might fall while transporting the body to the vehicle. Itemize other possessions and send them along with the body to the morgue for later release to the family if they are not evidence.

Although you may use a body bag, first wrap the body in a clean, white sheet. Evidence on the body that falls off is much easier to see on a sheet. The sheet also absorbs moisture.

Domestic Violence Homicide

Geberth (1998b, p. 51) explains:

Domestic violence homicides are those murders that occur between men and women, husbands and wives, boyfriends and girlfriends, boyfriends and boyfriends and girlfriends and girlfriends relationships. In fact, any murder between intimate partners would be considered a domestic violence homicide. They may also involve third-party relationships, such as "love triangles," former husbands and/or wives, and jilted lovers. The motive . . . is most often based upon . . . rage, hate, anger, jealousy or revenge.

As discussed in Chapter 10, many batterers eventually kill their intimate (one out of six murders are partner homicides), and women who leave their batterers face a 75 percent greater risk of being killed by their batterers than those who stay. In some cases batterers themselves become victims of homicide. Recall that four out of five murders by females are reported to be responses to domestic violence.

Law Enforcement Officers Killed

The risk of being killed in the line of duty "comes with the job." According to one source ("Officer Death Rate . . . ," 1999, p. 8): "Despite a seven-year declining crime rate in the United States, the rate of law enforcement fatalities has remained fairly steady." Another source ("Police Fatalities Drop . . . ," 2000, p. 8) reports: 130 federal, state and local law enforcement fatalities during 1999, compared to 156 during 1998. Of the 130 officers who died in 1999, 47 died in automobile accidents, 45 were shot to death, 15 succumbed to job-related illnesses, 10 drowned, 8 were struck by vehicles, 7 died in motorcycle accidents, 4 were killed in aircraft accidents, 2 were stabbed, 1 died in a fall, 1 was struck and killed by a train.

Although data from one year to the next may indicate a slight increase or decrease, overall the number of law enforcement officers killed has risen. Since the first recorded police death in 1794, more than 14,600 law enforcement officers have been killed in the line of duty ("Facts and Figures . . . ," 1999, p. 22). One possible explanation for the increase may be the fact that each year brings higher employment numbers in law enforcement—there are simply more cops ("Number of Police . . . ," 1998, p. A17).

Despite the apparent increase in the number of police killed on the job, recent years have shown a slight decline. Fox and Zawitz (p. 3) note: "The annual number of law enforcement officers killed in the line of duty declined mostly because of the decline in handgun murders." And although fewer than half of the officers killed on the job are gunned down or otherwise murdered, being shot and killed in the line of duty is still considered a very real risk of police work.

Witnesses

In violent criminal deaths, struggles often create noise and attract the attention of neighbors or passersby. Witnesses may know and name a suspect, or they may have seen the suspect or vehicle. Often, however, there are no witnesses, and information must be sought from family members, neighbors and associates.

St. Louis police have set up a homicide hotline with an untraceable number that murder witnesses can call to offer anonymous tips. The hotline is answered by a message machine and requires no staffing to implement. Figure 13.2 shows the card distributed to bystanders at homicide scenes.

Suspects

If the suspect is arrested at the crime scene, follow the procedures described in Chapter 1. If the suspect is known but is not at the scene, immediately disseminate the description to other investigators, field officers and police agencies.

If the suspect is not known, identification becomes a priority. Often several suspects are identified and eventually eliminated as information and evidence are obtained and the list is reduced to one or two prime suspects. In major cases any number of suspects may be developed from information at the scene, from informants and from intelligence files.

Discovering a motive is not a specific requirement in the investigation, but motive is so closely tied to intent and to developing a suspect that it should be determined. Murders are committed for many reasons. Common types of criminal homicide include the anger killing, the love-triangle killing, the revenge or jealousy killing, killing for profit, random killing, murder–suicide, the sex-and-sadism killing and felony murder. Anger killings often begin as assaults. The possibility of killing for profit almost always exists. Thus it is always critical to determine who would stand to profit from the victim's death.

Determine the motive for a killing because it provides leads to suspects and strong circumstantial evidence against a suspect.

Some murders are contracted or hired. This is frequently the case in murders of organized-crime figures.

FIGURE 13.2
The Card Handed Out to Bystanders at St. Louis Murder Scenes
Source: Courtesy of the St. Louis Police Department

"STOP THE KILLING"

If you have information regarding this or
any homicide investigation,
contact the

**HOMICIDE HOTLINE
444-5830**

*THE HOTLINE IS CONFIDENTIAL AND NONTRACEABLE
St. Louis Metropolitan Police Department

Mass Murderers

A **mass murder** occurs when multiple victims are killed in a single incident by one or a few suspects. The recent and well-publicized episodes of school shootings and attacks at community centers, in which a lone gunman or pair of gunmen opened fire on students or others within a building or institution, are examples. Frequently these killers unleash their murderous fury on total strangers. Holmes and Holmes (1999, p. 110) note: "Mass murderer George Hennard . . . drove his pick up truck through a restaurant and commenced his killings of unknown patrons. Mass killer Colin Wilson opened fire in a subway, killing six strangers. There were no relationships between Hennard and Wilson and their victims." A notable exception to this scenario occurs in school shootings.

Holmes and Holmes examined the school shootings in five communities—Littleton, Colorado; Paducah, Kentucky; Pearl, Mississippi; Springfield, Oregon; and Jonesboro, Arkansas—and provide a working profile of the typical school shooter (pp. 109–113):

In all these school shootings the killers are white males. Seldom are females involved in the shootings, although there are cases where there was a break-up in the relationship between the killer and his girlfriend. . . .

The school shooter is typically a student at the school where the murders occur. There is no stalking into the community for strangers to murder like adult mass killers. . . . The shooter and the victims are . . . often acquainted, if not on a personal basis at least in the sense that they have crossed paths in the hallways or classrooms.

The shooters told law enforcement they spent long hours on the Internet as well as played certain computer games . . . of intense violence, shooting, maiming and killing. . . .

School shooters were fascinated by exotic weapons and bombs . . . if for no other reason than to carry out their mission to kill. . . . Some learned how to construct bombs from the instruction available over the Internet.

The young shooters gave forewarnings of actions, but were not taken seriously by those privy to the comments. . . . The Colorado killers told fellow students that something was going to happen on Hitler's birthday. . . . Kinkel told a student he wanted to plant a bomb under the bleachers and block the doorway so students could not get out. . . .

The activities of the shooters prior to the fateful day is shrouded in secrecy. The killers, if alone, retreated to a personal space of aloneness, spending huge amounts of time playing video games and planning their attacks. If the killers murder with an accomplice, they share their time with each other. . . .

Because of the feelings experienced at the school, personal rejections, teasing, etc., the school shooter will eventually abandon his former friends. He will find acceptance, solace and comfort with the new members of his out group. . . . Some shooters attach themselves to groups that are devoted to a hate message, while others . . . [affiliate] with a group that was involved in the occult, particularly Satanism.

In many of these cases the killers take their own lives at the end of the shooting rampage, leaving investigators to wonder about possible motives. In other cases the shooters are easily identified and apprehended, sometimes quite boastful about what they have just "accomplished" and eager to provide authorities with their motives.

Another type of murder suspect who also kills multiple victims is the serial killer.

Serial Killers

Serial murder is the killing of three or more separate victims with a "cooling off" period between the killings. A number of serial killers in the United States have received national attention. These include Henry Lucas, who confessed to 188 murders in 24 states; the Green River murderer, 46 murders; Theodore (Ted) Bundy, 40 murders; and John Wayne Gacey, 33 murders. "Jack the Ripper," who killed at least seven prostitutes in London in 1888, is probably the best-known serial killer internationally. The 1997 cross-country murder spree of Andrew Cunanan, which culminated in the slaying of fashion designer Gianni Versace and the suicide of Cunanan a week later, is a more recent example of serial killings.

Investigating a murder committed by a serial killer may initially seem the same as investigating any other murder. As a case is investigated, however, and if no suspect can be developed, the investigator should consider reporting the crime to the FBI's National Center for the Analysis of Violent Crime (NCAVC) at Quantico, Virginia. NCAVC provides a profiling program as well as research and development, training and the Violent Criminal Apprehension Program (VICAP). Police departments investigating cases that they believe involve serial murder can submit their cases to VICAP.

Other cases with similar modus operandi submitted by other agencies are then compared, and information is furnished to the submitting agencies. As the Henry Lucas cases illustrate—where murders were committed in 24 states—VICAP is an important resource in investigating and prosecuting this type of killer. If VICAP determines that a serial murderer is probably involved, a multijurisdictional Major Crime Investigation Team may be assembled to handle the case.

Morrison (1998, pp. 68, 71) describes another tool used to track serial killers:

> Most serial criminals attack strangers at random, making it extremely difficult to put the connecting pieces together without some kind of help, whether it be luck, fate or a computer program. . . . The RIGEL system . . . is a geographic profiling system to help track violent criminals back to their homes. The software offers a powerful, flexible set of tools designed to assist law enforcement officers in geographic profiling. . . .
>
> The RIGEL system helps today's modern police instructor lose the old circle on the chalkboard and replace it with a better, high-tech way to find criminals where they hide.

Because of improved information sharing, interjurisdictional communication and media coverage, some homicide investigations that begin as single-incident investigations may now have the potential to develop into serial killing investigations. For example, Donald Blom, who confessed to abducting and murdering 19-year-old Katie Poirier in Minnesota is now a possible suspect in several other unsolved disappearances and murders around the state and in neighboring states. Carey Staner, a handyman suspected of the murder of a national park tourist, is suspected of three other killings. Authorities speculate that if Staner's last victim had not put up such a struggle, leaving behind a small but invaluable collection of physical evidence, his first three victims—and potentially more in the future—may have forever remained untraceable and unconnected to him.

Police officers who understand the psychology underlying serial killings will be more effective in investigating the murders and in interviewing the murderers. Profiles of

serial killers show they are extremely selfish and narcissistic and usually psychopathic. They know right from wrong—they simply do not care. They are often quite intelligent and very much in touch with reality, which partially explains their success in eluding capture.

Given these personality traits, bear in mind that when interviewing serial killers, any attempts to evoke sympathy for the victims or surviving relatives will probably be futile. Appeals to their ego, on the other hand, may succeed. It is also important not to display shock at the atrocities that may have been committed because this is often what serial murderers want.

Holmes et al. (1999), in seeking to identify and understand the reasons a serial murderer abandons normal modes of behavior and brutally takes the lives of others, have formulated the Fractured Identity Syndrome (FIS) theory:

> Serial killers are much like everyone else during the primary years of personality development. . . . What does happen, . . . often in the adolescent years, is that a social event, or a series of events, results in a fracturing of the personality of the serial killer.
>
> The term *fracture* . . . means that there is a small breakage of the personality. It is not a total destruction; the old personality is not ravaged. A small, but potent and destructive segment, takes its place alongside the total personality. . . . To the outside world, the serialist appears normal. . . . These serialists expose only their public faces. The fractured part of the personality is hidden from public view. . . .
>
> The only person to witness the fractured identity component of the actual social identity is the victim of the serial killer. . . . In essence, at the time of the murder, the killer exposes his actual social identity, laying bare his fractured identity. . . . The revelation of the fracture is comforting for the killer, and yet, it is also an experience of such vulnerability. . . . This is the reason why the witness to the fracture must be killed. After the killing, the fractured identity temporarily returns to comfort or a dominant state with the actual social identity where it once again lays [sic] in wait for the opportunity to manifest itself at the time of the next killing.

The acts of serial murderers seem incomprehensible to "normal" people. For example, in 1991 the killing and mutilation of 16 young men and boys by Jeffrey Dahmer made national headlines. When police entered Dahmer's stench-filled apartment, they found body parts of 11 males—painted human skulls, severed heads and body parts in cold storage and torsos disintegrating in an acid-filled vat. Dahmer's murders can also be classified as lust murders.

Lust Murderers

A **lust murder** is a sex-related homicide involving a sadistic, deviant assault. In lust murder the killer depersonalizes the victim, sexually mutilates the body and may displace body parts. Two types of lust murderers are often described—the organized and disorganized. The organized offender is usually of above-average intelligence, methodical and cunning. He is socially skilled and tricks his victims into a situation in which he can torture and then murder them. In contrast, the disorganized offender is usually of below-average intelligence, has no car and is a loner who acts on impulse. As Geberth (1998a, p. 98) notes: "The primary difference between organized and disorganized lust murderers is the inability of the disorganized offender to repeatedly escape apprehension."

Both the organized and disorganized offenders usually murder victims from their own geographic area, and the murders involve fantasy, ritual, fetishes and symbolism.

Physical Evidence

Physical evidence can be found on the body, at the scene or on the suspect.

- - - - - - - -

Physical evidence in a homicide includes a weapon, a body, blood, hairs and fibers.

- - - - - - - -

Any of the various types of evidence discussed can be present at a homicide scene. Especially important are the body and the weapon. In automobile homicides, physical evidence often consists of paint chips, glass fragments or tire impressions that can identify the vehicle involved. If the vehicle is located, it may contain evidence of the impact and usually has traces of the victim's blood, flesh, hair or clothing. Garner (p. 31) suggests:

Lay out your search areas by grids, strips, squares, rooms or regions, work them methodically, then swap areas of responsibility and search again. You are looking for anything that might even have a bearing on the death you are investigating. The evidence that you might collect is limited only by your eye for detail, but may include shell casings, spent projectiles, medicine or pill bottles, items of clothing, striking instruments and notes or other documents.

The Medical Examination

After the preliminary investigation, the body is taken to the morgue for an autopsy. Most large departments have medical examiners and forensic pathologists on staff or available as consultants for autopsies. The medical or forensic pathologist assists investigations by relating the evidence to the findings of the autopsy.

The main purpose of the coroner's or medical examiner's office is to determine the cause of death. If no unnatural cause is found, no crime exists. Much of the evidence that leads the examiner to conclude the death was murder also provides corroborating evidence for investigating and prosecuting the case; therefore, pathologists and investigators work together closely.

Certain types of death must be investigated. These include all violent deaths, whether homicide, suicide or an accident; sudden deaths not caused by a recognizable disease; deaths under suspicious circumstances; suspicious deaths of persons whose bodies will be cremated, dissected, buried at sea or otherwise made unavailable for further examination; deaths (other than from disease) of inmates in prisons or public institutions; deaths due to disease that may constitute a public threat; and deaths due to hazardous employment.

Before an autopsy, the body condition is kept intact. An investigator present at the autopsy records the location, date, time, names of those attending and the name of the person who performs the autopsy. The body is weighed, measured and photographed before the autopsy begins and is then periodically photographed as each stage is completed. Facial features and any marks, cuts, wounds, bruises or unusual conditions are photographed close up. The deceased, including clothing, is completely described. The clothing is tagged, marked for identification and sent to the police laboratory for examination. Fingerprints are usually taken, even if the body has been personally identified.

- - - - - - - -

The medical examination provides evidence related to the cause and time of death and to the presence of drugs or alcohol.

- - - - - - - -

After the autopsy is completed, the cause of death, if determined, is recorded. Deaths not recorded as natural, suicide or accidental are recorded as either undetermined or homicide. Before making a final determination, the medical examiner reads the police investigation reports to date. These reports indicate prior symptoms such as vomiting, a comatose state, partial paralysis, slow or rapid respiration, convulsions and various colorations. A close relationship between the pathologist and the investigator helps ensure effective exchange of information. During the investigation, report everything relating to the cause of death to the pathologist. Likewise, information discovered by the pathologist is immediately conveyed to the investigative team.

Pennsylvania has passed a law mandating that before any body is cremated, the coroner must approve the cremation. Although an autopsy is not done, the body is examined and X-rays are usually taken. This law is intended to decrease the likelihood of a murder going unnoticed.

Exhuming a Body for Medical Examination

It is not common procedure to exhume a body. Usually this is done to determine whether the cause of death stated on the death certificate is valid. It may also be done if the body is suspected of having been buried to conceal the cause of death or if the identity of the body is in question.

Exhuming a body requires adherence to strict legal procedures to prevent later civil action by relatives. First obtain permission from the principal relatives. If they do not grant it, it is necessary to obtain a court order to proceed. Arrange to have the coroner or medical examiner, a police representative, grave digger, cemetery official and family member present at the exhumation. Have the cemetery official or the person who placed the marker identify the grave. Photograph the general area, the specific grave with the marker and the coffin before exhumation.

At the morgue, the coroner, police, family, undertaker and pathologist are present at the lid opening. The body is then identified by the persons present if they knew the deceased, and the examination is conducted.

Collaborative Efforts

In addition to working with the medical examiner, investigators involved in homicide cases have other resources available to them and should collaborate with other agencies. Law enforcement agencies, particularly smaller departments with limited resources, are increasingly realizing the benefits of sharing information and expertise. As one police chief ("Regional Agencies Review. . . ," 1998, p. 39) noted: "The need is here for these agencies to coordinate, cooperate and communi-

cate. . . . People move around more now and many cases don't end at a border." A detective (p. 40) notes: "Many agencies have carefully guarded their turf for the past 20 to 30 years, but it's changing."

Death Notification

Death notification is one of the most difficult tasks in police work, yet, as Scott (1999, p. 11) states: "Death notifications remain one of the most important nonenforcement functions that officers perform." Notification may be made by a police dispatcher, police officer, police chaplain or a pastor of the religious faith of the deceased. Generally, if the police chaplain or another pastor accompanies the officer, the chaplain or pastor performs the initial notification, and the officer fills in the details. If the relative is in another community or state or is out of the country, ask police of that jurisdiction to make the notification.

Officers must be prepared for a wide range of emotional reactions people may have upon hearing such news. According to Scott (p. 11): "Denial, anger, hysteria, fainting, physical violence, shock, indifference, amnesia, and hostility represent typical responses." The officer should also carefully observe the person's reaction to the news, should they later become a suspect. As difficult as this task may be, Scott (p. 11) suggests: "Officers can lessen the negative stressful impact on themselves and the receivers of such painful news by following some simple, yet proven, procedures." He describes (p. 12) three basic steps in making death notifications: (1) gather all of the information, (2) decide who takes the lead (assuming more than one person attends the notification) and (3) deliver the news directly but sensitively. Scott's death notification overview (p. 13) advises the following:

- Always make the notification promptly and in person.
- Always try to have a two-person notification team.
- Always make the notification in private and with the receiver seated.
- Always remember that shock is a medical emergency.
- Always refer to the victim by name.
- Always offer to contact a support person and stay with the survivor until that person arrives.
- Always use clear, plain language.

- Always provide the next of kin with the procedures for obtaining the victim's personal effects; never deliver these items at the time of notification.
- Always be compassionate.

Leave a person's name or the name of an agency to contact for further information, and offer future assistance if needed. Scott (p. 14) adds: "Officers should keep survivors notified of the progress of the case, if the death resulted from violence."

Summary

Homicide investigations are challenging and frequently require all investigative techniques and skills. A basic requirement is to establish whether death was caused by a criminal action. The four basic types of death are death by natural causes, accidental death, suicide and homicide. Although technically you are concerned only with homicide, you frequently do not know at the start of an investigation what type of death has occurred; therefore, any of the four types of death may require investigation.

Homicide—the killing of one person by another—is classified as criminal (felonious) or noncriminal. Criminal homicide includes murder and manslaughter. Noncriminal homicide includes excusable homicide—the unintentional, truly accidental killing of another person—and justifiable homicide—killing another person under authorization of law. Premeditation is the essential element of first-degree murder, distinguishing it from all other murder classifications.

Special challenges in homicide investigations include pressure by the public and the media, difficulty in establishing that it is homicide rather than suicide or an accidental or natural death, identifying the victim and establishing the cause and time of death.

The first priority in a preliminary homicide investigation is to give emergency aid to the victim if he or she is still alive or to determine that death has occurred—provided the suspect is not at the scene. Signs of death include lack of breathing, lack of heartbeat, lack of flushing of the fingernail bed when pressure is applied and then released and failure of the eyelids to close after being gently lifted. After priority matters are completed, the focus of the homicide investigation is to identify the victim, establish the time of death and cause of death and the method used to produce it and to develop a suspect.

Homicide victims are identified by their relatives, friends or acquaintances; by personal effects, fingerprints, DNA analysis, skeletal studies including teeth, clothing and laundry marks; or through missing-persons files.

General factors used to estimate time of death are body temperature, rigor mortis, postmortem lividity, appearance of the eyes, stomach contents, stage of decomposition and evidence suggesting a change in the victim's normal routine. Body temperature drops 2 to 3 degrees in the first hour after death and 1 to 1 ½ degrees for each subsequent hour up to 18 hours. Rigor mortis appears in the head 5 to 6 hours after death; in the upper body after about 12 hours; and in the entire body after about 18 hours. After about 36 hours, rigor mortis usually disappears in the same sequence as it appeared. Any weapon tightly clutched in the victim's hand as the result of cadaveric spasm indicates suicide rather than murder. Postmortem lividity starts one-half to three hours after death and is congealed in the capillaries in four to five hours. Maximum lividity occurs within ten to twelve hours. The location of lividity can indicate whether a body was moved after death. A partial restriction of the pupil occurs in about seven hours. In twelve hours the cornea appears cloudy. The investigator should determine when and what the victim last ate. If any vomit is present, it should be preserved as evidence and submitted for examination. A dead body usually sinks in water and remains immersed for eight to ten days in warm water or two to three weeks in cold water. It then rises to the surface unless restricted. The outer skin loosens in five to six days, and the nails separate in two to three weeks.

Among the most common causes of unnatural death are gunshot wounds; stabbing and cutting wounds; blows from blunt instruments; asphyxia induced by choking, drowning, hanging, smothering, strangulation, gases or poisons; poisoning and drug overdoses; burning; explosions; electric shock; and lightning. In the case of a gunshot wound, suicide may be indicated if the gun was held against the skin, the wound is in the mouth or temple, the shot did not go through clothing or the weapon is present. Murder may be indicated if the gun was fired from more than a few inches away or from an angle or location that rules out self-infliction, if the victim was shot through clothing or if there is no weapon present. Stabbing and cutting wounds may be the result of suicide if the body shows hesitation wounds; if the wounds appear under clothing or on the throat, wrists or ankles; if the weapon is present; or if the body has not been moved. Defense wounds, cuts through clothing or to vital organs, disfigurement, the absence of a weapon and signs that the body has been moved indicate murder. Most cases of choking, drowning and smothering are accidental; most cases of hanging are suicides; most cases of strangulation are murder. Poisoning deaths can be accidental, suicide or murder. Most deaths caused by burning, explosions, electrocution and lightning are accidental, although burning is sometimes used in attempting to disguise murder.

The victim's background can also provide information about whether the death was an accident, a suicide or homicide. This background and the evidence on the victim's body often lead to a suspect.

Determine a motive for the killing to develop a suspect and to provide strong circumstantial evidence against the suspect. Physical evidence in a homicide includes a weapon, a body, blood, hairs and fibers.

A medical examination or an autopsy provides legal evidence related to the cause and time of death, and the presence of alcohol or drugs and corroborates information obtained during the investigation.

Checklist

Homicide

- How were the police notified? By whom? Date? Time?
- Was the victim alive or dead when the police arrived?
- Was medical help provided?
- If the victim was hospitalized, who attended the victim at the hospital? Are reports available?
- Was there a dying declaration?
- What was the condition of the body? Rigor mortis? Postmortem lividity?
- How was the victim identified?
- Has the cause of death been determined?
- Was the medical examiner notified? Are the reports available?
- Was the evidence technician team notified?
- Was the crime scene protected?
- Were arrangements made to handle the news media?
- Are all the elements of the offense present?
- What types of evidence were found at the scene?
- How was the time of death estimated?
- Was the complainant interviewed? Witnesses? Suspects? Victim if alive when police arrived?

- What leads exist?
- Was a description of the suspect obtained? Disseminated?
- Was a search or arrest warrant necessary?
- Was all evidence properly collected, identified and preserved?
- Were photographs taken of the scene? Victim? Evidence?
- Were sketches or maps of the scene made?

Application

A. Mary Jones, an 18-year-old high-school girl, quarreled with her boyfriend, Thomas Smith. At 3 A.M. following the evening of their quarrel, Mary went to Smith's home to return his picture. Smith stated that after receiving the picture, he went to his room, took a nap and awoke about 8 A.M. When he looked out his window, he saw Mary's car parked out front. Looking into the car, he discovered Mary sitting erect behind the steering wheel, shot through the chest, a .22 revolver lying beside her on the front seat. She was dead—apparently a suicide. The revolver had been a gift to Mary from her father. Smith called the police to report the shooting.

Mary had been shot once. The bullet entered just below the right breast, traveled across the front of her body and lodged near her heart. The medical examiner theorized that she did not die immediately. When found, she was sitting upright in the car, her head tilted slightly backward, her right hand high on the steering wheel, her left hand hanging limp at her left side.

When questioned, Smith steadfastly denied any knowledge of the shooting. Mary's clothing, the bullet from her body and the gun were sent to the FBI laboratory for examination. An examination of her blouse where the bullet entered failed to reveal any powder residues. The bullet removed from her body was identified as having been fired from the gun found beside her body.

Questions

1. Is the shooting likely to be a suicide or a homicide? What facts support this?
2. How should the investigation proceed?

B. Ten-year-old Denise was playing in a school parking lot with her nine-year-old stepbrother, Jerry. A car pulled up to the curb next to the lot, and the man driving the car motioned for Denise and Jerry to come over. When the man asked where they lived, Denise described their house. The man then asked Denise to take him to the house, saying he would bring her right back to the lot afterward. Denise got into the car with the man, and they drove away. When they did not return after an hour, Jerry went into the school and told a teacher what had happened. Denise did not return home that evening. The next day the police received a report that a body had been found near a lover's lane. It was Denise, who had been stabbed to death with a pocketknife.

Questions

1. What steps should be taken immediately?
2. Where would you expect to find leads?
3. What evidence would you expect to find?
4. Specifically, how would you investigate this murder?

Discussion Questions

1. Questions still remain regarding the assassination of President John F. Kennedy. Why is this murder so controversial? What special problems were involved in the investigation?

2. What special problems were encountered in investigating the shooting of Lee Harvey Oswald?

3. How many murders were committed in your community last year? In your state?

4. How do your state laws classify criminal homicide? What are the penalties for each classification? Are they appropriate? Are they more or less severe than in other states?

5. Are you for or against capital punishment for persons convicted of first-degree murder? Is execution of murderers a deterrent to crime? Is media publicity concerning such cases a deterrent to murder? Do TV shows and movies showing criminal violence contribute to such crimes? Would gun-control laws deter murder?

6. If patrol officers are dispatched to a murder scene, what are their duties and responsibilities there?

7. An investigator is called to a murder scene by the patrol officer at the scene. What are the duties and responsibilities of the investigator? What activities can be performed jointly by the patrol officer and the investigator? Who is in charge?

8. The investigation of murder is considered the classic crime investigation. Are there factors that make this crime more difficult to investigate, or is it basically the same as any other criminal investigation?

9. What investigative procedures are required in homicides resulting from drowning? Gunshot? Electrocution? Stabbing? Hanging? Poisoning?

10. Mass deaths in concentration camps during World War II, in Guyana involving a religious cult and the more recent mass deaths in Waco, Texas, introduce entirely new problems into homicide investigation. Who should be charged and with what degree of murder? What special problems are associated with such investigations?

References

Burke, Tod and Rigsby, Rhonda. "Suicide by Cop Revisited." *Law and Order,* Vol. 47, No. 6, June 1999, pp. 97–102.

Clark, Steven C. *National Guidelines for Death Investigation.* Washington, DC: National Institute of Justice, December 1997. (NCJ-167568)

"Ending Your Own Life Just Got Easier—Get a Cop to Do It." *Law Enforcement News,* Vol. XXV, Nos. 503, 504, January 15/31, 1999, pp. 1, 14.

"Facts and Figures from NLEOMF." *The Police Chief,* Vol. LXVI, No. 5, May 1999, p. 22.

Fox, James Alan and Zawitz, Marianne W. *Homicide Trends in the United States.* Washington, DC: Bureau of Justice Statistics Crime Data Brief, January 1999. (NCJ-173956)

Garner, Gerald W. "Investigating Death." *Police,* Vol. 21, No. 5, May 1997, pp. 26–33.

Geberth, Vernon. "Anatomy of Lust Murder." *Law and Order,* Vol. 46, No. 5, May 1998a, pp. 98–102.

Geberth, Vernon. "Domestic Violence Homicides." *Law and Order,* Vol. 46, No. 11, November 1998b, pp. 51–54.

Geberth, Vernon. "The Psychology of Suicide." *Law and Order,* Vol. 46, No. 10, October 1998c, pp. 163–166.

Holmes, Ronald and Holmes, Stephen. "School Shootings: A Country's Concern." *Law and Order,* Vol. 47, No. 6, June 1999, pp. 109–113.

Holmes, Stephen T.; Tewksbury, Richard; and Holmes, Ronald M. "Fractured Identity Syndrome: A New Theory of Serial Murder." *Journal of Contemporary Criminal Justice,* Vol. 15, No. 3, August 1999, pp. 262–272.

"Infrared Thermography Aids Crime Scene Detection." *Law and Order,* Vol. 46, No. 6, June 1998, p. 42.

Kennedy, Daniel B.; Homant, Robert J.; and Hupp, R. Thomas. "Suicide by Cop." *FBI Law Enforcement Bulletin,* Vol. 67, No. 8, August 1998, pp. 21–27.

"Kevorkian Says He Was Just Doing His Duty." (Minneapolis/St. Paul) *Star Tribune,* March 23, 1999, p. A4.

Kinchin, David. "Treating Fatal Road Accidents as Murders." *Law and Order,* Vol. 47, No. 3, March 1999, pp. 41–42.

MacDonald, John M.; Alpert, Geoffrey P.; and Tennenbaum, Abraham N. "Justifiable Homicide by Police and Criminal Homicide: A Research Note." *Journal of Crime and Justice,* Vol. XXII, No. 1, 1999, pp. 153–166.

Marcotty, Josephine and Smith, Dane. "Setting Straight the Facts behind Suicides." (Minneapolis/St. Paul) *Star Tribune,* October 8, 1999, pp. B1, B7.

Morrison, Richard D. "Tracking Serial Killers and Serial Rapists." *Law Enforcement Technology,* Vol. 25, No. 9, September 1998, pp. 68–71.

"Number of Police Killed on the Job Up 37%." (Minneapolis/St. Paul) *Star Tribune,* August 13, 1998, p. A17.

"Officer Death Rate Fails to Pace Crime Decline." *Police,* Vol. 23, No. 3, March 1999, p. 8.

Parent, Richard. "Suicide by Cop." *The Police Chief,* Vol. LXV, No. 10, October 1998, pp. 111–114.

"PDs Grope for Answers to Cop Suicides." *Law Enforcement News,* Vol. XXV, No. 514, June 30, 1999, p. 5.

"Police Fatalities Drop More than 15% in 1999." *Law Enforcement Technology,* Vol. 27, No. 2, February 2000, p. 8.

Quinnett, Paul. "QPR: Police Suicide Prevention." *FBI Law Enforcement Bulletin,* Vol. 67, No. 7, July 1998, pp. 19–24.

"Regional Agencies Review Homicide Cases, Share Resources." *Law and Order,* Vol. 46, No. 11, November 1998, pp. 39–40.

Scott, Brian J. "Preferred Protocol for Death Notification." *FBI Law Enforcement Bulletin,* Vol. 68, No. 8, August 1999, pp. 11–15.

Scoville, Dean. "Getting You to Pull the Trigger." *Police,* Vol. 22, No. 11, November 1998, pp. 36–44.

Strandberg, Keith W. "Suicide in Law Enforcement." *Law Enforcement Technology,* Vol. 24, No. 7, July 1997, pp. 38–40, 74–77.

Wells, Jeff. "Forensic Entomologist Uses Maggots to Blow Killers' Alibis." *Las Vegas Review Journal,* November 30, 1998, p. 6A.

Zamora, Jim Herron. "Suicide Prompts Review of Cop Stress." *San Francisco Examiner,* May 12, 1997, pp. A1, A9.

Investigating Crimes against Property

Most of the crimes discussed in this section do not involve force or violence against people and therefore are often not considered to be as serious as assault, robbery, rape or murder. However, according to the *Uniform Crime Reports,* crimes against property occur much more frequently than crimes against persons. For example, larceny/theft accounted for 59.1 percent of the crimes reported in 1998. The following figures present the percentage breakdown for 1998 Crime Index offenses. In 1998 a crime against property occurred every 3 seconds in the United States:

- One larceny/theft every 4 seconds
- One burglary every 14 seconds
- One motor vehicle theft every 25 seconds

**Crime Index
Offenses—1998**
Percent Distribution[1]

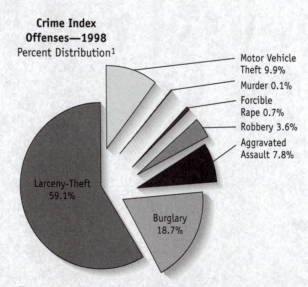

[1]Due to rounding, percentages do not add to 100.

Source: *Crime in the United States 1998.* The Uniform Crime Reports. Washington, DC: Department of Justice, FBI, 1999.

For the seventh consecutive year crimes against property decreased. In 1998, motor vehicle thefts dropped 8.4 percent, and larceny/theft dropped 4.8 percent.

Many property crimes are difficult to investigate because there is little evidence and there are usually no eyewitnesses.

Physical evidence in property crimes is often similar to that found in crimes against persons: fingerprints, footprints, tire impressions, hair, fibers, broken glass and personal objects left at the crime scene. Other important evidence in crimes against property includes tools, tool fragments, toolmarks, safe insulation, disturbance of paint and evidence of forcible entry. The modus operandi of a property crime often takes on added importance because there are no other significant leads. Further, crimes against property tend to occur in series, so solving one crime may lead to solving an entire series of similar crimes.

The chapters in this section discuss specific considerations in investigating burglary (Chapter 14), larceny/theft (Chapter 15), motor vehicle theft (Chapter 16) and arson (Chapter 17).

Burglary

Do You Know?

How to define *burglary?*

What the basic difference between burglary and robbery is?

What the two basic classifications of burglary are?

What three elements are present in laws defining burglary?

What additional elements can be included in burglary?

What determines the severity of a burglary?

What the elements of the crime of possession of burglary tools are?

How to proceed to a burglary scene and what to do on arrival?

What special challenges are involved in burglary investigations?

What is the most frequent means of entry to commit burglary?

How safes are broken into and what evidence to look for?

What physical evidence is often found at a burglary scene?

What modus operandi factors are important in burglary?

Where to search for stolen property?

What measures might be taken to prevent burglary?

Introduction

In a western city, police officers noticed what they believed was safe insulation on the steps of a cabin occupied by a known burglar. They obtained a warrant and searched the premises for evidence of a burglary. The substance found on the steps and some burglary tools found inside the home were mailed to a laboratory, where the substance was confirmed as safe insulation. The suspect was arrested and convicted of burglary. On appeal, the courts held that such knowledge on the officers' part was in effect an extension of the laboratory and was therefore probable cause even without the laboratory examination.

The verification by the laboratory only strengthened the probable cause, and the charge of burglary was sustained.

The FBI's *Uniform Crime Reports* define **burglary** as "the unlawful entry of a structure to commit a felony or theft, even though no force was used to gain entry." All such attempts also count as burglaries. The common-law definition of *burglary* (originating in sixteenth-century England) required that the breaking and entering be committed during the nighttime or "between sunset and sunrise." Many changes have been made in burglary statutes since that time, including eliminating the requirement that it occur between sunset and sunrise.

Burglary is the unlawful entry of a structure to commit a crime.

The word *burglar* comes from the German words *burg,* meaning "house," and *laron,* meaning "thief"; thus the meaning "house thief."

Burglary is reported by frequency and by the value of the property stolen and recovered. This is because many burglaries yield low losses, although a single burglary can yield a high loss. The public regards burglary as a major crime problem. Many people fear arriving home or at work and confronting a burglar, a situation that can develop into an assault. Moreover, it is traumatic for people to realize that they have been doubly victimized when someone has invaded the privacy of their home or business and stolen their possessions. Although the items taken may be covered by insurance, they may be irreplaceable because of their great sentimental value.

This chapter first explains the basic differences between burglary and robbery and presents a classification of various types of burglary. It then discusses the elements of the crime of burglary, how to determine its severity and the elements of the crime of burglary tools in possession. Next the chapter describes the "typical" burglar, how to respond to a burglary call and how to conduct the preliminary investigation. Then it explores precautions to take if explosives are discovered at the scene of a burglary. Next follows a description of modus operandi factors to consider and the possibility of fake burglaries. The chapter concludes with a discussion of effective case management, recovery of stolen property and burglary prevention. ■

Burglary vs. Robbery

A burglar seeks to avoid contact with people near the scene or on the premises.

Burglary differs from robbery in that burglars are covert, seeking to remain unseen, whereas robbers confront their victims directly. Burglary is a crime against property; robbery is a crime against a person.

Most burglaries occur in unoccupied homes and businesses; therefore, few witnesses exist, and few alarms are given to provide advance notice to the police. The best chances of apprehending a burglar in the act are when a silent alarm is tripped, a surveillance camera records the crime, a witness hears or sees suspicious activities and reports them immediately to the police or when alert patrol officers observe a burglary in progress. However, most burglaries are not solved at the crime scene but through subsequent investigation.

Classification

Burglaries are classified as residential or commercial.

Residential Burglaries

A **residential burglary** is one that occurs in buildings, structures or attachments that are used as or are suitable for dwellings, even though they may be unoccupied at the time of the burglary. Residential units include private homes, tenements, mobile homes, cabins, apartments, rooms within a house leased by a renter, houseboats used as dwellings and any other structure suitable for and used as a dwelling. About two-thirds of all burglaries are residential burglaries.

Burglars often ransack rooms looking for valuables, making it difficult for the victim to know what is missing. Often there are no leads and, therefore, little hope of apprehending the burglar or recovering the stolen property.

Residential burglaries are often committed by one or more juveniles or young adults who live in the same community. The targets are cash, items to convert to personal use or items to "fence" or sell, such as televisions, radios, computers, guns, jewelry, tools and other small household goods.

Whereas the study of burglary and related crime rates has historically focused on the offender, new theories shift the focus toward the victims and particular times and places. For example, the **lifestyle/exposure theory** links victimization risks to the daily activities of specific individuals. Robinson (1999, p. 29) states:

> Lifestyles are patterned, regular, recurrent, prevalent, or "routine activities." . . .
>
> Lifestyle . . . influences daily routines and vulnerability to criminal victimization, resulting in the fact that victimization is not evenly distributed randomly across space and time—there are high-risk locations and high-risk time periods. Lifestyle patterns influence (a) the amount of exposure to places and times with varying risks of victimization, and (b) the prevalence of associations with others who are more or less likely to commit crimes.

Another closely related hypothesis is the **routine activity theory,** which proposes that "crime results from the convergence of three elements in time and space: a presence of likely or motivated offenders; a presence of suitable targets; and an absence of capable guardians to prevent the criminal act" (Robinson, p. 31). Both theories acknowledge the role, however indirect, of victims in their own victimization and suggest that certain locations may be more susceptible to burglary at certain times because of the routine absence of residents.

Commercial Burglaries

A **commercial burglary** is one that involves churches, schools, barns, public buildings, shops, offices, stores, factories, warehouses, stables, ships and railroad cars.

Most commercial burglaries are committed in service stations, stores, schools, manufacturing plants, warehouses and office buildings. Burglars often specialize in one type of facility. Businesses located in out-of-the-way places are most susceptible to burglary because of a lack of police coverage and street lighting and because there are usually few witnesses to observe wrongdoing and notify the police.

Commercial burglaries are often committed by two or more people, depending on the type of premises, size and location of the building and the planned burglary attack. Some use a lookout who acts like a drunk, works on a stalled car or walks an animal near the location.

The building is "cased" in advance to learn about security devices, opening and closing times, employee habits, people in the neighborhood and the presence of a private security officer. Casing is also done by obtaining information from an employee or by posing as a worker, repairperson or salesperson to gain legitimate entrance.

Elements of the Crime: Burglary

Although burglary laws vary from state to state, statutes of all states include three key elements.

- - - - - - - -

Elements of the crime of burglary include:

- Entering a structure,
- Without the consent of the person in possession,
- With the intent to commit a crime therein.

- - - - - - - -

Entering a Structure Entry may be by walking through an open door, crawling through an open window or transom, reaching through an open door or window with a long stick or pole or climbing through a hole in the wall, through a tunnel or through a ventilation shaft. Entry can be made by jimmying a door or window, using a celluloid strip to open a door lock, climbing a ladder or stairs outside a building, descending through a skylight, hiding in an entryway or breaking a window and taking items from the window display, called **smash and grab.** Entry also includes remaining in a store until after closing time and then committing a burglary.

Some state laws include vehicles, trailers and railroad cars as structures.

Without the Consent of the Person in Possession To constitute burglary, the entry must be illegal and must be committed without permission of a person with lawful authority, that is, the owner of the property, the legal agent of such person or the person in physical control of the property such as a renter or part owner.

Entering a public place is done with consent unless consent has been expressly withdrawn. The hours for legal entry usually are posted on public buildings; for example, "Open Weekdays 9 A.M. to 5 P.M." Entrance at any other time is without consent. If a specific individual is restricted from entering a public place during its open hours, that individual must be notified orally or in writing that consent has been withdrawn.

With Intent to Commit a Crime Regardless of whether the burglary is planned well in advance or committed on the spur of the moment, intent must be shown. When the first two elements are present, the third is often presumed present; that is, if a person enters a structure without the owner's consent, the presumption is that it is to commit a crime, usually larceny or a sex offense.

Additional Elements

Three additional elements are found in the laws of some states.

- - - - - - - -

Elements of burglary can also include breaking into the dwelling of another during the nighttime.

- - - - - - - -

Breaking Into Actual "breaking" is a matter of interpretation. Any force used during the burglary to enter or leave the structure, even if a door or window is partly opened or closed, constitutes breaking. Entrance through trick or ruse or through threats to or collusion with any person residing in the building is also considered breaking.

Breaking and entering is strong **presumptive evidence** that a crime is intended, that is, it provides a reasonable basis for belief. Some laws include such wording as:

Every person who shall unlawfully break and enter a building or dwelling or other structure shall be deemed to have broken and entered or entered the same with intent to commit grand or petit larceny or a felony therein, unless such unlawful breaking and entering entry shall be explained by testimony satisfactory to the jury to have been made without criminal intent.

This, in effect, places the burden of proof on the defendant.

The Dwelling of Another Some states still require that the structure broken into be a dwelling, that is, a structure suitable for sheltering humans. This remnant from common law restricts burglary to residential burglaries.

During the Nighttime Common law also specified that burglary occur under the cover of darkness, an element still retained in some state laws. Nighttime is defined as the period from sunset to sunrise as specified by official weather charts.

Establishing the Severity of the Burglary

Most burglary laws increase the crime's severity if the burglar possesses a weapon or an explosive. Obtain the weapon and connect it with the burglar if possible. Check with the National Crime Information Center. If the weapon is stolen, a separate felony charge of theft or illegal possession of a weapon can be made.

A burglary's severity is determined by the presence of dangerous devices in the burglar's possession or the value of the property stolen.

If other crimes are committed along with the burglary or if the burglary is for the purpose of committing another crime such as rape, the additional crime is separate and must be proven separately.

Elements of the Crime: Possession of Burglary Tools

A companion crime to burglary is possession of burglary tools, an offense separate from burglary. The charge of possession of burglary tools can be made even if a burglary has not been committed if circumstances indicate that the tools were intended for use in a burglary.

Elements of the crime of possessing burglary tools include:

■ Possessing any device, explosive or other instrumentality.

■ With intent to use or permit their use to commit burglary.

Burglary tools include nitroglycerin, explosives and any engine, machine, tool, implement, chemical or substance designed for cutting or burning open buildings or protective containers.

A person with a large number of automobile keys probably intends to use them to open varied makes and models of vehicle doors. Portable key cutters, codes and key blanks such as those used in hardware stores and key-making shops are also classified as burglary tools, as are slam pullers, devices that look like an oversized screwdriver and are inserted in car locks to force them open.

Many other tools used in burglaries are commonly obtained in hardware stores. These include pry bars, screwdrivers, bolt cutters, extension cords, pipe wrenches, channel locks and tire irons. Lock picks and tension wrenches, lever-type wrenches, warded pass keys, pick guns, cylinder drill jigs and various types of metal blades to open car doors can also be used as burglary tools.

Because many people, especially mechanics and carpenters, have tools that might be used in a burglary in their car or on their person, circumstances must clearly show an intent to use or allow their use in committing a crime.

The Burglar

The burglar is often portrayed as a masked person with a bag over the shoulder loaded with silverware and candlesticks. In reality, burglars fit no set image; they are of all sizes, ages, races and occupations. They are either amateurs or long-time professionals whose sole income is derived from burglaries.

Most amateur burglars are between the ages of 15 and 25; most professionals are 25 to 55. The amateur is usually an unskilled, "infancy level" burglar who steals radios, televisions, cash and other portable property and who learns through trial and error. In contrast, the professional burglar usually steals furs, jewelry and more valuable items and has been carefully trained by other professional burglars.

Even though amateurs gain experience in committing burglaries, they are apt to make a mistake sooner or later and be observed by the police while committing a burglary. If caught and sentenced to prison, amateur burglars gain the opportunity to learn more about the "trade" from the professionals.

Professional burglars may have lookouts in communication through two-way radios. A getaway vehicle is usually close to the burglary site, and the lookout monitors police radio frequencies.

Although most burglars' motives are monetary or drug related, sometimes the excitement of committing burglary and evading detection is equally or more important. One burglar said it was a "thrill" not to know what was waiting for him and if he would get away with the crime.

Responding to a Burglary Call

Proceed to a burglary scene quietly. Be observant and cautious at the scene.

On the way to the burglary scene, watch for persons fleeing the area, suspicious-looking persons still at the scene and suspicious automobiles. Do not use a siren on the way to the scene. Cut your flashing lights some distance from the scene, and do not use a spotlight or flashlight to determine the address. Park several doors away from the address of the call, turn the radio down and close car doors quietly. Approach the immediate area with low-tone conversation and avoid jangling keys or coins or flashing lights.

The first two officers arriving place themselves at diagonally opposed corners of the building. This places them out of the other's line of fire but in position to protect each other.

Search the premises inside and outside for the burglar.

Use maximum cover and caution in going around corners. In a dark room, use a flashlight rather than room lights to prevent silhouettes. Hold the flashlight in front of you at a 45-degree angle. Have your gun drawn but not cocked.

Harris (1998b, pp. 157–160) summarizes the burglary response in five "s" steps:

- speed
- safety
- silence
- scanning
- strategic positioning

The Preliminary Investigation

Harris (1998a, p. 122) asserts: "With a national burglary clearance rate of only about 15%, it's time to get patrol officers more involved in fighting the problem from an investigative perspective." He adds (p. 119): "A preliminary investigation of a burglary should be recognized as an opportunity to investigate. On too many occasions, it is viewed as the distasteful chore of completing yet another form."

If no suspect is found, conduct the preliminary investigation as described in Chapter 1. Obtain detailed information about the type of structure burglarized, the means of entry, the time and date, the whereabouts of the owner, other persons recently on the premises, the property taken and the MO.

Determine who the occupants are and where they were at the time of the burglary. Were they on the premises? If not, when did they leave? Were the doors and windows locked? Who had keys? What visitors had recently been there? Obtain descriptions of peddlers, agents, service installers or maintenance people on the premises recently. Was the burglar familiar with the premises? Could the location of the stolen items be known only to a person who worked on the premises; that is, was it an inside job?

Obtain a complete list of the property taken. Estimate the value and find out where the property was obtained and where it was stored. Where and when did the owner last see it? What type of property was *not* stolen?

Harris (1998a, pp. 119–120) notes three basic leads most frequently solve burglaries:

- Interview witnesses—The victim is the most overlooked witness in a burglary. Many veteran detectives believe that in half of all burglaries there is a connection between the victim and the suspect. The suspect may have recently performed work or attended a party in the home. To locate other witnesses, conduct a neighborhood canvass. See if anyone saw anything. A canvass also serves to alert neighbors so they can take steps to avoid victimization.
- Check physical evidence—Evidence could be in the form of latent fingerprints, items brought and left on the premises by the burglar, or tool marks left by the instrument used to pry open a door or window. If no physical evidence is recovered at the scene, there is little chance of charging anyone.
- Follow up evidence—Check pawn shops to determine if any of the stolen items have been acquired. Articles with serial numbers are logged into NCIC. This lead is a long shot at best.

Residential Burglaries

The preliminary investigation of a residential burglary should include the following as a minimum:

- Contact the resident(s).
- Establish points and methods of entry and exit.
- Collect and preserve evidence.
- Determine the type and amount of loss, with complete descriptions.
- Describe the MO.
- Check for recent callers such as friends of children, salespeople and maintenance people.
- Canvass the neighborhood for witnesses, evidence, discarded stolen articles, etc.

Interviews of burglars have revealed that they prefer middle- to upper-class homes and corner homes that allow them to see people approaching from more directions. They may knock on doors before entering to determine if a dog is inside, and they may call in advance to see if anyone is home. The advent of Caller ID may bring about some change in this technique.

When processing the crime scene in a residential burglary, process the exit as well as the entry area. When looking for fingerprints, check the inside of drawers that have been ransacked, smooth glass objects, papers strewn on the floor, countertops and clocks. The same procedures are followed if the burglary has occurred in a multiple-dwelling or a commercial lodging establishment such as an apartment building or a hotel.

Commercial Burglaries

Preliminary investigation of a commercial burglary (for example, markets, shops, offices, liquor stores) should minimally include the following:

- Contact the owner.
- Protect the scene from intrusion by owners, the public and others.
- Establish the point and method of entry and exit.
- Locate, collect and preserve possible evidence.
- Narrow the time frame of the crime.
- Determine the type and amount of loss.
- Determine who closed the establishment, who was present at the time of the crime and who had keys to the establishment.
- Describe the MO.
- Identify friends of employees, maintenance people and any possible disgruntled employees or customers.
- Rule out a faked or staged burglary for insurance purposes.

Special Challenges in Investigation

- - - - - - - -

> Special challenges in investigating burglary include false alarms, determination of the means of entry into a structure as well as into objects such as safes or vaults and recovery of the stolen property.

- - - - - - - -

False Burglar Alarms False burglar alarms from personal security systems are a huge problem for law enforcement agencies. According to Spivey and Cobb (1997, p. 44): "Various surveys estimate that alarm calls account for 10 to 30 percent of all calls for police service; of these, 94 to 98 percent are false alarms." False alarms cost departments in wasted time and fiscal resources. One study estimated: "The direct annual cost of false alarms to police departments nationwide is at least $600 million, and achieving a major reduction in false alarm activations could free up as many as 60,000 officers in the United States" (Spivey and Cobb, p. 44). Not only are false alarms a waste of time for responding officers, but more important, they may cause officers to be caught off guard when a genuine alarm occurs.

Determining Entry into Structures

Burglary is a crime of opportunity and concealment. Entry is made in areas of a structure not normally observed, under the cover of darkness, in covered entryways, through windows screened by shrubbery or trees or through ruse and trickery. Sometimes, however, the burglar breaks a shop window, removes some items on display and rapidly escapes by jumping into a nearby vehicle driven by an accomplice.

- - - - - - - -

Jimmying is the most common method of entry to commit burglary.

- - - - - - - -

Almost every means imaginable has been used, including tunneling; chopping holes in walls, floors and ceilings; and using fire escapes. Some burglars have keys made. For example, some people leave their car at a repair shop along with their full set of keys—an open invitation to make a duplicate house or office key. At other times burglars hide inside a building until after closing. In such cases they often leave behind evidence such as matches, cigarette butts or candy wrappers because their wait is often lengthy. The **hit-and-run burglary,** also called smash-and-grab, in which the burglar smashes a window to steal merchandise, is most frequently committed by younger, inexperienced burglars. Jewelry and furs are the most common targets.

In recent years enterprising burglars have taken advantage of the prevalence of electric garage door openers. Using "code grabbers," burglars can record and replicate the electronic signal emitted from an automatic garage door opener. When a person leaves

Some burglars use a rock or brick to smash a display window and to then steal valuable merchandise. Such smash-and-grab burglaries often set off an alarm.

the house and activates the garage door opener, the burglar is able to capture the signal from up to several hundred yards away and reopen the door once the resident is safely out of sight. Some burglars are bold enough to back their own car into the garage, load it up with stolen items and drive away, leaving no sign of forced entry.

To combat the "code grabbing" technique to gain entrance into homes, a new device called a "code rotator" is now available. Each time an automatic door opener is used, the internal code rotates to a new one, rendering a "code grabber" useless.

Toolmarks, disturbed paint, footprints and finger-prints, broken glass or forced locks help determine how the burglar gained entry.

Determining Entry into Safes and Vaults

Safes are usually considered a good way to protect valuables, but most older safes provide little more than fire protection. Unless they are carried away or demolished by a burglar or lost in a fire, safes last many years; therefore, many old safes are still in use.

A **safe** is a semiportable strongbox with a combination lock. The size of the safe or lock does not necessarily correlate with its security. A **vault** is a stationary room of reinforced concrete, often steel lined, with a combination lock. Both safes and vaults are common targets of burglars.

Safes and vaults are entered illegally by punching, peel-ing, pulling, blowing, burning and chopping. Some-times burglars simply haul the safes away.

In **punching,** the burglar shears the dial from the safe door by holding a chisel to the dial and using a sledge to knock it off, exposing the safe mechanism spin-dle. Next the burglar holds a drift pin against the spindle and then uses the sledge to knock the spindle backward, releasing the tumblers.

In **peeling,** the burglar drills a hole in a corner of the safe and then makes this hole successively larger by using other drills until the narrow end of a jimmy can be inserted in the hole to pry the door partially open. The burglar then uses the larger end of the jimmy to com-plete the job. Although slow, this method is less noisy than other methods.

In **pulling,** also called **dragging,** the burglar inserts a *V* plate over the dial with the *V* in place behind the dial. The burglar then tightens the screw bolts one at a time until the dial and the spindle are pulled out. This method, the opposite of punching, works on many older safes but not on newer ones.

In **blowing,** the burglar drills a hole in the safe near the locking bar area or pushes cotton into an area of the safe door crack and puts nitroglycerin on the cotton. The bur-glar then places a primer cap against the cotton, tapes it in place and runs a wire to a protected area. Mattresses and blankets are often used to soften the blast. The burglar ignites the nitroglycerin, which blows the safe open. This danger-ous, noisy method requires experience and is rarely used.

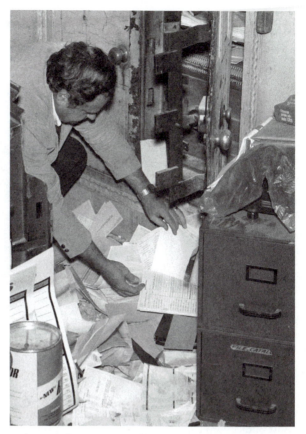

Safes are a frequent target of burglars.

The **burning** process often uses a "burning bar," a portable safe-cracking tool that burns a hole into the safe to gain entry. This hole may be burned near the safe's locking mechanism, or the safe may be tipped over and the hole burned through the bottom. An arc-air burning tool can punch a hole completely through a one-inch steel plate in about 10 seconds.

In **chopping,** the burglar uses chisels to chop a hole in the bottom of the safe large enough to remove the contents. This difficult, noisy process is seldom used.

Some burglars use one or more of the methods just explained at a site of their own choosing. They steal the entire safe, haul it away in a truck, and then open it.

The preceding methods are used on older safes still found in many smaller stores. Often the safe can be entered in under 15 minutes. Modern safes, however, do not have spindles and cannot be punched, peeled or pulled. Safes of newer steel alloys are highly resistant to burning and drilling.

A door frame at a burglary scene may contain evidence such as fingerprints and toolmarks.

Obtaining Physical Evidence

Most burglars are convicted on circumstantial evidence. Any physical evidence at the burglary scene is of the utmost importance.

- - - - - - - - -

Physical evidence at a burglary scene includes fingerprints, footprints, tire prints, tools, toolmarks, broken glass, safe insulation, paint chips and personal possessions.

- - - - - - - - -

Tools and toolmarks are especially important items of evidence that can connect one burglary with another. Be alert to the variety of containers used to carry burglary tools—handbags, suitcases, musical-instrument cases and packages that appear to contain merchandise. Tools can also be concealed under coats, inside pant legs or under car seats. Tools on the premises are also sometimes used to avoid being caught with burglary tools in possession.

Evidence at the scene of a safe burglary may also include safe insulation. The burglar often has some of this insulation on his or her clothing, either in pants, coat or jacket pockets or in the nailholes of shoes. Take comparison standards of safe insulation to be matched with particles found on the suspect, on tools the suspect used or in the vehicle used during the crime. In some cases safe insulation can also be matched with a series of burglaries.

DNA is also becoming important in burglary investigations. If a burglar gets cut breaking into a structure, he or she may leave blood behind that can be analyzed for DNA, perhaps linking the burglary to others.

Precautions for Explosives at the Scene

Sometimes explosives are encountered at a burglary scene. Use extreme caution in handling and preserving such evidence.

If a bomb threat is connected with a burglary, notify the FBI. If explosives are actually detonated, notify the Alcohol, Tobacco and Firearms Division of the U.S. Treasury Department. To dispose of explosives at the scene or in the suspect's possession, call the bomb squad of the nearest large metropolitan area or the explosives ordinance unit of the closest military installation. If an explosion has already occurred at the burglary scene, intentionally or accidentally, identify and preserve fragments from the explosive device and send them to a crime laboratory.

Modus Operandi Factors

Effective MO files are essential in investigating burglaries because most burglars commit a series of burglaries. Look for patterns in the location, day of week, time of day, type of property stolen and method of entry or exit. The burglar may commit vandalism, ransack, write with lipstick on mirrors, take only cash or jewelry, drink liquor from the scene or eat from the refrigerator. Such peculiarities can tie several burglaries to one suspect.

- - - - - - - - - -

> Important modus operandi factors include the time, type of victim, type of premises, point and means of entry, type of property taken and any peculiarities of the offense.

- - - - - - - - - -

Suspects often commit burglaries on only a certain day of the week, perhaps related to their day off from a regular job. The time of the burglary should be as accurate as possible, but when victims are gone on vacation, this is not easy to determine. Knowing the time also helps in checking alibis, interviewing witnesses and, in some states, determining the degree of the burglary.

Determine any peculiarities of the offense, including oddities of the suspect. What method of search was used? Was anything else done besides committing the burglary? Did the burglar telephone first to ensure that no one was home or pose as a delivery person? Did neighbors see such activities? Determine any trademarks of the burglar. Some burglars take such pride in their professionalism that they leave a calling card of some type to let the police know whose work it is.

Check the MO with local files. Talk to other officers, inquire at other agencies within a 100-mile radius and discuss the case at area investigation meetings. Other officers may have encountered a similar MO.

Fake Burglaries

Do not overlook the possibility of faked burglaries, especially in commercial burglaries where the owner appears to be in financial difficulty. Check the owner's financial status.

So-called combination safe jobs, in which the safe is opened by the combination without the use of external force, are usually due to the combination being found on the premises, the safe being carelessly left open or improperly locked, a dishonest present or former employee using the combination or selling it to the burglar or the employer faking a burglary to cover a shortage of funds.

Effective Case Management

Because burglary is predominantly a serial crime, the serial burglar should be the primary target of the burglary unit. This requires effective case management, including an effective system for prioritizing cases. Profiling may help, as Cook and Hinman (1999, p. 231) explain:

> Profilers study the evidence of the offender's activities with the victim and the offender's preparation and technical attention to details to develop a profile of the kind of person who is most likely to have committed the crime. When the profile is complete, the descriptors in it are compared to potential suspects as they are developed.

Effective case management also recognizes the mobility of burglars and makes assignments on the MO rather than on the geographic area—for example, burglaries involving forcible entry, daytime burglaries involving no force and nighttime residential burglaries. All information should be shared with the drug enforcement unit because many burglaries are drug related.

Using Computers to Investigate Burglaries

Kruse (1996, p. 66) describes the impact of computers on criminal investigations: "The computers have helped clear cases by discovering that some piece of evidence is duplicated in several different cases, sometimes a witness's name comes up several times and that information has been very helpful."

Using the computer's search capabilities, information retrieval is fast and simple, and investigations can proceed on information that in the past would have taken hundreds of hours to retrieve if indeed it could have been retrieved at all.

Showing Concern for Burglary Victims

Surveys indicate that victims' impressions of the police are related to how professionally investigators conduct the crime scene investigation. If officers are thorough, courteous, considerate, concerned and conscientious about keeping the victims informed of the progress of the investigation, victims generally express favorable opinions of the investigators. Solving the crime is first priority for the police, but the victims' feelings must be considered as well. They may feel devastated, violated, angry or completely dejected. Investigators must keep these feelings in mind as they conduct interviews with victims.

Recovering Stolen Property

Most burglars take money, jewelry, precious stones, negotiable bonds and other property that can be easily disposed of through a pawnshop, secondhand store or a **fence,** that is, a seller of stolen property.

- - - - - - - -

> Check with fences, pawnshops, secondhand stores, flea markets and informants for leads in recovering stolen property.

- - - - - - - -

One indicator of fencing activity is an operation that makes merchandise available to retailers at extremely low wholesale prices provided they pay cash. Another possible indicator is a small local outlet that offers significant savings to customers, conducts a large volume of business over a short period and then closes suddenly. Sales from fenced goods amounts to tens of billions of dollars annually.

Informants can often locate stolen property because they usually know who is active in the area. Surveillance of pawnshops and fences also is often productive. Circulate a list of the stolen property to all establishments that might deal in such merchandise in your own community and surrounding communities. If the property is extremely valuable, enter it into the FBI's NCIC files.

If property is recovered, determine how it got to where it was found. Have the owner identify the property. Although a fence does not normally identify a burglar, a pawnshop or secondhand store owner can often make such an identification.

There is often a higher ratio of property recovered than cases cleared by arrest because some property is discovered abandoned and some victims make deals with the burglars to recover their property when little hope of obtaining a conviction exists. The property recovery rate is between 25 and 40 percent in most communities.

Recovering stolen property and returning it to the rightful owner is aided by Operation Identification programs. In such programs homeowners mark all easily stolen property with a Personal Identification Number (PIN). The numbers are recorded and placed in a secure location.

Preventing Burglary

Officers who work with burglary victims can help them avoid future burglaries by conducting a security check of the premises. They can also assist their jurisdiction in reducing burglaries by having input into building codes that would require adequate locks, lighting and other security measures to deter burglaries.

- - - - - - - -

> Measures that deter burglaries include:

- Installing adequate locks, striker plates and door frames.
- Installing adequate indoor and outdoor lighting.
- Providing clearly visible addresses.
- Installing burglar-proof sidelight window glass beside doors.
- Installing a burglar alarm.

- - - - - - - -

Hoffman (1998, p. 151) notes how the institution of building codes has reduced burglaries significantly in some communities. For example, one area has experienced a 52 percent reduction in burglaries over 20 years, due in large part to the implementation of a building code.

Summary

Burglary is the unlawful entry of a structure to commit a crime. It differs from robbery in that burglars are covert, seeking to remain unseen, whereas robbers confront their victims directly. Burglary is a crime against property; robbery is a crime against a person.

Burglaries are classified as residential or commercial. The elements of the crime of burglary include (1) entering a structure (2) without the consent of the person in possession (3) with the intent to commit a crime therein. Additional elements of burglary that may be required include (1) breaking into (2) the dwelling of another (3) during the nighttime. A burglary's severity is determined by the presence of dangerous devices in the burglar's possession or by the value of the stolen property. Attempted burglary and possession of burglary tools are also felonies. The elements of the crime of possessing burglary tools include (1) possessing any device, explosive or other instrumentality (2) with intent to use or permit their use to commit burglary.

When responding to a burglary call, proceed to the scene quietly. Be observant and cautious. Search the premises inside and outside for the burglar. Special considerations in investigating burglary include the problem of false alarms, determination of the means of entry into a structure as well as into objects such as safes or vaults and recovery of the stolen property. Jimmying is the most common method to enter a structure to commit burglary. Attacks on safes and vaults include punching, peeling, pulling or dragging, blowing, burning, chopping and, for safes, hauling them away.

Physical evidence at a burglary scene often includes fingerprints, footprints, tire prints, tools, toolmarks, broken glass, safe insulation, paint chips and personal possessions. Important modus operandi factors include the time, the types of premises, the type of victim, point and means of entry, type of property taken and any peculiarities of the offense.

Check with fences, pawnshops, secondhand stores, flea markets and informants for leads in recovering stolen property. Measures to deter burglaries include installing adequate locks, striker plates and door frames; installing adequate indoor and outdoor lighting; providing clearly visible addresses; eliminating bushes or other obstructions to windows; securing any skylights or air vents over 96 inches; installing burglar-proof sidelight window glass beside doors; and installing a burglar alarm.

Checklist

Burglary

- Was a thorough preliminary investigation conducted?
- What is the address and description of the structure burglarized?
- What time and date did the burglary occur?
- What means was used to enter? Was it forcible?
- Who is the rightful owner? Was consent given for the entry?
- What visitors had recently been on the premises?
- Was the burglar familiar with the premises?
- What was taken (complete description and value of each item)?
- Where was the property located, and when was it last seen by the owner?
- What was *not* taken?
- What pattern of search did the burglar use?

- What was the burglar's MO?
- What physical evidence was found at the scene?
- Did any witnesses see or hear anything suspicious at the time of the burglary?
- Does the owner have any idea who might have committed the burglary?
- Have the MO files been checked?
- Have neighboring communities been informed of the burglary?
- Have you checked with fences, pawnshop owners and secondhand stores for the stolen property? Have you circulated a list to the owners of such businesses?
- Might this be a fake burglary?

Application

Read this account of a criminal investigation and evaluate its effectiveness:

In a California city two janitors were met at the door of the restaurant they were cleaning by two armed men. One janitor was taken inside; the other escaped and notified the police. When the police arrived, both suspects were outside the building in different areas and claimed they knew nothing of a crime being committed. Inside, the one janitor was tied up in the kitchen, unharmed. The safe had been punched open. A substance believed to be safe insulation, along with paint chips, was found in the trouser cuffs and shoes of both suspects. Both janitors made a positive field identification of the two suspects. Laboratory analysis of the substance found in the suspects' clothing and shoes matched a comparison sample of the safe insulation, and the paint chips matched the top two layers of paint on the safe. The men were charged with burglary.

Questions

1. Was it legal to take the men into custody?
2. Was field identification appropriate?
3. Was it legal to submit the safe insulation and paint chips for laboratory analysis?
4. Was the charge correct?
5. What additional evidence should have been located and seized?

Discussion Questions

1. Many people think of *burglary* and *robbery* as interchangeable terms. What is the principal difference between these two offenses from an investigative viewpoint?

2. Describe the following methods of entering a safe: a pull job; a peel job; a chopping; blowing a safe; burning.

3. What types of evidence would you expect to find at the scene of a safe burglary? How would you collect and preserve it?

4. What are the elements of burglary in your state? What is the penalty?

5. How frequent is burglary in your community? Your state? Has burglary been increasing or decreasing in the past five years?

6. If you are investigating a burglary, which persons would you be most interested in talking to at the scene? Away from the scene?

7. What other crimes are often committed along with burglary?

8. Is it legal to "steal back" your own property if someone has stolen it from you?

9. If the object stolen in a burglary is valued below $100, is the crime a misdemeanor?

10. What can the police do to increase the reporting of burglaries? What can they do to help the public prevent burglaries?

References

Cook, Patrick E. and Hinman, Dayle L. "Criminal Profiling." *Journal of Contemporary Criminal Justice,* Vol. 15, No. 3, August 1999, pp. 230–241.

Harris, Wesley. "Improving Patrol Response to Burglary Investigations." *Law and Order,* Vol. 46, No. 7, July 1998a, pp. 119–123.

Harris, Wesley. "A Look at Responding to Burglary Calls." *Law and Order,* Vol. 46, No. 10, October 1998b, pp. 157–160.

Hoffman, John. "Building Codes Help Reduce Burglaries." *Law and Order,* Vol. 46, No. 10, October 1998, pp. 149–151.

Kruse, Warren. "2001—A Computer Odyssey." *Law Enforcement Technology,* April 1996, pp. 63–66.

Robinson, Matthew B. "Lifestyles, Routine Activities, and Residential Burglary Victimization." *Journal of Crime and Justice,* Vol. XXII, No. 1, 1999, pp. 27–56.

Spivey, Katherine and Cobb, Renee. "False Alarms." *The Police Chief,* Vol. LXIV, No. 6, June 1997, pp. 44–50.

Chapter 15

Larceny/Theft, Fraud, White-Collar and Environmental Crime

Can You Define?

Do You Know?

How to define *larceny/theft?*

How larceny differs from burglary and robbery?

What the elements of larceny/theft are?

What the two major categories of larceny are and how to determine them?

What legally must be done with found property?

What the common types of larceny are?

When the FBI becomes involved in a larceny/theft investigation?

What the elements of the offense of receiving stolen goods are?

What fraud is and how it differs from larceny/theft?

What the common means of committing fraud are?

What the common types of check fraud are?

What the elements of the crime of larceny by credit card are?

What white-collar crime is and what specific offenses are included in this crime category?

Introduction

Larceny/theft is one of the eight Part One Index Crimes. Although fraud, white-collar crime and environmental crime are not Index Crimes, they are so closely related to larceny/theft that they are included in this chapter. All three have elements in common and are investigated in similar ways.

Some states eliminate the distinctions between larceny, fraud and white-collar crimes, combining them into the single crime of *theft*. However, because many states do have separate offenses, this chapter discusses them separately. The distinction may be unimportant in your jurisdiction.

This chapter begins with an overview of larceny/theft, a discussion of the elements of the crime of larceny/theft, classification of such crimes and how "found property" fits. Then follows a description of the preliminary investigation, the various types of larceny/theft that might be investigated, proving the elements of the crime and an explanation of recovering stolen property and receiving stolen goods. The chapter then focuses on the various types of fraud investigators might encounter and concludes with a discussion of white-collar and environmental crime. ■

Larceny/Theft: An Overview

Reported larcenies exceed the combined total of all other Part One Index Crimes (59 percent) and have increased more rapidly than any other Index Crime.

- - - - - - - - -

Larceny/theft is the unlawful taking, carrying, leading or driving away of property from the possession of another.

- - - - - - - - -

Larceny is committed through the cunning, skill and criminal design of the professional thief or as a crime of opportunity committed by the rank amateur. The adage that "there is a little larceny in everyone" has considerable truth. Although some thefts result from revenge or spite, the motive for most larcenies is the same for the professional and amateur thief—monetary gain—either actual cash or articles that can be converted to cash or to personal use.

- - - - - - - - -

Both larceny and burglary are crimes against property, but larceny, unlike burglary, does not involve illegally entering a structure. Larceny differs from robbery in that no force or threat of force is involved.

- - - - - - - - -

Elements of the Crime: Larceny/Theft

The crime of larceny/theft takes many forms, but the basic elements of the offense are similar in the statutes of every state.

- - - - - - - - -

The elements of the crime of larceny/theft are:

- The felonious stealing, taking, carrying, leading or driving away,
- Of another's personal goods or property,
- Valued above (grand) or below (petty) a specified amount,
- With the intent to permanently deprive the owner of the property or goods.

- - - - - - - - -

Felonious Stealing, Taking, Carrying, Leading or Driving Away This element requires an unlawful, wrongful or felonious removal of the property; that is, the property is removed by any manner of stealing. Taking items such as fuel and electricity is also included in this element. Withholding property is a form of larceny by a failure to return, or to properly account for the property or to deliver the property to the rightful owner when it is due. Failure to pay a debt is *not* larceny, even though there is a failure to pay. Civil remedies are sought for this type of theft.

The Personal Goods or Property of Another Goods or **property** refers to all forms of tangible property, real or personal. It includes valuable documents; electricity, gas, water and heat supplied by municipalities or public utility companies; and domestic animals such as cats, dogs and farm animals. It also includes property in which the accused has co-ownership, a lien, pledge, bailment, lease or other subordinate interest. Larceny laws also cover cases in which the property of a partnership is converted to personal use adverse to the partner's rights, except when the accused and the victim are husband and wife.

In the definition of larceny/theft, *another* refers to an individual, a government, corporation or an organization. This element refers to the true owner or the one authorized to control the property. Care assignment, personal custody or some degree of legal control is evidence of possession. In numerous cases ownership of property

A security guard monitors the facilities of a California computer company using multi-image closed-circuit television sets.

has been questioned. Ownership usually means the true owner or the person who has superior rights at the time of the theft. The owner must support the charge of larceny; otherwise, there is no prosecution.

Of a Value Above or Below a Specified Amount

Value determines whether the offense is grand or petty larceny. Value means the market value at the time of the theft. Determine value by learning the replacement cost, legitimate market value, value listed in government property catalogues, fair market value or reasonable estimates.

If the property is restored to the owner, value means the value of the property's use or the damage it sustained, whichever is greater, while the owner was deprived of its possession. However, this cannot exceed the original value declared.

If several items are stolen in a single crime, the value of *all* items combined determines the value of the loss, even if the property belonged to more than one owner. Identical items stolen from different larceny locations are not combined but are treated as separate offenses.

With the Intent to Permanently Deprive the Owner of the Property or Goods

Intent either exists at the time the property was taken or is formed afterward. The person may have intended only to borrow the property but then decided to keep it permanently. This element is usually the most difficult to prove. Establish ownership through documents of pur-

chase, statements describing how the property was possessed, the length of time of possesion and details of the delegation of care and control to another by the true owner.

Because of its frequency, much police time is devoted to larceny, and individual merchants and private security forces are also involved. Millions of dollars in losses go unreported each month. Those that are reported are usually reported to collect insurance rather than in the hope of recovering the property or clearing the case.

Classification of Larceny/Theft

Most statutes have two major categories of larceny/theft based on the total value of the property stolen.

- - - - - - - - -

The categories of larceny/theft are **grand larceny,** a felony, and **petty larceny,** a misdemeanor—based on the value of the property stolen.

- - - - - - - - -

In many states the amount for grand larceny is $100 or more; any lesser amount is petty (petit) larceny. Check the laws in your jurisdiction for the dollar value that distinguishes petty and grand larceny. It is important to know whether the crime is a misdemeanor or a felony before proceeding with the investigation.

Found Property

Keeping or selling property lost by the owner is a form of theft.

In most states taking found property with the intent to keep or sell it is a crime.

Although the finder has possession of the property, it is not legal possession. Thieves apprehended with stolen property often claim to have found it—an invalid excuse. A reasonable effort must be made to find the owner of the property, for example, by making inquiries or advertising in a newspaper. The owner, if located, must pay the cost of such inquiries before the property is returned.

If the owner is not located after reasonable attempts are made to do so and after a time specified by law, the finder of the property can legally retain possession of it.

The Preliminary Investigation

Investigating larceny/theft is similar to investigating a burglary, except that in a larceny/theft even less physical evidence is available because no illegal or forcible entry occurred. Physical evidence might include empty cartons or containers, empty hangers, objects left at the scene, footprints and fingerprints.

Do not give the complainant or victim the impression that the investigation of the reported theft is unimportant. If there is little hope of recovering the property or finding the thief, inform the complainant of this but only after you obtain all the facts.

Types of Larceny/Theft

Common types of larceny are purse snatching, picking pockets, theft from coin machines, shoplifting, bicycle theft, theft from motor vehicles, theft from buildings, theft of motor vehicle accessories and jewelry theft.

The *Uniform Crime Report* for 1998 indicates the relative frequency of these types of larceny (see Figure 15.1).

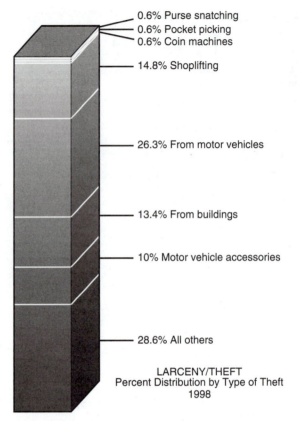

0.6% Purse snatching
0.6% Pocket picking
0.6% Coin machines
14.8% Shoplifting
26.3% From motor vehicles
13.4% From buildings
10% Motor vehicle accessories
28.6% All others

LARCENY/THEFT
Percent Distribution by Type of Theft
1998

FIGURE 15.1 *Larceny*

Source: *Crime in the United States 1998.* The Uniform Crime Reports. Washington, DC: Department of Justice, 1999, p. 47.

Pickpockets and Purse-Snatchers

Pickpockets are difficult to apprehend because the victim must identify the thief. This is difficult to do unless the thief is observed by someone else or is caught in the act. The purse-opener and purse-snatcher are modern versions of the pickpocket. These thieves use force if necessary but rely on their skills to avoid the use of force and to evade identification. Lost wallets and purses, often the work of the pickpocket, are not reported as thefts because the victims do not realize that theft has occurred.

Obtain from the victim a description of what was stolen and its value. Ask if the victim recalls being jostled or distracted momentarily, and, if so, obtain complete details. Keep careful records of pickpockets and purse-snatchers, as often they are caught.

Employee Theft

Shrinkage refers to the "unexplained or unauthorized reduction of inventory from a retail establishment"

(Jaeger, 1999, p. 6). In 1997 shrinkage accounted for a $26-billion loss to the nation's retail industry. Although many assume the majority of this loss is due to shoplifting, most thefts and losses from stores are internal, committed by employees of the establishment. The 1998 National Retail Security Survey (Jaeger, p. 6) recently reported that 42.7 percent of the total losses in the retail industry were due to employee thefts. Shoplifting accounted for 34.4 percent, bookkeeping or administrative errors for 17.6 percent and other types of problems, such as vendor fraud, for 6.3 percent. Employee theft is a serious and growing problem. Employee embezzlement has bankrupted some smaller corporations. In surveys conducted by loss specialists, 30 percent of the employees interviewed admitted to stealing from their employers.

One recommendation for reducing employee theft is to keep the more expensive items under security lock and to have frank discussions with employees regarding the problem. Employees who are aware of management's policy regarding employee theft are less likely to steal. Some companies attempt to eliminate potential employee thieves by informing job applicants that a drug test is required, even if it is not. This announcement alone may weed out applicants who have a drug habit and therefore are more prone to steal to support the habit.

Shoplifting

Shoplifting, also known as *boosting,* involves taking items from retail stores without paying for them. It is usually committed by potential customers in the store during normal business hours. It does *not* include thefts from warehouses, factories or other retail outlets or thefts by employees.

Shoplifting has increased with the modern merchandising techniques that display goods for sale, remove barriers between customer and merchandise and permit potential buyers to pick up and handle goods. Most shoplifted items are on the main floor, where it is easy to leave the store.

Shoplifting losses are astronomical. In 1997 retail losses due to shoplifting totaled nearly $9 billion (Jaeger, p. 6). Unfortunately, customers ultimately pay because prices are usually increased by 1 or 2 percent to compensate for losses due to theft. The amount not recovered is part of the business's operating expenses, resulting in lower profits. These losses may be enough to force a small business to go out of business.

To fight the increasing threat posed by shoplifting, Slater (1998, p. 4B) notes: "Retailers are spending millions of dollars on high-tech electronic security devices just to keep the nation's estimated 23 million shoplifters at bay." She adds:

> Clever, futuristic anti-theft weapons are being deployed in the war against "industry shrinkage."
>
> Plastic electronic article surveillance (EAS) tags that consumers now find locked onto clothing are giving way to thin label-like electronic circuits that could be hidden anywhere on a garment or a product.
>
> In tandem with new tags and labels, microwave security systems long used in stores are being replaced by state-of-the-art acousto-magnetic technology that is nearly impossible to fool. . . .
>
> Some companies . . . can actually manufacture a fabric label in the neck of a shirt that has an electronic device embedded in it.

DeFranco (1999, p. 111) explains how this new antitheft technology is broadening protection options:

> Beginning [in May 1999], retailers in the previously underserved optical and jewelry categories will be able to join the ranks of EAS users. . . . Ultra Lock is a hybrid EAS/benefit-denial system that incorporates . . . acousto-magnetic anti-shoplifting technology into smaller tags that allow customers better access to products, thereby increasing the potential both for sales and safety.

According to DeFranco (p. 111), EAS tags on eyeglasses, sunglasses and watches were, in the past, so large and awkward that they not only discouraged theft but sales as well. However, newer EAS labeling allows customers to try on products without the distraction and discomfort of bulky tags.

Despite advancing technology the apprehension rate for shoplifters remains extremely low compared with the total number of shoplifting offenses committed. Police

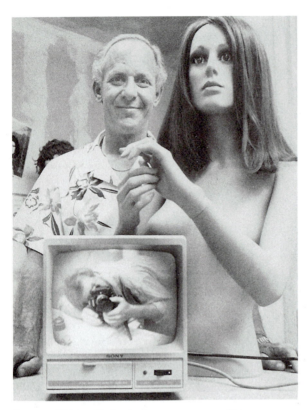

Inventor F. Jerry Gutierrez demonstrates one of his surveillance mannequins designed to watch for shoplifters. They are being photographed by the photographer shown on the TV monitor.

officers usually catch shoplifters only by luck or after being tipped off to a professional group operating in a community. Most apprehensions are by private security forces working for department stores and shopping centers or by floorwalkers or supervisory personnel.

Stores that detect and apprehend shoplifters often do not prosecute for fear of losing a good customer, of being humiliated and embarrassed in court or of facing a false arrest suit. Other reasons for not prosecuting are the cost of attorney's fees, the hope that a reprimand will cure the problem or the belief that notifying a juvenile shoplifter's parents will control the situation.

Managers sometimes call the police for the chastening effect it will have on the shoplifter, but if the property is recovered, they often decline to sign a formal complaint. If a charge is made by a merchant or merchant's employee, officers may arrest a suspected shoplifter without a warrant if reasonable cause exists for believing that person has attempted or actually committed shoplifting. In some states store personnel themselves are encouraged to interview the suspect because they are

not police officers and thus do not have to warn suspects of their rights.

Elements of Larceny by Shoplifting The elements of shoplifting are very similar to those required for general larceny:

- Intentionally taking or carrying away, transferring, stealing, concealing or retaining possession of merchandise or altering the price of the merchandise
- Without the consent of the merchant
- With intent to permanently deprive the merchant of possession or the full purchase price

- - - - - - - - -

Altering the price of an item is considered larceny. It is usually not required that the person leave the premises with the stolen item before apprehension.

- - - - - - - - -

Early laws required that a shoplifter leave a store before an apprehension could be made. However, many laws have been changed to permit apprehension after the suspect has passed the last cashier's counter in the store for the particular level or department. The farther the suspect is from the normal place of payment, the greater the degree of intent that is shown to permanently deprive the merchant of the item. After being told why, the suspect may be detained for a reasonable length of time and then delivered to a police officer, parent or guardian.

Because intent is absent, it is not a crime for a person to walk out of a store after simply forgetting to pay for an item. This is a common problem for individuals who suffer from Alzheimer's disease. Such people may forget they have picked up an item, may forget to pay for it or may honestly believe they have paid for it when in fact they have not. Such incidents require officers to exhibit patience, understanding and excellent communication skills in resolving the situation.

Because shoplifting can be either petty or grand larceny, a misdemeanor or a felony, you must establish the value of the property. If the shoplifter is placed under arrest, recover and retain the stolen item as evidence. Whether the individual is prosecuted depends on the individual's attitude, the policy of the store and the police department, the value of the property taken and how many of the legal requirements for prosecution are fulfilled. Evidence to support shoplifting or altering a price requires an eyewitness or proof that the item could not have been removed except by the person charged. The property must be carried away or removed but not necessarily to outside the store.

Have the manager or clerk identify the property and show proof of the store's ownership.

Proving the intent to permanently deprive is the most difficult problem in investigating shoplifting. Show this intent by the shoplifter's actions from the time the item was stolen until the arrest was made.

Stores are legally within their rights to recover items taken from a store if there is no proof of purchase. This does not mean the person is guilty of shoplifting. It may be impossible to prove an intent to steal.

If a store manager wants to prosecute, review the store's reports to determine whether a crime has been committed. If it has, take the shoplifter to the police station, book and search him or her for additional property. The person making the arrest must sign a complaint. Most shoplifters never reach the stage of arrest and release to the police. When it does occur, encourage store cooperation because good arrests by store personnel aid convictions and can deter shoplifting in the particular store.

Overcrowded courts have become a problem to retailers who want to prosecute for shoplifting. Prosecutors have difficulty obtaining convictions. Forty-three states have passed statutes providing for civil fines instead of, or in combination with, criminal penalties. Retailers are not satisfied with the criminal prosecution approach because of the delays, low conviction rate and lack of restitution for the lost property. The civil approach permits the retailer to sue in small claims court, even in cases in which the offender is not convicted of a crime. Penalties under civil action range from $50 to $500 or in some cases actual damages plus five times the value.

Bicycle Theft

As bicycles have increased in popularity, so has bicycle theft. Identification of bicycles is difficult due to failure to have a registration system or to use one that exists, the complex method of providing serial numbers and the fact that stolen bikes are often altered, dismantled, repainted and resold.

Bicycles are most frequently stolen from schoolyards, college campuses, sidewalk parking racks, driveways and residential yards. Juveniles are responsible for the majority of thefts, although some professional bike theft rings operate interstate, even exporting stolen bicycles out of the country. In many bicycle thefts, the crime is grand larceny due to the high value of many bicycles.

A single bike theft is best investigated by the patrol force. Determine the bicycle's value and have the owner sign a complaint. A juvenile apprehended for a single

theft can be prosecuted, especially with a prior record of similar or other offenses. Restitution for damage and an informal probation are usually initiated. If multiple thefts have occurred, the offender usually goes to juvenile court. Adults are prosecuted by the same procedures used for other larcenies.

The investigative division compiles a list of bike complaints organized by make of bike, serial number and color. Bike thefts are also entered into the police computer system. Patrol officers are given a bike "hot sheet" similar to that for stolen vehicles and periodically check bike racks at parks, schools and business areas against this sheet.

Bikes are sometimes reported stolen to defraud insurance companies. Even if the bike is recovered, the owner has already collected its value, and there will seldom be a prosecution.

Large numbers of thefts in a short time may indicate an interstate ring has moved into the community. These use covered trucks to transport bicycles from the area, making recovery almost impossible.

Stolen bicycles are used for transportation or are sold to bike stores, repair shops or bargain hunters. The professional thief, often using a van or covered truck, steals several expensive bikes at one time, takes them to a garage and repaints or dismantles them for parts.

Bicycles are easy to disguise by painting over or removing ID tags. Many are immediately disassembled and sold for parts, easily taken from one location to another by riding them or placing them into a vehicle trunk, van or truck. One problem in identifying stolen bikes is the lack of a uniform state or national registration system such as that used for motor vehicles.

Mail Theft

In the quest for new and easier ways to steal money, thieves are now targeting sites used daily as repositories for hundreds of thousands of dollars, sites often left unsupervised for hours—mailboxes. On certain days of the month, with tremendous predictability, many households receive government assistance checks. Others mailboxes hold numerous applications for credit cards or the actual cards themselves.

Mailboxes are used not only to receive money but to submit payments as well. Millions of people leave their bills, accompanied by checks, for pickup in their mailboxes. Thieves known as **flaggers** go around neighborhoods targeting mailboxes with their flags up, searching for envelopes containing checks and other forms of payment. Thieves may also raid the large blue mailboxes used by people who may not trust leaving their own flag up. For example, in Seattle:

> Thousands of blue streetside mailboxes are being replaced after thieves duplicated the master key and embarked on a months-long check- and credit-card-stealing spree. . . .
>
> The blue boxes on the curb aren't the only targets. The stolen master key also opens an estimated 35,000 apartment mailboxes throughout the region ("Mailless in Seattle . . . ," 1998, p. 20A).

Once thieves have a check, they may call the bank posing as a legitimate business to confirm the funds are available, or they may simply go ahead and alter the check, assuming it will clear. The thieves protect the check signer's signature using "liquid skin" and then use another solution to strip off the remaining ink, thus enabling them to rewrite the check payable to another source and for another amount.

Jewelry Theft

Jewelry, most often stolen by professional thieves, is also the target of armed robbers and burglars. Jewel thieves know the value of jewels, that they are extremely difficult to identify once removed from their settings and that the rewards are higher for the amount of risk involved than in other types of larceny. They also have ready outlets for disposition.

Most jewelry thefts are from vehicles owned by jewelry salespeople, who typically carry thousands of dollars in jewels, and from private individuals known to be careless about the security of their jewelry. Jewel thieves also operate in stores, distracting the salesperson and then substituting a cheap facsimile for expensive jewelry. Jewel thieves tend to operate interstate and to use locally known fences. They have many ingenious methods to steal and hide jewelry.

Because jewel thieves operate interstate, the FBI becomes involved. The local FBI office maintains files of known jewel thieves and their last known operations; their pictures, descriptions and modus operandi; and information about whether they are in or out of prison.

- - - - - - - -

Always inform the FBI of jewel thefts, even without immediate evidence of interstate operation.

- - - - - - - -

FBI jurisdiction is attained under Title 18, Sections 2314 and 2315. Section 2314 gives jurisdiction when the value exceeds $5,000 and the items are transported interstate or in foreign commerce and when the criminal knows the goods to be stolen, converted to personal use or obtained fraudulently. Section 2315 gives jurisdiction when buyers of the goods know they are stolen, that they have been transported interstate or by foreign commerce and that they are worth more than $5,000. Mailing packages that contain illegally obtained jewels to another state also constitutes interstate operation.

Investigating jewelry theft is the same as for any other larceny. To obtain physical evidence, search the crime scene as you would in a burglary. Obtain the names of people in neighboring rooms at motels and hotels. Interview employees and other possible witnesses. Review the victim's account of the theft. Obtain a complete description of the jewelry, the value of each item and the amount of insurance carried. Contact informants and have them be on the alert for information about the thieves and also the location of the stolen items.

Art Theft

Art theft is increasing, and to cope with the problems resulting from the interstate and international nature of these thefts, the FBI created the National Stolen Art File in 1979. Objects must have a value of at least $2,000 to be entered into this file. Local FBI offices have the reporting forms that a police agency—not the owner—must submit.

Slahor (1996, p. 181) reports: "More than $5 billion worth of art and antiquities [is] stolen each year. And the trade in these items is skyrocketing." This offense usually comes to the attention of law enforcement through an art gallery's report of a burglary or theft. In other instances art objects are recovered during the investigation of another crime, or the theft is reported by another police agency. Two unique factors in art thefts are that the objects are frequently held for a long time and are then sold or moved coast to coast or internationally for disposition. Baker (1996, p. 19) suggests: "Art theft and related crime are almost always international. Art stolen in one country typically ends up in another—after passing through numerous hands." In fact, theft of art objects is considered a major international criminal activity, second only to drug trafficking.

- - - - - - - -

Thefts of valuable art should be reported to the FBI and to INTERPOL, which also has an international stolen art file.

- - - - - - - -

Few police officers have any training in identifying art, so they should conduct only the normal burglary, theft or fraud investigation. Then an authenticity check of the art object should be conducted by the FBI and national art dealers. People who own art objects rarely have adequate descriptions or photos of each piece, and the pieces rarely have identification numbers. Investigators should submit to the FBI all known information concerning the theft and a photograph of the art if available.

Numismatic Theft: Coins, Metals and Paper Money

Thefts of coins, metals of various types and paper money have also been increasing. Coin collections are typically stolen during commercial and residential burglaries. Obtain the exact description of the coins, the condition, any defects, scratches, dye breaks, how they were jacketed and any other identifying information. The condition of coins determines their value; a coin in mint condition may be worth twice the value of a coin in poor condition. Stolen coins may be taken from one coast to the other for disposition. Large coin shows are held throughout the year in larger cities, usually at convention centers or hotels. If interstate transportation is suspected, notify the FBI.

Metals such as gold, copper, silver and aluminum are valuable. Copper is obtained from electrical and telephone lines or from storage yards of these companies. Thieves have been known to cut down telephone lines and to strip electrical lines in remote areas. A weekly check of scrap yards may be advisable in some jurisdictions.

Agricultural Theft

In certain areas of the country, agricultural theft is an increasing problem that requires investigation. Such crimes may include theft of timber, livestock, farm equipment and chemicals.

Timber Theft The U.S. Forestry Service estimates $100 million in lumber is stolen annually through illegal logging. Tree "rustlers" harvest **burls,** the large gnarly root at the base of walnut trees. Burls can weigh as much as 2,000 pounds and are used to make fine woodwork. Tree "tippers" harvest the tips of pine trees to make into wreaths. According to Windsor (1999, p. 19):

> Every crime scene contains evidence, regardless of the location, and a timber theft crime scene is no exception. Each scene will always contain traceable evidence of the timber's being taken, such as tire tracks, occasional paint transfers, stumps, and various other items that the thief may have purposely discarded or accidentally left behind. . . .
>
> Before investigators begin the search for stolen timber, they should have an idea of how it may be

used. For example, . . . Douglas fir and hemlock are harvested for commercial firewood, and cedar is harvested for shake shingles and fence posts. . . .

> Once officers determine the suspected use, they can begin to look at various mills in their area. . . .
>
> By making contact with area mills; state, national, and private foresters; timber buyers; and other timber industry personnel, officers can gain valuable knowledge that will save them crucial time when a timber theft occurs and will help them in apprehending the thief more quickly.

Livestock Just as in the days of the old wild west, cattle rustlers are still around, stealing more than 20,000 cattle annually. Most livestock is stolen from the open range and consequently may go undetected for weeks or even months. Investigators may need the help of stock auctioners, slaughter houses, feedlot operators and livestock associations when looking into these crimes. Cattle rustlers are almost always armed because they often slaughter the animals on the spot, butcher them and load them into refrigerated trucks. Evidence in such cases again includes shoe and tire impressions, soil samples and perhaps forged bills of sale.

Horse rustling is another problem, with over 50,000 horses stolen annually. Sometimes after the desired horses are loaded onto a truck, the rustlers break down the fence and scatter the remaining horses. Owners may then think the horses broke out themselves and those not recovered are simply lost. Most stolen horses are slaughtered, and the meat is sold in Europe and Japan. The United States is the world's leading exporter of horsemeat, which is considered better than our best steaks.

Both cattle and horses are usually stolen at night and are fairly easy to lure away because they are herd animals— once rustlers get one animal to come, the rest soon follow.

Farm Equipment and Chemicals Farm equipment and chemicals are also targets for thieves. Because of their expense, pesticides and herbicides are especially attractive. Farmers themselves may be the thieves, or they may buy their chemicals and equipment at ridiculously low prices from such thieves. Evidence of this crime may be uncovered by examining purchasing records.

Fish and Wildlife Theft

Poaching is the illegal taking or possession of fish, game or other wildlife, including deer, elk, bear, pheasant, ducks, wild turkeys and grouse. This crime may be committed by the amateur—the usually law-abiding hunter who is faced with an unexpected opportunity to poach, such as coming across an animal not in season to hunt while hunting another animal that is in season—or the professional poacher who, in contrast, sets out to hunt prey illegally, often as a "trophy hunter." Hunting license verifications and vehicle stops to check limits are two means of detecting poachers. Yet the challenges to investigators are many, as Doherty (1999, p. 111) acknowledges:

> Local police departments face a number of handicaps when confronting such [wildlife crime] incidents; many officers are unfamiliar with the laws governing hunters, with hunting techniques, and processing wildlife-related crimes. However, every state in the nation has a law-enforcement agency dedicated to such incidents. Whether they are called game wardens, conservation officers or environmental police, they can be an effective resource for local police departments.

Doherty (p. 112) notes that many game wardens carry crime scene equipment, and the U.S. Fish and Wildlife Service maintains a wildlife forensic lab. Wardens may be familiar with many of the local hunters and poachers and may be aware of certain poachers' MOs. Wardens know the hunting and wildlife laws, for example, most states do not require probable cause to check a hunter's license; also, in some states spotlighting is legal (p. 113). Wardens can also help gather evidence. For example (p. 112): "Many poachers take only the antlers; such antlers may later turn up in a taxidermy shop and be matched to the skull from which they were taken. The portion of the esophagus left in the gutpile can be matched to the remaining portion inside a carcass at a suspect's home. Likewise, if only the head is taken, vertebrae can be matched to a carcass left behind."

Toft (1999, pp. 119–120) describes a powerful new computerized database, Green Parrot, which can be used in the "never-ending war against wildlife smugglers." Developed in the UK, the data base has about "3,300 images, textual data for about 7,000 animal and 15,000 plant species, information on skins, trophies and Oriental medicines made from animal parts, including bones, penises, blood, semen and gall bladders" (p. 119). Says Toft (p. 120): "The Green Parrot data base should enable police and customs authorities worldwide to make life increasingly difficult for those who illegally trade in endangered species of wildlife."

Cargo Theft

With the United States producing and transporting ever increasing amounts of goods and products, Stedman (1998, p. 20) notes: "Cargo theft is becoming a problem of monumental proportions, rivaling only terrorism and drug interdiction as a priority for federal law enforcement officials." The National Cargo Security Council reports that criminal gangs in this country are costing Americans nearly $10 billion every year, making it one of the United States' most serious property crimes. According to Badolato (1998, p. 14): "The theft of cargo has become so widespread that it constitutes a serious threat to the flow of commerce in the United States." He continues (p. 14):

> There are a number of key reasons for this rapid increase, including the emergence of a new breed of cargo crook, the predominant use of cargo to support various criminal activities, the reluctance to effectively prosecute and sentence cargo crooks, the rapid structural changes in the transportation industry, the lack of an effective nationwide cargo theft reporting system and the lateness of the U.S. security technology industry to address this problem.

The increasing popularity of cargo theft is due to two primary features: It is low risk (few thieves are apprehended, prosecuted or incarcerated), and it is extremely profitable. Stedman (p. 21) reports: "The value of the average [cargo] theft has risen from a range of from $5,000 to $10,000 to from $50,000 to $500,000 on average." Badolato (p. 15) adds: "The widespread use and availability of computer-generated cargo shipping information to insiders is another recent factor affecting the increase in cargo crime."

One problem in the investigation of such offenses is that cargo theft is not an indexed crime. Stedman (p. 21) states: "It can be listed in a number of ways: theft, robbery, fraud, etc." Hence there may be little continuity from one jurisdiction to another when interstate cargo theft rings are involved. Efforts, however, are being made to overcome this inconsistency. Neeley (1998, p. 16) notes: "The FBI will soon unveil a database designed to track cargo thefts and other crimes. Called the Criminal Intelligence Support Program (CISP), it will serve as a clearinghouse for information from other government agencies and private industry." Other challenges also exist in investigating cargo theft. According to Stedman (p. 22):

> The problems posed by tracking and nabbing the perpetrators of cargo theft are formidable. The thieves can be very inventive. For instance, when law enforcement begins to unravel the distribution pattern of a gang, they have switched their methodologies in mid-stream. One agent said, "Today we see bartering between the thieves and the trade, the gray market. This makes it a lot tougher to follow the money trail."

Stedman (p. 22) notes that, although arresting thieves is still a goal, many agencies, including the FBI, are now focusing on finding the source—the organized crime rings and their front businesses. Approximately half of all domestic cargo thefts are the result of organized crime (Dolan, 1999, p. 27), and law enforcement is now using criminal statutes that target money laundering to shut down cargo theft rings: "To further tighten its grip, the Department of Justice intends to strip the gangs of their assets, using RICO conspiracy law and a combination of civil penalties involving the IRS and other federal agencies." Other agencies getting involved in cargo theft include the Immigration and Naturalization Service because, as Stedman (p. 22) points out: "Many of the cargo theft gangs in the U.S. are of foreign origin . . . , primarily illegal immigrants."

The shipping of merchandise through retail distribution centers has been an area plagued by theft. As Kelly (1999, p. 78) notes:

> It was not unusual for a shipment to take seven days to move through a facility. By the time an order was ready to be shipped, it would have been touched, counted, ticketed, repacked and handled in one form or another by several people, each having ample opportunity to steal from the order. . . .
>
> Presently, there is a movement among retailers to change their focus in distribution to become faster and more accurate in handling freight. This will be accomplished by a drive toward the use of UCC-128 barcode technology, and through the advanced receipt of carton content information via EDI (electronic data interchange) systems.

Trash Theft

Lehman and Dion (1996, p. 39) call stealing trash a "**gray-collar crime.**" They note: "The national average cost to haul and dispose of a ton of trash is estimated at $125. This means that the trash disposal industry is a $67 million per day—$24.5 billion per year—operation in the United States. This is big business and a big opportunity for theft." They cite as an example a trash hauler who claims the garbage he is dumping is residential rather than commercial, meaning the city pays for it. A typical 25-yard compactor truck hauling 10–13 tons of trash a day would cost $500 to $650—an "instant theft of the same amount from

the town." They note that if this happens once a day, five days a week, in a year the hauler has stolen $130,000 to $160,000, and that's just *one* truck. Lehman and Dion (p. 44) conclude:

> Policing trash crime hardly has the glamourous aura of traditional police work. Yet this form of theft is just as real as taking cash from the till of the corner store. The difference is that there is a lot more money in the trash industry, and the crime is a lot more insidious.

Proving the Elements of the Crime

To prove the felonious stealing, taking, carrying, leading or driving away of property, you must gather enough evidence to prove the property is missing—not simply misplaced. Obtain proof of ownership through bills of sale or receipts or through evidence that the owner had custody or possession of or responsibility for the item. Determine the item's value by ascertaining its replacement cost, legitimate market value or reasonable estimates. The owner can testify to the actual value if he or she is familiar with the specific item and its quality and condition at the time of the theft. Persons with business knowledge of the value of similar items can help determine value. If certain items obviously exceed the petty larceny limitation, it is not necessary to know their exact value. Take statements from the owner regarding where the property was located and what security was provided. Also obtain evidence that the owner no longer possesses the property.

Intent to permanently deprive the owner of the property is shown by the suspect's selling, concealing, hiding or pawning the property or converting it to personal use. Intent is proven by a motive of revenge, possession under circumstances of concealment, denial of possession where possession is proven or flight from normal residence.

Recovering Stolen Property

Stolen property is disposed of in many ways. Often it is sold on the streets to obtain a higher profit than would be paid by a fence and to avoid a record of the sale. Because many people are looking for a bargain, thieves can usually dispose of the property on the streets, but they risk being reported to the police by someone who sees the transaction.

If property is sold to pawnshops or secondhand stores or is left at a store on consignment for sale, most states and communities have statutes or ordinances requiring a permanent record of the transaction. The seller must be given a receipt describing the property purchased, the seller's name and address and the amount paid. A copy of the transaction is often sent to the police department of the community listed as the seller's home address. If the property is identified as stolen, the police contact the shop owner and, upon proof that the property is stolen, can recover it. Shop records are open to police inspection at all times. Information in these records can lead to the arrest of the seller as the person who committed the theft.

When you recover stolen property, record the date the property was recovered, where it was recovered, who turned it in and the circumstances surrounding the recovery. List the names and addresses of anyone present at the time of recovery. Mark the property as evidence and take it into custody. In some states, it is legal to return the property as long as its identification is recorded and a photograph is taken. There is no reason the original property must be produced in court unless it was an instrument that caused death or serious injury.

Receiving Stolen Goods

A go-between who receives stolen goods for resale is referred to as a **fence.**

- - - - - - - - -

The elements of the offense of receiving stolen goods are:
- Receiving, buying or concealing stolen or illegally obtained goods.
- Knowing them to be stolen or otherwise illegally obtained.

- - - - - - - - -

Receiving stolen property for resale is a crime, as is concealing stolen property, even though not purchased. A thief does not have to personally sell goods to a fence. An "innocent" third party can sell the property for the thief, but it is still an offense if the buyer knows the property was stolen.

It is difficult to prove that a buyer knew the purchased goods were stolen. The property must be found in the receiver's possession and identified as the stolen property by the owner's testimony, marks, serial numbers or other positive identifying marks. Knowing can then be proved by the very low price paid for the goods in comparison with the true value.

Usually evidence of the sale is provided through an informant who either made the sale or knows who did. The property may have been resold, and the person buying the item may be the informant who identifies the receiver of stolen goods. This person assists the police in making another sale or identifying property in the receiver's possession.

The receiver of stolen goods is often discovered when the person who stole the property is arrested and identifies the receiver. It is necessary to show that the receiver could not legitimately own the item unless he or she had bought it from a thief. Show that it was not purchased through a normal business transaction. The character of the person selling the property or any indication that the property was being concealed is evidence. Evidence that markings or serial numbers have been altered or removed indicates concealment and intent to deprive the rightful owner of the property. The seller can testify to conversations with the receiver about the property and the fact that it was stolen. The receiver's records may not show the transaction, which would be evidence of intent to conceal. The charge of receiving stolen goods can be used when possession of stolen items can be shown but there is not sufficient evidence to prove theft.

Sting Operations Many cities have established sting operations, in which the police legally establish a fencing operation. A suitable shop is set up as a front for the operation. Normally, secondhand stores, repair shops, salvage dealers, appliance dealers or pawnshops make good front operations. The store is stocked with items to support the type of business selected.

Word is spread through informants and the underworld that the business will "buy anything." Attractive prices are paid to get the business started. Closed-circuit television records all transactions between the fence and the seller of stolen goods. The camera is usually focused on an area in which a calendar and clock are clearly visible to establish the date and time of each transaction. Video equipment records the transaction, the actual sale and the person selling the stolen goods. A parking lot surveillance camera shows the vehicle used to transport the property and its license number.

When an item is presented at the counter, the seller, the amount paid for the property and the buyer are recorded. The property is then dusted for fingerprints to further prove the seller's possession. The stolen goods are checked through normal police channels to determine where they were stolen.

The shop is run for two to three months and then discontinued. Arrest warrants are then issued for those implicated during the store's operation.

Fraud

Fraud is a general term used for deceit, trickery and cheating as well as to describe the activity of individuals who pretend to be what they are not. Legally, however, fraud has a narrower meaning.

Fraud is an intentional deception to cause a person to give up property or some lawful right. It differs from theft in that fraud uses deceit rather than stealth to obtain goods illegally.

Wells (1999, p. 70) notes data from the Association of Certified Fraud Examiners (ACFE) that reveal that: "Internal fraud is a growing problem that costs corporate America an estimated $400 billion a year." Slotter (1999, p. 1) adds: "Fraud and abuse cost U.S. employers an average of $9 a day per employee. . . . Median losses committed by executives represent 16 times more damage than those committed by their employees, and the most costly abuses occur in companies with fewer than 100 employees."

Phelps (1999, p. D1) reports: "As the booming stock market makes more people richer, a growing number of economic criminals are trying to cheat them out of their money." Advances in technology and, in particular, the proliferation of electronic commerce have given innovative criminals yet another way to commit fraud. As one U.S. Attorney notes (Phelps, p. D7): "We're well aware . . . there is a convergence between your typical con artist and your technical expert, which is a very scary proposition."

Fraud victims are in a good position to provide information regarding suspects because they have had firsthand dealings with the suspects.

Fraud is committed in many ways, including through the use of checks, credit cards, confidence games and embezzlement.

Check Fraud

Holland (1999, p. 76) notes: "Aided by better and less expensive technology, fraud artists have increased their focus on the humble bank check." Losses from bad-check operations cannot be determined exactly because no single clearinghouse gathers statistics on this offense. Hansen (1999, p. 10) states: "Various sources have estimated that the total economic impact of check fraud on financial institutions, private businesses, and the public ranges from $815 million to between $5 and $10 billion annually." Holland (p. 76) adds:

> The *American Banker* has projected that check fraud will grow by 25 percent annually in coming years. According to the American Banker's Association (ABA) 1998 Check Fraud Survey . . . , financial institutions alone incurred $512.3 million in check fraud losses, before recoveries, in 1997. When losses to all businesses are factored in, that figure rises to more than $13 billion. . . . These figures were debated at a recent check fraud conference, with several security professionals arguing that they might well be higher, because many check fraud losses are never reported or are misclassified by companies as policy losses.

Checks used to defraud include personal, business, counter, draft and universal checks as well as money orders. Fraudulent checks are made to appear genuine in many ways. The check blank can be similar to the one normally used and difficult to detect. In fact, many fraudulent and forged checks are written on stolen check blanks. Handwriting is practiced to look authentic. Various stamps, checkwriters, date stamps and cancellation stamps are placed on the front and back of the check to give it a genuine appearance.

In some cases, the checks are not stolen but handed over willingly to thieves—for a price. According to Holland (p. 81): "The latest scam involves buying account data from owners and instructing them to report their wallet stolen." The checking account owner benefits by being paid more money than is actually in the account, while the thief is allowed to cash checks or purchase merchandise for a few days before the bank is notified of the check "theft."

Common types of check fraud are insufficient-fund checks, issuing worthless checks and forgeries.

The *insufficient-* or *nonsufficient-fund check* falls into one of two categories: (1) accidental, in which people carelessly overdraw their checking account and are generally not prosecuted unless they do so habitually or (2) intentional, in which professionals open a checking account with a small deposit, planning to write checks well in excess of the amount deposited. This is intent to defraud—a prosecutable offense.

Most bad checks are not written with intent to defraud. They may have been mistakenly drawn against the wrong bank, the account balance may have been less than the writer thought, two or more people may have used the same account without knowing the actual balance or the bank may have made an error.

Issuing a worthless check occurs when the issuer does not intend the check to be paid. Proof of intent is shown if the issuer has no account or has insufficient funds or credit or both. A worthless check is normally prosecuted the same as one for insufficient funds. Obtain the check as well as statements from the person who accepted it, any other witnesses and bank representatives. Also obtain a signed complaint.

Forgery is signing someone else's name to a document with the intent to defraud. This includes actually signing the name and using a rubber stamp or a check-writing machine. To prosecute, obtain the forged check or document, statements from the person whose name is forged, any witnesses to the transaction and the testimony of a handwriting expert if necessary. Blank checks are often obtained through burglaries or office thefts committed by professionals. The check is authentic and therefore easier to cash once the endorsement is forged.

It is also forgery to alter the amount on a check or to change the name of the payee. The person who initially draws the check must testify as to the authorized amount and payee. It is also forgery to change a name on a charge account slip.

Investigating bad or fraudulent checks requires precise details about the check and the entire transaction. The check itself is the main evidence. Carefully examine the front and back of the check and note peculiarities. Describe the check: type, firm name and whether it is personal, payroll, federal or state. Was it written in pencil or ink or typed? Were any special stamps used? Was anything altered: the payee, the date, the amount? Was the signature forged? Were there erasures or misspellings? Were local names and addresses used? Put the check in a protective polyethylene envelope or plastic container so that it can also be processed for fingerprints at the laboratory.

Where was the check passed? Who took it? Were there other witnesses? If so, obtain their names and addresses. If currency was given, what were the denominations?

Obtain an exact description of the check passer. Was the suspect known to the person taking the check? Had he or she ever done business with the store before? What identification was used: driver's license, social security card, bank identification card, credit card? Was the suspect left- or right-handed? Was the suspect alone? If with others, what did they look like? What approach was used? What words were spoken? If the check passer used a car, did anyone notice what it looked like or the license number? Hansen (p. 11) advises: "Confidential informants with knowledge of underworld trafficking in stolen and counterfeit identification documents can help investigators identify check passers and others involved

in organized check fraud." Hansen (p. 13) lists some red flags that may signal check fraud:

- Customer attempts to open an account with a corporate check or other third-party check.
- Customer tries to flatter, hurry or confuse the teller to draw attention away from the transaction.
- Customer delays endorsing a check or producing identification during peak hours to frustrate the teller and hurry the transaction.
- Customer presents for cash a low-numbered check drawn on a new account.
- Customer offers foreign documentation (birth certificate, passport or visa) or nonphoto identification (Social Security card, credit card) in lieu of photo identification to open an account or cash a check.
- Customer offers altered or damaged identification to open an account or cash a check.
- Customer attempts to cash or convert several small checks into wire transfer, gold or other tender.
- Customer requests an exception to established rules to force the transaction.

Law enforcement can not only develop their own preventive strategies to combat check fraud but also support innovative techniques used by other institutions, such as the inkless fingerprinting campaigns launched by some banks. As Hansen (p. 16) notes:

> Banks in Nevada, Arizona, and Texas experienced remarkable reductions in check fraud losses after they began requiring that noncustomers provide inkless fingerprints when cashing checks at the teller line. . . . Modern innovations in automated fingerprint processing and aggressive marketing by financial institutions resulted in . . . recent loss reductions of between 43 and 59 percent.

If the check passer is apprehended, look for devices used to make checks such as check writers, ink pads, typewritten date stamps or other rubber stamps on the person or in the vehicle.

The National Fraudulent Check File Professional check passers who write several checks in a city in a short time and then move to another city or state often use the same technique. The FBI's National Fraudulent Check File helps identify such persons and often shows a pattern of travel. The FBI maintains other files that assist in tracing bad-check writers. These include files on check-writer standards, watermarks, confidence operators, safety paper standards, rubber stamps, anonymous letters and typewriter standards.

Counterfeiting

Counterfeiting of money generally comes to the attention of the police through a retailer or a bank. The Secret Service publishes pamphlets on identifying counterfeit money. The most common denominations of counterfeit money are $10, $20 and $50. The paper of authentic bills has red and blue fibers imbedded in it, and the bills have intaglio printing. The portrait is detailed and lifelike; the Treasury seal is clear and distinct on sawtooth points; the borders are clear and unbroken; and serial numbers are distinct, evenly spaced and the same color as the Treasury seal.

Chatzky (1998, p. 12) notes that with counterfeiting on the rise, the Treasury Department has modified some of the most commonly copied bills. In September 1998 a supposedly counterfeit-proof $20 went into circulation, with several redesigned features to make counterfeiting extremely difficult, including:

- A security thread with the words "USA TWENTY" and a flag embedded along the left side of the front of the bill, which can be viewed when held up to the light. The thread also glows green under ultraviolet light.
- A larger, off-center, more detailed portrait of Andrew Jackson to make fakes easier to spot.
- Color-shifting ink in the numeral 20 in the bottom right corner, which looks green when viewed straight on but black at an angle.
- A watermark of a duplicate image of Jackson to the right of the center image, which is visible when held up to a light but cannot be photocopied.

A newly developed felt-tip marker can instantly detect even the finest-quality counterfeit money with a single stroke. With the felt-tip marker, a dot or short line is made on the suspected bill. If the "ink" remains gold, the bill is authentic. If the "ink" turns black, the bill needs scrutiny.

If a bill is suspect, give a receipt to the retailer or bank, and turn the bill over to the nearest Secret Service office to determine its authenticity. Obtain details of how the bill came into the complainant's possession as well as an accurate description of the bill passer.

Commercial Counterfeiting Currency is not the only item targeted for counterfeiting. According to Barry (1999, p. 14): "Commercial counterfeiting is the economic crime of this century, and indicators suggest it will continue to grow well into the next. The current $200 billion figure is up from $60 billion just 10 years ago." Commercial counterfeiting includes trademark counterfeiting and copyright pirating.

Trademark counterfeiting is illegally reproducing cheaper counterfeit "knock-offs" of well-known pricier products such as Rolex watches, Gucci handbags or Mont Blanc fountain pens.

Wessells (1999, p. 20) reports that some companies are helping other companies combat trademark and patent counterfeiting:

> Web.Sweep [is] a new proprietary software that performs an exhaustive, real-time search of the Internet for critical intelligence about your company and its competitors.
>
> Web.Sweep searches the entire Internet . . . for references to your protected property, products or brands and pertinent competitive intelligence. If it belongs to you, and it's being used online without your consent, Web.Sweep will find it.

Another technology being developed to combat both Internet and street fraud is a state-of-the-art, patent-pending, proprietary system for authenticating goods through the use of a unique fiber-placement algorithm. The technology . . . can be used with virtually everything—jewelry, artwork, event tickets, clothes labels and so on (Wessells, p. 20).

A secret service agent compares a counterfeit $100 bill, top, and a genuine one, bottom, in his Richmond, Virginia, office in May 1996. At least 14 fake $100 bills were passed at fast-food restaurants, grocery stores, convenience shops and discount outlets in Chesterfield County, Petersburg and Hopewell, Virginia. Local counterfeiters are apparently using computers, image scanners and full-color copiers or printers.

Copyright pirating is making—for trade or sale—unauthorized copies of copyrighted material, including print and sound media. Morrison (1998, p. 109) reports: "Every year, the United States sound recording industry loses almost $300 million dollars in lost revenue as a result of piracy. . . . Artists, writers, publishers and, ultimately, the record buyers also lose money as a result." In contrast to trademark counterfeiting, however, where products are sold far below the retail value of their legitimate counterparts, with pirated music the consumer often faces much steeper prices to obtain illegal underground versions. Morrison notes three forms of piracy:

- Counterfeiting—knock-off copies of legitimate releases
- Pirate recordings—usually one or more cuts by various artists on an unauthorized compilation
- Bootleg recordings—unauthorized recordings of radio or television broadcasts or live concerts

It is a felony in 33 states to pirate sound recordings, and nearly every state has some type of law related to pirated recordings. Despite the illegalities of this business, Morrison (p. 110) notes: "If you get on the Internet and type in bootleg CD, you will find people advertising their bootleg CDs for trade or sale. . . . In fact, Alta Vista listed about 20,000 sites on the subject of bootleg CDs. The list is awesome, and these people are not hiding." Morrison (p. 110) continues: "Clearly enforcement will have to be directed at the manufacture, import and distribution channels in order to be effective."

Credit-Card Fraud

Credit card refers to any credit plate, charge plate, courtesy card or other identification card or device used to obtain a cash advance, a loan or credit or to purchase or lease property or services on the issuer's credit or that of the holder. The **holder** is the person to whom such a card is issued and who agrees to pay obligations arising from its use.

Use of credit cards has become a way of life in the United States. The credit card has also opened a new avenue for criminals to obtain goods and services by theft and fraud. Carnes (1999, p. 13) notes:

Nationwide losses from stolen credit cards are in the billions of dollars. Blank or embossed, new credit card stock sells for anywhere from $3,000 to $5,000 per card "on the street." The "take" on a card is typically $10,000. Even then the stolen card might be recycled a year or so later.

Despite these losses the credit card, like the check, reduces cash thefts from individuals and reduces the amount of cash-on-hand in places such as filling stations, as well as the amount of cash transferred to banks from businesses. Use of credit cards also aids in identifying criminals who have the cards in their possession, more so than does cash, which is not as easily identifiable.

Levi (1998, p. 368) reports that frauds involving credit cards "can be committed by a continuum of organizational forms, from lone thieves who use the cards they have stolen to global organized crime syndicates." Because credit-card fraud is often spread throughout many jurisdictions, many police departments place low priority on this type of offense. Further complicating this crime, many businesses accept credit-card telephone purchases. Fraudulent orders are placed, and if the victims do not review their bills, the fraud can go completely undetected.

Most people involved in credit-card fraud are also involved in other types of crimes. The credit cards are obtained principally by muggers, robbers, burglars, pickpockets, purse-snatchers, thieves and prostitutes. They can also be obtained through fraudulent application or by manufacturing counterfeit cards.

Credit cards can be stolen by mailbox thieves who may have been tipped off by a postal employee, at apartment boxes or by dishonest employees of the card manufacturer. Cards from the manufacturer are desirable because they are unsigned. The criminal can sign the holder's name in his or her own handwriting. These cards also provide more time for use before the theft is discovered. For the same reasons, these cards are more valuable for resale to other fraudulent users.

To take maximum advantage without being detected, the criminal obtains the card by fraud, theft or reproduction, uses it for a short time and then disposes of it.

The elements of the crime of larceny by credit card include:

- Possessing a credit card obtained by theft or fraud,
- By which services or goods are obtained,
- Through unauthorized signing of the cardholder's name.

To use another person's credit card illegally, the criminal must either forge the cardholder's signature on sales slips or alter the signature on the card. The latter is made difficult by colored or symbol undertones that indicate when erasures and alterations are attempted.

The criminal must also operate under the floor-release limit to avoid having a clerk check the card's validity. The **floor-release limit** is the maximum dollar amount that may be paid with a charge card without getting authorization from the central office unless the business assumes liability for any loss. The limit is set by each company and is subject to change. It can be $50 or $100; in some gas stations, it is only $10. **Zero floor release** means that all credit card transactions must be checked. A suspicious merchant usually runs a check regardless of the amount of credit requested. Often the criminal is asked for additional identification, which is difficult to produce unless other identification was also obtained in the theft.

New techniques and instruments are being researched and devised in hopes of improving the verification of cardholder legitimacy, but advancements are slow. Levi (p. 382) explains: "In the future, technology may generate enhanced cardholder verification by methods such as iris scans, finger scans, or (as in France) having the customer tap in the PIN at point of sale against data encoded on the chip cards." Such technology, however, presumes the card was stolen from a consumer who had previously registered an iris scan, finger scan or PIN with the issuing credit institution.

Credit cards are attractive to criminals who operate interstate. Such criminals know that few companies will pay the witness fees for out-of-state prosecutions and that extradition is difficult to obtain unless the losses are great.

Many laws cover larceny or fraudulent use of credit cards. Possessing a forged credit card or one signed by a person other than the cardholder is the basis for a charge of possession of a forged instrument. Possessing two such cards is the basis for presuming intent to defraud. Illegally making or embossing a credit card or changing the expiration date or account number also subjects the person to a charge of intent to defraud. In most jurisdictions it is not necessary to prove that the person possessing the card signed it. Persons who have machinery or devices to counterfeit or forge credit cards can be charged with possession of forgery devices.

It is larceny to fail to return a found credit card or to keep one that is sent by mistake if the finder or recipient uses the card. Airline tickets bought with a stolen or forged credit card are also stolen property. The degree of larceny, petty or grand, is determined by the ticket's value. It is also larceny to misrepresent credit information or identity to obtain a credit card. If a person sells his or her credit card to someone who uses it and the original cardholder then refuses to pay, the cardholder can be charged with larceny.

Not all merchants and businesspeople are the victims of credit-card fraud. Some of them commit such fraud themselves. For example, a merchant may direct an employee to make more than one authorized record of charge per sale and then forward the charges for payment or raise the amount on the credit-card charge slip. This is larceny, with the degree determined by the difference between the actual charge and that forwarded for payment. It is also forgery because a document was altered. It is an attempt to commit larceny if such actions are not completed because of intervening circumstances such as the cardholder's becoming suspicious.

Most large credit-card issuers assign personnel to work with local police in cases of credit-card larceny. These people can be contacted for help or for information on the system used to manufacture and issue the cards.

When investigating credit-card fraud, obtain samples of handwriting from sales slips signed by the suspect. If a card is obtained by false credit application, handwriting is available on the credit application form. If the card is used for a car rental, other information about the rented vehicle is available. Gas stations often record the state and license number of vehicles they service. Drivers' licenses are used for identification. If a suspect is arrested, obtain a warrant to search the suspect's vehicle and residence for copies of sales slips or tickets obtained with the card, even though it has been discarded or sold.

Examine credit cards for alteration of the signature panel; the numbers or name can be shortened by using a razor blade to shave them off. New numbers can be entered to defeat the "hot card" list. Merchandise on sales slips found in the criminal's possession can provide further proof of illegal use. If the service obtained is a motel room, telephone calls can be traced to pinpoint accomplices. Clerks who handle the transactions often initial the sales slip, which enables the company or store to furnish the name of a witness.

Identity Fraud

A relatively new type of theft that can wreak havoc on a person's credit and financial security is identity fraud. According to a U.S. Public Interest Research Group, approximately 40,000 people have their identities stolen each year (Wexler, 1999, p. 39), and that figure is projected to rise. Wexler (p. 39) notes: "Computer crime experts point to the Internet as one of the chief reasons for the increase in identity theft." Hall (1999, p. 6) states: "Internet commerce is booming—millions are shopping on the net and it's not all secure, despite what the merchants say—credit card issuance is explosive and tech-thieves are always finding new, innovative methods to assume your identity and ruin your day."

Wexler (p. 39) maintains: "Credit-worthy consumers with high incomes are often the preferred prey of identity thieves." He further explains:

> Once the perpetrators identify their victims, they seek out their Social Security numbers. The Social Security number is the one piece of information that can open the doors to an individual's financial life . . . [and] can be gathered from a variety of sources, including motor vehicle and medical insurance records, voter registration lists, student transcripts, survey response forms, and even warranty cards.
>
> With a Social Security number and a few personal tidbits, thieves can assume identities to apply for driver's licenses, telephone numbers, car loans, and charge cards. They can also use the stolen identities to steal benefits such as pensions and Social Security payments.

In response to the growing problem of identity theft, Congress has enacted the Identity Theft and Assumption Deterrence Act. This Act makes it a federal crime to steal another person's identity for economic gain and allows for prison sentences up to 25 years for those convicted of the offense. It also enables victims to seek restitution for identifiable losses and for expenses related to restoring their credit rating. Oldenburg (1997, p. E5) offers the following suggestions to protect against identity theft:

- Never give anyone your personal information, including your address, bank account, credit card numbers, phone numbers or birth date.

- Do not write account numbers on the outside of payment envelopes.

- Do not keep PIN numbers written down.

- Guard your Social Security number.

- Destroy any records, canceled checks, receipts, deposit slips, etc., before throwing them away.

Any of the preceding, when found in possession of an identity thief, offers evidence of the offense.

Real Estate Fraud

In many areas of the country, populations are booming, and the corresponding real estate market is also thriving. In some communities, however, real estate scams, such as phantom down payments and "flipping," are costing lenders and home buyers tremendous amounts of money. In a real estate transaction, **flipping** "involves a middleman who buys a property near its estimated market value, then resells it—often within minutes—for a greatly increased price. Many deals rely on fraudulent appraisals that inflate the value of the property" ("Complaints of Inflated . . . ," 1998, p. B1). Brandt (1999, p. A1) notes that even though flipping itself is not illegal, if it is built on mortgage fraud, it is a prosecutable offense.

One area plagued by flipping has been the Twin Cities of Minneapolis and Saint Paul, Minnesota. Brandt (p. A1) offers several examples of flips: One house sold at $40,000 on August 7, 1997, and resold the same day at $94,000. Another house a few blocks away sold on September 12, 1997, for $35,000 and resold the same day for $86,000. Diaz (1998, p. A9) states: "The scam seems prevalent in the minority community . . . , where the desperate search for low-cost housing collides with property owners who sometimes are desperate to sell. Enter the 'flippers'—middle men who help swing the deals and pocket the difference between the original sale prices and the inflated ones they broker." According to one source ("Schemes Could Corrupt . . . ," 1998, p. A9):

> Such practices have been investigated for months by the Minnesota Department of Commerce and, more recently, by the state attorney general, the FBI, and the U.S. Department of Housing and Urban Development (HUD).
>
> Authorities say that the schemes threaten to:
>
> - Drive underfunded buyers into default, damaging their credit even more.
> - Cost lenders large sums, driving up credit costs for everyone.
> - Corrupt the Twin Cities area's valuation data, driving up property taxes and inflating the price of low-end houses beyond poor people's reach.

Telephone Fraud

Telemarketing fraud and other types of fraud using the telephone have also proliferated. In one such scam, a "representative" informs potential victims that they have won a sweepstakes prize and that the company needs their name, address and Social Security number to process the award. The company then uses the Social Security number for fraudulent purposes.

Cellular-phone and personal communication services (PCS) fraud are growing problems police must be prepared to deal with. According to the Cellular Telecommunications Industry Association (CTIA), cellular fraud cost carriers an estimated $710 million in 1996 (O'Brien, 1998, p. 22). Cellular phone and PCS

While talking on a cell phone, a person is vulnerable to having the phone's number "grabbed" and used by someone illegally.

fraud may be classified as low-tech or high-tech. As O'Brien (p. 21) notes:

> Subscription fraud is the least sophisticated and most common form of fraud. [It is] estimated that subscription fraud accounts for 80 percent of all PCS fraud. Individuals establish service using false credentials, including their names, social security numbers, credit references, and salary information. They use the service but never pay for it. . . .
>
> The most prevalent form of high-tech fraud is cloning fraud. Individuals acquire legitimate account information either by outright theft from a carrier or by on-the-air interception. . . . Armed with someone else's account numbers, the thief programs them into a cellular or PCS telephone, creating a clone of the legitimate phone.

O'Brien (p. 20) concludes:

> Despite the advanced technology used by some offenders, law enforcement agencies can combat these crimes using traditional methods. Successful resolution of cases involving telecommunications fraud often depends on partnerships with service providers, combined with an understanding of the nature of the crimes.

Caller ID can both enhance *and hinder* fraud investigations. It can identify perpetrators of fraud, but it can also pose a danger to officers who work undercover. They may be exposed by having their telephone numbers revealed to the criminals they telephone.

Mail Fraud

Mail fraud involves the perpetuation of scams through use of the mail, for example, bogus sweepstakes entries and notices. If mail fraud is suspected, police officers should contact the Postal Inspector through their local post office. Postal authorities can assist in investigating if the fraud scheme uses the mails to obtain victims or to transport profits from crime.

Confidence Games

Confidence games have separated people from their money for centuries; in fact, con games were known as early as 100 B.C. Changing times require changing techniques, but four basic elements are always present: locating a mark from whom to obtain the money, selecting the game, conducting it and then leaving the area as rapidly as possible.

A **confidence game** obtains money or property by a trick, device or swindle that takes advantage of a victim's trust in the swindler. The confidence game purports to offer a get-rich-quick scheme. The victim is sworn to secrecy and told that telling anyone could cause the deal to fall through or the profits to be divided among more people. The game may require the victim to do something dishonest or unethical, thus making the victim less apt to report the swindle to the police. It is often conducted away from the victim's hometown so that the victim cannot obtain advice from friends.

A particular type of person is needed to make the con game work. Con artists develop cunning, guile and skills through their own systems of learning and education. They are taught by older persons in the "trade," usually starting as the "number two" or "straight man." As they gain experience, they work their way up until they are the "number one" in a swindle of their own. Con artists understand human nature, are extremely convincing with words, lack conscience, have an uncanny ability to select the right victim and have no mercy for their victims, often extracting the life savings of elderly people.

Two basic approaches are used in con games: the short con and the long con. **Short-con games** take the victims for whatever money they have with them at the time of the action. For example, "Three-Card Monte," similar to the old shell game, entices victims to bet on whether they can select one card from among three. "Huge Duke" involves betting on a stacked poker hand, with the victim dealing the final hand. "The Wipe" involves tying money into a handkerchief for safekeeping and then switching it with one containing newspaper bits.

Long-con games are usually for higher stakes. For example, in "The Wire," the original long-con game, the victim is enticed to bet on horse races, convinced through an elaborate telegraph office setup that the manager can beat the bookmaker by delaying the results of the race long enough to let the victim and other cohorts in the scheme make bets. After allowing the victim to win a few games at low stakes, the "big bet" is made in which the victim may lose thousands of dollars.

When investigating con-game fraud, obtain a complete description of the confidence artists and the type of fraud, trick or false pretense they used, as well as the exact amount of money involved.

Because the victim usually sees and talks with the con artists, it is often easy to identify them, but unless the police are notified quickly, the suspects will be gone from the area. Obtain descriptions of the perpetrators and their MO. Keep this information on file for future reference. The FBI maintains a confidence artist file to assist in locating such suspects, as well as a general appearance file of con artists (even though photographs are not available). The FBI assists in investigating violations that occur on interstate conveyances such as planes, boats and trains. It also assists if there is evidence that radio, television or telegraph was used in committing the crime or if a money order was sent to a person in another state. If the swindle exceeds $5,000, the FBI has jurisdiction under the Interstate Transportation of Stolen Property Act. (Many con games exceed this amount.) As with mail fraud, postal authorities may assist investigators in cases in which confidence artists use the mails in the execution of their crimes.

Most states include con games in laws relating to larceny by trick and to obtaining money under false pretenses. Check the laws in your jurisdiction for the specific elements that must be proven.

One type of fraud that may be unfamiliar to law enforcement is called "gypsy crime." According to Harman (1996, p. 97): "A crime family specializing in fraud has operated successfully throughout the world for almost 2,000 years. Millions of dollars are lost each year to these perpetrators, but fewer than 5% of the victims ever complain—and those that do are most often met with laughter." Harman explains that the gypsy population is a close-knit family, superb at keeping secrets and speaking their own language. In addition to fortune-telling fraud, gypsies also operate major welfare frauds and are often involved in extortion schemes.

Other Scams

Other scams investigators might be summoned to examine include:

■ Easy-credit scams—Con artists target people who seek to repair damaged credit ratings by offering credit cards in exchange for advanced payments or deposits.

■ Bogus prize offers—Mail or phone announcements proclaim that "You're a big winner!" The winner is instructed to wire money to cover taxes or fees in order to receive their grand prize.

■ Phony home repairs—Workmen knock on a door and explain that they are finishing several jobs (roofing, siding, driveways) in the neighborhood. They have leftover material and can offer to fix anything at a great discount. They may take a deposit or the entire payment and never return to complete the job, or they may begin the work and then claim the job is more involved than they had

thought and state they will need additional payment to finish the job.

■ Fake phone services—Also known as "cramming," this scam involves adding charges to a phone bill for services the customer never requested. The vendor levies the charge against a phone number, and the phone company is required by law to pass the charges on to the customer. Because the amounts are typically quite small, many customers never even notice they have been scammed.

■ Travel scams—Victims are promised an exciting, free vacation in an exotic location but must first provide a credit-card number for "verification."

■ Cyber-scams—The Internet offers numerous sites to sell or trade merchandise, and con artists are taking advantage of this lucrative virtual swap shop to sell defective or nonexistent products.

Although it may be hard to believe people would fall for some of these scams, the con artists are extremely well versed and tend to target more vulnerable and trusting victims, such as the elderly.

White-Collar Crime

The FBI Academy defines **white-collar crime** as "illegal acts characterized by fraud, concealment, or a violation of trust, which are not dependent upon the actual or threatened use of physical force or violence" (Robertson, 1999, p. 24). White-collar crime is big business. According to Burkhart and Lantz (1996, p. 3): "Estimates start at $40 billion a year and growing." Robertson (p. 24) adds: "On the U.S. federal level, every agency with white-collar crime jurisdiction has experienced a dramatic increase in the number and types of white-collar crime cases." Furthermore (p. 24): "The FBI's white-collar crime program has grown extensively, now representing the largest investigative program within the bureau's Criminal Investigative Division."

"National White Collar Crime Center" (1996, p. 11) notes: "While its impact on the economy may be measured in the hundreds of billions of dollars, the crime known as white-collar, economic or financial, is often misperceived as victimless." The article explains:

Typically, there is no body and no blood. The individual involved in economic criminal activity is generally smarter and more sophisticated than his or her street crime counterpart, and the victim, for a number of reasons, doesn't report the crime. Fighting economic crime is a complicated undertaking involving tedious financial research and analysis.

Many instances of larceny/theft and fraud can also be classified as white-collar crime. In some cases perpetrators of white-collar crime do not "look like" criminals—they are often highly educated, socially accepted people who hold high-level positions of trust within a company. Because of such positions, they are able to commit crimes involving millions of dollars. However, the profile of the white-collar criminal has changed in recent years. Robertson (p. 24) notes:

> When most people hear the term "white-collar crime," they picture a person in a business suit who works as a bookkeeper or accountant. . . . While that may have been the case 30 years ago, it is certainly not true now—nor has it been in a significant way for the past 10 years. Today's white-collar criminals are organized crime members, drug dealers, juveniles and members of violent criminal groups.

He adds (p. 26): "Alarmingly, the number of juveniles involved in and prosecuted for white-collar crime has grown dramatically. . . . An estimated 11, 300 juveniles were arrested in 1997 for fraud, . . . a 58 percent increase from 1988 to 1997."

Much white-collar crime is never reported because it involves top-level executives whose reputations their organizations do not want to damage. White-collar crimes may be committed by individuals against other individuals such as family members, lawyers, real estate agents, insurance agents and physicians. They may be committed against organizations by insiders such as business partners, office managers, computer programmers and senior executives. White-collar crimes may also be committed by individuals with no relationship to the victim, such as corporate spies, forgers, counterfeiters, computer hackers and information pirates.

The United States Chamber of Commerce has identified nine categories of white-collar crime:

- - - - - - - - -

White-collar or business-related crime includes (1) securities theft and fraud, (2) insurance fraud, (3) credit-card and check fraud, (4) consumer fraud, illegal competition and deceptive practices, (5) bankruptcy fraud, (6) computer-related fraud, (7) embezzlement and pilferage, (8) bribes, kick-backs and payoffs and (9) receiving stolen property.

- - - - - - - - -

Investigate these crimes as you would any larceny case. Whether they are felonies or misdemeanors depends on the value involved.

White-collar crimes can be committed by any employee within a business or organization. However, low-level employees usually do not have the opportunity to steal a large amount from their employer. Most often their crimes consist of pilferage from the employer. Many employees do not see taking office supplies or placing personal long-distance phone calls from a work phone as dishonest. However, they would not think of doing the same thing in a place where they did not work. Over time, the losses from pilferage are often much more than what a high-level employee might embezzle.

Few law enforcement agencies are equipped to investigate white-collar crime, encouraging such investigations to be conducted internally by in-house or contracted private investigators. The National White Collar Crime Center (NWCCC) links criminal justice agencies across international borders and also bridges the gap between local and state criminal justice agencies. This center provides assistance in preventing, investigating and prosecuting economic crime. Kruchten (1999, p. 9) also notes:

> Law enforcement officers can turn to the Financial Crimes Enforcement Network (FinCEN), a division of the U.S. Department of the Treasury, which serves as an information clearinghouse. . . .
>
> FinCEN's financial database contains a wealth of information that law enforcement can use in any criminal investigation where the suspects have access to large sums of money.

FinCEN's database stores information collected under the Bank Secrecy Act (BSA) and contains more than 20 million reports from banks and other financial institutions.

Sloan (1999, p. 8) describes an application of computer technology that allows investigators to "follow the money" in economic crimes:

> Project Gateway, developed . . . by FinCEN, . . . has helped uncover important financial clues and attack criminal proceeds. Following the money trail of criminals can produce tremendous opportunities in terms of the identification of suspects and assets, as well as the ability to attack money launderers and other criminals at their source. . . .
>
> Another useful feature of Gateway is the "alert" mechanism that automatically alerts FinCEN when two agencies have an interest in the same subject.

Embezzlement

Embezzlement is the fraudulent appropriation of property by a person to whom it has been entrusted. The property is then used by the embezzler or another person contrary to the terms of the trust. The owner retains title to the property during the trust period. The property so entrusted may be real or personal property. Even though the title remains with the owner, the embezzler usually has control through appointment as agent, servant, bailee or trustee. Because of the relationship between owner and embezzler, the embezzler has custody of the property. Most embezzlements involve employees. Most bank losses are from embezzlement, often involving large sums of money.

Bank embezzlement is jointly investigated by the local police and the FBI.

Bank embezzlements often start small and gradually increase. Surprisingly, many embezzlements are not committed for the benefit of the embezzler. Many start by providing unauthorized credit extensions to customers. As the amount increases, the employee is afraid to make the error known to the employer and attempts to cover the losses. In other cases, the employee uses funds to start other businesses, fully intending to replace the borrowed funds, but the businesses often fail. Other motives for embezzlement are to cover gambling debts, to support a drug habit, to make home improvements, to meet heavy medical expenses or to get even with the employer for real or imagined grievances.

Businesses, industries and other financial institutions are also victims of embezzlement. Embezzlement includes committing petty theft over a period of time, "kiting" accounts receivable, overextending credit and cash returns, falsifying accounts payable records and falsifying information put into computers—a highly sophisticated crime. (Computer-related crimes are discussed in Chapter 18.)

Embezzlement is increasing at 15 percent per year and has an estimated annual cost of $4 billion. The prosecution rate is low because of adverse publicity for both the individual and the company. Often the employee has been trusted for many years, and sympathy overrules justice.

Embezzlement losses may be discovered by accident, by careful audit, by inspection of records or property, by the embezzler's abnormal behavior, by a sudden increase in the embezzler's standard of living or by the embezzler's disappearance from employment. Because police training rarely includes accounting courses, investigating embezzlement cases often requires help from professional accountants. In embezzlement cases, prove fraudulent intent to convert property contrary to the terms of a trust by establishing how and when the property was converted, what the exact amount was and who did the converting. Establish that a financial loss did in fact occur. Determine the amount of the loss. Describe the property accurately if it is not money. Describe and prove the method of obtaining the property. Establish the nature of the trust. Seize all relevant books and financial records as evidence. It is necessary to determine the motive to prove fraudulent intent.

Environmental Crime

Environmental crime investigation is a new area of specialization that mixes elements of law, public health and science. Contrary to what many believe, environmental crime is not victimless—the victims are our children and our children's children. Environmental crime is far-reaching and pervasive, and its consequences are often hidden for years or even decades.

The most common environmental crimes prosecuted involve illegal waste disposal. The most common substances involved in such offenses are hazardous wastes. The collection and processing of evidence in these cases often requires special training and equipment. Many law enforcement officers lack the scientific background needed to put together an environmental pollution case or to deal safely with the illegal disposal of hazardous waste. Indeed, walking into a hazardous waste site without proper protective gear or skills for handling the material may be just as deadly as facing an armed robber in a dark alley.

Furthermore, most officers have little or no idea of the existence of the complex array of environmental control laws with all their exceptions, changes and omissions. For example, Congress and administrative agencies are continuously amending environmental laws and regulations to increase punishments for environmental criminal offenses, in many cases making them felonies rather than misdemeanors. Among such acts are the following:

- Comprehensive Environmental Response, Compensation and Liability Act (CERCLA)
- Resource Conservation and Recovery Act (RCRA)
- Federal Water Pollution Control Act (FWPCA)
- Clean Air Act (CAA)

tance from an environmental regulatory agency. Collaboration with specially equipped environmental labs, as opposed to crime labs, may also be necessary. According to Laska (1997, p. 52):

> Environmental investigations are a growing facet of law enforcement. Many of those cases, especially where hazardous waste is involved, will require chemical analysis of suspect materials. For the law enforcement officer, a cooperative effort with environmental labs will lead to results that will be useful to an appropriate disposition of the case.

Laska (1996, p. 94) states: "Environmental investigations bring together varied professionals and permit each to use his or her unique skills." He suggests: "To the law enforcement officer, these cases are intimidating because of the technical facets involved. By working together with administrative regulators, officers can solve the technical aspects unique to the investigation." Laska (p. 96) concludes: "Just as a white collar investigator will call upon an accountant or computer specialist for technical assistance, so will the environmental investigator use the regulator for the technical aspects of the investigation. The skillful investigator will then fit the technical expertise into the developed case, just as in a burglary, drug or murder investigation."

Some jurisdictions have designated specially trained law enforcement officers to investigate environmental crimes. Although many such officers are derisively being called "the garbage police," one agency's Sanitation Police are gaining respect and recognition for their efforts in keeping the city clean and free of environmental wrongdoings (Dyment, 1998, p. 127):

> The New York City Department of Sanitation maintains the only municipal police force in the nation dedicated to environmental concerns. . . .
>
> For the 1996 fiscal year, the Sanitation Police, along with their civilian enforcement agents, issued 308,329 citations. The fines ranged from $25 for recycling improperly to $20,000 for illegal dumping.

In one case, a lethal acid was left on the street with regular garbage, with a death resulting when someone was exposed to the chemical. Dyment (p. 129) notes:

> Members of the Sanitation Police worked closely with the New York City Police Department and the Department of Environmental Protection to find the people who illegally left the deadly hydrofluoric acid. . . . In addition to this high profile murder investigation, their other duties are more mundane, catching illegal dumpers and nabbing the dog owner who doesn't clean up after his pet.

In July 1999, Royal Caribbean Cruises, Ltd. agreed to pay a record $18 million criminal fine for dumping oil and hazardous chemicals in U.S. water and lying about it to the Coast Guard.

In each of these acts, amendments were made converting misdemeanors to felonies.

In 1990 the Pollution Prosecution Act was enacted, making enforcement of environmental crimes a new concern for law enforcement. Violations of various environmental crime acts call for penalties of up to $25,000 per day for noncompliance or imprisonment up to 10 years.

Civil regulatory agencies are knowledgeable in these laws and have the resources to document evidence of a violation. For these reasons, in addition to the safety issues, many investigators find it beneficial to seek assis-

Many of the problems associated with investigating environmental crime are similar to investigating computer-related crime and other crimes that became more prevalent during the end of the twentieth century. Definitions of environmental crimes vary from state to state. Statistics are not uniformly compiled. The suspects are often otherwise upstanding business people who often do not feel they are committing crimes.

Premeditation or malice are not required to prove an environmental crime. All that must be proved is that an act that violated the law was done knowingly rather than by mistake. For example, the owner of a company makes a conscious decision to dump hazardous materials into a waterway or unload a truck full of construction and demolition (C & D) debris in a remote location off a desolate road under cover of darkness. Evidence of "knowing" may include tire tracks in remote locations and documented "after hours" activities, for it may be concluded such "detours" are made to illegally dump and are not in fact accidental.

Of special concern in environmental crime investigations is the search warrant. Investigators must know what substances they may seek and how they should collect such samples to avoid becoming contaminated. Again, regulatory personnel may provide assistance.

Through criminal prosecution of environmental crimes, local prosecutors have a crucial function and can assume the role of protector of the public health.

Summary

Larceny/theft is the unlawful taking, carrying, leading or driving away of property from another's possession. It is synonymous with theft. Both larceny and burglary are crimes against property, but larceny, unlike burglary, does not involve illegally entering a structure. Larceny also differs from robbery in that no force or threat of force is involved.

The elements of the crime of larceny/theft are (1) the felonious stealing, taking, carrying, leading or driving away of (2) another's personal goods or property (3) valued above or below a specified amount (4) with the intent to permanently deprive the owner of the property or goods. The two major categories of larceny/theft are grand larceny—a felony based on the value of stolen property (usually more than $100)—and petty larceny—a misdemeanor based on the value of the property (usually less than $100). In most states taking found property with the intent to keep or sell it is also a crime.

Among the common types of larceny are purse snatching, picking pockets, theft from coin machines, shoplifting, bicycle theft, theft from motor vehicles, theft from buildings, theft of motor vehicle accessories and jewelry theft.

When dealing with shoplifters, remember that altering the price of an item is considered larceny. Also remember that it is not usually required that a shoplifter leave the premises with the stolen item before apprehension. When investigating jewelry theft, inform the FBI of the theft even if there is no immediate evidence of interstate operations. The elements of the offense of receiving stolen goods are (1) receiving, buying or concealing stolen or illegally obtained goods (2) knowing them to be stolen or illegally obtained.

Fraud is intentional deception to cause a person to give up property or some lawful right. It differs from theft in that fraud uses deceit rather than stealth to obtain goods illegally. Fraud is committed in many ways, including through the use of checks, credit cards, confidence games and embezzlement. Common types of check fraud are insufficient-fund checks, issuance of worthless checks and forgeries.

Elements of the crime of larceny by credit card include (1) possessing credit cards obtained by theft or fraud (2) by which services or goods are obtained (3) through unauthorized signing of the cardholder's name.

White-collar or business-related crime includes (1) securities theft and fraud, (2) insurance fraud, (3) credit-card and check fraud, (4) consumer fraud, illegal competition and deceptive practices, (5) bankruptcy fraud, (6) computer-related fraud, (7) embezzlement and pilferage, (8) bribes, kick-backs and payoffs and (9) receiving stolen property. Bank embezzlements are investigated jointly by the local police and the FBI.

Checklist

Larceny

- What are the name, address and phone number of the complainant or the person reporting the crime?
- What are the name, address and phone number of the victim if different from the complainant?
- Has the victim made previous theft complaints? If so, obtain all details.
- What were the date and time the crime was reported and the date and time the crime was committed if known?

- Who owns the property or has title to it or right of possession?

- Will the owner or person in control or possession sign the complaint?

- Who discovered the loss? Was this the logical person to discover it?

- Where was the item at the time of the theft? Was this the usual place for the item, or had it been recently transferred there?

- When was the item last seen?

- Has the area been searched to determine whether the property might have been misplaced?

- What security precautions had been taken? Were these normal?

- Exactly what property was taken? Obtain a complete description of each item, including number, color, size, serial numbers or other identifying marks.

- What was the value of the items? How was the value determined: estimated original price, replacement price or estimated market value?

- How easily could the items be sold? Are there likely markets or buyers?

- Were there any witnesses to the theft or persons who might provide leads?

- Who had access to the property before and during the time of the theft?

- Who were absentee employees?

- Who are possible suspects and why? What might be the motive?

Application

A cash box was left on top of a desk at a university office. Some students had registered early that day, so there was about $600 in the box. The box was closed but not locked. The office manager went to lunch, leaving a college student in charge. The student took a phone call in the dean's office, and the box was out of her sight for about five minutes. Later she heard a noise in the hallway outside the office. She went out to see what had happened and discovered that a student had been accidentally pushed through a glass door across the hallway from the main office. She observed the scene in the hallway for about five minutes and then went back to the registration office, where she did not notice anything out of order.

After a half hour the office manager returned from lunch and helped register two students at the front counter. When she went to the cash box to make change, she found that the $600 was missing. She immediately notified the administrator's office, and a controller was sent over to the registration office. The controller conducted a brief investigation and then notified the police.

You are the investigator arriving at the registration office.

Questions

1. What procedure would you use upon arrival?
2. What steps would you take immediately?
3. What evidence is likely to be located?
4. What questions would you ask?
5. What is the probability of solving the case?

Discussion Questions

1. Larceny has been called the most unreported crime in the United States. What factors might account for failure to report larceny? Is there a way to determine how many larcenies actually occur when you consider shoplifting, bicycle thefts and minor thefts of property that victims may regard as simply losing or misplacing things?

2. What are possible motives for committing larcenies such as bicycle theft? Shoplifting? Embezzlement? Thefts from autos? Gasoline thefts? Theft by check or credit card?

3. How does the receiver of stolen goods (fence) fit into the larceny crime problem? Is the fence's role more or less serious than that of the person who initially steals the property?

4. How do petty and grand larceny differ in your state? Do the elements that must be proved for each of these crimes differ in your state?

5. A con artist has bilked a senior citizen in your community out of $2,000. The senior citizen has filed a complaint in the hopes of having his money returned and the perpetrator arrested. What crime has been committed under your state laws, and what is the procedure for following up the complaint?

6. A man has been arrested for shoplifting and taken to the police station for booking. During the search for this offense, the police discover several credit cards that are not issued in the name of the person arrested. What offense is involved? Is there a separate offense from the original offense of shoplifting? Can the person be tried on both offenses? What procedure is necessary to prove the second charge?

7. Embezzlement is most frequently associated with white-collar crime. Has it been a problem in your community?

8. How do the following differ: stealing a suitcase from the baggage claim area at an airport, from an automobile and from a retail store?

9. If a customer knows an article is priced much higher in the store where she is shopping than in another store and can prove it, is it legal for her to change the price on the article?

10. What can the police do to reduce the number of larcenies in a community? Does your community have an antishoplifting program? An antibike-theft program? Do banks send literature to senior citizens concerning con games? What other measures have been initiated in your community? What additional measures might be taken?

References

Badolato, Edward. "Current and Future Trends in Cargo Security." *Security Technology and Design,* Vol. 8, No. 8, August 1998, pp. 14–18.

Baker, Thomas J. "Combating Art Theft: International Cooperation in Action." *The Police Chief,* Vol. LXIII, No. 10, October 1996, pp. 19–23.

Barry, Marc. "All the Rage." *Security Technology and Design,* Vol. 9, No. 1, January 1999, pp. 14–21.

Brandt, Steve. "Reeling from Deals." (Minneapolis/St. Paul) *Star Tribune,* September 12, 1999, pp. A1, A20.

Burkhard, Bob and Lantz, Brad. "Are Your Computers Safe?" *Talking Business,* October 1996, p. 3.

Carnes, W. Robert. "Don't Forget to Check Environment for Compromising Conditions." *Access Control and Security Systems Integration,* May 1999, p. 13.

Chatzky, Jean. "Can You Spot a Counterfeit?" *USA Weekend,* September 18, 1998, p. 12.

"Complaints of Inflated Real Estate Deals Draw State, Federal Probes." (Minneapolis/St. Paul) *Star Tribune,* July 13, 1998, pp. B1, B2.

DeFranco, Liz Martinez. "New Anti-Theft Technology Broadens Protection Options." *Security Technology and Design,* Vol. 9, No. 5, May 1999, pp. 110–113.

Diaz, Kevin. " 'Flip' Scams Prey on the Poor, Unknowing." (Minneapolis/St. Paul) *Star Tribune,* July 14, 1998, p. A9.

Doherty, Michael. "Game Wardens: A Resource for Local Police." *Law and Order,* Vol. 47, No.5, May 1999, pp. 111–113.

Dolan, Thomas G. "Cargo Theft: Out of Control." *Security Technology and Design,* Vol. 9, No. 9, September 1999, pp. 26–30.

Dyment, Robert. "Police Force Dedicated to Environmental Crimes." *Law and Order,* Vol. 46, No. 5, May 1998, pp. 127–129.

Hall, Dennis. "Sign Here for a New Approach to Problem of Identity Fraud." *Police,* Vol. 23, No. 1, January 1999, p. 6.

Hansen, Walter N. "Combating Check Fraud: A Multifaceted Approach." *FBI Law Enforcement Bulletin,* Vol. 68, No. 5, May 1999, pp. 10–17.

Harman, Alan. "Gypsy Crime." *Law and Order,* Vol. 44, No. 5, May 1996, pp. 97–100.

Holland, Thomas G. "Checks and Balances." *Security Management,* Vol. 43, No. 8, August 1999, pp. 76–82.

Jaeger, Sandy. "The Case of the Pilfered Profits." *Security Technology and Design,* Vol. 9, No. 2, February 1999, pp. 6, 74.

Kelly, Michael J. "The New Era of Shortage Control in a Retail Distribution Center." *Security Technology and Design,* Vol. 9, No. 7, July 1999, pp. 78–80.

Kruchten, Gary J. "The Bank Secrecy Act: A Powerful Weapon for Law Enforcement." *FBI Law Enforcement Bulletin,* Vol. 68, No. 8, August 1999, pp. 8–10.

Laska, Paul. "Environmental Investigations: A New Way of Thinking." *Law Enforcement Technology,* October 1996, pp. 94–99.

Laska, Paul R. "Environmental Crime, Evidence and the Lab." *Law Enforcement Technology,* Vol. 24, No. 3, March 1997, pp. 51–52.

Lehman, Peter and Dion, Mark. "Stealing Trash: Gray-Collar Crime." *The Police Chief,* Vol. LXIII, No. 8, August 1996, pp. 39–44.

Levi, Michael. "Offender Organization and Victim Responses: Credit Card Fraud in International Perspective." *Journal of Contemporary Criminal Justice,* Vol. 14, No. 4, November 1998, pp. 368–383.

"Mailless in Seattle: Thieves Raid Boxes." *Las Vegas Review Journal,* November 24, 1998, p. 20A.

Morrison, Richard D. "The Sounds of Crime." *Law and Order,* Vol. 46, No. 5, May 1998, pp. 109–110.

"National White Collar Crime Center." *Security Concepts,* January 1996, pp. 11, 17.

Neeley, Dequendre. "FBI Steps Up Cargo Security." *Security Management,* Vol. 42, No. 1, January 1998, p. 16.

O'Brien, John T. "Telecommunications Fraud: Opportunities for Techno-Criminals." *FBI Law Enforcement Bulletin,* Vol. 67, No. 5, May 1998, pp. 20–25.

Oldenburg, Don. "How to Prevent Identity Theft." (Minneapolis/St. Paul) *Star Tribune,* November 11, 1997, p. E5.

Phelps, David. "New Growth Industry: Fraud." (Minneapolis/St. Paul) *Star Tribune,* September 6, 1999, pp. D1, D7.

Robertson, Jim. "The Changing Face of White-Collar Crime." *The Police Chief,* Vol. LXVI, No. 9, September 1999, pp. 24–26.

"Schemes Could Corrupt Area's Valuation Data, Authorities Say." (Minneapolis/St. Paul) *Star Tribune,* July 14, 1998, p. A9.

Slahor, Stephenie. "Society to Prevent Trade in Stolen Art." *Law and Order,* Vol. 44, No. 10, October 1996, pp. 181–182.

Slater, Pam. "Clever Anti-Theft Weapons Used to Fend Off Shoplifters." *Las Vegas Review Journal,* September 20, 1998, p. 4B.

Sloan, James F. "Using Computer Technology to 'Follow the Money.'" *The Police Chief,* Vol. LXVI, No. 9, September 1999, p. 8.

Slotter, Keith. "Investigative Assets: The CPA's Role in Detecting and Preventing Fraud." *FBI Law Enforcement Bulletin,* Vol. 68, No. 7, July 1999, pp. 1–6.

Stedman, Michael J. "Cargo Security: Optimal Options for Defense." *Security Technology and Design,* Vol. 8, No. 8, August 1998, pp. 20–24.

Toft, Ron. "New Parrot Power: A New Weapon against Illegal Wildlife Trading." *Law and Order,* Vol. 47, No. 10, October 1999, pp. 119–120.

Wells, Joseph T. "A Fistful of Dollars." *Security Management,* Vol. 43, No. 8, August 1999, pp. 70–75.

Wessells, Fred P. "Www.ripoff.com." *Security Technology and Design,* Vol. 9, No. 1, January 1999, p. 20.

Wexler, Sanford. "Recovering Stolen Identities." *Law Enforcement Technology,* Vol. 26, No. 4, April 1999, pp. 36–39.

Windsor, David L. "Timber Theft: A Solvable Crime." *FBI Law Enforcement Bulletin,* Vol. 68, No. 9, September 1999, pp. 17–19.

Motor Vehicle Theft

Do You Know?

What a VIN is and why it is important?

What the five major categories of motor vehicle theft are?

What the elements of the crime of unauthorized use of a motor vehicle are?

What types of vehicles are considered "motor vehicles"?

What embezzlement of a motor vehicle is?

What the Dyer Act is and how it assists in motor vehicle theft investigation?

Why false reports of auto theft are sometimes made?

What two agencies can help investigate motor vehicle theft?

How to improve effectiveness in recognizing stolen vehicles?

How to help prevent motor vehicle theft?

Introduction

It is not unusual for an American family to finance or own more than $20,000 in motor vehicles. Yet the motor vehicle, even though highly vulnerable, is the least protected of all property subject to theft. The vehicle, its accessories and the property inside are all targets for thieves.

Most people use motor vehicles to travel to work and for pleasure. Thousands of recreational vehicles are also targets for theft and burglary. Aircraft and watercraft thefts add to the problems facing police investigators.

According to Siuru (1996, p. 69): "Of all things stolen, vehicles top the list in total dollar losses." Burke (1996, p. 42) adds: "The Federal Bureau of Investigation [notes] that more than 1.5 million vehicles are stolen annually (nationally, one vehicle is stolen every 20 seconds) at an estimated cost of 8 billion dollars." Ragavan and Kaplan (1999, p. 118) state: "According to the FBI, vehicle thefts have added an average of $85 to a family's annual insurance premium." Table 16.1 summarizes the cities with the highest vehicle theft rates and the most commonly stolen vehicles in the United States.

Table 16.1	Vehicle Theft in the United States
Cities with the highest vehicle theft rates	*Most commonly stolen vehicles in the U.S.*
1. Miami, FL	1. Honda Accord
2. Jersey City (Hudson Co.), NJ	2. Toyota Camry
3. Fresno, CA	3. Oldsmobile Cutlass
4. Memphis, TN	4. Honda Civic/CRX
5. New York, NY	5. Ford Mustang
6. Tucson, AZ	6. Toyota Corolla
7. Phoenix-Mesa, AZ	7. Chevrolet Full-Size Pickup
8. Albuquerque, NM	8. Nissan Maxima
9. Sacramento, CA	9. Jeep Grand Cherokee (SUV)
10. New Orleans, LA	10. Ford F-150 Series Pickup

Source unknown.

This chapter begins with an explanation of motor vehicle identification and motor vehicle theft classification. This is followed by descriptions of the elements of the crimes of unauthorized use of a motor vehicle, embezzlement and interstate transportation of motor vehicles. Next the chapter describes the preliminary investigation as well as the problem of insurance fraud and names various agencies that might cooperate in investigating and/or preventing motor vehicle theft. Following this is a discussion of how to recognize a stolen motor vehicle or an unauthorized driver, how to recover an abandoned or stolen motor vehicle and efforts to prevent motor vehicle theft. The chapter concludes with a discussion of thefts of other types of motor vehicles. ■

Motor Vehicle Identification

Given the millions of motor vehicles operating on our roads, an identification system is imperative. The most important means of vehicle identification is the **vehicle identification number,** or **VIN.**

The vehicle identification number (VIN) is the primary nonduplicated, serialized number assigned by a manufacturer to each vehicle made. This number—critical in motor vehicle theft investigation—identifies the specific vehicle in question.

VINs are often vandalized or altered after a vehicle theft.

The Motor Vehicle Theft Law Enforcement Act of 1984 requires manufacturers to place the 17-digit VIN on 14 specified component parts including the engine, the transmission, both front fenders, the hood, both front doors, both bumpers, both rear quarter-panels, both rear doors and the deck, lid, tailgate *or* hatchback. Some manufacturers position the labels in plain view; others hide them. Car thieves often attempt to change or replace VINs to conceal vehicles' true identities. The National Institute of Justice notes: "The majority of auto theft investigators agree that it's extremely rare for all anti-theft VIN labels to be successfully removed from a vehicle. It takes only one component part with an intact anti-theft label to trace the vehicle owner, prove the vehicle was stolen and make arrests" ("A Job Well Done," 1997, p. 103). As one investigator puts it: "I often refer to the labels as our guardian angels—you can't see them, but you know they're constantly working in your favor."

Manufacturers also use numbers to identify engines and various vehicle components.

Classification of Motor Vehicle Theft

Motor vehicle thefts are often classified by the thief's motive or purpose, recognizing that it is impossible to determine the motive for thefts in which the vehicle is abandoned.

- - - - - - - - -

Classifications of motor vehicle theft based on the motive of the offender include:

■ Joyriding.

■ Transportation.

■ Commission of another crime.

■ Stripping for parts and accessories.

■ Reselling for profit.

- - - - - - - - -

Joyriding

The joyrider and the person stealing for transportation are sometimes grouped together, but there is an important distinction between them. The joyrider is generally a younger person who steals for thrills and excitement.

Joyriders look for cars with keys in the ignition that can be started and driven away rapidly. The vehicle is taken for a comparatively short time and then abandoned near the location of the theft or near the joyrider's destination. A vehicle taken to another community is generally left there, and another vehicle is then stolen for the return trip.

Stolen vehicles are often found where young people congregate: fast food places, skating rinks, malls and athletic events. Several vehicle thefts within a short time may follow a pattern, providing clues for investigators. For example, most cars stolen by the same individual or group in a short period are the same make, entered in the same manner and stolen and dropped off in the same general area. Juvenile informants can be extremely helpful in investigating such auto thefts.

Motor vehicle thefts by juveniles are often not regarded seriously by the courts, even though they account for most vehicle thefts and can cause injury or death to others. It is not unusual for juveniles to be involved in up to a hundred car thefts before apprehension. Vehicle theft by juveniles is a serious problem. In fact, in some states joyriding is a separate offense.

Transportation

Theft of a motor vehicle for transportation can involve a joyrider but is more apt to involve a transient, hitchhiker or runaway. The objective is to travel from one point to another at no cost. These offenders are generally older than joyriders. Late fall and winter are peak periods for this type of theft.

A vehicle stolen for transportation is kept longer than one stolen for joyriding. Frequently it is operated until it runs out of gas or stops running. It is then abandoned and another vehicle is stolen. The vehicle is often dumped to avoid suspicion. The license plates may be changed, or a plate may be stolen and put on the rear of the vehicle.

Commission of Another Crime

Automobiles are used in most serious crimes. Robberies of banks, bank messengers, payroll offices, businesses and service stations as well as criminal escapes almost always involve a getaway in a stolen vehicle. Vehicles provide both rapid transportation and a means to transport the loot. Other crimes frequently committed while using stolen vehicles include rapes, kidnappings, burglaries, larcenies to obtain gas and assaults of police officers attempting to apprehend a suspect. Records indicate that many habitual criminals have stolen at least one car in their criminal career. Some began as car thieves.

Stolen cars are used in committing other crimes to escape detection at the crime scene and to avoid being identified by witnesses. Therefore, the criminal normally uses the stolen vehicle for only a brief time. In fact, a stolen vehicle report may not yet have been made when the crime is committed. Stolen plates are often used to cause confusion in identification. The vehicle used in committing the crime—the "hot" car—is usually soon abandoned for a "cold" car—a vehicle used to escape from the crime scene vicinity.

Stolen vehicles played a major role in the search for serial killer Andrew Cunanan. As O'Connor and Graves (1997) report, authorities were able to re-create the route taken by Cunanan in his cross-country killing spree by locating one victim's vehicle in the vicinity of the next victim's body. Cunanan's homicidal rampage began in late April 1997 in Minnesota with the killing of two men. Cunanan then stole one of the victims' Jeep Grand Cherokee, which police later discovered near the home of a third victim in Chicago. The Chicago victim's Lexus was reported missing and was later found in New Jersey at the murder scene of Cunanan's fourth victim. In continuing the pattern, the fourth victim's pickup truck was stolen and later turned up in a Miami Beach parking ramp, several blocks from where designer Gianni Versace had been murdered in front of his home by Cunanan.

A stolen motor vehicle driven by a criminal is 150 to 200 times more likely to be in an accident than one driven by a noncriminal, therefore, regard as suspicious any damaged, abandoned vehicles you observe. Conditions contributing to this high accident rate include operating the vehicle on unfamiliar streets and roads, driving at high speeds in an attempt to escape police pursuit, testing the vehicle's speed, unfamiliarity with the vehicle and use of drugs.

A criminal apprehended with a stolen vehicle after committing another crime is usually prosecuted for only the major crime, not the auto theft.

Stripping for Parts and Accessories

Many vehicles are stolen by juveniles and young adults who strip them for parts and accessories to sell: transmissions, rear ends, motors and wheels. Batteries, radiators and heaters are sold to wrecking yards, used car lots and auto repair shops. Expensive accessories such as car phones, stereo tape decks, radios, CB radios and CD players also are removed for resale. The stripped vehicle is often crushed for scrap metal. The profit is extremely high.

Sometimes thieves steal specific items for friends, other vehicle owners or themselves. These are often parts that are impossible to buy or are very expensive.

Stealing for Chop Shops A "chop shop" is a business, usually a body shop, that disassembles stolen autos and sells the parts. The chop shop deals with car thieves who steal the cars specifically for them, often on demand, stealing the exact make, model and color. The vehicle may

This vehicle was dumped by car thieves in Sunset Park, a working-class immigrant neighborhood in Brooklyn. For days, visitors came by to strip parts until the sanitation department arrived to take the vehicle away.

triple in value when sold for parts. There is no waiting period and no tax to the customer. The cars are dismantled, and the parts are cataloged. In some cities this business is so big that network organizations dispose of the stolen parts. Auto parts are also sought outside the United States, as Ragavan and Kaplan (p. 119) note: "Chop shops have discovered a whole new foreign market for car parts."

The chop shop may also deal directly with the owner of a vehicle who wants to dispose of it for insurance purposes due to dissatisfaction with its performance. The owner leaves the registration with the chop shop. The shop returns the registration to the owner after the vehicle is dismantled and crushed. The insurance company has no chance of recovery.

Reselling

Auto thefts are also committed by professional thieves who take an unattended vehicle, with or without the keys, and simply drive it away. They may go to a used car lot, posing as a buyer, and drive the vehicle away on a no-return test drive. Another method is to answer an ad in the paper for a particular car, try it out and then never return it. This gives the thief time to escape because the owner gave permission to take the vehicle—which makes the case one of embezzlement. Cars are also stolen by using bad checks.

U. S. Attorney Michael Stiles shows the extent of an international car-theft operation that netted $40 million over a nine-year period and involved conspirators from Pennsylvania to China.

Very few vehicles stolen by professional car thieves are recovered. Moreover, such thieves are difficult to detect and prosecute. As specialists in automobiles, the thieves know how to steal cars and how to alter them or the documents needed to make them eligible for resale. The professional is rarely the actual thief; rather, the professional hires others to steal cars and bring them to a specified location, usually a garage, for making the necessary alterations.

Alterations include repainting, changing seat covers, repairing existing damage and altering the engine number. The car is also completely searched to eliminate any items that connect it with the former owner. The VIN is almost always altered or replaced. The most common method of changing the VIN is to buy a similar vehicle from a salvage lot and then remove and replace the entire dash, making the change undetectable. If the VIN is not located on the dash, the car thief has a much more difficult time. In some cases the VIN plate itself is removed and carefully altered, or the car thief can make embossed tape with a hand-tape numbering device and place it over the regular VIN plate. Unless the inside of the car is investigated, a false VIN plate is not usually detected.

After all number changes on the motor and the VIN plate are completed, the vehicle is prepared for resale with stolen or forged titles, fictitious bills of sale or titles received with salvage vehicles bought by the thieves. When the mechanical alterations and paperwork are completed, the vehicle is registered through the Department of Motor Vehicles and resold, usually at a public car auction, to a used car dealer or to a private individual.

Many stolen cars are exported for resale in other countries. According to Ragavan and Kaplan (p. 119):

> Illegal exports took off in the early 1990s, with the opening of markets in the former Soviet Union and China and the easing of border controls in Europe. Car thieves quickly realized that immense profits could be made overseas, where buyers pay two to three times a vehicle's retail price. . . .
>
> Most stolen American cars end up in Mexico, officials say, despite treaties on áuto theft that date back to the 1930s. . . . For years, Mexican police have been seen driving stolen cars, some still bearing U.S. license plates. . . .
>
> But Mexico is not the only hot destination. In 1998, investigators tracked stolen U.S. vehicles to 47 countries.

One international car-theft ring was indicted by a federal grand jury for illegally obtaining vehicles from Reno car dealers and transporting them to the Port of Long Beach in California, where the cars were loaded onto freighters and shipped to China to be sold at three to four times their original price. The ring members then reported the cars stolen to police and insurance companies for reimbursement of their losses. Charges against ring members included making false statements on loan and credit applications, mail fraud, interstate and foreign transportation of stolen property, aiding and abetting, and attempting to evade financial reporting requirements. The FBI estimated the scheme involved total losses of up to $6 million.

Elements of the Crime

Unauthorized Use of a Motor Vehicle

Most car thieves are prosecuted not for auto theft but for unauthorized use of a motor vehicle. Prosecution for auto theft requires proof that the thief intended to permanently deprive the owner of the vehicle, which is often difficult or impossible to establish.

The elements of the crime of unauthorized use of a motor vehicle are:

- Intentionally taking or driving,
- A motor vehicle,
- Without the consent of the owner or the owner's authorized agent.

Intentionally Taking or Driving *Intent* is often described in state laws as "with intent to permanently or temporarily deprive the owner of title or possession" or "with intent to steal." Intent can be inferred from the act of taking or driving, being observed taking or driving or being apprehended while taking or driving. Laws often include any person who voluntarily rides in a vehicle knowing it is stolen.

A Motor Vehicle **Motor vehicle** is not restricted to automobiles. It includes any self-propelled device for moving people or property or pulling implements, whether operated on land, on water or in the air.

Motor vehicles include automobiles, trucks, buses, motorcycles, snowmobiles, vans, self-propelled watercraft and aircraft.

Homemade motor vehicles are also included.

Without the Consent of the Owner or the Owner's Authorized Agent Legitimate ownership of motor vehicles exists when the vehicle is in the factory being manufactured, when it is being sold by an authorized dealership or when it is owned by a private person, company or corporation. *Owner* and *true owner* are not necessarily the same. For example, the true owner can be a lending agency that retains title until the loan is paid.

Usually the owner or the owner's authorized agent reports the theft. Thus, it can be determined immediately whether consent was given. Previous consent is not a defense although it may be considered.

If you stop a suspicious vehicle and the driver does not have proof of ownership, check with the State Department of Motor Vehicle Registration to determine who the legal owner is. If that person is not the driver, check with the legal owner to determine whether the driver has permission to use the vehicle.

Motor Vehicle Embezzlement

Motor vehicle embezzlement exists if the person who took the vehicle initially had consent and then exceeded the terms of that consent.

This most frequently occurs when a new or used car agency permits a prospective buyer to try out a vehicle for a specific time. The person decides to convert the vehicle to personal use and does not return it. This is fraudulent appropriation of property. Motor vehicle embezzlement can also occur under rental or lease agreements or when private persons let someone test drive a vehicle that is for sale.

Interstate Transportation

In 1919 the need for federal control of motor vehicle theft was recognized, and Congress approved the National Motor Vehicle Theft Act, commonly known as the *Dyer Act.*

The **Dyer Act** made interstate transportation of a stolen motor vehicle a federal crime and allowed for federal help in prosecuting such cases.

The act was amended in 1945 to include aircraft and is now called the *Interstate Transportation of Stolen Motor*

Vehicles Act. Since the Dyer Act was passed, more than 300,000 vehicles have been recovered, and more than 100,000 criminals have been convicted in interstate car theft cases.

The elements of the crime of interstate transportation of a motor vehicle are that:

- The motor vehicle was stolen.
- It was transported in interstate or foreign commerce.
- The person transporting or causing it to be transported knew it was stolen.
- The person receiving, concealing, selling or bartering it knew it was stolen.

The vehicle thief may be prosecuted in any state through which the stolen vehicle passed. Prosecution is normally in the state in which the vehicle was stolen, but sometimes it is in the state in which the person was arrested.

Intent is not required. The stolen vehicle could accidentally be driven over the state line or forced to detour into another state. If the vehicle is transported by train or truck through another state, prosecution is also possible.

The Anti-Car Theft Act of 1992 provides tougher legislation on auto theft, previously a low-profile crime. The penalty for importing or exporting stolen vehicles was increased from five to ten years as was the penalty for interstate transportation of stolen vehicles. The Act provides the U.S. Customs new authority in checking for stolen vehicles and provides funds to states that participate in the National Motor Vehicle Title Information System. It also made armed carjacking a federal offense (Kime, 1993, pp. 25–26).

The Preliminary Investigation

When a motor vehicle theft is reported, initial information obtained by police includes the time, date and location of the theft; the make, model and color of the vehicle; the state of issue of the license plate; license plate number; direction of travel; description of any suspect; and the complainant's present location.

The complainant is asked to remain at his or her present location, and a police officer is dispatched to obtain further information and to complete the proper complaint form (see Figure 16.1).

False motor vehicle theft reports are often filed when a car has been taken by a family member or misplaced in a parking lot, when the driver wants to cover up for an accident or crime committed with the vehicle or when the driver wants to provide an alibi for being late.

It is also possible that the vehicle has been reclaimed by a loan company—a civil matter.

A preliminary description is provided to patrol officers, who are told the theft has not been verified; therefore, no all-points bulletin is issued. During this time patrol officers are alerted, but they make no move if they see the stolen vehicle because the report has not been validated. The officer in the field obtains information to determine the validity of the theft charge: the circumstances surrounding the alleged theft, identifying characteristics of the stolen vehicle, any details of items in the car and any possible suspects. Interviews with witnesses are another crucial aspect of the preliminary investigation. Frequent false reports impair cooperation from other agencies, especially when the errors should have been detected by the investigating officers.

Recovered vehicles must be examined for usable latent prints and other physical evidence. If a vehicle is found with accident damage, it is necessary to determine whether the damage occurred before or after the report. Vehicles involved in a hit-and-run accident are sometimes abandoned by the driver and then reported as stolen. Younger persons sometimes report a car stolen if they have an accident and are afraid to tell their parents.

Computerized police files can assist in searching for suspects. Investigators can enter data concerning past suspects and other individuals in the vehicle, types of vehicles stolen, the manner in which they were entered or stolen, the types of locations from which they were stolen (apartment complexes, private residences or commercial parking lots, for example), where the vehicles were abandoned and where the vehicles were if the suspects were arrested in them.

Common Tools and Methods

Investigators must be familiar with the tools and methods commonly used to commit vehicle theft, including car openers, rake and pick guns, tryout keys, impact tools, key way decoders, modified vice grips, tubular pick locks, modified screw drivers and hot wiring. Be familiar with these items and techniques and know what evidence to collect to prove their use.

FIGURE 16.1

Sample Motor Vehicle Report

Source: Courtesy of the St. Louis Park, Minnesota, Police Department

ST. LOUIS PARK POLICE DEPT. MN0272100	SUPERVISOR APPROVED S/A	MOTOR VEHICLE REPORT	
	DATE & TIME REPORT MADE 4-5-00 1330	FOR ALL ATTEMPTS AND THEFTS OF MOTOR VEHICLES	PAGE

DATE/TIME COMPLAINT RECEIVED 4-5-00 1245

UDC   GRID NO.   COMPLAINT NO.

HOW COMPLAINT RECEIVED   FOUND BY POLICE ☐   RADIO ☐   CITIZEN ☐   STATION ☐   LETTER ☐   PHONE ☒

Date of Theft (DOT) 4-5-00 1115   Time of Theft, Between 4-4-00   and   4-5-00

Owner Jerald Combs   Person Reporting same

Address: 646 13th Street   Address:

Telephone: Res.: 293-2415   Bus.:   Telephone: Res.:   Bus.:

License No. (LIC) AMU 345   State of Issue (LIS) Minnesota   License Plate Yr.: (LIY) 1994   License Plate Type: (LIT) P

Vehicle Serial No. (VIN) 643210   Vehicle Year (VYR) 1992   Vehicle Make: (VMA) Chev   Vehicle Model: (VMO) 4 cyl

Vehicle Style (VST) 4 dr   Vehicle Color (VCO) Beige   Other Ident. Characteristics (MIS)

Special Equipment: Spotlight-left side   Odometer Reading 18,000

Damage to Vehicle prior to theft none   Where?

Personal Property in Vehicle Little value   Value of Vehicle 7,500

Car was Parked at 646 13th St.   Vehicle Locked Yes X No   Location of Keys in house

Is anyone Permitted to use vehicle? wife   Under What Conditions? all times

Do you have Absolute Ownership? Yes   Name of Finance Co. none   Name of Insurance Co. Farmers Life

Will Owner Prosecute? Yes   Does Owner Suspect Anyone? No

I Hereby Certify That The Foregoing Statement is True and Correct   X

Date (DOR) Recovered 4-6-00   Time Recovered 2330   Where Recovered accident-St. Louis Park

Vehicle Impounded At St. Louis Park PD   Owner Notified By St. Louis Park   Date of Notice 4-6-00

Vehicle Recovered By St. Louis Park PD

Vehicle NCIC Entered into MINCIS Yes   Date of Entry 4-5-00   NCIC MINCIS No.: 162345

Recovery NCIC Cancelled-MINCIS Yes   Date of Cancel 4-5-00   NCIC MINCIS No.: 162345

Officer Taking Report Milo Prins   Date of Report: 4-6-00   Time of Report: 0015

Case Investigated By: Det. Thomas Strong, St. Louis Park PD   Disposition of Case:

DETAILS OF OFFENSE: Vehicle was parked on street at about 8:30 PM, 4-4-00 and was missing at early morning 4-5-00. Didn't report until several hours after checking with friends.

DEFENSE CLEARED BY ARREST ☒   EXCEPTIONALLY ☐   CASE UNFOUNDED ☐   INACTIVE (Not Cleared) ☐   OTHER ☐

PERSONS ARRESTED, SUSPECTS, WITNESSES & ADDITIONAL DETAILED REPORT ON SUPPLEMENTARY

Douglas Amherst, 1614 College Street, St. Louis Park, Minnesota

Insurance Fraud

Vehicle insurance fraud is a major economic crime that affects every premium payer through increased insurance rates.

Many police departments facilitate insurance fraud by allowing car theft reports to be phoned in or by taking them "over the counter" at the police station and then never investigating the reports. The primary reason the auto theft is reported is often for insurance purposes. To avoid this situation law enforcement agencies should investigate all auto theft reports and should not discount the possibility that the "victim" is actually committing insurance fraud.

For example, a luxury car stolen from a suburban mall parking lot was found four days later on fire on a rural road. The case seemed routine until a detective began an investigation to eliminate the car's reported owner. The detective found that there were three pending lawsuits against the "victim" and that the "victim" had filed for bankruptcy shortly after the lawsuits and months before the car was stolen. He had filed an affidavit claiming he no longer owned the car because he had sold it six months before. Investigation revealed that the buyer was a friend who let the car be transferred into his name so it would not be involved in the bankruptcy proceedings.

This was a clear case of filing false information with the police. Further, after a fire investigator and mechanic inspected the car, they reported that the lab tests showed ongoing engine failure. The victim wanted the insurance company to pay for a replacement—an obvious case of fraud.

Cooperating Agencies in Motor Vehicle Theft

Police most frequently use state motor vehicle bureaus to check owners' registrations. They also use driver's license bureaus to compare the driver of a vehicle with the registered owner. When vehicle registration and driver's registration checks are completed, further checks can be made in the FBI's National Crime Information Center files to determine whether the vehicle is stolen and whether the driver has a criminal record.

> The FBI and the National Insurance Crime Bureau provide valuable help in investigating motor vehicle thefts.

The FBI

The FBI assists local and state authorities who notify the bureau that a stolen motor vehicle or aircraft has been transported interstate—which places it within the provisions of the Interstate Transportation of Stolen Motor Vehicles Act. The FBI works with local authorities to find the vehicle and the person who stole it. The FBI can also examine suspicious documents relating to false sales or registrations. The Bureau's NCIC contains information on stolen vehicles and stolen auto accessories. Its National Automobile Altered Numbers File is an additional resource.

The National Insurance Crime Bureau (NICB)

In 1992 the National Auto Theft Bureau was incorporated into the National Insurance Crime Bureau (NICB), a nonprofit organization supported and maintained by hundreds of automobile insurance companies. The organization helps law enforcement agencies reduce and prevent auto thefts and investigate questionable or fraudulent vehicle fires and thefts.

The NICB also disseminates reports on stolen cars to law enforcement agencies and serves as a clearinghouse for information on stolen cars. Computer files are maintained for several million wanted or stolen cars, listed by make, engine number, VIN and component part number. This information is available free upon request to law enforcement agencies. The bureau can also trace cars from the factory to the owner. Its staff of specialists and technicians are experts in identifying stolen cars and restoring mutilated, changed or defaced numbers. They also restore altered or obliterated VINs.

The bureau publishes and distributes to police agencies their *Manual for the Identification of Automobiles.* This publication describes the location of identifying numbers, gives license plate reproductions and provides a short legal digest of each state's motor vehicle laws. In an emergency, call the bureau collect. Otherwise, send a letter requesting specific assistance.

Recognizing a Stolen Motor Vehicle or an Unauthorized Driver

As with other crimes, a suspicious nature and an alert mind help an officer detect motor vehicle thefts. Detection is sometimes improved by an instinct developed through training, observation and experience. Police officers develop individual techniques for recognizing stolen cars. No absolute, single peculiarity identifies a stolen car or its driver, but either one can draw the attention of an observant officer.

> To improve your ability to recognize stolen vehicles:
>
> ■ Keep a list of stolen vehicles in your car.
> ■ Develop a checking system to rapidly determine whether a suspicious vehicle is stolen.
> ■ Learn the common characteristics of stolen vehicles and car thieves.
> ■ Take time to check suspicious persons and vehicles.
> ■ Learn how to question suspicious drivers and occupants.

A *potential car thief on foot* usually appears nervous. He or she may be looking into cars on the street or in parking lots, trying door handles and carrying some sort of entry tool. Observe such an individual from a distance until an overt act is committed.

Characteristics of a driver of a stolen vehicle include sudden jerks or stops, driving without lights or excessively fast or slow, wearing gloves in hot weather and attempting to avoid or outrun a squad car. Any unusual or inappropriate driving behavior may be suspicious.

Characteristics of a stolen vehicle include having one license plate when two are required or two when one is required. Double or triple plates with one on top of the other can indicate lack of time to take off the original plates. A set of old plates with new screws, wired-on plates, altered numbers, dirty plates on a clean car or clean plates on a dirty car, differing front and rear plate numbers, plates bent to conceal a number, upside-down or hanging plates and homemade cardboard plates are all suspicious. Observe whether the trunk lid has been pried or whether side windows or door locks are broken. Look for evidence of a broken steering column or of tampering with the ignition switch. Abandoned vehicles are also suspicious.

When *questioning a driver and any occupants of a car* you have stopped on suspicion of motor vehicle theft, observe their behavior. Watch for signs of nervousness, hesitancy in answers, overpoliteness and indications that the driver does not know the vehicle. Request the driver's license and the vehicle registration papers for identification. Examine the driver's license and ask for the driver's birthdate. The driver will probably not know the correct date unless it is his or her license. Compare the description on the license with the person. Compare the state of issuance of the license with the car's license plates. Ask the driver to sign his or her name and compare the signature with that on the driver's license.

Ask the driver the year, make and model of the car and compare the answers with the registration papers. Ask the mileage. The driver of a stolen car rarely knows the mileage, whereas the owner or regular driver knows within a reasonable number of miles. Ask the driver to describe the contents of the car's trunk and glove compartment.

Check inside the vehicle for an extra set of license plates, bullet holes or other damage, bloodstains and service stickers showing where and when the car was last serviced. Inspect the VIN plate for alterations. A roll of adhesive tape can indicate it was used to tape windows before breaking them. Wire or coat hangers bent straight to open doors, rubber gloves, jumper cables or tools for breaking into a car are also alerting signals.

Parked cars may have been stolen if debris under the car indicates it has been in the same place for a long time. Check with neighbors to determine how long the vehicle has been parked there. The neighborhood canvass is one of the most effective techniques in investigating abandoned cars. Check for illegal entrance, for open car windows in inclement weather and for dirty vehicles indicating lack of care. A citation under the wiper can indicate when the car was abandoned. Keys left in the ignition and lack of license plates are also grounds for checking.

A warm or running motor and firearms or valuables left in the car may indicate that the thief has temporarily parked the car and intends to return. Stake out stolen vehicles (identified by license number or description) because the thief will very likely return. Consider partially immobilizing the vehicle to prevent an attempted escape.

Recovering an Abandoned or Stolen Motor Vehicle

Most motor vehicle thefts are local problems involving a locally stolen and recovered vehicle. Sixty-nine percent of stolen vehicles are recovered, most of them within 48 hours, especially those stolen by juveniles. Stolen vehicles are recovered when patrol officers observe a vehicle on a hot list, a suspicious vehicle or driver or an apparently abandoned vehicle or when private citizens report an abandoned vehicle.

Although patrol units are responsible for more than 90 percent of the stolen vehicles recovered, investigative personnel play a major role in furnishing information to the uniformed patrol on all areas of motor vehicle theft.

The initial patrol officer at the scene examines recovered and abandoned vehicles unless there is reason to believe the vehicle was involved in a serious crime. Investigators assigned to such a crime may want to look for specific items in the vehicle that might not be known to the patrol officers. In these cases the vehicle is protected until the specialists arrive.

Once recovery and impound reports have been completed, the car is removed from the hot list, and the owner is notified of the recovery. A vehicle recovery report, such as the one in Figure 16.2, should be completed and filed.

If a crime has recently been committed in the area or if the vehicle's position and location suggest that the suspect may return, drive by and arrange for a stakeout. If the car is locked and the keys are gone, if heavy rain or fog exists and the windshield wiper marks indicate they were recently used or if no dry spot appears under the car, the vehicle was probably used recently and the driver may return. Round rain spots on the vehicle mean it has been parked for a longer period than if there are elongated rain drops, which indicate recent movement. A quick check of heat remaining on the hood, radiator or exhaust pipe also indicates whether the car was recently parked. Consider attempting to apprehend the criminal on return to the vehicle.

On the other hand, if a car has an empty gas tank, a rundown battery or a flat tire, it is probably abandoned and can be immediately processed either at the scene, the police station or a storage location. Consider the possibility that the vehicle was used in committing another crime such as robbery, burglary, murder, hijacking, abduction or kidnapping. Search the vehicle's exterior first and then the interior as described in Chapter 4. Many car thieves have been located through items left in a vehicle.

If you suspect the vehicle was used in another crime, take it to a garage or lock and seal it with evidence tape; then notify the proper authorities. After processing, notify the rightful owner.

Technology is facilitating the recovery of stolen vehicles. LoJack, a Massachusetts company, has developed a system that places a homing device in an obscure place on a vehicle. If the vehicle is reported stolen, the device is activated and a tracker picks up a signal that is displayed on a lighted compass. An illuminated strength-meter tells operators when they are nearing the stolen vehicle. The display also shows the model and color of the car. Domash (1999, p. 50) reports: "The LoJack Company boasts a recovery rate of more than 90 percent and a 20 to 25 percent arrest rate." In comparison, nonequipped cars have only a 64 percent recovery rate and a 5 percent arrest rate. The system may, however, indirectly help protect and recover nonequipped vehicles, as Domash (p. 52) notes:

DISTRICT NUMBER | **St. Louis Park Police Department** **VEHICLE RECOVERY REPORT** | COMPLAINT NUMBER

LICENSE ___ STATE ___ YR. ___ SERIAL ___
MAKE ___ YR. ___ TYPE ___ RECOVERED BY ___ DATE ___ TIME ___
WHERE RECOVERED ___ ON STREET - ALLEY - PARKING LOT - GARAGE
RECOVERED ON INFORMATION FROM: RADIO - CITIZEN - FOUND BY POLICE - OTHER ___
REASON FOR IMPOUNDING: INVOLVED IN ACCIDENT -ARREST - ABANDONED - OTHER ___
EXTENT OF DAMAGE TO VEHICLE ___
VEHICLE LOCKED? ___ TRUNK LOCKED? ___ WERE KEYS IN CAR? ___
PERSON ARRESTED ___ CHARGE ___
TOW TRUCK ORDERED AT ___ ARRIVED ___ TOW COMPANY ___ DRIVER (SIGNATURE) ___
VEHICLE OWNER ___ ADDRESS ___
VEHICLE DRIVER ___ ADDRESS ___
O.K. TO RELEASE YES ☐ NO ☐ TO OWNER ☐ DRIVER ☐ OTHER ☐

LIST VEHICLE EQUIPMENT				INVENTORY OF PERSONAL PROPERTY IN VEHICLE
	LICENSE PLATES		BATTERY	
	WHEELS		HEAD LIGHTS	
	TIRES		TAIL LIGHTS	
	RADIO		BUMPERS	
	EXPOSED AERIAL		TAPE PLAYER	

OTHER EQUIPMENT ___ | DISPOSITION OF PROPERTY:
IF RELEASED PRIOR TO VEHICLE, HAVE RECEIVER SIGN HERE:
RELEASED BY ___ RECEIVER ___
DATE ___ TIME ___
REPORT MADE BY ___ DATE ___ TIME ___ REMARKS ___
HOLD ☐ AUTHORITY ___ REASON ___
RELEASED BY ___ | I HEREBY ACKNOWLEDGE RECEIPT OF ABOVE DESCRIBED VEH. & PROP.
DATE ___ TIME ___ | NAME ___
AUTHORIZED BY ___ | ADDRESS ___
CERT. OF REGISTRATION ☐ BILL OF SALE ☐ INS. POLICY ☐ | TELEPHONE ___ DATE ___ TIME ___

FIGURE 16.2 ***Vehicle Recovery Report Form***

Source: Courtesy of the St. Louis Park, Minnesota, Police Department

"In many cases, the [LoJack] technology has led officers to chop shops, where major operations were put out of business."

The system is not without its drawbacks, however. First, unless police departments across the country install tracking devices in their squad cars, the devices are ineffective. Second, the lag time between a car theft and its report may be hours or even days. Third, there are some dead spots—locations where transmitted radio signals will not be detected. Fourth, some departments hesitate to become a partner with a private company. Finally, some departments worry that the public will perceive them to be focused on preventing car theft from the more affluent members of the community, those who can afford the $600 auto recovery system.

Other systems also are available, some of which activate automatically. If someone drives off in the car without deactivating the system, an alarm is sent to the tracking center. Such systems might, however, result in false alarms and pose as great a problem as false burglar alarms pose. Other systems provide a personal alert service that allows motorists to signal authorities in case of emergencies. One system allows controllers to shut off a stolen car's engine by remote control if police tracking the car believe it would be safe to do so.

Preventing Motor Vehicle Theft

Effective preventive measures could eliminate many motor vehicle thefts. Vehicle theft requires both desire and opportunity, and it is often difficult to know which comes first. An unlocked automobile with keys in the ignition is a temptation. A parked vehicle with the motor running is also extremely inviting. Many juveniles take cars under such conditions and then boast of their ability to steal.

Numerous motor vehicle thefts can be prevented by effective educational campaigns and by installing antitheft devices in vehicles during manufacture.

Educate motor vehicle owners about the importance of removing their keys from the ignition and locking their vehicles when parked. Public education campaigns might include distributing dashboard stickers with the reminder "Have you removed your keys from the ignition?" or "Don't forget to take your keys and lock your car."

Automobile manufacturers have helped by installing ignition and door locking devices as well as buzzer systems that warn the driver that the keys are still in the vehicle. **Keyless doors**—by which the owner enters a combination by pushing numbered pads in a programmed sequence to gain access to the car—may make it harder for thieves to break into vehicles to steal them.

One manufacturer has developed an antitheft system that can prevent the theft even of a car left running. Such technology is desirable for those in law enforcement, who must occasionally bail out of their vehicles without turning off the ignition, thus rendering their idling car a temptation for thieves. Kanable (1999, p. 62) explains:

> Trem Products Company's anti-theft system . . . is designed to lock up the shifter lever automatically every time the shift lever is placed in the park position. To release the anti-theft system the driver has to depress a covert actuator. The system is equipped with an on/off switch to turn the system off when it is necessary for civilians to drive the vehicle.

To deter theft some automakers have developed ignition systems and keys that use microchips with electronic codes embedded in them. However, car thieves have been able to duplicate these antitheft keys by using code grabbers similar to the devices used to duplicate codes that open garage doors. In response, as with garage door makers, some auto manufacturers are now using rolling codes and encrypted systems that use randomly generated codes to defeat thieves. According to Siuru (p. 69): "Ford is one of the first U.S. automakers to offer a theft deterrent system that should be virtually impossible to defeat. There are some 72 quadrillion possible electronic codes available."

Burke (p. 38) describes a silent antitheft system, the Smoke Defense Machine (SDM), designed to be a "proactive" deterrent against auto theft:

> The SDM unit relies on dual sensors designed to detect tampering and/or intrusion to the vehicle. . . . In case of an intrusion attempt, the radar sensor will sense the movement of the intruder and alert the system to be triggered the instant the shock senses any further violation. A non-toxic and odorless dense white smoke is then released to cover the inside of the vehicle (within five seconds) before the intrusion can occur. This is designed to prevent auto theft and/or theft of the vehicle's contents by fully clouding its interior to hinder vision. The smoke will remain in the vehicle for approximately 50 seconds . . . and then dissipate if no further intrusion is detected. . . . Smoke will continue to be launched every 90 seconds if the door remains ajar making driving impossible.

Police departments are using several strategies to combat rising auto theft levels:

- Setting up sting operations—for example, a body shop that buys stolen vehicles
- Providing officers with auto theft training
- Coordinating efforts across jurisdictional lines
- Instituting anti-car-theft campaigns
- Increasing penalties for stealing vehicles

In Atlanta, where the auto-theft rate increased 20 percent during the first quarter of 1996, an Auto Theft Task Force (ATTF) was initiated to target high-risk areas at high-risk times. Moss (1998, p. 107) notes the predominant approach involved high visibility uniformed patrol, members' making frequent traffic stops and heavy reliance upon field investigative interviews. The efforts of the task force paid off, with the seven ATTF officers making 2,500 arrests in the first year and recovering more than 400 vehicles (p. 108). According to Moss (p. 108): "Team members attribute their success to aggressive traffic enforcement and extensive training."

To combat the rising auto theft rate at Newark International Airport in New Jersey, airport police have

taken several crucial steps (Slattery, 1997), including the following:

- Increasing the candlepower of parking lot lights
- Conducting weekly inspections of the lot perimeter to locate access points for thieves (e.g., broken or cut fences)
- Offering monetary rewards to the public for information leading to the arrest of car thieves
- Securing unused remote entrances
- Touring the lots with marked and unmarked patrol cars

In one area of the United Kingdom, where van thefts have been a particular problem, the police department used a decoy vehicle to catch auto thieves. According to Kinchin (1998, p. 31), the decoy has played a crucial role in the arrest of more than 50 offenders:

> The van . . . has been designed to be stolen. It is equipped with electronic tracking gear that has allowed police to trail the vehicle to the operations and headquarters of a number of prolific auto-crime gangs.

Kinchin (p. 32) notes the deterrent effect the decoy has had on vehicle thefts in the local area:

> Use of this "Trojan horse" van has helped smash three major gangs of "cut and shut" operators [chop shops] in the last year. Theft of motor vehicles has plummeted by 32% in the area and theft from vehicles has dropped by about 1/5. At the same time, arrests linked to vehicle crime are up by 10%. In the six weeks that followed the deliberate leaking to the press about the "Trojan horse" being used in the Stockton area of Cleveland not a single motor vehicle was stolen!

In areas where police have made special efforts to educate the public and to assign extra squads to patrol high auto theft areas, auto theft has significantly decreased.

New York City has instituted a Combat Auto Theft (CAT) Program that has been highly successful. Participating car owners sign a form indicating they do not normally operate their automobiles between 1 A.M. and 5 A.M., the peak auto theft hours. They also sign a consent form that authorizes the police to stop their vehicle during these hours without probable cause. Owners are given a CAT program decal to affix prominently on the inside of the car's rear window. Officers may stop any car having the decal without probable cause if they see it traveling on city streets between 1 A.M. and 5 A.M.

Minnesota's Help Eliminate Auto Theft (HEAT) program offers up to $5,000 for information leading to the arrest and trial of suspected auto-theft-ring members or chop shop operators. The program's toll-free number is answered by the Minnesota Highway Patrol.

The increased use of alarms and protective devices may in part account for the rise in armed carjackings, as explained in Chapter 9. Unwilling to give up their lucrative "trade," car thieves may use force against a vehicle operator to gain control of the vehicle rather than risk being thwarted by antitheft devices.

Whereas carjacking is treated as quite a severe crime, regular unarmed auto theft remains a relatively minor offense and, from a criminal perspective, a "safe crime to commit." Walsh (1998, p. A10) explains: "Police tell victims they'll probably never make an arrest, prosecutors admit they seldom push cases to conviction and legislators say state laws don't really intend to lock car thieves away."

Routine Activities and Motor Vehicle Theft

The routine activity approach to crime suggests that the daily routine activities of populations influence the availability of targets of crime. Copes (1999, p. 125) reports that: "Results from multiple regression analysis show that measures of potential offenders, suitable targets, and guardianship explain variation in the rate of motor vehicle theft." Copes (p. 129) further reports that city blocks with bars have almost twice as many auto thefts as city blocks without bars and that blocks adjacent to high schools have higher levels of auto theft than blocks that are not near high schools. In addition, parking lots with attendants have lower rates of auto theft than similar lots with no attendants on duty. Such findings might be used in designing auto theft prevention programs.

Thefts of Other Types of Motor Vehicles

Investigating stolen trucks and trailers, construction vehicles and equipment, recreational vehicles, motorized boats, snowmobiles, motorcycles, motor scooters, mopeds and aircraft is similar to investigating auto thefts.

Trucks and Trailers

Usually trucks and trailers are stolen by professional thieves although they are also stolen for parts. A "finger-man" often provides information to the thief. In most cases the fingerman is an employee of the company that owns the truck. A "spotter" locates the truck after getting information from the fingerman and then follows the truck to the point where it is to be stolen. A driver experienced in operating the targeted vehicle then commits the actual theft.

Truck trailers are usually stolen by simply backing up a tractor to the trailer and hauling it away. The trailer's cargo is generally the target.

Stolen trucks and trailers are identified much as passenger vehicles are—by the manufacturer or through the *Commercial Vehicle Identification Manual* published by the National Insurance Crime Bureau.

Construction Vehicles and Equipment

Expensive construction vehicles whose parts are easily sold are often parked at unprotected construction sites. There is no organized identification system for the numerous types of construction equipment. However, many construction companies have formed protection programs, have identified their equipment with special markings and have offered rewards for information about thefts. Contact the manufacturers or sellers of the equipment for identification information. Local construction firms can also provide information about possible outlets for stolen parts.

Recreational Vehicles

More than 450 makes and models of recreational vehicles (RVs) are marketed in the United States. Because there are so many makes and models, contact the manufacturer for any special numbers not readily visible. Recreational vehicles are also targets for vehicle burglaries because many contain CB radios, televisions and appliances. Many false theft claims are made because of the high cost of operating these vehicles.

Motorized Boats

Since 1972 many states have required licensing of boats, including an identification number on the boat's hull. Most such identification numbers are 10 to 13 digits. The first several digits are the manufacturer's number. This is followed by four or five identification numbers and several certification numbers. Because boats also are the objects of many fraudulent insurance claims, determine whether the theft claim is legitimate.

Snowmobiles

Snowmobiles are easy to steal because they can be transported inside vans and trucks. Most of the major snowmobile manufacturers in the United States and Canada use chassis and engine numbers that aid in identification.

Motorcycles, Motor Scooters and Mopeds

Motorcycles, motor scooters and mopeds are easy to steal because they lack security devices and are often left unprotected. The lock number is easily identified, and substitute keys can be made. These cycles can be driven away or loaded on trailers or into vans and transported, perhaps several at a time.

Identifying such cycles is difficult because of the many types and the fact that parts are not readily identifiable. However, identification numbers can often be obtained through the National Insurance Crime Bureau, local dealers and manufacturers.

Aircraft

Aircraft theft, although infrequent, is a high-value theft. Such thefts are jointly investigated with the FBI and the Federal Aviation Administration. Many stolen aircraft are used in narcotics smuggling so the plane can be sacrificed at no cost if there is danger of apprehension.

Aircraft identification consists of a highly visible *N* identification number painted on the fuselage. Many aircraft parts, including the engine, radio equipment, landing gear and tires, also have individual serial numbers. Aircraft identification can be verified through the manufacturer.

Summary

Motor vehicle thefts take much investigative time, but they can provide important information on other crimes under investigation. The vehicle identification number (VIN), critical in motor vehicle theft investigations, identifies the specific vehicle in question. This number is the primary nonduplicated, serialized number assigned by the manufacturer to each vehicle.

Categories for motor vehicle theft based on the offender's motive include (1) joyriding, (2) transportation, (3) stripping for parts and accessories, (4) commission of another crime and (5) reselling for profit.

Although referred to as "motor vehicle theft," most cases are prosecuted as "unauthorized use of a motor vehicle" because a charge of theft requires proof that the thief intended to deprive the owner of the vehicle permanently, which is often difficult or impossible to establish. The elements of the crime of unauthorized use of a motor vehicle are (1) intentionally taking or driving (2) a motor vehicle (3) without the consent of the owner or the owner's authorized agent. Motor vehicles include automobiles, trucks, buses, motorcycles, motor scooters, mopeds, snowmobiles, vans, self-propelled watercraft and aircraft. Embezzlement of a motor vehicle occurs if the person who took the vehicle had consent initially and then exceeded the terms of that consent.

The Dyer Act made interstate transportation of a stolen motor vehicle a federal crime and allowed for federal help in prosecuting such cases. False motor vehicle theft reports are often filed because a car has been taken by a family member or misplaced in a parking lot, to cover up for an accident or a crime committed with the vehicle or to provide an alibi for being late. The FBI and the National Insurance Crime Bureau provide valuable help in investigating motor vehicle theft.

To improve your ability to recognize stolen vehicles, keep a list of stolen vehicles in your car, develop a checking system for rapidly determining whether a suspicious vehicle is stolen, learn the common characteristics of stolen vehicles and car thieves, take time to check suspicious persons and vehicles and learn how to question suspicious drivers and occupants.

Numerous motor vehicle thefts can be prevented by effective educational campaigns and by manufacturer-installed security devices.

Checklist
Motor Vehicle Theft

- Description of vehicle: year, make, color, body type.
- Anything unusual about the vehicle such as color combination or damage?
- Identification of vehicle: VIN, engine number, license number by state and year.
- Registered owner and legal owner, address, telephone number.
- What were the circumstances of the theft: date and time reported stolen, location of theft? Were doors locked? Was the key in the ignition?

- Was the vehicle insured and by whom?
- Was the vehicle mortgaged and by whom? Are payments current?
- Did anyone have permission to use the vehicle? Have these persons been contacted?
- Was the owner arrested for another crime or suspected in a crime?
- Does the owner have any motive to falsely report the vehicle stolen?
- Was the owner involved in a hit-and-run accident or driving while intoxicated?
- Did the spouse report the vehicle missing?
- What method was used to take the vehicle?
- Has the vehicle been recovered? Where?
- Were crimes committed in the area where the vehicle was stolen or recovered?
- Was anybody seen near where the vehicle was stolen or found? When? How were they dressed? Approximate age?
- Was the vehicle seen on the street with suspects in it? Description of the suspects?
- Does the owner have any suspects?
- Were police field interrogation cards checked for the day of the theft and the days after to determine whether the vehicle had been stopped by police for other reasons?
- Were pawnshops checked for items that were in the vehicle?
- If the vehicle was a motorcycle, were motorcycle shops checked?
- If the vehicle was a truck, have there been other truck thefts in the area or labor problems?
- Is the vehicle suspected of going interstate? Was the FBI notified?
- Has a check been made with the National Insurance Crime Bureau?
- Have junkyards been checked?
- Have known auto thieves been checked to determine whether they were in the area at the time of the theft?
- Was a check made with the motor vehicle department to determine the registered owner?

Application

A. On July 2 an internist finished his shift at a Veterans Administration hospital and went to the hospital parking lot to find that his TR4A was missing. He called the local police, but they refused to come, saying that because the theft occurred on federal property, it was the FBI's problem. The doctor called the FBI, which first said it would not investigate a car theft unless the car was transported out of the state. The doctor's insurance company finally convinced the FBI to investigate the theft, which it did. Two days later, local police in a town 529 miles away discovered the TR4A abandoned in the parking lot at a race track. Because the car had been hot-wired, they assumed it was stolen and made inquiries to the state department of vehicle registration about its ownership. The car was towed to a local storage garage. When it was learned who owned the TR4A, local police contacted the police in the doctor's city. Because that police department had no record of a stolen TR4A, officers there assumed the message was in error. It was a holiday weekend, they were busy and the matter was dropped. Eight months later the storage garage called the doctor to ask him when he was coming to get his car.

Questions

1. What mistakes were made in this incident?
2. Who is primarily to blame for the eight-month delay in returning the car to the owner?

B. Samuel Paris parked his 1999 Corvette in front of his home shortly after midnight when he and his wife returned from a party. He locked the car and took the keys with him. He discovered the vehicle missing the following morning about 7:45 A.M. when he was leaving for work. He immediately called the police to report an auto theft.

Questions

1. Were his actions correct?
2. What should the police department do upon receiving the call?
3. What should the officer who is assigned to the case do?

Discussion Questions

1. How do you identify a stolen vehicle so that you can prove in court that it was in fact stolen?

2. What evidence do you need to charge a suspect with unauthorized use of a motor vehicle? Embezzlement of a vehicle?

3. Where would you start looking for a stolen vehicle used in a crime? For joyriding? For transportation? For stripping and sale of parts?

4. How large a problem is auto theft in your community? Are such thefts thoroughly investigated?

5. What agencies besides local police are involved in investigating auto thefts, and under what circumstances can their services be requested? Who would be contacted in your area? What services can they perform?

6. How do juvenile and professional auto thieves differ with regard to motive and type of vehicle stolen? Are there different methods for locating each?

7. A CD player has been taken from a stolen motor vehicle abandoned on a city street. Is this burglary or larceny in your state? Does it make any difference if the car door was closed but unlocked?

8. Does the value of the stolen vehicle affect the charge made? The punishment?

9. What other crimes are frequently committed along with motor vehicle theft?

10. What measures does your community take to prevent motor vehicle theft? What else might it do?

References

Burke, Tod W. "Where There's Smoke . . . There's the Smoke Defense Machine." *Law Enforcement Technology,* Vol. 23, No. 9, September 1996, pp. 38–42.

Copes, Heith. "Routine Activities and Motor Vehicle Theft: A Crime Specific Approach." *Journal of Crime and Justice,* Vol. 22, No. 2, 1999, pp. 125–146.

Domash, Shelly Feuer. "Keeping Track with LoJack." *Police,* Vol. 23, No. 6, June 1999, pp. 50–52.

"A Job Well Done." *Law and Order,* Vol. 45, No. 7, July 1997, pp. 103–105.

Kanable, Rebecca. "Anti-Theft Systems Keep Criminals in Park." *Law Enforcement Technology,* Vol. 26, No. 5, May 1999, pp. 62–65.

Kime, Roy C. "Section-by-Section Analysis of the 'Anti-Car Theft Act of 1992.'" *The Police Chief,* Vol. LXV, 1993, pp. 25–26.

Kinchin, David. "Catching a Car Thief." *Law and Order,* Vol. 46, No. 11, November 1998, pp. 31–32.

Moss, Calvin W. "An Auto Theft Task Force." *Law and Order,* Vol. 46, No. 9, September 1998, pp. 107–109.

O'Connor, Anne and Graves, Chris. "Cunanan Eludes Manhunt." (Minneapolis/St. Paul) *Star Tribune,* July 17, 1997, p. A1.

Ragavan, Chitra and Kaplan, David. "Why Auto Theft Is Going Global." *U.S. News and World Report,* June 14, 1999, pp. 116–120.

Siuru, William D. "Smart Keys Outsmart Code Grabbers." *Law Enforcement Technology,* Vol. 23, No. 9, September 1996, pp. 69–70.

Slattery, William. "Reducing Auto Theft." *Law and Order,* Vol. 45, No. 8, August 1997, pp. 89–91.

Walsh, James. "Auto Thieves Rarely Caught, Convicted." (Minneapolis/St. Paul) *Star Tribune,* April 20, 1998, pp. A1, A10.

Arson

Do You Know?

What *arson* is?

How fires are classified?

What presumption is made when investigating fires?

What the elements of arson are?

What constitutes aggravated arson? Simple arson?

What degrees of arson the Model Arson Law establishes?

Who is responsible for detecting arson? Investigating arson?

What special challenges exist in investigating arson?

What the fire triangle is and why it is important in arson investigations?

What accelerants are and which are most commonly used in arson?

What common igniters are used in arson?

What common burn indicators are?

How to determine a fire's point of origin?

How fires normally burn?

What factors indicate the likelihood of arson?

When an administrative warrant is issued? A criminal warrant?

When a warrant is needed for investigating a fire scene and what the precedent case is?

What to check when investigating suspected arson of a vehicle?

What to pay special attention to when investigating explosions and bombings?

Introduction

Arson is one of the oldest crimes known. It has probably been practiced since soon after fire was discovered. Arson is a combination crime against persons and property, threatening life and causing immense property losses. In October 1978 Congress mandated that the FBI reclassify arson as a Part One Index Crime in its Uniform Crime Reporting Program, effective March 1979.

In June 1999, three synagogues in Sacramento, California, were damaged by arson attacks. The worst damaged synagogue was B'Nai Israel, which sustained $800,000 in damage and lost 5,000 books on Jewish history in the blaze.

Arson is the malicious, willful burning of a building or property.

Davis and Lauber (1999, p. 273) state: "Deliberate firesetting, or incendiarism, is one of the most malevolent and potent forms of maladaptive behavior that is spawned by the criminal mind." They further note (p. 282):

> Arson, unlike other crimes, is unique in the sense that the magnitude of its power is often unknown, even to the arsonist. A gunman can choose the number of rounds to expend, and a knife-wielding perpetrator can make a conscious choice as to the number of wounds to inflict, but an arsonist surrenders the power of choice once the fire takes on a mind of its own. Fire chooses its own course of destiny based on several environmental factors; it is no longer dictated by the malevolent wishes of the individual who gave it life.

Arson is difficult to prove because in many fires the evidence is consumed and there are few witnesses. Few police officers or investigators have extensive training in investigating arson, and they are often confused by the complications involved in securing evidence and cooperating with other agencies. Mentzer (1997, p. 30) states: "Arson investigators are a unique branch of the law enforcement community: part firefighter, part detective, but all cop when investigating arsons, bombings and fraud cases."

Many sources gather statistics on fires, including the FBI, the National Fire Protection Association, insurance companies, state fire marshals' offices, state crime bureaus, sheriffs' offices and local police and fire departments. Although statistics vary, all reporting agencies agree that arson is a major problem. Mentzer (p. 31) points out: "Aside from the risk to life and limb, arson fires cause millions of dollars in property damage every year and can also significantly affect insurance rates. Rarely considered is the cost to taxpayers of police and private investigative work expended on these cases." A Department of Justice study states: "Arson, next to war, is humanity's costliest act of violence."

This chapter begins with a classification of arson crimes, the elements of the crime of arson and the Model Arson Law. This is followed by a profile of the typical arsonist and a description of the need for police and fire department cooperation as well as the availability of other sources of assistance. Next is a discussion of the special challenges in investigating arson, the preliminary investigation and the types of search warrants that might be required. The challenges of investigating vehicle arson and prosecuting arsonists are covered next. The chapter concludes with an in-depth look at investigating explosions caused by bombs. ■

Classification

- - - - - - - -

Fires are classified as natural, accidental, criminal (arson), suspicious or of unknown origin.

- - - - - - - -

A *natural fire* is one set intentionally to destroy refuse, weeds or waste products in industrial processes or to provide warmth. It is easy to determine that such fires are natural.

An *accidental fire,* as the name implies, is not intentional. Fires can be accidentally ignited by the heat of the sun's rays, lightning, faulty wiring, leaking gas, a carelessly tossed cigarette, overheated Christmas tree lights, children playing with matches and many other causes. Arsonists usually try to make their fires appear accidental.

A *criminal fire* (arson) is ignited intentionally and maliciously to destroy property or buildings. Proof must be obtained that the fire was not natural or accidental.

A *suspicious fire* is one suspected as arson even though proof is lacking.

A fire of *unknown origin* is one in which there is no evidence to indicate whether the fire was natural, accidental or criminal. The cause is simply not known.

- - - - - - - -

Fires are presumed natural or accidental unless proven otherwise.

- - - - - - - -

The prosecution has the burden of proving that a fire is not accidental or natural. Because arson cases are hard to prove and require a great deal of work, they are unattractive to prosecutors. Moreover, a prosecutor may feel uneasy with the large amount of expert scientific testimony required.

Exercise caution in investigating fires. The vast majority are not the result of arson. Do not unduly suspect property owners who have already been subjected to fire losses.

Elements of the Crime: Arson

Under common law, the *crime of arson* was defined as the malicious, willful burning of another's house or outbuilding. It was considered such a serious offense that the penalty was death. Laws have now extended arson to cover other buildings, personal property, crops and the burning of one's own property. As in other crimes, arson laws vary from state to state but share some common elements.

- - - - - - - -

The elements of the crime of arson include:

- Willful, malicious burning of a building or property,
- Of another, or of one's own to defraud,
- Or causing to be burned, or aiding, counseling or procuring such burning.

- - - - - - - -

Attempted arson is also a crime in most states.

Willful, Malicious Burning of a Building or Property *Willful* means "intentional." If a motive is determined, intent can be proven; therefore, when possible, show motive even if it is not required by law. Merchandise or household goods moved in or out immediately before the fire help to establish motive and intent.

Malicious denotes a "spiteful, vindictive desire to harm others." Malice is shown by circumstantial evidence such as statements of ill will, threats against persons or property, a recent increase in insurance coverage or past property burned.

Burning is the prime element in the corpus delicti. There must be more than an exposure to heat although flames need not have been visible nor the property destroyed. Heating to the ignition point is sufficient even if the fire extinguishes itself.

Of Another, or of One's Own to Defraud The motive for burning another's property can range from revenge to economic gain. The burning of one's own property, however, is almost always to defraud. Prove the property was insured and show a motive for desiring the insurance money. Copies of the insurance policies obtained from the victim after serving proper notice show whether an excessive amount of insurance was taken out, whether recent additions or changes were made in the policy or whether the insurance was soon to expire. Businesses are sometimes burned because they are failing financially, which can be established by business records or employee statements.

Causing to be Burned, or Aiding, Counseling or Procuring the Burning A person who hires a professional (a "torch") to commit arson is also guilty of the crime. Seek evidence connecting this person with the actual arsonist.

Aggravated and Simple Arson

Some laws categorize arson as either aggravated or simple.

> **Aggravated arson** is intentionally destroying or damaging a dwelling or other property by means of fire or explosives or other infernal device—creating an imminent danger to life or great bodily harm, which risk was known or reasonably foreseeable to the suspect. **Simple arson** is an intentional destruction by fire or explosives that does not create imminent danger to life or risk of great bodily harm.

Fire does not require visible burning or an actual flame, but it must involve some extent of burning. *Explosives* include any device, apparatus or equipment that causes damage by combustion or explosion such as time bombs, Molotov cocktails, missiles, plastic explosives, grenades and dynamite. *Destruction or damage* does not require total destruction or consummation. Damage that affects the value or usefulness of the property is sufficient.

Creating an imminent danger to life or risk of great bodily harm is assumed whenever the burned structure is a dwelling or is likely to have people within it. People need not be there at the time. *If the danger or risk was known or reasonably foreseeable* means that even if the suspect did not intend to harm anyone, the risk should have been known or reasonably anticipated. If a person dies in a fire set by an arsonist, the death is first-degree murder, an additional offense to be prosecuted.

Attempted Arson

The elements of attempted arson are the intent to set a fire and some preparation to commit the crime. The intent is normally specific, and the act must be overt. It must be shown that the fire would have occurred except for some intervention. Attempted arson also includes placing any combustible or explosive material or device in or near any property with the intent to set fire, to destroy or to otherwise damage property. Putting materials together at a location where they could not cause a fire does not constitute attempted arson.

Setting Negligent Fires

Setting a negligent fire is causing a fire to burn or to get out of control through culpable negligence, creating an unreasonable risk and the likelihood of damage or injury to persons or property. This charge is often brought against people who leave smoldering campfires that cause forest fires.

The Model Arson Law

The Model Arson Law was written and promoted in the 1920s by the National Fire Protection Association. The latest revision is included in *The Fire Almanac*, published annually by the same organization. Many states do not classify fires as aggravated or simple but instead have adopted the Model Arson Law, which specifies four degrees of arson:

> The Model Arson Law divides arson into the following degrees:
>
> - First-degree: burning of dwellings
> - Second-degree: burning of buildings other than dwellings
> - Third-degree: burning of other property
> - Fourth-degree: attempting to burn buildings or property

The Model Arson Law includes within each degree not only the actual act but also anyone who aids, counsels or procures the act.

The Arsonist

In arson, unlike other crimes, the victim is often the prime suspect. Motivation, although it need not be proved, has great significance in arson investigations.

Motivation

Common motives for arson include revenge, spite or jealousy; vandalism and malicious mischief; crime concealment and diversionary tactics; profit and insurance fraud; intimidation, extortion and sabotage; and psychiatric afflictions, pyromania, alcoholism and mental retardation.

Revenge, spite and jealousy motivate jilted lovers, feuding neighbors, disgruntled employees, quarreling spouses, people who feel cheated or abused and those who feel racial or religious hostility. Some have called the rash of arsons at African-American churches across the southern United States during the mid- to late-1990s a symptom of the race relations problem in this country ("Federal Probe of Arsons . . . ," 1996, p. 3). In other parts of the country, especially in rural areas, disagreements often result in the burning of homes or barns.

Vandalism and malicious mischief are frequent motives for juveniles who burn property merely to relieve boredom or as a general protest against authority. Garry (1997, p. 1) reports: "Juveniles are arrested for a greater share of [arson] crimes than any other." Many fires in schools, abandoned autos, vacant buildings and trash containers are caused by this type of arsonist.

Crime concealment and diversionary tactics motivate criminals to set fires to destroy evidence of a crime or evidence connecting them to the crime. In murder cases arson can be used to attempt to make it impossible to identify a victim. In other cases people set fires to destroy records containing evidence of embezzlement, forgery or fraud. Arson is also used to divert attention while criminals commit another crime or cover their escape.

Profit and insurance fraud are frequent motives for arson. A business person may wind up in financial straits and decide that the easiest way out is to burn the business and collect the insurance. Some people overinsure property and then burn it, collecting far more than the

property was worth. For example, a St. Louis property owner received more than $415,000 in insurance payments for 54 fires occurring within a two-year period. In large cities professional arson rings defraud insurance companies of millions of dollars.

Other methods of obtaining profit have used arson to stimulate business, to eliminate business rivals or to secure employment. For example, security guards, firefighters or police officers might set fires to obtain a job. In South Carolina five firefighters were charged with arson "believed to be motivated not by profit but by a desire to practice fighting fires" ("Firefighters Charged with Arson," 1995, p. 16A). In other cases firefighters have set fires and then responded to the alarm, receiving attention and praise at having "played the hero." Mentzer (p. 32) calls these "vanity" arsons. Law enforcement has a name for such firefighters gone bad— **strikers.**

It is not always firefighters who seek to become heros. In December 1999 a male nurse set a fire that killed billionaire banker Edmond Safra, stating he hoped to emerge as the hero who saved his employer's life ("Nurse Confesses. . . ," 1999, p. A7). Safra was terrified that assailants were after him and locked himself in his Monaco penthouse bathroom, refusing to leave even when police and firefighters arrived. He died of asphyxiation.

Intimidation, extortion and sabotage are motives of striking workers and employers to apply pressure during a strike. Criminals, especially mobsters, use arson to intimidate witnesses and to extort money. Protesters have also used arson as a way of sending a message. For example: "An environmental group has claimed responsibility for a series of fires that caused $12 million in damage . . . saying it started the fires in protest of Vail Associates moving forward with its controversial 885-acre Category III ski expansion" ("Group Claims it Set . . . ," 1998, p. 10A).

Psychiatric afflictions, pyromania, alcoholism and mental retardation account for many other fires. Pyromaniacs start fires because of an irresistible urge or passion for fire. Some derive sexual satisfaction from watching fires. Others become arsonists to show power over their environment or because they believe they are acting with divine guidance. Davis and Lauber (p. 274) state: "The estimates on the percentage of deliberate firesetters who are pyromaniacs are extremely varied and controversial. Some estimates are as high as 40% . . . , whereas others claim that pyromania is very rare, especially cases involving those individuals who obtain sexual gratification from the act."

Several studies reveal the same pattern: Revenge is the most common motive. Nonetheless, many arson investigators believe insurance fraud is the most prevalent motive for arson. It may be that arson intended to defraud is often hired out to a professional who is less likely to get caught and who, if apprehended, is more likely to have better legal counsel.

The professional "torch," the arsonist for hire, is extremely difficult to identify because such individuals have no apparent link to the fire. Also under suspicion, however, is the victim in many instances. A guilty victim typically has an iron-clad alibi. Also to be considered is the unintentional firesetter, that is, the individual who accidentally sets a fire and then is too embarrassed to admit it or who fears that insurance may not cover the loss if the accident is made known.

Computer software can play a pivotal role in identifying serial arsonists by allowing investigators to efficiently organize and manage tips, evidence and other information related to related fires. Such case management can shorten investigations by months.

Profiling

Research by Davis and Lauber reveals the following arsonist characteristics (p. 277):

- Predominantly Caucasian
- Male
- Reared in disruptive, frustrating, harsh, broken or unstable homes
- Have extensive criminal histories
- Below average in intelligence
- Socially maladjusted or loners
- Lacking in marital ties
- Typically unemployed or working in unskilled positions
- Intoxicated at the time they set the fire

Police and Fire Department Cooperation

Arson is investigated by many agencies with joint jurisdiction: state fire marshals, state police, county sheriffs and local police and fire departments. In addition, insurance investigators often become involved.

Lack of trained personnel to investigate arson is a major problem in both police and fire departments, except in large cities that have their own arson investi-

gation squads. Although arson is a crime, police tend to give it low priority, believing the fire department should investigate. However, many firefighters are volunteers who are not trained in arson investigation. Many full-time departments do not train their personnel to investigate arson. Rural areas and cities of up to 75,000 in population rely heavily on the state fire marshal's office, which usually does not have enough staff to conduct full investigations throughout the state. State fire marshals' offices can help local police and fire agencies by providing advice, coordinating activities and supplying information on suspect profiles. They cannot, however, assume full responsibility for the investigation. Even fire departments that provide training in arson detection seldom include training on the criminal procedures followed in prosecuting arson.

Attitudes about the responsibility for investigating arson vary. Some fire departments feel arson investigation and prosecution are their responsibility; others feel just as strongly that arson is a police matter.

- - - - - - - - -

Logic suggests that the fire department should work to detect arson and determine the fire's point of origin and probable cause, whereas the police department should investigate arson and prepare the case for prosecution.

- - - - - - - - -

Fire Department Expertise

Recognizing factors concerning smoke and fire conditions, detecting arson evidence and determining the cause of a fire are specific areas of expertise for the fire department, which investigates many accidental and natural fires. To delegate this responsibility to the police department would be an unnecessary duplication of skill, especially because only a small number of fires are due to arson.

Trained fire personnel know about buildings, how fires are started and the various components necessary for ignition. Fire marshals also have extralegal powers to summon witnesses, subpoena records and take statements under oath that police officers do not have. Moreover, fire personnel may enter buildings after a fire without a warrant, a benefit to criminal investigations. They also work closely with insurance companies and are apt to recognize people frequently present at fires.

The fire department's basic role is fire investigation and arson detection, not arson investigation. Once the cause of the fire is determined to be arson, the police are notified and the process becomes a joint investigation.

Police Department Expertise

Police on patrol duty and investigators, through intelligence files, are likely to know possible arson suspects. Field interview cards can include names of people present in an area where arson fires are being set. Specialized techniques such as interviewing witnesses and interrogating suspects are normal police operations. Moreover, police have contacts with informants and arrest power.

Coordinating Efforts

Regardless of the actual agency assigned to an arson investigation, someone must coordinate the efforts of everyone involved. A full-time arson squad has the potential for conducting the best arson investigation. The next-best arrangement is to have a well-trained arson investigator from local jurisdictions or the state fire marshal's office. However, police personnel trained in criminal investigation working with fire personnel trained in arson detection can do an effective job if they mutually agree about who is in charge.

Other Sources of Assistance in Investigating Arson

Other sources of assistance in investigating arson are the Bureau of Alcohol, Tobacco and Firearms (ATF), the news media, insurance companies and arson task forces.

The Bureau of Alcohol, Tobacco and Firearms

The Bureau of Alcohol, Tobacco and Firearms (ATF) has extensive resources for investigating arsons, including an ATF National Response Team ready to investigate within 24 hours of receiving a call. Other ATF resources include arson profilers; national laboratories in Georgia, Maryland and California; an Explosives Incidents Systems (EXIS) database, an Intelligence Division; financial auditors; accelerant-detecting canines; photograph examiners; and Certified Fire Investigators ("Investigating African-American . . . ," 1996, p. 54).

News Media

One source of assistance frequently overlooked is the news media, which can publish profiles of arsonists and seek the public's help in identifying them. They may also have photographs or videotapes of in-progress fires that can be extremely useful in investigations.

Insurance Companies

Insurance companies can be very helpful in an arson investigation. Insurance companies usually request the insured to sign a release authorizing the company to obtain private records such as income tax returns, financial audits, bank accounts, credit reports, telephone records and utility company records. Without this release, obtaining such records is a long, complex process.

Private insurance company investigators can assist fire and police efforts in investigating fire losses. Many insurance companies have full-time fire loss investigators, whereas many smaller fire and police agencies do not. The objective is the same for both—obtaining the truth. For fire and police authorities, the goal is to locate the suspect. If the suspect in a fire-for-profit is arrested, fire loss problems for the insurance company are resolved.

The property owner must work with the fire, police and insurance company to collect the insurance money. Consequently, interviewing and interrogating efforts are much enhanced. Background checks, bank and credit inquiries and financial status are also easier to verify.

Insurance investigators have the additional advantage of being able to enter the fire scene without a warrant in their efforts to examine the damage and to determine the cause of the fire.

Further, several index bureaus gather insurance-claim information in attempting to determine whether the same claim is being made to more than one company or whether a pattern of claims exists. Law enforcement investigators can benefit from information gathered by these bureaus as well. Most states provide limited civil immunity to insurance companies that provide information to law enforcement agencies in their investigations.

Arson Task Forces

The development of arson task forces made up of fire and police department personnel; community leaders; insurance representatives; city, county and district attorneys; federal agency personnel; and others has a powerful impact on coordinating existing forces and developing new sources for combating arson and arson-related problems in any community, county or state. Arson has the lowest clearance by arrest of the major crimes, primarily due to inadequate training for fire and police department personnel, the difficulty of locating and preserving evi-

dence and a lack of coordination of personnel of the various organizations involved.

Special Challenges in Investigation

- - - - - - - - -

Special challenges in investigating arson include:

- Coordinating efforts with the fire department and others.
- Determining whether a crime has in fact been committed.
- Finding physical evidence, most of which is destroyed by the fire.
- Finding witnesses.
- Determining whether the victim is a suspect.

- - - - - - - - -

Investigating arson often requires even more persistence, thoroughness and attention to minute details than do other crimes. Arson is a difficult crime to investigate because there are seldom witnesses and because the evidence needed to prove that a crime has been committed is usually consumed in the fire. Moreover, arson is an easy crime to write off without being publicly criticized because the victim and the suspect are often the same person. However, the innocent victim of arson is frequently frustrated by the lack of evidence and witnesses and by the police's inability to prove that a crime was committed.

The Preliminary Investigation

The fire department usually receives the initial fire call unless the departments have a joint dispatcher or are merged into a public safety department. Fire personnel make out the reports and forward them to the state fire marshal. Insurance companies are also represented, and their efforts are coordinated with those of fire and police personnel.

The scene of a fire is dirty, messy and complicated, making it difficult to obtain evidence of possible arson. An arson scene may be the most contaminated crime scene you will ever encounter. The Law Enforcement Assistance Administration describes the scene:

> No other type of crime scene except bombing is characterized by as much destruction and disorder as arson. Investigators must search through piles of debris and rubble, often on their hands and knees. Ashes, soot, and char make fire scenes filthy and malodorous. . . .
>
> The fire scene search is further aggravated by water and foam remaining from the extinguishment. The scene may be a quagmire, making the rubble wet and heavy to move out of the way. Plaster fallen from walls and ceilings mixes with the water, forming a grey slush retarding the investigator's movements. In cold weather, there is the additional pressure of completing the work before everything freezes and the investigation is severely impeded.
>
> The fire scene may be dangerous to work in because of the imminent collapse of upper parts of the structure. It may be exposed to the elements, making work in foul weather difficult and unpleasant.
>
> In addition to the destruction of the fire, there are further problems caused by firefighter mop-up and salvage operations immediately following the fire. The mop-up process involves finding and eliminating any smoldering spots that might rekindle the fire. This involves tearing open walls, ceilings, roofs, and other partitions, and throwing objects like mattresses and sofas out of the building. The salvage process involves removing any salvageable items, such as furnishings or machinery, to a safe place and covering them from the elements. This process hampers efforts to reconstruct the fire scene and the sequence of events that led to the arson.

Although the fire department is responsible for establishing that arson has occurred, you must verify those findings by understanding what distinguishes an accidental fire from arson and by knowing what evidence and information are available for proving the elements of the crime.

The Fire Triangle

The fire triangle is a basic concept critical to an arson investigation.

- - - - - - -

The **fire triangle** consists of three elements necessary for a substance to burn: air, fuel and heat. In arson one or more of these elements is usually present in abnormal amounts for the structure.

- - - - - - -

Extra amounts of *air* or oxygen can result from opened windows or doors, pried-open vents or holes knocked in walls. Because firefighters often chop holes in structures, determine whether any such openings were made by the firefighters or by someone else. *Fuel* can be added by piling up newspapers, excelsior or other combustible materials found at or brought to the scene. Gasoline, kerosene and other accelerants add sufficient *heat* to the fire to cause the desired destruction after it has been ignited.

Arson Indicators

Accelerants

- - - - - - - -

Evidence of **accelerants,** substances that promote combustion, especially gasoline, is a primary form of physical evidence at an arson scene.

- - - - - - - -

Most arson cases involve a flammable liquid, and in 80 percent of these cases, it is gasoline. Perhaps this is because gasoline is easily obtained and widely known to arsonists or because gasoline's familiar odor makes it easier for investigators to detect. Other common accelerants are kerosene, charcoal lighter, paint thinner and lacquer solvent.

Look for residues of liquid fire accelerants on floors, carpets and soil because the liquid accelerants run to the lowest level. In addition, these areas often have the lowest temperatures during the fire and may not have enough oxygen to support complete combustion of the accelerant. Accelerants may seep through porous or cracked floors to underlying soil that has excellent retention properties for flammable liquids. Accelerants can also be found on the clothes and shoes of the suspect if apprehended. You can also identify fire accelerants at the scene either by your own sense of smell or by using portable equipment that detects residues of flammable liquids.

Olfactory detection, the sensitivity of the human nose to gasoline vapor, is ineffective if the odor is masked by another strong odor such as that of burned debris. Moreover, it is often inconvenient or impossible to sniff for accelerant odors along floors or in recessed areas.

Catalytic combustion detectors are the most common type of flammable vapor detector used by arson investigators. Commonly known as a *sniffer,* a *combustible gas indicator,* an *explosimeter* or a *vapor detector,* this detector is portable, moderately priced and fairly simple to operate. Basically, vapor samples are pumped over a heated,

platinum-plated wire coil that causes any combustible gas present to oxidize. The heat from the oxidation raises the coil's electrical resistance, and this change is measured electrically.

Although fire accelerants are the most frequent type of evidence submitted to laboratories for analysis (80 percent), explosives (13 percent) and incendiary devices (4 percent) are also frequently submitted.

Igniters **Igniters** are substances or devices used to start fires. The most common igniters are matches. To be carrying matches is not damaging evidence unless some have been removed from the book or box and the parts found at an arson scene match those found in the suspect's possession.

- - - - - - - -

Common igniters include matches; candles; cigars; cigarettes; cigarette lighters; electrical, mechanical and chemical devices; and explosives.

- - - - - - - -

Electrical devices left in the "on" position, kerosene-soaked papers in waste baskets, time fuses, shorted light switches, magnifying glasses, matches tied around a lighted cigarette and numerous other igniters have been used to commit arson.

Candles are often used in arsons because they give the suspect time to leave the scene. The average candle burns about 30 to 45 minutes per inch, depending on its size, shape, composition and the amount of air in the room. Tapered candles burn faster at the top and slower toward the base. The arsonist may control the length of time by cutting off part of the candle before lighting it. The candle can be set in a material that will ignite once the candle burns down, or the hot wax may be allowed to drip onto a surface to start a fire. The candle's flame can also be used to ignite other materials in the room.

Regardless of whether arsonists use direct or delayed ignition, they usually plan for the fire to consume the igniter; however, this often does not happen. Moreover, in their haste to leave the scene, arsonists may drop parts of the igniter in an area unaffected by the fire. Any igniter not normally present at the location is evidence.

Burn Indicators **Burn indicators** are visible evidence of the effects of heating or partial burning. They indicate various aspects of a fire such as rate of development, temperature, duration, time of occurrence, presence of flammable liquids and points of origin. Interpreting burn indicators is a primary means of determining the causes of fires.

Arson investigations are extremely challenging. The alligatoring at this fire scene will provide important information to the investigator.

Common burn indicators include alligatoring, crazing, the depth of char, lines of demarcation, sagged furniture springs and spalling.

Alligatoring is the checking of charred wood that gives it the appearance of alligator skin. Large, rolling blisters indicate rapid, intense heat. Small, flat alligatoring indicates slow, less-intense heat.

Crazing is the formation of irregular cracks in glass due to rapid, intense heat, possibly caused by a fire accelerant.

The **depth of char,** or how deeply wood is burned, indicates the length of burn and the fire's point of origin. Use a ruler to measure depth of char.

A **line of demarcation** is a boundary between charred and uncharred material. A puddle-shaped line of demarcation on floors or rugs can indicate the use of a liquid fire accelerant. In a cross-section of wood, a sharp, distinct line of demarcation indicates a rapid, intense fire.

Sagged furniture springs usually occur when a fire originates inside the cushions of upholstered furniture (as from a lighted cigarette rolling behind a cushion) or when a fire is intensified by an accelerant.

Spalling is the breaking off of surface pieces of concrete or brick due to intense heat. Brown stains around the spall indicate use of an accelerant.

A photograph of a line of demarcation, seen in this carpet, is important evidence in an arson investigation.

This church arson fire was started by two juveniles using altar candles and caused $80,000 damage.

Point of Origin Knowing the fire's point of origin helps to establish how the fire spread and whether it followed a normal burning pattern. The more extensive the destruction, the more difficult it is to determine the fire's point of origin.

- - - - - - - -

The point of origin is established by finding the area with the deepest char, alligatoring and usually the greatest destruction. More than one point of origin indicates arson.

- - - - - - - -

Incendiary (igniter) evidence might be discovered at the point of origin. In addition, information from witnesses who saw the fire can establish where the flames began.

Burning Pattern

- - - - - - - -

Fires normally burn upward, not outward. They are drawn toward ventilation and follow fuel paths.

- - - - - - - -

Given adequate ventilation, a fire will burn upward. If a door or window is open, it will be drawn toward that opening. If the arsonist places a path of flammable liquid, the fire will follow that path, known as a **trailer.** Trailers can be made of paper, hay, flammable compounds or any substance that burns readily, and they result in an abnormal pattern. The char marks will follow the trailer's path. Areas of uneven burning can also indicate the presence of an incendiary or that a great amount of flammable material was already at the scene.

Appearance of Collapsed Walls Notice how walls seem to have collapsed, especially if you smell gas. Lighter gases tend to explode walls outward from the top of the room; heavier gases explode walls out from the bottom of the room. Fast-exploding gases such as hydrogen, acetylene or butane give the appearance of the walls caving in. If odors or the walls' appearance suggests gas as the igniter or accelerator, determine whether the gas is normally on the premises.

Smoke Color Generally, blue smoke results from burning alcohol; white smoke from burning vegetable compounds, hay or phosphorous; yellow or brownish yellow smoke from film, nitric acid, sulfur, hydrochloric acid or smokeless gunpowder; and black smoke from petroleum or petroleum products.

Notice the smoke's color if the fire is still in progress. If it has been put out when you arrive, ask the firefighters or witnesses what color the smoke was. Determine whether substances likely to produce smoke of that color were on the premises before the fire.

Summary of Arson Indicators

Arson is likely in fires that:

- Have more than one point of origin.
- Deviate from normal burning patterns.
- Show evidence of trailers.
- Show evidence of having been accelerated.
- Produce odors or smoke of a color associated with substances not normally present at the scene.
- Indicate that an abnormal amount of air, fuel or heat was present.
- Reveal evidence of incendiary igniters at the point of origin.

Professional arsonists use a variety of methods to ignite fires, including the following:

- Connecting magnesium rods to timed detonators and placing them in a building's electrical system. The rods burn with extreme intensity and cause a fire that looks as though it was caused by faulty wiring.
- Connecting a timed explosive charge on one or more barrels of gasoline or other highly flammable liquid. This method is often used when large areas such as warehouses are to be burned.
- Pouring acid onto key support points in steel-structured buildings to make certain the building will collapse during the fire.

Photographing and Videotaping an Arson Fire

Pictures of a fire in progress show the smoke's color and its origination as well as the size of the fire at different points and times. Pictures are especially useful if there appears to be acceleration of the fire at a specific time that would indicate arson or the presence of highly combustible substances. Many fire departments take such in-progress photographs. Smaller departments may seek help from television or newspaper photographers who may take pictures that can be of immense help. Photographs or videotapes of the fire scene are also ideal to show the judge and jury.

Pictures taken of people at the fire scene might reveal the presence of a known arsonist or may show a person who repeatedly appears in photos taken at fires and is therefore an arson suspect.

After the fire take enough pictures to show the entire scene in detail. Start with the outside of the structure, showing all entries and exits. Also show any obstructions that were placed in front of windows to prevent seeing inside the building. Persons familiar with the structure can review the pictures for anything out of the ordinary.

Take inside pictures to show the extent of burning. These will prove the corpus delicti. Take close-up pictures of extra papers, rags, gas cans or other suspicious substances as well as examples of alligatoring and deep charring. Take pictures at each stage of the search to show the point of origin, the nature of the burning and the direction and speed of the fire's spread.

Physical Evidence

Preserving evidence is a major problem because much of the evidence is very fragile. Follow carefully the procedures described in Chapter 5. Use disposable cellulose sponges to sop up accelerants for transfer to a container. Use hypodermic or cooking syringes to suck up accelerants between boards or crevices. Sift ashes to detect small objects such as the timing device from an igniter.

Incendiary evidence at the point of origin can be part of a candle, an empty flammable liquid container, excessive amounts of unburned newspaper folded together or a number of unburned matches.

Paper exposed to high temperatures and sufficient air burns with little ash to examine. However, with a limited supply of air, only partial combustion occurs, leaving charred paper evidence that can be collected for laboratory examination. Paper in a fireplace or stove may be only partially burned, even if the building was totally consumed. These papers may provide a motive for the arson. If the paper is not destroyed, a laboratory may be able to recover any messages on it.

As mentioned, murderers may use arson in an attempt to destroy evidence or conceal the crime. However, they may erroneously assume blood evidence will be consumed in the fire. Mentzer (p. 32) points out that: "DNA in 'baked' blood is not always destroyed and may be used to identify the suspect."

An important step in an arson investigation is identifying potential accelerants at a fire scene. The accepted method is to use gas chromatography with a flame ionization detector (GC-FID), which can make an identification in 95 percent of the cases.

Using K–9s in Arson Investigations

Dogs can be of great assistance in arson investigation. One former ATF agent (Pilant, 1997b, pp. 18–19) maintains: "The detection dog is one of our biggest assets. . . . They're better than any mechanical device. They save time."

Connecticut's K–9 accelerant-detection program, for example, is the result of collaboration of the ATF, the New Haven County State's Attorney's Office, the State Police Science Laboratory, the Emergency Services Division Canine Unit and the Bureau of the State Fire Marshal. Their first dog, Mattie, was trained to detect extremely small quantities of highly diluted flammable and combustible liquids including paint remover, lacquer thinner, charcoal lighter fluid, paint thinner, kerosene, naphtha, acetone, dry gas, heptone, gasoline, number 2 fuel, diesel fuel, gum turpentine, Heritage lamp oil, transmission fluid, octane and Jet-A-Fuel.

Mattie is now a lab-certified accelerant-detection canine. She helps detect accelerants at fire scenes and can also search a crowd for possible suspects, search a suspect's clothing and vehicle for the presence of accelerants and search areas for accelerant containers.

The ATF is the only federal agency that offers arson detection training for canines, a process that can be quite expensive. Yet, as Pilant (1997b, p. 22) notes: "The cost (about $3,500) can easily be justified because the dog is the one tool that can reduce the number of samples collected. When a dog 'hits,' it is usually a good sample because dogs will not mistake hydrocarbon-based plastic burn compounds for accelerants."

Evidence on a Suspect, at a Residence or in a Vehicle

If you have a suspect, look for any burns he or she may have received while setting the fire. The suspect may have scorched hair, torn clothing, stains, cuts and other injuries, or his or her clothing or shoes may have traces of accelerants. The suspect's residence or vehicle may contain clothes noticed at the fire by a witness, objects removed from the scene of the fire or incendiary devices. You may also find insurance documents or business or financial records that provide a motive.

Observing Unusual Circumstances

Suspicious circumstances implying arson include suddenly emptied premises, the presence of materials not normally part of the business, holes in the plaster or plasterboard that expose the wood, disconnected sprinkler systems, blocked-open interior doors, nailed-open fire doors and other alterations that would provide more air, heat or fuel to the area.

Interviewing the Victim, Witnesses and Firefighters

Ask questions such as: How was the fire discovered? Who discovered it? Who were witnesses? What did they see? What color was the smoke, and where was it coming from? What direction was the wind? Did the fire appear to suddenly accelerate? Did anything out of the ordinary occur before the fire? Were there unusual odors? Were the shades up or down? Did obstructions prevent seeing into the building? Were suspicious persons or vehicles observed at the scene before, during or after the fire?

Also try to learn who had an opportunity to set the fire and who might benefit from it. Determine who had keys and how the property was normally guarded or protected. Check the victim's financial status and find out how much insurance was carried on the property. Interview the firefighters assigned to the fire and obtain copies of their reports.

Search Warrants and Fire Investigations

The United States Supreme Court requires a two-step warrant process for investigating fires involving crimes. The initial search may require an **administrative warrant** for searching the premises for cause of fire and origin determination *and* a criminal warrant when evidence of a crime is discovered. Both require probable cause for issuance.

An administrative warrant is issued when it is necessary for a government agent to search the premises to determine the fire's cause and origin. A criminal warrant is issued on probable cause when the premises yield evidence of a crime.

Both require an affidavit in support of the warrant that states the location and legal description of the property, the purpose (to determine the fire's cause and origin), the area and time of the search, the use of the building and the measures taken to secure the structure or area of the fire. Searches are limited to the items specified in the warrant. Found evidence may be seized, but once the officers leave after finding the evidence, they must have a criminal warrant to return to the premises for a further search.

Administrative warrants allow civil inspections of private property to determine compliance with city ordinances such as fire codes. The Court has established guidelines for arson investigators. In *Michigan v Clifford* (1984), the Court held:

> If a warrant is necessary, the object of the search determines the type of warrant required. If the primary object is to determine the cause and origin of a fire, an administrative warrant will suffice . . . and if the primary object is to gather evidence of criminal activity, a criminal search warrant may be obtained only on a showing of probable cause to believe that relevant evidence will be found in the place to be searched.

In *Coolidge v New Hampshire* (1971), the Court held that evidence of criminal activity discovered during a search with a valid administrative warrant may be seized under the plain view doctrine. Any evidence so seized may be used to establish the probable cause needed to obtain a criminal search warrant.

- - - - - - - - - -

Entry to fight a fire requires no warrant. Once in the building, fire officials may remain a reasonable time to investigate the cause of the blaze. After this time an administrative warrant is needed, as established in *Michigan v Tyler* (1978).

- - - - - - - - - -

Guidelines on the current legal status of searches conducted during fire investigations include the following:

- Warrants are not required when an authorized individual consents to the search. The consent must be written and must specify the areas to be searched and the purpose of the search. This consent can be revoked at any time.

- Warrants are not required when investigators enter under "exigent circumstances," that is, if investigators enter the premises while firefighters are extinguishing the blaze or conducting overhaul. The scope of the search must be limited to determining the cause and origin. If evidence of a crime is discovered, a criminal warrant is required to continue the search.

- Without consent or an exigency, warrants are required if the premises are subject to a "reasonable expectation of privacy." This includes commercial businesses as well as private residences. Exceptions would be premises that are so utterly devastated by the fire that no expectation of privacy is reasonable or property that has been abandoned.

- Evidence of a crime discovered during an administrative search may be seized if in plain view.

- Once evidence of arson is discovered, the fire's cause and origin are assumed to be known. The scope of the administrative warrant has been exhausted. A criminal warrant is required to continue the search.

When in doubt, obtain a warrant.

Investigating Vehicle Arson

Although vehicle fires can be caused by accident, vehicles usually do not burn readily. Accelerants are used on many vehicles to accomplish arson. A quart to a half-gallon of flammable liquid is required to cause a major vehicle fire.

- - - - - - - - - -

When investigating vehicle fires, look for evidence of accelerants and determine whether the vehicle was insured.

- - - - - - - - - -

Motives for vehicle arson include the desire to collect insurance, inability to make needed repairs after an unreported accident, desire to eliminate a loan on the vehicle, desire to cover up another crime committed in or with the vehicle, general dissatisfaction with the vehicle's performance and desire to resolve arguments over the vehicle's use.

A close correlation exists between insurance coverage and vehicle arson; few arsons are committed when there is no insurance coverage. Obtain proof that the vehicle was insured against fire, that the fire was willfully set, that damage resulted and that there was intent to defraud.

Prosecuting Arsonists

Some studies indicate that well over 90 percent of arsonists go unpunished, probably because arson is most often committed without the benefit of witnesses. According to the International Association of Arson Investigators, approximately 25 percent of all fires in the United States—about 500,000 per year—result from arson, but only about 2 percent of all arsonists are ever arrested and convicted for their crimes ("Did You Know That . . . ," 1999, p. 18).

The difficulty of investigating arson has been discussed as has the need for cooperation between law enforcement investigators and firefighters. Equally difficult is prosecution. Cooperative investigation and prosecution are required if the losses from arson are to be stemmed.

Many prosecutors fail to bring charges because all they have is circumstantial evidence. However, circumstantial evidence can be used to successfully prosecute a case. Look for evidence of planning, such as increasing insurance coverage, removing items or making off-hand remarks or unusual changes. Also look for evidence of disabled or turned off alarms or sprinkler systems and doors left open. Finally, look for evidence of motive.

Preventing Arson

To prevent arson, efforts have been made to identify various properties at risk of being set on fire. Lutz (1998, pp. 51–52) describes how computer mapping has helped identify arson targets:

> Recognizing that many arson fires are targets of opportunity, we reviewed the tax assessment records and identified a negative-equity trend among properties considered to be vacant. . . .
>
> With targets determined, the focus shifted to finding the catalyst for the fires and pinpointing probable arson zones. Prior crime analysis determined that the majority of the properties that had experienced an arson fire during the course of previous events were either abandoned or vacant properties located near or adjacent to notably high-crime locations. . . .
>
> A total of six key layers were collated and merged into one master map:

- abandoned properties;
- negative-equity properties;
- properties whose gas and/or electric were shut off;
- prior-year fires;
- gang locales; and
- CDS [Controlled Dangerous Substances] locations.

Lutz (p. 52) asserts that such mapping has proven accurate in identifying target arson zones and summarizes how it can help prevent arson: "With predictions this accurate, officers can be stationed within or adjacent to targeted zones, thus expediting response time and reinforcing future deterrence through proactive policing."

Bombs and Their Effects

Following the highly publicized bombings of military barracks in Saudi Arabia and numerous sites around the United States, it should come as no surprise that bombs have become a high-profile, almost routine, weapon of mass destruction. Bombs generate substantial media attention and provide an impersonal means of causing considerable damage while allowing a bomber to be a safe distance away when detonation occurs. Bombs are also relatively easy to build from directions that can even be found on the Internet. Pilant (1997b, p. 38) comments:

> Experts say the Internet has been the single most powerful influence on explosive incidents in the past several years. This is especially true for teen-agers who take bomb-building information from the Internet—information that at one time was buried in dusty library stacks.

Abshire (1997, p. 74) notes:

> According to the Bureau of Alcohol, Tobacco and Firearms (ATF), for the period 1991 through 1995, there were 8,567 actual bombings classified as explosive and 2,078 attempts in the United States. There were 2,468 incendiary bombings and 782 attempts, and a total of 192 bomb accidents. All together, they accounted for 456 fatalities, 3,859 injuries, and $1.25 billion in property damage. . . .
>
> Over that same five-year period, according to the ATF, 26,969 pounds of dynamite was reported stolen nationally, along with 199 pounds of military C-4; 221,609 feet of Det-Cord; and 42,713 detonators.

Morris (1996, p. 77) describes the following types of common bombs (reprinted by permission of Bobit Publishing, Redondo Beach, CA.):

- **Dry ice**—All that is involved here is a 2-liter plastic soda bottle, dry ice and some water. Depending on the condition of the bottle, the amount of ice and the weather, the device will explode in three to seven minutes. These dangerous and loud explosions are favorites of youngsters for blowing up trash cans, dumpsters and mailboxes.
- **Mailbox bomb**—All the bomber needs is a 2-liter bottle of chlorine, a touch of sugar and some water. The somewhat humble explosion can launch an average mailbox 20 feet into the air.
- **Car bomb**—Traditional bombers have been known to "wire" cars, but according to information on the Internet, a common method of making a car bomb is to wrap a fuse around the car's

exhaust manifold. The fuse is ignited by the heat of the manifold, detonating the explosion.

- **Pipe bomb**—These simple bombs, which are detonated by a spark or some heat source, consist of pipe, end caps and smokeless powder. The pipe bomb that caused two deaths in Atlanta's Centennial Park bombing was laced with nails and other hardware to increase fragmentation.

The bomb, more than any other weapon, makes people feel vulnerable. Unlike a gun, a bomb does not have to be aimed. Unlike poison, it does not have to be administered. Bombs are weapons of chance. Victims are simply in the wrong place at the wrong time. Consider this example: The 1993 World Trade Center bombing in New York resulted in six dead, more than a thousand injured and millions of dollars in property damage. The "mastermind" of this bombing, Ramzi Ahmed Yousef, received a life sentence without possibility of parole ("Mastermind of the Trade . . .," 1998, p. A4).

The 1995 bombing at the Murrah Federal Building in Oklahoma City claimed 169 lives, caused nearly 500 injuries and resulted in losses of $651 million. Bomber Timothy McVeigh was found guilty of the crime and sentenced to death. More recently the pipe bomb that exploded in Atlanta's Centennial Park during the Olympics festivities captured the media's attention.

National attention has also focused on the Unabomber case. After 18 years of investigation, 29 injuries and 3 deaths, Theodore Kaczynski, "a Montana hermit filled with rage against a technological society," was arrested, found guilty and sentenced to life in prison without possibility of release ("Kaczynski Admits . . .," 1998, p. A1). Evidence found in Kaczynski's cabin included scrap metal and wood, batteries and electric wire, ten three-ring binders filled with writings and diagrams about constructing and concealing explosive devices, and two manual typewriters investigators believe Kaczynski used to type his "Unabomber Manifesto" ("After 17 Years . . .," 1996, p. 11).

Abshire (p. 73) observes: "Over the years, American bombers have sorted themselves out into three general categories: fanatics, nuts, and crooks." Fanatics are those motivated by religious, philosophical, or atavistic national or ethnic vendettas, such as Yousef, McVeigh and Kaczynski. The "nuts" are those whose mental pathology feeds a perverse desire to blow things up. Abshire (pp. 73–74) states: "Far and away, the largest category of bombers, like arsonists, is that of crooks, most commonly motivated by greed or revenge. . . . Crooks

use bombs to eliminate rivals, intimidate extortion victims, conceal evidence of other offenses, or defraud insurance companies."

Responding to a Bomb Threat

Special safety precautions must be taken when responding to a bomb threat. Fuller (1999, p. 29) cautions:

> The most important rule in handling suspect packages remains: DO NOT TOUCH the package. If at all possible, officers should not approach suspect packages; they should observe them from a distance—the greater the distance, the better. Officers should remember that bomb squad personnel, with the benefit of specialized training and equipment, will not approach a suspect package until one of them has donned a bomb suit and helmet.

Fuller (pp. 29–30) notes other precautions first-responding officers should take:

- Clear the area—evacuate the area immediately and ensure no one reenters. An initial "exclusion area" of a 300-foot radius is a good rule to follow.
- Alert emergency personnel—notify fire and emergency medical personnel quickly and instruct them on how to approach the scene safely.
- Turn off the radios—curtail all radio use within 300 feet of a suspected improvised explosive device (IED). Some bombs use an electric firing system, and radio transmitters may produce enough electromagnetic energy to detonate such fuses.

Finally, Fuller (pp. 30–31) advises: "Additional questions officers should ask witnesses include many similar to those they would ask at other crime scenes:

- Has someone recently threatened the area or anyone associated with it?
- Does anyone have a grudge to settle that might manifest itself in such a manner?
- Who found the package? When?
- Has anyone approached the package? If so, by what route?
- Does anyone have any suspects?
- Do any of the suspects identified in the initial investigation have the knowledge to build such a device?"

Investigating Bomb Explosions

- - - - - - - -

When investigating explosions and bombings, pay special attention to fragments of the explosive device as well as to powder present at the scene. Determine motive.

- - - - - - - -

Bomb-scene investigations must progress logically, and the first step is to determine the scene's parameters. In general, once the furthest piece of recognizable evidence is located, a radius 50 percent wider is established. For example, in the Oklahoma City bombing, the rear axle of the truck carrying the explosives was located three blocks from the blast site, so the scene parameters were approximately four and a half blocks in all directions.

Using K–9s in Detecting Explosives

As with arson investigations, dogs have become increasingly useful in bomb detection and in searches for evidence following explosions. Pilant (1997a, p. 39) notes:

> To help combat the worldwide explosives threat, ATF has developed the Canine Explosives Detection Program (CEDP). To be certified through this program, ATF canines must identify 20 explosive compounds—in quantities from 1.7 to 15 grams—with 100 percent accuracy. Canines who pass this test can be expected to identify the majority of the 19,000 different explosive compounds, including smokeless powders and other explosive fillers used in firearms and ammunition.

Following the precaution of not handling the explosive, bomb dogs are trained to alert the handler by sitting near a suspect package without touching it. Pilant (1997a, p. 42) reports: "[Bomb dogs] can identify black powder, smokeless powder, flash powder, TNT, C4, Dexcop, ammonium nitrate, nitrate dynamite, sodium and potassium chlorate, Data Sheet, Flex-X, booster charge, detonation cord, time fuse, and military and civilian detonation cord and time fuse."

Using Robots

Bomb squads in larger departments are using robots to approach and detonate suspected packages. For example, Miami's bomb squad has a REMOTEC Mark VI Robot they use for recon, sending it in to open such packages. Strandberg (1998, p. 46) notes: "The robots have all kinds of gear mounted on them, from remote cameras to water cannons, and everything in between." Water cannons shoot a slug of water that goes right through a package without detonating the bomb. Other features of bomb robots include portable X-ray machines and devices to remotely cut open a car door.

Importance of the Team Approach

The teamwork of field investigators and laboratory specialists in investigating bombings is critical. Such teamwork followed a California pipe-bombing incident that killed the driver of a vehicle to which a bomb had been attached. The Rialto Police Department, the San Bernardino Sheriff's Office and the ATF combined their efforts. They investigated and forwarded evidence from the scene to the ATF laboratory for examination. Chemists identified the type and brand of powder used in the bomb by examining intact powder particles found in the bomb's end caps. A subsequent search at the suspect's home uncovered a can of smokeless powder identical to the identified powder. Additional evidence obtained during the search provided further links between the suspect and the bombing. The suspect was arrested and charged with murder.

Investigators with technical questions about commercial explosives can receive assistance from the Institute of Makers of Explosives (IME) in Washington, DC. This nonprofit safety organization has 31 member-companies and 80-plus subsidiaries and affiliates, which together produce more than 85 percent of the commercial explosives used in the United States. Also of help is the ATF National Response Team (NRT), which can be deployed in the most urgent, difficult bomb cases.

Another source of assistance is the Interpol Explosives Incident System (IEXIS), an explosives index containing

A bomb squad robot carries a pipe bomb out of a house in Columbus, Ohio, where Peter Langan, a suspect in a string of Midwest bank robberies, was arrested after a shootout with the FBI and local police in 1996.

descriptions of all explosives materials manufactured throughout the world. A primary objective of IEXIS is to immediately determine whether a bombing or an attempted bombing in one country is significantly similar to bombings in the same or another country. This combination of explosives-theft information, IED componentry and manner of construction, along with modus operandi of the criminal or terrorist groups, should greatly assist in investigating all forms of explosives-related crimes.

Summary

Arson is the malicious, willful burning of a building or property. Fires are classified as natural, accidental, criminal (arson), suspicious or of unknown origin. They are presumed natural or accidental unless proven otherwise.

The elements of the crime of arson include (1) the willful, malicious burning of a building or property (2) of another, or of one's own to defraud (3) or causing to be burned, or aiding, counseling or procuring such burning. Attempted arson is also a crime. Some states cat-egorize arson as either aggravated or simple. Aggravated arson is intentionally destroying or damaging a dwelling or other property by means of fire or explosives, creating an imminent danger to life or great bodily harm, which risk was known or reasonably foreseeable to the suspect. Simple arson is intentional destruction by fire or explosives that does not create imminent danger to life or risk of great bodily harm. Other states use the Model Arson Law, which divides arson into four degrees: first-degree involves the burning of dwellings; second-degree involves the burning of buildings other than dwellings; third-degree involves the burning of other property; and fourth-degree involves attempts to burn buildings or property.

Logic suggests that fire departments should *detect* arson and determine the point of origin and probable cause, whereas police departments should *investigate* arson and prepare cases for prosecution.

Special challenges in investigating arson include coordinating efforts with the fire department and others, determining whether a crime has been committed, finding physical evidence and witnesses and determining whether the victim is a suspect.

Although the fire department is responsible for establishing whether arson has occurred, law enforcement investigators must be able to verify such findings. To do so requires understanding the distinction between an accidental fire and arson. Basic to this understanding is the concept of the fire triangle, which consists of three elements necessary for a substance to burn: air, fuel and heat. In arson, at least one of these elements is usually present in abnormal amounts for the structure. Evidence of accelerants at an arson scene is a primary form of evidence. The most common accelerant is gasoline. Also important as evidence are igniters, which include matches; candles; cigars and cigarettes; cigarette lighters; electrical, mechanical and chemical devices; and explosives.

Burn indicators that provide important information include alligatoring, crazing, depth of char, lines of demarcation, sagged furniture springs and spalling. The point of origin is established by finding the area with the deepest char, alligatoring and (usually) the greatest destruction. Fires normally burn upward and are drawn toward ventilation and follow fuel. Arson is likely in fires that:

- Have more than one point of origin.

- Deviate from normal burning patterns.

- Show evidence of trailers.

- Show evidence of having been accelerated.

- Produce odors or smoke of a color associated with substances not normally present at the scene.

- Indicate that an abnormal amount of air, fuel or heat was present.

- Reveal evidence of incendiary igniters at the point of origin.

An administrative warrant is issued when it is necessary for a government agent to search the premises to determine the fire's cause and origin. A criminal warrant is issued on probable cause when the premises yield evidence of a crime. Entry to fight a fire requires no warrant. Once in the building, fire officials may remain a reasonable time to investigate the cause of the blaze. After this time an administrative warrant is needed, as established in *Michigan v Tyler*.

When investigating vehicle fires, look for evidence of accelerants and determine whether the vehicle was insured. It is seldom arson if there is no insurance. When investigating explosions and bombings, pay special attention to fragments of the explosive device as well as to powder present at the scene. Determine motive.

Checklist

Arson

- Who first noticed the fire?

- Who notified authorities?

- Who responded from the fire department?

- Did the fire department record the color of the smoke? The color of the flame?

- What was the fire's point of origin? Was there more than one point of origin?

- What material was used to ignite the fire?

- Was there an explosion before the fire? During the fire? After the fire?

- How did the building explode: inward or outward?

- Was the fire's burn time normal? Did it appear to be accelerated?

- Were any accelerants (newspapers, rags or gasoline) found at the scene?

- What was the weather: dry, windy, snowy?

- What property was destroyed that was unusual for the premises?

- Were there any unusual circumstances?

- Was anyone injured or killed? Was an autopsy done to determine whether there were other causes for death than fire? Were carbon monoxide tests made of the victim to determine when death occurred— whether before or during the fire?

- Were regular informants checked to determine possible suspects?

- Who had access to the building?

- What appeared to be the motive for the fire? Who would benefit?

- Who owns the property destroyed? For how long?

- Was there insurance and, if so, how much?

- Who was the insurance payable to?

- What is the name of the insurance company? Obtain a copy of the company's report.

- Does the owner have any record of other property destroyed by fire?

- Does the owner have a criminal record for this or other types of crimes?

- Were any suspicious people or vehicles observed at the scene before, during or after the fire?

- Was the state fire marshal's office notified? Did it send an investigator? If so, obtain a copy of the investigator's report.

- Were photographs or videos taken? Are they available?

Application

A. It is midafternoon on a Sunday. The fire department has just received a call to proceed to the Methodist Church on St. Anthony Boulevard. Smoke has been reported coming out of the church's windows by a nearby resident. When the fire department arrives, the church is engulfed in flames. By the time the fire is brought under control, the church is gutted with damage estimated at $320,000. Suspecting arson, the fire department asks for help from the local police department.

Questions

1. Was the request for assistance justified at this point?

2. What are the responsibilities of the investigator assigned to respond to the call?

B. Investigators Ron McNeil and Brett Joyce worked together as part of Boston's special arson task force. Just before midnight they received a call from the dispatcher and were told to proceed to a certain address. They arrived minutes later at a small, one-story frame house and pulled in behind the first fire rig. Orange flames were shooting from every window of the house.

While the firefighters fought the blaze, McNeil and Joyce walked among the bystanders, asking if anyone had seen anything suspicious before the fire, but no one had. When the fire was out and the smoke cleared, floodlights illuminated the house and McNeil and Joyce started their investigation. Beginning in the small front room, they noticed extensive burning and windows totally blackened from the fire. They proceeded through a small alcove, where the top portion had been destroyed, and then entered the kitchen. The glass in a window over the kitchen sink had broken and melted, with a series of intricate cracks running through each fragment. After shoveling out layers of debris and dragging in a fire hose to wash the floor, McNeil and Joyce noticed the floor was deeply charred and spongy with water. Inspection of the wooden cabinets around the sink revealed large, rolling blisters. They also discovered the electricity to the structure had been disconnected. Then they began to photograph the fire scene.

Shortly afterward the owner and his wife arrived. The owner calmly answered questions, informing the investigators that he had been letting a carpenter live in the house in exchange for fixing up the place. But when the tenant failed to make the repairs and instead stole the construction materials, much of the furniture and many appliances, the owner kicked him out. The carpenter threatened to "make him sorry." The owner had no fire insurance because he had intended not to live in the house but to use it as an investment property.

After filing their report, McNeil and Joyce returned to the property at 4 A.M. A heavy rain the day before had soaked the ground, and the mud in the backyard was crisscrossed with footprints. Joyce noticed some boot prints leading from the back door and took a plaster cast of them. Just then a neighbor stopped over to say he had seen a green pickup parked behind the house with the motor running just before the fire. McNeil photographed all the tire tracks in the dirt alley where the pickup was reportedly parked. The next morning the inves-

tigators learned that the carpenter, now their prime suspect, had been in jail when the fire broke out. The green pickup was registered to a friend of his, a man who had been previously arrested for arson.

They obtained a search warrant and executed it later that morning. The tires of the carpenter's friend's truck and his boot soles resembled the impressions found at the fire scene, but the impressions were so spongy it was difficult to match them exactly. The investigators found no further evidence linking the man to the fire. (Adapted from Kevin Krajick's "Seattle: Sifting through the Ashes.")

Questions

1. Where did the fire probably originate? What factors indicate this?

2. What indicated that the fire was probably arson?

3. Did the investigators have probable cause to arrest the carpenter's friend? Would the owner also be a possible suspect? Why or why not?

4. What aspects of this case illustrate an effective arson investigation?

Discussion Questions

1. Do you agree that investigation of arson cases is the joint responsibility of police and fire departments? Which department should be in charge?

2. What are the respective roles of the police and fire departments in your community during an arson investigation?

3. Arson has a low conviction rate. What factors make an arson investigation difficult? What factors make prosecution difficult?

4. Imagine that you are called to the scene of a fire to determine whether it was accidental or of criminal origin. What initial steps would you take in making this determination?

5. What types of evidence are material to the crime of arson? Where do you find such evidence at a fire scene? How do you collect it? Where do you send it for examination in your area?

6. What are common motives for arson? How do these motives help an investigator locate suspects?

7. Arson was added to the Part One Index Crimes in the Uniform Crime Reporting Program. Is arson

serious enough to be in this category along with murder and rape? Are there other reasons it should or should not be a Part One Index Crime?

8. What agencies outside the police and fire departments can assist in an arson investigation? Who would you contact? What services could they provide?

9. What other types of crimes might be involved along with arson?

10. Organized crime has used arson to bring pressure on uncooperative persons and businesses. Why is arson effective for this purpose? Why is it difficult to prosecute such cases?

References

Abshire, Richard. "Raising the Stakes in a Deadly Game." *Law Enforcement Technology,* Vol. 24, No. 10, October 1997, pp. 72–78.

"After 17 Years, the End of the Bloody Road." *Law Enforcement News,* December 31, 1996, p. 11.

Davis, Joseph A. and Lauber, Kelli M. "Criminal Behavioral Assessment of Arsonists, Pyromaniacs, and Multiple Firesetters." *Journal of Contemporary Criminal Justice,* Vol. 15, No. 3, August 1999, pp. 273–290.

"Did You Know That . . . ." *Security Management,* Vol. 43, No. 7, July 1999, p. 18.

"Federal Probe of Arsons at Black Churches Turns Up Suspects, But No Conspiracy." *NCJA Justice Bulletin,* November 1996, pp. 3–5.

"Firefighters Charged with Arson." *Las Vegas Review Journal,* November 1995, p. 16A.

Fuller, T. C. "Bomb Threat: A Primer for the First Responder." *FBI Law Enforcement Bulletin,* Vol. 68, No. 3, March 1999, pp. 28–31.

Garry, Eileen M. *Juvenile Firesetting and Arson.* Washington, DC: Office of Juvenile Justice and Delinquency Prevention Fact Sheet #51, January 1997. (FS-9751)

"Group Claims It Set Series of Vail Fires." *Las Vegas Review Journal,* October 28, 1998, p. 10A.

"Investigating African-American Church Fires." *The Police Chief,* Vol. LXIII, Vol. 11, November 1996, pp. 52–54.

"Kaczynski Admits He's Unabomber." (Minneapolis/ St. Paul) *Star Tribune,* January 23, 1998, pp. A1, A12.

Lutz, William E. "Computer Mapping Helps Identify Arson Targets." *The Police Chief,* Vol. LXV, No. 5, May 1998, pp. 50–52.

"Mastermind of Trade Center Bombing Gets Life Sentence." (Minneapolis/St. Paul) *Star Tribune,* January 9, 1998, p. A4.

Mentzer, Alan. "Working in the Line of Fire." *Police,* September 1997, pp. 30–37.

Morris, Cole. "Explosive Situation." *Police,* September 1996, pp. 44–46, 70–77.

"Nurse Confesses in Banker's Death, Prosecutor Says. Arson Went Awry in Monaco." (Minneapolis/ St. Paul) *Star Tribune,* December 7, 1999, p. A7.

Pilant, Lois. "Building a Better Bomb Squad." *The Police Chief,* Vol. LXIV, No. 9, September 1997a, pp. 37–42.

Pilant, Lois. "Investigating Arson." *The Police Chief,* Vol. LXIV, No. 3, March 1997b, pp. 17–22.

Strandberg, Keith W. "Bomb Squads." *Law Enforcement Technology,* Vol. 25, No. 6, June 1998, pp. 42–48.

Other Challenges to the Criminal Investigator

The two preceding sections discussed investigating crimes against persons and property. Many crimes do not fall neatly into one of the eight Part One Index Crimes but involve a combination of illegal acts related to both people and property. Unique investigative challenges are presented by investigating computer crime (Chapter 18); organized crime, gang-related crime, bias/hate crime and ritualistic crime (Chapter 19); and drug buyers and sellers (Chapter 20). Investigating the illegal activities related to these groups is more difficult because the elements of the crimes are not neatly spelled out and statistics are not available as they are for the Index Crimes.

Computer crime is relatively new, but organized crime, gang-related crime, bias/hate crime and ritualistic crime have existed in one form or another for centuries. Not until recently, however, have they had such an impact on law enforcement, straining already limited resources and resulting in what many view as "war" on such crimes. A further complication is that the areas overlap; people involved in organized crime, drugs and gangs are often the same people—but not necessarily. Although each type of crime is discussed separately, you should always keep this overlap in mind. Further, moral and ethical issues are raised by the activities of these organizations that are not raised by the activities of, say, bicycle thieves, rapists and murderers. Stealing, raping and murdering are clearly wrong in our society. This is not necessarily true for gambling, worshiping Satan or smoking pot.

Computer Crime

Do You Know?

What the three key characteristics of computer crime are?

What computer crime can involve?

What types of computer crime are most frequently committed?

How an investigator with a search warrant should execute it in a computer crime investigation?

How evidence of computer crime differs from evidence of other felonies?

What form evidence usually takes in computer crimes?

What precautions you should take when handling computer disks?

How computer disks taken as evidence should be stored?

What approach is often required in investigating computer crime?

Who the "typical" suspect is in a computer crime?

What the most frequent motive is in such crimes?

How computer crimes can be prevented?

Introduction

Two computer programmers for an oil company plant who were responsible for the company's purchasing files created a fictitious supply company. They altered the company's computer database so that the oil company bought its supplies twice, once from the real supplier and once from the fictitious supply company, resulting in an embezzlement of several million dollars over a two-year period. The crime was discovered during a surprise audit, but the company declined to prosecute, not wanting to publicize how vulnerable its database was or how long it took to discover the embezzlement. Ironically, rather than being dismissed, the two embezzlers were promoted and placed in charge of computer security.

In another instance, a New York bank hired an outside consultant to work with its computer technicians on transferring funds electronically. In the course of his work, the consultant observed the access code being used to transfer the funds. He later used this access code to transfer a large sum of money to his own bank account. When the loss was finally discovered, management insisted that everyone in the section take a polygraph test, including the consultant. All except the consultant complied, and all passed. Although management was convinced the consultant had stolen the money, they did not prosecute. They simply changed their access code.

These cases illustrate three key characteristics of computer crimes.

- Computer crimes are relatively easy to commit and difficult to detect.
- Most computer crimes are committed by "insiders."
- Most computer crimes are not prosecuted.

Computers are becoming increasingly common in the home, workplace and school. In fact, according to one report ("House Passes Measure . . . ," 1998, p. 5): "Computer industry experts have estimated that . . . by the year 2002, 45 million children will use the Internet to do homework assignments." Sullivan (1999, p. 19) notes: "As history has proven, freedom and technological and societal advances usually come with a price." That price is manifested in the high cost of computer crime. Strandberg (1999, p. 24) predicts: "Cyber crime is the wave of the future. The computer world and the Internet frontier are perfect for criminal activities." Williams (1999, p. 18) adds: "With a dollar cost estimated as high as $100 billion annually, electronic crime presents NCTP [the National Cybercrime Training Partnership] and law enforcement at all levels with an urgent task."

Schmidt (1998, p. 38) asserts: "Investigating and prosecuting violations of law involving computers are formidable challenges." In fact, Wiles (1999, p. 72) estimates: "Ninety-seven percent of all high-tech [computer] crimes go undetected." It is not surprising, then, that officers assigned to investigate computer crimes must possess specific knowledge and skills. Meyer and Short (1998, p. 35) provide a job description for the "ideal" computer crime investigator:

> The officer chosen to investigate computer crime should be an experienced, competent investigator with the ability to think analytically. He should have a complete understanding of computer/fraud-related laws as well as their application. He should receive advanced training in the investigation of computer crime as well as being familiar with the major operating systems. This investigator should develop professional contacts that would assist in conducting investigations.

This chapter begins with a discussion of the scope of the computer crime problem as well as an explanation of the classification of such crimes and relevant terminology. This is followed by a discussion of the preliminary and the follow-up investigations. Next the subjects of suspects and evidence are presented. The chapter concludes with a discussion of the security of police department computers and the prevention of computer crime. ■

The Scope of the Problem

The current hot crime tool is the personal computer. Experts predict that the use of computers in homes, small and large offices, businesses and government installations will steadily increase; therefore, it can be expected that computer-related crimes will remain a serious police investigative problem. Sullivan (p. 21) states: "Internet crime represents a real and serious threat to the well-being of the public." Strandberg (p. 29) forecasts: "As more people get online, [computer] crime will grow exponentially."

The types of crimes committed with computers range from students changing school records and grades to thieves embezzling millions of dollars from large corporations to pedophiles luring unsuspecting children into child pornography. All types of offenses are increasing, and each presents unique challenges to investigators. Leary (1998, p. 100) observes:

> Many information technology (IT) professionals in product manufacturing and research and development continually worry about abuse, fraud and theft of intellectual property due to unauthorized access. Unauthorized access of PCs, workstations or networks containing mission critical information is a tangible corporate threat. A recent survey by the American Society for Industrial Security noted that losses due to intellectual theft have reached almost $300 billion.

Big business is not the only target of computer criminals. The rising numbers of at-home web "surfers" has opened the door to a whole new realm of cybercriminal. Sullivan (p. 18) explains:

> Every day, adults and children alike invite strangers into their home. By signing on to the Internet, they give strangers the opportunity to crash their computers, access and misuse personal information, manipulate their finances, and threaten their safety. . . .
>
> The Web offers anonymity and a buffer from getting caught, which, in turn, creates an opportunity for the "perfect" crime. Indeed, the Internet has become a breeding ground for crime. Thieves transfer funds from victims' bank accounts to their own. Vandals send computer viruses to destroy computers. Pedophiles exchange child pornography with others or chat with minors, building their trust so they can set up meetings under false pretenses.

Huycke (1997, p. 34) notes: "There is unprecedented growth in child pornography in the United States largely because of the Internet, which provides child sexual predators with a virtually undetectable means of sending and receiving illicit images of children." Armagh (1998, p. 11) adds: "The stark truth about the Internet is that it can expose children to vile and degrading materials in the sanctity of their homes and open the door to dangerous child sexual predators." Another report ("House Passes Measure . . . ," p. 5) emphasizes the dangers the Internet can pose to children: "Children who have been persuaded to meet their new on-line friend face to face have been kidnapped, raped, photographed for child pornography, and worse. Some children have never been heard from again."

Legislation

With the proliferation of on-line child pornography and other crimes involving the computer, new legislation is arising. For example ("House Passes Measure . . . ," p. 5):

> The House of Representatives has approved a package of tougher penalties for sex crimes against children, particularly those facilitated by the use of the Internet. H.R. 3494, the Child Protection and Sexual Predator Punishment Act, was passed on June 11, [1998], after members of Congress cited horror stories involving sexual predators making initial contact with young children through the Internet.

Enormous sums of money and tremendous quantities of information are transferred by computer daily. These transfers present a unique opportunity for the computer thief. In October 1986 then-President Reagan signed a bill to modernize the federal wiretap law to protect the privacy of high-tech communications. This bill makes it illegal to eavesdrop on electronic mail, video conference calls, conversations on cellular car phones and computer-to-computer transmissions. Other federal statutes relevant to computer-related crimes include patent laws, espionage and sabotage laws, trade secret laws, the Copyright Act of 1976 and the Financial Privacy Act of 1978.

Rasch (1996, p. 59) notes: "Computer technology has changed the nature of crime. And now legislatures and the courts are racing to catch up." He gives as an example the fact that one element of the crime of larceny requires proof of "taking away" the property, but in the case of computer crime, the stolen data may still be where they were originally. According to Rasch (p. 65): "Every state except Vermont has enacted a computer crime statute."

States address computer crime either by modifying existing statutes such as those pertaining to theft or by adding computer-crime chapters to their criminal codes. For example, some statutes state that disclosing the password of a computer system without the owner's consent is considered "unlawful use of a computer." Additionally, many existing state statutes are applicable to crimes involving computers (see Table 18.1). Well-defined statutes are critical to investigating and prosecuting computer crimes successfully.

Terminology and Classification

To fully understand and effectively investigate computer crime, officers need a working knowledge of relevant terminology and the categorization of such crimes.

Terminology

The FBI defines **computer crime** as "that which involves the addition, deletion, change or theft of information" (Pilant, 1999, p. 48). To effectively investigate computer crime, officers must be familiar with basic computer terminology as well as terms specifically related to computer crime:

- **Boot.** To start up a computer.
- **Byte.** The amount of space needed to store one character of information.
- **Cybercop.** An investigator involved in computer forensics. Also called a *cybersleuth*.
- **Cybercrime.** Any crime that is committed or helped by the use of a computer.

Table 18.1	Computer Crime and Current Statutes
Arson	Intentionally setting fire to a computer center
Burglary	Entering a computer center illegally with the intent to commit a crime therein
Extortion/blackmail	Making threats against the operator of a computer center to obtain money
Collusion	Working with others to commit a crime
Conspiracy	Several persons agreeing to commit an illegal act
Counterfeit	Copying or imitating computer documents
Embezzlement	Fraudulently converting property to personal use
Espionage	Stealing secret documents or information
Forgery	Issuing false documents
Fraud	Altering accounts or illegally transferring funds
Larceny	Theft of computer parts and materials
Malicious destruction of property	Destroying computer hardware or software
Murder	Tampering with life-sustaining computerized equipment resulting in the death of a patient
Receiving stolen property	Accepting goods or information stolen by computer, knowing they were stolen
Sabotage	Intentionally destroying computer information, programs or hardware
Theft	Stealing goods or money by use of a computer or stealing computer parts and materials

■ **Cyberpunk.** An antiestablishment rebel in cyberspace.

■ **Cyberspace.** The air that "exists" between two computers. Also called the *information superhighway*.

■ **Disk drive.** Physical location of disks on a computer (internal hard drives are usually labeled as C drive; floppy drives are generally identified as A or B drive).

■ **DOS.** Disk Operating System.

■ **Download.** To receive data, files or pictures from another computer. (Opposite of *upload*)

■ **E-mail.** Electronic mail.

■ **Floppy disk.** Magnetic media capable of storing large amounts of information (a 3 ½" disk can hold as much information as 470 sheets of paper).

■ **Gigabyte** (GB). One billion bytes.

■ **Hacker.** A person who specializes in unauthorized access into computer networks and other computer systems, primarily for the challenge and status. Not necessarily a negative term.

■ **Hard disk.** A nonremovable means of data storage located inside a computer.

■ **Hardware.** The computer equipment, such as hard drives, memory, CPUs, the monitor and so on.

■ **Kilobyte** (KB). One thousand bytes.

■ **Logic bomb.** Secretly attaches another program to a company's computer system. The attached program monitors the input data and waits for an error to occur. When this happens, the new program exploits the weakness to steal money or company secrets or to sabotage the system. For example, if a specific name fails to appear in the payroll system, the logic bomb would delete the entire payroll database.

■ **Megabyte** (MB). One million bytes (a typical 240MB hard drive could hold up to 27 four-drawer filing cabinets of information).

■ **Modem.** A device linking a computer to telephone or cable lines so that information can be exchanged with computers at different locations.

■ **Network.** Two or more computers connected for the purpose of sharing data and resources.

■ **PC.** A personal computer.

■ **Piracy.** The copying and use of computer programs in violation of copyrights and trade secret laws.

- **Program.** A series of commands instructing a computer to perform a desired task.
- **Scanner.** A device that can look at a typed page or photograph, convert it to digital format and copy it onto a disk.
- **Script.** A text file containing a sequence of computer commands.
- **Software.** Computer programs.
- **Trashing.** To scavenge through a business's garbage looking for useful information.
- **Trojan horse.** Uses one computer to reprogram another for illegal purposes. For example, the computer log-on process could log on a user but also record the user's password.
- **Upload.** To transfer data, files or pictures to another computer. (Opposite of *download*)
- **Virtual reality.** An artificial, interactive world created by computer technology (usually involving some kind of immersion system, such as a headset).
- **Virus (computer).** A program that attacks computer hardware and either replaces or destroys data.

Classification

As computer crime evolves and specific offenses emerge, different categories are being identified. Barrett and Joyce (1998, p. 34) note: "The more significant types of computer crimes include:

- stealing tangible or intangible assets
- destroying or altering data
- embezzling funds
- destroying or altering software
- defrauding consumers, investors or users
- stealing computer software
- producing/distributing child pornography."

Wiles (p. 73) states:

Unfortunately, computers are susceptible to more types of crime than just about anything else in your home or office. Not only do they face the old standby crimes of physical theft, destruction and vandalism, the newer more high-tech crimes may be even more damaging . . . , [including] software piracy, stealing source code, stealing credit card numbers, stealing passwords and login IDs, industrial espionage, PBX fraud, intentional insider damage and many others.

According to Meyer and Short (p. 28): "At their most basic level, computer crimes can be divided into

two general categories: 'computer as tool' and 'computer as target.' " The first category includes crimes in which the computer is used to commit fraud, embezzlement and other offenses by misusing passwords and access codes that protect information. For example, instead of using a gun to commit armed robbery, criminals use code-breaking programs and a computer to steal money or information from businesses and private parties. Schmidt (p. 38) notes:

An example of a computer's being used as an instrument of a crime would be [using] automated dialing programs, called war dialers. For example, a program might be set to automatically dial every phone number from 234-0000 to 234-9999 and identify phone lines that are connected to a computer system via modem. Once . . . identified, the hacker will then attempt to connect to the system using common techniques, such as logging in as "guest" with the password "1234." If not changed, this typical default combination permits a hacker to easily gain control of the user's computer system—including law enforcement records systems.

Strandberg (p. 26) reports: "[One man] used a 486 home computer, and stole 86,000 credit cards that had about 1 billion dollars worth of credit." He also states (p. 26): "The best way to steal from a bank is to get in and take a penny off every transaction, and that way you get a lot of money. All it takes is a computer to open up an account, access the bank's coding system and tell it to deposit a penny off of every transaction into an account." One factor that makes these crimes difficult to investigate and stop is the reluctance of victims to report the offense in the first place. Joyce and Barrett (1999, p. 35) point out: "The majority of hacker attacks that result in financial loss go unreported. There appear to be several reasons why financial organizations are reluctant to report cyber crime, but chief among them is the potential loss of the public's trust in the financial institution."

The second category includes crimes in which the computer itself or the information stored on it is the target. Thieves may burglarize homes and businesses, stealing computer systems and turning them over to computer "chop shops," where parts are changed, fake serial numbers are attached and the systems are resold to the public. This category of computer crime also includes offenses in which criminals break into systems to intentionally destroy data or steal information contained in the computer's storage banks. Williams (p. 25) notes:

In 1988, Cornell University graduate student Robert T. Morris, Jr., unleashed the Morris "worm," which attacked computers throughout the Internet, consumed their memories and crippled over 6,000 computers at a cost of $98 million in about 48 hours. . . . In 1990, a hacker group known as the Legion of Doom penetrated Bell South and gained the ability to alter and disrupt local telephone service, including the 911 emergency phone system.

Viruses

A **computer virus** is a program created to infect other programs with copies of itself. Viruses can be transmitted through communication lines or by an infected disk and can infect any PC. Just as human viruses are spread from one person to another, so computer viruses are spread from program to program. Viruses can be accidentally introduced into a system by disks carried between home and work.

An example is the "Melissa" computer virus, "which disguises itself as an 'important message' from a friend" and wreaked havoc on companies nationwide in March 1999 ("Ecolab, Honeywell among . . . ," 1999, p. A5):

The Computer Emergency Response Team (CERT) at Carnegie Mellon University in Pittsburgh estimated that more than 100,000 computers and 250 companies had been infected.

The FBI said military and government computers were sabotaged, along with thousands of other institutions' systems. . . .

The virus can crash e-mail systems because it directs computers to send more infected documents into cyberspace in great numbers. . . . All new Word documents created on an infected computer will also contain the virus. . . .

The fact that Melissa came via e-mail and was attached to address books made it more insidious than most viruses, said Jason Tschetter, a computer systems architect. . . . "Everybody has an address book, which interconnects so many lives and businesses," Tschetter said.

Another problem is distinguishing the genuine viruses from the hoaxes. Although nonsense viruses do nothing to disrupt or damage a computer system, they can cause short-term panic to spread and needless efforts

Jeff Carpenter of the Software Engineering Institute at Carnegie Mellon University in Pittsburgh works on an advisory warning regarding the Melissa computer virus.

to be spent in trying to contain them. McCumber (1999, p. 120) tells of one nonsense virus he received an e-mail warning about:

> DON'T BE TEMPTED Someone is sending out a very desirable screen-saver, the Budweiser Frogs—"BUDDYLST.ZIP." If you download it, you will lose everything!!! Your hard drive will crash and someone from the Internet will get your screen name and password!
>
> DO NOT DOWNLOAD THIS UNDER ANY CIRCUMSTANCE!!! . . . This is a new, very malicious virus and not many people know about it. The information was announced yesterday morning from Microsoft.
>
> Please share it with everyone who might access the Internet. Once again, pass this along to EVERYONE in your address book so this may be stopped.

According to McCumber, such warnings can keep an Information Technology (IT) department busy "putting out fires:"

> The problem for the IT security staff is the time and energy expended in an effort to debunk the bogus alert. Once the prank gains some momentum, management is forced to send out organization-wide messages asking people to refrain from forwarding the alerts to others both inside and outside the company. This anti-hysteria activity is also part of the insidious nature of these false warnings.

Normally, a discerning eye can quickly pick out the essential elements of a virus hoax: the overuse of exclamation points, the reliance on hyperbole and the unquoted references to reputable companies like AOL and Microsoft who should know about such things.

Nature of the Crimes

Computer crimes may involve the input data, the output data, the program, the hardware or computer time.

Input data may be manipulated. For example, fictitious suppliers may be entered as in the case of the oil company mentioned previously; figures may be changed or data may be removed. Some universities have experienced difficulties with student grades being illegally changed through use of a computer.

Output data may be obtained by unauthorized persons through wiretapping, electromagnetic pickup and theft of data sheets. In one case a Charles County, Maryland, teenage hacker used a home PC to access a list of credit card account numbers and then charged $2,000 worth of computer equipment from seven computer firms in California, Georgia, Michigan, Minnesota, New York, Ohio and Wisconsin. The crime was discovered when one computer firm became suspicious of fraud because several orders were received using different names but the same mailing address. The firm contacted the U.S. Secret Service. The youth was subsequently charged with seven counts of theft. Typically, however, output data are misused by an employee, not an outsider.

The *computer program* itself might be tampered with to add costs to purchased items or to establish a double set of records. In one instance a programmer feared he was about to lose his job, so he altered the computer's payroll program in such a way that if he was not issued a paycheck, all the payroll records would be scrambled (a logic bomb). The *computer hardware,* either the entire machine or some of its components, may be stolen or sabotaged. Williams notes (p. 20): "The trade in high-value computer chips has inspired such crimes as violent factory invasions and truck hijackings to steal the chips, and stolen chips have become barter in criminal drug transactions." Morrison (1999, p. 87) reports: "Nearly 2 billion dollars worth of personal computers is stolen in the United States each year, and only 3 percent of the equipment is ever recovered." Technology to assist in equipment recovery is discussed later in the chapter.

Computer time may be used for personal use.

The most common types of computer crime are misuse of computer services, program abuse and data abuse.

For the police to deter such crimes, they must be reported, thoroughly investigated and, when the evidence is sufficient, prosecuted. Too often, however, investigators assigned to computer-related crimes have not been trained to investigate these felonies. Those who commit these crimes are usually more technologically sophisticated than the investigators assigned to the cases. The technological disadvantage of many law enforcement agencies is painfully obvious.

Law enforcement at all levels needs additional training in the following areas: the unique requirements of computer-related crimes; computer evidence; identifying, marking and storing this evidence; the capabilities of present private and state agencies to analyze this evidence; and the procedures for developing teams to conduct investigations of computer-related crimes.

The Preliminary Investigation

When a report of a possible computer-related crime is received by a police department, the departmental report procedure is followed for the initial information. The officer assigned to the case interviews the reporting person to obtain the information necessary for determining whether a crime has been committed.

Overloading of the computer system or a lack of accessibility to records that the system was designed for may indicate illegal use of the computer. This type of crime may occur more frequently in a small computer operation, where greater opportunity exists. However, this makes the investigator's task easier because the number of suspects is reduced.

Employees are a good source of information unless they are suspected of collusion. Internal reporting of this type of crime is the same as for any other crime within an organization. It normally begins at the lowest level and reports upward to the supervisor and then to management. However, supervisory or management personnel are conceivably part of the collusion, so care must be used in the initial stages to eliminate those capable of being involved.

Normal or special audit procedures may have brought the crime to the attention of the proper persons, much the same as in embezzlement cases. Because computer operations require contact with other employees in collecting computer-input information, suspicion develops when employees appear to withdraw from other normal relationships.

If a crime is suspected or determined, further interviewing of the complainant and witnesses should continue. It is essential that information be obtained as soon as possible because evidence is easily destroyed. The principles in investigating computer crimes are basically the same as in other felonies. However, the investigator must have extensive knowledge of computers or seek the assistance of a computer expert.

Important Steps at the Crime Scene

Because of the highly technical nature of computer crimes, officers must receive "first responder" training, what Meyer and Short (p. 32) describe as "training in how to secure a computer system until more knowledgeable personnel arrive to retrieve the data." They note: "Inexperienced officers (and, occasionally, victims) sometimes damaged key evidence or rendered it inadmissible in court simply by accessing the computer to 'look around.'" Pilant (pp. 43–44) offers more specific suggestions on how investigators should proceed at a computer crime scene:

As with all crime scenes, first responders should refrain from touching anything, but should be aware that a computer may hold untold amounts of related information. Don't overlook it. In the case of a missing child, detectives asked the family about the child's hobbies and were told he spent a great deal of time on the computer. By examining the computer files, detectives learned that the child had been contacted by a pedophile and had unwittingly arranged a meeting. Detectives went to the meeting site and found the child with the pedophile.

Do not immediately seize the computer, turn it on or off, or start poking around with the mouse. Have someone on-scene who knows how to collect, tag and safely transport computer-related evidence.

If there is a modem, consider disconnecting it. Some criminals have been known to dial in and destroy evidence while police are searching the scene.

Keep your eyes open for passwords written on scrap paper or sticky notes and stashed around the crime scene.

Never work with the suspect's hard drive. Make a duplicate of it, and examine that. Examiners with the postal inspection service have even stricter guidelines; they do not work with the duplicate, but make copies of it for examination. Be sure to protect the original drive so no one can write to it.

Always boot the computer using your software, not the suspect's. Starting up a computer can change the data—changes that are time- and date-stamped on the files. If these dates are subsequent to the seizure of the computer, a defense attorney could use it to cloud the case or confuse a jury.

If you do not know what you're doing, find someone who does. Do not delude yourself into believing that noodling around on your home computer qualifies you as a computer forensics expert. If you're in over your head, admit it and get help.

Kopelev (2000, p. 65) suggests three "absolutes" for law enforcement professionals handling computer evidence:

1. Be certain that no changes have been made to the information.

2. Take precautions while gathering evidence. . . . Original evidence (that which is actually seized) should never be examined before a bit-level image has been made.

3. Be able to testify technically to the integrity of the evidence.

Follow-Up Investigation

Once the initial report has been completed and the general information has been obtained, a plan is made for the remaining investigation. The plan will assist in a directed investigation even though deviations from the plan may occur because exigencies may not be known at the beginning. The plan should identify the problem, the crime that has been committed, areas and people involved in the crime, equipment used, internal and external staffing needs, approximate length of time required for the investigation, a method of handling and storing evidence and the assignment of personnel. Motive, opportunity, means of commission, the type of security system bypassed and known bypass techniques must be ascertained. It is also necessary to determine which federal, state or local laws are applicable to the specific type of computer crime committed.

Sometimes it is necessary to develop an undercover operation within the organization. This operation must be headed by a computer expert and coordinated with the nonsuspects. Lists must be prepared of all persons to be used in the case and the evidence to be obtained. Furthermore, if search warrants are necessary, those arrangements must be made.

Search Warrants

You may have to obtain a search warrant to locate the evidence necessary to prosecute successfully. Searches may also be conducted by consent; in other words, the owner of the materials may give voluntary consent for a search. However, if the suspect is unknown, this is not desirable because it could alert the person who committed the crime. In such cases, you must obtain a search warrant. Privacy issues surrounding some or all of the information contained in the computer evidence desired may pose a legal technicality. If the organization involved is the victim of the crime, its management normally grants permission. If it is not the victim, it may be necessary to obtain permission from persons contained in the file, which could be an enormous task. It may be better to take the evidence to a court and obtain court permission if possible.

Investigators may have in their possession both a consent search form and a search warrant, thus avoiding the possibility of destruction of evidence. Consent is better than a search warrant in that it avoids the usual attack by the defense in search-warrant cases.

- - - - - - - - -

Request the consent initially, and if that fails, use the search warrant—in that order.

- - - - - - - - -

If the order is reversed, the consent is bastardized because the search warrant was used as a threat in obtaining voluntary consent. The areas of search and the sought items must be specified in the warrant. A person connected with the computer operation in question should assist with the search warrant to provide information to the investigators, and this person should accompany the investigators with the affidavit for warrant in case the judge requires technical explanations that the investigator cannot provide regarding the equipment and the evidence desired.

Evidence

Regarding computer crimes, interviewing and interrogating techniques are basically the same as for other felonies, as are search techniques and patterns used. The major difference is in the types of evidence involved. Pilant (p. 43) cautions: "The biggest difference between traditional, tangible evidence and computer evidence is its fragility. Electronic evidence can be altered, damaged or destroyed simply by turning the computer on or off at the wrong time." McEwan (1995, p. 93) suggests the following when dealing with computer evidence (excerpt used by permission of the publisher):

1. Obtain a search warrant, including the computers and related items to be seized.

2. To secure the site, remove all persons and prevent further access.

3. Immediately evaluate any possible evidence displayed on the monitor. If possible, photograph the screen and then unplug the system from the wall. Unplug any phone lines leading to the computer. NEVER use the toggle switch to turn off the machine; always unplug from the wall. [Unplugging without first shutting down the system risks losing any open documents!]

4. Photograph the rear of the machine to record the cabling configuration.

5. Label the cabling system (using masking tape and pen) before disconnecting cables. Label all ports and slots for proper reconstruction later.

6. If more than one system is seized, keep the components separate. For example, label the monitor from the first system #A1. The monitor from the second system #B1.

7. Collect all operating manuals and software found at the scene, including collections of floppy disks and peripheral components such as printers and

keyboards. Pay attention to scraps of paper nearby that may contain passwords.

8. In boxing the system for transport, avoid static charges. Do not wrap the unit in plastic and keep the unit away from electromagnetic sources such as a radio transmitter in the trunk of your car. This could cause loss of electronically stored data.

9. The property room should be temperature and climate controlled. Again, keep the unit away from magnetic sources such as stereo speakers.

Mendell (1999, p. 38) notes the importance of photographing physical evidence:

> The investigator should take pictures of any damaged equipment and transmission lines. He or she should . . . include pictures of tools, materials, chemicals, accelerant residues, paints, associated containers, and electronic equipment used in the crime. In addition, these items should be secured for the police department's forensics unit. . . .
>
> If there are slogans spray-painted on walls or equipment, security managers should . . . use color film to capture the hues and shades employed by the vandals or extremists. The colors may be an important part of the perpetrator's "statement." . . .
>
> If any communications or transmissions lines have been cut or spliced, investigators should photograph the cut with a high-magnification lens. The cut patterns on the wires may match unique metal imperfections on tools found later in the case.

Other procedures for processing and caring for evidence differ from those for the traditional crime scene because of the nature of the evidence, but many of the approaches suggested in Chapter 5 are applicable. Obtaining evidence in computer cases is unique in that the evidence is not as readily discernible as in most other criminal cases. Computer disks, although visible in the physical sense, contain "invisible" information.

- - - - - - - - -

Computer evidence is often contained on disks, is not readily discernible and also is highly susceptible to destruction.

- - - - - - - - -

Start the investigation as soon as possible to obtain the physical evidence. Destruction of the program or of information files may be programmed in so that any attempt to access the information or to print it will cause it to self-destruct. Determine early on the computer system used and the types of physical evidence available from this system. Include this information in the application for a search warrant.

In more complex cases, the volume of evidence is significant because large amounts of information can be stored on a single disk or CD. In the majority of felony investigations, the amount of evidence is not a major problem, but in the case of computer crimes, the evidence may involve hundreds of disks or CDs. Copying this amount of evidence can be costly and time consuming. In addition, taking equipment into evidence can be a major problem because some equipment is heavy and bulky.

To overcome some of these evidence-collection challenges, new cybercop tools are being developed. Dees (1999, p. 14) describes one such device:

> A new portable hard drive duplication tool is now available that will permit investigators to quickly create a mirror image of one or more hard drives in the field without removing the original to a remote site. The Datafast D-101 is a handheld device, about the size of a hardcover novel, that is capable of transferring data at speeds in excess of 400 megabytes per minute.

Investigators must determine whether backup copies of existing file materials are available, thus eliminating the necessity of copying or reproducing them. If backup copies are available, the chance of the same crime being committed against the copies is diminished, and continued use of the computer during the investigation is permitted. Obviously, copying disks must conform to the rules of evidence specified in Chapter 5.

The condition in which evidence is found may also reveal important clues about possible suspects. Mendell (pp. 38, 40) explains:

> Certain physical clues [suggest] that the incident was the work of an insider. . . . Investigators should seek answers to the following questions:
>
> ■ Do conditions make it clear that the offending party knew how to bypass security controls— where to get keys, what time of day to attack, and exactly where to go?
>
> ■ Was the incident orderly? The element of randomness is rarely present when the offender is an insider. . . .
>
> ■ Did tools that aided in the crime belong to the company?

Types of Evidence

Some form of documentation is the most frequent type of computer evidence.

Evidence is normally in the form of disks, data reports, programming or other printed information run from information in the computer.

In a very few cases the evidence is the computer equipment. Also, it may be necessary to keep the equipment operating to continue business. Investigators must work with management to determine how to best accomplish this. If the evidence cannot be moved from the premises, management may have to provide on-premises security with their own guards or with temporarily hired security until the evidence can be copied or otherwise secured by court order or by police security.

Mendell (pp. 38–43) summarizes the basic types of evidence in computer crimes cases:

- Physical evidence—the computer equipment itself (consoles, terminals, monitors, cables, etc.)

- Software evidence—error reports, access reports, system crashes, financial records, code changes, corrupt media, etc.

- Human evidence—assessment of the employee population for signs of persons who are not adjusting well to the work environment (may include access control, entry logs, video surveillance, changes in job assignments, vacation log, overtime logs, etc.)

Legal Aspects of Obtaining Computer Evidence

Stolen information is difficult to evaluate. The question is whether such intangible property *can* be stolen. Investigation is hampered by a lack of precedents or clear definitions in this area. As Schmidt (p. 42) observes:

In dealing with . . . [computer evidence] issues, numerous legal and technical aspects must be addressed. Many of the laws pertaining to evidence search and seizure were written years ago, . . . and often have not kept pace with technological advances. Since computer data can't be seen, like paper documents, special language must be included in search warrants and affidavits to allow seizure of computer equipment and peripherals that might contain evidence.

As in all cases, the evidence must follow the best-evidence rule. Individuals must testify in court to the authenticity of the disks, CDs or printouts. The materials must be proven to be either the originals or substitutes in accordance with the best-evidence rule. This evidence must be tied to its source by a person qualified to testify about it. Because computers often use magnetically produced signals, printouts must be made of these signals, and computer experts must verify that the printouts are copies of the original data.

Searching for and Processing Physical Evidence

Search techniques and patterns described in Chapter 4 are applicable to computer-related crime searches. Seal the area and search it according to the type and location of the evidence necessary for prosecution. Avoid pressures to speed up the search because of a desire for continued use of the system, but at the same time, return the equipment as soon as possible.

Information about the hardware should include all identification data such as the manufacturer, model, identification numbers and the language used by the system such as Fortran or Cobol. Does it include a modem?

Information about the software is also important. The software must usually be copied or printouts made. This can often be an extremely time-consuming task: "Gathering information from a computer disk is like going through someone's trash—it's tedious and demanding work" ("Finding Needles in . . . ," 1999, p. 5). If a department's forensics unit is untrained in analyzing computer hard drives, you may obtain outside help, but the turnaround time is often prohibitive to the course of the investigation. For example, "The average wait for the U.S. Attorney's office in Louisville to have a computer hard drive analyzed by the FBI is seven months. . . . The average hard drive can take an expert two months to read" ("Finding Needles in . . . ," p. 5).

Fortunately, as computer crime gains momentum, technical companies are realizing the benefits to law enforcement of tools that expedite the examination and investigation process. Harrington (1999, p. E15) reports that One Tough ComputerCop Professional is a program that "find[s] hidden or trashed files, bypass[es] password protection and automatically restore[s] erased documents." He notes the software "allows law enforcement to zip through a computer's hard drive in a matter of hours or even minutes to scan for incriminating words or images."

Investigators must reproduce the material within the rules of evidence. Identification should include the case number, date, time and the initials of the person taking the evidence into custody. To mark a metal container, use a carbide metal scribe such as that used in marking items in the Operation Identification program. Use a permanent black-ink marker or felt-tip pen to identify disks. If the evidence is in a container, both the container and the inside disks should be identified in the same way. Marking both identically avoids interchangeability and retains the credibility of the item as evidence. Use normal evidence tape to mark containers and to seal them.

> Avoid contact with the recording surfaces of computer tapes and disks. Never write on disk labels with a ballpoint pen or pencil or use paper clips or rubber bands with disks. To do so may destroy the data they contain.

Usually printouts must be made of data contained on computer disks or CDs. These printouts should be clearly identified and matched with the software they represent.

Storage problems can arise because of the nature of the evidence in computer-related crimes. Store disks in the manufacturers' containers, and store all computer evidence in areas away from strong sources of light. Computers and the information stored in them and on disks are sensitive to temperature extremes and dust. Exposing magnetic media to any magnetic field such as radio waves, motors, degaussers or speakers can alter or destroy data. Disks should be stored vertically, not stacked one on top of another. In addition, do not use plastic bags to store computer equipment or disks because they can cause static electricity and condensation, both of which can damage electronically stored data.

If possible, obtain from management the procedures normally used for storing their disks and other materials. If this is not possible, contact the manufacturer for this information.

> Store computer disks vertically, at approximately 70°F and away from strong light, dust and magnetic fields. Do not use plastic bags.

Laboratory Examination of Evidence

Crime laboratories, either public or private, have much of the equipment necessary to examine computer evidence. Computer hardware has individual characteristics, much the same as other items of evidence such as tools. The hardware might also contain fingerprints, but frequently the perpetrator's fingerprints are not unusual because he or she has legal access to the hardware. Printers have individual characteristics, much the same as typewriters. Document examinations of printouts can be made, and these printouts can also be analyzed for fingerprints. Fragments of software may be compared. And, as discussed, the entire file content of a computer's hard drive may be analyzed for incriminating text or images.

Data Recovery

Data recovery is a computer forensic technique that requires not only an extensive knowledge of computer technology and storage devices but also an understanding of the laws of search and seizure and the rules of evidence. Software programs can help investigators restore data on damaged hard drives or disks or recover information that has been deleted. Stites (1991, p. 165) provides some basic rules for data recovery:

- Develop a plan. Don't hurry and don't allow others to rush you. Identify the hardware and software needed. Pick a quiet site where you will not be interrupted.
- Do not use the original seized disks or hard disk for examination. Make copies of the seized data.
- Write-protect the diskettes and hard disk.
- Do not process the data on the seized computer because the suspect may have set up a booby trap to destroy data, the hard drive or both.
- Examine the data using a utility program designed for this purpose.
- Print all files.

Special Challenges in Investigation

Special challenges in investigating computer crimes include the scarcity of investigators, attorneys, probation officers and judges who understand computers and computer crimes and the tremendous proliferation of computer crimes and losses. Strandberg (p. 28) remarks: "Law enforcement, from the start, is behind the eight ball. Police don't have the money, the time, or the technology to keep pace with the bad guys. Cyber criminals often have unlimited resources, unlimited access to the newest technology, and unlimited time to devote to criminal action." Meyer and Short (p. 28) concur: "Criminals are more computer-literate than the investigators who track them." Williams (p. 25) adds:

> Surveys taken in 1997 and 1998 . . . revealed that public awareness of the problem [of computer crime] remains low. Most seriously of all, there is a greater demand for training than there is training available— especially for seizure, handling and processing of computer-based evidence—and even when there is training, there is often no clear career path to effectively utilize the trained officer's skills.

Difficulties exist in determining jurisdiction when the equipment is located in one community and the computer that is illegally entered electronically is in another state or even another country. For example, in 1994 a 28-year-old in St. Petersburg, Russia, hacked into Citibank's cash-management system in New York City and stole millions of dollars. As Joyce and Barrett (p. 35) note: "The Internet's ability to make physical distance irrelevant causes many problems for law enforcement. Where did [the] crime take place—St. Petersburg or New York City? Who has jurisdiction?"

Other major challenges in investigating computer-related crimes include the needs to determine the exact nature of the crime and to gather evidence in ways that do not disrupt an organization's operation. Furthermore, many victims are reluctant to press charges, and the length of time needed to investigate computer crimes may extend to a year or longer for thorough investigations.

The Investigative Team

Based on the information received, a plan of action is developed that includes assigning personnel and obtaining specialists for the investigative team. Police agencies that must investigate complex art thefts, bank embezzlements or other types of thefts in which they have had little expertise seek the advice and services of experts. For computer-related crimes this is also true because the evidence may involve highly technical database systems, operational systems and equipment that are unfamiliar to police officers.

- - - - - - - -

Investigating computer crime often requires a team approach.

- - - - - - - -

The investigative team is responsible for assigning all team personnel according to their specialties, including securing outside specialists if necessary; securing the crime scene area; obtaining search warrant appli-

cations; determining the specific hardware and software involved; searching for, obtaining, marking, preserving and storing evidence; obtaining necessary disks, printouts and other records; and preparing information for investigative reports.

In the majority of computer-related crimes, investigators seek assistance from the victim who owns the equipment, database processing technicians, auditors, highly trained computer experts or programmers and others. If necessary, the team contacts the manufacturer of the equipment, the consulting services of a local university or a private computer-crime investigative agency.

To assist in combatting increasing computer-related crimes, government and private businesses are developing computer crime teams similar to the FBI's kidnapping crime teams and the BATF's arson investigation specialist teams. The FBI's Computer Analysis Response Team (CART) helps not only federal agents but also state and local law enforcement. CART helps write and execute search warrants, seize and catalog evidence, and perform routine examinations of digital evidence. Pilant (p. 38) reports: "At CART headquarters are 26 highly trained people doing the kind of lab examinations of digital evidence that field agents are not trained to do, or that are too massive to do in the field."

As Robinson (2000, p. 6) notes: "Cyber-crime poses a unique challenge to law enforcement . . . . To successfully overcome this challenge, law enforcement agencies at all levels of government must work in partnership to develop the capabilities that will be necessary to detect, investigate, and apprehend cyber-criminals."

Police agencies in many states are forming cooperative groups and providing training seminars on investigating computer crimes. Such groups are especially helpful for small departments, which are less likely to have the needed expertise in-house. For example, Florida's law enforcement agencies can submit computer evidence to the Computer Evidence Recovery (CER) program, which also trains the state's law enforcement agencies to prepare warrants to search computers and to follow specific procedure when seizing computer-crime evidence.

Training in computer crimes investigation is also available from other sources, notes Williams (p. 18):

> Working in partnership with state, local, federal and international law enforcement agencies, the U.S. Department of Justice has developed the National Cybercrime Training Partnership (NCTP) [to address] . . . the problem of electronic crime. . . . NCTP will work with all levels of law enforcement to

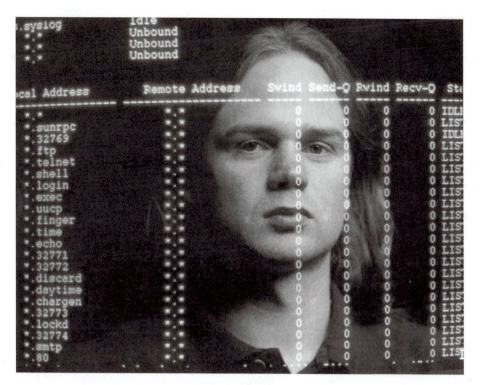

Professional computer hacker Steve Turcich is shown in this double-exposure photograph. Turcich works for companies that actually pay him to break into their computers, helping them perfect security systems.

- develop and promote a sound long-range strategy for high-tech police work in the 21st century, including interagency and interjurisdictional cooperation, information networking and technical training;

- garner public and political understanding of the problem and generate support for solutions; and

- serve as a proactive force [to] focus the momentum of the entire law enforcement community to ensure that proposed solutions are fully implemented.

The NCTP is open to any law enforcement agency involved in electronic crime investigation, prosecution or training (p. 26). Another resource to help law enforcement handle computer crimes is the High-Technology Crime Investigation Association (HTCIA), reports Wiles (p. 75): "The HTCIA chapters offer some of the best training available for both law enforcement agencies and corporate security specialists."

Suspects

A major difference in computer crime investigation, other than the involvement with high technology and complex equipment, is the type of person who commits such crimes.

- - - - - - - - - -

Those involved in computer crimes are most commonly technical people such as data entry clerks, machine operators, programmers, systems analysts and hackers.

- - - - - - - - - -

These people have the necessary knowledge of and access to the computer system. Although some computer users may feel they are free to do whatever they please on the computer, a Florida resident learned differently. Although he claimed that, only as a joke, he e-mailed a friend telling him that weasels would rip the flesh off his corpse, he was convicted under the state's stalking laws for threats by computer.

People who commit computer crimes are often regarded as honest, hardworking employees and as respected members of the community. They are not criminal types in the usual sense of the word, nor are they repeat offenders in this or other criminal endeavors. More than likely they have no prior criminal record. Therefore, normal criminal record checks and modus operandi comparisons are not usually useful in determining suspects. Profiling the typical computer criminal poses a special challenge, as it is a very eclectic group.

The suspect may act alone or in collusion in committing the crime. In cases of internal abuse, commission normally occurs during authorized use or during periods of overtime when the employee is working alone. Developing a suspect's work history assists in locating past opportunities for committing the offense. The suspect's training will provide information about his or her knowledge of computers and computer languages. Comparisons of these factors with the equipment at the crime scene will help determine whether the suspect was capable of the crime.

A complete review of everyone within the organization who has access, type of access, technical capability or opportunity greatly assists the investigation if the crime is internal. Check for employees who have a history of computer crimes.

Investigators will often find that computer-related thefts originate from agencies that already have highly trained computer personnel on their staffs. If the theft is internal, the investigator may confidentially involve personnel of that agency who are not suspect. In internal crimes of this nature, the number of suspects will necessarily be limited, as opposed to a crime such as a residential burglary in which the suspect could be a local or an outsider. In computer crimes for theft, supervisory and management personnel may use computers to hide their offenses and then misdirect the investigative team toward subordinate staff who have committed relatively minor transgressions.

Internal auditing procedures are normally started with the security director involved. If an employee is suspected at this point, management must decide whether to handle the matter internally or proceed with prosecution. If the decision is to handle the matter internally, then the case is closed. If not, the investigation contin-

ues, often involving state or private investigators. Such individuals may have the expertise and anonymity not available to local police departments.

Motivations

Research has found four motivations for internal abuse, fairly evenly distributed in frequency.

Frequent motives for computer crimes are ignorance of proper professional conduct, misguided playfulness, personal gain and maliciousness or revenge.

Revenge is a motive when a suspect feels that management has committed injustices or when militants destroy computer centers that deal with controversial issues or products. In contrast, computer hackers gain entrance to computer information simply for the challenge of breaking the code. A number of these types of crimes have been reported nationally by the news media.

Hackers

Although a significant amount of computer crime is perpetrated by employees within a victim company, another threat comes from the outside—from hackers. Joyce and Barrett (p. 28) report: "The typical hacker . . . is a white male, aged 15 to 34, who began using the computer underground between the ages of 10 and 25." Other profiles of hackers reveal the average number of hours per week

Tsutomu Shimomura, computational physicist and computer security expert, helped to break the Kevin Mitnick cybertheft case. Mitnick, until apprehended, was cyberspace's most wanted hacker.

involved with computer crime is 11.7, the average number of victims is 154.2, and the average age when introduced to computer crime is 15 years (p. 28). Joyce and Barrett state:

> With the hacking tools and methods . . . readily available on the Internet—many of which require little technical expertise—hackers access others' computers to . . . [steal] information, [launch] attacks on other computer systems or simply [explore] the target computer system.

They (p. 32) identify various motivations for hackers: "Breaking into computer systems motivates malicious hackers because it provides an ego-boosting sense of power and control. . . . The cat-and-mouse game between hackers and system administrators is the motivation that currently drives most of today's hackers."

Hackers are continually seeking new challenges, including that of breaking into supposedly secure government systems, including those of law enforcement.

Security of the Police Department's Computers

When considering computer crime, law enforcement officers should not overlook the possibility that their own computers may be accessed by criminals. Any computer attached to a telephone line is accessible by unauthorized persons outside the department, even thousands of miles away on a different continent. Schmidt (p. 38) warns: "Police record computers connected to phone lines or to the Internet are especially vulnerable to those wishing to obtain or alter criminal justice information." The only way to ensure that confidential data stay that way is to keep computers disconnected from phone or cable lines.

Preventing Computer Crime

Although computers and related technologies have added immeasurable benefits and value to our quality of life, this technology has opened up new avenues of crime and exploitation. According to Parsons (1998, p. 7): "Computer hackers and other cyberspace criminals have grown better able to penetrate computer systems once thought secure. . . . In response to this growing threat, . . . the U.S. Department of the Navy [has] established the Computer Investigations and Operations Department (CIOD). . . . Members of the CIOD work by the motto, 'A bit of prevention is worth a gigabyte of cure.'" The CIOD publishes and distributes a variety of

pamphlets, each geared to a specific audience. Examples of these publications are "Protecting Your Children in Cyberspace," "Taking a Byte Out of Computer Crime," "Protecting Our Networks: Electronic Triage for System Administrators," and a pamphlet highlighting CIOD's Computer Crime Prevention Hotline.

One reason computer crime has proliferated among businesses in the private sector is that many managers are unprepared to deal with it. They may be ignorant, indifferent or both. They also frequently lack control over their information. Without standards to violate, there is no violation.

- - - - - - - - -

> Computer crimes can be prevented by educating top management and employees and by instituting internal security precautions. Top management must make a commitment to defend against computer crime.

- - - - - - - - -

Management must institute organization-wide policies to safeguard its databases, and it must educate employees in these policies and any security measures that are implemented. Management should also take internal security precautions. Data disks and CDs should have backup copies and be kept in locked files. One of the most important, yet most frequently overlooked, security measures is to use a paper shredder for all sensitive documents once they are no longer needed. Schmidt (p. 45) recommends:

> Community services or crime prevention functions can also [help address] the computer crime problem. . . . Computer safety information can be easily incorporated into existing block-watch programs to increase awareness among both parents and children. Local businesses need to understand how they can protect themselves from electronic break-ins. . . . Publications, awareness meetings and crime prevention pamphlets are needed to inform citizens of the dangers of those who would use this new technology against them.

Middleton (1999, p. 59) advises:

> In the physical world, a [hired] security professional . . . will look over the property as if "casing the joint" to spot and shore up weaknesses before a criminal can exploit them. The same approach makes sense for a company's computer network. Security can best assess the system's exposures by focusing on the perspective of a potential intruder. In many cases, security practitioners . . . [run] automated programs that look for system vulnerabilities.

One technique gaining momentum in the effort to increase computer security is biometrics. According to

Leary (p. 100): "Increased manageability, scalability and dropping costs have renewed interest in using biometric devices as a form of computer and network access control." He further notes (p. 101):

> Biometric devices offer an advantage over traditional passwords since they authenticate users through characteristics the user can't lose or give away. . . . Currently, biometrics making the greatest impact on computer and network access controls are facial, voice and fingerprint recognition, mainly due to their dramatic drop in cost.

Other technological advances have helped curb computer crime and loss from computer theft. For example, a new tracking device called CompuTrace helps locate and recover lost or stolen personal computers in much the same way the Lo Jack device tracks stolen cars. According to Morrison (pp. 87–88):

> When a user installs CompuTrace software on his computer, a monitoring program called an "Agent" is hidden on the hard drive. The "Agent" remains undetectable to anyone using the computer. As soon as CompuTrace is installed and registered with Absolute Software [the designer of the program], it continuously monitors the location of the user's equipment. . . .
>
> If the computer is stolen, the owner of the computer simply notifies Absolute Software that his machine is missing. The company alerts the CompuTrace server. The next time the "Agent" calls in, the source of the call is tracked and immediately reported to local law enforcement. . . .
>
> CompuTrace primarily is marketed toward the business community. The price per computer is about $89 per year.

Morrison (p. 88) notes another computer theft recovery software program called Stealth 95/98, which operates like CompuTrace but is targeted toward individual users and retails for $29. Stealth 95/98 Theft Recovery Software can provide the location of a stolen PC notebook or desktop running Windows 95, 98 or NT. This information is passed on to the owner and to the proper authorities.

Summary

Computer crimes are relatively easy to commit and difficult to detect. Most computer crimes are committed by insiders, and few are prosecuted.

Computer crimes may involve input data, output data, the program, the hardware or computer time. The most common types of computer crime are misuse of computer services, program abuse and data abuse.

If investigators possess a search warrant and wish to conduct a search, they should first request permission for the search. If consent is given, the search can proceed right away. If it is not given, then the warrant can be served and the search conducted.

Evidence in computer crimes is often contained on disks or CDs, is not readily discernible, and is highly susceptible to destruction. In addition to information on disks or CDs, evidence may take the form of data reports, programming or other printed materials based on information from computer files.

Investigators who handle computer disks should avoid contact with the recording surfaces. Never write on computer disk labels with a ballpoint pen or pencil and never use paper clips on or rubber bands around computer disks, for to do so may destroy the data they contain. Computer disks taken as evidence should be stored vertically, at approximately 70°F and away from bright light, dust and magnetic fields. CDs should be handled by their edges and, as with disks, kept away from extreme heat, direct sunlight, dust and magnetic fields.

Investigating such crimes often requires a team approach. Persons involved in computer crimes are usually technical people such as data entry clerks, machine operators, programmers, systems analysts and hackers. Common motivators for such crimes are ignorance, misguided playfulness, personal gain and maliciousness or revenge.

Computer crimes can be prevented by educating top management and employees and by instituting internal security precautions.

Checklist
Computer Crime

- Who is the complainant?
- Has a crime been committed?
- What is the specific nature of the crime reported to the police?

- What statutes are applicable? Can the required elements of the crime be proven?

- Has the crime been terminated, or is it continuing?

- Is the origin of the crime internal or external?

- Does the reported crime appear to be a cover-up for a larger crime?

- What barriers exist to investigating the crime?

- What are the make, model and identification numbers of the equipment involved? The hardware? The software?

- Is the equipment individually or company owned?

- Is an operations manual available for the hardware?

- Is a flowchart of computer operations available? Is a computer configuration chart available?

- Is documentation for the software available?

- What computer language is involved? What computer programs are involved?

- What is the degree of technicality involved? Simple or complex?

- What are the input and output codes?

- What accounting procedures were used?

- What is the database system? What are the system's main vulnerabilities?

- Is there a built-in security system? What is it? How was it bypassed?

- What are the present security procedures? How were they bypassed?

- Can the equipment be shut down during the search and investigation or for a sufficient time to investigate the portion essential to obtaining evidence?

- Can the computer records be "dumped" without interfering with the ongoing operations, or must the system be closed down and secured?

- Does the equipment need to be operational to conduct the investigation?

- Does the reporting person desire prosecution or only disciplinary action?

- Are there any suspects? Internal or external?

- If internal, are they presently employed by the reporting organization or person?

- Is a list of current employees and their work histories available? Are all current computer-related job descriptions available?

- What level of employees is involved? Is an organizational table available?

- How can the investigation be carried out without the knowledge of the suspect?

- What is the motive for the crime?

- What competitors might be suspect?

- What types of evidence are needed or likely to be present?

- What external experts are needed as part of the search team?

- Does the available evidence meet the best-evidence requirement?

- What are the main barriers to the continued investigation? How can they be overcome?

Application

A. (From "Marijuana Buyers Club Sets Up Site on Internet." *Las Vegas Review Journal,* November 14, 1996, p. 14E.)

After voters in one state approved a proposition legalizing marijuana use "for medicinal purposes," an Internet site began offering marijuana to severely ill or disabled people who need it requiring proof of a doctor's recommendation to use marijuana. The site's director states, "I don't want people trying to order marijuana without the proper authorization. I'm really trying to do this in keeping with the proper spirit of [the proposition]."

A police sergeant from the jurisdiction from which the marijuana is being shipped contends the operation is clearly illegal. "Along with supplying and selling marijuana, which are felonies, I imagine you could cook up something extra for using the Internet," he said.

The site is receiving orders from all over the state, as well as from people outside the state who are using in-state mailing addresses.

Questions

1. What crime is being committed, if any?
2. Who has jurisdiction?
3. What steps would you take to conduct this investigation?
4. How would you prepare a search warrant?
5. What types of evidence would you look for?

B. A local firm contacts your police department concerning theft of customer credit-card and Social Security numbers from their computer records. This operation and theft is suspected to be internal, so present and past employees are the prime suspects.

Questions

1. How would you plan to initiate the investigation?
2. What statements would you obtain?
3. Would you use internal or external assistance?
4. What types of evidence would you need?

Discussion Questions

1. What do you perceive to be the differences between investigating computer crime and investigating other felonies?

2. What are the differences in interviewing and interrogating individuals involved in computer crime?

3. What are the legal differences between a computer crime investigation and other felony investigations?

4. If you were in charge of a computer crime investigation team, what would you include in your plan?

5. Do you have a computer crime law in your municipality? Your state?

6. Is anyone in your police department trained specifically in computer crime investigation? If so, where was this training obtained?

7. Do you have a computer? If so, how do you store your information?

8. What type of computer security is used in your local police department?

9. Of all the various types of computer crime, which do you think is the most serious?

10. What do you consider the greatest challenge in investigating computer crimes?

References

Armagh, Daniel. "A Safety Net for the Internet: Protecting Our Children." *Juvenile Justice,* Vol. V, No. 1, May 1998, pp. 9–15.

Barrett, Shawn and Joyce, Matt. "Computers and Crime: Are You Prepared to Meet the Challenge?" *The Police Chief,* Vol. LXV, No. 5, May 1998, p. 34.

Dees, Tim. "Translators, Facial Composite Software and the Cybercop Tool." *Law and Order,* Vol. 47, No. 8, August 1999, pp. 13–14.

"Ecolab, Honeywell among Companies Hit by 'Melissa.' " (Minneapolis/St. Paul) *Star Tribune,* March 30, 1999, p. A5.

"Finding Needles in a Computer Haystack." *Law Enforcement News,* Vol. XXV, No. 513, June 15, 1999, p. 5.

Harrington, Mark. "Computer Cop Finds Evidence for Real Cops." (Minneapolis/St. Paul) *Star Tribune,* July 15, 1999, p. E15.

"House Passes Measure to Bar Child Abuse through the Internet." *Criminal Justice Newsletter,* Vol. 29, No. 10, May 15, 1998, p. 5.

Huycke, D. "Protecting Our Children: U.S. Customs Service Child Pornography Enforcement Program." *Police Chief Journal,* February 1997, p. 34.

Joyce, Mattias and Barrett, Shawn. "The Evolution of the Computer Hacker's Motives." *The Police Chief,* Vol. LXVI, No. 2, February 1999, pp. 28–35.

Kopelev, Sergio D. "Cracking Computer Codes." *Law Enforcement Technology,* Vol. 27, No. 1, January 2000, pp. 60–67.

Leary, Mark. "Biometrics Increase Computer Security." *Security Technology and Design,* Vol. 8, No. 8, August 1998, pp. 100–102.

McCumber, John R. "Hoaxes, Scams, and the Nonsense Virus." *Security Technology and Design,* Vol. 9, No. 3, March 1999, pp. 120–121.

McEwan, Tom. "Cybercops." *Law and Order,* March 1995, pp. 93–94.

Mendell, Ronald L. "Matching Wits against Bits." *Security Management,* Vol. 43, No. 5, May 1999, pp. 36–43.

Meyer, Jon'a F. and Short, Charles. "Investigating Computer Crime." *The Police Chief,* Vol. LXV, No. 5, May 1998, pp. 28–35.

Middleton, Bruce. "Using the Hacker's Toolbox." *Security Management,* Vol. 43, No. 6, June 1999, pp. 59–65.

Morrison, Richard D. "PC Call Home: Program Tracks Stolen PCs." *Law Enforcement Technology,* Vol. 26, No. 4, April 1999, pp. 87–89.

Parsons, Matt. "Crime Prevention and the Electronic Frontier." *FBI Law Enforcement Bulletin,* Vol. 67, No. 10, October 1998, pp. 7–10.

Pilant, Lois. "Electronic Evidence Recovery." *The Police Chief,* Vol. 23, No. 2, February 1999, pp. 37–48.

Rasch, Mark D. "Legal Lessons in the Computer Age." *Security Management,* April 1996, pp. 59–67.

Robinson, Michael D. "Law Enforcement Response to Cyber-Crime." *The Police Chief,* Vol. LXVII, No. 1, January 2000, p. 6.

Schmidt, Howard. "The Changing Face of Computer Crime." *The Police Chief,* Vol. LXV, No. 5, May 1998, pp. 38–45.

Stites, Clyde M. "PCs: Personal Computers, or Partners in Crime?" *Law and Order,* September 1991, pp. 161–165.

Strandberg, Keith W. "Cyber Crime." *Law Enforcement Technology,* Vol. 26, No. 4, April 1999, pp. 24–29.

Sullivan, Scott. "Policing the Internet." *FBI Law Enforcement Bulletin,* Vol. 68, No. 6, June 1999, pp. 18–21.

Wiles, Jack. "High-Tech Crime: A New Type of Disaster." *Security Technology and Design,* Vol. 9, No. 1, January 1999, pp. 72–75.

Williams, Wayne P. "The National Cybercrime Training Partnership." *The Police Chief,* Vol. LXVI, No. 2, February 1999, pp. 17–27.

Useful Resources

Federal Law Enforcement Training Center, Glynco, GA: 800-74-FLETC

Florida Department of Law Enforcement, Computer Crime Center: 850-488-8771

FBI Computer Analysis Response Team, Washington, DC: 202-324-9307

NIJ/National Law Enforcement and Corrections Technology Centers, El Segundo, CA: 888-548-1618; Rome, NY: 888-338-0584

National White Collar Crime Center, Computer Crime Center, Fairmont, WV: 800-221-4424

National Cybercrime Training Partnership, Washington, DC: 202-514-0823

Chapter 19

Organized Crime, Gang-Related Crime, Bias/Hate Crime and Ritualistic Crime

Can You Define?

Antichrist
Beelzebub
bias crime
Black Mass
Bloods
bookmaking
coven
Crips
cult
gang
graffiti
Hand of Glory
hate crime
incantation
loan-sharking
magick
money laundering
moniker
occult
organized crime
ritual
ritualistic crime
sabbat
street gang
swarming
turf

Do You Know?

What the distinctive traits of organized crime are?

What organized crime activities are specifically made crimes by law?

What the major activities of organized crime are?

What the investigator's primary role in dealing with the organized crime problem is?

What agencies cooperate in investigating organized crime?

What a street gang is?

What types of crimes gangs typically engage in?

How to identify gang members?

What kinds of records to keep on gangs?

What special challenges are involved in investigating illegal activities of gangs?

What two defense strategies are commonly used by gang members' lawyers in court?

What bias or hate crimes are?

What a cult is?

What a ritualistic crime is?

What may be involved in cult or ritualistic crime?

What are indicators of cult-related or ritualistic crimes?

What special challenges are involved in investigating cult-related or ritualistic crimes?

Introduction

A mob-influenced vendor sets up a dummy trucking company and charges a retail chain nearly a million dollars for deliveries that never took place. On a busy Brooklyn street during broad daylight, a former champion Russian boxer turned hard-hitting businessman is gunned down "mob-style" by a lone assassin, who retreats unnoticed into a neighborhood restaurant and flees the country the next day.

In Minneapolis, a 12-year-old boy and an 18-year-old man, both with ties to a local gang, are shot to death while sitting in a car parked behind an apartment building, allegedly by a reputed member of a rival gang. In Denver, Colorado, a 16-year-old girl tries to break free from gang life and is stabbed to death a month later by a rival gang member.

In Jasper, Texas, a black man is chained by his ankles to a pickup truck and dragged to his death, his head and arm ripped from the rest of his body during the incident. In Laramie, Wyoming, a gay college student is beaten, tied to a fence and left to die alone. In Littleton, Colorado, two students open fire in a high school, killing 12 students and a teacher before turning their guns on themselves, allegedly because of biases the gunmen held against the victims.

On a lonely rural road in Wisconsin, a pharmacist who was a member of a voodoo cult arranges to have himself shot and killed by two friends, also cult members. In Rancho Santa Fe, California, 39 members of a high-tech cult pack their bags and commit mass suicide, believing that in death they will rendezvous with a UFO that was trailing the Hale-Bopp comet. In Tavares, Florida, members of a teen-age "vampire clan" use cigarettes to burn a "V" onto the body of a man they had just bludgeoned to death.

Scenes from the movie of the week? Unfortunately, no—they are actual events that have occurred across the country and reflect the everyday reality of orga-

nized crime, gang-related crime, hate crime and ritualistic crime in the United States.

This chapter begins with a discussion of organized crime in the United States, including its characteristics, applicable laws, major activities, role in corruption and its challenge to law enforcement. The discussion then looks at agencies that cooperate in investigating organized crime, investigative aids including asset forfeiture and the current status of organized crime.

The next major topic is gang-related crime, a continuous challenge to law enforcement. The discussion provides some definitions of gangs and a look at their extent within society. Next, gang leadership, membership and organization are presented, followed by a discussion of gang activities, including their relationship to drugs, their turf and their graffiti. Next the discussion focuses on ways to identify gang members, the records to keep, ways to investigate illegal gang activity and the police response to the gang problem.

The third major topic in the chapter is bias/hate crimes, a type of crime that has only recently been making the headlines and presenting major problems for law enforcement. The last topic in the chapter is ritualistic crime and the police's role in investigating it. ■

Organized Crime

The FBI defines **organized crime** as "a continuing criminal conspiracy, having an organized structure, fed by fear and corruption and motivated by greed" (Das, 1999, p. 1). It is most frequently thought of as a highly secretive, sophisticated criminal organization called *the Mafia* or *La Cosa Nostra*. A number of state laws define organized crime for prosecution purposes.

Even though no agreed-on definition of organized crime exists, several characteristics distinguish it from crimes committed by individuals or unorganized groups.

Characteristics of Organized Crime

Distinctive characteristics of organized crime include:

■ Definite organization and control.

■ High-profit and continued-profit crimes.

■ Singular control.

■ Protection.

The *organization* provides direct *control,* leadership and discipline. The leaders are isolated from the general operations through field or area leaders who, in turn, control the everyday activities that bring in the profits. Organized crime deals primarily in *high-profit* crimes that are susceptible to organizational control and that can be developed into larger operations that will provide the continued profit necessary for future existence.

Organized crime functions through many forms of corruption and intimidation to create a *singular control* over specific goods and services that ultimately results in a monopoly. Monopoly provides the opportunity to set higher prices and profits for that product or service. Organized crime flourishes most where *protection* from interference and prosecution exist. The first line of immunity is the indifference of the general public and their knowing or unknowing use of the services or purchase of the goods offered by organized crime. Through such activities, citizens provide the financial power that gives organized crime immunity from legal authorities.

Moreover, organized crime uses enforcement tactics to ensure compliance with its decrees. Paid enforcers intimidate, brutalize and even murder those who fail to obey the dictates of organized crime bosses.

In the early 1960s Joseph Valachi made public for the first time the awesome power of organized crime and dispelled many misconceptions about it. First, organized crime is not a single entity controlled by one superpower. Although a large share of organized crime is controlled by the Mafia, other organizations throughout the United States also operate as organized crime syndicates. According to Das (p. 3): "The La Cosa Nostra, LCN, is the most well-known domestic organized crime enterprise operating in the United States today." However, Asian and Russian/Eurasian criminal groups have been springing up across the country in recent years.

Second, organized crime does not exist only in metropolitan areas. Although organized crime operates primarily in larger metropolitan areas, it has associate operations in many smaller cities, towns and rural areas.

Third, organized crime does not involve only activities such as narcotics, prostitution, racketeering and gambling. In fact, organized crime is involved in virtually every area where profits are to be made, including legitimate businesses. According to Williams (1998, p. 36): "Organized crime continues to make its money the old fashioned way—through intimidation and infiltration of legitimate commercial operations."

Fourth, citizens are not isolated from organized crime. They are directly affected by it through increased prices of consumer goods controlled by behind-the-scenes activities of organized crime. In addition, citizens who buy items on the black market or who bet through a bookie, take chances on punch boards or participate in other innocent betting operations directly contribute to the financial success of organized crime. Millions of citizens support organized crime by knowingly or unknowingly taking advantage of the goods and services it provides. Das (p. 6) asserts: "Organized crime is made possible by crooked politicians and crooked companies. . . . Organized crime would not exist without widespread public participation in prohibited activities and services."

Applicable Laws

In addition to various state laws, two other distinct groups of laws seek to control organized crime: criminal laws that attack the criminal act itself and laws that make violations a criminal conspiracy. Charges have also been brought against some types of organized crime through prosecution under the Internal Revenue laws and through initiation of civil lawsuits.

The major federal acts specifically directed against organized crime are the 1946 Hobbs Anti-Racketeering Act, the 1968 Omnibus Crime Control and Safe Streets Act and the Organized Crime Control Act of 1970. These acts make it permissible to use circumstantial rather than direct evidence to enforce conspiracy violations. They also prohibit the use of funds derived from illegal sources to enter into legitimate enterprises (commonly known as *laundering* money). Title 18, U.S. Code, Section 1962, defines three areas that can be prosecuted.

It is a prosecutable conspiracy to:

■ Acquire any enterprise with money obtained from illegal activity.

■ Acquire, maintain or control any enterprise by illegal means.

■ Use any enterprise to conduct illegal activity.

Joseph 'Skinny Joey' Merlino, the reputed head of Philadelphia's organized crime family, was arrested in the summer of 1999 on drug-related charges.

The Racketeering Influenced and Corrupt Organizations Act (RICO), passed in 1970, is often used to prosecute many white-collar crimes in which organized crime is involved.

Major Activities

Organized crime is involved in almost every legal and illegal activity that makes large sums of money with little risk.

Organized crime is heavily involved in gambling, drugs, pornography, prostitution, loan-sharking, money laundering, fraud and infiltration of legitimate businesses.

Most reports on organized crime indicate that illegal gambling is the backbone of organized crime activities and its largest source of income. **Bookmaking**—soliciting and accepting bets on any type of sporting event—is the most prevalent gambling operation. In addition, various forms of numbers, policy and other lottery games net substantial portions of the financial gain from gambling.

Loan-sharking—lending money at exorbitant interest rates—is supported initially by the profits from gambling operations. The hierarchy lends money to people in lower echelons, charging them 1 to 2 percent interest on large sums of money. These people in turn lend the money to customers at rates of 20 to 30 percent or more. The most likely customers are people who cannot obtain loans through legitimate sources, often to pay off illegal gambling debts.

Fencing operations are used by organized crime figures to dispose of large quantities of stolen goods. Sometimes a business is purchased and operated as a legitimate enterprise, with stolen goods provided along with standard products. The merchandise is stolen on order or acquired through cargo thefts and truck hijackings, or it is taken from semiorganized, smaller criminal groups of shoplifters or burglars.

Be aware of such businesses in the community and be suspicious of delivery vehicles carrying merchandise that does not fit the place of delivery. Be alert to mention of purchases made at ridiculously low prices, which suggests that the items were stolen and sold by people associated with organized crime.

The relation of organized crime to *street crimes* is not always clear. Some crimes such as prostitution and narcotics selling are initiated in the streets and are organized and directly controlled by organized crime. Other crimes such as burglary or robbery can be committed by amateurs to support narcotics or illegal gambling habits. The stolen goods are often disposed of through fences associated with organized crime.

Money laundering, another activity frequently engaged in by organized crime, is converting illegally earned cash to one or more alternative forms to conceal its illegal origin and true ownership. As Horowitz (1997, p. 51) puts it: "Money launderers use a bogus trail to give illegal earnings a legal pedigree." Drug traffickers and other racketeers who accumulate large cash inventories face serious risks of confiscation and punishment if considerable, unexplained cash hoards are discovered. For these criminals to fully benefit from their illicit activities, they must first convert those cash proceeds to an alternative medium—one that is both easier than cash to use in everyday commerce and avoids pointing, even indirectly, to the illegal activity that generated it. The chief of the FBI's Economic Crimes Unit asserts (Strandberg, 1997b, p. 28):

> Money laundering occurs ancillary to other criminal activity. You have a violent crime [bank robbery], a white collar crime with fraud that generates illicit proceeds, or you have a terrorist group that has to fund their activities. Wherever you have a crime that generates money or needs money to function, you will have money laundering present.

One form of money laundering is *structuring,* which breaks transactions larger than $10,000 into smaller increments by making several deposits or withdrawals. This tactic avoids the reporting requirements by financial institutions of transactions over $10,000, although it may not always escape the filing of SARs (suspicious activity reports) with the federal government.

The amount of money laundered in financial institutions and other companies across the country has been estimated at hundreds of billions of dollars and, despite efforts to curb such criminal practices, many expect money laundering to continue to increase as both domestic and international enforcement challenges. In light of the ever expanding potential of the Internet, Strandberg (1997b, p. 32) cautions: "Cyberpayments, or electronic cash (e-cash), could change the face of money laundering completely. Though the system is not completely worked out yet, the potential for immediate payment and receipt is there, as is the potential for criminal activity."

Investigating money laundering usually uses white-collar crime investigative techniques such as financial auditing and accounting, undercover operations (perhaps through "sting" operations) and electronic surveillance.

In recent years organized crime has become increasingly involved in *legitimate business.* The vast profits from illegal activities are given legitimacy by being invested in legal business. This is another way of "turning dirty money into clean money," or "laundering" it. For example, a medium-sized company experiences a lack of business and is unable to get credit. Convinced that an infusion of money will turn the business around, the president turns to a loan shark and borrows at an inter-

est rate of 50 percent per week. Within months organized crime has taken over the company. The crime boss keeps the president as a figurehead and uses his reputation to order goods worth thousands of dollars, yet never intending to pay for them. Within a few months the company files for bankruptcy.

Although the history of organized crime is filled with bloodshed, violence and corruption, organized crime bosses no longer wield power through a Thompson submachine gun. They manipulate the business economy to their benefit. Such crimes as labor racketeering, unwelcome infiltration of unions, fencing stolen property, gambling, loan-sharking, drug trafficking, employment of illegal aliens and white-collar crimes of all types can signal syndicate involvement.

Investigators must be aware that some criminal groups are more involved than others in particular activities. Familiarity with a crime group's "specialties" or crimes of preference will greatly assist in investigations and will help identify the presence of new organized crime factions.

The Rise of New Organized Crime Groups

Whereas Italian crime syndicates may have predominated in the early days of organized crime in the United States, groups from other parts of the world are now cashing in on America's reputation as the "land of opportunity." The rise of Asian, Mexican and Russian gangs requires the government to redesign the fight against organized crime.

Asian Organized Crime Asian Organized Crime (AOC) groups are involved in murder, kidnapping, extortion, prostitution, pornography, loan-sharking, gambling, drugs, money laundering, alien smuggling and various protection schemes. Asian organized crime is often global, well run and hard to crack. Strandberg (1997a, p. 58) states: "Shrouded in legend but rooted in violence, Asian crime groups, whether it be the Yakuza, the Chinese Triads, the Black Hand, or street gangs, are threats to law enforcement and the maintenance of order in U.S. cities."

Japanese Organized Crime is sometimes known as *Boryokudan* but is more commonly known as the *Yakuza.* The term *boryokudan* means "violent ones," which quite accurately describes these groups, who concentrate on robberies and business extortions.

Triads are the oldest of the *Chinese Organized Crime* (COC) groups. The Triads engage in a wide range of criminal activities, including money laundering, drug

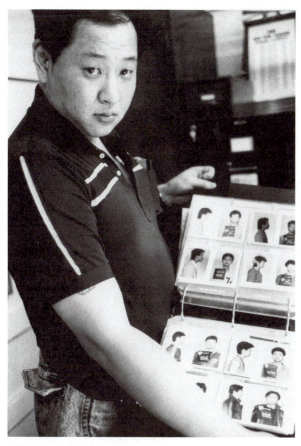

The Chinese Mafia may be the most secretive in the world. Some organized crime experts believe it is an even greater threat since Hong Kong again became part of China in 1997. Here a police sergeant from New York's 5th precinct task force in Chinatown shows Chinese gang members' mug shots.

trafficking, gambling, extortion, prostitution, loansharking, pornography, alien smuggling and numerous protection schemes.

Vietnamese Organized Crime is generally one of two kinds: roving or local. As the name suggests, roving bands travel from community to community, have a propensity for violence and have no permanent leaders or group loyalty. They lack language and job skills and have no family in the United States. Local groups, in contrast, tend to band together in a certain area of a specific community and to have a charismatic leader. They also have a propensity for violence and tend to engage in extortion, illegal gambling and robbery.

AOC investigations present some unique challenges, due primarily to cultural and social differences. Many Asians are suspicious of the police and the U.S. criminal justice system because, as Valdez (1997b, p. 50) notes: "In their old countries the police were often corrupt and worked with local organized crime figures." Asian criminals exploit this distrust by preying on other Asians, secure in the knowledge that their crimes will most likely go unreported. Another challenge is the fact that many Asian groups are very mobile and have associates or family scattered throughout the United States.

According to Valdez (2000b, p. 64): "The nation's largest Asian street gang is probably the 'Tiny Rascal Gang'" or TRG. The TRG is highly mobile and very monetarily motivated. It has been involved in extortions, home invasion robberies, burglaries, auto thefts, assaults, drug sales and murders.

Mexican Organized Crime Because of Mexico's proximity to the United States, Mexico's organized crime groups are becoming an increasing threat to the United States. Valdez (2000a, p. 56) suggests: "Hispanic gangs are among the fastest growing gangs in the country." Many of these gangs claim Sureño or Sureño-13 allegiance. Sureño gang members sentenced to state prison often start Sureño prison gangs there. According to Constantine (1997, p. 178):

> [There is] growing concern [that] organized crime groups from Mexico are having a negative impact on many aspects of American life. These international drug trafficking organizations have eclipsed organized crime groups from Colombia as the premier law enforcement threat facing the United States today.
>
> [The Colombian and Mexican drug trafficking organizations] are, in fact, the most sophisticated, violent and powerful organized crime groups ever to confront American law enforcement. They have used their immense wealth to corrupt institutions, law enforcement and government officials so they might continue their illicit activities. When they have found they could not secure their goals by corruption, they have used violence freely and ruthlessly.

The international nature of these crime groups poses a serious challenge to U.S. law enforcement. Constantine (p. 178) further notes:

> Today, even when our law enforcement agencies penetrate the operations of these drug syndicates and secure sufficient evidence to indict and prosecute the leadership, we often find them beyond the reach of our criminal justice system. . . . The inability to arrest, imprison or extradite [members of Mexican organized crime groups] to face their charges has hampered our enforcement efforts.

Russian Organized Crime A relatively new threat to U.S. justice is that of Russian Organized Crime (ROC). Ekberg (1998, p. 47) states: "Governments and law enforcement agencies in Europe and in the United States have become increasingly concerned about the risks posed by such trans-border criminality as illegal migration, drug smuggling, money laundering, illegal transfer of nuclear material and much more—all with roots in the former Soviet Bloc." McGovern (1999, p. 66) notes: "Today, Russian organized crime represents a major threat to not only the economic status of the United States, but also its national security." FBI director Louis Freeh contends the Russian Mafia "is the fastest growing criminal organization in the United States" (Wexler, 1998b, p. 57). According to Zalisko (1999, pp. 219–220):

> Common criminal activities committed by ROC include burglary, credit card forgery, auto theft, insurance and medical fraud, fuel tax fraud, arson, prostitution and narcotics trafficking.
>
> The ROC syndicates conduct the most sophisticated criminal operations ever seen in the United States, based on their access to expertise in computer technology, encryption techniques and money-laundering facilities that process hundreds of millions of dollars.

Investigating Russian organized crime is challenged by several factors. According to Wexler (1998b, p. 56): "Unlike long established crime families, the Russian mob is composed of hundreds of groups, all acting independently." McGovern (p. 67) asserts:

> Russian organized crime differs greatly from other forms of organized crime previously encountered by United States law enforcement. One of the most unique features was their lack of oppressing their own people upon arrival to the United States. It is believed this was due to the fact that most mobsters, upon their arrival, were already hardened criminals, and as a result were ready to prey upon the American society as a whole.
>
> Another fact was [that] the education level was far above that of previous new immigrants. These new American mobsters began calling themselves the *Organizatsiya,* or Organization.

Wexler (1998b, p. 58) adds: "Besides the Organizatsiya, the FBI has identified another Russian organized crime syndicate called the Russian-Armenian Mafia. Based in New York and Southern California, the criminal enterprise is involved in arms smuggling, prostitution, drug trafficking, and carrying out murders for hire."

As with other immigrant organized crime groups, language presents a challenge to investigators. Wexler (1998b, p. 59) states: "One of the greatest obstacles that the FBI faces in gathering intelligence on Russian mobsters is the language barrier. . . . Another stumbling block in fighting Russian mob activity is locating their so-called parent organizations." Yet another problem lies in the cooperation among and pooling of resources between Russian and other organized crime groups. For example, as noted by Wexler (1998b, p. 58):

> Recently American and Russian law enforcement authorities have teamed up to investigate Colombian drug cartels who are allied with Russian mobsters. It is believed that Russian and Colombian groups are shipping drugs to Europe and weapons to the United States and Latin America. The Russian groups have reportedly set up more than a dozen Offshore banks on Antigua and other Caribbean islands to launder money for the operations.

Organized Crime and Corruption

One of the greatest threats posed by organized crime is the corruption it engenders throughout the entire legal system. Although the police are interested in any corruption by public officials, they are especially concerned about corruption in their own department. Bribes of police officers can take many forms: outright offers of money, taking care of medical bills or providing free merchandise or free vacations. Any police officer who is offered a bribe must report it immediately to a superior and then attempt to make an arrest that will involve the person making the offer as well as those responsible higher in the organization.

Some officials repay organized crime figures by providing inside information that can be used to manipulate securities or to purchase real estate in areas of future development that can be sold for a much higher price. However, as Beare and Martens (1998, p. 412) suggest:

> In the United States, by divesting authority to organized crime control among the legislative, judicial, and executive branches of government, no one branch of government is given the ultimate and exclusive authority to investigate and prosecute complex crime. This, in turn, minimizes the extent to which corrupting influences can thwart an investigation or prosecution, or perhaps more important, it reduces the likelihood that civil rights and civil liberties can be intruded on without the knowledge of other responsible authorities.

Organized Crime and the Police Officer

It is frequently difficult for local law enforcement officers to understand their role in investigating or controlling organized crime. But there is a direct relationship between what officers do on assignment and investigation of organized crime activities. Local law enforcement officers are the first line of defense in the control of all crime, and organized crime is no exception. Because of the highly structured nature of organized crime, law enforcement officers can seldom break into the hierarchy, but they can remain the "eyes" and "ears" of the information and intelligence system essential to combat organized crime.

The daily observations of local law enforcement officers provide vital information for investigating organized crime. Report all suspicious activities and persons possibly associated with organized crime to the appropriate person or agency.

Because organized crime is involved in a great number of activities, information can arise from many sources. Thus, your street-level observations can be critical. Every day you observe many conditions related to crime and deal with individuals who are part of the community's activities. Seemingly unimportant details can fit into an overall picture that an intelligence unit is putting together.

Ways to become aware of people and conditions that suggest organized crime activity are provided by the International Association of Chiefs of Police (reprinted from *Criminal Intelligence,* Training Key #223, with permission of the International Association of Chiefs of Police):

A retail establishment seems to be doing a brisk business—many customers coming and going. But the customers do not remain in the store very long and do not leave with packages or other evidence that purchases were made. The store may have a meager selection of merchandise, which raises the question of how it can attract so many customers day after day. This could indicate the presence of a policy operation at the writer level or the place of business of a bookmaker's commissionman.

At about the same time each day, a package is delivered to a newsstand, bar, or other location. Later the package is picked up by another individual. The location could be a policy drop—the place to which a policy writer sends his slips and/or day's receipts.

You are called to investigate a beating in a bar or at a location near a factory or other place of employment. The incident may occur on a payday or within a couple of days thereafter. The beating may have resulted from the impatience of a loan shark who has not been paid on schedule.

A shopkeeper complains about poor business and notes that as a result he had to borrow money recently. A few comments by the patrol officer about the high interest rates and the shopkeeper might disclose the imposition of an interest above the legal maximum. If so, the shopkeeper may have been dealing with a loan shark.

After arriving at the scene of an assault, a patrol officer learns that the victim is a union official. This information should be noted because if there have been other similar assaults in the city, the overall total, when analyzed by an organized crime intelligence unit, may strongly indicate an attempt by racketeers to gain control over a local union.

Merchants complain about another price rise by the cartage company that removes their garbage or trash. They also mention that there is either no competitor to deal with or if there is one, it will not accept their business. Not infrequently, this is an indication that an organized crime group is trying to monopolize the cartage business or limit competition through territorial agreements.

A rash of vandalism strikes a number of establishments engaged in the same type of business—such as dry cleaning. Racketeers may be trying to coerce reluctant owners into joining an association or into doing business with mob-controlled vendors.

Make a habit of checking out new businesses that set up shop in the area. If the enterprise is one that requires a license, such as a bar, ask to see it if for no other reason than to observe who the owners are, ascertain the identity of the company which distributes or services the jukeboxes, etc. If, for example, the distributor of the jukeboxes or vending machines is a company controlled by the organized underworld, so also might be the bar in which they are located.

Report in writing all information pertaining to such activities when time permits or immediately if the activity involves an imminent meeting. Report as nearly as possible exact conversations with victims of assaults who are suspected of associating with organized crime members. These conversations can include names or organizations responsible for violence and crime in the community.

Agencies Cooperating in Investigating Organized Crime

Under the authority of the 1968 Omnibus Crime Control Act, the Safe Streets Act and the Organized Crime Control Act of 1970, the U.S. Justice Department established the Organized Crime and Racketeering Unit. Organized-crime strike forces were formed throughout the country, mostly in major cities.

Organized-crime strike forces coordinate all federal organized crime activities and work closely with state, county and municipal law enforcement agencies.

Other agencies that play important roles in investigating organized crime are the *Federal Bureau of Investigation,* which often has a member on the strike forces; the *Postal Inspector,* who is in charge of mail fraud, embezzlements and other crimes involving material distributed through the mails; the *United States Secret Service,* which investigates government checks and bonds as well as foreign securities; the *Department of Labor,* which investigates organized crime activities related to labor practices and pension funds; the *Securities and Exchange Commission,* which investigates organized crime activities in the purchase of securities; and the *Internal Revenue Service,* which investigates violations of income tax laws.

In addition to these agencies, the state attorney general's office and the district attorney's office can assist the police in building a case against organized crime figures who violate local and state laws.

Methods to Combat Organized Crime

Because organized crime groups often have extremely abundant resources and international connections to help protect their interests, law enforcement must deploy a wide variety of tactics to conquer the threat. Das (pp. 4–5) lists several methods the criminal justice system as a whole should use to combat organized crime:

- International cooperation—Various countries (the Netherlands, South Africa, USA, Canada, Australia and so on) are making extensive use of assigning police officers in foreign countries to strengthen international police cooperation.

- Interagency cooperation—Integrated Anti-Drug Profiteering Units (IADP) and Integrated Proceeds of Crime Units (IPOC) and other task forces that include the police from different jurisdictions or different types of investigators, computer and electronic specialists, multilingual interpreters, and so forth . . . illustrates interagency cooperative efforts.

- Proactive police initiatives—Includes allowing the police greater technological facilities for surveillance, eavesdropping, wiretapping, targeting specific ethnic criminal gangs and increased internal vigilance against police corruption. Also includes keeping track of large monetary transactions and having a witness protection program available.

- Police use of community resources—For example, in fighting Russian organized crime groups in the USA, it is recommended by a Senate Sub-Committee that open lines of communication must be introduced and maintained by the police and the public.

To prevent organized crime, Hicks (1998, p. 334) contends that we must think globally and act locally:

A number of commentators have acknowledged that policy makers, law enforcement, and other agencies (e.g., health, social services) have not coordinated their efforts at the international, state, or local level, and they have not mobilized citizens in the fight against organized crime.

Hicks further asserts (pp. 335–336) that citizens, police and local businesses can effectively be recruited to tackle problems that directly threaten the interests of their communities:

Sustainable success can be achieved in stemming the tide of drugs, violence, and young offenders through the use of targeted situational and social development approaches to crime prevention. Broadly based problem-solving partnerships—involving local authorities, citizens, police, social services, and housing authorities—are perhaps the most potent mechanism for effectively preventing both the situational and social causes of crime. . . .

Community mobilization against local drug markets, car theft prevention, and credit card fraud prevention are also problems that have profound effects at the local level, but increasingly these crimes involve the influence of organized crime.

Investigative Aids

Electronic surveillance of suspects is essential in investigating organized crime. Organized crime leaders often avoid direct involvement in criminal acts by planning and coordinating criminal activity over the telephone or the Internet. Consequently, electronic surveillance can be used to build an effective case based on a criminal's own words while avoiding the risks associated with using informants or undercover agents.

A federally protected witness testifies at a hearing about mob involvement in the garbage/toxic waste industry as a federal officer keeps watch nearby.

Pen registers also are important in investigating sophisticated criminal networks. Pen registers record the numbers dialed from a telephone by monitoring the electrical impulses of the numbers dialed. In *Smith v Maryland* (1979) the Supreme Court held that using a pen register does not constitute a search within the meaning of the Fourth Amendment, so neither probable cause nor a warrant is required to use the device. Several state courts, however, have held that using a pen register *is* a search under the respective state statutes and that a warrant supported by probable cause *is* needed. Investigators must be familiar with their state's statutes in this area.

The same situation exists for trap-and-trace devices, which reveal the telephone number of the source of all *incoming* calls to a particular number. Their use may or may not require a warrant, depending on the specific state.

Asset Forfeiture

One weapon against organized crime is the asset forfeiture program, which allows law enforcement agencies to seize funds and property associated with criminal activity. In effect, asset forfeiture subjects criminals to 100 percent tax on their earnings. This program not only deprives criminals of their illegally gained profits but also provides the criminal justice system with resources with which to continue the fight against crime. According to Farley (1995, p. 6):

Asset forfeiture is one of the most powerful and effective law enforcement tools we have to combat drug trafficking and other forms of organized crime. If

we are to achieve the maximum use of our Federal and State forfeiture laws, then we need to pursue forfeiture aggressively while protecting individual rights.

Asset forfeiture is not without its critics, however, as some argue the pockets of organized crime are too deep to be significantly affected by the seizing of assets. In thinking about organized crime prevention, Hicks (p. 325) asserts: "Crime fighting heroics associated with 'get tough' approaches to traditional organized crime policing are not working. Aggressive enforcement measures aimed at detection, seizure, and confiscation of assets, and prosecution of offenders are not substantially hurting organized criminal enterprises or diminishing the overall threat of organized crime."

The Decline of Organized Crime?

Certainly one hopes that tougher legislation, improved investigative techniques and increased use of tools such as asset forfeiture have brought about a decline in organized crime. Wexler (1998a, p. 45) states:

Armed with the comprehensive Racketeer Influenced and Corrupt Organizations (RICO) Act, stiff federal sentencing guidelines and a new willingness of informers to talk, the Department of Justice has had unprecedented success in prosecuting organized crime figures. Not one of the nation's 24 mafia families has escaped successful prosecution in recent years, and only a few have sustained their top leadership.

Law enforcement and the criminal justice system won a significant victory in the battle against organized crime in April 1992 when John Gotti, the country's most notorious mobster since Al Capone and known as the "Teflon Don" because charges would not stick, was found guilty on 13 counts and sent to prison for life. His arrest resulted in the breakup of the 400-member Gambino crime family. However, FBI officials acknowledged that others would move quickly to acquire the family's lucrative operations.

It is sometimes difficult to determine whether criminal events are the work of organized crime or of gangs. In fact, many of the defining characteristics of organized crime groups are strikingly similar to those of better-organized gangs.

Gang-Related Crime

Gangs have been of interest and concern for centuries. Street gangs have existed in the United States for most of the country's history and have been studied since the 1920s. The number and types of street gangs have increased dramatically since then.

Belonging to a gang is *not* illegal; however, many activities that gangs engage in are illegal. Gangs traffic in drugs; commit shootings, assaults, robbery, extortion and other felonies; and terrorize neighborhoods. Once loosely knit groups of juveniles and young adults engaged in petty crimes have become powerful, organized gangs, presenting a form of domestic terrorism. Gang wars, drive-by shootings and disregard for innocent bystanders have a chilling effect. Gangs now exist in almost every community. McCorkle and Miethe (1998, p. 41) report:

> The past decade has witnessed increasing concern about street gangs and their role in violent crime and drug trafficking. According to a recent national survey, more than 80 percent of prosecutors in large cities now acknowledge that gangs are a problem in their jurisdiction, that their numbers are growing, and that levels of gang-related violence are increasing.

To investigate such crimes effectively, law enforcement personnel must understand the makeup of these organizations, what types of crimes to expect, how to identify their members and how to deal with the special challenges of investigating such crimes.

Gangs Defined

A **gang** is a number of people associated in some way, an organized group of criminals or a group of youths from the same neighborhood banded together for a social reason.

Minnesota statutes define a *gang* as "an association of three or more persons, with a common name and established hierarchy, formed to encourage gang members to perpetrate crimes or to provide support to gang members who do commit crime." A gang has the main characteristics of leadership and organization for the purpose of committing illegal acts or crimes, either as individuals or as a group.

A **street gang** is a group of individuals who form an allegiance, have a name and recognizable symbols, claim a geographic territory and engage in continuous unlawful or criminal activity.

Extent of Gangs

Gangs range in size from small groups of three to five up to several thousand. Nationally known gangs such as the Crips number around 50,000 and the Bloods number about 20,000 to 30,000. Large gangs are normally broken down into smaller groups but are known collectively under one name. More than 90 percent of gangs have between 3 and 100 members, and only 4 percent have more than 100 members. The number of gangs in large cities ranges from 1,200 to 1,500.

Huff (1998, p. 1) asserts: "By all accounts, the number of youth gangs and their members continues to grow." However, the actual number of gangs and gang members in the United States remains uncertain and varies from survey to survey. According to the 1998 National Street Gang Survey Report, in which 373 law enforcement agencies responded, more than 13,700 gangs and 750,000 gang members were identified ("National Street Gang Survey," 1999, p. 21). Huff (p. 1) reports: "There are an estimated 23,388 youth gangs with 664,906 members in all 50 states. These numbers are probably conservative estimates because many jurisdictions deny, often for political and image reasons, that there is a problem." According to Howell (1998, p. 1), in 1996 more than 31,000 gangs existed in nearly 4,800 jurisdictions and had a combined membership of approximately 846,000. The National Youth Gang Center reports: "Youth gangs are present and active in nearly every state, as well as in Puerto Rico and other territories. Few large cities are gang-free" (Jackson, 1999, p. 62). A survey conducted by the Office of Juvenile Justice and Delinquency Prevention (OJJDP) found ("Police Reporting Juvenile . . . ," 1999, p. 6):

> Police in almost three-fourths of all cities with populations over 25,000 reported some type of youth gang problem, and most suburban counties have youth

gangs as well. . . . In the largest cities, with populations over 250,000, *all* of the responding police agencies reported gang problems. . . .

Responding law enforcement agencies reported an estimated 850,000 gang members active in nearly 31,000 gangs.

According to Valdez (1998b, p. 49), California leads the nation in number of gang members with 254,618, followed by Illinois (75,226) and Texas (57,060).

Proliferation and Migration Two trends linked to the extent of gangs are the increasing proliferation and migration of such groups. As Maxson (1998, p. 2) explains and as the previously discussed statistics support: "The term 'gang proliferation' indicates the increase in communities reporting the existence of gangs and gang problems." Gangs have proliferated for several reasons, including the following:

- Increasing academic failure
- Increasing substance abuse
- An apathetic society
- An acceptance of violence as a way to deal with conflict

Gangs proliferate when new gangs form within a community or when existing gangs relocate to a new location. As society in general has become more mobile, gangs and gang members have also increased their mobility, contributing to gang migration. Whereas early gangs tended to exist primarily in large cities near the country's borders (Los Angeles, New York, Miami, Chicago), gangs are now sending members across the country and into the nation's heartland to take advantage of new territory, diminished competition from other gangs and law enforcement agencies who are less experienced in dealing with gang activity. In a survey of police officers that examined why gang members migrated to their cities, Maxson (p. 8) found:

> The most frequently cited reason was that gang members moved with their families. When this was combined with the reason of staying with relatives and friends, 57 percent of the survey respondents believed that migrants relocated primarily for social reasons. Drug market expansion was the second most frequently cited motivation . . . for migrating. When this was combined with other criminal opportunities, it created a larger category of illegal attractions, or "pull" motivators, in 32 percent of cities reporting an influx of migrant gangs. "Push" motivators that forced gang members to leave cities, such as law enforcement crackdowns, court-ordered relocation, or a desire to

escape gangs, were cited in 11 percent of migrant-recipient cities.

Maxson (p. 8) offers a final observation regarding gang proliferation and migration: "Gang member migration, although widespread, should not be viewed as the major culprit in the nationwide proliferation of gangs. Local, indigenous gangs usually exist prior to gang migration, and migrants are not generally viewed by local law enforcement as the cause of gang problems."

Gang Characteristics

Gangs are typically structured around race or nationality. For example, Minneapolis has two Native American street gangs, the Naturals and The Club, with membership estimated at several hundred. This is in addition to black gangs, primarily the Vice Lords and the Disciples, and to Hmong youth gangs. Table 19.1 describes characteristics of youth gangs.

The gang establishes its **turf,** or *geographic* area of domination, and then other gangs challenge its reputation and turf. In the past this took the form of gang fights. Today, however, it often takes the form of "drive-by shootings" from a moving vehicle, many of which have killed innocent citizens as well as rival gang members. Attacks on police officers by snipers or by ambushes in which assault weapons are used have also occurred. In addition, gangs are heavily involved in drug use, abuse and sales.

Several types of gangs present unique challenges to law enforcement due to the specific defining characteristics of gang members. Examples of such gangs include biker or motorcycle gangs, female gangs, Asian gangs and correctional or prison gangs.

Motorcycle Gangs One type of gang that has been a problem for decades is the motorcycle gang, which typically consists of individuals older than street gang members. These gangs function throughout the United States and internationally. Smith et al. (1998, p. 54) report: "There are an estimated 500 motorcycle gangs throughout the world involved in criminal activity."

The FBI has recognized the connection between the Outlaws gang and organized crime. Other known motorcycle gangs are the Free-Wheelers, Renegades, Bandidos, Misfits, Hells Angels, Pagans and Dirty Dozen. Some of these gangs are involved in money laundering, narcotics trafficking, murder, extortion, prostitution, rapes and bombings. They often use cellular phones, pagers, computers and sophisticated weaponry in their criminal activities. Trethewy and Katz (1998, p. 53) note

Table 19.1	Characteristic Groups of Youth Gangs
Black Gangs	Origins in Los Angeles, Chicago, New York, Miami and other major urban ghettos. Crips, Bloods, Players, Untouchables and Vice Lords are some of the more prominent gangs.
Jamaican Posses	Immigrant Jamaicans in the U.S. with roots in Jamaica. Groups have been identified in New York, Boston, Philadelphia, Washington, DC, Houston, Atlanta, Detroit, Seattle and Anchorage among other locations.
Hispanic Gangs	Origins in Los Angeles, valleys of California, New York (Puerto Rico), Miami (Mariel Cubans, Dominicans), Washington, DC, and other urban barrios. Tend to use highly stylized graffiti lettering.
Asian Gangs	Origins among recent emigres from Vietnam, Hong Kong and Philippines. Activity centered in New York; New Orleans; Los Angeles and Orange County, California; Portland, Oregon; Seattle; San Francisco; and Houston.
Pacific Islander Gangs	Primarily Samoans who have migrated to Western urban areas, i.e., Los Angeles, San Francisco, Portland.
White "Stoner" Gangs	Caucasian groups identified with Heavy Metal and Punk Rock music preferences and with some British working-class gangs. Sometimes involved with Satanic rites and symbols.
Neo-Nazi Gangs	Tend to articulate white supremacy, racism and Nazi symbols. Some call themselves "skinheads" and sport close-cut hair or shaved heads.
Motorcycle Gangs	Dominantly Caucasians, branches of Hells Angels and other notorious motorcycle groups. Tend to be heavily involved with the manufacture and sale of methamphetamine.

Source: Metropolitan Court Judges Committee Report. *Drugs—The American Family Crisis: A Judicial Response: 39 Recommendations,* August 4, 1988.

the increasing sophistication of biker gangs, stating: "Once considered nothing more than rowdy toughs on two-wheelers, motorcycle gangs have evolved into crime units that are sufficiently well-oiled and well-organized to rival the Mafia." They further note (p. 55):

> Better dressed and better educated, many of today's biker gang members and associates are earning college-level degrees in computer science, finance, business, criminal justice and law. These curricula improve the gang's expertise in highly profitable criminal enterprises. Education has allowed gang associates to entrench themselves in government positions (including the military) and other legitimate professions.

International gang rivalries pose a serious challenge to law enforcement in all countries. Smith et al. (p. 54) note:

> A gang war between the Hell's Angels in Canada and a rival drug distribution gang called the Rock Machine is [an] example of U.S.-based motorcycle gang affiliates fighting for control of drug trafficking in another country. To date, it has been estimated that 84 people have been murdered and 88 bombs have been exploded in Quebec since 1984.

Female Gangs Female gangs present their own challenges to law enforcement. People in general, including some police officers, unfortunately tend to assume—incorrectly, even fatally—that females are less violent and therefore less dangerous than males. However, according to Laflin (1996, p. 87): "Gangs consisting of female members, whether it be auxiliary branches of male gangs or fully autonomous female organizations, are fully capable and disposed to commit as many crimes as any male gang." Valdez (1997a, p. 40) notes: "No longer strictly affiliated with male gangs, female gang members have come into their own. But whether they belong to a male gang, female gang or coed gang, they can be lethal for unwitting officers." Huizinga (1997) adds that although female gang members constitute only a small percentage of all active gang members, studies show they commit more violent crimes than nongang boys. Researchers Esbensen and Winfree (1998, p. 521) report:

> Our findings do not support the notion that gang girls are mere sex objects with no involvement in the violent acts that the gang boys commit. The gang girls commit the same variety of offenses as the boys, but at a slightly

This girl gang, posed in front of a wall of their graffiti, is named "Tiny Diablas of the South Side Grape Street Watts." The gang color is purple, and their hand signal is similar to sign language "g."

lower frequency. Further, the gang girls are two to five times more delinquent than the nongang boys.

Their research also found (p. 520) that 38 percent of gang members in their study sample were female, a fact they claim "contributes to the growing body of research reporting greater rates of female participation in gangs than was previously acknowledged." Howell (1998, p. 3) echoes: "Among all adolescents, female involvement [in gangs] may be increasing proportionally with male gang involvement." Mendez (1996, p. 8B) reports:

More and more girls are joining gangs in mid-sized cities, and now—instead of hanging out with other girls—they increasingly are hooking up with male gangs that tend to be more violent. . . .

But ties with male gangs can put girls in life-threatening situations and lead to unwanted pregnancies, sexually transmitted diseases and jail time.

When girls decide to leave gang life, . . . breaking ties can be difficult because rival gangs remember faces, places, colors, hand signs and slights, both real and perceived.

Many girls enter gang life through their brothers or other males from their neighborhood, making it even more difficult to break away.

Asian Gangs

A serious development has been the increase of Asian gangs, many of which are committing vicious drug-related crimes. As with Asian organized crime groups, Asian gangs tend to target other Asians as victims because of the tendency for Asian immigrants to distrust law enforcement and consequently to let victimization go unreported. One kind of Asian gang is the Home Invasion Crew. According to Dunlap (1997, p. 311): "Home invasion crews tend to have the following characteristics:

- The majority are Vietnamese males between the ages of 18 and 22.

- Most are close friends who have shared living quarters, food, money, cars, jail cells, and common life experiences (e.g., being Vietnamese in America).

- They have a strong family-like bond.

- They normally have experience in committing robberies and this knowledge has been passed down from the older members to the younger members.

- They may all be members of the same street gang, or they may not be a street gang at all, but merely close friends. These friends may get together to do a home invasion in Houston on Monday and then two or three may splinter off from the first group to do a business robbery in New Orleans on Wednesday."

Correctional Gangs

Because many gang members serving time in correctional facilities will one day return to the streets, such gang members are of concern not only to their host facilities but also to law enforcement. Godwin (1999, p. 98) contends: "If we wish to put our 'finger on the pulse' of the level of gang activity in our society, there is no better place to do so than within the confines of our detention facilities, prisons and jails." Howell (1998, p. 4) notes a survey of juvenile correctional facilities found gangs to be a problem in more than three-fourths of responding institutions. Furthermore: "Fifty-two percent of the responding institutions reported that more than 10 percent of confined youth were involved in gangs. More than one-third (40 percent) reported gang involvement of female inmates."

Even while behind bars, gang members may wield tremendous power and pose a serious threat to public safety. According to Godwin (p. 96): "Nearly every major street gang that is active in the United States receives direction from persons incarcerated in correctional facilities. This includes violent gangs with national affiliations, such as Latin Kings, Black Gangster Disciples, Vicelords and many others."

Incarcerated gang members may also serve as valuable sources of information for investigators. Godwin (p. 94) notes:

> Corrections often is forgotten as a source of information during traditional law enforcement investigations. . . .
>
> Drive-by shootings, robberies and even homicides that involve suspects who have gang affiliates or social acquaintances serving time should automatically generate an inquiry to correctional agencies to determine if any intelligence is available.

Gang Membership, Leadership and Organization

According to Howell (1998, p. 2): "The average age of youth gang members is about 17 to 18 years old, but tends to be older in cities in which gangs have been in existence longer, like Chicago and Los Angeles." Sometimes gang members are multigenerational—that is, father and son may have been members of the same gang.

Gang membership generally emerges among people who live in specific areas of a community. They start out small and grow in relation to the purpose and desire of the group. Most gangs are of limited numbers, sufficient for the entire group to meet and discuss things in person. Incidents that happen to them or that are expressly initiated by them cause them to identify as a group. This bonding normally takes place over a period of time.

Most gang members are unemployed or work at part-time jobs. Many are most active at night and sleep during the day. Some stay with their gangs into adulthood, and others may go back to school or gain full-time employment, usually in jobs with very low pay.

Most gang members are weak academically because they lack good study habits although they are mentally capable. This is an important factor because gangs are essentially self-operated and self-governed. Some operate by consensus, but the majority have leaders and a subgoverning structure. Leadership may be single or dual. Status is generally obtained by joining the gang, but equal status within the gang once joined is not automatically guaranteed.

Gang members have differing levels of commitment and involvement in gang activities. According to Lanata (1998, p. 87): "Most gang members can be identified as either hard-core, associate or peripheral members." The hard-core members are those most dedicated to the gang. Lanata (p. 87) states:

> The hard-core member lives for the gang. The gang constitutes his total identity and therefore is what he most values in life. The hard-core member's name will appear frequently on field contact cards, indicating his presence during or after the commission of gang-related crimes. He also will be the subject of citizen complaints and hotline calls.
>
> Gang leadership, fluid as it may be, normally emerges from the ranks of the hard-core membership. Various titles are used for gang leaders: "boss," "veterano," "original gangster" ("OG"), or "shot caller," depending upon the type of gang.

Knowing how a gang is organized and what level of involvement a member has can be of great assistance to investigators. For example, as Lanata (p. 87) explains:

> Hard-core street gang members have associates. The associate has a full knowledge of the gang activities and often is involved in the same criminal acts as hard-core members. However, the commitment level of the associate member is different from that of the hard-core member. The hard-core member's life is the gang. The associate has another life. . . .
>
> The associate member is . . . more likely than the hard-core member to provide statements to law enforcement, especially if he thinks he is in danger of losing access to the people or things he values more than the gang.
>
> Peripheral members are the best sources of information. They are the younger kids that live in "the neighborhood." Although they are ripe for hard-core recruitment, they tend to live on the fringe of the gang and are least likely to be involved in heavy violence.

Some gangs are highly disorganized and do not specifically recognize or identify different levels of membership, nor do they have designated leadership. According to Decker et al. (1998, p. 402):

> Differentiation within the organization is an important indicator of the level of gang organization.

In general, the less differentiation between roles or levels of membership within the gang, the less highly developed the organization, and the less effective it can be in generating goals and producing compliance among members in the pursuit of those goals.

In examining the differences between two Chicago gangs and two San Diego gangs, Decker et al. (p. 402) found that the more established Chicago gangs had a much greater degree of gang organization, including specific levels of membership, leaders, regular meetings, written rules and dues. Furthermore, the Chicago gangs were more likely to be involved in political activities and legitimate businesses and to have consequences for leaving the gang.

Gang Activities

Many gang activities are similar to those of other segments of society and are *not* illegal. Gangs gather informally on streets and street corners, in parks, homes, abandoned buildings, vehicles, vacant lots or recreational areas and buildings. Indeed, many of the defining characteristics of a gang could be applicable to any other organization in society, with the exception of the purpose, which is to engage in antisocial or criminal behavior. Not all gangs engage in criminal behavior, however. Some "gangs" form out of normal relationships in a neighborhood or a school. If they do not engage in antisocial behavior, nothing ever happens that causes them to feel a need to "band together" to protect their group from outside activity or threats. The gang remains a social group or club.

However, when a gang forms for social reasons and then outside activities occur that endanger one or more of the members, the group may "close ranks" and act as a group in their defense. For example, the group may be having a meeting in the park, and an outside group beats up a few of the members. The group may report this to the police, or they may decide to "take things into their own hands" and seek revenge.

Other gangs form for the express purpose of committing antisocial behavior or criminal activities, starting with the manner of initiation into the group, which may require shoplifting or a more serious illegal activity.

Regardless of how or why gangs form, society views them as undesirable. The public often associates drinking and sexual promiscuity with gangs, and this is often the reality. Drinking is associated with becoming an adult. Gangs offer a sense of belonging and importance to their members that society and family do not provide. Gang members gradually dissociate from social conformity

and become responsible only to themselves and their group activities.

Each gang develops its own culture and activities over time. Most of their activity consists of "hanging around" together, as the gang provides identification, self-esteem, self-worth, status, reputation, a stable relationship, protection, economic support and emancipation from parental and social control and institutions such as schools and churches. Yet, gangs desire status and recognition, and a major recognition factor seems to be criminal activity. Crime may progress from petty theft to rolling drunks, mugging, pickpocketing and drug dealing. The types and frequencies of crimes gang members commit differ noticeably from those committed by other at-risk youths not in gangs. Huff (p. 4) notes:

> Gang members are far more likely to commit certain crimes, such as auto theft; theft; assaulting rivals; carrying concealed weapons in school; using, selling, and stealing drugs; intimidating or assaulting victims and witnesses; and participating in drive-by shootings and homicides than nongang youths, even though the latter may have grown up under similar circumstances.

Youth gang homicides are a serious concern to both law enforcement and the community at large because innocent bystanders are often unintentional casualties of shootings. According to one report ("Police Reporting Juvenile . . . ," p. 6): "Juvenile gang members were estimated to have been involved in 2,364 homicides in large cities and another 561 homicides in suburban areas during 1996." Howell (1999, p. 210) states:

> Youth gang homicides are unique in several respects. . . . [They] occur in spurts and thus do not correspond with [a] city's overall homicide trend line. Youth gang homicides are also distinct from nongang homicides in terms of settings in which they occur and participant characteristics. Drive-by shootings and the use of firearms also distinguish them from other homicides committed by adolescents and young persons.

Howell (1999, p. 211) notes that youth gang homicides "are generally more chaotic, with more people, weapons, offenses, and injuries out in the open, among people less familiar with each other."

Howell (1998, p. 11) comments: "Gang-related drive-by shootings have increased in certain cities. Interestingly, killing is a secondary intent; promoting fear and intimidation among rival gangs is the primary motive." Table 19.2 compares gang and nongang behavior.

Although gang crime often involves only a few members at a time, occasionally the entire gang, or a

Table 19.2	Comparison of Gang and Nongang Criminal Behavior (Cleveland)	
Crime (p¹)	Gang N = 47	Nongang N = 49
Auto Theft (***)	44.7%	4.1%
Assault Rivals (***)	72.3	16.3
Assault Own Members (*)	30.4	10.2
Assault Police (n.s.)	10.6	14.3
Assault Teachers (n.s.)	14.9	18.4
Assault Students (n.s.)	51.1	34.7
Mug People (n.s.)	10.6	4.1
Assault in Streets (*)	29.8	10.2
Theft-Other (***)	51.1	14.3
Intim/Assault-Vict/Wit (***)	34.0	0.0
Intim/Assault Shoppers (*)	23.4	6.1
Drive-by Shooting (***)	40.4	2.0
Homicide (**)	15.2	0.0
Sell Stolen Goods (*)	29.8	10.2
Guns in School (***)	40.4	10.2
Knives in School (***)	38.3	4.2
Concealed Weapons (***)	78.7	22.4
Drug Use (**)	27.7	4.1
Drug Sales (School) (n.s.)	19.1	8.2
Drug Sales (Other) (***)	61.7	16.7
Drug Theft (***)	21.3	0.0
Bribe Police (n.s.)	10.6	2.0
Burglary (Unoccupied) (*)	8.5	0.0
Burglary (Occupied) (n.s.)	2.1	2.0
Shoplifting (n.s.[.058])	30.4	14.3
Check Forgery (n.s.)	2.1	0.0
Credit Card Theft (n.s.)	6.4	0.0
Arson (*)	8.5	0.0
Kidnapping (n.s.)	4.3	0.0
Sexual Assault/Molest (n.s.)	2.1	0.0
Rape (n.s.)	2.1	0.0
Robbery (*)	17.0	2.0

* *Level of statistical significance: * p<.05; ** p<.01; *** p<.001; n.s. = no significant difference.*

Source: C. Ronald Huff. *Comparing the Criminal Behavior of Youth Gangs and At-Risk Youths.* National Institute of Justice Research in Brief, October 1998, p. 4.

large portion of it, participates in the illegal activity. For example, a surveillance video from a Las Vegas minimarket showed more than 40 teenagers flooding into the tiny store. Three youths jumped the counter and robbed the cashier at gunpoint while the others flocked to coolers. Teens clogged the doorways as they rushed out, carrying cases of beer and handfuls of food. The whole incident took less than 90 seconds. Police call this technique **swarming.**

The community, the schools and law enforcement each have a somewhat different perspective on gang activity. From the community's view, gang activity includes vandalism in the form of graffiti and the wanton destruction of public and private property. Customers stay away from businesses in gang areas; insurance rates go up; citizens become afraid to leave their homes. In essence, the streets belong to the gangs.

Similarly, in the schools, vandalism and graffiti pose a problem as does violence—including stabbings, shootings and sometimes arson. Teachers and students are intimidated, and learning is disrupted. In fact, if several gang members are in a class, the teacher may be powerless to enforce discipline or to teach. Gang problems in the Clark County, Nevada, school system (much the same as in most other school systems throughout the United States) led to a five-point system for dealing with the problem:

1. Permanent expulsion from the school system of hard-core and violent gang members.

2. Identification cards for junior and senior high students to keep nonstudent gang members off school grounds.

3. Criminal prosecution of students who commit violent acts.

4. Adoption of a schoolwide emergency procedure system to be initiated when a violent crime is committed on school grounds.

5. Creation of a computerized list of active gang members to be distributed to each school.

- - - - - - - -

In addition to drug dealing, gang members often engage in vandalism, arson, shootings, stabbings, intimidation and other forms of violence.

- - - - - - - -

Figure 19.1 describes the type of gang-related crime by percentage.

Gangs and Drugs

Until the early 1980s, when crack, or rock cocaine, hit the market, gangs engaged primarily in burglary, robbery, extortion and car theft. Although drug trafficking existed, it was nowhere near current levels. The reason: enormous profit.

Economic gain is often the reason youths join gangs. It is hard to convince a youth that $5.50 an hour for busing tables is preferable to making $400 for two hours' work as a drug courier. In a recent survey, police estimated that 43 percent of the illegal drug sales in their jurisdiction involved gang members ("Police Reporting Juvenile . . . ," p. 6). According to the 1998 National Street Gang Survey Report, more than 80 percent of the 1,250 significant gangs identified are involved in drug trafficking (p. 21).

Some, however, caution that drug trafficking by gangs is not as rampant as others might claim. For example, Howell (1998, p. 11) asserts:

> Empirical research has not documented extensive networks of drug trafficking as an organized activity managed by youth gangs. The consensus among the most experienced gang researchers is that the organizational structure of the typical gang is not particularly suited to the drug-trafficking business.

Aside from expert opinions that most gangs lack the discipline, leadership and crime skills necessary to sustain a successful drug operation, those gangs that are successful are serious forces to be reckoned with. Baker (1999, p. 192) calls such large, well-organized

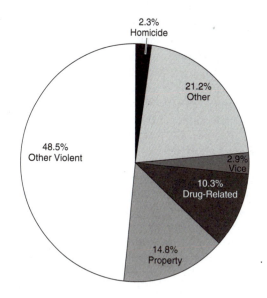

FIGURE 19.1 *Gang-Related Crime by Type as a Percentage of the Total Recorded*
Source: NIJ Gang Survey.

Table 19.3	Common Differences between Street Gangs and Drug Gangs	
Street Gangs		*Drug Gangs*
Versatile ("cafeteria-style") crime		Crime focused on drug business
Larger structures		Smaller structures
Less cohesive		More cohesive
Looser leadership		More centralized leadership
Ill-defined roles		Market-defined roles
Code of loyalty		Requirement of loyalty
Residential territories		Sales market territories
Members may sell drugs		Members do sell drugs
Intergang rivalries		Competition controlled
Younger on average, but wider age range		Older on average, but narrower age range

Source: James C. Howell. *Youth Gangs: An Overview.* OJJDP Juvenile Justice Bulletin, August 1998, p. 13.

gangs "supergangs" and compares them to organized crime groups, adding: "Supergangs have an organizational structure that supports drug trafficking. . . . Criminal analysis, organized crime and narcotics investigation techniques should be applied to supergang drug marketing." Table 19.3 compares characteristics of street gangs and drug gangs.

Gangs often purposely exploit the difference between juvenile and adult law in their drug dealing, using younger gang members whenever possible to avoid adult sanctions. Most states will not allow youths under age 15 to be certified as adults, and most states have statutory restrictions on placing youths under age 18 into adult correctional facilities.

Turf and Graffiti

Gang members establish a specific territory, or turf, that they will defend to the death. The turf includes the schools, businesses, residential areas, streets and alleys in the area, all controlled through fear, intimidation and violence.

Gangs identify their turf through **graffiti,** called "throwing a placa." Police officers who deal with gangs can learn much by understanding wall graffiti. The center of a gang's turf will have the most graffiti. It may name members of the gang, often in order of authority, listed in neat rows under the gang's logo. Unchallenged graffiti affirms the gang's control.

Understanding the messages behind gang graffiti can greatly assist investigators. Graffiti can:

- Identify turf boundaries.
- Insult rival gangs.
- Warn of impending death.
- List fallen comrades.
- Announce a gang's presence in a certain area of a city.
- Show gang alliances (Valdez, 1998c, p. 39).

Other gangs may challenge the turf claim by writing over or crossing out the graffiti, replacing it with their own. Such crossouts are usually found at the edge of a gang's territory. Gang members caught in the act of crossing out graffiti in a rival's territory may be killed. In examining the threat posed by gang graffiti, one article (*Addressing Community Gang . . .* , 1998, p. 34) notes that graffiti are "a territorial claim, a communication, and even a challenge to other gangs. Outside gangs may read them as an invitation to attack."

With the increasing mobility of society, graffiti no longer has to necessarily remain within a gang's turf. As Ferrell (1998, p. 587) explains:

In the widespread and growing hip hop graffiti underground, a new subcultural practice has recently become popular: the illegal painting of graffiti on outbound freight trains as a means of sending graffiti images out from their initial, circumscribed points of production into wider circulation.

Hispanic graffiti is highly artistic and very detailed. It frequently refers to group or gang power. Black-gang graffiti, in contrast, shows less flair and attention to detail and often is filled with profanity as well as expressions of individual power. The symbolism is more obvious and often includes weapons.

Investigators should be aware of and familiar with the differences between "tagger" graffiti and gang graffiti (*Addressing Community Gang . . .* , p. 34):

> Taggers often form into groups, sometimes called "crews," and adopt crew tags.
>
> Taggers who move in tag crews can achieve more daring feats. They can help each other get to difficult places, like overhead signs, which are referred to as "heavens." They have been known to help fellow crew members rappel down blank walls to put tags in apparently unreachable places.
>
> The larger a tag crew, the more it begins to look and act like a street gang. While street gangs look down on individual taggers with disdain, they are more likely to regard large crews as a threat that must be dealt with. Then the two begin to act like rival street gangs, even though the crew may have started out with a less dangerous purpose.

Gang graffiti is a source of frustration and expense to property owners and local governments.

Identifying Gang Members

The first step in dealing with the gang problem is to identify the gang members. Valdez (1996a, p. 20) suggests: "Photos, jewelry, hairstyles and body piercing are among the obvious physical traits investigators look for when profiling gangs." Tattoos (sometimes called body art) are another means of identifying gang members. The most respected tattoos are those earned by serving a prison sentence.

Gang members may be identified by their names, symbols (clothing and tattoos) and communication styles, including graffiti and sign language.

The **Crips,** for example, are associated with blue or purple bandanas, scarves or rags. The **Bloods** are identified by red or green colors. Mexican gangs often wear brown bandanas as a symbol of ethnic pride. Some gangs wear jackets and caps identified with professional sports teams, posing a problem for those youth who

wear them because of actual loyalty to the particular team. Gang members may also be identified by the hand signals they use.

Often, the stylized dress and haircuts, tattoos, graffiti, slang, hand signs and jewelry used by other street gangs are also used by Southeast Asian gangs. However, Valdez (1996b, p. 20) describes a trend that started among the Southeast Asian gang community—burns and scars on the arms and hands:

> Displaying these body modifications or inflicting them in the presence of other gang members gives the wearer instant respect among his or her peers. The marks also serve as a kind of silent advertisement to the rest of the population. Without saying a word, a person wearing these marks or tattoos can walk into a cafe or restaurant and intimidate the owner into providing free food or paying for protection.

Another characteristic of Southeast Asian street gangs is that they do not claim turf but rather are very mobile, with informal networks throughout the United States. Table 19.4 summarizes the criteria that some jurisdictions use to define gangs.

Police also need to identify the gang leaders and the "tough guys." Reducing the effectiveness of the leaders is important but is often difficult and can be accomplished only by having sufficient evidence to convict the leader of a crime that results in a prison sentence.

Records to Keep

Information on gangs is an essential tool for law enforcement. The following *gang file* information should be recorded and filed by name separately and alphabetically:

■ Number of active and associate members

■ Type of gang

■ Ethnic composition

■ Territory

■ Hideouts

■ Types of crimes usually committed

■ Method of operation (MO)

■ Choice of victims

■ Leadership

■ Violent members

Included within the record system should be a *gang member pointer file* that cross-references the names of suspected gang members with the gang file. This may be a cardex or computerized file.

Table 19.4	Criteria for Defining Gangs	
Criteria Used	Large Cities*	Smaller Cities*
Use of Symbols	93%	100%
Violent Behavior	81%	84%
Group Organization	81%	88%
Territory	74%	88%
Leadership	59%	48%
Recurrent Interaction	56%	60%

*Of the cities surveyed, 70 (89%) of the large cities and 25 (58%) of the smaller cities indicated the criteria used to define gangs.

Source: *1994 National Institute of Justice Gang Survey*. Washington, DC.

A *moniker file* connects suspected gang members' street names with their legal names. A **moniker,** or nickname, is the name gang members use among their peers and often during the commission of crimes. Wilson (1997, pp. 14–15) notes: "Several different styles of monikers exist. Many reflect a distinctive aspect of a gang member's personality, physical characteristics, reputation, or other trait. Some convey boldness or devotion to the gang lifestyle. Others reinforce the gang member's ego." Although no two members of the same gang will have the same moniker, several gangs may have members with the same moniker. Therefore, one card should have on it the moniker and all gang members who use it. Wilson (p. 15) asserts: "Gang members now use monikers . . . so dependably that these pseudonyms can provide a reliable source of investigative information."

A *photograph file* is of great help in conducting photographic identification sessions. A *gang vehicle file* can be maintained, arranged alphabetically by vehicle *make*. Include color, year, body type, license number, distinguishing features, known drivers and usual parking spots. An *illegal activities file* can also be maintained, arranged alphabetically, listing the gangs known to engage in the activities.

Maintain records on gangs, gang members, monikers, photographs, vehicles and illegal activities. Cross-reference the records.

Computers are helping law enforcement recognize gang members. As Quarantiello (1996, p. 80) suggests:

"For officers attempting to cope with the ever-increasing number of gang members throughout the country, the ability to execute a computerized records search based on very little known input is a godsend. It is often the difference between a case that remains open and one that is cleared."

Baker (1998, p. 62) explains how computer programs are creating instant photos to help gang crime fighters:

A baby has just been kidnapped in Atlanta. Her teenage baby sitter, a suspected gang member, agrees to cooperate with the police investigation. With the nickname she provides of the gang member allegedly involved in the crime, Atlanta Police Department (APD) puts its Gang Intelligence System (GANGIS) database into action. GANGIS cross-references the name and physical characteristics of the alleged kidnapper and, moments later, provides a short list of potential suspects and their corresponding photos. APD personnel compose and present an electronic lineup of six juveniles for the baby sitter to review. She IDs the alleged suspect out of the lineup and, within six hours of the crime's being reported, the kidnapper is apprehended and the infant is returned safely to her parents.

A police map marking the boundaries of South Los Angeles's gang war zone. The officer points out grid 64, turf of "the Rolling 60s," one of the worst areas in the city.

Investigating Illegal Gang Activity

Gang investigations should proceed like most other criminal investigations. Uniformed officers should establish personal contacts with the gangs in the community and become familiar with their size, the names of as many members as possible and each gang's identifying symbols, colors and graffiti. Godwin (pp. 98–99) notes that some of the more common sources of gang intelligence include documents (charters, constitutions and recruiting documents), phone monitoring, mail cover, financial transactions, visitation records and graffiti. Lanata (p. 86) adds:

> Through traditional investigative techniques, such as informant and associate interviews, record checks, physical and electronic surveillance, etc., investigators can gain insight into an individual subject's value system. When an investigator understands what a person cares about, he can formulate a line of questioning that will elicit meaningful responses.

A mutual understanding between the police and the gang members can reduce violence. The police know what gangs do, and the gangs know what police do. However, gangs do not like the police because they interfere with the gang's unlawful gatherings and criminal activities. Gang members try to avoid the police but at times engage in open confrontation because of police interference with their territory and the criminal activities they carry on.

Some disenchanted gang members may become police informants. Children know what is going on among their peers even though they may not be gang members themselves. Teachers and school counselors are other sources of information on acceptable and unacceptable youth activities. In addition, recreation department personnel know what is going on in the youth community and are therefore sources of information.

Obtaining information from gang members is difficult because of the unity of gang membership. The same techniques police use to obtain information about organized crime and other serious criminal activity can produce information about gang activity. Obtaining witness information from nongang members is difficult because they feel threatened by the gang and have obvious concerns about their personal safety.

The immediate area in which a crime occurs may yield much information. Any graffiti present indicates which gang controls the territory. Keep in mind that gang members do not like to be on foot in a strange area, especially one dominated by their enemies; therefore, commando-type raids on foot are very rare. If a crime suggests that no vehicles were involved, odds are good the suspects are local, possibly members of the same gang as the victim. These crimes generally reflect intragang conflicts involving narcotics, girlfriends or family disputes.

- - - - - - - -

Special challenges in investigating the illegal activities of gangs include the multitude of suspects and the unreliability or fear of witnesses.

- - - - - - - -

Illegal activities of gangs usually involve multiple suspects, which makes investigation much more difficult. Evidence may link only a few of the suspects with the crime, and, as with organized crime figures, gang members maintain fierce loyalty to each other.

A further difficulty is that many "witnesses" may actually be gang members or people who at least sympathize with the gang, so their information is usually unreliable. In addition, others within the neighborhood may have information but may be afraid to become involved. Because they live in the neighborhood with the gang and may fear for their lives, they may provide information and then later deny it. For this reason, tape record or videotape all such interviews.

Evidence obtained in gang investigations is processed the same as in other crimes. Photograph graffiti for later identification. File field interview cards on members, vehicles, territory, locations, crimes committed, drug activities and any other information.

Gang members may usually be located within their territory even after they commit a crime—because this is their "home."

Throughout the investigation of illegal gang activities, be aware of the most common defenses gang members use in court.

- - - - - - - -

The two most often used defense strategies are pleas of diminished capacity and self-defense.

- - - - - - - -

Although some states have eliminated "diminished capacity" as a defense, many have not. Therefore, document whether the suspect was under the influence of alcohol or other drugs at the time of the crime. Likewise, document whether the suspect was threatened by the victim and could possibly have been acting in self-defense.

Table 19.5 summarizes difficulties in prosecuting gang-related crimes. In both large and small jurisdictions, obtaining cooperation of victims and witnesses and intimidation of victims and witnesses presented the most problems.

Police Response

Some police departments have established neighborhood substations where the primary purpose of assigned officers is to prevent gang activities, protect the innocent youth of the area and make necessary arrests. This is a viable form of community policing. Additionally, the police departments in many larger cities have specialized gang squads that cover the entire city.

Even though law enforcement unquestionably plays a major role in effectively combating the gang problem, partnerships with the community, parents and schools significantly increase the likelihood of a successful response. Police antidrug programs, such as the Drug Abuse Resistance Education (DARE) program in the schools, may help reduce gang influence by reducing the demand for drugs. Police become involved in prevention, control, arrests, prosecutions and the promotion of proper laws to restrict drug and gang activity. Panther (1999, p. 119) describes an effective community-based gang-prevention program in Arlington County, Virginia:

Police officers recognized that many of the parents and guardians of young people who were most susceptible to gang recruitment within their communities were very naive about recognizing potential gang activity and involvement within their homes. In response, [the] officers created a comprehensive program unofficially referred to as GRIP (Gang Resistance Involving Parents) to identify at-risk youth and educate them and their families on gang activity, the lure of gang recruitment and the consequences of gang involvement.

Another program aimed at stopping gang violence before it starts is GREAT—the Gang Resistance Education and Training Program—which:

. . . was developed to supplement law enforcement's efforts to eradicate youth violence. It is a pro-active approach to deter violence before it even begins. Just as teachers work to develop a solid foundation of basic skills upon which to build the structure of their students' future, G.R.E.A.T. builds a foundation focused on teaching children the life skills needed to avoid violence and gang membership ("A G.R.E.A.T. Program," 1999, p. 73).

Many cities have passed laws to create "safe school zones" that prohibit drug possession or sales on school property and within 1,000 feet of school property. Violations of these laws have been upgraded from misdemeanors and gross misdemeanors to felonies, and sentencing is mandatory. Possession of beepers or pagers is also prohibited within the "safe school zone" area. Some schools have removed pay phones because students were using them to make drug contacts and sales during school hours.

Table 19.5	Prosecution Problems by Size of Jurisdiction

Problem	Large Jurisdictions (n = 118)			
	Not a Problem	Minor Problem	Moderate Problem	Major Problem
Obtaining cooperation of victims and witnesses	2.6%	8.8%	27.2%	61.4%
Intimidation of victims and witnesses	1.8%	17.0%	30.4%	50.8%
Lack of appropriate sanctions for juvenile gang members who commit crimes	9.7%	22.2%	21.2%	46.9%
Lack of early intervention for youth at risk of gang involvement	9.7%	11.5%	32.8%	46.0%
Lack of resources for witness protection	6.1%	20.2%	31.6%	42.1%
Victim and witness credibility	6.2%	16.8%	46.9%	30.1%
Inadequate police preparation of crime reports	33.3%	41.2%	20.2%	5.3%

Problem	Small Jurisdictions (n = 74)			
	Not a Problem	Minor Problem	Moderate Problem	Major Problem
Obtaining cooperation of victims and witnesses	10.1%	15.9%	30.4%	43.5%
Intimidation of victims and witnesses	13.2%	19.2%	25.0%	42.6%
Lack of appropriate sanctions for juvenile gang members who commit crimes	2.9%	27.5%	37.7%	31.9%
Lack of early intervention for youth at risk of gang involvement	15.7%	18.6%	34.3%	31.4%
Lack of resources for witness protection	7.1%	27.1%	37.2%	28.6%
Victim and witness credibility	1.4%	30.0%	41.4%	27.2%
Inadequate police preparation of crime reports	34.8%	39.2%	13.0%	13.0%

Source: Claire Johnson, Barbara Webster and Edward Connors. *Prosecuting Gangs: A National Assessment.* National Institute of Justice Research in Brief, February 1995, pp. 6–7.

Other tactics are being employed to suppress gang activity and the violence that often accompanies it. Fritsch et al. (1999, p. 122) report that an experimental antigang initiative in Dallas produced the following results: "Aggressive curfew and truancy enforcement led to significant reductions in gang violence, whereas simple saturation patrol did not." Regini (1998, p. 29) states: "Several municipalities have used civil injunctions to abate gang activity under the theory that ongoing gang activity is a public nuisance." Other communities have passed loitering ordinances specifically aimed at keeping gang members from congregating in public places. How-

ever, use of such measures has opened the door to challenges of unconstitutional interference with individuals' First Amendment rights of association and violation of the Fourteenth Amendment's guarantee of due process. Spector (1999, p. 11) notes:

In 1992, the Chicago City Council enacted the Gang Congregation Ordinance, prohibiting criminal street gang members from loitering with one another or others in public places. Loitering was defined as "remaining in any one place with no apparent purpose."

Before enacting the ordinance, the council held hearings during which concerned citizens testified as to how gangs disrupted their lives to the point where they feared leaving their homes to go to work, school or shop. The council found that an increase in criminal street gang activity was largely responsible for the city's rising murder rate and an escalation of drug-related crimes.

Despite the many justifications for the ordinance, its constitutionality was challenged and, according to Schofield (1999, p. 28): "On June 10, 1999, in the case of *City of Chicago v. Morales,* the U.S. Supreme Court held by a 6-3 vote that Chicago's Gang Congregation Ordinance is unconstitutional." Justice John Paul Stevens wrote that the ordinance did not provide sufficient guidance to police officers enforcing it and, thus, was unconstitutionally vague and in violation of the Fourteenth Amendment due process clause ("Supreme Court Strikes . . . ," 1999, p. 1). However, since the Court's primary objection to the ordinance was its obscure wording, Spector (p. 11) notes: "The U.S. Supreme Court left the door open for the use of loitering ordinances to control gang activity if the ordinance is properly crafted and enforced."

A Violent Gang Task Force (VGTF) has been instituted by the Immigration and Naturalization Service (INS) to deal with gang members who come here from other countries. This task force has 130 special agents who have conducted over 100 criminal investigations since its inception.

Gangs of the Future?

McCort (1996, p. 33) describes the evolution of street gangs and their apparent shift toward organized crime:

Over the past 15 years, street gangs have undergone a swift and dramatic change. . . . The problem that was once restricted to large cities is now shared by small suburban and rural communities as well. These gangs have become a driving influence on violent crime, drug trafficking and community stability. . . .

An examination of recent developments in street gang activity . . . reveals an evolutionary process that has been characteristic of ethnic gangs throughout American history. . . .

Where the evolution will lead today's gangs is not completely understood. It is certain, however, that law enforcement must consider the potential emergence of a new organized crime system. . . .

For the most part, street gangs will likely remain loose-knit social entities, involved primarily in street-level crime. However, individuals or elements of the subculture are evolving into a more sophisticated level of organized crime.

Bunker (1996, p. 54) presents a different view of the future of gangs:

The expanding presence of street gangs in the United States can be linked both to military trends in the non-Western world and to future warfighting concerns—particularly in terms of the disruption of a society's social organization.

The increasing diversity of the U.S. population is also reflected in the makeup of gangs today. Valdez (1999a, p. 60) notes the emerging presence of a South American import gang, the Mara Salvatrucha (MS), in certain parts of the United States such as southern California and Washington, DC. The gang is composed of refugees and immigrants with ties to La Mara, a violent street gang in El Salvador, and members of the Farabundo Martí National Liberation Front (FMNL), which include El Salvadoran peasants trained as guerilla fighters and adept at using firearms, explosives and booby traps.

Immigration alone does not account for the rise of new gangs in this country. Some are evolving from groups that were present before the United States was colonized. Valdez (1998d, p. 47) comments on the spread of Native American gangs:

Today . . . the gang lifestyle has an ideal target recruitment group in young Native Americans, males and females alike, especially those who live on the reservations. . . .

No one knows why, but throughout the country the Crip and Blood street gangs . . . seem to have the greatest influence on Native Americans who do become involved in the gang subculture on reservations. . . .

Unfortunately, Native American gang members have adopted the same types of criminal gang activities and gang-motivated violent attacks we see throughout the United States.

Valdez (1999b, p. 46) further notes the increasing membership in a white supremacist gang called the Nazi Low Riders:

Around 1995, California law enforcers saw a gang growing in numbers and gaining strength through the lucrative methamphetamine trade. Considered both a prison and street gang, the Nazi Low Riders (NLR) have developed a reputation for being cold-blooded and ruthless. . . . NLR members have been linked to murders, home-invasion robberies, witness intimidation, drug sales and assaults on police officers.

Another emerging type of gang is the train gang, as Howard (1998, p. 117) warns: "Any community with railroad tracks is at risk of having members of this new type of gang infiltrate their neighborhoods. The leading gang goes by the name of Freight Train Riders of America (FTRA)." Three main factions of the FTRA have been identified (p. 119):

> Low riders—who ride the rails in the south from Texas to California. They wear red bandanas around the neck.
> Mid riders—who ride the rails across the Midwest. They wear blue bandanas around the neck.
> High riders—who ride the northern rails from Minnesota to Northern California. They wear black bandanas.

As with many other gangs, the FTRA has a unique style of graffiti and is involved in drug use, their drugs of choice being methamphetamine and marijuana. Not all emerging gangs, however, actively condone vandalism (through graffiti) and drug use. Harris (1999, p. 69) notes the emergence of a new "clean-living gang" called Straight Edge:

> An offshoot of the punk movement, . . . its adherents are mostly young white males from middle and upper class families. Most Straight Edge youth are not involved in gangs or terrorism, embracing a non-violent philosophy. Straight Edgers proclaim their movement is the only youth counterculture to actively discourage drug use, alcohol use and promiscuous sex.
>
> But apparently a hardcore minority of Straight Edgers are giving the movement a bad name. They have been accused of using chains, clubs and pepper spray to enforce their abstinent lifestyle on others in schools, at concerts and other public places.

Some gangs, such as white supremacist groups, specialize in crimes known as bias or hate crimes.

Bias/Hate Crime

Generically, a **bias crime** or **hate crime** is a criminal act committed because of someone's actual or perceived membership in a particular group (Levin, 1999, p. 8). Specifically, as Gondles (1999, p. 6) notes:

The definition for hate crimes is contained in Section 28003 (a) of the 1994 Crime Act, which calls it: "a crime in which the defendant intentionally selects a victim, or in the case of a property crime, the property that is the object of the crime, because of the actual or perceived race, color, national origin, ethnicity, gender, disability or sexual orientation of any person."

Crimes range from verbal intimidation and harassment to destruction of property, physical violence and even murder.

Bias or hate crimes are motivated by bigotry and hatred against a specific group of people.

Petrosino (1999, p. 22) states: "Hate crimes are despicable acts. Their toll only begins with the victim. Harm expands to the victim's family, group, and society itself." Neubauer (1999, p. 6) adds: "The impact of hate crime on a community can be devastating; it can polarize citizens to divert their energy and attention away from other important issues. Unlike burglary or larceny, hate crimes perpetuated against one individual will affect the entire community."

However, hate crime is not a new development in our country. According to Petrosino (p. 23): "Substantial evidence exists to suggest that hate crime as a behavior has existed in America for more than 300 years; however, only recently—relatively speaking—has it become recognized as a violation of the law." Nor is hate crime unique to our country. Gondles (p. 6) notes: "Around the world, in places like Kosovo, the Middle East, Northern Ireland and Rwanda, we witness unspeakable inhumane acts simply because people are different."

Motivators for Hate Crime

Race is usually the primary motivation, and blacks are most often the victims. According to the FBI ("Racial Prejudice Most . . . ," 1999, p. 12A):

> Racial prejudice motivated more than half of the 8,049 hate crimes in 1997 that were reported to the FBI. . . .
>
> In order of magnitude, other reported motivations were 1,385 incidents attributed to prejudice about religion, 1,102 sexual orientation, 836 ethnic or nation origin, 12 to disability and four to multiple prejudices. (See Figure 19.2.)

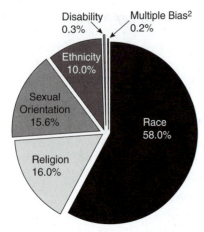

FIGURE 19.2 *Bias-Motivated Offenses 1998, Percent Distribution[1]*

[1]Due to rounding, percentages do not add to 100.
[2]Category represents offenses associated with multiple-bias incidents.
Source: *Crime in the United States 1998.* The Uniform Crime Reports. Washington, DC: Department of Justice, 1999, p. 59.

Regarding hate crimes against gay individuals, a recent study has found self-defense, ideology, thrill seeking and peer dynamics to be the key motivating factors ("Study Reveals Motivations . . . ," 1998, p. 1).

The groups most likely to be victims of hate crime are (in alphabetical order) African-Americans, Arabs, Asians, gay males, Jews, Latinos, lesbians, Native Americans, and white women in interracial relationships. Some characteristics typical of hate-motivated violence are relatively rare in other crimes of violence:

■ *The relationship of the victim to the perpetrator.* Most assaults involve two people who know each other well. The opposite is true of hate-motivated assaults, which are very likely to be "stranger crimes," in which the perpetrator and victim are completely unknown to each other.

■ *The number of perpetrators.* The majority of assaults typically involve one victim and one perpetrator or two "mutual combatants." Hate crime generally involves an average of four assailants for each victim, although the ratio varies.

■ *The uneven nature of the conflict.* In addition to the frequently unfair dynamic of ganging-up on the victim, hate crime perpetrators often attack younger or weaker victims or arm themselves and attack unarmed victims.

■ *The amount of physical damage inflicted.* Hate crime is extremely violent. In fact, victims of hate crime are

three times more likely to require hospitalization than normal assault victims.

■ *The treatment of property.* In a very large fraction of property crimes something of value is taken. In hate-motivated crimes, perpetrators are more likely to damage or destroy something of value.

■ *The apparent absence of gain.* Gain is absent in most hate crimes. For example, although property may be damaged, it is not usually stolen. In hate crime, no personal score is settled; no profit is made.

■ *The places in which hate crimes occur.* Hate crime frequently takes place at churches, synagogues, mosques, cemeteries, monuments, schools, camps and in or around the victim's home (Bodinger-deUriate, 1991, p. 2).

Hate Crime Offenders

According to Tischler (1999, p. 76):

> The typical hate crime offender is a first-time offender, or a teen-ager who goes out on Saturday night looking for someone to bash. . . . [While it is estimated] no more than 5 percent of hate crimes are committed by organized hate groups, . . . these groups are most likely to be involved in the most serious crimes, such as homicide.

Clayton (1999, p. 8) observes: "There are a number of organized hate groups in America, including the Ku Klux Klan (our nation's oldest hate group); the National Alliance; the Aryan Nation; World Church of the Creator and Neo-Nazi Skinheads." According to the Southern Poverty Law Center, the number of hate groups nationwide reached 537 in 1998 ("Internet Blamed for . . . ," 1999, p. 3A). One article ("Number of Hate Groups . . . ," 1998, p. A4) reports: "The increase [in hate groups] comes primarily from growth in the number of chapters of preexisting groups, such as the Ku Klux Klan, and in the number of churches belonging to the Christian Identity movement, which cites biblical foundations for white supremacy and anti-Semitism."

The increasing popularity of personal computers and easy access to the Internet is being blamed for the recent growth surge of hate groups. When Klan member Don Black created his "Stormfront" site on the World Wide Web in 1995, it was the first of its kind; now there are more than 250 sites advocating hatred (McCafferty, 1999, p. 7). According to a report issued by the Southern Poverty Law Center ("Hate Groups Increase . . . ," 1998, p. 10): "The Internet offers hate groups many advantages, including the ability to build a strong sense

Some 30 graves scribbled with swastikas and other graffiti in a Jewish cemetery.

of community through encrypted messages, chat room talk, electronic mail communication, and propaganda displayed on Web sites." One researcher for the Center states: "The Internet is allowing the white supremacy movement to reach places it has never reached before—middle-and upper-middle class, college-bound teens" ("Internet Blamed for . . . ," p. 3A). Furthermore, many of these sites are aimed directly at children.

Campbell (1999, p. 40) notes that websites of hate groups usually have a disclaimer that allows them to report criminal acts without actually advocating them, for example:

> We do not support, condone, promote or encourage criminal activity of any sort. However, we refuse to condemn any who take independent action for the benefit of the white race.

Campbell suggests that the KOF (Knights of Freedom) web page is a good place for officers beginning to study such groups.

Music containing messages of hate and intolerance has also been identified as fueling the spread of hate groups (" 'Hate Rock' Spreads . . . ," 1999, p. 8):

> As rock groups with "white-power" themes join the mainstream music scene through the Internet and on some college radio stations, organized hate groups are finding it easier to recruit teen-agers to their cause. . . .

"Music is the most effective propaganda tool ever," says one community activist. "It brings racists together into a so-called 'music scene' that lets them spread their message almost innocently."

Neo-Nazi Groups Especially troublesome to law enforcement has been the rise of neo-Nazi "skinhead" groups. Indeed, as Miller (1998, p. 39) stresses: "An understanding of these people and their philosophy is a critical part of the arsenal police officers should carry when dealing with suspected skinheads." The skinheads are shaven-headed youths who sport Nazi insignia and preach violence against Blacks, Hispanics, Jews, Asians and homosexuals. The intense hatred between skinheads and African-Americans was dramatically depicted in the movie *American History X.*

Skinheads often wear dark leather jackets or greenish flight jackets, blue or black jeans or camouflage army fatigues, and black military boots or the British high-top boots called "Doc Martens." Their clothing often displays American flags, German crosses and swastikas or expressions such as "White Power," "Skins Rule," "KKK" or "WAR." Their bodies are frequently covered with tattoos of skulls, swastikas or words such as "Skinhead" and "SWP" (Supreme White Power).

Some reports indicate that there are more than 3,500 skinhead members in the United States. The increased number of skinheads has been accompanied by an increase in the number of violent crimes (including homicides, shootings, beatings and stabbings) they have committed against members of minority groups. The skinheads have also been linked with drug use and Satanism. Police departments find themselves walking a tightrope between protecting the safety and property of citizens and protecting the rights of assembly and free speech.

The Police Response

Respond promptly to reports of hate crime, attempt to reduce the victims' fears and determine the exact type of prejudice involved. Then provide follow-up information to the victims. Include in the report the exact words or language used, reflecting racial, religious, ethnic or sexual orientation bias; the perpetrators' actions; symbols; colors; dress or any other identifying characteristics or actions.

Reporting Bias Crimes

In 1990 the Federal Hate Crime Statistics Act (HCSA) was passed, mandating that the Justice Department collect data on crimes related to religion, race, sexual orientation or ethnicity. In addition to the federal statute, 46 states have passed statutes that address prejudicial hate crimes and, as of 1997, 21 states and the District of Columbia have passed statutes requiring collection of hate crime data. The FBI has also published manuals concerning the types of statistics needed and has established training programs in major cities. Nonetheless, it is difficult to establish hate crime records because some hate crimes involve groups rather than individuals.

Given the rising number of hate crimes reported, it is difficult to know how much is attributable to a true increase in crime and what amount is simply due to more thorough reporting of such crimes. For example, data from the FBI's UCR shows a 52 percent increase in the number of hate crimes reported against African-Americans from 1992 to 1996. Yet, as Torres (1999, p. 52) states: "Although the federal government has made a substantial effort to initiate a statistical baseline of hate crime in the United States, considerable uncertainty continues regarding whether the hate crime rate is increasing or decreasing."

Despite higher reported numbers of hate crime, many believe such crime remains seriously underestimated. Murphy (1999, p. 88) contends:

> Reports of bias violence are low. Bias violence is severely underreported by victims, particularly gay

men, lesbians and members of immigrant groups, primarily because of ignorance of the law, distrust and fear of law enforcement officials, and language and cultural barriers. Bias violence incidents also are underrecorded by law enforcement agencies.

According to Nolan and Akiyama (1999, p. 115):

> A number of social forces . . . might prevent individuals and agencies from fully participating in a program to identify and report hate crimes. Some forces are based within the organization (e.g., resources, policies, and organizational culture). Others are based outside the organization (e.g., the political climate, local laws, or social norms). Still others are based on individual convictions (e.g., religious beliefs and personal commitment). Social forces that encourage participation also seem to lie both inside and outside the law enforcement organization.

Table 19.6 summarizes the variables that may encourage or discourage an agency from reporting hate crimes.

Efforts to Combat Bias/Hate Crimes

Regardless of how an agency or individual officer views hate crime, it remains a criminal offense that requires a law enforcement response. Martin (1996, p. 455) observes: "The apparent substantial increase in hate crime . . . has led to two responses: legislation to expand the scope of the law and severity of punishment for such offenses, and police-initiated efforts to focus attention on and more fully investigate such crimes." Other efforts include community-based programs to increase awareness of and offer solutions to the problem of hate crime.

Legislation McMillan (1999, p. 3) asserts: "In a civil society, we cannot allow predators to roam the streets preying on individuals who do not fit what others feel is acceptable. These violators should be punished more severely." Senator Orrin Hatch states: "As much as we condemn all crime, hate crime can be more sinister than non-hate crime. A crime committed not just to harm an individual, but out of the motive of sending a message of hatred to an entire community, is appropriately punished more harshly" ("Senate Moving to . . . ," 1999, p. 2). Indeed, as Dunbar (1999, p. 64) notes: "Hate crime laws have resulted in the promulgation of additional sentencing options and penalty enhancements for convicted perpetrators." McMillan (p. 3) adds: "With hate crimes many law enforcement agencies have created policies that provide additional care for the victims—similar to domestic violence victims."

Table 19.6	Variables That Affect Whether Agencies Report Hate Crimes

Agency Encouragers	Agency Discouragers
Ability to assess intergroup tensions in community	Not deemed important by department
Desire to give support to communities	Perception on part of police that no problem exists
Belief that hate crime reporting will improve police/community relations	Insufficient support staff to process, record, and submit hate crime data
Belief that police help set level of acceptable behavior in the community	Perceived as not being real police work
Understanding that community wants police to report hate violence	A belief that reporting hate crimes will make things worse for victim
Need to know extent of problem as first step to developing solutions	A belief that reporting hate crimes will make things worse for communities
Lets community know that department takes hate crimes seriously	Perception that some minority groups complain unnecessarily
A belief that victims will get help	Not a priority of local government
Will help diffuse racial tensions within the police department	A belief that identifying a crime as a hate crime will have no effect on the outcome
The right thing to do politically	A belief that it is wrong to make these types of crimes special
The right thing to do morally	A belief that hate crime reporting will result in negative publicity for the community
Will help maintain department's good relationship with diverse groups	A belief that hate crime reporting supports the political agendas of gay and minority groups (which is seen as a negative thing)
Consistent with values of department	It creates too much additional work
A belief that identifying problem will keep others safe	Hate crimes are not as serious as other crimes (i.e., a lower priority)
Citizens appreciate the hate crime reporting efforts of the police	Agency does not have the adequate technological resources

Source: James J. Nolan and Yoshio Akiyama. "An Analysis of Factors That Affect Law Enforcement Participation in Hate Crime Reporting." *Journal of Contemporary Criminal Justice,* Vol. 15, No. 1, February 1999, p. 118. Reprinted by permission.

Grigera (1999, p. 69) states: "The primary rationale for hate crime legislation is that harassment and intimidation, assault and property destruction assume a particularly dangerous and socially disruptive character when motivated by prejudice." The most common elements of hate crime legislation include:

■ Enhanced penalties.

■ Criminal penalties for vandalism of religious institutions.

■ Collection of data.

Legislation must also keep up with the technology used to spread messages of hate. For example, the Anti-Defamation League (1999, p. 106) notes a legal precedent for prosecuting those who send racist threats via e-mail:

In 1998, a former student was sentenced to one year in prison for sending e-mail death threats to 60 Asian-American students at the University of California, Irvine. His e-mail was signed "Asian hater" and threatened that he would "make it my life career [sic] to find and kill everyone one [sic] of you personally." That same year, another California man pleaded guilty to Federal civil rights charges after he sent racist e-mail threats to dozens of Latinos throughout the country.

Despite such legislation, those who propagate messages of bigotry, intolerance and hatred claim they have a constitutionally protected right to do so. Israel (1999, p. 97) states:

A cornerstone of democracy is the First Amendment's protection of free speech. The founding fathers saw this as contributing to democratic government. Ironically, contemporary free speech protects groups such as Nazis, White and Black supremacists, pornographers, gangster rappers, TV violence, and gratuitous film profiteers; in short, these are agents of disorder, and have practically nothing of discourse value.

Grigera (p. 72) notes:

Critics of statutes aimed at punishing hate violence contend that it would be wrong to say that a crime against one person is more serious than a crime against his or her neighbor. According to some, the law must remain blind to specific motives and should concentrate solely on the acts themselves. Opponents of bias crime legislation often attempt to validate their positions by relying on constitutional challenges to such statutes.

Such objections include free speech, due process and equal protection challenges. Grigera (p. 74) concludes, however: "Overall, despite criticism of hate crime statutes, 41 states and the District of Columbia have adopted legislation that enhances penalties for hate-motivated violence and state courts have upheld their constitutionality."

Programs Communities throughout the country are making efforts to address the problem of hate violence. As Mahoney (1999, p. 82) reports:

Massachusetts recognizes the seriousness of these crimes and is increasing prevention efforts within the school system. Since many perpetrators of hate crimes are under the age of 20, it is imperative that we identify incidents in schools and colleges. To meet this challenge, the Governor's Task Force on Hate Crimes created the Student Civil Rights Project to provide assistance and support for students, parents, educators and law enforcement by creating school environments that are safe and free of harassment and violence.

In other communities, civil rights lawyers are organizing a national response to hate crime. According to Murphy (p. 88):

In 1963, the Lawyers' Committee for Civil Rights Under Law Inc. was founded . . . to create an organization through which members of the private bar could take the fight for equal rights out of the streets and into the courts. . . .

As early as 1982, the Lawyers' Committee began to respond to hate crimes. In June 1999, the committees announced the formation of a coordinated response, . . . through which they will work with the U.S. Department of Justice (DOJ) to eradicate this destructive and insidious problem.

Murphy (p. 90) elaborates on this initiative:

To combat bias violence, attorneys and other advocates must work with law enforcement officials to ensure input from survivors and to see that perpetrators are brought to justice. Advocacy to improve laws and policies is necessary. Police officers and prosecutors must be trained to enforce the laws effectively. Community education to inform people of their rights and available remedies is necessary, as is community organization to change the environment that allows such conduct to flourish.

The International Association of Chiefs of Police has developed a pamphlet: "Responding to Hate Crimes: A Police Officer's Guide to Investigation and Prevention," available via the Internet at www.theIACP.org. This pamphlet asserts ("Responding to Hate Crimes," 2000, p. 1): "Police officers and their agencies can accomplish much by working in partnership with citizens to implement the American vision of diverse and tolerant communities that offer freedom, safety and dignity for all."

Sometimes, the hideous nature of hate crimes leaves investigators wondering whether the offense is truly based on bias or whether some type of ritualistic torture was involved.

Ritualistic Crime

Ritualistic crimes are most often associated with cults. For this discussion it is necessary to distinguish between cults and "cults." In general, *cult* refers to a system of religious beliefs, rituals and believers. In this text and in law enforcement, cult denotes a group of people whose beliefs and rituals appear to the majority of society to be socially deviant or even violent and destructive. Such cults are commonly connected with the occult, paganism, witchcraft, demonism and Satanism or devil worship.

- - - - - - - - - - -

A **cult** is a system of religious beliefs and rituals. It also refers to those who practice such beliefs.

- - - - - - - - - - -

One informal definition of a *cult* is "any religion other than your own." The term is often applied to religious or mystical groups that society does not understand. Most cults involve some form of worship and followers who are dedicated to the concepts promoted by the leader.

Normally cults have a charismatic leader who develops an idea that attracts people looking for fulfillment. The leader is usually self-appointed and claims the right of rule because of a supernatural power of appointment. Cult membership may include males and females, and there is normally no room for democratic participation. Leadership is most often exerted through fear and mysticism. Charles Manson and Jim Jones are notorious examples of cult leaders.

A cult in Waco, Texas, the "Branch Davidians," headed by David Koresh, clashed with federal agents attempting a raid in February 1993. The raid turned into a gun battle in which four federal agents and at least two cult members were killed. Sixteen agents were wounded. Weapons inside the compound included at least one tripod-mounted .50-caliber machine gun and many semi-automatic weapons. A child who was released from the compound and who had lived with the cult for four years said she had been taught to put a gun into her mouth and told how to commit suicide by taking cyanide.

A 51-day standoff between the federal government and Koresh's armed cult ended in April 1993, when fire engulfed the compound. The FBI had sent an armored combat vehicle to ram holes into the buildings and pump tear gas into them. The FBI asserted that cultists started the blaze, which killed at least 80, including women and children. Survivors of the fire, however, insisted the fire was caused by the tank's hitting a barrel of propane and tipping over lit camping lanterns. In 1999 evidence that the FBI may have fired incendiary devices into the compound surfaced. As this text goes to press, the incident is under investigation.

Terminology

Over the years a number of terms have been associated with cults. Among the terms law enforcement officers should be familiar with are the following:

- **Antichrist**—the son of Satan
- **Beelzebub**—a powerful demon, right under Satan
- **Coven**—a group of witches or Satanists
- **Hand of Glory**—the left hand of a person who has died
- **Incantation**—verbal spells

- **Magick**—the "glue" that binds occult groups. It is a supernatural act or force that causes a change in the environment
- **Occult**—secret knowledge of supernormal powers
- **Ritual**—prescribed form of religious or mystical ceremony
- **Sabbat**—a gathering of witches

Symbolism

Among the satanic and occult symbols are the *circle,* which symbolizes totality and wholeness and within which ceremonies are often performed; the *inverted cross,* which mocks the Christian cross; the *goat's head,* symbolizing the devil; the *heart,* symbolizing the center of life; the *hexagram* (six-pointed star), purported to protect and control demons; the *pentagram* (five-pointed star), representing the four elements of the earth surmounted by "the Spirit"; and the *horned hand,* a hand signal of recognition used between those who are members of a cult. This is similar to the hand signals used by street gangs. Figure 19.3 illustrates symbols commonly associated with satanic and occult groups.

Colors also have significance to many cults:

- Black—darkness, night, sorrow, evil, the devil
- Blue—water, tears, sadness
- Green—vegetation, nature, restfulness
- Red—blood, physical life, energy, sexuality
- White—cleanliness, purity, innocence, virginity
- Yellow—perfection, wealth, glory, power

The Nature of the Crimes

Cults and the occult have created great interest because of recurring stories from children and adults in different areas of the United States concerning bizarre satanic rituals and behaviors. Although some may be fantasies, there appears to be some truth, especially regarding the danger to children of the members of satanic groups.

- - - - - - - -

A **ritualistic crime** is an unlawful act committed with or during a ceremony. Investigate the crime, not the belief system.

- - - - - - - -

Strandberg (1998, p. 53) states:

There are basically three levels of activity in [occult] groups.

FIGURE 19.3
Common Satanic and Occult Symbols

AC/DC	ANTICHRIST/ DEVIL CHILD
ZOSO	THREE-HEADED DOG THAT GUARDS GATE TO HELL
S	SATAN/STONER
MARKOS	ABRACADABRA
FFF	ANTICHRIST
666	ANTICHRIST
	ANTICHRIST
NATAS	SATAN REVERSED
6, 9, 13, XIII	OCCULT NUMBERS
	HORN AND TAIL ADDED TO ANY LETTER
	LIGHTNING BOLT HEAVEN TO HELL STRENGTH
	SWASTIKA
	ANTICHRIST CROSS OF CONFUSION

PENTAGRAM WHITE MAGIC

PENTAGRAM UPSIDE-DOWN STAR SIGN OF OCCULT

HEXAGRAM CIRCLE

INFINITY- CONTAINMENT CONTROL OF EVIL POWER

ANK

LUCIFER MORNING STAR

The first level is fun and games, "dabblers," and it is not a sign of serious activity, though it is a symptom of a deeper problem. Teenagers playing with the occult, really trying to make more of a statement of rebellion than worship the devil, are examples of this stage. . . .

Serious involvement is the next level, and these people are convinced that the supernatural really exists and they make serious attempts to become involved in satanic activity.

The final level is criminal involvement, the only level where law enforcement can be actively involved. The individuals involved believe that they must engage in criminal activity to reach the reality of the supernatural. . . . It is not illegal to be in a satanic group, but some of their activities are illegal, [such as] underage liquor and drugs, animal mutilation, kidnapping, child abuse and murder.

According to Kail (1999, p. 139), occult crime is committed for a number of reasons, including:

- Recruitment—Many criminal occult groups require new members to commit crimes such as grave robbing, vandalism or animal cruelty to show they are serious.

- To preach the group's "theology" to the world—For example, Charles Manson's group committed the Tate-Labianca murders to start a race war.

- As an appeasement to a group's deity—commonly in the form of an animal or human sacrifice.

- "Divine inspiration" from the group's deity, spirit or demon—For example, in 1990 a female cult member was told by a "spirit" to kill the next person she met.

- To finance a group's activities—through participation in prostitution, child pornography, drug trafficking, the sale of human remains and murder for hire.

Cult or ritualistic crimes include vandalism, destruction or theft of religious artifacts; desecration of cemeteries; the maiming, torturing or killing of animals and humans; and the sexual abuse of children.

The "Black Masses" of Satanism often incorporate religious articles stolen from churches. A **Black Mass** mocks the Christian ritual of communion by substituting blood and urine for the wine and feces for the bread. The cross is usually inverted, and candles and cups may be used in sexual acts. "Hymns" that are either obscene or that praise Satan may be sung, and heavy-metal music may be played.

The Black Mass frequently involves animal mutilation and sacrifice and sometimes torture and sacrifice of humans, preferably babies or virgins. The sacrifice often incorporates ritualistic incantations. Victims, animal or human, are tortured and mutilated because it is believed that while the victim struggles, the life forces given off can be captured and stored for later use. Such sacrifices may be followed by a dance and an orgy.

"Stoner" gangs consist of middle-class youths involved in drugs, alcohol and often Satanism. Although stoners are not as apt to engage in the violent crimes associated with other street gangs, they may mutilate animals, rob graves and desecrate churches and human remains. Their graffiti frequently depict satanic symbolism such as inverted crosses and the number *666*.

Who Commits Ritualistic Crime?

Valdez (1998a, p. 27) asserts: "Crimes associated with occult religion are often, in fact, the work of unbalanced individuals." A psychological profile of males and females involved in the occult reveals they tend to be creative, imaginative, curious and daring. They also tend to be intelligent and well educated yet are frequently underachievers. Although they are egocentric, they also have a low self-esteem and have suffered peer rejection or persecution. They come from various social and economic backgrounds, can be any age (although the age range of 13 to 24 is the most common), and are of a variety of races, nationalities and religions. Interestingly, few Jews are involved in Satanism because they do not believe in the devil.

A number of factors may lead an individual to occult involvement including family alienation, insecurity and a quest for personal power, unfulfilled ambitions, a spiritual search for answers, idealism, nonconformity, adolescent rebellion, a desire for adventure and excitement, a need for attention and recognition, a need to escape reality or their own birth in the occult group.

Although the personal appearance of those involved in occult activity is often quite normal, others adopt a less mainstream look. For example, they may dress entirely in black or other dark clothing; pierce various parts of their bodies; grow their hair long and dye it; wear chains as implements of confinement; wear heavy eyeshadow and white makeup to appear more ashen or deathlike; wear heavy boots; display tattoos depicting serpents, skulls or other occult symbols; and have scars indicating cuttings, burnings or whippings.

People are drawn to a variety of occult groups, and different groups perform different rituals. Investigators should be familiar with various types of occult religions being practiced in their jurisdictions and the propensities of such groups for engaging in specific ritualistic crimes. For example, as Kail (p. 141) notes:

American Satanism has many different traditions and interpretations. Researchers of this movement have classified Satanists in three categories. The "religious" Satanist is one who usually publicly declares his/her affiliation with a legally recognized church. Criminal acts are seldom with these groups. The "Traditional" Satanist is usually criminally active, many times involved with underground groups . . . involved in narcotics distribution, prostitution, arson, and even murder for hire organizations. Many of these groups are generational in nature. The "Self-Styled" Satanist is usually a young adult who creates a "homemade" religion using aspects of occultism found in books, movies, and music. Criminal acts are sometimes evident in this category.

Meissner (1999, p. 48) describes seven types of Satanists: the proclaimed Satanist (bona fide church), black magic practitioners (devil worshippers), generational (passed through family), psuedo-Satanists ("Wannabes"), solitary (self-styled), theatrical Satanists (dabblers) and experimental Satanists.

Kail (p. 142) lists some other occult religions and their involvement, if any, in criminal activity:

- Wicca—A pantheistic religion focused on goddess worship and working with the four basic elements of earth, wind, water and fire. This is a basically nonviolent, noncriminal religion.

- Santeria—A form of African paganism with thousands of followers in the United States. The only evident criminal activity within the traditional practice of Santeria is animal sacrifice.

- Palo Mayombe—From the Kongo region of Africa, this religion centers on the use of "magickal sticks" and a cauldron containing "spirits" that are revered through rituals and sacrifices. Because much of Palo deals with the dead, grave robbing has been used to acquire ritual implements. Palo has also been found in many criminal cases involving drug related criminal groups.

- Voodoo—Also from Africa, the practice has been westernized in the United States. Animal sacrifice, however, is used by many voodoo houses.

Investigating Ritualistic Crimes

Cult and occult reports and activities are investigated in much the same way as any other crime. Interview the people who report these incidents, and prepare reports concerning witnesses or alleged victims of criminal activity. Take photos, sketch symbols, describe colors found and measure objects. Preserve all objects at the scene as evidence. Work from the outside perimeter to the center or the focus point of the site.

Strandberg (1998, p. 55) offers the following advice to those investigating ritualistic crime: "Remain vigilant. . . . Get to know the groups in your jurisdiction. Make an effort to understand their belief systems, and find out who are the major players in these groups." He (p. 55) also notes: "The Internet has expanded the reach of these groups, and made it harder to follow any group's recruitment activities. . . . The Internet can be used against these groups, however, because it offers an opportunity to learn more about these groups, and watch them."

Numerous books on the beliefs and rituals of various cults are available. The background contained in such books is beyond the scope of this book, but investigators should be alert to signs that criminal activity may be cult related.

Signs of Cult-Related Activity The following items may be important indicators of satanic or cult activity. If you suspect ritualistic crime, list these items in any search warrant sought: altars (stone or metal); animal parts (anus, heart, tongue, ears, front teeth, front legs, genitals); ashes; bells; blood; body paint; body parts (may be in a freezer); bones used or taken from graves (femur, fibula, index finger, skull and other large bones. The upper right leg and joints of the right-hand fingers are valued); booby traps; books on Satanism (especially *Book of Shadows*); bottles containing blood (may be in refrigerator); bowls with powder, colored salt, drugs or herbs; bullwhips; cages; candles, candle holders or candle drippings; cat-o'-nine-tails whips; cauldron for a fire; chalices; circle with a 9-foot diameter (may contain a pentagram); coffin; cords (colored and knotted); crystals; daggers or double-edged short sword; drums; effigylike clay figures, voodoo dolls stuck with pins or otherwise mutilated; flash powder; glove (black satin or velvet) for the right hand; gongs; hoods, hats or helmets; hypodermic needles (for removing blood); incense; inverted crosses; jewelry such as amulets or medallions with satanic symbols; knives; ligatures; martial arts weaponry and clothing; masks; nondiscernible alphabet; occult games; Ouija board; painted rocks; parchment (for making contracts); pillows; robes (especially red, white or black); rooms draped in black or red (or nail holes in walls and ceiling indicating that such drapes may have been used); Satanic symbols painted on rocks or trees; skulls; smoke bombs; swords; Tarot cards; unusual drawings or symbols on walls or floors (hexagrams, pentagrams, horns of death, etc.); vandalized Christian artifacts; and a wooden stand for an altar.

-- -- -- -- -- -- --

Indicators that criminal activity may be cult related include symbols, candles, makeshift altars, bones, cult-related books, swords, daggers and chalices.

-- -- -- -- -- -- --

If evidence is found to support the commission of a crime, submit the case to the prosecuting attorney's

Texas Attorney General Jim Mattox (center) views a cauldron of bones found at a ranch where 12 bodies were found buried.

office, as in other crimes. Also as with other crimes, if illegal acts are being committed in the presence of an officer who arrives at the scene, an immediate arrest may be executed. However, many authorities on cult activity warn that no one, including a police officer, should ever approach or try to stop an occult ritual alone because in all probability, the officer would be dealing with mentally deranged people high on drugs.

Investigating Animal Deaths Unusual circumstances surrounding animal deaths may be important indicators of satanic or cult activity. The following circumstances connected with dead animals should be noted:

- No blood—The blood has been drained from the animal.
- An inverted cross carved on the animal's chest.
- Surgically removed head.
- Intestines or other body organs removed.

If a rash of missing animal reports occurs, gather information on the kind of animals they are, when they disappeared and from what area. Look for patterns, and coordinate efforts with the local humane society and veterinarians.

Investigating Homicides At the scene of a homicide investigation, the following may suggest a ritualistic death:

- Missing body parts—heart, genitals, left hand, tongue, index finger
- Scarring between index finger and thumb or inside the wrist from past rituals involving members' blood
- Blood drained from body
- Ritualistic symbols such as a pentagram associated with satanic worshipers carved on the body or surrounding area
- Tattoos on armpits or the bottom of feet
- Wax drippings, oils, incense or powders of ritual on the body
- Urine or human/animal feces smeared on body or found in body cavities
- Semen inside, on or near body cavities or smeared on the body
- Victim undressed
- Body painted or tied up
- Neck wounds, branding-iron marks or burn marks on body
- Colored strings near the body

Cult murders are usually stabbings or cuttings—seldom are they gunshot wounds—and many of the victims are cult members or former members. The person who commits the murder is typically a white male from a middle- to upper-class family with above-average intelligence. Some form of drug use is characteristic.

Guard against reacting emotionally when confronted with ritualistic crime, for they tend to be emotionally and spiritually repulsive. Also bear in mind that unusual crimes are also committed by individuals with mental problems who are not connected with cults.

During postmortem examination, the stomach contents can be of great importance in determining what occurred just before death.

In many ritualistic homicides the body is not available because it has been burned, leaving no evidence. Further, most juries disbelieve seemingly outlandish charges of Satanism and human sacrifice, and most judges do not regard Satanism as a real problem. Hence, most cases are dismissed.

Investigating Satanic Serial Killings

Serial killings may be linked to satanic-like rituals in the murder act itself as well as in the killer's behavior following the murder. Serial killings frequently linked to Satanism include the following:

Charles Manson had links with the Process, a satanic group. Many of the murders committed by Manson and his followers had ritualistic overtones.

The "Son of Sam" murders involving David Berkowitz are claimed by author Maury Terry in *The Ultimate Evil* to have been a conspiracy among satanic cult members of the Process group.

Some brutal, vicious serial killers find Satanism a justification for their bizarre antisocial behavior.

"Night Stalker" Richard Ramirez had a pentagram on the palm of his hand, wrote satanic graffiti on the walls of some of his victims' homes and was obsessed with AC/DC's *Highway to Hell* album featuring the song "Night Stalker." Ramirez shouted "Hail, Satan" as he left the courtroom.

Investigating Youth Suicides

Increasingly, law enforcement has been faced with satanic "overtones" to suicides committed by young people. Lyle Rapacki of Flagstaff, Arizona, has compiled a list of indicators that a youth is involved in cult or occult activities:

- Withdrawal from family and friends
- Changing of friends and associates
- Sudden lack of interest in church and the Bible
- New friends who are loners, nonacademic and problematic for school officials
- Change of dress to darker, more subdued color; more jewelry

- Increased rebellion, depression or aggressive behavior
- Negative change in moral behavior; also a change in priorities to a more "I"-centered pattern
- Drop in grades, lack of interest in school or lack of concentration
- Interest in occult literature; may start their own "Book of Shadows"—a notebook containing personal symbols and rituals, often written in code
- Magazines focusing on death, violence, secrecy and sexual acting-out
- Increasing involvement in fantasy role-playing games such as Dungeons and Dragons (D&D)
- Increased viewing of occultic movies and TV
- Collection of occultic paraphernalia such as bones, skulls, ritual knives and candles
- Rock, punk and heavy-metal music
- Nightmares; shades drawn during the day
- Preoccupation with death, destruction or harming things
- Sudden missing pets or animals in neighborhood

Investigators dealing with youth suicides that they suspect may be occult related should inquire into the kind of music the youths listened to, the kinds of games they played, whether they had Ouija boards or tarot cards and whether they dabbled in astrology or seances.

Special Challenges

Just as law enforcement officers may have a difficult time relating to gang members and not reacting negatively to them because of their gang associations, they may also have difficulty relating to those who engage in ritualistic activity. This is also true of the general public and the media, which frequently sensationalize cases involving ritualistic or cult-related crimes, particularly sexual abuse of children and homicides.

- - - - - - - - -

Special challenges involved in investigating ritualistic or cult-related crimes include separating the belief system from the illegal acts, the sensationalism that frequently accompanies such crimes and the "abnormal" personalities of some victims and suspects.

- - - - - - - - -

Frequently the "victims" of occult-related crimes are former participants in the cult. Many have been or are currently undergoing psychological counseling, which makes their testimony less than credible to some people. Likewise, many of the suspects are outside what most would consider to be normal and consequently may be treated differently because of how they look and what they believe rather than because of their actions.

Strandberg (1998, p. 57) concludes with a warning: "As people continue to feel more and more disenfranchised, the capacity of new religious groups to recruit more and more people grows exponentially. The threat of violence is always there."

Summary

Distinctive characteristics of organized crime include definite organization and control, high-profit and continued-profit crimes, singular control and protection. It is a prosecutable conspiracy to acquire any enterprise with money obtained from illegal activity; to acquire, maintain or control any enterprise by illegal means; or to use any enterprise to conduct illegal activity. Organized crime is continuously attempting to do all of the preceding with money obtained through its heavy involvement in gambling, drugs, pornography, prostitution, loan-sharking, money laundering, fraud and infiltration of legitimate businesses.

The daily observations of local law enforcement officers provide vital information for investigating organized crime. All suspicious activities and persons possibly associated with organized crime must be reported to the appropriate person or agency. Organized-crime strike forces coordinate all federal organized crime activities and work closely with state, county and municipal law enforcement agencies.

Belonging to a gang is not illegal; however, the activities of gang members frequently *are* illegal. A street gang is a group of people who form an alliance for a common purpose and engage in unlawful or criminal activity. In addition to drug dealing, gang members often engage in vandalism, arson, shootings, stabbings, intimidation and other forms of violence. Gang members may be identified by their names, symbols (clothing and tattoos) and communication styles, including graffiti and sign language. Maintain records on gangs, gang members, monikers, photographs, vehicles and illegal activities. Cross-reference the records.

Special challenges in investigating the illegal activities of gangs include the multitude of suspects and the unreliability or fear of witnesses. The two most often used defense strategies are pleas of diminished capacity and self-defense.

Bias or hate crimes are motivated by bigotry and hatred against a specific group of people.

A cult is a system of religious beliefs and rituals and those who practice them. A ritualistic crime is an unlawful act committed within the context of a ceremony. Investigate the crime—not the belief system.

Ritualistic crimes have included vandalism; destruction and theft of religious artifacts; desecration of cemeteries; the maiming, torturing and killing of animals and humans; and the sexual abuse of children. Indicators that criminal activity may be cult related include symbols, candles, makeshift altars, bones, cult-related books, swords, daggers and chalices. Special challenges in investigating ritualistic or cult-related crimes include separating the belief system from the illegal acts, the sensationalism that frequently accompanies such crimes and the "abnormal" personalities sometimes found in both victims and suspects.

Checklist
Organized Crime

- Have people recently moved into the city and purchased businesses that obviously could not support their standard of living?
- Do any public officials appear to live beyond their means?
- Does a public official continuously vote in favor of a business that is suspected of being connected with organized crime?
- Have business owners complained of pressure to use a specific service or of threats to close the business if they do not hire certain people?
- Does a business have high-level executives with police records?
- Have there been complaints of someone on the premises operating as a bookie?
- Have families complained about loss of wages paid to a loan shark?
- Have union officials suddenly been replaced by new, nonlocal persons?
- Has there been damage or injury to property during union problems?

- Are goods being received at a store that do not fit with merchandise sold there?

- Has a discount store suddenly appeared without a clear indication of true ownership?

- Has arson suddenly increased?

- Do nonemployees hang around manufacturing plants or nonstudents hang around a school? (This could indicate a bookie operation or drug sales.)

- Is the same person using a pay telephone at the same time each day?

- Is evidence of betting operations being left in public wastebaskets or trash containers on the streets?

- When assaults occur, what are the motives? Could they be a result of gambling debts owed to a loan shark?

- Are people seen going into and out of certain businesses with which they are not ordinarily associated?

- Are known gamblers or persons with other criminal records repeatedly seen in a specific location?

Gangs

- What illegal activities have been committed?
- Who reported the activities?
- What evidence is there?
- Who are the suspects?
- What signs tend to implicate a specific gang?
- Who are the leaders of this gang?
- What records exist on this gang?
- Who might provide additional information?

Cults

- What type of activity brought the cult to the attention of the police?
- Is the activity illegal?
- What statutes or ordinances are applicable?
- Who reported the activity? What is their connection to the cult?
- What evidence is there that the illegal activity is part of a ritual?
- Who are suspected members of the cult?
- What records exist on the cult?
- Who might provide additional information?

Application

A. Determine how each of these situations might indicate organized crime activity (Reprinted from *Criminal Intelligence,* Training Key #223, with permission of the International Association of Chiefs of Police).

You note pickets outside one or two stores in the same line of business. The picketing may be a perfectly legitimate tactic.

A cheap hotel appears to be doing a reasonably brisk business. Its patrons travel light—many do not carry luggage. A bar has a reputation for being a "clip joint"; charges of watered-down liquor are frequent.

A truck is loaded at a location other than a depot or shipping dock. Goods are transferred from a truck of a well-known company to an unmarked truck. A warehouse that is almost always empty is now full. Unusual activity at an unusual time occurs in a warehouse area. Merchandise is transferred from a truck to the garage of a residence.

A group begins to congregate at a certain street location at certain times each day.

A business establishment suspected of being mob-controlled burns to the ground.

Certain people always seem to frequent a certain bar although none of them live in the neighborhood.

A club shuts down at irregular times—sometimes early in the afternoon, other times at midevening. Do these times coincide with the completion of racing or when the results of other sporting events become available?

A known racketeer frequently meets with certain unidentified individuals.

B. Graffiti has suddenly appeared in increasing amounts in specific areas on walls, public buildings, telephone poles and street lights in your community. Some are in blue paints and some are in red. Groups in the local park have been seen wearing blue bandanas, whereas in another park they are wearing red kerchiefs. Some of them have been seen flashing particular hand signals to each other. Some of the graffiti symbols represent animals and insects. A blue word *Crips* has the letter *C* crossed out with a red *X*.

Question

If graffiti is truly the "newspaper of the street gangs," what information should the preceding description give to a police officer?

C. While looking for a stolen safe in a wooded area, the police discover a circular open area about 200 feet in diameter with candles placed around the circumference. A rough altar has been constructed with a cross. A fire has been burned beneath the cross. A five-pointed star is scratched in the dirt, and the word *NATAS* is scrawled on several trees and on the cross. The number *6* also appears on several trees. What appears to be bones are found in the ashes of the fire below the altar.

Question

What do these findings suggest? Is this something the police should investigate further? Why or why not?

Discussion Questions

1. Most experts believe that organized crime can flourish only in areas where it has corrupted local officials. Do you agree?
2. What is your perception of the prevalence of organized crime in your community? Your state? The country?
3. Has organized crime become more or less of a problem for police in the past decade?
4. How would you define *gang? Cult?* What is the difference between them?
5. Are there gangs in your community? If so, in what activities do they engage?
6. What are the signs of occult influence among teenagers?
7. What can parent groups do about community gangs? Cults?
8. What does gang membership provide for its members that society does not?
9. What is the police responsibility with regard to investigating gang activity? Cult activity? Hate crimes?
10. Is there evidence of ritualistic crime or hate crime in your community? Your state?

References

Addressing Community Gang Problems: A Practical Guide. Washington, DC: Bureau of Justice Assistance, May 1998. (NCJ-164273)

Anti-Defamation League. "Poisoning the Web: Hatred Online." *Corrections Today,* Vol. 61, No. 5, August 1999, pp. 102–114.

Baker, A. Morgan. "Instant Photos Offer Gang Crime Fighters Compelling Evidence." *The Police Chief,* Vol. LXV, No. 4, April 1998, pp. 62–64.

Baker, Thomas E. "Supergangs—or Organized Crime?" *Law and Order,* Vol. 47, No. 10, October 1999, pp. 192–197.

Beare, Margaret E. and Martens, Frederick T. "Policing Organized Crime." *Journal of Contemporary Criminal Justice,* Vol. 14, No. 4, November 1998, pp. 398–427.

Bodinger-deUriate, Cristina. *Hate Crime: The Rise of Hate Crime on School Campuses.* Bloomington, IN: Phi Delta Kappa, 1991.

Bunker, Robert J. "Street Gangs—Future Paramilitary Groups?" *The Police Chief,* Vol. LXIII, No. 6, June 1996, pp. 54–59.

Campbell, R.K. "Investigating Hate Groups on the Internet." *Law and Order,* Vol. 47, No. 11, November 1999, p 40.

Clayton, Susan L. "Learning Not to Hate." *Corrections Today,* Vol. 61, No. 5, August 1999, p. 8.

Constantine, Thomas A. "Mexico's Organized Crime Groups." *The Police Chief,* Vol. LXIV, No. 4, April 1997, p. 178.

Criminal Intelligence. Training Key #223. International Association of Chiefs of Police, p. 19.

Das, Dilip. "Organized Crime: A World Perspective." *ACJS Today,* Vol. XVII, Issue 4, January/February 1999, pp. 1, 3–7.

Decker, Scott H.; Bynum, Tim; and Weisel, Deborah. "A Tale of Two Cities: Gangs as Organized Crime Groups." *Justice Quarterly,* Vol. 15, No. 3, September 1998, pp. 395–425.

Dunbar, Edward. "Defending the Indefensible: A Critique and Analysis of Psycholegal Defense Arguments of Hate Crime Perpetrators." *Journal of Contemporary Criminal Justice,* Vol. 15, No. 1, February 1999, pp. 64–77.

Dunlap, Russell W. "Asian Home Invasion Robbery." *Journal of Contemporary Criminal Justice,* Vol. 13, No. 4, November 1997, pp. 309–319.

Ekberg, Christer. "Cooperation in Baltic Sea Area Addresses Organised Crime." *The Police Chief,* Vol. LXV, No. 9, September 1998, pp. 47–49.

Esbensen, Finn-Aage and Winfree, L. Thomas. "Race and Gender Differences between Gang and Nongang Youths: Results from a Multisite Survey." *Justice Quarterly,* Vol. 15, No. 3, September 1998, pp. 505–526.

Farley, Terrence P. "New DOJ State and Local Asset Forfeiture Training Initiative." *BJA Bulletin: Asset Forfeiture Series.* Washington, DC: Bureau of Justice Assistance, August 1995. (NCJ-152056)

Ferrell, Jeff. "Freight Train Graffiti: Subculture, Crime, Dislocation." *Justice Quarterly,* Vol. 15, No. 4, December 1998, pp. 587–608.

Fritsch, Eric J.; Caeti, Tory J.; and Taylor, Robert W. "Gang Suppression through Saturation Patrol, Aggressive Curfew, and Truancy Enforcement: A Quasi-Experimental Test of the Dallas Anti-Gang Initiative." *Crime and Delinquency,* Vol. 45, No. 1, January 1999, pp. 122–139.

Godwin, Cory A. "Applying Correctional Intelligence to Law Enforcement Investigations." *Corrections Today,* Vol. 61, No. 5, August 1999, pp. 94–100.

Gondles, James A., Jr. "Hate Crime: Not New, but Still Alarming." *Corrections Today,* Vol. 61, No. 5, August 1999, p. 6.

"A G.R.E.A.T. Program." *Law and Order,* Vol. 47, No. 2, February 1999, pp. 73–74.

Grigera, Elena. "Hate Crimes: State and Federal Responses to Bias-Motivated Violence." *Corrections Today,* Vol. 61, No. 5, August 1999, pp. 68–74, 80.

Harris, Wesley. "Straight Edge: America's Newest Gang?" *Law and Order,* Vol. 47, No. 2, February 1999, pp. 69–70.

"Hate Groups Increase by 20 Percent, According to Southern Poverty Law Center." *NCJA Justice Bulletin,* Vol. 18, No. 4, April 1998, pp. 10–11.

" 'Hate Rock' Spreads Its Musical Message." *Law Enforcement News,* Vol. XXV, No. 508, March 31, 1999, p. 8.

Hicks, David C. "Thinking about Organized Crime Prevention." *Journal of Contemporary Criminal Justice,* Vol. 14, No. 4, November 1998, pp. 325–350.

Horowitz, Richard. "The Low Down on Dirty Money." *Security Management,* Vol. 41, No. 10, October 1997, pp. 50–57.

Howard, Christine. "Train Gangs Today." *Law and Order,* Vol. 46, No. 10, October 1998, pp. 117–120.

Howell, James C. *Youth Gangs: An Overview.* Washington, DC: Office of Juvenile Justice and Delinquency Prevention, Juvenile Justice Bulletin, August 1998. (NCJ-167249)

Howell, James C. "Youth Gang Homicides: A Literature Review." *Crime and Delinquency,* Vol. 45, No. 2, April 1999, pp. 208–241.

Huff, C. Ronald. *Comparing the Criminal Behavior of Youth Gangs and At-Risk Youths.* Washington, DC: National Institute of Justice, Research in Brief, October 1998. (NCJ-172852)

Huizinga, D. "Gangs and the Volume of Crime." Presented at the annual meetings of the Western Society of Criminology, Honolulu, 1997.

International Association of Chiefs of Police. "Responding to Hate Crimes: A Police Officer's Guide to Investigation and Prevention." 1999.

"Internet Blamed for Growth of Hate Groups." *Las Vegas Review Journal,* February 1999, p. 3A.

Israel, Michael. "Hate Speech and the First Amendment." *Journal of Contemporary Criminal Justice,* Vol. 15, No. 1, February 1999, pp. 97–110.

Jackson, Lonnie. "Understanding and Responding to Youth Gangs." *Corrections Today,* Vol. 61, No. 5, August 1999, pp. 62–66, 112.

Kail, Tony. "The Occult: Still a Police Problem." *Law and Order,* Vol. 47, No. 7, July 1999, pp. 138–142.

Laflin, Melanie. "Girl Gangs." *Law and Order,* March 1996, pp. 87–89.

Lanata, John. "Identifying and Interviewing Gang Members." *Law Enforcement Technology,* Vol. 25, No. 10, October 1998, pp. 86–93.

Levin, Brian. "Hate Crimes: Worse by Definition." *Journal of Contemporary Criminal Justice,* Vol. 15, No. 1, February 1999, pp. 6–21.

Mahoney, Jeremy. "Stop the Hate: Massachusetts Task Force Creates Student Civil Rights Project to Combat Problem." *Corrections Today,* Vol. 61, No. 5, August 1999, pp. 82–86.

Martin, Susan E. "Investigating Hate Crimes: Case Characteristics and Law Enforcement Responses." *Justice Quarterly,* Vol. 13, No. 3, September 1996, pp. 455–480.

Maxson, Cheryl L. *Gang Members on the Move.* Washington, DC: Office of Juvenile Justice and Delinquency Prevention, Juvenile Justice Bulletin, October 1998. (NCJ-171153)

McCafferty, Dennis. "WWW.Hate.Comes to Your Home." *USA Weekend,* March 26–28, 1999, pp. 6–7.

McCorkle, Richard C. and Miethe, Terance D. "The Political and Organizational Response to Gangs: An Examination of a 'Moral Panic' in Nevada." *Justice Quarterly,* Vol. 15, No. 1, March 1998, pp. 41–64.

McCort, Michael C. "The Evolution of Street Gangs: A Shift toward Organized Crime." *The Police Chief,* Vol. LXIII, No. 6, June 1996, pp. 33–38, 51–52.

McGovern, Glen P. "The Growing Threat of Russian Organized Crime." *Law and Order,* Vol. 47, No. 2, February 1999, pp. 66–68.

McMillan, Gloria. "Editorial." *Journal of Contemporary Criminal Justice,* Vol. 15, No. 1, February 1999, pp. 3–5.

Meissner, Craig S. "Satanism and Crime: Look at the Whole Picture." *Police,* Vol. 23, No. 12, December 1999, pp. 48–49.

Mendez, Deborah. "Girls in Gangs Find that Life is Tough Both on, off the Street." *Las Vegas Review Journal,* November 10, 1996, p. 8B.

Miller, R. K. "Skinheads: The New Nazis." *Police,* Vol. 22, No. 12, December 1998, pp. 39–41.

Murphy, Clyde E. "Civil Rights Lawyers Organize a National Response to Hate Crime." *Corrections Today,* Vol. 61, No. 5, August 1999, pp. 88–93, 144–145.

"National Street Gang Survey." *FBI Law Enforcement Bulletin,* Vol. 68, No. 7, July 1999, p. 21.

Neubauer, Ronald S. "Hate Crime in America— Summit No. 5." *The Police Chief,* Vol. LXVI, No. 2, February 1999, p. 6.

Nolan, James J. and Akiyama, Yoshio. "An Analysis of Factors that Affect Law Enforcement Participation in Hate Crime Reporting." *Journal of Contemporary Criminal Justice,* Vol. 15, No. 1, February 1999, pp. 111–127.

"Number of Hate Groups Is Rising despite Good Economy, Report Finds." (Minneapolis/St. Paul) *Star Tribune,* March 3, 1998, p. A4.

Panther, Thomas M. "Gang Violence: Getting a GRIP on Gangs." *The Police Chief,* Vol. LXVI, No. 10, October 1999, pp. 119–121.

Petrosino, Carolyn. "Connecting the Past to the Future: Hate Crime in America." *Journal of Contemporary Criminal Justice,* Vol. 15, No. 1, February 1999, pp. 22–47.

"Police Reporting Juvenile Gangs in Cities and Towns of All Sizes." *Criminal Justice Newsletter,* Vol. 30, No. 9, May 3, 1999, p. 6.

Quarantiello, Laura E. "Tracking the Homeboys." *Law and Order,* Vol. 44, No. 6, June 1996, pp. 80–82.

"Racial Prejudice Most Frequent Motive for Hate Crimes, FBI Says." *Las Vegas Review Journal,* January 22, 1999, p. 12A.

Regini, Lisa A. "Combating Gangs: The Need for Innovation." *FBI Law Enforcement Bulletin,* Vol. 67, No. 2, February 1998, pp. 25–32.

"Responding to Hate Crimes." *Community Policing Exchange,* Phase VII, No. 30, January/February 2000, p. 1.

Schofield, Daniel L. "Gang Congregation Ordinance: Supreme Court Invalidation." *FBI Law Enforcement Bulletin,* Vol. 68, No. 9, September 1999, pp. 28–32.

"Senate Moving to Expand Law on Prosecution of Hate Crimes." *Criminal Justice Newsletter,* Vol. 30, No. 6, March 16, 1999, pp. 2–3.

Smith, Bruno W.; York, James T.; Forster, Paul E.; and Bjorngaare, Wenche. "Interpol's 'Project Rockers' Helps Disrupt Outlaw Motorcycle Gangs." *The Police Chief,* Vol. LXV, No. 9, September 1998, pp. 54–56.

Spector, Elliot B. "Loitering Ordinances to Control Gang Activity." *The Police Chief,* Vol. LXVI, No. 10, October 1999, pp. 11–12.

Strandberg, Keith W. "Investigating Asian Crime." *Law Enforcement Technology,* Vol. 24, No. 9, September 1997a, pp. 58–62.

Strandberg, Keith W. "Money Laundering." *Law Enforcement Technology,* Vol. 24, No. 7, July 1997b, pp. 28–33.

Strandberg, Keith W. "Investigating Satanism and Cults." *Law Enforcement Technology,* Vol. 25, No. 6, June 1998, pp. 52–57.

"Study Reveals Motivations behind Antigay Hate Crimes." *NCJA Justice Bulletin,* Vol. 18, No. 11, November 1998, pp. 1, 6.

"Supreme Court Strikes Down Chicago Anti-Gang Ordinance." *Criminal Justice Newsletter,* Vol. 30, No. 3, February 2, 1999, pp. 1–2.

Tischler, Eric. "Can Tolerance Be Taught?" *Corrections Today,* Vol. 61, No. 5, August 1999, pp. 76–79.

Torres, Sam. "Hate Crimes against African Americans." *Journal of Contemporary Criminal Justice,* Vol. 15, No. 1, February 1999, pp. 48–63.

Trethewy, Steve and Katz, Terry. "Motorcycle Gangs or Motorcycle Mafia?" *The Police Chief,* Vol. LXV, No. 4, April 1998, pp. 53–60.

Valdez, Al. "Easing Investigations on the Gang Battlefield." *Police,* Vol. 20, No. 3, March 1996a, pp. 20–21.

Valdez, Al. "A New Gang Threat Rears Its Ugly Head." *Police,* Vol. 20, No. 7, July 1996b, pp. 20–21.

Valdez, Al. "Girls in the Hood: Dangerous Liaisons." *Police,* Vol. 21, No. 9, September 1997a, pp. 40–41.

Valdez, Al. "Southeast Asian Gangs." *Police,* Vol. 21, No. 4, April 1997b, pp. 50–51.

Valdez, Al. "Beating the Devil." *Police,* Vol. 22, No. 6, June 1998a, p. 27.

Valdez, Al. "Gangs: Migration or Imitation?" *Police,* Vol. 22, No. 1, January 1998b, pp. 48–49.

Valdez, Al. "Interpreting That Writing on the Wall." *Police,* Vol. 22, No. 4, April 1998c, pp. 39–40.

Valdez, Al. "Native American Gangs Spreading." *Police,* Vol. 22, No. 2, February 1998d, p. 47.

Valdez, Al. "Getting to Know the Mara Salvatrucha." *Police,* Vol. 23, No. 6, June 1999a, pp. 60–62.

Valdez, Al. "Nazi Low Riders." *Police,* Vol. 23, No. 3, March 1999b, pp. 46–48.

Valdez, Al. "Shoes and Sureños: Tracking a Gang." *Police,* Vol. 24, No. 2, February 2000a, pp. 56–59.

Valdez, Al. "The Tiny Rascal Gang: Big Trouble." *Police,* Vol. 24, No. 1, January 2000b, pp. 64–67.

Wexler, Sanford. "Bringing Down the Mob." *Law Enforcement Technology,* Vol. 25, No. 1, January 1998a, pp. 42–45.

Wexler, Sanford. "The New Wiseguys: The Russian Mafia." *Law Enforcement Technology,* Vol. 25, No. 5, May 1998b, pp. 56–59.

Williams, Richard H. "Holding the Line against Organized Crime." *Security Management,* Vol. 42, No. 4, April 1998, pp. 36–41.

Wilson, Craig R. "What's in a Name? Gang Monikers." *FBI Law Enforcement Bulletin,* Vol. 66, No. 5, May 1997, pp. 14–17.

Zalisko, Walter. "Russian Organized Crime." *Law and Order,* Vol. 47, No. 10, October 1999, pp. 219–227.

Drug Buyers and Sellers

Do You Know?

How drugs are commonly classified?

What drugs are most commonly observed on the street, in the possession of users and seized in drug raids, and what the most frequent drug arrest is?

When it is illegal to use or sell narcotics or dangerous drugs and what physical evidence can prove these offenses?

How to recognize a drug addict? What the common symptoms are?

What the major legal evidence in prosecuting drug sale cases is?

When an on-sight arrest can be made for a drug buy?

What precautions to take in undercover drug buys and how to avoid a charge of entrapment?

What hazards exist in raiding a clandestine drug laboratory?

What agency provides unified leadership in combatting illegal drug activities and what its primary emphasis is?

Introduction

The traditions of American democracy affirm our commitment to both the rule of law and individual freedom. Although government must minimize interference in the private lives of citizens, it cannot deny people the security on which peace of mind depends. Drug abuse impairs rational thinking and the potential for a full, productive life. Drug abuse, drug trafficking, and their consequences destroy personal liberty and the well-being of communities. Drugs drain the physical, intellectual, spiritual, and moral strength of America. Crime, violence, workplace accidents, family misery, drug-exposed children, and addiction are only part of the price imposed on society. Drug abuse spawns global criminal syndicates and bankrolls those who sell drugs to young people. Illegal drugs indiscriminately destroy old and young, men and women from all racial and ethnic groups and every walk of life. No person or group is immune (*The National Drug Control Strategy*, 1998, p. 1).

The Federal Drug Enforcement Agency (FDEA) estimates that 5 percent of the population, or nearly 10 million Americans, are involved in drug abuse of some sort. Deputy Chief Robert Warshaw, associate director of the Office of National Drug Control Policy's (ONDCP) Bureau of State and Local Affairs, states: "Drugs cost our society $110 billion a year and kill 16,000 people a year" (deGroot, 1998, p. 90). Gondles (1998, p. 6) adds:

> Drug usage and drug addiction suck the very life out of our society. They drain us of our most important asset—our kids. Medical costs. Incarceration costs. Victim costs. Psychological costs. Lost wages costs. Welfare costs. Insurance costs—it goes on and on and on.
>
> Seeing your son or daughter, or brother or aunt, whomever waste away because of the scourge of substance abuse is like watching life itself seep, drop by drop, toward the final step of death.

Walchak (1996, p. 6) highlights the seriousness of the drug problem.

> When crack cocaine was introduced in the United States in the mid-1980s, violent crime rates began to soar. In fact, much of the violent crime in America is linked to drug trafficking and drug abuse. Over one-third of all violent acts and almost half of all homicides are drug-related. According to a recent report from DEA, the two causes most frequently cited for the growth of violent crime are drug lords protecting and expanding their drug turf, and drug users seeking to obtain money for drugs.

A recent survey of police chiefs across the country revealed (Hall, 1998, p. 72): "Drugs—and the crime often associated with street narcotic activity—was cited more often as a 'problem' than anything else—in both small and medium-sized towns, cities and in the heartland—by 48 percent of the chiefs." The violence inspired by drug-related activities translates into murders, arsons, drive-by shootings, car bombs and other random acts that threaten and terrorize a community. Drug gangs have turned many communities into virtual war zones. Sometimes these acts are gang reprisals or witness intimidation; others are designed simply to frighten innocent citizens enough to ensure that they refrain from calling the police. As Strandberg (1997, p. 28) states: "The experts agree that drugs, guns, and youth crime are inexorably interconnected. . . . Youths get involved with the drug trade, and soon they

are carrying guns for protection; then they are using guns for violent crimes. It's a natural progression, and one that is seen by law enforcement every single day."

Law enforcement agencies have encountered all types of technology used by drug sellers, ranging from two-way radios and cellular phones to robot planes. One seller of two-way radios stated that drug dealers were his biggest customers. If a radio was confiscated in an arrest, another was immediately purchased.

Drug dealers use personal computers, sophisticated encryption systems that even federal agencies have difficulty deciphering, night vision equipment, police frequency jamming equipment, scanners and networking systems. The main advantages drug dealers have over government in using technology are the availability of almost unlimited funds and a lack of bureaucratic approval systems.

Law enforcement officers must understand the drug problem, know when drugs are being used, recognize a wide variety of drugs by sight and know the procedures for seizing drug evidence and making an arrest. Local officers have a responsibility not only to their community but also to other jurisdictions and to agents of other levels of government that enforce drug laws.

Street officers have an important responsibility, even in large departments that have special narcotic units. Drugs are a major problem because users often commit crimes to support their habit. Law enforcement personnel seek to minimize the flow of drugs and to control their sale and use. Unquestionably, drugs and illicit drug trafficking are intertwined with the general crime problem. Many criminals who formerly confined their activities to other crimes turn to the higher profits available from drug sales. Others commit crimes simply to support a drug habit.

This chapter explains the classification of controlled drugs and discusses illegal possession or use of controlled substances, as well as the illegal sale and distribution of controlled substances. Then it presents investigative aides and the hazards involved in investigating clandestine drug laboratories. This is followed by a look at agency cooperation and the role of drug asset forfeitures in combatting the drug problem. The chapter concludes with an exploration of where efforts might be concentrated in the future. ■

Classification of Controlled Drugs

A major problem for law enforcement officers is to recognize drugs found in a suspect's possession. Because of the many different types, colors, sizes, trade names and strengths of commercial drugs, many officers use a pharmaceutical reference book. The *Physicians' Desk Reference* (PDR), used widely by health-care providers, is the basis for PDR I.D., a drug identification tool used by criminal investigators.

The portable, easy-to-use "fan-deck" of cards contains colored, actual-size photographs of 1,700 capsules and tablets and gives information about each drug (see Figure 20.1). Street drugs, on the other hand, can be identified by using a field test kit to provide probable cause for the officer to arrest and can then be sent to a laboratory for comprehensive testing. Officers should be familiar with the commonly used "street" terms for drugs and drug paraphernalia, including the following:

Acid	Crack	Ice	Short
Angel	Crank	Joint	Snow
Dust	Dexies	Lid	Speed
Bag	Drop	Lumbo	Spike
Barbs	Dust	Meth	Spoon
Boy	Fit	PCP	Stash
Cap	Girl	Rainbows	Stick
Christmas	Gold	Red	"T"
Trees	Grass	Red Devils	Tea
CMT	"H"	Reds	Window Pane
Coke	Horse	Shit	Yellow Jackets

Seven categories of drugs are frequently used:

- Central nervous system depressants (alcohol, barbiturates and tranquilizers)
- Central nervous system stimulants (cocaine, amphetamines and methamphetamines)
- Narcotic analgesics (heroin, codeine, Demerol and methadone)
- Hallucinogens (LSD, peyote and psilocybin)
- Phencyclidine (PCP and its analogs)
- Cannabis (marijuana, hashish and hash oil)
- Inhibitants (model airplane glue and aerosols)

Drugs can be classified as depressants, stimulants, narcotics, hallucinogens, phencyclidine, cannabis or inhibitants.

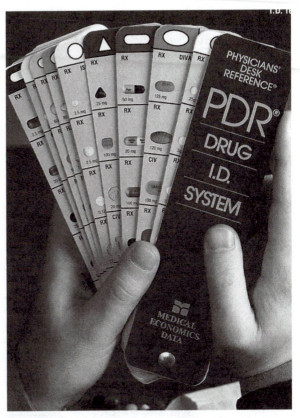

The PDR Drug I.D. System is a valuable aid to investigators involved in drug-related investigations.

Stimulants and depressants are controlled under the Drug Abuse Control Amendments to the Federal Food, Drug and Cosmetic Act (United States Code Title 21).

The most commonly observed drugs on the street, in possession of users and seized in drug raids are cocaine, codeine, crack, heroin, marijuana, morphine and opium. Arrest for possession or use of marijuana is the most frequent drug arrest.

Larger cities experience a broad spectrum of drug sales, use and abuse. A particular drug will achieve popularity over other drugs for a time and then lose popularity because it becomes difficult to obtain, is found to produce ill effects or increases in cost. The drug may then return to a lower level of use or fall into disuse. At different times opium or its derivatives, LSD, cocaine and crack have been heavily used drugs. However, marijuana has always been the most frequently used drug because of its lower cost, ease of use and mild effects.

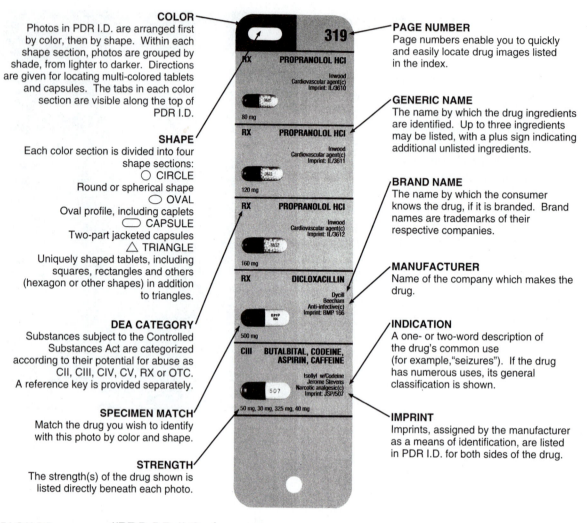

COLOR — Photos in PDR I.D. are arranged first by color, then by shape. Within each shape section, photos are grouped by shade, from lighter to darker. Directions are given for locating multi-colored tablets and capsules. The tabs in each color section are visible along the top of PDR I.D.

SHAPE — Each color section is divided into four shape sections:
○ CIRCLE Round or spherical shape
◯ OVAL Oval profile, including caplets
⬭ CAPSULE Two-part jacketed capsules
△ TRIANGLE Uniquely shaped tablets, including squares, rectangles and others (hexagon or other shapes) in addition to triangles.

DEA CATEGORY — Substances subject to the Controlled Substances Act are categorized according to their potential for abuse as CII, CIII, CIV, CV, RX or OTC. A reference key is provided separately.

SPECIMEN MATCH — Match the drug you wish to identify with this photo by color and shape.

STRENGTH — The strength(s) of the drug shown is listed directly beneath each photo.

PAGE NUMBER — Page numbers enable you to quickly and easily locate drug images listed in the index.

GENERIC NAME — The name by which the drug ingredients are identified. Up to three ingredients may be listed, with a plus sign indicating additional unlisted ingredients.

BRAND NAME — The name by which the consumer knows the drug, if it is branded. Brand names are trademarks of their respective companies.

MANUFACTURER — Name of the company which makes the drug.

INDICATION — A one- or two-word description of the drug's common use (for example, "seizures"). If the drug has numerous uses, its general classification is shown.

IMPRINT — Imprints, assigned by the manufacturer as a means of identification, are listed in PDR I.D. for both sides of the drug.

FIGURE 20.1 *"PDR I.D." Card*

Source: Reprinted by permission of *Medical Economics Data*.

Cocaine and Crack

Cocaine and its derivative, crack, are major problems for law enforcement officers. **Crack,** also called *rock* or *crack rock,* is produced by mixing cocaine with baking soda and water, heating the solution in a pan and then drying and splitting the substance into pellet-size bits or chunks. These are put into small plastic vials and sold for $10 to $25 per vial, substantially less expensive than cocaine which, in similar amounts, would sell for $100 or more. For the past two decades the cocaine supply in the United States has been controlled by the Medellin and Cali mafias.

Crack is smoked in glass pipes and has 10 times the impact of cocaine. The user experiences a rapid high because the drug is absorbed through the lungs and travels directly to the brain within seconds. It is described as "cocaine intensified or amplified" in terms of its effects on the human body, which include the following:

■ Brain—creates a craving for the drug, irritability, euphoria followed by severe depression, convulsions, sleeplessness, inability to feel normal pleasures, paranoia, psychosis and a tendency to suicide.

■ Heart—increases the heart rate and blood pressure, which can result in arrhythmia or heart attack. Death can result from heart failure.

■ Lungs—causes damage similar to emphysema and may cause respiratory arrest or death.

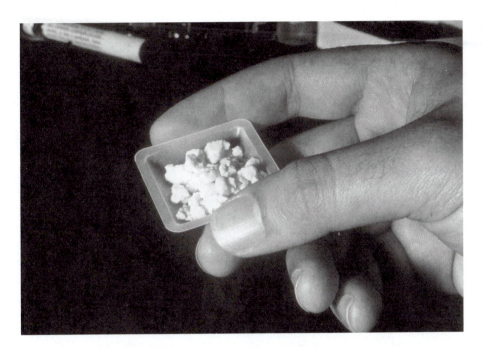

A container of rock cocaine, more commonly known as crack. *Crack is much less expensive than cocaine and has 10 times the impact.*

- Throat—causes sore throat and hoarseness.
- Skin—creates the sensation of bugs crawling on the skin.
- Appetite—reduces the desire for food, which can result in malnutrition.

The intense high produced by crack is usually followed by a severe depression or "crash" and a deep craving for more of the drug. It is more addictive than cocaine, at a much earlier stage of use, sometimes after the first use.

Some users "space base" the drug; that is, they lace it with PCP or other drugs. PCP causes out-of-control behavior, an added hazard to the already dangerous effects of crack itself. Moreover, the buyer of crack cannot visually determine whether the crack purchased has been laced with PCP because PCP is colorless. Thus the user runs a much increased risk of physical, emotional and mental damage.

According to the ONDCP (*Drug Use Trends,* 1999, p. 2):

> In 1997, an estimated 0.7% (1.5 million persons) of the population age 12 and older reported using cocaine, including crack, at least once in the past month. . . .
>
> [However,] overall, no significant increase has occurred in reporting current use of cocaine, including crack, since 1991.

Heroin

Heroin, a commonly abused narcotic, is synthesized from morphine and is up to 10 times more powerful in its effects. Heroin is physically addictive and expensive. It may cause an easing of fears, followed by euphoria and finally stupor. Heroin available in the United States is produced in Southeast Asia, Southwest Asia/Middle East (Turkey, Pakistan and Lebanon), Mexico and South America (Colombia). According to a government report ("Heroin Surpasses Cocaine . . . ," 1999, p. A10):

> The number of Americans checking into treatment centers for heroin and other opiates has surpassed the number of those seeking help for cocaine, . . . offering further evidence of heroin's spread.
>
> The rise is fueled by users who snort and smoke heroin—proof, experts say, that these methods can be just as addictive as injecting the drug.
>
> The number of treatment-center admissions for heroin and other opiates rose by 29 percent—from 180,000 to 232,000—between 1992 and 1997. . . .
>
> But there was some good news: In that same five-year period, cocaine admissions declined by 17 percent from 267,000 to 222,000.

Marijuana

Marijuana is variously classified as a **narcotic,** a **depressant** and a **hallucinogen** and is the most controversial of the dangerous drugs. Its use was outlawed by the Federal Marijuana Tax Act of 1927.

A wide spectrum of opinions exists regarding the harmfulness of marijuana. Some feel it should be legalized; others feel it is a very dangerous drug. Many surveys document *psychological* addiction from continued use of marijuana, as is true for most drugs. Like alcohol, marijuana is used socially. Although research does not indicate that marijuana is *physically* addictive, some users claim withdrawal symptoms similar to those resulting from discontinuance of hard narcotics.

Whether marijuana abusers progress to hard narcotics or other controlled substances has not been totally researched. The vast majority of hard-narcotics users once used marijuana, but how many marijuana users proceed to hard drugs is unknown. Marijuana is frequently used with alcohol, barbiturates and amphetamines. The marijuana user may be more susceptible to experimenting with other drugs while under the influence of marijuana.

The wide availability of marijuana makes it less costly, but the potency ("quality") of the drug varies greatly depending on where it is grown and how. Much marijuana is now grown by hydroponic methods indoors, often in abandoned barns or other buildings in rural areas. Such controlled cultivation increases its potency—by three to ten times—which increases its value and thus the growers' profits. Known as **sinsemilla,** homegrown marijuana has become extremely popular.

One good indication of indoor marijuana growing operations is excessive use of electricity. The plants need lots of light and obviously cannot be placed near windows, so artificial light is required. In one case, police were alerted to a residence that had been using 10 times the normal amount of electricity. Based on this information and observations of the type and amount of traffic to and from the house, police were able to obtain a search warrant and to break up a large marijuana-growing operation.

Another way to find targets for indoor marijuana-cultivation investigations is the Green Merchant List. This DEA document shows recipients of cultivation materials sold by and shipped from retailers, what was ordered, delivery date, weight and cost.

Marijuana has been, and continues to be, popular with all ages. According to the ONDCP (*Drug Use Trends,* p. 2): "In 1997, the percentage of Americans reporting use of marijuana at least once in the past month was 5.1% (11.1 million persons) of the population age 12 and older, which was statistically unchanged from 1996." The same report reveals, however, a rise in marijuana use among youth: "The increase in the use of marijuana has been especially pronounced. Between 1991 and 1998, past month use of marijuana increased from 13.8% to 22.8% among high school seniors, 8.7% to 18.7% among 10th graders and 3.2% to 9.7% among 8th graders." Despite the larger number of people smoking marijuana, the drug apparently leads a lower percentage of its users to treatment than other drugs: "Although other surveys indicate marijuana is by far the most popular illegal drug, it accounted for just 13 percent of admissions to treatment centers in 1997 ("Heroin Surpasses Cocaine . . . ," p. A10).

Methamphetamine

Methamphetamine—also known as meth, ice, crystal, glass, crank or speed—is another big problem drug and getting bigger. It is a synthetic stimulant that looks like cocaine but is made from toxic chemicals, including drain cleaner. It is taken primarily by snorting or smoking, but it can also be swallowed or injected. The typical users are high school and college students and working-class white men and women. A **tweaker** is a methamphetamine addict.

Although methamphetamine was developed in 1887 and introduced in the United States in 1932 as the nasal decongestant, Benzedrine, its popularity as an illicit drug has sprung to life only recently. Now, as Graves (1998, p. A10) notes: "It threatens to become a serious public health and law enforcement problem because it's cheaper [than cocaine], it's not sold as openly, its high makes users more violent, and it's hitting rural and suburban communities in ways that crack never did."

Meth labs have been cropping up across the country. Graves (p. A10) continues: "Clandestine labs have been found in suburban hotel and motel rooms, in middle-class homes, in trailers, in cars, in barns." Furthermore, concocting the drug is a relatively simple and inexpensive endeavor. Graves states (p. A10): "Making methamphetamine doesn't take a chemistry degree. It's as easy as cruising the Internet for a recipe, strolling into a discount store for the ingredients and setting up shop. An initial outlay of about $150 will produce meth with a street value of $2,000 to $4,000, officials estimate." Another way people are making money is by becoming meth-making consultants. For example: "Narcotics officers in Dakota County [Minnesota] are investigating a woman who, for $500, will allegedly provide a customer with her meth recipe, come to the customer's home, set up the equipment and make the first batch" (Graves, p. A10).

Rohypnol

One drug making news recently is the "date rape" drug, Rohypnol, also known as "roofies." Available by prescription outside of the United States, Rohypnol is a central nervous system depressant 10 times more potent than Valium (*Rohypnol,* 1998, p. 1). Sold in pill form, usually for less than $5 per tablet, it is taken orally or by snorting or injecting:

> The effects of Rohypnol begin within 30 minutes of administration, peak within 2 hours, and may persist for at least 8 hours, depending on the amount ingested. . . . When taking Rohypnol, individuals may experience a slowing of psychomotor performance, muscle relaxation, decreased blood pressure, sleepiness, and/or amnesia. Some of the side effects associated with Rohypnol use are drowsiness, headaches, memory impairment, dizziness, nightmares, and tremors.

As it became known that Rohypnol was being slipped into unwary victims' drinks and used as an aid for committing sexual assault, the manufacturer of the drug reformulated it to increase its detectability in clear fluid and to retard its dissolution rate.

GHB

Another drug used to commit sexual assault is gamma-hydroxybutyric acid, or GHB. Recognized by a variety of street names, including cherry menth, easy lay, Liquid X, salty water and scoop, GHB is a colorless, odorless, slightly salty liquid or white powder. It is taken orally and costs $5 to $20 per dose (capful or ounce). Asante (1999, p. 21) states:

> A hypnotic, anesthetic agent, gamma-hydroxybutyric acid (GHB) has drawn considerable media attention for its recent rise in illicit use. Since 1990, party and nightclub attendees have abused GHB for its euphoric and sedative effects, while body builders have misused it as an unproven anabolic steroid.

Investigating cases involving GHB may be very challenging, and investigators have started referring to it as a "stealth drug" because of the difficulty in detecting its use. Asante (p. 23) notes:

> As a clear, colorless liquid, [GHB] can be combined readily with water, alcohol, or a host of other common liquids and placed in any number of generic bottles. . . . No field test currently exists for detecting GHB. . . .
> GHB in the body presents an even greater problem. The body processes GHB in a manner

similar to alcohol; it converts the drug almost completely to carbon dioxide within hours. Most state medical examiners cannot detect GHB through standard drug tests.

Because GHB causes unconsciousness, victims may be unable to provide much useful information to investigators regarding any attack that may have occurred following ingestion of the drug. According to Asante (p. 24): "To date, only 11 states have criminalized GHB possession, most recently, California. Taking note of the resurgence of GHB, the FDA has renewed its warning that GHB remains an unapproved and potentially dangerous drug that cannot be legally marketed, sold, or manufactured in the United States."

Other Narcotics and Drugs

Designer drugs are so named because they can be created by adding to or omitting something from an existing drug. In many instances the primary drug is not illegal. The drugs are called *analogs* of the drug from which they are created, for example, meperidine analog or mescaline analog. These drugs may cause the muscles to stiffen and give the appearance of someone suffering from Parkinson's disease. Because designer drugs are difficult for amateurs to manufacture, they are high-profit drugs for dealers. Due to their complex natures, these drugs must be submitted to a laboratory for analysis.

Prescription Drugs

Many narcotics and dangerous drugs can be legally obtained with a prescription from a physician and legally sold or distributed by licensed manufacturers and pharmacies. Beary et al. (1996, p. 33) suggest: "One-third of the drug abuse problem in the United States can be linked to prescription controlled drugs." They list the following drugs as frequently involved in prescription fraud: narcotics, stimulants, barbiturates, benzodiazepines, tranquilizers and other psychoactive substances manufactured for use in legitimate medical treatment. Law enforcement officers spend a significant amount of time investigating cases involving prescription fraud, many of which also involve insurance, Medicare or Medicaid fraud.

Table 20.1 summarizes the various narcotics and dangerous drugs. As you study it, pay special attention to each drug's effects. This information is important in investigating the sale and use of drugs.

Table 20.1	Summary of Controlled Substances	

Drug	Trade or Other Names	Usual Methods of Administration
Narcotics		
Opium	Dover's powder, paregoric, Parepectolin	Oral, smoked
Morphine	morphine, pectoral syrup	Oral, smoked, injected
Codeine	Tylenol with Codeine, Empirin Compound with Codeine, Robitussan A-C	Oral, injected
Heroin	diacetylmorphine, horse, smack	Injected, sniffed, smoked
Hydromorphone	Dilaudid	Oral, injected
Meperidine (pethidine)	Demerol, Merpergan	Oral, injected
Methadone	Dolophine, methadone, Methadose	Oral, injected
Other narcotics	LAAM, Leritine, Numorphan, Percodan, Tussionex, Fentanyl, Darvon, Talwin, Lomotil*	Oral, Injected
Depressants		
Chloral hydrate	Noctec, Somnos	Oral
Barbiturates	phenobarbital, Tuinal, Amytal, Nembutal, Seconal, Lotusate	Oral
Benzodiazepines	Ativan, Azene, Clonopin, Dalmane, diazepam, Librium, Xanax, Serax, Tranxene, Valium, Verstran, Halcion, Paxipam, Restoril	Oral
Methaqualone	Quaalude	Oral
Gluethimide	Doriden	Oral
Other depressants	Equanil, Miltown, Noludar, Placidyl, Valmid	Oral
Stimulants		
Cocaine*	coke, flake, snow	Sniffed, smoked, injected
Amphetamines	Biphetamine, Delcobese, Desoxyn, Dexedrine, Mediatric	Oral, injected
Phenmetrazine	Preludin	Oral, injected
Methylphenidate	Ritalin	Oral, injected
Other stimulants	Adipex, Bacarate, Cylert, Didrex, Ionamin, Plegine, Pre-Sate, Sanorex, Tenuate, Tepanil, Voranil	Oral, injected
Hallucinogens		
LSD	acid, microdot	Oral
Mescaline and peyote	mesc, buttons, cactus	Oral
Amphetamine variants	2,5-DMA, PMA, STP, MDA, MDMA, TMA, DOM, DOB	Oral, injected
Phencyclidine	PCP, angel dust, hog	Smoked, oral, injected
Phencyclidine analogs	PCE, PCP, TCP	Smoked, oral, injected
Other hallucinogens	Bufotenine, Ibogaine, DMT, DET, psilocybin, Psilocyn	Oral, injected, smoked, sniffed
Cannabis		
Marijuana	pot, Acapulco gold, grass, reefer, sinsemilla, Thai sticks	Smoked, oral
Tetrahydrocannabinol	THC	Smoked, oral
Hashish	hash	Smoked, oral
Hashish oil	hash oil	Smoked, oral

*Designated a narcotic under the CSA (Controlled Substance Act)

Table 20.1 continued

Possible Effects	Effects of Overdose	Withdrawal Syndrome
Euphoria, drowsiness, respiratory depression, constricted pupils, nausea	Slow and shallow breathing, clammy skin, convulsions, coma, possible death	Watery eyes, runny nose, yawning, loss of appetite, irritability, tremors, panic, chills and sweating, cramps, nausea
Slurred speech, disorientation, drunken behavior without odor of alcohol	Shallow respiration, clammy skin, dilated pupils, weak and rapid pulse, coma, possible death	Anxiety, insomnia, tremors, delirium, convulsions, possible death
Increased alertness, excitation, euphoria, increased pulse rate and blood pressure, insomnia, loss of appetite	Agitation, increase in body temperature, hallucinations, convulsions, possible death	Apathy, long periods of sleep, irritability, depression, disorientation
Illusions and hallucinations, poor perception of time and distance	Longer, more-intense "trip" episodes, psychosis, possible death	Withdrawal syndrome not reported
Euphoria, relaxed inhibitions, increased appetite, disoriented behavior	Fatigue, paranoia, possible psychosis	Insomnia, hyperactivity and decreased appetite occasionally reported

- - - - - - - -

It is illegal to possess or use narcotics or dangerous drugs without a prescription and to sell or distribute them without a license.

- - - - - - - -

Most narcotics laws prohibit possessing, transporting, selling, furnishing or giving away narcotics. Possession of controlled substances is probably the most frequent charge in narcotics arrests. Actual or constructive possession and knowledge by a suspect that a drug was illegal must be shown. If the evidence is not on the person, it must be shown to be under the suspect's control.

Legal Definitions and Problems

The legal definitions of *narcotics* and *controlled substances* as stated in local, state and federal laws are lengthy and technical. The laws define the terms that describe the drugs, the various categories and the agencies responsible for enforcement.

Laws generally categorize drugs into five Schedules of Controlled Substances, arranged by the degree of danger associated with the drug. The five schedules contain the official, common, usual, trade and chemical names of the drugs. The laws also establish prohibited acts concerning the controlled substances. Basically, these laws state that no person, firm or corporation may manufacture, sell, give away, barter or deliver, exchange, distribute or possess these substances with intent to do any of the prohibited acts. The schedules establish penalties in ratio to the drug's danger, with Schedule I drugs being the most dangerous. Possessing a small amount of marijuana is a felony in some states, a misdemeanor in others and not a crime at all in a few states.

Laws also define the type of activity drug traffickers are involved in and can be used to impose criminal sanctions even when the intended act is unsuccessful. According to Hendrie (1999, p. 32):

Drug trafficking usually involves an agreement between two or more people to cooperate in the illegal drug enterprise. One effective way to address the drug trafficking problem is through the conspiracy laws. Drug traffickers can be charged and convicted of conspiracy, even though they have not completed the drug crime they have agreed to commit. In addition, in many jurisdictions, a person who is a member of a conspiracy is vicariously guilty of any reasonably foreseeable crimes committed by the members of the conspiracy even though those crimes were not part of the plan.

Investigating Illegal Possession or Use of Controlled Substances

Leshner (1998, p. 3) states:

Research has shown that drug abuse is a duel-edged health issue as well as a social issue. . . . But drug abuse and addiction also have tremendous implications for the health of the public, since drug use, directly or indirectly, is now a major vector for the transmission of many serious infectious diseases, particularly HIV/AIDS, hepatitis, and tuberculosis—and for the infliction of violence as well.

If you observe someone using a narcotic or other dangerous drug, you may arrest the person and seize the drugs as evidence. The arrested person may be searched incidental to the arrest. If a vehicle is involved but the suspect was not in the vehicle, post a guard at the vehicle or impound it. Drugs found on a person during a legally conducted search for other crimes may also be seized, and additional charges may be made.

Take the suspect into custody quickly. Then make sure the suspect does not dispose of the drugs by swallowing them, putting them between car seat cushions or placing them in other convenient hiding places. While in custody, the suspect may experience withdrawal pains and other bodily ills that can create special problems for the arresting officers.

Recognizing the Drug Addict

In drug crimes the victims are implicated; thus, they usually avoid contact with the police, conspiring with the sellers to remain undetected. If apprehended and faced with charges, however, the drug addict may be willing to work with the police. Therefore, many drug investigations involve identifying those who buy drugs illegally and who can thus provide information about sources of supply.

Congress has defined a **drug addict** as "any person who habitually uses any habit-forming narcotic drug so as to endanger the public morals, health, safety or welfare, or who is or has been so far addicted to the use of habit-forming narcotic drugs as to have lost the power of self-control with reference to the addiction."

Drug addiction is a progressive disease. The victim uses increased amounts of the same drug or harder drugs. Each increase has a corresponding cost increase—thus the frequent necessity for committing crime. In addition, as the addiction increases, the ability to control the habit decreases. Drug addicts become unfit for employment as their mental, emotional and physical condition deteriorates.

- - - - - - - -

Common symptoms of **drug abuse** include:

- Sudden, dramatic changes in discipline and job performance.
- Unusual degree of activity or inactivity.
- Sudden, irrational outbursts.
- Significant deterioration in personal appearance.
- Dilated pupils or wearing sunglasses at inappropriate times or places.
- Needle marks or razor cuts or constant wearing of long sleeves to hide such marks.
- Sudden attempts to borrow money or to steal.
- Frequent association with known drug abusers or dealers.

- - - - - - - -

The addict generally is unkempt, appears drowsy, does not feel well, has copious quantities of tears or mucus in the eyes and nose and suffers from alternating chills and fever. Needle marks resembling tattoos may be present in the curve of the arm at the elbow or, after prolonged drug use, in other areas of the body. Because addicts often help each other obtain drugs, exercise extreme caution when addicts are in jail to prevent visitors from getting drugs to them.

Once a person is addicted, it is extremely difficult to quit using drugs without special assistance. Drugs preoccupy the addict; nothing and nobody else matters. Institutional rehabilitation of drug addicts has not had much long-term success because the drugs have such a powerful influence over the individual's mental, emotional and physical being. A high percentage of addicts eventually return to their drug habit, their familiar setting and their old associates in drug abuse.

Drug Recognition Experts

Police officers are adept at recognizing and legally charging individuals who are under the influence of alcohol, especially if they are driving. They are not so able to recognize drug-impaired individuals. However, a Drug Recognition Projects Unit has an impressive 97 percent conviction rate.

Officers begin by using the standard field sobriety tests. If impairment is noticeable, the subject is given a breath test. If the blood alcohol reading is inconsistent with the perceived impairment, a drug recognition expert (DRE) evaluates the individual's appearance, performance on psychological tests, eyes and vital signs.

The initial interview includes questions about the subject's behavior; response to being stopped; attitude and demeanor; speech patterns; and possible injury, sickness or physical problems. Physical evidence such as smoking paraphernalia, injection-related material and needle marks on the subject is sought.

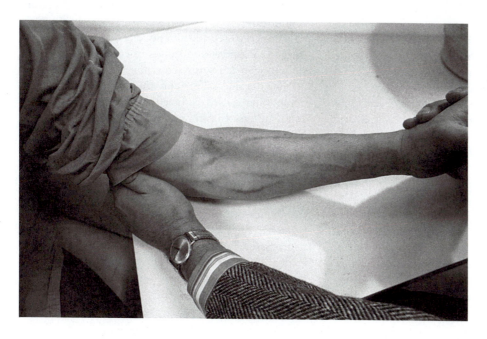

The arm of a heroin addict in the methadone program at New York's Beth Israel Hospital shows the track marks of needles.

The physical examination includes an eye examination, an improved walk-and-turn test, the Rhomberg Standing Balance test and the one-leg stand test, as well as the finger-to-nose test. Also tested are vital signs (blood pressure, pulse rate and temperature) and muscle rigidity. If warranted, a toxicological examination is also conducted.

Physical Evidence of Possession or Use of Controlled Substances

The suspect's clothing may conceal drugs, which have been found in neckties, shirt collars, coat and pants linings and seams, shoe tongues, soles of shoes or slippers, hat or cap bands and, naturally, in pockets. Suspects are usually strip-searched because drugs can be concealed in any body opening including the rectum or vagina, in the hair, behind the ears and between the toes. Drugs can also be attached to the body with tape.

Objects in the suspect's possession can also contain drugs, depending on the suspect's ingenuity. Cigarette cases, lighters, holders and packages as well as chewing gum wrappers, fountain pens, jewelry, glasses cases, lockets, pencil erasers and many other objects can conceal illegal drugs.

Vehicles have innumerable hiding places, including under seat covers, behind cushions or seats, in heater pipes, hubcaps, glove compartments, under floor mats, in false auto batteries and oil filters, as well as secret compartments devised for great amounts of smuggled drugs. Put the vehicle on a hoist and examine the undercarriage.

In a residence or building, do not give the suspect a chance to flush the toilet or turn on the water in a sink to destroy evidence. Look for drugs in drawer bottoms, fuse boxes, bedposts, behind pictures, in tissue boxes, in overhead light fixtures, under rugs and carpets, in and under furniture and in holes in walls. If you find evidence, attempt to locate the owner of the property and inform him or her of the arrest. Gather all correspondence addressed to the person arrested if it is not in a mailbox. Obtain rent receipts, utility bills and other evidence that establishes that the suspect resides at that location.

One initial problem is identifying the suspected substance. As noted earlier, pharmaceutical manuals and physicians' desk manuals provide information needed to identify various drugs. Field tests can be conducted to serve as the basis for a search warrant,

Some of the drug paraphernalia collected by Sharry Heckt-Deszo, an anti-drug activist. Nearly all of this equipment was confiscated from teenagers. Heckt-Deszo uses the real-life props for "The Bong Show," a show-and-tell program about drug abuse reserved for adults-only audiences of parents and teachers.

but such tests must always be verified by laboratory examination.

A recently developed residue detection swab can be used to test surfaces for traces of cocaine. Investigators simply wipe the swab across the area to be tested. If cocaine residue is present, the swab instantly turns color. Individually wrapped in foil packaging, these swabs are easy to carry and to use and have a relatively long shelf life.

If evidence of narcotics or other dangerous drugs is found on an arrested suspect, as a result of a search of the premises or even by accident, immediately place it in a container, label it and send it to a laboratory. If it is already in a container, leave it there and process the container for fingerprints. Package uncontained drug evidence carefully to avoid a challenge to its integrity as evidence. Use special precautions to avoid contaminating or altering the drugs by exposure to humidity, light or chemicals.

Table 20.2 | **Indicators of Drug Abuse**

Drug	Physical Evidence	Observable Conditions
Morphine	Burning spoon, candle, hypodermic needle, actual substance	Needle marks, euphoria
Heroin	Burning spoon, candle, hypodermic needle, razor blade, eyedropper, actual substance	Needle marks or razor cuts, euphoria, starry look, constricted pupils, profuse perspiration
Cocaine	White or colorless crystalline powder, hypodermic needle, pipe	Needle marks, dilated pupils, increased heart rate, convulsing
Crack	Pellets, glass pipes, plastic bottle	Depression, euphoria, convulsions
Stimulants	Pills of various shapes and sizes	Restlessness, nervousness, hand tremor, dilated pupils, dry mouth, excessive perspiration
Depressants	Pills of various shapes and sizes	Symptoms resemble those of drunkenness: slurred, indistinct speech and loss of physical coordination
Hallucinogens	Hypodermic needle, eyedropper, spoon, bottle caps, tourniquets, cotton balls, actual substances	Needle marks on inner elbow, extreme emotionalism, noticeable dilation of pupils, often causing persons to wear dark glasses even at night
Marijuana	Roach holder, pipe with a fine screen placed halfway down the bowl, actual substance	Sweet smoke odor; symptoms resemble those of mild intoxication: staring off into space, glassy eyes, semiconsciousness, drowsiness

---

Physical evidence of possession or use of controlled substances includes the actual drugs, apparatus associated with their use, the suspect's appearance and behavior and urine and blood tests.

Often found along with drugs are various types of pipes, syringes, cotton, spoons, medicine droppers, safety pins, razor blades, hypodermic needles and the like—common components of a drug addict's "outfit."

A suspect's general appearance and signs such as dilated pupils, needle marks or razor cuts in the veins, confusion, aggressiveness, watery eyes, runny nose and profuse perspiration provide additional evidence of drug use. Table 20.2 lists indicators of drug abuse. To establish that an arrested person is under the influence of drugs, a urine and blood test, a medical examination and a report of personal observations are used along with an alcoholic or drug influence test form.

In-Custody Deaths

One serious problem that you may encounter in dealing with drug users is what Benner and Isaacs (1996, p. 20) call **excited delirium,** a term that describes the "manifestations of extreme drug abuse." This condition may be related to the sudden, seemingly inexplicable deaths of some suspects being held in police custody. A common cause of sudden death in police custody is cocaine toxicity. Benner and Isaacs (p. 21) cite the following published symptoms attributed to "excited delirium":

- Bizarre and/or aggressive behavior
- Violence toward others
- Shouting
- Unexpected physical strength
- Paranoia
- Sudden tranquility
- Panic

Reak and Gunta (1996, p. 10) note that hog-tying a person under the influence of cocaine might result in toxic reaction to cocaine (TRTC). People who ingest cocaine and then engage in bizzare, violent behavior are at high risk of dying in the custody of police if they are restrained.

Investigating Illegal Sale and Distribution of Controlled Substances

Because addiction depends on drug availability, drug control must be directed toward the supplier. This is often a joint effort among law enforcement agencies at all levels. Drug users and sellers know the local police, so it is difficult to operate locally. Outsiders are frequently brought in by the police to make buys and arrests. However, local patrol officers are still responsible for investigating drug offenses because they see the users and sometimes observe drug sales. Actions they take against users can put pressure on sellers because their market is hurt when users are arrested and jailed.

Moreover, drug users often become sellers to support their habit. Many such individuals, called **mules,** sell or transport drugs for a regular dealer in return for being assured of a personal drug supply. Whereas some remain in small operations sufficient to support their needs, others see the profit they can make in large operations and go into business on a larger scale. Further, many drug pushers become users—an occupational hazard. This sometimes occurs accidentally as the result of testing the quality of the merchandise over an extended period.

Investigating the illegal sale and distribution of drugs requires all the basic techniques used for other crimes, plus special investigative skills related to the behavior of drug users and sellers, both of whom can be dangerous and unpredictable. The wide variety of drugs makes it difficult to identify them under street conditions, and special types of searches are required to locate minute amounts of drugs that may be hidden ingeniously.

Investigators also encounter special problems in finding drugs smuggled across national borders in a variety of ways and in identifying those who transport and distribute them. It takes much time and expense to develop informants and to make a purchase or otherwise discover and confiscate drugs while ensuring that the evidence will stand up in court. Luitweiler (1998, p. 41) notes:

> Over the past few years, drug gangs' capabilities have become far more threatening, as two new factors have emboldened international drug lords.

First, political and economic barriers have been lowered . . . encouraging the free flow of people and products across international borders. . . .

A second factor is drug traffickers' easy access to sophisticated communications technology, including fax machines, pagers, cell phones, personal communications systems and networks that are frequently changed to evade law enforcement.

The actual transfer of drugs from the seller to the buyer is the major legal evidence in prosecuting drug sale cases.

A patrol officer may see the transfer by chance or observe it after long surveillance or when an undercover officer makes a planned buy. Some transfers are quite intricate. In one case, a drug seller put drugs on a dog's back, and the dog brought them to the buyer and then returned to the seller with the payment. Even though the seller did not personally hand the drugs to the seller, there was a sale. In other cases, the seller leaves drugs at a predetermined location and picks up payment at another location. Such subterfuge is countered by personal testimony.

If either the buyer or seller throws the drugs away to avoid being caught with them in possession, the drugs can be recovered as abandoned property and taken into custody. If the suspect was seen discarding the drugs, they can be used as evidence.

Narcotics cases begin with a report of suspicious drug activity, a search warrant obtained on information from a reliable informant or an on-sight observation of a drug buy. Undercover officers and informants then become central figures in obtaining evidence.

On-Sight Arrests

Strandberg (1998, p. 62) states: "Street level drug trade is important for law enforcement to stop because it is how U.S. customers buy their drugs." Patrol officers witnessing a suspected drug buy should obtain as complete a description as possible of the persons and vehicles involved. There is usually no urgency in making a drug arrest because the seller and buyer continue to meet over time.

If you observe what appears to be a drug buy, you can make a warrantless arrest if you have probable cause. Often, however, it is better to simply observe and gather information.

Crack and cocaine dealers in action.

Probable cause is established through knowledge of the suspect's criminal record, by observing other people making contact with the suspect and finding drugs on them, by knowing of the suspect's past relationships with other drug users or sellers and through observing actions of the suspect that indicate a drug buy. The courts usually give weight to officers' experience and to their information about the suspect and the circumstances of the arrest, including actions by the suspect before the arrest that are commonly associated with drug selling.

If probable cause is based on information supplied by an informant, check the information for accuracy against intelligence files. If no prior intelligence information exists, add the facts provided to the file. Check the informant's reliability by asking about other suspects in drug cases. Are these suspects already in the files? Has the informant helped before? How many arrests or convictions were based on the information? You might ask the informant to obtain a small amount of the drug if possible.

Surveillance

It is frequently best simply to watch and obtain information if you witness a drug buy. The suspected seller or the location of the buy can then be put under surveillance, an especially important technique in narcotics investigations. Surveillance can provide protection for planned buys, protect the money used to make the buy, provide credibility for the buyer, provide information regarding the seller's contacts and provide information to establish probable cause for an arrest or search warrant. It is not necessary to make an arrest on the first surveillance. In fact, it is generally advisable to make several surveillances to gather evidence.

Surveillance officers must have patience because many planned drug buys necessitate a long period of surveillance before the actual sale, or bust, is made. The drug dealer is concentrating on making the sale. No sale, no profit. At the same time the dealer is trying to avoid being "busted." It is essentially a cat-and-mouse game. Drug dealers often feel they are being observed when they are not, and surveillance officers often feel they have been "burned" when they have not. Pre-arranged signals and communications between surveillance officers and undercover officers are essential to prevent untimely drug busts. A detailed plan of action is mandatory. The surveillance team must be prepared with adequate equipment, food and drink for the estimated surveillance period. Surveillance officers should have specialized training and detailed briefing prior to actual assignment.

Planned Buys

Planned buys usually involve working an undercover agent into a group selling or buying drugs or having an informant make the buy. Before using an informant to buy drugs, determine why the person is involved and keep a strict log of his or her activities. Use care in working with drug users as buyers because they are known by the courts to be chronic liars.

The enormous number of drug buys by undercover agents and informants have made drug sellers wary of new customers. Informants often introduce the undercover officer. Informants are often involved in criminal narcotics as users or sellers and are "turned" by the police for providing information in exchange for lesser charges. The prosecutor's office usually makes the decision to use an informant in this manner. Most people arrested for dealing drugs who are given the option of either going to jail or becoming an informant choose the latter. Police departments should have written policies on the use of informants.

Undercover agents are usually police officers of the investigating agency (in large cities) or of cooperative agencies on the same level of government in an exchange operation or a mutual-aid agreement that provides an exchange of narcotics officers.

If working undercover, be thoroughly conversant with the language of the user and the seller, know the street prices of drugs and have a tight cover. Talk little and listen much. Observe without being noticed. Also devise an excuse to avoid using the drugs. Work within the seller's system. Drug pushers, like other criminals, tend to develop certain methods for making their sales. Asking them to change their method can cause suspicion, whereas going along with the system establishes your credibility for subsequent buys. Avoid dangerous situations by insisting that you do not want to get into a situation where you could be ripped off, injured or killed.

- - - - - - - -

Undercover drug buys are carefully planned, witnessed and conducted so that no charge of entrapment can be made.

- - - - - - - -

Make careful plans before a drug buy. Select a surveillance group and fully brief them on the signals to use and their specific assignments. Small transmitters are important communications devices for members of the surveillance team. Have alternative plans in case the original plan fails.

Careful preparation includes searching the buyer immediately before the transaction to avoid the defense that drugs were planted on the suspect. Any items on the buyer other than the money are retained at the police station or with other police officers until after the buy.

Prepare the buy money in advance—marked, identified, counted and recorded by serial number, date, time and denomination. Have this procedure witnessed by one or more people. The money is not given to the buyer until immediately before the buy. Fluorescent powders can be used, but some drug sellers check money for these powders before making a transaction. All buys should be observed from a location where the movements of both the seller and the buyer can be seen by the surveillance team.

At the meeting, record the seller's description, the vehicles used, telephone numbers called to set up the buy and observations about the seller's personal statements and habits. If the informant and the undercover officer are both present, the officer makes the buy to protect the informant's identity if an arrest is planned. If no arrest is planned, both the undercover officer and the informant make buys, providing additional evidence.

If several buys are made from the same seller over a period of time, the seller may relax security and include others higher in the organization. Even if this is not the case, the seller usually visits his or her drug source frequently. The route to or the actual location of the supplier can then be put under surveillance. Such an opportunity seldom arises on the first contact because sellers usually devise very clever ruses to cover their tracks.

The FBI's Drug Enforcement Administration (DEA) has adapted the traditional triangle used in tactical training to illustrate the dynamic balance between the drug dealer and the police officer (Figure 20.2).

The three things valued by dealers are the drugs, the money the drugs can bring and their freedom to do business. In the middle of the triangle is the officer. When both the money—that is, the **flashroll**—and the drugs are present at the same time, the undercover officer faces the greatest danger.

The ability to negotiate is essential for an undercover officer. Almost everything is negotiable in a drug deal. Remaining cool and collected during the actual buy is absolutely necessary. If the situation does not look right or appears to be too dangerous, walk away from the deal; there is always another time and place. Because of the prevalence of weapons in drug trafficking, undercover officers can be in extreme danger, usually alone.

If the buy is successful, an arrest can be made immediately, or a search warrant can be obtained on the basis of the buyer's observation of other drugs on the premises. After the buy, the buyer is searched again and the exact amount of money and drugs on the buyer recorded.

- - - - - - - -

Make two or more buys to avoid the charge of entrapment.

- - - - - - - -

FIGURE 20.2 *Drug Dealer-Officer Dynamics*

Although police are responsible for investigating narcotics offenses and arresting violators, they are equally responsible for making every reasonable effort to avoid arresting an innocent person. The illegal act involved in the sale should be voluntary, without special urging or persuasion. An agent who knows that a seller is in business and merely asks for, pays for and receives drugs is not using entrapment. But continued requests for drugs from a person who does not ordinarily sell them *is* entrapment. If there has been more than one voluntary drug transaction, no basis for a defense of entrapment exists.

Stings

A **sting** is a complex operation organized and implemented by undercover agents to apprehend criminals, especially drug dealers. In a recent sting, federal and local drug-enforcement officers arrested 93 suspects in an effort to dismantle the operations of drug trafficker Amado Carillo Fuentes, who died in 1997 ("Sting Dismantles Drug . . . ," 1999, p. A6). The investigation had the cooperation of the Mexican government and targeted alleged "cell heads" running the drug operations after Carillo's death. Carillo was "considered Mexico's No. 1 drug lord until he died in July 1997 while recovering from plastic surgery meant to help him evade law enforcement."

Narcotics Raids

Surveillance frequently provides enough information for obtaining a no-knock search or arrest warrant. Successful narcotics raids are rarely spontaneous; they are planned on the basis of information obtained over an extended period. They can be designed to occur in two, three or more places simultaneously, not only in the same community but in other communities and even in other states.

Narcotics raids are often dangerous; therefore, before the raid, gather information about the people involved and the premises where the drugs are located. Also determine how many police officers are needed, the types of weapons needed and the location of evidence, as discussed in Chapter 7.

The raid itself must be carried out forcefully and swiftly because drugs can easily be destroyed in seconds. All confiscated drugs are taken to a laboratory for examination. Disposition of confiscated drugs is carefully controlled to avoid tainting the integrity of the police.

Clandestine Drug Laboratories

An increase in clandestine drug laboratories has occurred as more emphasis has been placed on reducing illegal foreign drug imports into the United States. These laboratories pose serious health hazards to law enforcement agencies conducting raids on the premises. Heiskell (1996, p. 32) cautions: "Clandestine drug labs can be deadly chemical time bombs if you do not take appropriate and immediate precautions." He (p. 33) warns: "Knowledge of clandestine drug lab hazards and safety procedures could mean the difference between life and death." In fact, according to Heiskell: "Clandestine laboratories are considered the largest single source of on-the-job injuries to narcotics officers."

Specific hazards that may exist in clandestine drug laboratories include:

- *Physical hazards.* Improper ventilation, few access routes, poor lighting, booby traps, potential for explosions, fire and assaults from attack dogs or violent drug "cooks" under the influence of their products.

- *Chemical hazards.* Many of the substances are explosive and extremely flammable. They often are unidentified or misidentified.

- *Toxic hazards.* Irritants and corrosives, asphyxiants and nerve toxins may be encountered.

Clandestine drug laboratories present physical, chemical and toxic hazards to law enforcement officers engaged in raids on the premises.

According to Doane and Marshall (1998, p. 36): "A Schedule II controlled substance, methamphetamine is the most prevalent controlled substance clandestinely synthesized in the United States. . . . During the first

Officers investigating clandestine drug laboratories wear fire- and chemical-resistant suits, gloves and boots and use self-contained breathing devices for protection.

nine months of 1997, 98 percent of the clan labs seized by DEA were producing methamphetamine." Calling such labs "toxic timebombs" because of the presence of highly flammable materials and deadly chemicals, Cashman (1998, p. 42) cautions: "A clandestine methamphetamine laboratory investigation is one of the few investigations where the evidence and crime scene can hurt or possibly kill the investigator. When working clandestine laboratories, the key word is safety." He adds (p. 45):

> [Clan labs] are located everywhere—hotel rooms, apartments, houses, storage lockers and vehicles of all types. An officer can come into contact with a lab when he responds to a domestic violence call. A deputy can become exposed to a deadly clan lab after initiating a traffic stop.

Because of their volatility, these labs pose a significant public safety threat. Manning (1999, p. 11) states: "The danger to children becomes obvious when a methamphetamine lab explodes, killing or injuring them, or when authorities discover neglected children as a result of their parents' methamphetamine use." Table 20.3 outlines the methamphetamine production process and identifies the various hazards generated at each stage.

When encountering a drug lab or its components, do not use matches, lighters or items that could ignite fumes. Do not turn switches on or off because the electric connection could produce sparks and cause an explosion. Do not taste, smell or touch any substance, and check for booby traps before moving or touching containers.

A safety program developed by the DEA and the California Bureau of Narcotics Enforcement following OSHA and NIOSH recommendations has four basic elements: policies and procedures, equipment and protective clothing, training, and medical monitoring.

Policies and procedures are aimed at ensuring officer safety through a certification process. Only certified individuals are allowed to seize, process and dispose of clandestine laboratories. Their procedure for conducting a raid has five stages: planning, entry, assessment, processing and exit. During the planning stage, certified agents and chemists identify the chemicals that may be present and arrange for the proper safety *equipment and protective clothing*.

Entry has the most potential for danger. The entry team faces the possibility of armed resistance by owners and operators, booby traps and exposure to hazardous chemicals. Still, the entry team wears the least protection because the gear limits mobility, dexterity, vision and voice communications.

Once entry has been successful, the assessment team—an agent and a chemist—enter the site to deal with immediate hazards, to ventilate the site and to segregate incompatible chemicals to halt reactions. Assessment team members wear fire-protective, chemical-resistant suits, gloves and boots. They also use self-contained breathing devices for respiratory protection. This team determines what safety equipment and clothing the processing team will need.

The processing team then enters, identifies and collects evidence. They photograph and videotape the site

Table 20.3	Methamphetamine Production Process			
Stage	*Steps in Process*	*Chemicals Added*	*Process*	*Hazards Generated*
Cooking	Initial Mixing and Heating	Ephedrine Hydriodic Acid Red Phosphorous	Chemicals are mixed and heated for about 12 hours to form D-meth in an acidic mixture.	Fires Explosions Toxic Gas
	Straining	None	Mixture is strained through a bed sheet or pillowcase to remove the red phosphorous.	Discarded bed sheets/pillowcases contaminated with red phosphorous and hydriodic acid
Extraction	Converting to a Base	Sodium Hydroxide (lye/caustic soda) Ice	Sodium hydroxide is added to convert the acidic mixture to a basic one. Ice is then added to cool the resulting exothermic reaction to prevent evaporation or loss of product. After this step, the mixture is transferred to a separatory vessel, most often a 55-gallon drum with a spigot at its base.	Spills
	Extracting D-meth	Freon (cooks have been known to use Coleman fuel or other solvents)	Freon is added to aid in the extraction of the D-meth from the sodium hydroxide solution. The Freon will drag the D-meth to the bottom of the vessel, and the clandestine lab cook will drain it off. If another solvent is used, the D-meth base floats to the top because this solvent is lighter than water.	Large amounts of sodium hydroxide waste
Salting	Salting and Drying	Hydrogen Chloride Gas	When treated with hydrogen chloride gas, the D-meth oil will convert into a white crystalline powder. Presses or mop buckets are used to remove excess Freon.	Discarded solvents Flammable hazards

Information obtained from U.S. Department of Justice, National Drug Intelligence Center, *Hazards of D-Methamphetamine Production,* June 1995.

Source: Tom Manning. "Drug Labs and Endangered Children." *FBI Law Enforcement Bulletin,* Vol. 68, No. 7, July 1999, p. 13. Reprinted by permission.

and collect samples of the various chemicals. The final step involves removing and disposing of hazardous materials, decontaminating and posting the site.

Training involves 40 hours of classroom instruction followed by a 24-hour in-service training course at the field level. *Medical monitoring* has two stages: medical screening of potential team members and annual monitoring to learn whether any team members have developed adverse health effects as a result of working with hazardous chemicals. Guidelines and training for clandestine drug laboratory investigations are available through the National Sheriffs Association.

Because hotel rooms are a commonly sought site for those planning to set up "clan" labs, some law enforcement agencies are now training hotel managers and employees on the dangers such labs pose and ways to identify suspected "meth cooks." Thompson (1999, pp. 138–139) notes:

There may be hidden danger in needles tossed into a trash can or on the floor containing HIV, hepatitis, or other health risks. Another danger is the chemicals used can make the carpet dangerous—the friction sparks of walking across the floor could ignite an explosion. The red phosphorous used becomes airborne as a dust and will burn the lungs.

The lab has to be vented so the vapors don't kill the cook. One solution is to vent the lab into the ceiling of the room, which allows the deadly vapors to spread throughout the entire hotel.

Thompson (p. 138) also states:

DEA agents profiled a typical local meth cook as "male, white, trashy looking, with rotting teeth (the meth cook look), and a skinny, also trashy looking girlfriend. Both will likely have poor quality tattoos, and they will have a local address on their identification. . . .

The agents explained the chemicals used in the production are corrosive, such as Drano, and the cooks usually don't get all of them out prior to using the drug. Consequently they suffer the effects of corrosion on their teeth and skin.

Armed with information on how to prevent meth cooks from setting up shop on their premises, hotels are now taking specific action, including:

- Not accepting cash for a room from a local resident without a credit card and photo ID with matching names.

- Calling the police when guests register for a week or longer but have no luggage, or when a guest registers for only one night and brings an inordinate amount of luggage.

- Notifying police if a guest makes and receives numerous phone calls shortly after check-in.

- Notifying police if a guest has the "meth cook look" (Thompson, p. 139).

Not only do clan labs pose a danger to officers and the public, they can be very expensive to clean up. The Comprehensive Methamphetamine Control Act (MCA) of 1996 helps offset this cost. Doane and Marshall (p. 40) explain: "The law allows the courts to order a defendant convicted of manufacturing methamphetamine to pay the cost of cleanup of the lab site. Last year, DEA alone spent $4 million on clan lab clean-up—double the expenditure of the previous year."

Despite efforts to detect and shut them down, clan labs continue to proliferate. Cashman (p. 47) concludes: "Clandestine labs are a growing menace, requiring a comprehensive and well-orchestrated response by properly trained and equipped personnel. Without such a response, we run the risk of being decimated by an enemy within our own borders."

Investigative Aids

The National Institute of Justice has funded development of a computerized Drug Market Analysis Program (DMAP) to aid in drug investigations. This sophisticated information and mapping system helps law enforcement target retail drug sellers. Figure 20.3 illustrates the automated pin map used in the program.

FIGURE 20.3

DMAP's Automated Pin Map

The automated pin map allows narcotics and patrol officers to use computers to zoom to particular neighborhoods—and even particular streets—to get an up-to-date picture of drug trafficking activity. Information about narcotics arrests, calls for service, crimes known to police and drug hotline calls is consolidated onto one map.

Source: Courtesy of the National Institute of Justice.

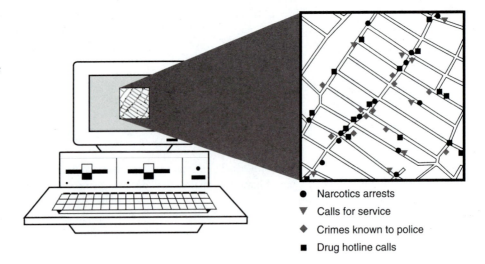

- ● Narcotics arrests
- ▼ Calls for service
- ◆ Crimes known to police
- ■ Drug hotline calls

Another tool to help federal, state and local law enforcement agencies investigate drug trafficking is the DEA's National Drug Pointer Index (NDPIX), a nationwide database that became operational across the United States in 1997. Constantine (1998, p. 28) notes the objectives of the NDPIX include enhanced agent/officer safety, elimination of duplication, increased information sharing and coordination, minimization of costs through use of existing technology and 24-hour/seven-day access to information through an effective, secure law enforcement telecommunications system.

Yet another investigative aid is the Internet. Although communicating information about drugs on the Internet can be problematic for law enforcement, it can also be a source of assistance. As Sclabassi (1996, p. 62) notes: "Trading drug information is nothing new, but keeping this illegal business off the Internet is tough to tackle." She (p. 63) states: "Everything from the side effects of using a particular drug to how to best grow marijuana plants indoors can be discussed on the Internet by drug users and dealers." Sclabassi suggests that rather than trying to stop these communications, investigators use the information to their advantage.

Some investigative aids are not so high-tech. For example, using dogs to detect drugs has been common for decades because their keen sense of smell enables them to detect minute traces of illicit drugs: "Two police dogs have been credited with the seizure of two more suitcases of marijuana at the Greyhound bus depot. Authorities said the 100 pounds of marijuana had an estimated street value of $150,000 to $300,000" ("Drug-Sniffing Dogs . . . ," 1997, p. 6B). Bulzomi (2000, p. 28) notes: "A dog's positive alert alone generally constitutes probable cause to search a vehicle under the motor vehicle exception to the search warrant requirement." Bulzomi suggests drug detection dog handlers should be prepared to establish a dog's reliability by providing prosecutors with the following:

■ Verification that the dog was trained to detect the odors for particular drugs

■ The dog's success rate

■ The method used to train the dog to indicate an alert

■ Proof of the dog's certification

■ Proof that the dog has continued to meet certification requirements and receive necessary training regularly

Drug-sniffing pot-bellied pigs have also been used because they have a keen sense of smell, are the third-smartest land mammals behind humans and apes and can be trained much more quickly than dogs.

Researchers have developed mechanical "sniffers" that detect vapors and take vacuum samples, doing essentially the same job as detector dogs or pigs. Strandberg (1999, p. 37) explains:

> Drugs leave behind residue and vapors. . . . [Any surface that comes] into contact with narcotics and/or explosives . . . [is] covered with the ions.
>
> Ion Track is being used by law enforcement for drug interdiction. . . . It's hand-held with a pump that sucks air through it . . . [and] can search the carpet or the floorboards [of a vehicle.] . . .
>
> Ion Track also has a vapor tracer being used for undercover buys. The undercover officers keep it in a small duffel bag—and it's about the size of a half gallon of milk. This way, the officers can check their undercover buys quickly, to make sure it's drugs, and do a larger buy within minutes of the test purchase.

Another technology that allows for on-the-spot drug detection is AccuPRESS, described by Brandenstein (1997, p. 33):

> The inexpensive, palm-size, evidence collection and surface drug test kit, "AccuPRESS," . . . allows officers in the field [to positively identify] trace amounts of cocaine or opiates in minutes. . . .
>
> AccuPRESS has already been instrumental in sting operations leading to indictments and linking of suspects to major drug trafficking conspiracies, arrests leading to convictions, and seizure of assets totaling millions of dollars.

Finding secret compartments that might contain drugs is now easier with a special high-accuracy laser rangefinder developed for the U.S. Customs Service. Investigators use the unit to measure the interior dimensions of cargo containers in their search for hidden compartments in which drugs may be smuggled. The small laser beam allows measurements of loaded containers in which physical access to the rear wall is limited. The handheld, battery-operated, laser rangefinder measures distances from 6 to 85 feet with an accuracy of one inch.

Strandberg (1999, p. 37) describes another handheld device called a Mini Buster, which helps detect anomalies in vehicles and storage areas, indicating whether something unusual is behind a wall or under the hood of a car.

Other advances in technology are assisting narcotics investigators in identifying persons under the influence of drugs. For example, Strandberg (1999, p. 37) describes one noninvasive drug detection device: "The EyeCheck . . . measures the pupilary response to a light stimuli, and . . . shows a great deal of promise." Mieczkowski and Lersch (1997, p. 13) explain other emerging, noninvasive drug detection technologies, including hair, sweat and saliva testing:

> Hair analysis has been suggested as a supplement to urine testing because, by offering a longer "window" of detection, and for other reasons, it makes evasion more difficult. . . .
>
> The scientific basis of hair analysis is the capacity of the growing hair to absorb drugs and their metabolites (the products of the body's metabolism). Once a metabolite is embedded in the hair shaft, it appears to remain there almost permanently. . . .
>
> Since sweat [eliminates] waste from the body, it contains drugs and drug metabolites much like urine and can be analyzed with similar technologies. But much time is needed to collect quantities sufficient for analysis. The adhesive patch is a mechanism that can overcome this problem because it is worn for an

extended time before being removed and subjected to analysis. . . .

> Looming on the horizon are "smart patches," which conceptually are similar to the standard patch but produce results instantly. Embedded micro-electronic chips create this advantage. . . .
>
> One of the most compelling aspects of saliva specimens is that they are readily available, relatively simple to collect, and do not pose problems of privacy and intrusion as does urine testing. . . .
>
> Although saliva has shown its utility in detecting drugs of abuse—it has been used to identify cocaine and cannabinoids—its full potential has still to be realized.

Agency Cooperation

Investigating illegal drug activities requires the cooperation of all law enforcement agencies, including the exchange of suspect car lists and descriptions of sellers and buyers. Local police assist state and federal narcotics investigators by sharing their knowledge of drug users and sellers in their community. In addition, many narcotics officers exchange vehicles and personnel with other agencies to have less-identifiable operators and equipment.

The federal government has mobilized an all-out attack on illegal drug activities. Before 1973 several federal agencies were involved in investigating illegal drug activities. These included the Bureau of Narcotics and Dangerous Drugs (BNDD), the Office for Drug Abuse Law Enforcement, the Office of National Narcotics Intelligence, the drug investigative and intelligence units of the Bureau of Customs and the drug enforcement sections of the Office of Science and Technology. In 1973 all these agencies were merged into the Federal Drug Enforcement Administration (FDEA), often called simply the DEA.

- - - - - - - - -

The Federal Drug Enforcement Administration (FDEA) provides unified leadership in attacking narcotics trafficking and drug abuse. Its emphasis is on the source and distribution of illicit drugs rather than on arresting abusers.

- - - - - - - - -

The DEA's emphasis is on stopping the flow of drugs at their foreign sources, disrupting illicit domestic commerce at the highest levels of distribution and helping state and local police to prevent the entry of illegal drugs

In August 1999 dozens of American Airlines employees and contract workers were arrested by the Bureau of Alcohol, Tobacco and Firearms (ATF) and Drug Enforcement Administration (DEA) agents. Those arrested were accused of using the airline's planes to smuggle drugs into the United States.

into their communities. The DEA's Mobile Enforcement Team (MET), established in 1995, consists of more than 200 agents deployed across the nation to help fight the drug war (Quinn, 1996, p. 36).

The DEA, however, relies heavily on cooperation from other agencies. For example: "Customs inspectors are the front line of drug interdiction, searching baggage and people" ("Customs Chief Wants . . . ," 1999, p. 13A). Customs agents are also involved in training U.S. corporations on how to detect and avoid getting entangled in complex money laundering schemes by drug traffickers (Gordon, 1999, p. D1).

U.S. agencies must cooperate with law enforcement in other countries because much of the U.S. domestic drug problem actually originates across national borders. According to Ronderos (1998, p. 385):

> Organized criminals dealing with drugs have often been successful because of the lack of coordinated law enforcement efforts among nations and because even when there is the political will on the part of all of the involved countries, transnational law enforcement is a "patchwork quilt of overlapping and competing agencies."

To overcome interjurisdictional competition and duplication of effort, multijurisdictional drug task forces

have been implemented across the country. Jefferis et al. (1998, pp. 85, 87) state:

> Multijurisdictional drug task forces formalize cooperative ventures and dedicate attention to drug crimes with the assumption that such will lead to more effective drug law enforcement. . . .
>
> A primary objective of drug task forces is to coordinate resources and activities of multiple agencies in an effort to accumulate the evidence needed to arrest and prosecute known drug dealers.

LaBrasseur (1998, p. 32) describes a task force in Massachusetts that consists of representatives from the DEA, Immigration and Naturalization Services (INS), the Massachusetts State Police, local probation officers and the Essex County District Attorney's Office:

> Code-named Operation Overdose, the strategy [targets] drug dealers and buyers at the street level—specifically, at their contact telephones. . . .
>
> Tactical advantages were gained when INS and the local probation departments came on board. . . . Any illegal alien could be detained by INS, while anyone on probation faced a possible arrest for violating that probation. . . .
>
> In the end, the program's success justified the expense: 484 arrests were made, 36 search warrants

were executed, $43,687 in cash was confiscated, and drug seizures totaled 20,102 dosage units of heroin, 3.7 pounds of cocaine and 2 pounds of marijuana.

Sometimes task forces and programs are created not out of a desire to cooperate but out of a need to eliminate dissention. Hoffmann (1999, pp. 121, 124) explains:

> The lack of cooperation between federal and local law enforcement agencies is legendary, but when the feds couldn't get along among themselves fighting drug trafficking in Miami or fighting for appropriation dollars in the Congress, High Intensity Drug Trafficking Area (HIDTA) was created to get law enforcement refocused toward criminals. . . .
>
> Before HIDTA, federal agencies competed to make the same arrests and seizures. Customs, DEA, Border Patrol, Coast Guard and FBI often had separate investigations going after the same traffickers. There was additional competition with local law enforcement.
>
> The HIDTA takes funding out of the hands of individual agencies and forces it to be shared. . . .
>
> A big advantage of the HIDTA program is that it shows federal agents [that] some of the best investigators in the nation are on local police departments.

One benefit of working with a task force is shared forfeiture revenues.

Drug Asset Forfeitures

The asset-forfeiture program was introduced in the preceding chapter as it relates to the seizing of assets of organized crime figures. This program is also operative in drug-related cases. Kash (1998, p. 56) asserts: "One of the best weapons law enforcement has in the war on drugs is its capability to seize and forfeit assets that have been used to violate the laws of the United States."

The Federal Comprehensive Crime Control Act of 1983 initiated procedures for asset forfeitures as a result of drug arrests. Confiscating drug dealers' cash and property has been effective in reducing drug trafficking and is providing local, state and federal law enforcement agencies with assets they need for their fight against drugs. The asset forfeiture laws provide for the confiscation of cash and other property in possession of a drug dealer at the time of the arrest. Seized vehicles, boats or airplanes may be used directly by the agency or sold at auction to generate funds. Monetary assets may be used

to purchase police equipment, to hire additional law enforcement personnel or to provide training in drug investigation.

Precise recording of all proceedings is necessary to avoid allegations of abuse or misuse of these funds. Because of the required legal and judicial proceedings regarding these confiscations, it is often six months or longer after an arrest before the assets are available for police agency use. Domash (1997, p. 69) cautions: "It is essential, according to forfeiture experts, that [law enforcement] departments know that unlike many court decisions that continually control the extent of police investigations, asset forfeiture is not a black and white procedure but one that is always changing. . . . If done right, asset forfeiture [is] an effective way of dealing with criminals."

A common defense to asset seizure is the Innocent Owner Defense. If an owner can prove that he or she had no knowledge of the prohibited activity, the property is not subject to forfeiture.

According to Warchol and Johnson (1996, p. 49): "While arrest, prosecution and incarceration can incapacitate drug dealers, forfeiture can destroy their illegal organizations by undermining their economic foundation. Forfeiture has also been used successfully to eliminate crack houses, money-laundering facilities and clandestine drug labs." They (p. 53) conclude: "Used equitably, it [asset forfeiture] is an effective method of destroying criminal organizations and deterring aspiring criminals, while providing much-needed revenue to fight drug trafficking."

The program has not been without problems and misunderstandings. The confiscated funds may be used only for police department efforts to increase their fight against drugs. Police budgets cannot be reduced because of the availability of the asset-forfeiture funds.

Focus of the Future

Tremendous national, state and local efforts are being directed to meeting the challenges of drug use and abuse in the United States. A national drug czar serves at the direction of the president, and many states appoint people to similar positions to direct state and local efforts. Federal funding is available through state agencies. Federal, state and local agencies with roles in the drug war coordinate their efforts. Thousands of volunteers, groups and agencies have joined the fight against illegal drugs. For example, Operation Weed and Seed is a national initiative for marshaling the resources of a number of federal agencies to strengthen law enforcement and revitalize communities. It is a comprehensive, coordinated approach to controlling drugs and crime in targeted high-crime neighborhoods. The Weed and Seed program links concentrated law enforcement efforts to identify, arrest and prosecute violent offenders, drug traffickers and other criminals and community policing (weeding) with human services such as after-school, weekend and summer youth activities; adult literacy classes; parental counseling; and neighborhood revitalization efforts to prevent and deter further crime (seeding).

An evaluation conducted by the National Institute of Justice found that: "Implementation strategies that relied on bottom-up, participatory decision-making approaches, especially when combined with efforts to build capacity and partnership among local organizations, proved the most effective" ("Weed and Seed Evaluation," 1999, p. 7). But crime control is only one of several drug-control strategies individual communities and the nation as a whole have available. Figure 20.4 depicts the multifaceted drug-control strategies competing for funds and support now and into the future.

Many communities have adopted community-wide programs for dealing with drug abuse, guided by people who represent community organizations and agencies. An example of such community change is the adoption of drug-free zones around schools. Anyone who commits a drug violation within this zone—typically a 1,000-foot radius—may be charged with a felony. Public telephones have been removed from some schools, and many no longer allow students to carry pagers or radios on the school grounds.

Some communities are developing specific programs to address the drug problem and are recognizing the need for innovative approaches. For example, according to Harrell et al. (1998, pp. 9–10):

> In 1997, Birmingham, Alabama, became the first major U.S. city to take a comprehensive approach to the challenge of addressing offender drug abuse. . . . This initiative, Breaking the Cycle (BTC), . . . is designed to apply the lessons learned over the past two decades. . . . When substance abuse treatment is reinforced by the coercive power of the criminal justice system, defendant outcome improves. BTC fully integrates drug testing, referral to treatment, judicial supervision of treatment, and graduated sanctions.

A community's efforts to control drug use and sales have the potential to reduce crime in general. In fact, in many instances, substance abuse can be linked with most of the criminal acts discussed in this text. According to LaBrasseur (p. 32), the Massachusetts task force code-named Operation Overdose, while targeting street-level drug sales, had other far-reaching effects:

> The most significant result may well be found in the dramatic reduction in the city's crime statistics: compared to the same period in the previous year, robberies dropped 40 percent, assaults 20 percent, breaking-and-entering 10 percent and homicides 50 percent. Although not an intended effect of the operation, the reduction in crime was clearly driven by the number of arrests made.

The International Association of Chiefs of Police, in conjunction with the Drug Enforcement Administration, a division of the U.S. Department of Justice, has published a manual for police chiefs and sheriffs, *Reducing Crime by Reducing Drug Abuse*. The Office of National Drug Control Policy has implemented a 10-year plan called the *National Drug Control Strategy* to help guide national efforts to reduce substance abuse and more effectively handle the consequences of such abuse. The *Strategy* (pp. 21–22) consists of five basic goals:

- Educate and enable America's youth to reject illegal drugs as well as alcohol and tobacco.
- Increase the safety of American citizens by substantially reducing drug-related crime and violence.
- Reduce health and social costs to the public of illegal drug use.
- Shield America's air, land, and sea frontiers from the drug threat.
- Break foreign and domestic drug sources of supply.

Despite the tremendous effort to win the war on drugs, many have criticized the ineffectiveness of the endeavor, with some declaring it an all-out failure. Hall (1999, p. 6) cites statistics from the *1999 National Drug Control Strategy* that demonstrate how our federal drug policy has failed:

> Drug-related deaths (accidental, suicide and other) have risen more than 60 percent since 1990.
>
> Cocaine and heroin hospital emergency room mentions (i.e., admissions) have risen steadily almost every year since 1978.

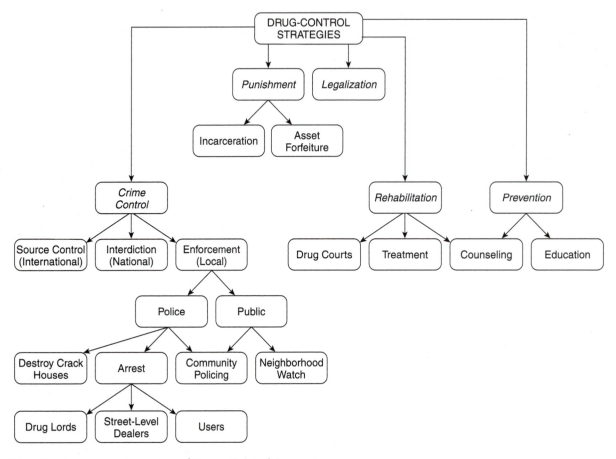

FIGURE 20.4 *Overview of Drug-Control Strategies*

Source: Henry M. Wrobleski and Kären M. Hess. *Introduction to Law Enforcement and Criminal Justice,* 6th edition. Belmont, CA: Wadsworth/Thomson Learning, 2000, p. 281. Reprinted by permission.

Total incarcerations in local, state and federal jails and prisons recently reached an all-time high of 1.8 million Americans (thanks to the Drug War). . . .

Current drug use overall among Americans for any illicit drugs has remained fairly steady for nearly a decade, *despite* all the money thrown at the problem and all the people jailed behind drug laws during the same period.

Defenders of the drug control strategy maintain that the policy itself is valid; rather, it is how people see the challenge that is flawed:

The metaphor of a "war on drugs" is misleading. Although wars are expected to end, drug control is a continuous challenge. . . .

Cancer is a more appropriate metaphor for the nation's drug problem. Dealing with cancer is a long-term proposition. It requires the mobilization of support mechanisms—medical, educational, and societal—to check the spread of the disease and improve the prognosis. The symptoms of the illness must be managed while the root cause is attacked. The key to reducing both drug abuse and cancer is prevention coupled with treatment (*The National Drug Control Strategy,* pp. 3–4).

Anti-illegal-drug programs must be a total national, state and local government effort, combined with local community programs. Law enforcement interdiction efforts must combine with these drug reduction efforts. This requires leadership, cooperation and coordination at all levels to succeed.

Summary

Drugs can be classified as depressants, stimulants, narcotics, hallucinogens, phencyclidine, cannabis or inhibitants. The most common drugs on the street, in possession of users and seized in drug raids are heroin, opium, morphine, codeine, cocaine, crack and marijuana. Arrest for possession or use of marijuana is the most frequent drug arrest.

It is illegal to possess or use narcotics or other dangerous drugs without a prescription; it is illegal to sell or distribute them without a license. Investigators learn to recognize drug addicts by knowing common symptoms of drug abuse, such as sudden, dramatic changes in discipline or job performance; unusual degrees of activity or inactivity; sudden, irrational outbursts; significant deterioration in personal appearance; dilated pupils or wearing sunglasses at inappropriate times or places; needle marks, razor cuts or constant wearing of long sleeves to hide such marks; sudden attempts to borrow money or to steal; and frequent associations with known drug abusers or pushers.

Physical evidence of possession or use of controlled substances includes the actual drugs, apparatus associated with their use, the suspect's appearance and behavior and urine and blood tests.

Evidence of the actual transfer of drugs from the seller to the buyer is the major legal evidence required for prosecuting drug sale cases. If you observe what appears to be a drug buy, you can make a warrantless arrest if you have probable cause. Often, however, it is better simply to observe and gather information. Undercover drug buys are carefully planned, witnessed and conducted so that no charge of entrapment can be made. Two or more buys are made to avoid the charge of entrapment.

Clandestine drug laboratories present physical, chemical and toxic hazards to law enforcement officers who raid them.

The Federal Drug Enforcement Administration (FDEA) provides unified leadership in attacking narcotics trafficking and drug abuse. The FDEA's emphasis is on the source and distribution of illicit drugs rather than on arresting abusers.

Checklist

Drugs and Controlled Substances

- How did the complaint originate? Police? Victim? Informant? Neighbor?

- What is the specific nature of the complaint? Selling? Using? Possessing? Overdose? Are all required elements present?

- What type of narcotics are suspect?

- Is there enough evidence of sale to justify planning a buy?

- Were obtained drugs tested with a department drug-detection kit?

- Has the evidence been properly collected, identified and preserved?

- Has the evidence been sent to a laboratory for examination?

- Has the drug been determined a controlled substance?

- Has everyone involved been interviewed or interrogated?

- Do those involved have prior arrests for similar offenses?

- Is surveillance necessary to obtain evidence for an arrest and/or a search warrant?

- Is a raid called for? (If so, review the checklist for raids, Chapter 7, p. 203.)

- Have cooperating agencies been alerted?

Application

A. *The Stakeout* (Adapted from an account of an actual narcotics investigation written by David Peterson.)

It is dark as the five men emerge from the plane. They haul out their luggage and walk to the parking lot of the tiny, one-strip airport. The pilot enters a white shack that is trimmed in red. When the pilot leaves, the others gather around a young man who has driven out to meet them. His name is Bruce Preece, and he looks like an outdoorsman. Bearded, he wears a suede hat and red plaid jacket.

Moments later, a camper occupied by two more men pulls into the parking lot, and most of the group piles into the back. Seated along foam-rubber benches, they are dim in the shadows as the camper moves through the empty town.

"That guy sure was an inquisitive one," the pilot remarks, referring to the man in the shack. "He knew we were here last week, and he wanted to know what we were up to."

"Tourists," someone else replies, his head silhouetted against a window. Everyone looks like a visitor—a hunter, perhaps, or a fisherman. They carry small bags and wear down jackets and jeans.

The clothing is deceptive.

Four narcotics agents, or *narcs,* and four agents from the Federal Drug Enforcement Administration are staked out in a camper outside the home of a man who works for a chemical firm. They suspect that at home he is manufacturing illegal drugs in a clandestine laboratory. The agents call him "No. 1."

They suspect another man is getting illegal drugs and distributing them in nearby towns. They call him "No. 2."

No. 1 came under suspicion when a chemical supply company in Connecticut notified the feds that someone in this little town was ordering chemicals often used to make illegal substances. No. 2 came under suspicion when he told a local deputy sheriff he would be paid $2,000 if he notified him of any narcotics investigations.

The two men have been under surveillance for several weeks. One agent has even been inside the house by taking a shipment of chemicals from the Connecticut firm and making a "controlled delivery"—that is, he pretended to be the mailman and hauled the heavy boxes inside the house.

The agents have noticed a pattern. On Wednesdays, No. 1's wife goes into town and No. 2 stops by. It is Wednesday night. The plan is to watch No. 2 enter and leave the house and arrest him before he reaches his car. Assuming he is carrying illegal drugs, the agents will arrest No. 1 as well, search his home and seize the contents of the lab. Both men are known to be armed.

By 7 P.M. surveillance has begun in earnest. The eight are waiting for something to happen. Two agents sit in an unmarked car along the highway leading to the house. Two others are in the woods, within view of the house. The other four are in the camper, parked just off the highway. Even from inside, the camper looks normal. But its cabinets contain an array of radios, cameras, lenses, firearms and other gear. From the camper's bathroom, one agent takes out a telephoto lens the size of a small wastebasket and attaches it to a "night scope."

At about 7:15, the woman leaves.

Each of the three groups of agents has a radio. However, No. 1 is believed to have a police scanner, which would allow him to monitor their conversation. So they speak in a rough sort of code, as though they were squad cars checking for speeders. "401," for example, will mean that No. 2 has arrived.

Hours pass. None of the agents has eaten since noon. They pass around a bag of Halloween-sized Snickers bars and start telling narc stories.

At 10, a sober, low voice over the radio says, "You may have three visitors shortly." A few minutes later, three agents climb into the camper, shivering. One agent, who has been watching No. 1 through his kitchen window with binoculars, says, "He's busy in there. He's

pouring stuff, and he's running something, like a tableting machine."

The agents know that if they could just bust into that house, they'd find a guilty man surrounded by evidence. No. 2 doesn't show. Another night wasted?

Questions

1. Do the agents have probable cause to conduct a raid at this time?
2. Could they seize the materials No. 1 is working with as plain-view evidence? Why or why not?
3. What aspects of the surveillance illustrate effective investigation?
4. Have the agents made any mistakes?
5. What should their next step be?
6. Is there likely to be a link between the suspects and organized crime? Why or why not?

B. The 1992 *LET* Challenge (Adapted and reprinted by permission from *Law Enforcement Technology,* July, August and September 1992.)

The Investigation

Interior Anytown Police Department—Day One. You are the detective lieutenant in charge of a large drug operation, the largest you've ever conducted. You've been on the force 12 years. It is up to you to make all the right calls, make sure all the evidence is there, plan the complete operation, organize the surveillance and orchestrate the tactical operation. At the end of the operation, if you do everything correctly, the result will be a huge drug bust and seizure, all the officers involved will come out safely and you will put a major drug supplier behind bars.

As you are sitting behind your desk, Rogers, the undercover officer whom you have assigned to this case enters without knocking and sits down. He fills in the details about the buy, which was set up by an informant that your department arrested previously. Introduced by this informant, Rogers has been able to set up the buy, and now all you have to do is supply the necessary "show money"—$100,000—100 big ones that your department definitely does not have in its budget!

Questions

1.1. Where should you obtain the needed money?
    A. The Department   C. The state
       of Justice   D. None of the above
    B. The DEA   E. All of the above

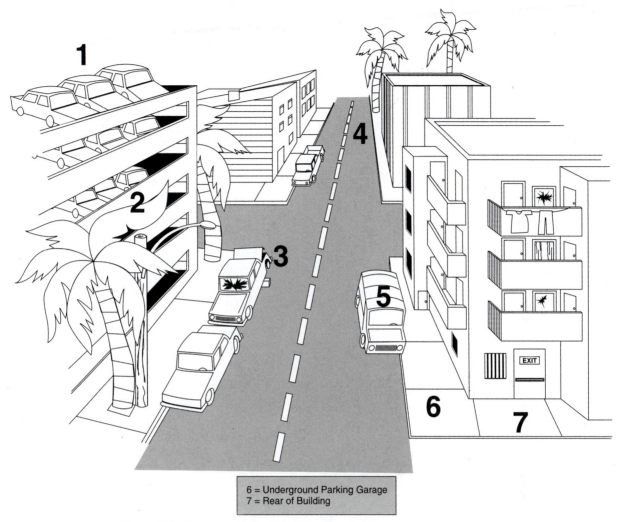

6 = Underground Parking Garage
7 = Rear of Building

FIGURE 20.5 *Map of the Longwood Gardens Housing Project*

Putting together this investigation has definitely been a great deal of work. You think back on what you have done to get this far: You knew your informant had proven unreliable in the past, so you decided to run all known information about the principals through your department's computer system. Entering the key subject's alias and the strange tattoo on his shoulder into the database, the computer turned up the following information about the subject and the group he travels with:

■ The subject has three prior convictions for drug dealing and distribution.

■ The group has a propensity for violence, particularly with high-powered automatic weapons.

■ They regularly make trips to drug distribution cities.

Rogers has already set up the buy, so you head to the D.A.'s office to arrange the warrant.

1.2 Do you have enough to obtain a search warrant?
  A. Yes   B. No

Next you request and receive from Rogers a building plan of the apartment complex in question, the "Longwood Gardens Housing Project," shown in Figure 20.5. Study it carefully.

After a trip to town hall for the blueprints, Rogers learns the following about the location:

■ The exact apartment in which the buy is going down—on the third floor

■ Steel apartment doors

■ Windows open out

- Sewer system bypass information
- No fire escapes; stairways on exterior with private entrances
- Exits (front exit; one on each side; rear exit; one from the underground garage)

1.3 Do you also need a search warrant for the apartment next door?
A. Yes   B. No

1.4 Should you set up a phone tap for the apartment in which the deal is going down?
A. Yes   B. No

1.5 Would you need a separate warrant to tap the phone?
A. Yes   B. No

The week before the actual buy, the sellers contact Rogers and demand a "flashroll" (pre-buy)—they want to see the money to make sure Rogers is serious. What should you do?

1.6 Agree to the "flashroll"?
A. Yes   B. No

If you answered "yes" to the preceding question, please answer the following two questions. If you answered "no," skip questions 1.7 and 1.8.

1.7 Do you take the entire $100,000 to the "flashroll"?
A. Yes   B. No

1.8 Where should the pre-buy be held?
A. A public place   B. The apartment in question

The Surveillance

You arrive at the scene of the impending drug bust with your response team of nine officers. Using the map in Figure 20.5, place your three surveillance officers in strategic points so all exits are covered and you are faced with no surprises.

2.1 There are five exits: Where do you place your three officers? (Use the numbers on the map.)
A. #3, 6 and 7   C. #4, 5 and 7
B. #2, 5 and 6   D. #1, 4 and 6

You have separate officers to operate the surveillance/command center.

2.2 Where is the best place for the command center?
A. #1   C. #4
B. #2   D. #5

Because it is early morning, there is little activity in the apartment building. As the sun rises higher, activity increases. Kids start to come out into the open hallway/balconies, and people are mingling in the stairwells and the hallways. Sight lines are being obstructed as the balconies fill, and telling the good guys from the bad guys is becoming increasingly difficult.

2.3 You should clear the building.
A. True   B. False

2.4 You should cut off electricity to restrict movement of those living in the apartment.
A. True   B. False

2.5 You should mark the apartment door.
A. True   B. False

2.6 You should disable the sewage system.
A. True   B. False

2.7 Please eliminate the one unnecessary piece of knowledge from the following list:
A. Which way the windows open (in or out)
B. Where the stairways are located
C. Where the fire escapes are
D. The number of people inside the apartment building
E. What weapons the sellers have

2.8 You need to arrange a battering ram or hydraulic tool to get through the apartment door.
A. True   B. False

2.9 Here are some ways to find out more about the apartment in question. Which answer does not belong?
A. Get blueprints of the building
B. Wiretaps
C. Surveillance on the building
D. Send Rogers in before the buy to check it out
E. Talk to the apartment manager

Your communications system finally indicates a caller from the command center.

2.10 Your mode of communication should be:
A. Cellular phone   B. Radio

You switch it on to hear that Rogers is going in. He is wired. You sign off and review your surveillance choices as you wait for the signal that everything is in place and your team is ready to go in.

The Bust

The officers in your command are in place on the walkway around the corner of the building, waiting for the drug bust to go down. Your communication system signals to you to "take 'em!"

4 = **Bedroom**
5 = **Windows**
6 = **Outside**

FIGURE 20.6 *Map of the Drug Bust Room*

3.1 Using three of your officers for backup, divide your six officers into the following teams:

Entry:

Arrest:

Evidence:

Evidence/entry:

3.2 What equipment should your team be carrying? Of the following list, eliminate two items your team would not need:
A. Shields
B. Bullet-resistant vests
C. Diversionary devices (flash bangs, etc.)
D. Tear gas
E. Dogs
F. Evidence kits

You give the order to go in, and your entry team, backed up by the evidence team, is heading for the door. Just as they turn the final corner to the apartment door, three small children come walking up the open hallway, laughing and singing.

Seeing the team and their guns, the children *freeze* right in front of the apartment door. They are ready to scream.

3.3 What do you do with the kids?
A. Yell for them to "get down" and storm the door?
B. Have a member of the entry team take them away?
C. Have a member of the evidence team take them away?
D. Ignore them and hope for the best?

The kids are taken care of, and your team goes up to the door. If you had chosen a battering ram to get through the door, you'd be in trouble because you are faced with a thick steel door. Luckily you had already arranged for a master key, which you pull from your pocket and slip into the lock. The door opens easily, and you are inside the apartment.

There are six people inside, including the informant, your officer and a pregnant woman. They are all huddled in the center of the room, leaning over a table. They freeze for a second when "flash bang" explodes as you open the door, but they break and scatter quickly. Drugs are in evidence everywhere, as is a pile of weapons.

3.4 It is correct to use either tear gas or pepper mixture to incapacitate the occupants of the apartment.
A. True   B. False

As your team enters, they shout loudly for everyone to get down and stay down. Some comply, while others are *screaming* and *yelling* at your team. In the midst of the confusion, your team fans out to cover the room, and one of the entry team heads for the bathroom.

3.5 Place your officers strategically within the room so that all possible eventualities are covered. (Use map of room [Figure 20.6].)
A. #1, 2, 4 and 5   C. #2, 4 and 6
B. #1, 2, 5 and 6   D. #1, 5 and 6

The team leader announces, "Police officers! Everybody down! Right now!"

3.6 Is it reasonable to place a pregnant woman on the floor?
A. Yes   B. No

One of the bad guys gets to the bathroom first, and you hear the toilet flushing. Luckily, during the previous section, you chose to divert the sewage system, so all that he is flushing down the drain is going straight to your evidence people. Finally the chaos in the room calms down, and the arrest team goes to work, cuffing the occupants and reading them their rights.

3.7 Your team should treat the undercover officer and the informant as just two of the arrestees.
A. True   B. False

Your arrest team takes the bad guys out of the apartment, while the evidence team collects all the drugs and the money, including the $100,000 you have to return. It's been a good day all around, and you and your officers share a smile.

Discussion Questions

1. How serious do you feel the drug problem is nationally? Statewide?

2. Would legalizing drugs be a feasible solution to the problem?

3. Why should alcohol abuse be considered an illness and drug abuse a crime?

4. Does your high school have a drug awareness program?

5. How are drug raids treated by the media in your community?

6. Do you know anyone with a drug abuse problem? How has it affected that person's life?

7. To what extent are drugs used in your community? What types are most prevalent? Are they used primarily by adults or juveniles? (You may also want to consider legally prescribed drugs, alcohol and tobacco in this discussion.)

8. Should the penalty for use of marijuana be reduced to a misdemeanor as it has been in some states? Should it be legalized, or should it remain a felony? In what amounts should the determination be made?

9. Is the drug abuse problem too large for the police to handle? Has it reached a status of social acceptance such that drug laws should not be enforced? Who makes this determination?

10. What effect do educational campaigns have in reducing or controlling drug abuse? Do you have such a campaign in your community? How successful is it?

References

Asante, John S. "GHB: Grievous Bodily Harm." *FBI Law Enforcement Bulletin,* Vol. 68, No. 4, April 1999, pp. 21–25.

Beary, Kevin; Murdi, John P.; and Dorsch, Linda. "Countering Prescription Fraud." *The Police Chief,* Vol. LXIII, No. 3, March 1996, pp. 33–35.

Benner, Alan W. and Isaacs, S. Marshall. " 'Excited Delirium': A Two-Fold Problem." *The Police Chief,* Vol. LXIII, No. 6, June 1996, pp. 20–22.

Brandenstein, Albert. "Advanced Technologies Bolster Law Enforcement's Counterdrug Efforts." *The Police Chief,* Vol. LXIV, No. 1, January 1997, pp. 32–34.

Bulzomi, Michael J. "Drug Detection Dogs: Legal Considerations." *FBI Law Enforcement Bulletin,* Vol. 69, No. 1, January 2000, pp. 27–31.

Cashman, Michael. "Meth Labs: Toxic Timebombs." *The Police Chief,* Vol. LXV, No. 2, February 1998, pp. 42–47.

Constantine, Thomas A. "NPDIX: The National Drug Pointer Index." *The Police Chief,* Vol. LXV, No. 4, April 1998, pp. 24–30.

"Customs Chief Wants Intelligence Unit to Stop Drug Runners." *Las Vegas Review Journal,* March 5, 1999, p. 13A.

deGroot, Gabrielle. "Interview with ONDCP." *Corrections Today,* Vol. 60, No. 10, October 1998, pp. 90–93.

Doane, George and Marshall, Donnie. "Responding to the Methamphetamine Problem." *The Police Chief,* Vol. LXV, No. 2, February 1998, pp. 36–40.

Domash, Peter. "The Assets of Asset Forfeiture." *Police,* Vol. 21, No. 10, October 1997, pp. 69–72.

Drug Use Trends. Washington, DC: Office of National Drug Control Policy, Fact Sheet, June 1999. (NCJ-175050)

"Drug-Sniffing Dogs Assist in Depot Bust." *Las Vegas Review Journal,* March 2, 1997, p. 6B.

Gondles, James A., Jr. "Human Heartache: The Other Side of Drugs." *Corrections Today,* Vol. 60, No. 10, October 1998, p. 6.

Gordon, Marcy. "Currency Schemes Enmesh U.S. Firms." (Minneapolis/St. Paul) *Star Tribune,* November 2, 1999, pp. D1, D8.

Graves, Chris. "Meth: The New Drug of Choice." (Minneapolis/St. Paul) *Star Tribune,* September 27, 1998, p. A10.

Hall, Dennis. "Chiefs' Survey: Drugs, Gangs, Domestic Violence Top List." *Police,* Vol. 22, No. 8, August 1998, pp. 72–76.

Hall, Dennis. "Fed Report Again Shows: Our Drug Policy Just Isn't Working." *Police,* Vol. 23, No. 10, October 1999, p. 6.

Harrell, Adele; Cook, Foster; and Carver, John. "Breaking the Cycle of Drug Abuse in Birmingham." *National Institute of Justice Journal,* July 1998, pp. 9–13.

Heiskell, Lawrence E. "Danger: Clandestine Drug Labs." *Police,* Vol. 20, No. 9, September 1996, pp. 32–35, 73.

Hendrie, Edward M. "Drug Conspiracies." *FBI Law Enforcement Bulletin,* Vol. 68, No. 6, June 1999, pp. 26–32.

"Heroin Surpasses Cocaine as Cause for Treatment-Center Admissions." (Minneapolis/St. Paul) *Star Tribune,* August 26, 1999, p. A10.

Hoffmann, John. "Dissention Results in HIDTA." *Law and Order,* Vol. 47, No. 6, June 1999, pp. 121–124.

Jefferis, Eric S.; Frank, James; Smith, Brad W.; Novak, Kenneth J.; and Travis, Lawrence F., III. "An Examination of the Productivity and Perceived Effectiveness of Drug Task Forces." *Police Quarterly,* Vol. 1, No. 3, 1998, pp. 85–107.

Kash, Douglas A. "The Federal Forfeiture Adoption Option." *Police,* Vol. 22, No. 11, November 1998, pp. 56–59.

LaBrasseur, John. "Operation Overdose." *The Police Chief,* Vol. LXV, No. 4, April 1998, pp. 32–35.

Leshner, Alan I. "Addiction Is a Brain Disease—and It Matters." *National Institute of Justice Journal,* October 1998, pp. 2–6.

Luitweiler, David M. "International Cooperation Key to Success in Drug Wars." *The Police Chief,* Vol. LXV, No. 9, September 1998, pp. 41–46.

Manning, Tom. "Drug Labs and Endangered Children." *FBI Law Enforcement Bulletin,* Vol. 68, No. 7, July 1999, pp. 10–14.

Mieczkowski, Tom and Lersch, Kim. "Drug Testing in Criminal Justice: Evolving Uses, Emerging Technologies." *National Institute of Justice Journal,* Issue #24, December 1997, pp. 9–15.

The National Drug Control Strategy, 1998: A Ten Year Plan. Washington, DC: Office of National Drug Control Policy, 1998.

Quinn, Steve. "DEA: Metropolitan Enforcement Teams." *Police,* Vol. 20, No. 9, September 1996, pp. 36–38, 79–82.

Reak, Keven P. and Gunta, S. C. "Cocaine, Restraints and Sudden Death." *The Police Chief,* Vol. LXIII, No. 6, June 1996, p. 10.

Rohypnol. Washington, DC: Office of National Drug Control Policy, Fact Sheet, June 1998. (NCJ-161843)

Ronderos, Juan G. "Transnational Drugs Law Enforcement: The Problem of Jurisdiction and Criminal Law." *Journal of Contemporary Criminal Justice,* Vol. 14, No. 4, November 1998, pp. 384–397.

Sclabassi, Mary A. "Drug Users on the Net." *Police,* Vol. 20, No. 12, December 1996, pp. 62–70.

"Sting Dismantles Drug Cartel, Officials Say." (Minneapolis/St. Paul) *Star Tribune,* September 21, 1999, p. A6.

Strandberg, Keith W. "Drugs, Guns and Youth Crime." *Law Enforcement Technology,* Vol. 20, No. 1, January 1997, pp. 28–30.

Strandberg, Keith W. "Waging War on the Street." *Law Enforcement Technology,* Vol. 25, No. 9, September 1998, pp. 62–66.

Strandberg, Keith W. "Non-Invasive Testing." *Law Enforcement Technology,* Vol. 26, No. 5, May 1999, pp. 36–42.

Thompson, Jon. "Preventing Clandestine Labs." *Law and Order,* Vol. 47, No. 10, October 1999, pp. 137–140.

Walchak, David G. "Drugs and Violent Crime." *The Police Chief,* Vol. LXIII, No. 3, March 1996, p. 6.

Warchol, Greg L. and Johnson, Brian R. "Ensuring the Future of Asset Forfeiture Programs." *The Police Chief,* Vol. LXIII, No. 3, March 1996, pp. 49–53.

"Weed and Seed Evaluation." *FBI Law Enforcement Bulletin,* Vol. 68, No. 12, December 1999, p. 7.

Death Scene Checklist

This form is to be used as a supplementary source sheet for readily available information and is not intended to replace conventional reports. Copies should be distributed to investigating officers and medical examiners.

Name of deceased:

First   Middle   Last

Address:

Age: **Race:** White   Black   Hispanic   Asian   Native American   Unknown

Sex: Male   Female

Telephone number:

Marital status: S   M   W   D   Separated   Unknown

Next-of-kin:

Name:

Address:

Telephone number:

Police notified by:

Date: Time:

Name:

Address:

Telephone number:

Relationship to deceased:

Deceased found:

Date: Time:

Address: (if different from above)

Location: Apartment   House   Townhouse   Other (describe)

Entrance by: Key   Cutting chain   Forcing door   Other (describe)

Type of lock on door:

Condition of other doors and windows: Open   Closed   Locked   Unlocked

Body found:

Living Room   Dining Room   Bedroom   Kitchen   Attic   Basement   Other (describe)

Location in room:

Position of body: On back   Face down   Other:

Condition of body:

Fully clothed   Partially clothed   Unclothed

Preservation: Well preserved   Decomposed

Estimated Rigor: Complete   Head   Arms   Legs

Livor: Front   Back   Localized

Color:

Blood: Absent   Present   Location

Ligatures: Yes   No

Apparent wounds: None   Gunshot   Stab   Blunt force

Number:

Location: Head   Neck   Chest   Abdomen   Extremities

Hanging: Yes   No   Means:

Weapon(s) present: Gun (estimate caliber)

Type:

Knife:

Other (describe)

Condition of surroundings: Orderly   Untidy   Disarray

Odors: Decomposition   Other

Evidence of last food preparation:

Where:

Type:

Dated material:

Mail:

Newspapers:

TV guide:

Liquor bottles:

Last contact with deceased:

Date:

Type of contact:

Name of contact:

Evidence of robbery: Yes   No   Not determined

Identification of deceased: Yes   No

If yes, how accomplished:

If no, how is it to be accomplished:

Evidence of drug use: (prescription and nonprescription) Yes   No

If drugs present, collect them and send with body.

Evidence of drug paraphernalia: Yes   No

Type:

Evidence of sexually deviant practices: Yes   No

Type: (collect and send with body)

Name and telephone number of investigating officer:

Source: James C. Beger, M.D., and William F. Enos, M.D. *FBI Law Enforcement Bulletin.* August 1981, pp. 16–18. Reprinted by permission of the FBI.

Associations That Provide Support in Investigating Computer-Related Crimes

Law Enforcement Electronic Technology Assistance Committee (LEETAC)

Office of the State Attorney

2725 Judge Fran Jamieson Way, Bldg. D; Viera, FL 32940

407–617–7510

Alan Diamond

The organization is composed of five prosecutors from the State Attorney's office, thirteen officers representing each municipality in the county, and two representatives from the sheriff's department. The organization provides technical assistance and expertise to law enforcement regarding computer crimes.

Information Systems Security Association (ISSA)

1926 Waukegan Rd, Suite 1; Glenview, IL 60025

800–370–4772

847–657–6746

Carl B. Jackson

Founded 1982; 300 members. Computer security practitioners whose primary responsibility is to ensure protection of information assets on a hands–on basis. Members include banking, retail, insurance, aerospace and publishing industries. The association's objective is to increase knowledge about information security. ISSA sponsors educational programs, research, discussion and dissemination of information. The association has regional and state chapters.

The Institute of Internal Auditors

Established in 1941, The Institute of Internal Auditors (IIA) serves nearly 75,000 members in internal auditing, governance and internal control, IT audit, education and security in approximately 129 countries. The world's leader in certification, education, research and technological guidance for the profession, the Institute serves as the profession's watchdog and resource on significant auditing issues around the globe.

Presenting important conferences and seminars for professional development, producing leading-edge educational products, certifying qualified auditing professionals, providing quality assurance reviews and benchmarking, and conducting valuable research projects through the IIA Research Foundation are just a few of the Institute's many activities.

The IIA also provides internal auditing practitioners, executive management, boards of directors and audit committees with standards, guidance and information on internal auditing best practices.

IIA Customer Service Center
249 Maitland Avenue; Altamonte Springs, FL 32701-4201
Tel: 1-407-830-7600, Ext. 1
Fax: 1-407-831-5171
E-mail: custserv@theiia.org
Web site: www.theiia.org

National Center for Computer Crime Data (NCCCD)

1222 17th Ave., Suite B
Santa Cruz, CA 95062
408-475-4457
Jay Bloom Becker, Director

Founded 1978. The center disseminates data and documents to facilitate the prevention, investigation and prosecution of computer crime. The center sponsors speakers and seminars, conducts research and compiles statistics.

Sample Form for Reporting Bias Crimes

PS-21410-01 (9/92)

BIAS OFFENSE REPORT*

AGENCY IDENTIFIER (ORI)_____

AGENCY NAME_____

MONTH AND YEAR_____

This form is to be used to report any bias motivated crimes in violation of Minnesota State Statute 626.5531. The chief law enforcement officer for an agency must complete form and return to the Department of Public Safety, Office of Information Systems Management, 314 Transportation Building, 395 John Ireland Blvd., St. Paul, Minnesota 55155 within 30 days (Laws of Minnesota, 1996, Chapter 643).

A. GENERAL OFFENSE INFORMATION

1) Agency Case Number: _____   2) Date of Offense: _____

3) Bias offense base on: ❏ Officer's belief   ❏ Victim's belief

4) *Description of Offense: _____   5) *Disposition: _____

6) *Type of Bias and Description: _____ /_____

　　　　　　　　　　　　　　　Type Code　　　　　　　　　　　Description Code or Literal

7) *Target: _____   8) Place of Occurrence: _____

*Reprinted by permission of the Minnesota Bureau of Criminal Apprehension.

B. VICTIM/OFFENDER INFORMATION

9) VICTIMS				10) OFFENDERS			11) *RELATIONSHIP TO VICTIM	12) AFFILIATION (if any)
#	Age	Sex	Race	Age	Sex	Race		
1								
2								
3								
4								
5								
6								
7								
8								
9								
10								
11								
12								
13								
14								
15								

COMMENTS: _____

*Use code tables on reverse

Return to: DPS/OISM
314 DOT Building
395 John Ireland Blvd.
St. Paul, MN 55155

CODE TABLES

4) *DESCRIPTION of OFFENSE:*

To be used in further identifying offense
01-Cross Burning
02-Swastika
03-Bombing
04-Hanging in Effigy
05-Disturbing Public Meeting
06-Graffiti
07-Spitting
08-Letter
09-Verbal Abuse (Person to Person)
10-Telephone
11-Homicide
12-Criminal Sexual Conduct
13-Robbery
14-Burglary
15-Aggravated Assault
16-Arson
17-Larceny Theft
18-Disturbing the Peace
19-Property Damage
20-Simple Assault
00-Other (Describe)

5) *DISPOSITION:* Based on CJRS Reporting System—Major Offenses
A-Arrest of Adult and/or Adult & Juvenile
J-Arrest of Juvenile
E-Exceptionally Cleared
U-Unfounded
P-Pending

6) *TYPE of BIAS and DESCRIPTION:*

Type	Description
01-Racial	W-White
	H-White/Hispanic Origin
	N-Negro/Black
	B-Black/Hispanic Origin
	I-Indian or Alaskan Native
	M-Indian w/Hispanic Origin
	O-Asian or Pacific Islander
	A-Asian or Pacific Islander
	w/Hispanic Origin
02-Religious	01-Catholic
	02-Hindu/Buddhist
	03-Islamic/Moslem
	04-Jewish
	05-Protestant
	06-Fundamentalist
	07-Other (Describe)
03-National Origin	Specify

04-Sex	M-Male
	F-Female
05-Age	Specify age(s)
06-Disability	Specify disability
07-Sexual Orientation	01-Homosexual Male
	02-Homosexual Female
	03-Heterosexual Male
	04-Heterosexual Female

7) *TARGET CODES:*

01-Person
02-Private Property
03-Public Property

8) *PLACE of OCCURRENCE:*

01-Residence
02-Hotel, Motel or Other Commercial Short-Term Residence
03-Parking Lot Areas
04-Business
05-Vehicle
06-Street/Sidewalk
07-Highway/Freeway
08-Park/School Ground
09-Vacant Lot
10-Jail
11-Rural Area/Country Road
12-Cemetery
13-Religious Building
14-Government Building
15-School Building
16-Private Club
17-Other (Describe)

11) *RELATIONSHIP of OFFENDER to VICTIM:*

01-Family Member
02-Neighbor
03-Acquaintance
04-Boyfriend/Ex-Boyfriend
05-Girlfriend/Ex-Girlfriend
06-Ex-Husband
07-Ex-Wife
08-Employee
09-Employer
10-Friend
11-Homosexual Relation
12-Other-Known to Victim
13-Stranger
14-Gang Member
15-Peace Officer Related
16-Unknown
17-Other (Describe)

★Reprinted by permission of the Minnesota Bureau of Criminal Apprehension.

Glossary

The number in parentheses is the chapter in which the term is discussed.

ABANDONMENT The act of parents deserting their children. (12)

ACCELERANTS Substances that cause fires to burn faster and hotter. (17)

ACCESSORY Anyone except a husband, wife or member of the offender's family who knows the offender has committed a felony or is liable to arrest and yet harbors, conceals or helps the offender avoid or escape arrest, trial, conviction or punishment.

ACTIVE VOICE The subject performs the action of the sentence. In contrast to passive voice. (3)

ADIPOCERE Soapy appearance of a dead body left for weeks in a hot, moist location. (13)

ADMINISTRATIVE WARRANT Official permission to inspect a given property to determine compliance with city regulations; for example, compliance with fire codes. (17)

ADMISSION Statement containing information about the elements of a crime but falling short of a full confession. (6)

AGGRAVATED ARSON Intentionally destroying or damaging a dwelling or other property, real or personal, by means of fire or explosives, creating an imminent danger to life or great bodily harm, which risk was known or reasonably foreseeable to the suspect. (17)

AGGRAVATED ASSAULT (FELONIOUS ASSAULT) An unlawful attack by one person on another to inflict severe bodily injury. (10)

ALLIGATORING Checking of charred wood that gives the appearance of alligator skin. Large, rolling blisters indicate rapid, intense heat; small, flat blisters indicate long, low heat. (17)

AMPHETAMINE A stimulant. (20)

ANTICHRIST The son of Satan. (19)

ARREST Taking a person into custody in the manner authorized by law. (7)

ARSON The malicious, willful burning of a building or property. *See also* **AGGRAVATED ARSON.** (17)

ASPHYXIATION Death or unconsciousness resulting from insufficient oxygen to support the red blood cells reaching the body tissues and the brain. (13)

ASSAULT Unlawfully threatening to harm another person, actually harming another person or attempting to do so. Formerly referred to threats of or attempts to cause bodily harm but now usually includes *battery*. (10)

ASSOCIATIVE EVIDENCE Evidence that links a suspect with a crime. (5)

AUTOEROTIC ASPHYXIATION Accidental death from suffocation, strangulation or chemical asphyxia resulting from a combination of ritualistic behavior, oxygen deprivation, danger and fantasy for sexual gratification. (13)

AUTOMATED FINGERPRINT IDENTIFICATION SYSTEM (AFIS) A computerized system of reviewing and mapping fingerprints. (5)

BACKING Marking photographs on their back with a felt-tip pen or label to indicate the photographer's initials, date photo was taken, brief description of what it depicts and the direction of north. Evidence can be circled on the back of the photo in the same way. (2)

BAIT MONEY Currency whose serial numbers are recorded and that is placed so it can be added to any robbery loot. (9)

BARBITURATE A depressant drug. (20)

BARCODES Identification symbols affixed to an item that can be scanned into a computer; now used in property control systems. (5)

BASELINE (PLOTTING) METHOD Establishes a straight line from one fixed point to another from which measurements are taken at right angles. (2)

BATTERY Actually hitting or striking someone. (10)

BEELZEBUB A powerful demon, right below Satan, according to Satanists. (19)

BEST EVIDENCE The original object, or the highest available degree of proof that can be produced (*Cheadle v Bardwell*). (3)

BIAS CRIME A crime motivated by bigotry and hatred against a specific group of people. (19)

BIGAMY Marrying another person when one or both of the parties are already married. (11)

BIOMETRICS The statistical study of biological data such as fingerprints. (5)

BLACK MASS Diabolical communion ritual performed by Satanists that mocks and desecrates the Christian mass. (19)

BLIND REPORTING Allows sexual assault victims to retain their anonymity and confidentiality while sharing critical information with law enforcement. It also permits victims to gather legal information from law enforcement without having to commit immediately to an investigation. (11)

BLOODS A black gang; associated with the colors red and green. (19)

BLOWING A SAFE Opening a safe using cotton, primer cap, copper wire and nitroglycerine. (14)

BOOKMAKING Soliciting and accepting bets on any type of sporting event. (19)

BOOT To start up a computer. (18)

"BUGGING" Using a machine to record conversations within a room without the consent of those involved. (7)

BURGLARY The unlawful entry of a structure to commit a felony or theft. (14)

BURLS The large gnarly root at the base of walnut trees, sought after by tree "rustlers." (15)

BURN INDICATORS Visible evidence of the effects of heating or partial burning. (17)

BURNING A SAFE Opening a safe using a burn bar or an oxyacetylene tank, a hose and a torch. (14)

BYTE The amount of space needed to store one character of information on a computer. (18)

CADAVERIC SPASM A condition occurring in certain muscle groups that can indicate suicide. It usually occurs when the victim is holding something at the time of death and the hand closes tightly around the object due to the stress and tension of dying. Does not disappear as rigor mortis does. (13)

CARJACKING Taking a motor vehicle from a person by force or the threat of force. A new category of robbery. (9)

CARROLL DECISION Established that vehicles may be searched without a warrant if there is probable cause for the search and if the vehicle would be gone before a search warrant could be obtained. (4)

CAST To make an impression using plaster of Paris or a similar substance. Also, the physical reproduction of such an impression. (5)

CERTIORARI When the U.S. Supreme Court agrees to review a case it is called *granting certiorari*. (4)

CHAIN of EVIDENCE Establishes each person who has custody of evidence. (5)

CHICKEN HAWK An online pedophile. Uses chatlines and member profiles to locate potential victims. (12)

CHILD MOLESTATION The violation of a child by lewd or lascivious acts, indecent exposure, incest or rape. Usually a felony. (11)

CHILD SEXUAL ABUSE Sexually molesting a child, performing sexual acts with a child and statutory rape and seduction. (12)

CHIMEL DECISION Established that a search that is incidental to a lawful arrest must be made simultaneously with the arrest and confined to the area within the suspect's immediate control. (4)

CHOP SHOP An auto body shop that disassembles stolen vehicles and sells the parts. (16)

CHOPPING A SAFE Opening a safe by chopping a hole in it. (14)

CHRONOLOGICAL ORDER In time sequence. (3)

CIRCLE SEARCH (PATTERN) Begins at the center of a crime scene and spreads out in ever-widening concentric circles. (4)

CIRCUMSTANTIAL EVIDENCE A fact or event that incriminates a person in a crime, for example, being seen running from a crime scene. (5)

CIVIL LIABILITY A person's risk of being sued. Anyone who acts under the authority of law who violates another person's constitutional rights can be sued. (1)

CLASS CHARACTERISTICS Features that place an item into a specific category, for example, the size and shape of a tool. (5)

CLOSE TAIL Moving surveillance by which a subject is kept constantly in view. Also called a *tight tail*. (7)

COGNITIVE INTERVIEW Interviewing technique that helps victims or witnesses to imagine themselves at the scene of a crime. (6)

COMMERCIAL BURGLARY One that involves churches, schools, barns, public buildings, shops, offices, stores, factories, warehouses, stables, ships or railroad cars. (14)

COMMERCIAL EXPLOITATION Having as a direct or an indirect goal monetary or other material gain. (12)

COMMUNITY POLICING A philosophy or orientation that emphasizes working with citizens to solve crime-related problems and to prevent crime. Also called *community-oriented policing*. (1)

COMPASS-POINT (PLOTTING) METHOD Measures the angles between two lines. (2)

COMPETENT EVIDENCE Evidence that has been properly collected, identified, filed and continuously secured. (5)

COMPETENT PHOTOGRAPH A photograph that accurately represents its subject and is properly identified and placed in the chain of evidence and secured until court presentation. (2)

COMPLAINANT The person who requests an investigation or that action be taken. Often a crime victim. (6)

COMPUTER CRIME That which involves the addition, deletion, change or theft of information. (18)

COMPUTER VIRUS A computer program created specifically to "infect" other programs with copies of itself. (18)

CONCLUSIONARY LANGUAGE Nonfactual; drawing inferences; for example, "The man was *nervous.*" To be avoided in police reports. (3)

CONFESSION Information that supports the elements of a crime that is provided and attested to by anyone involved in committing the crime. Can be oral or written. (6)

CONFIDENCE GAME Obtains money or property by a trick, device or swindle that takes advantage of a victim's trust in the swindler. The confidence game offers a get-rich-quick scheme. (15)

CORPUS DELICTI The elements of a specific crime. Evidence that establishes that a specific crime has been committed. (5)

CORPUS DELICTI EVIDENCE All evidence that establishes that a crime was committed. (5)

COVEN A group of witches or Satanists. (19)

COVER Assumed identity used while on an undercover assignment. (7)

CRACK Cocaine mixed with baking soda and water, heated in a pan and then dried and split into pellet-size bits or chunks, which are smoked to produce effects reportedly ten times greater than cocaine at a tenth the cost. (20)

CRAZING Formation of irregular cracks in glass due to rapid, intense heat. It can indicate arson or the use of an accelerant. (17)

CREDIT CARD Any credit plate, charge plate, courtesy card or other identification or device used to obtain a cash advance, a loan or credit or to purchase or lease property or services on the issuer's or holder's credit. (15)

CRIME An act or omission forbidden by law and punishable by a fine, imprisonment or even death. Crimes and their penalties are established and defined by state and federal statutes and local ordinances. (1)

CRIMINAL HOMICIDE Includes murder and manslaughter and is a felony. (13)

CRIMINAL INTENT Performing an unlawful act on purpose, knowing the act to be illegal. (1)

CRIMINAL INVESTIGATION Seeking all facts associated with a crime to determine the truth: What happened and who is responsible. (1)

CRIMINAL NEGLIGENCE Acts of commission or omission creating situations that result in unreasonable risk of death or great bodily harm. (13)

CRIMINAL PROFILING Method of suspect identification that attempts to identify a person's mental, emotional and psychological characteristics. Also called *psychological profiling.* (7)

CRIMINAL STATUTE Legislative act relating to crime and its punishment. (1)

CRIMINALISTICS *see* **FORENSIC SCIENCE.** (1)

CRIPS A black gang; associated with the colors blue and purple. (19)

CROSS-CONTAMINATION Allowing evidence to become mixed together. (5)

CROSS-EXAMINATION Questioning by the opposite side in a trial that attempts to assess the validity of testimony given under direct examination. (8)

CROSS-PROJECTION SKETCH A sketch that presents the floor and walls of a room on the same surface. (2)

CULT A system of religious beliefs and rituals and its body of adherents. (19)

CUNNILINGUS Sexual activity involving oral contact with the female genitals. (11)

CURTILAGE The portion of the residence that is not open to the public and is reserved for private owner or family use—in contrast to sidewalks and alleys, which are used by the public. (4)

CUSTODIAL ARREST *see* **IN CUSTODY.** (6)

CUSTODIAL INTERROGATION Questioning by law enforcement officers after a person has been taken into custody or otherwise deprived of freedom in a significant way. Requires that the Miranda warning be given. (6)

CYBERCOP Name given to investigator involved in computer forensics. (18)

CYBERCRIME Any crime that is committed or helped by the use of a computer. (18)

CYBERPUNK An antiestablishment rebel in the computer universe. Also refers to an entire counterculture existing in cyberspace. (18)

CYBERSPACE The thin air that "exists" between two computers. (18)

CYBERSTALKING Preying on a victim via computer. (10)

DANGEROUS WEAPON Any firearm, loaded or unloaded; any device designed as a weapon and capable of producing great bodily harm or death; or any other device or instrument that is used or intended to be used in a way likely to produce great bodily harm or death. (10)

DATE RAPE Type of sexual assault in which the victim knows the suspect. (11)

DEFENSE WOUNDS Nonfatal wounds incurred by victims as they attempt to ward off attackers. Indicative of murder. (13)

DEPRESSANT Drug that reduces restlessness and emotional tension and induces sleep; most common are the barbiturates. (20)

DEPTH OF CHAR How deeply wood is burned. (17)

DESIGNER DRUGS Substances created by adding to or taking something away from an existing drug. (20)

DIRECT EVIDENCE see *PRIMA FACIE* EVIDENCE. (5)

DIRECT EXAMINATION The initial questioning of a witness or defendant during a trial by the lawyer who is using the person's testimony to further his or her case. (8)

DIRECT QUESTION A question that is to the point with little chance of misinterpretation, for example, "What time did you leave?" (6)

DISK DRIVE Physical location of disks on a computer (internal hard drives are usually labeled as C Drive; floppy drives are generally identified as A or B drive). (18)

DNA Deoxyribonucleic acid. An organic substance found in the nucleus of living cells that provides the genetic code that determines a person's individual characteristics. (5)

DNA PROFILING Analysis of blood, hair, saliva, semen or cells from almost any part of the body to determine a person's identity. (5)

DOMESTIC VIOLENCE (DV) A pattern of behaviors involving physical, sexual, economic and emotional abuse, alone or in combination, by an intimate partner often for the purpose of establishing and maintaining power and control over the other partner. (10)

DOS Disk operating system. (18)

DOWNLOAD To receive transferred data, files or pictures from another computer. Opposite of *upload*. (18)

DRAGGING A SAFE see **PULLING**. (14)

DRUG ABUSE Use of illegal drugs. (20)

DRUG ADDICT A person who habitually uses habit-forming narcotic drugs and thus endangers the public morals, health, safety or welfare; or who is or has been so far addicted to habit-forming narcotic drugs as to have lost self-control. (20)

DYER ACT Made interstate transportation of a stolen motor vehicle a federal crime and allowed for federal assistance in prosecuting such cases. (16)

ELDER ABUSE The physical or mental mistreatment of a senior citizen. May include fraud as well as assault, battery and even murder. (10)

ELECTRONIC SURVEILLANCE Use of wiretapping and/or bugging to obtain information. (7)

ELEMENTS OF THE CRIME Conditions that must exist and be proven to exist for an act to be called a specific kind of crime. (1)

"ELEPHANT-IN-A-MATCHBOX" DOCTRINE The doctrine that requires that searchers consider the probable size and shape of the evidence they seek, for example, large objects cannot be concealed in tiny areas. (4)

ELIMINATION PRINTS Fingerprints taken of everyone whose prints are likely to be found at a crime scene but who are *not* suspects. (5)

E-MAIL Electronic mail. (18)

EMBEZZLEMENT Fraudulent appropriation of property or money by a person to whom it was entrusted. (15)

EMERGENCY A dangerous suspect at or near a crime scene and/or a gravely injured person at the scene. (1)

EMOTIONAL ABUSE Causing fear or feelings of unworthiness in others by means such as locking them in closets, ignoring them or constantly belittling them. (12)

ENTRAPMENT Tricking someone into committing a crime that they would not normally commit. (7)

EVIDENCE Anything that helps to establish the facts related to a crime. (5)

EXCEPTIONAL FORCE More than ordinary force. (7)

EXCITED DELIRIUM A term that describes the manifestations of extreme drug abuse. (20)

EXCLUSIONARY RULE Established that the courts cannot accept evidence obtained by unreasonable searches and seizures, regardless of its relevance to the case (*Weeks v United States*). (4)

EXCULPATORY EVIDENCE Physical evidence that would clear one of blame, for example, having a blood type different from that found at a homicide. (5)

EXCUSABLE HOMICIDE Unintentional, truly accidental killing of another person. (13)

EXHIBITIONIST A person who gains sexual satisfaction by exposing himself or herself. (11)

EXPERT WITNESS A person who has special knowledge not known to persons of moderate education and/or experience in the same field. (8)

EXPLOITATION Taking unfair advantage of people or using them illegally. (12)

FACT Something known to be true. (1)

FELLATIO Sexual activity involving oral contact with the male genitals. (11)

FELONIOUS ASSAULT see **AGGRAVATED ASSAULT**. (10)

FELONY A major crime such as homicide, aggravated assault or robbery. Usually carries a penalty of imprisonment in a state penitentiary or death. (1)

FENCE A seller of stolen property. (14,15)

FIELD IDENTIFICATION On-the-scene identification of a suspect by the victim of or witnesses to a crime, conducted within minutes of the commission of the crime. (7)

FIELD INTERVIEW Spontaneous questioning at the scene. (6)

FINISHED SCALE DRAWING see **SCALE DRAWING**. (2)

FIRE TRIANGLE The three elements necessary for a substance to burn: heat, fuel and air. (17)

FIRST PERSON The use of *I, me, we* and *us* in speaking and writing. This is in contrast to the second person (*you*) and the third person (*he* or *this officer*). (3)

FIRST-DEGREE MURDER Premeditated killing of another person or killing someone while committing or attempting to commit a felony. (13)

FIXED SURVEILLANCE *see* **STATIONARY SURVEILLANCE.** (7)

FLAGGERS Thieves who go around neighborhoods hitting mailboxes with their flags up, searching for envelopes that contain checks and other forms of payment. (15)

FLASHROLL Money used in an undercover drug buy. (20)

FLIPPING In a real estate transaction, it involves a middleman who buys a property near its estimated market value, then resells it—often within minutes—for a greatly increased price. (15)

FLOOR-RELEASE LIMIT Maximum dollar amount that may be paid with a check or credit card without authorization from the central office. (15)

FLOPPY DISK Magnetic medium capable of storing large amounts of information (a 3 ½" disk can hold as much as 470 sheets of paper). (18)

FORCIBLE RAPE Sexual intercourse against a person's will by use or threat of force. (11)

FORENSIC SCIENCE (CRIMINALISTICS) Application of the physical sciences and their technology to examining physical evidence of crimes. (1)

FORGERY Signing someone else's name to a document or altering the name or amount on a check or document with the intent to defraud. (15)

FRAUD Intentional deception to cause a person to give up property or some lawful right. (15)

FRISK An external search of an individual's clothing. Also called a *patdown.* (4)

FRUIT-OF-THE-POISONOUS TREE DOCTRINE The doctrine that evidence obtained as a result of an earlier illegality must be excluded from trial. (4)

GANG A group of people who form an allegiance for a common purpose and engage in unlawful or criminal activity. (19)

GENETIC FINGERPRINT Using DNA analysis to identify a person. (5)

GEOGRAPHIC PROFILING Uses the locations of past crimes and a complex mathematical algorithm to calculate the probabilities of where a suspect lives. (7)

GIGABYTE One billion bytes. (18)

GOOD-FAITH DOCTRINE A doctrine that states that illegally obtained evidence may be admitted into trial if the police were truly not aware that they were violating the suspect's Fourth Amendment rights. (4)

GOODS Property, including anything that is tangible and has value, for example, gas, clothing, money, food. (15)

GRAFFITI Wall writing; sometimes called the "newspaper of the street." (19)

GRAND LARCENY A felony based on the substantial value of the stolen property. (15)

GRAY-COLLAR CRIME Stealing trash. (15)

GRID (SEARCH PATTERN) Adaptation of the lane search pattern in which the lanes are traversed and then cross-traversed. *See also* **LANE SEARCH PATTERN.** (4)

HACKER A person who specializes in unauthorized access into computer networks and other computer systems, primarily for the challenge and status. (18)

HALLUCINOGEN A mind-expanding drug, for example, LSD, DMT and PCP or angel dust. (20)

HAND OF GLORY The left hand of a person who has died. (19)

HARD DISK A nonremovable means of data storage located inside a computer. (18)

HARDWARE (COMPUTER) Computer equipment, including the keyboard, monitor and printer. (18)

HATE CRIME A crime in which the defendant intentionally selects a victim, or in the case of a property crime, the property that is the object of the crime, because of the actual or perceived race, color, national origin, ethnicity, gender, disability or sexual orientation of the person. Also called *bias crime.* (19)

HEAT OF PASSION Extremely volatile emotional condition. (13)

HEBEPHILE A person who selects high-school-age youths as sex victims. (12)

HESITATION WOUNDS Less severe cutting marks caused by an individual's attempts to build up courage before making a fatal cutting wound. Indicates suicide. (13)

HIT-AND-RUN BURGLARY Theft in which a window is smashed to steal merchandise. Also called *smash-and-grab.* (14)

HOLDER Person to whom a credit card is issued. (15)

HOMICIDE The killing of one person by another. (13)

HYPNOSIS A trancelike condition psychically induced in which the person loses consciousness but responds to a hypnotist's suggestions. (6)

ICE Smokable methamphetamine. (20)

IDENTIFYING FEATURES *see* **INDIVIDUAL CHARACTERISTICS.** (5)

IGNITERS Substances or devices used to start a fire. (17)

IMMEDIATE CONTROL   Within a person's reach. (4)

IN CUSTODY (CUSTODIAL ARREST)   The point at which an officer has decided a suspect is not free to leave, there has been considerable deprivation of the suspect's liberty or the officer has in fact arrested the suspect. (6)

IN LOCO PARENTIS   Having the authority to take the place of a parent. Teachers usually have this right. (10)

INCANTATION   Verbal spell. (19)

INCEST   Sexual intercourse with another person known to be nearer of kin than first cousin, in some states whether biological or adopted. (11)

INDECENT EXPOSURE   Revealing oneself to such an extent as to shock others' sense of decency. (11)

INDIRECT QUESTION   Question that skirts the issue, for example, "How do you and the victim get along?" Should be used sparingly if at all. (6)

INDIVIDUAL CHARACTERISTICS   Features that set one item apart from others of the same type. Also called *identifying characteristics.* (5)

INEVITABLE-DISCOVERY DOCTRINE   The doctrine that if the evidence would in all likelihood eventually be discovered anyway, it may be used even if it was obtained illegally. (4)

INFERENCE   A judgment based on reasoning. (1)

INFORMANT   Any individual who can provide information related to a case and who is not a complainant, witness, victim or suspect. (6)

INFORMATION AGE   Period of time driven by information rather than by agriculture or industry (as in the past). (6)

INFRARED ENERGY   The invisible energy beyond the red end of the color spectrum. Used in photography to see through a haze, to read smeared or deteriorated writings and erasures and to distinguish among inks, dyes and other pigments. (5)

INKLESS FINGERPRINTS   A fingerprinting procedure that uses pretreated or special card stock or standard cards to retain nonsmearable, nonerasable fingerprints that can be read by a computer. (5)

INTEGRITY of EVIDENCE   Refers to the requirement that any item introduced in court must be in the same condition as when it was found at the crime scene. (5)

INTERROGATION   Questioning persons suspected of direct or indirect involvement in the crime being investigated. (6)

INTERVIEW   Questioning persons not suspected of being involved in a crime but who know about the crime or the individuals involved in it. (6)

INTIMATE PARTS   Usually refers to the primary genital areas, groin, inner thighs, buttocks and breasts. (11)

INTUITION   The "time of knowing" without any conscious reasoning or apparent logic. Based on knowledge and experience or what is commonly called "street sense." An intangible urge; a "gut feeling" developed by experience. (1)

INVESTIGATE   To observe or study closely; to inquire into something systematically in a search for true information. (1)

INVISIBLE FINGERPRINTS   Fingerprints that are not readily seen but that can be developed through powders or chemicals. (5)

INVOLUNTARY MANSLAUGHTER   Killing someone through extreme, culpable negligence. Unintentional homicide. (13)

JUDGE   An official who is authorized to hold or preside over a court of record. (8)

JUSTIFIABLE HOMICIDE   Killing another person under authorization of the law. (13)

KEYLESS DOORS   Doors that are unlocked by entering a set combination by pushing numbered pads in a programmed sequence. Used on some newer automobiles. (16)

KIDNAPPING   Taking a person to another location by force, often for ransom. (12)

KILOBYTE   One thousand bytes. (18)

KLEPTOMANIACS   Compulsive thieves. (15)

LANE   Narrow passage or strip. (4)

LANE-SEARCH PATTERN   A search pattern that divides a crime scene into lanes by using stakes and strings or by having officers walk shoulder to shoulder or at arm's length. (4)

LARCENY/THEFT   The unlawful taking, carrying, leading or driving away of property from another's possession. (15)

LASER-BEAM PHOTOGRAPHY   A photographic process that reveals evidence indiscernible to the naked eye, such as a footprint in a carpet. (2)

LATENT FINGERPRINTS   Fingerprint impressions caused by perspiration on the ridges of the fingers being transferred to a surface or occurring as residues of oil, dirt or grease. (5)

LAWFUL AUTHORITY   Any person who owns, leases or controls property by an act of the courts or the person who owns the property. (15)

LEGEND   That part of a crime scene sketch containing the case number, name of victim or complainant, location, date, time, investigator, person assisting, scale, direction of north and any other identifying information required by the department. (2)

LEWDNESS (WITH A MINOR)   Touching a minor so as to arouse, appeal to or gratify the perpetrator's sexual desires; the touching may be done by the perpetrator or by the minor under the perpetrator's direction. (12)

LIFESTYLE/EXPOSURE THEORY Links victimization risks to the daily activities of specific individuals. (14)

LINE OF DEMARCATION (FIRE) A boundary between charred and uncharred material. (17)

LINEUP IDENTIFICATION Having victims or witnesses identify suspects from among at least five people presented to them. Used when the suspect is in custody. (7)

LIVIDITY *see* **POSTMORTEM LIVIDITY.** (13)

LOAN-SHARKING The lending of money at exorbitant rates. (19)

LOGIC BOMB Secretly attaches another program to a company's computer system. The attached program monitors the input data and waits for a certain type of error to occur. When this happens, the new program exploits the weakness to steal money or company secrets or to sabotage the system. (18)

LONG-CON GAMES Schemes in which the victims are sent for whatever money they can raise. (15)

LOOSE TAIL Moving surveillance in which it does not matter if the subject is temporarily lost. (7)

LUST MURDER A sex-related homicide involving a sadistic, deviant assault, in which the killer depersonalizes the victim, sexually mutilates the body and may displace body parts. (13)

MACROPHOTOGRAPHY Photographic enlargement of a subject to show details of evidence such as fingerprints or toolmarks. (2)

MAGICK The "glue" that binds occult groups; the supernatural act or force that causes a change in the environment. (19)

MAGISTRATE A judge. (8)

MALICIOUS INTENT (MALICE) Ill will, wickedness, cruelty or recklessness; an evil intent, wish or desire to annoy or injure another person. Can be inferred from an act done in willful disregard for the rights of another, an act done without just cause or excuse or an omission of a duty by willful disregard. (13)

MANSLAUGHTER Unlawful killing of another person with no prior malice. Can be voluntary or involuntary. (13)

MARKER (PHOTOGRAPHIC) An item included in a photograph to show accurate or relative size. (2)

MASS MURDER The killing of multiple victims in a single incident by one or a few suspects. (13)

MATERIAL EVIDENCE Evidence that is relevant to the specific case and forms a substantive part of the case or that has a legitimate and effective influence on the decision of the case (*Porter v Valentine*). (5)

MATERIAL PHOTOGRAPH A photograph that relates to a specific case and the subject. (2)

MEGABYTE One million bytes. (18)

METALLURGY The study of metals and alloys. Frequently used in police laboratories in analyzing metallic materials. (5)

MICROPHOTOGRAPHY Taking pictures through a microscope to help identify minute particles of evidence, (for example, hair or fiber). (2)

MIRANDA WARNING A warning that informs suspects of their right to remain silent, to have counsel present and to have the state appoint and pay for counsel if the suspects cannot afford one. It also warns suspects that anything they say can be used against them in court. (6)

MISDEMEANOR A minor crime such as shoplifting or pilferage. Usually carries a fine or a short sentence in a county or municipal jail. (1)

MISOPED A person who hates children, has sex with them and then brutally destroys them. (12)

MOBILITY Capable of being easily moved. (4)

MODEM A device that links a computer to a telephone line so that messages can be sent between computers at different locations. (18)

MODUS OPERANDI (MO) The characteristic way a criminal commits a specific type of crime. (1)

MOLESTATION (SEXUAL) Acts motivated by unnatural or abnormal sexual interest in another person that would reasonably be expected to disturb, irritate or offend the victim. Touching of the victim is unnecessary. (12)

MONEY LAUNDERING Converting illegally earned cash to one or more alternative forms to conceal its illegal origin and true ownership. (19)

MONIKER Street name; nickname. (19)

MOTOR VEHICLE Any self-propelled device for moving people or property or pulling implements, whether operated on land, water or air. Includes automobiles, trucks, buses, motorcycles, snowmobiles, vans, construction equipment, self-propelled watercraft and aircraft. (16)

MOVING SURVEILLANCE Following people or vehicles on foot or in a vehicle to observe their actions or destinations. Also called *tailing*. (7)

MUG SHOTS Photographs of those who have been taken into custody and booked. (2)

MULES Individuals who sell or transport drugs for a regular dealer in return for being assured of a personal drug supply. (20)

MUMMIFICATION Complete dehydration of all body tissues that occurs when a cadaver is left in an extremely dry, hot area. (13)

MÜNCHAUSEN SYNDROME Involves self-induced or self-inflicted injuries. (12)

MÜNCHAUSEN SYNDROME BY PROXY (MSBP) A form of child abuse in which a parent or adult caregiver deliberately stimulates or causes medical distress in a child. (12)

MURDER *see* **FIRST-, SECOND-** and **THIRD-DEGREE MURDER.** (13)

NARCOTIC A drug that is physically and psychologically addicting; examples include heroin, morphine, codeine and cocaine. (20)

NARRATIVE A technical report that is structured in chronological order and that describes a sequence of investigative events. (3)

NATIONAL CRIME INFORMATION CENTER (NCIC-2000) The FBI clearinghouse for criminal fingerprint records and information on wanted criminals, stolen property and vehicle information. (7)

NEGLECT Failure to properly care for a child, property or one's actions. (12)

NETWORK Relationships, links between people, and between people and their beliefs. (6,18)

NIGHTCAP PROVISION Provision that an arrest or search warrant may be carried out at night. (7)

NO-KNOCK WARRANT Search warrant that contains a special provision that permits officers to execute the warrant without first announcing themselves. (4)

NONCRIMINAL HOMICIDE Classification that includes excusable and justifiable homicide. (13)

NONVERBAL COMMUNICATION Messages conveyed by dress, eye contact, posture, gestures, distance, mannerisms, rate of speech and tone of voice. (6)

OCCULT Secret knowledge of supernormal powers. Many cults claim to have such knowledge. (19)

OPINION A personal belief. (1)

ORAL COPULATION The act of joining the mouth of one person with the sexual organ of another person. *See* **CUNNILINGUS** and **FELLATIO.** (11)

ORDINANCE An act of the legislative body of a municipality relating to all the rules governing the municipality, inclusive of misdemeanor crimes (*Bills v Goshen*). (1)

ORGANIZED CRIME Two or more persons conspiring to commit crimes for profit and using fear and corruption to obtain immunity from the law. (19)

OSTEOGENESIS IMPERFECTA (OI) A genetic disorder characterized by bones that break easily, often from little or no apparent cause. Also called *brittle bone disease.* (12)

OVERLAPPING A photographic technique whereby the entire scene is photographed in a clockwise direction so that a specific object is on the right side of the first photograph; on the next photo the same object is on the left side of the photo and so on until the entire scene is photographed. (2)

PAST TENSE Use of verbs that indicates that the action has already occurred, for example, *lived* rather than *lives.* (3)

PATDOWN *see* **FRISK.** (4)

PC Personal computer. (18)

PEDOPHILE A person who is sexually attracted to young children. (11)

PEELING A SAFE Opening a safe using a breast drill, a set of graduate drills and a jimmy. (14)

PENETRATION *see* **SEXUAL PENETRATION.** (11)

PENTAGRAM Five-pointed star. (19)

PERSON Legally includes not only individuals, but any corporation or joint stock association or any state, government or country that can lawfully own property. (15)

PETTY (PETIT) LARCENY A misdemeanor based on the value of the stolen property. (15)

PHARMACOLOGY The study of drugs. Applied in analyzing and identifying drugs submitted as evidence. (5)

PHOTOGRAPHIC IDENTIFICATION Having victims or witnesses identify suspects from among pictures of people of comparable general description. Used when a suspect is not in custody or when a fair lineup cannot be conducted. (7)

PHYSICAL ABUSE Beating, whipping, burning or otherwise inflicting physical harm. (12)

PHYSICAL EVIDENCE Anything real—that has substance—and helps to establish the facts of a case. (5)

PIRACY The copying and use of computer programs in violation of copyrights and trade secret laws. (18)

PLAIN-VIEW EVIDENCE Unconcealed evidence that is seen by an officer engaged in a lawful activity. (4)

PLANT *see* **STATIONARY SURVEILLANCE.** (7)

PLASTIC FINGERPRINTS Impressions left in soft substances such as putty, grease, tar, butter or soft soap. *See also* **VISIBLE PRINTS.** (5)

PLOTTING METHODS Systematic methods for finding the exact location of objects by using fixed points, including rectangular coordinates, base lines, triangulation and compass points. (2)

POACHING Illegal taking or possession of fish, game or other wildlife. (15)

POLYGRAPH Lie detector. Scientifically measures respiration and depth of breathing, changes in the skin's electrical resistance and blood pressure and pulse. (6)

POSTMORTEM LIVIDITY Dark blue or purple discoloration of the body where blood has drained to the lowest level after death. Also called simply *lividity.* (13)

PREDICATION A brief statement justifying the opening of a case. (1)

PREMEDITATION Considering, planning or preparing for an act, no matter how briefly, before committing it. (13)

PRESUMPTIVE EVIDENCE Evidence that provides a reasonable basis for belief. (14)

PRIMA FACIE **EVIDENCE** Evidence that is made so by law, for example, the blood alcohol level for intoxication. Also called *direct evidence.* (5)

PRINCIPAL Every person involved in committing a crime, whether directly committing the act constituting the offense or aiding in its commission, whether present or absent. It includes every person who directly or indirectly advises, encourages, pays, commands or otherwise induces another to commit a felony.

PROBABLE CAUSE Evidence that warrants a person of reasonable caution to believe that a crime has been committed. (4)

PROBATIVE EVIDENCE Evidence that is vital for the investigation or prosecution of a case. Tending to prove or actually proving guilt or innocence. (5)

PROCESSING EVIDENCE Includes discovering, recognizing and examining evidence; collecting, recording and identifying it; packaging, conveying and storing it; exhibiting it in court; and disposing of it when the case is closed. (5)

PROFILING *see* **GEOGRAPHICAL** or **PSYCHOLOGICAL PROFILING.** (7)

PROGRAM A series of commands that instruct a computer to perform a desired task. (18)

PROPERTY All forms of tangible property, real and personal, including valuable documents, electricity, gas, water, heat and animals. (15)

PROSTITUTION Soliciting sexual intercourse for pay. (11)

PROTECTIVE SWEEP Authority for the police to search areas immediately adjoining the place of arrest, justified when reasonable suspicion exists that another person might be present who poses a danger to the arresting officers. (4)

PSYCHOLOGICAL PROFILING Indicates the type of person most likely to have committed a crime that has certain unique characteristics. Also called simply *profiling.* (7)

PUBLIC SAFETY EXCEPTION Ruling that police may interrogate a suspect without first giving the Miranda warning if a public threat exists that might be removed by having the suspect talk. (6)

PULLING (DRAGGING) A SAFE Opening a safe with a heavy plate of steel by using a V-cut and drilling holes in the corners in which to insert bolts. (14)

PUNCHING A SAFE Opening a safe with a short-handled sledge, a steel chisel and a drift pin. (14)

RAID A planned, organized invasion that uses the element of surprise to recover stolen property, seize evidence and/or arrest a suspect. (7)

RAPE Having sexual intercourse with a person against his or her will. (11)

RAPPORT A harmonious relationship between individuals created by genuine interest and concern. (6)

REASONABLE FORCE The amount of force a prudent person would use in similar circumstances. (7)

RECTANGULAR-COORDINATE (PLOTTING) METHOD Uses two adjacent walls of a room as fixed points from which distances are measured at right angles from each wall. (2)

RELEVANT EVIDENCE Evidence that applies to the matter in question (*Barnett v State*). (5)

RELEVANT PHOTOGRAPH A photograph that assists or explains testimony regarding the matter in question. (2)

RES GESTAE **STATEMENT** Spontaneous statement made at the time a crime is committed. Considered more truthful than planned responses. (1)

RESIDENTIAL BURGLARY A burglary that occurs in buildings, structures or attachments that are used as or are suitable for dwellings even though they may be unoccupied at the time of the burglary. (14)

RIGOR MORTIS A stiffening of portions of the body after death, presumably due to enzyme breakdown. (13)

RITUAL Prescribed form of religious or mystical ceremony. (19)

RITUALISTIC CRIME An unlawful act committed with or during a ceremony. (19)

ROBBERY The felonious taking of another's property, either directly from the person or in the person's presence, through force or intimidation. (9)

ROGUES' GALLERY Mug shots gathered in files and displayed in groups. (2)

ROHYPNOL The "date rape drug"; a sedative that dissolves rapidly when placed in a carbonated drink and acts quickly (20 to 30 minutes) to produce physical as well as mental incapacitation after ingestion. (11)

ROUGH SKETCH The first, pencil-drawn outline of a crime scene, which shows the location of objects and evidence. Basis for the finished *scale drawing.* (2)

ROUGH TAIL Moving surveillance in which it does not matter if the surveillant is detected. (7)

ROUTINE ACTIVITY THEORY Crime results from the convergence of three elements in time and space: a presence of likely or motivated offenders; a presence of suitable targets; and an absence of capable guardians to prevent the criminal act. (14)

SABBAT A gathering of witches. (19)

SADIST Person who receives sexual gratification from causing pain to others, often through mutilation. (11)

SADOMASOCHISTIC ABUSE Fettering, binding or otherwise physically restraining, whipping or torturing for sexual gratification. (11)

SAFE Semiportable strongbox with combination lock. (14)

SCALE Used in sketching, determined by taking the longest measurement at the scene and dividing it by the longest measurement of the paper. (2)

SCALE DRAWING (FINISHED DRAWING) The final drawing, drawn to scale using exact measurements, done in ink and usually on a better grade of paper. (2)

SCANNER A device that converts a typed page or photograph to digital format and copies it onto a disk. (18)

SCRIPT A text file that contains a sequence of computer commands. (18)

SEARCH An examination of a person's house or other buildings or premises or of the person for the purpose of discovering contraband, illicit or stolen property or some evidence of guilt to be used in prosecuting a criminal action with which the person is charged (*Elliot v State*). (4)

SEARCH PATTERNS Systematic approaches to seeking evidence at a crime scene, for example, by using lanes, concentric circles or zones. (4)

SECOND-DEGREE MURDER Intent to cause the death of another but without premeditation. (13)

SECTOR (SEARCH PATTERN) *see* **ZONE SEARCH PATTERN.** (4)

SERIAL MURDER The killing of three or more victims with emotional time breaks between the killings. (13)

SERVICES As an economic term, includes labor, professional services, hotel and restaurant services, entertainment, gas, electricity, water and transportation. (15)

SEXUAL CONTACT (ILLEGAL) Any sexual act committed without the complainant's consent for the suspect's sexual or aggressive satisfaction. (11)

SEXUAL EXPLOITATION (OF A MINOR) To employ, use, persuade, induce, entice or coerce a minor to engage or assist in engaging in any sexually explicit conduct, for example, prostitution and pornography. (12)

SEXUAL PENETRATION Includes sexual intercourse, cunnilingus, fellatio, anal intercourse or any other intrusion, no matter how slight, into the victim's genital, oral or anal openings by the suspect's body or by an object. An emission of semen is not required. (11)

SEXUAL SEDUCTION (OF A MINOR) Ordinary sexual intercourse, anal intercourse, cunnilingus or fellatio committed by a nonminor with a consenting minor. (12)

SEXUALLY EXPLICIT CONDUCT General term referring to any type of sexual intercourse between persons of the same or opposite sex, bestiality, sadomasochistic abuse, lewd exhibition or masturbation. (11)

SHOPLIFTING Taking an item from a retail store without paying for it. (15)

SHORT-CON GAMES Victims are taken for whatever money they have on their person at the time of the swindle. (15)

SHRINKAGE The unexplained or unauthorized reduction of inventory from a retail establishment. (15)

SHYLOCKING *see* **LOAN-SHARKING.** (19)

SIMPLE ARSON Intentional destruction by fire or explosives that does not create imminent danger to life or risk of great bodily harm. (17)

SIMPLE ASSAULT Intentionally causing another person to fear immediate bodily harm or death or intentionally inflicting or attempting to inflict bodily harm on another. Usually a misdemeanor. (10)

SINSEMILLA Homegrown marijuana. (20)

SKETCH A drawing. May be a rough or a finished sketch. (2)

SMASH AND GRAB In burglary, breaking a window and taking items from the window display. (14)

SODOMY Any form of unnatural sex. (11)

SOFTWARE (COMPUTER) The programs run by a computer. (18)

SOLVABILITY FACTORS Those crucial to resolving criminal investigations. (7)

SOURCES OF INFORMATION FILE A file that contains the name and location of persons, organizations and records that can assist in a criminal investigation. (6)

SPALLING The breaking off of surface pieces of concrete, cement or brick due to intense heat. (17)

SPECTROGRAPHIC ANALYSIS Using a laboratory instrument that rapidly analyzes color and coloring agents in small samples of material to determine what elements they contain. (5)

STAKEOUT *see* **STATIONARY SURVEILLANCE.** (7)

STALKER A person who intentionally and repeatedly follows, attempts to contact, harasses and/or intimidates another person. (10)

STALKING Harassing or threatening behavior that an individual engages in repeatedly. (10)

STANDARD OF COMPARISON An object, measure or model with which evidence is compared to determine whether both originated from the same source. (5)

STATEMENT A legal narrative description of events related to a crime. (6)

STATIONARY SURVEILLANCE Observing a location from a fixed location. Also called *fixed surveillance, plant* and *stakeout*. (7)

STATUTORY RAPE Sexual intercourse with a minor, with or without consent. (11)

STIMULANT Drug that peps people up; the most common is the *amphetamine*. (20)

STING A complex operation organized and implemented by undercover agents to apprehend criminals, especially drug dealers. (20)

STOCKHOLM SYNDROME A psychological phenomenon in which hostages bear no ill feelings toward the hostage takers and in fact fear the police more than their captors. (9)

STREET GANG A group of individuals who form a social alliance and engage in unlawful or criminal activity. (19)

STRIKERS Firefighters who set fires to become heroes in putting them out. (17)

STRIP-SEARCH PATTERN An adaptation of the lane search pattern that is used when only one officer is available to search. (4)

SUBJECT What is observed during surveillance, for example, a person, place, property, vehicle, group of persons, organization or object. (7)

SUDDEN INFANT DEATH SYNDROME (SIDS) A condition, whose cause is uncertain, that causes death in young children and for which parents may become suspected of child abuse. (12)

SUICIDE Intentionally taking one's own life. (13)

SUICIDE BY POLICE A situation in which a person decides he or she wants to die but does not want to pull the trigger and so creates a situation in which police are forced to shoot. (13)

SURVEILLANCE The covert, discreet observation of people, places or objects. (7)

SURVEILLANT An investigator assigned to surveillance. (7)

SUSPECT Person considered to be directly or indirectly connected with a crime, either by overt act or by planning and/or directing it. If charged and brought to trial, the person is called a *defendant*. (6)

SWARMING A theft technique in which a group of people rapidly enter, steal from and exit an establishment, overwhelming employees' capabilities to do anything about the situation. (19)

TAIL *see* **MOVING SURVEILLANCE.** (7)

TEMPLATE A pattern, often used by architects and drafters. (3)

TEMPORARY CUSTODY WITHOUT HEARING Removing a child from the custody of parents or guardians for a brief period, usually 48 hours. (12)

TERRY DECISION Established that a patdown or frisk is a protective search for weapons and, as such, must be confined to a scope reasonably likely to discover guns, knives, clubs and other hidden instruments for the assault of a police officer or others. (4)

THEFT *see* **LARCENY.** (15)

THIRD DEGREE The use of physical force, threats of force or other physical, mental or psychological abuse to cause a suspect to confess. (6)

THIRD-DEGREE MURDER Death that results from an imminently dangerous act but does not involve premeditation or intent. (13)

TIGHT TAIL *see* **CLOSE TAIL.** (7)

TOOLMARK An impression left by a tool on a surface. (5)

TOXICOLOGY The study of poisons. Toxicologists are consulted if food or drink poisoning is suspected. (13)

TRACE EVIDENCE Extremely small physical matter. (5)

TRAILER A path, consisting of paper, hay, flammable compounds or any other substance that burns and is set down for a fire to follow. Indicates arson. (17)

TRAP PHOTOGRAPHY Photos that prove an incident occurred, can assist in identifying suspects and the weapons used and can corroborate witness testimony and identification. Also called *surveillance photography*. (2)

TRASHING To scavenge through a business's garbage looking for useful information. (18)

TRIANGULATION (PLOTTING METHOD) Uses straight line measurements from two fixed objects to the location of the evidence, creating a triangle. The evidence is in the angle formed by the two straight lines. (2)

TROJAN HORSE Uses one computer to reprogram another for illegal purposes. (18)

TRUE (UNCONTAMINATED) SCENE Crime scene in which no evidence has been introduced or removed except by the person committing the crime. (4)

TRUTH SERUMS Fast-acting barbiturates that produce sleep at the approximate level of surgical anesthesia for the purpose of releasing a person's inhibitions so that he or she will give information not available otherwise. Most commonly used are sodium amytol and sodium pentathol. (6)

TURF Geographic area claimed by a gang. Often marked by graffiti. (19)

TWEAKER A methamphetamine addict. (20)

ULTRAVIOLET LIGHT The invisible energy at the violet end of the color spectrum that causes substances to emit visible light. Commonly called *fluorescence*. Used to detect secret inks, invisible laundry marks, seminal fluid stains, marked buy money or extortion packages. (5)

ULTRAVIOLET-LIGHT PHOTOGRAPHY Uses the low end of the color spectrum, which is invisible to human sight, to make visible impressions of bruises and injuries long after their occurrence. In addition, the type of weapon used can often be determined by examining its impression developed using ultraviolet light. (2)

UNCONTAMINATED SCENE *see* **TRUE SCENE.** (4)

UNDERCOVER Using an assumed identity to obtain information and/or evidence. (7)

UPLOAD To transfer data, files or pictures to another computer. Opposite of *download*. (18)

VAULT Stationary security chamber of reinforced concrete, often steel-lined, with a combination lock. (14)

VEHICLE IDENTIFICATION NUMBER *see* **VIN** (16)

VICTIM The person injured by a crime. (6)

VICTIMLESS CRIME Crime in which the victim is a willing participant in the illegal activity, for example, a person who bets. (19)

VIN (VEHICLE IDENTIFICATION NUMBER) The primary nonduplicated, serialized number assigned by a manufacturer to each vehicle manufactured. Formerly called *serial number* or *motor vehicle identification number*. (16)

VIRTUAL REALITY An artificial, interactive world created by computer technology (usually involving an immersion system such as a headset). (18)

VIRUS, COMPUTER A program created specifically to infect other programs with copies of itself. (18)

VISIBLE FINGERPRINTS Prints made when fingers are dirty or stained or when they leave their impression on a soft substance. (5)

VISUAL MEDIUM Any film, photograph, negative, slide, book, magazine or other visual medium. Also called *visual print*. (12)

VOICEPRINT Graphic record of an individual's voice characteristics made by a sound spectrograph that records energy patterns emitted by speech. (5)

VOLUNTARY MANSLAUGHTER Intentionally caused death of another person in the heat of passion. (13)

VOYEURISM Window peeking; peeping tomism. (11)

WAIVER Giving up of certain rights. (6)

WHITE-COLLAR CRIME Business-related or occupational crime, for example, embezzlement, computer crimes, bribery, pilferage. (15)

WIRETAPPING Intercepting and recording telephone conversations by a mechanical device without the consent of either party in the conversation. (7)

WITNESS A person who saw a crime or some part of it being committed or who has relevant information. (6)

X-RAY DIFFRACTION Laboratory instrument that compares unknown crystalline substances and mixtures of crystals. (5)

ZERO FLOOR RELEASE The requirement that all transactions by credit card be authorized. (15)

ZONE (SEARCH PATTERN) Search pattern in which an area is divided into equal squares and numbered and then each square is searched individually. Also called *sector search pattern*. (4)

Author Index

Subject Index

Photo Credits

Page 4: AP Photo/Joseph S. Picior; **9:** Stock Boston/© Cary Wolinsky; **10:** Stock Boston/© Cary Wolinsky; **11:** Archive Photos/Reuters/Stephen Jaffe; **15:** AP/Wide World Photos/Michael Tweed; **20:** Joel Gordon; **24:** Impact Visuals/Thor Swift; **31:** Associated Press, AP; **32:** UPI/Bettmann; **35:** AP/Wide World Photos; **37:** James L. Shaffer; **38:** Associated Press, AP; **41:** © Joel Gordon; **44:** AP/Wide World Photos; **59:** Joel Gordon; **61:** © Monkmeyer/Conklin; **70:** Photo Edit/Elena Rooraid; **75:** Associated Press, AP; **79:** Stock, Boston/© N.R. Rowan; **86:** Gamma Liaison/Craig Filipaccohi; **92:** Gamma Liaison/Craig Filipaccohi; **98:** Associated Press, AP; **98:**Corbis; **101:** ODV, Inc., South Paris; **103:** Associated Press, The Natchex Democrat; **113:** Bettmann/© Reuters; **123:** Gamma Liaison/© Stephen Ferry; **137:** Associated Press, Sacramento County Sheriff's Dept.; **142:** Matrix/Stephen Shames; **159:** Paul Conklin/Photo Edit; **172:** Associated Press, AP; **179:** Photo Edit/James L. Shaffer; **187:** Photo Researchers/© Mark C. Burnett; **189:** Impact Visuals/Andrew Lichtensten; **191:** 1993 Star Tribune/Minneapolis–St. Paul. Staff photo by Jerry Holt; **193:** Stock Boston/David Woo; **199:** Photo Edit/James L. Shaffer; **209:** AP/Wide World Photos/Kathy Willens, Pool; **214:** Jim Laurie/Review-Journal; **226:** Associated Press, AP; **228:** IPP/H. Armstrong Roberts; **230:** AP/Wide World Photos/Kathy Willens, Pool; **241:** Archive Photos/Reuters/Ho; **253:** © Donna Ferrato/Domestic Abuse Awareness, Inc. (NYC); **261:** Associated Press, AP; **269:** Joanne Brandon; **276:** PWI 1997/Leslie McGehee; **277:** Contact Press Images/Mark Richards; **290:** Associated Press, AP; **299:** Courtesy Eymann Dolls, Sacramento, CA, **302:** AP/Wide World Photos/Alan Diaz; **315:** Associated Press, Henry County Police Department; **325:** Gamma Liaison/Jim Pozarik; **327:** Maricopa County Medical Examiner; **330:** Maricopa County Medical Examiner; **332:** Maricopa County Medical Examiner; **349:** Superstock; **354:** Stock, Boston/© Barbara Alper; **355:** James L. Shaffer; **356:** Stock, Boston/© Joseph Schuyler; **363:** Stock, Boston/© Spencer Grant; **366:** AP/Wide World Photos; **376:** AP/Wide World Photos/Richmond Times–Dispatch, Masaaki Okada; **379:** © Joel Gordon; **384:** Associated Press; **390:** National Insurance Crime Bureau; **390:** National Insurance Crime Bureau; **392:** Impact Visuals/Michael Kaufman; **393:** Associated Press, AP; **407:** Associated Press, AP; **415:** Stock, Boston; **415:** Courtesy of Winona Fire Department; **416:** Archive Photos/Reuters/Jeff Mitchell; **423:** AP/Wide World Photos/Columbus Dispatch, Jeff Hinckley; **433:** Associated Press, AP; **441:** AP/Wide World Photos/The Keene Sentinel, Michael Moore; **442:** Saba/Associated Press, Najlah Feanny; **451:** Associated Press, AP; **453:** Magnum Photos/Patrick Zachmann; **457:** The Image Works/Kathy McLaughlin; **461:** Gamma Liaison: Deborah Copaken; **469:** UPI Bettmann; **475:** Archive Photos/Reuters/Andre Pichette; **483:** PI/Corbis-Bettmann/Richard Carson; **493:** Medical Economics Anatomically Correct Data; **495:** Saba/Steve Starr; **501:** UPI/Corbis-Bettmann; **502:** AP/Wide World Photos/Journal American; **505:** The Image Works/Jim Mahoney; **508:** AP/Wide World Photos; **513:** Associated Press, AP